Rules for Predicate Logic

In using the rules **UI**, **EI**, and **UG**, let the expression (. . . *w* . . .) denote any sentence or sentence form which results from replacing all occurrences of *u* free in the sentence or sentence form (. . . *u* . . .) by occurrences of *w* free in (. . . *w* . . .), and let *u* and *w* be any variables or constants, unless otherwise specified. Let the same be true for rule **EG**, except that the expression (. . . *w* . . .) must denote a sentence form which results from replacing *one or more* (but not necessarily all) occurrences of *u* free in (. . . *u* . . .) by occurrences of some variable *w* free in (. . . *w* . . .).

UI: (*u*)(. . . *u* . . .) /∴ (. . . *w* . . .)

EI: (∃*u*)(. . . *u* . . .) /∴ (. . . *w* . . .)

Provided:

1. *w* is not a constant.
2. *w* does not occur free previously in the proof.

UG: (. . . *u* . . .) /∴ (*w*)(. . . *w* . . .)

Provided:

1. *u* is not a constant.
2. *u* is not free in a line obtained by **EI**.
3. *u* is not free in an assumed premise within whose scope (. . . *u* . . .) occurs.
4. To each *w* free in (. . . *w* . . .) there corresponds a *u* free in (. . . *u* . . .).

EG: (. . . *u* . . .) /∴ (∃*w*)(. . . *w* . . .)

Provided:

1. To each *w* free in (. . . *w* . . .) there corresponds a *u* free in (. . . *u* . . .).

QN:

(*u*)(. . . *u* . . .) :: ~(∃*u*)~(. . . *u* . . .)

(∃*u*)(. . . *u* . . .) :: ~(*u*)~(. . . *u* . . .)

(*u*)~(. . . *u* . . .) :: ~(∃*u*)(. . . *u* . . .)

(∃*u*)~(. . . *u* . . .) :: ~(*u*)(. . . *u* . . .)

ID:

(. . . *u* . . .)

u = *w* /∴ (. . . *w* . . .)

IR: /∴ (*x*)(*x* = *x*)

Logic and Philosophy
A Modern Introduction
Fifth Edition

Howard Kahane

University of Maryland Baltimore County

Wadsworth Publishing Company
Belmont, California
A Division of Wadsworth, Inc.

Philosophy Editor: Kenneth King
Production Editor: Robin Lockwood
Designers: Lois Stanfield and Hal Lockwood
Copy Editor: Linda Purrington
Technical Illustrator: Larry Blanton

Printed in the United States of America
3 4 5 6 7 8 9 10—90 89 88 87

ISBN 0-534-05652-0

Library of Congress Cataloging-in-Publication Data

Kahane, Howard, 1928–
Logic and philosophy.

Bibliography: p.
Includes index.
1. Logic. I. Title.
BC108.K3 1986 160 85–22714
ISBN 0-534-05652-0

Preface to the Fifth Edition

The purpose of this fifth edition is the same as the first: to provide students with a clear, concise, comprehensible introduction to a complete system for sentential and first order predicate logic; the fundamentals of the traditional syllogistic logic; an empiricist account of the logic of scientific inference; and related material on logic and philosophy. This great variety of material (more than in any other introductory logic text) enables instructors to choose topics of most interest to them and best suited to their students.

This fifth edition includes many minor improvements and several major revisions:

1. The chapter on probabilities has been completely revised so as to make it more comprehensible and up to date—much new material has been added (for example, concerning Bayes' Theorem and Dutch books).
2. Chapters on modal, epistemic and deontic logics, removed from the third edition, have been restored in response to popular demand.
3. The improved chapter on scientific method includes new material on Popper's falsification theory and Goodman's "new riddle of induction".
4. A section on Christine Ladd-Franklin's antilogisms has been added to Chapter Eleven.
5. The direct coupled tree method has been added to the chapter on the tree method for proving validity.
6. A section has been added to Chapter Five on adding new valid argument forms to the system.
7. Some of the material from the fourth edition has been moved to new, more appropriate locations (for instance, the material on logical paradoxes has been moved to Chapter Nine, and the material on truth trees from an appendix to Chapter Seventeen).
8. Seventeen new exercise sets have been added, containing hundreds of new exercise items.

The key to understanding logic is still the same. The student who fails to grasp the material (assuming modest effort) almost always does so because of a failure to understand the difference between variables and constants and thus between sentence forms and sentences. That is why Exercise 2-2 is still the most important one in the book. (Failure to grasp the idea of truth functionality is the next most important reason for failure to grasp the material in general.)

I learned my logic from the late Hans Reichenbach, and my debt to him is obvious. I am also indebted to several other teachers, in particular Nelson Goodman, although our differences of opinion on several subjects tend to cloud this fact. I must also mention my debt to Carl Hempel, since the viewpoint on philosophy of science expressed in this text more nearly resembles his than that of any other eminent philosopher.

I would also like to thank the many students in my logic classes at Whitman College, the University of Kansas, Baruch College, and U.M.B.C. for their invaluable aid; my colleagues at these schools—especially Richard Cole, Warner Morse, Douglas Lackey, and in particular Arthur Skidmore and Parviz Morewedge—for their expert advice and assistance; and my friend Alan Hausman, Ohio State University. I'm also indebted to the publisher's readers: Sid Gendin, Eastern Michigan University; Thomas McKay, Syracuse University; Robert Schwartz, University of Wisconsin-Milwaukee; R. V. Dusek, University of New Hampshire; Patrick Maher, University of Illinois at Urbana-Champaign; Thomas O'Kelley, St. Petersburg Junior College; Rex Hollowell, Spokane Falls Community College; Frank Leavitt, Wright State University; James Roper, Michigan State University; Joseph Gilbert, SUNY Brockport; Robert Barrett, Washington University; Thomas Blakeley, Boston College; Nino Cocchiarella, Indiana University; Arthur Lord, Centralia College; Kenneth H. Small, University of Washington; William Bonis, California State University, Long Beach; Christopher Boorse, University of Delaware; George Gale, University of Missouri, Kansas City; Emily Groscholz, Pennsylvania State University; Harrison Hall, University of Delaware; Wesley Morriston, University of Colorado at Boulder; Paul Roth, University of Missouri at St. Louis; and especially Walter O'Briant, University of Georgia and Robert Burch, Texas A & M University; to the three Wadsworth philosophy editors who have helped develop this text, Robert Gormley, Michael Helm, and Ken King (who in the words of another Wadsworth author exercised his "remarkable ability to stroke and poke at just the right times"); and to several others at Wadsworth, in particular Mary Arbogast and Diane Sipes.

Many instructors who have used previous editions of this text have sent me suggestions that have been incorporated into this text. I would like to thank all of them, in particular, Kenneth E. Haas, Hamline University; Mark A. Brown and John D'Onofrio, Syracuse University; Norman A. Krebs, Whitworth College; Nelson Pole, Cleveland State University; David L. Hitchcock, McMaster University; Erwin Theobold, California State College at Los Angeles; David Hill, Augustana College; Harry J. Gensler, Loyola University; Eva H. Cadwallader, Westminster College; John Titchener, University of Maryland Baltimore County; Stephen C. LaFever, Castleton State College; Tom Grimes, Arkansas State University; and Jon Wulff, Bellevue Community College.

Finally, just in case they're listening somewhere, my thanks to Leon Satinoff, who first gave me the idea of writing a logic text, and to Edward Schouten Robinson.

Howard Kahane
Mill Valley, California

Contents

To Art, Betsy, Charles, Don, Edward,
Frank, George, Harry, and . . . Nancy!

Part One

Sentential Logic

Chapter One

Introduction

1 *Reasoning and Arguments*

Consider the following simple example of reasoning:

> Identical twins often have different IQ test scores. Yet such twins inherit the same genes. So environment must play some part in determining IQ.

Logicians call this kind of reasoning an **argument.** (But they don't have in mind shouting or fighting. Rather, their concern is *arguing for* or presenting reasons for a conclusion.) In this case, the argument consists of three statements:

1. Identical twins often have different IQ test scores.
2. Identical twins inherit the same genes.
3. So environment must play some part in determining IQ.

The first two statements in this argument give *reasons* for accepting the third. In logic talk, they are said to be **premises** of the argument, and the third statement is called the argument's **conclusion.**

In everyday life, few of us bother to label premises or conclusions. We usually don't even bother to distinguish one argument from another. But we do sometimes give clues. Such words as *because, since,* and *for* usually indicate that what follows is a premise. And words like *therefore, hence, consequently, so,* and *it follows that* usually signal a conclusion. Similarly, expressions like "It has been observed that . . . ", "In support of this . . ." and "The relevant data . . ." generally introduce premises, while expressions like "The result is . . . ," "The point of all this is . . . ," and "The implication is . . ." usually signal conclusions. Here is a simple example:

> *Since* it's wrong to kill a human being, *it follows that* abortion is wrong, *because* abortion takes the life of (kills) a human being.

In this example, the words *since* and *because* signal premises offered in support of the conclusion signalled by the phrase *it follows that*. Put into textbook form, the argument reads:

1. It's wrong to kill a human being.
2. Abortion takes the life of (kills) a human being.

/∴ 3. Abortion is wrong.*

(Of course, an argument may have any number of premises and may be surrounded by or embedded in other arguments.)

But not all groups of statements form arguments. Only those do that provide *reasons* for believing something. Thus, anecdotes are generally not arguments, nor are most other forms of *exposition* or *explanation*. It's important to understand the difference between rhetoric that is primarily expository or explanatory and rhetoric that is basically argumentative. A passage that contains only exposition gives us no reason to accept the "facts" in it other than the authority of the writer or speaker, whereas passages that contain arguments allege to give reasons for some of their claims (conclusions) and call for a different sort of evaluation than merely an evaluation of the authority of the writer.

Examples:

Here are some examples of groups of statements that do not constitute arguments:

1. Wow! Indian food sure is hot. Pass the water pitcher.
2. Every time something goes wrong around here, people blame me. Wonder what it's like in other offices.
3. Well, our vacation was just great. We flew to Paris. Then we went over to Vienna, Budapest, Bucharest, and then Athens, before flying back to the States. All in ten days. What a wonderful trip.

Exercise 1-1

Here are twelve passages (the first six are from student papers and exams, modestly edited). Determine which contain arguments and which do not. Label the premises and conclusions of those that do, and *explain*

* The symbol "/∴" is used to indicate that a conclusion follows.

your answers. Paraphrase if that makes things clearer. (Even-numbered items in most exercise sets are answered in a section at the back of the book.)

1. I don't like big-time college football. I don't like pro football on TV either. In fact, I don't like sports, period.
2. My summer vacation was spent working in Las Vegas. I worked as a waitress at the Desert Inn and made tons of money. But I guess I got addicted to the slots and didn't save too much. Next summer my friend Hal and I are going to work in Reno, if we can find jobs there.
3. Well, I have a special reason for believing in big-time college football. After all, I wouldn't have come here if Ohio State hadn't gone to the Rose Bowl, because that's how I heard about this place in the first place.
4. At the present rate of consumption, the oil will be used up in 20–25 years. And we're sure not going to reduce consumption in the near future. So we'd better start developing solar power, windmills, and other "alternative energy sources" pretty soon.
5. The abortion issue is blown all out of proportion. How come we don't hear nearly as much about the evils of the pill? After all, a lot more potential people are "killed" by the pill than by abortion.
6. I've often wondered how they make lead pencils. Of course, they don't use lead, they use graphite. But I mean how do they get the graphite into the wood? That's my problem. The only thing I can think of is maybe they cut the lead into long round strips and then cut holes in the wood and slip the lead in.
7. Punishment, when speedy and specific, may suppress undesirable behavior, but it cannot teach or encourage desirable alternatives. Therefore, it is crucial to use positive techniques to model and reinforce appropriate behavior that the person can use in place of the unacceptable response that has to be suppressed.

   —Walter and Harriet Mischel, *Essentials of Psychology*

8. There was no European language that Ruth could not speak at least a little bit. She passed the time in the concentration camp, waiting for death, by getting other prisoners to teach her languages she did not know. Thus did she become fluent in Romany, the tongue of the gypsies.

   —Kurt Vonnegut, *Jailbird*

9. How do education and training affect lifetime income? Are they worth their cost? The evidence answers, decidedly yes. Men who never finish eight grades of school earn scarcely $3,800 annually; college graduates do three times as well. Unemploy-

ment among school dropouts exceeds that of graduates by a growing margin.

—Paul Samuelson, *Economics* (7th ed.)

10. There are two main reasons why someone might buy a six-month bank certificate instead of going for the higher yields of a money-market fund. The first is that these certificates are insured by an agency of the federal government. The second is that a certificate enables you to lock up your 9 percent, or whatever rate you are getting for the next six months.

—Richard Blodgett, *McCall's* magazine

11. A senior Soviet editor said yesterday that Mikhail Gorbachev plans to attend the U.N. General Assembly session in September, an occasion that could provide an opportunity for a meeting with President Reagan. . . . No official announcement has been made of Gorbachev's plans, and diplomats in Moscow cautioned that the Soviet leader could alter them if conditions changed. But the *Pravda* editor was quoted as saying: "I know for sure that Mr. Gorbachev will go to the General Assembly session".

—*San Francisco Chronicle,* 23 April 1985

12. You can choose to fight them in the morning—they'll kill you or enslave you. You can choose to hide from them—they'll find you. Or you can take their victory from them. They will remember you.

—ABC dramatization *Masada*

---

2 *Deduction and Induction*

There are two basic kinds of good arguments or reasonings. The first kind are often called *deductively valid* arguments or *valid deductive* arguments or simply *valid* arguments, and the second kind *inductively correct, inductively strong,* or *inductively valid* arguments.

The fundamental property of a **deductively valid argument** is this: *If all of its premises are true, then its conclusion must be true also.* To put it another way, if all of the premises of a deductively valid argument are true, then its conclusion *cannot be false*. The truth of its premises "guarantees" the truth of its conclusion.

The question naturally arises as to why the premises of a deductively valid argument, if true, guarantee the truth of its conclusion. Unfortunately, no easy answer can be given.* Perhaps the best we can say at this point is that the information contained in the conclusion of a deductively valid argument is already "contained" in its premises. We are not usually aware of this fact, because it is usually contained in the premises implicitly, along with other information not contained in the conclusion.

Examples:

We know that if the premises of the deductively valid argument

1. If Bonny had her appendix out, then she doesn't have to worry about getting appendicitis.
2. Bonny had her appendix out.

/∴ 3. She doesn't have to worry about getting appendicitis.

are true, then the conclusion (sentence 3) must be true also. For in asserting that if Bonny had her appendix out, then she doesn't need to worry about appendicitis (premise 1) *and* that Bonny has in fact had her appendix out (premise 2), we implicitly assert that Bonny doesn't have to worry about appendicitis.

Here is another example:

1. All wars are started by miscalculation.
2. The Vietnam conflict was a war.

/∴ 3. The Vietnam conflict was started by miscalculation.

Having said in the first premise that all wars are started by miscalculation, and in the second that the Vietnam conflict was a war, we implicitly say that the Vietnam conflict was started by miscalculation.

Good inductive arguments are said to be **inductively correct,** or **inductively strong.** Unlike the case of deductively valid reasoning, an inductively strong argument does not guarantee that if its premises are true then its conclusion must be true also. An inductive argument, however strong, only provides good, never conclusive evidence in support of its conclusion. At best such an argument only makes its conclusion *probable,* never certain, no matter how much supporting evidence it presents.

* Indeed, we cannot give an answer acceptable even to a majority of philosophers. In philosophy, fundamental questions such as this one tend to be the most controversial. In Parts One and Two of this text we shall avoid taking sides in such controversies whenever this can be done without seriously affecting the intent and validity of the material presented.

A perfectly good inductive argument, containing nothing but true premises, *may* turn out to have a false conclusion, and occasionally one does.

Example:

The following argument could have been constructed before the 1984 Democratic National Convention:

1. No woman has ever won the vice-presidential nomination of a major U.S. political party.

/∴ 2. The next Democratic party vice-presidential candidate will not be a woman.

Anyone who had no other pertinent information at that time would have been justified in accepting the conclusion of this (modestly) inductively strong argument, although in fact the conclusion turned out to be false, since the Democrats nominated Geraldine Ferraro.

The reason an inductively strong argument with true premises sometimes has a false conclusion is that its conclusion is *not* contained in its premises, either explicitly or implicitly. (This difference is the major one between a deductively valid argument and an inductively correct one.) There is a "gap" between premises and conclusion in such an argument, a gap bridged by an inductive "leap".

Good and bad inductive reasoning and argument are considered in some detail in Part Four of this text, where the "logic" of scientific reasoning is discussed; the first two parts of this text deal exclusively with deductive validity and invalidity. However, let's say here that, roughly speaking, induction is the process of finding *patterns* or *resemblances*—the more all encompassing, the better—that fit our experiences (and in particular have never been contradicted by any of our experiences).

3 *Argument Forms*

Consider the following argument:

1. Art is an Abadab or he's a Glubphlab.
2. It's not true that Art is an Abadab.

/∴ 3. He's a Glubphlab.

In this argument, if premises 1 and 2 are both true, then the conclusion must be true also. But are both premises true? We have no way of knowing, since, presumably, we don't know anything about Abadabs or Glubphlabs and consequently don't know whether Art is or is not an Abadab. But in spite of this, it is clear that *if* the premises are true (that is, *if* Art is either an Abadab or a Glubphlab, but he's not an Abadab) *then* the conclusion must be true (that is, Art must be a Glubphlab). We know this because of the form of the argument and not because of its content; its form makes this argument a valid argument.* Any argument having the same form—that is, any argument of the form

1. ________ or _ _ _ _ _ _ .
2. It's not true that ________ .

/∴ 3. _ _ _ _ _ _ .

where each pair of similar lines (solid lines, dashed lines) is filled in with the same expression—is deductively valid. (Of course, there are many other valid argument forms.)

Examples:

Arguments (1) through (4) all have the same form. So do arguments (5) through (8), but the form they share is different from that of (1) through (4):

(1) 1. It will rain or it will snow.
2. It's not true that it will rain.
/∴ 3. It will snow.

(2) 1. A Democrat will win or a Republican will win.
2. It's not true that a Democrat will win.
/∴ 3. A Republican will win.

(3) 1. There's a devil or there's a God.
2. It's not true that there's a devil.
/∴ 3. There's a God.

(4) 1. There's complete justice, or there's a devil.
2. It's not true that there's complete justice.
/∴ 3. There's a devil.

(5) 1. If Art is an Abadab, then he's a Glubphlab.
2. Art is an Abadab.
/∴ 3. He's a Glubphlab.

(6) 1. If a Republican wins, then a Democrat loses.
2. A Republican wins.
/∴ 3. A Democrat loses.

(7) 1. If a Democrat wins, then a liar wins.
2. A Democrat wins.
/∴ 3. A liar wins.

(8) 1. If a Republican wins, then a thief wins.
2. A Republican wins.
/∴ 3. A thief wins.

---

* We shall see later that, in general, arguments have several forms; a valid argument is one that has at least one valid form.

Logic is concerned primarily with **argument forms,** and only secondarily with arguments, for all arguments that have a valid argument form are valid, and all other arguments are invalid. Thus, the principal task of deductive logic is to provide a method for distinguishing deductively valid argument forms from deductively invalid argument forms.

4 *Sentences, Propositions, Statements*

Consider the sentences "Snow is white", "Der Schnee ist weiss", and their equivalents in many other languages. Although they are different **sentences** (for example, the first has eleven letters, the second seventeen), they seem to have something in common, for they seem to "say the same thing, only in different words". Sentences of this kind are said to express the same **proposition.**

Some philosophers claim that logic deals with propositions, others that it deals with sentences, and still others that it deals with **statements** (where a *statement* is what one asserts in uttering a sentence). In Parts One and Two of this book, we shall speak of sentences (having in mind declarative sentences) or statements but not of propositions. We do so not to take sides on the proposition-sentence issue, but simply because some words must be used, and "sentence" and "statement" are as well understood as any.*

5 *Truth and Validity*

In Section 3, we mentioned valid and invalid arguments and argument forms, but it makes no sense to speak of valid or invalid *sentences.* Validity and invalidity are properties of arguments, inferences, and the like, not of sentences. Sentences are either *true* or *false;* they are not valid or invalid.

It is important to realize that a deductively valid argument can have a false conclusion, if one or more of its premises are false. Similarly, an invalid argument can have a true conclusion. In fact, every combination of validity-invalidity and truth-falsehood can occur, except one: *a deductively valid argument with true premises cannot have a false conclusion.*

Examples:

Valid Arguments

(1) *True premises and true conclusion:*

---

* See Chapter Nine, Section 6, for more on the proposition-sentence issue.

1. If Ronald Reagan won, then George Bush did also.
2. Ronald Reagan won.

/∴ 3. George Bush did also.

(2) *True premises and false conclusion:*

(This cannot occur; an argument with true premises and a false conclusion must be invalid.)

(3) *False premises and true conclusion:*

1. If Ronald Reagan was once a peanut farmer, then he won in 1980.
2. Ronald Reagan was once a peanut farmer.

/∴ 3. He won in 1980.

(4) *False premises and false conclusion:*

1. If Walter Mondale was once a movie star, then he won in 1984.
2. Walter Mondale was once a movie star.

/∴ 3. He won in 1984.

Invalid Arguments

(5) *True premises and true conclusion:*

1. If Ronald Reagan was a candidate in 1984, then he stretched the truth.
2. He stretched the truth.

/∴ 3. Ronald Reagan was a candidate in 1984.

(Notice that argument (5) has a different form than the first four arguments.)

(6) *True premises and false conclusion:*

1. If Jackie Onassis was a senate candidate in 1984, then a woman was a senate candidate that year.
2. A woman was a senate candidate that year.

/∴ 3. Jackie Onassis was a senate candidate in 1984.

(The existence of an argument of this form with true premises and a false conclusion indicates that *all* arguments of this form are invalid, even those—such as argument (5) above—that have true conclusions. The fact that (5) has a true conclusion is an accident, a contingent fact not guaranteed by logic. The premises of arguments having the same form as (5) do *not* provide good deductive grounds for their conclusions.)

(7) *False premises and true conclusion:*

1. If Nixon was President in 1970, then he won in 1960.
2. He won in 1960.

/∴ 3. Nixon was President in 1970.

(8) *False premises and false conclusion:*

1. If Rhode Island is larger than Texas, then it's larger than California.
2. It's larger than California.

/∴ 3. Rhode Island is larger than Texas.

(In this example, premise 1 is true, but premise 2 false. Thus, *taken as a unit,* the premises are false.)

6 *Soundness*

Valid arguments that contain only true premises (and thus also have a true conclusion) are said to be **sound arguments.** Invalid arguments and valid arguments containing at least one false premise are said to be **unsound arguments.** Thus, example (1) above is sound, because it has true premises and a valid form; all the other examples above are unsound, because they have false premises or an invalid form.

In general, logic is not concerned with the soundness of arguments, because, with one exception, logic alone cannot determine whether the premises of an argument are true or false. (The one exception concerns premises that are *logically* true or false. See Chapter Eight, Section 4.)

7 *Contexts of Discovery and Justification*

When someone states that something is true, two important kinds of questions can be asked. First, what psychological factors led that person to think of such a conclusion (what made him think of it), and second, what reasons are offered for accepting it as true? Questions of the first kind are said to be in the area or context of **discovery,** those of the second kind in the area or context of **justification.**

In general, logic does not deal with the context of discovery. The mental processes used in thinking of hypotheses or conclusions are of interest to the psychologist, not the logician. The logician is interested in reasons that are, or might be, presented in support of conclusions. In other words, the logician is interested in the context of *justification.*

The difference between discovery and justification is illustrated by the difference between the sometimes agonizing thought processes necessary to "figure out" solutions to difficult problems and the arguments we then present in their defense. The discovery process, the figuring out, often is long and involved, while the argument presented to justify the conclusion arrived at by this long process is elegantly simple.

For instance, a scientist may first think of a scientific theory in a dream. But the arguments that he presents to his fellow scientists to support his theory would not refer to the dream. The dream and its contents are part of the process of discovering the theory, not part of the process of justifying it. (Of course, sometimes the processes of discovery and justification overlap.)

Exercise 1-2:

1. Can an argument have all true premises and a true conclusion and yet not be deductively valid?
2. Can an inductively strong argument have all true premises and a false conclusion?
3. Can a deductively valid argument have false premises?
4. A false conclusion?
5. Can a deductively invalid argument have a true conclusion?
6. Can a deductively valid argument have all true premises and a false conclusion?
7. Can an argument be sound but not valid?
8. Can a deductively valid argument be sound and yet have a false conclusion?
9. Have we proved that the conclusion of a deductively valid argument is true when we have established that its premises are all true?
10. Do the words "must" and "therefore" typically signal premises or conclusions of arguments?
11. Do the words "for", "since", and "because" typically introduce premises or conclusions of arguments?
12. What is the difference between the context of discovery and the context of justification? Which one is the concern of logic?

Key Terms Introduced in Chapter One

Argument: A list of sentences (premises-reasons) offered in support of another sentence (the conclusion).

Argument form: The form or structure of an argument.

Deductively valid argument: An argument such that if its premises are true, then its conclusion must be true. The premises of a valid deductive argument provide conclusive evidence for its conclusions. (*Synonyms:* **Valid deductive argument, valid argument**.)

Discovery, context of: The context in which thought processes take place that result in the discovery of new conclusions. (See **Justification, context of**.)

Inductively correct argument: An argument whose premises, if true, provide good but not necessarily conclusive evidence for its conclusion. An inductively correct argument *may* have true premises and a false conclusion. (*Synonym:* **Inductively strong argument**.)

Justification, context of: The context with which formal logic is concerned, that is, the context of rational justifications of conclusions. (See **Discovery, context of**.)

Proposition: The meaning or sense common to all sentences that have the same meaning; for example, the meaning common to the sentences "John took the ball", "The ball was taken by John", and so on. (Whether or not there are such things as propositions is in dispute.)

Sentence: A linguistic expression that is either true or false.

Sound argument: A deductively valid argument with true premises. Arguments that have a false premise or are invalid are *unsound*.

Statement: That which is asserted or expressed when one utters a sentence. (See **Proposition**.)

Chapter Two

Sentential Logic—I

1 Atomic and Compound Sentences

It is a familiar fact about language that sentences can be combined to form longer sentences by means of **sentence connectives** such as "and" and "or".

Examples:

1. Reagan won in 1980 and he also won in 1984.
2. God's on our side or He's on their side.
3. Either we reduce the birthrate or soon there won't be any room to sit down.

Sentences built from shorter sentences by means of sentence connectives are called **compound sentences.** All others are said to be **atomic,** or **simple.** Thus, the two sentences "God's in his heaven" and "All's right with the world" are atomic, while "God's in his heaven and all's right with the world" is compound. (Note, however, that an atomic sentence may be quite long, as is the atomic sentence "On the 23rd of September, 1945, the Reverend Maurice Klotzman filed a name-changing petition in Superior Court before Judge Bonny Robbins".)

Chapters Two through Five of this text are concerned with the part of logic that can be developed without considering the interior structure of atomic sentences, the part that's called **sentential logic, propositional logic,** or **the logic of truth functions.** (Sentential logic, along with the *predicate logic* to be discussed in Part Two of this text, forms what is often called **symbolic logic,** to distinguish it from the older, Aristotelian system discussed in Part Three.)

2 *Conjunctions*

We now introduce a few symbols to save time and effort and to increase our ability to handle complex arguments. Use of these symbols also helps to eliminate a great deal of the vagueness and ambiguity of many English words and sentences. The power of a symbolic notation to increase our ability to handle complex arguments is illustrated by the use of symbols in arithmetic. Imagine how hard it would be to multiply, say, eighty-six thousand three hundred seventy-seven by ninety-four without using the symbols 0, 1, 2, 3, and so on.

Compound sentences formed by use of the sentence connective "and" are called **conjunctions,** and the two sentences joined together by the "and" are called **conjuncts** of the conjunction.

Let's abbreviate the sentence "Art went to the show" by the capital letter *A*, the sentence "Betsy went to the show" by the capital letter *B*, and the connective "and" by the **dot,** "·". (The symbol "&" often is used instead of "·".) Then the sentence "Art went to the show and Betsy went to the show" can be symbolized as $A \cdot B$. Now consider all of the possible **truth values** of the two conjuncts of this sentence. First, if *A* and *B* both are true (that is, if Art and Betsy both went to the show), then it is obvious that the compound sentence $A \cdot B$ is true. Second, if *A* is true and *B* is false, then $A \cdot B$ is false. Third, if *A* is false and *B* true, then $A \cdot B$ is false. And finally, if *A* and *B* both are false, then $A \cdot B$ is false. There are no other possible combinations of truth values for the sentences *A* and *B*. So anyone who is given the actual truth values of *A* and *B* can "figure out" the truth value of the compound sentence $A \cdot B$, because (as was just illustrated) the truth value of that compound sentence is *determined by* (is a function of) the truth values of its component parts. The same is true for any compound sentence formed from two shorter sentences by using the sentence connective "·". Therefore, it can be said that "·" is a **truth-functional** sentence connective, since the truth values of the compound sentences formed by its use are uniquely determined by the truth values of their two conjuncts.

The information about the compound sentence $A \cdot B$ contained in the above paragraph can be put into the form of a table, called a **truth table,** as follows:

	A	*B*	$A \cdot B$
1.	True **(T)**	True **(T)**	True **(T)**
2.	True **(T)**	False **(F)**	False **(F)**
3.	False **(F)**	True **(T)**	False **(F)**
4.	False **(F)**	False **(F)**	False **(F)**

Line 1 of this truth table indicates that if A and B both are true, then $A \cdot B$ is true. Line 2 indicates that if A is true and B false, then $A \cdot B$ is false, and so on.

Not all uses of the word "and" are to be translated by the dot symbol. It would be wrong, for instance, to symbolize the sentence "Art and Betsy are lovers" as $A \cdot B$, for that would say that Art is a lover and Betsy is a lover, but not that *they love each other*. Similarly, it would be wrong to symbolize the sentence "Tom Seaver and Dave Kingman were teammates" as $S \cdot K$, for that would say that Tom Seaver was a teammate and Dave Kingman was a teammate, but not that *they were teammates of each other*.

However, some sentences that look like the two we have just considered are logically quite different. For instance, the sentence "Art and Betsy are intelligent" looks just like "Art and Betsy are lovers", and indeed it has the same grammatical structure. But it does not have the same *logical* structure.* The sentence "Art and Betsy are intelligent" *does* say the same thing as "Art is intelligent and Betsy is intelligent", and thus can be correctly symbolized as $A \cdot B$.

Several other common English words often are used to connect sentences in the same way as the word "and". Thus, the word "but" often means "and on the contrary" or "and on the other hand". For example, the word "but" in the compound sentence "Art is smart, *but* he's a poor athlete" informs the reader that the information to follow is significantly different from what came before. In this case, the information preceding the word "but" is favorable to Art; so this use of the word prepares us for unfavorable information to follow. When the word "but" is symbolized by the dot, the part of its meaning that signals a switch of this kind is lost. However, only the *truth-functional* part of its meaning is important for logic and that part is captured by the dot symbol. Therefore, in this case, symbolization of the word "but" by the dot is acceptable for our purposes.

In addition to "and" and "but", the expressions "however", "yet", "on the other hand", "still", "although", "despite the fact that", and many others often are correctly symbolized by the dot.

Exercise 2-1:

Which of the following are logically compound sentences and thus correctly symbolized using the dot? Explain.

---

*Thus grammatical structure is not a sure guide to logical structure; we cannot automatically move from grammatical to logical structure, but always have to reflect on what the sentences in question *mean*.

1. Betsy went to the movies and Art to the jazz session.
2. A large star is large, but a large flea is small.
3. Bonny and Eugene were classmates.
4. Wine, women, and song are a deadly combination.
5. We'll always have death and taxes.
6. In the twenties alcohol was prohibited, but now pot is.
7. Art and Betsy are music lovers.
8. Two and two are four.
9. Though he loved her, he left her.
10. Everything that's great fun is illegal, immoral, and fattening.

---

3 Variables and Constants

The truth table on page 15 concerns the sentences A, B, and $A \cdot B$. But clearly, what it says about these sentences is equally true of any two sentences connected by the dot. For example, we can construct a similar truth table for the sentences C ("Charles is a logician"), D ("Don is a mathematician"), and $C \cdot D$, as follows:

	C	D	$C \cdot D$
1.	T	T	T
2.	T	F	F
3.	F	T	F
4.	F	F	F

Obviously, the truth table for *any* two sentences and their conjunction will be just like the two truth tables already presented. This fact can be expressed in the form of a general truth table in the following way:

	______	- - - - -	______ · - - - - -
1.	T	T	T
2.	T	F	F
3.	F	T	F
4.	F	F	F

In each use of this truth table, the blanks are to be filled in by *any* sentences, atomic or compound, provided only that whatever sentence is placed in the first solid line blank is also placed in the second, and whatever sentence is placed in the first dashed line blank is also placed in the second.

It is customary to use letters instead of solid and dashed lines. Thus, the above truth table would normally be written as follows:

	p	q	$p \cdot q$
1.	T	T	T
2.	T	F	F
3.	F	T	F
4.	F	F	F

This truth table indicates that given any two sentences p and q:

1. If p and q both are true, then their conjunction, $p \cdot q$, is true.
2. If p is true and q false, then their conjunction, $p \cdot q$, is false.
3. If p is false and q true, then their conjunction, $p \cdot q$, is false.
4. If p and q both are false, then their conjunction, $p \cdot q$, is false.

Since this truth table specifies the truth value of any conjunction, given the truth values of its two conjuncts, it can be said to *define* or *specify the meaning of* the dot symbol.

It is important to understand that in the above truth table, the small letters p and q *are not abbreviations for specific sentences*. Rather they serve as place holders. It is only when we replace them by capital letters (abbreviations for specific sentences) that we get expressions which are sentences. Place holders such as p and q are called *variables,* in this case **sentence variables** (because they are to be replaced by abbreviations for sentences).*

Except where otherwise specified, we shall conform to the convention that the small letters p, q, r, and so on are to be used as sentence variables, and the capital letters A, B, C, and so on as sentence abbreviations, referred to as **sentence constants.**

4 *Negations*

Sentence connectives are a kind of operator. That is, they operate on sentences to produce longer, compound sentences, the way the dot performs

---

* Actually, we will use p, q, and so on both as place holders *and* as what are called *metalinguistic variables*. (This distinction is made clear in Appendix B, where axiom systems and the distinction between object language and metalanguage are discussed.)

the operation of joining the sentence A and the sentence B to produce the compound $A \cdot B$.

The sentence connective dot operates on two sentences to produce a third. But some operators generate a new sentence out of just one starting sentence. For instance, the operator *being well known* operates on the sentence "Ronald Reagan was a movie star" to produce the compound "It's well known that Ronald Reagan was a movie star".

A great many operators operate on a single sentence to produce a new, compound sentence. But only one of these, *denial,* or **negation,** is used in standard sentential logic (perhaps because almost all of the others are non-truth-functional—as is the operator *being well known*).

Let's introduce the symbol "~", called **tilde,** to abbreviate expressions of negation. Then we can symbolize, say, the statement "It's not the case that Walter Mondale was a movie star" or, more colloquially, "Walter Mondale was not a movie star", as $\sim S$ (where "S" = "Walter Mondale was a movie star"). And let's expand the concept of a sentence connective so that we can call the negation operator a sentence connective.

Now let's consider the possible truth values for compound sentences formed by adding a negation sign. Unlike the case for conjunctions, there are only two possibilities. Take the sentence "Art is smart", abbreviated as A. Either A is true, in which case $\sim A$ is false, or A is false, in which case $\sim A$ is true. This information can be put into the form of a truth table, as follows:

A	$\sim A$
T	F
F	T

Of course, we again can generalize because the truth table for *any* sentence and its negation will be just like the one for A and $\sim A$. We can express this general fact by constructing a truth table using the variable p, as follows:

p	$\sim p$
T	F
F	T

This truth table indicates that given any sentence p:

1. If p is true, then its negation is false.
2. If p is false, then its negation is true.

5 *Parentheses and Brackets*

Consider the mathematical expression $6 \div 3 \times 2 = 1$. Is this expression true or false? If it states that 6 divided by the result of multiplying 3 times 2 (that is, 6 divided by 6) equals 1, then it is true. But if it states that 6 divided by 3 (which equals 2) multiplied by 2 equals 1, then it is false. As it stands, the expression is *ambiguous* (has more than one distinct meaning). In mathematics, ambiguity of this kind is removed by using parentheses and brackets. Thus, $(6 \div 3) \times 2 = 4$, while $6 \div (3 \times 2) = 1$.

Similarly, parentheses, "(" and ")", brackets, "[" and "]", and braces, "{" and "}", are used to remove ambiguity in logic. Consider once again the sentences "Art went to the show", A, and "Betsy went to the show", B. To deny A and assert B, we can write $\sim A \cdot B$. To deny A *and* deny B, we can write $\sim A \cdot \sim B$. But to deny the *combination* (the conjunction) $A \cdot B$, we need to use parentheses and write $\sim(A \cdot B)$, using the parentheses to indicate that it is the combination or conjunction of A and B that is being denied.

To summarize: The sentence $\sim A \cdot B$ asserts that Art did not go to the show, but Betsy did. The sentence $\sim A \cdot \sim B$ asserts that Art did not go and Betsy didn't either (that is, neither Art nor Betsy went). And the sentence $\sim(A \cdot B)$ asserts that it is false that both Art and Betsy went. Notice that the sentences $\sim A \cdot \sim B$ and $\sim(A \cdot B)$ are not equivalent, as proved by the fact that if Art went to the show but Betsy didn't, then the sentence $\sim A \cdot \sim B$ is false while the sentence $\sim(A \cdot B)$ is true.

When symbolizing more complex sentences, brackets may be used in addition to parentheses. For instance, we can symbolize the sentence "It is not the case both that Art will go and that Betsy and Charles won't" either as $\sim(A \cdot \sim(B \cdot C))$ or as $\sim[A \cdot \sim(B \cdot C)]$.

In addition, parentheses or brackets may be placed around an entire symbolization, or omitted, as we wish. Thus, the sentence "Billie Jean King wears glasses, but Jimmy Connors and Chris Evert Lloyd do not" is correctly symbolized as $[K \cdot (\sim C \cdot \sim E)]$ or as $K \cdot (\sim C \cdot \sim E)$.

6 *Sentences and Sentence Forms*

Expressions such as $p \cdot q$ containing only sentence variables and sentence connectives are called **sentence forms.** Of course, sentence forms are not sentences (and so are neither true nor false). But if we replace all of the variables in a sentence form by expressions (atomic or compound) that are sentences, then the resulting expression will be a sentence. For instance, if we replace the variables p and q in the sentence form $p \cdot q$ by the sentence constants A and B, respectively, then the resulting expression, $A \cdot B$, will be a sentence. The sentence $A \cdot B$ is said to be a **substitution instance** of the sentence form $p \cdot q$. (Of course, in replacing sentence variables with sentence constants, we must make sure that every occurrence of a given sentence variable is replaced by the *same* sentence constant. Thus, $A \cdot \sim(B \cdot A)$ and $\sim C \cdot \sim(B \cdot \sim C)$ are correct substitution instances of $p \cdot \sim(q \cdot p)$, but $A \cdot \sim(B \cdot C)$ and $\sim C \cdot \sim(B \cdot C)$ are not.)

Compound sentences are substitution instances of more than one sentence form. For instance, the sentence $A \cdot B$, which is a substitution instance of the sentence form $p \cdot q$, also is a substitution instance of the sentence form p (because replacement of p, the one variable in the sentence form p, by the compound sentence $A \cdot B$ results in the sentence $A \cdot B$).

Because sentence forms are not sentences, they are neither true nor false. But all of their substitution instances are sentences, and hence all of their substitution instances are either true or false.

Understanding the difference between sentences and sentence forms and between variables and constants is the key to understanding the correct use of the rules of logic.

7 *Disjunctions*

Another frequently used sentence connective is the English word "or" (and its variants, particularly "either . . . or"). Two sentences connected by the word "or" form a compound sentence called a **disjunction,** and the two sentences so connected are called **disjuncts** of the disjunction.

There are two different senses of this connective in common use. One, the **exclusive** sense, is illustrated by the sentence "Art took the makeup exam on Tuesday or on Wednesday". The implication of this sentence is that Art took the makeup exam on Tuesday or on Wednesday, *but not on both Tuesday and Wednesday*. The other sense of the term "or" is called its **inclusive** sense, or sometimes its *nonexclusive* sense. If a football coach exclaims, "We'll beat either Notre Dame or Army", his assertion is not false if the team wins both of these games. The coach means to say that either we'll beat Notre Dame, or we'll beat Army, *or we'll beat both Notre Dame and Army*.

In legal documents, the inclusive sense of the term "or" usually is expressed by the phrase "and/or". Thus a contract may state that "Repairs will be made by the lessor and/or his agent", meaning that repairs will be made by one or the other, or both.

The symbol "$\vee$", called **vee,** or **vel,** is introduced to symbolize the *inclusive* sense of the word "or" and, like the dot, "$\vee$" is a truth-functional connective. Abbreviating the sentence "We'll beat Notre Dame" by the capital letter N, and the sentence "We'll beat Army" by the capital letter

A, we can symbolize the sentence "We'll beat Notre Dame or Army" as $N \vee A$.

Now let's consider all of the possible combinations of truth values of N and A. First, if both N and A are true, then $N \vee A$ is true. Second, if N is true and A false, then $N \vee A$ is true. Third, if N is false and A true, then $N \vee A$ is true. Finally, if both N and A are false, then $N \vee A$ is false. The following truth table summarizes our findings:

N	A	$N \vee A$
T	**T**	**T**
T	**F**	**T**
F	**T**	**T**
F	**F**	**F**

And once again, we can generalize. The truth table for *any* two sentences connected by "$\vee$" will be the same as the one for N and A. Using the variables p and q, we indicate this in a truth table, as follows:

p	q	$p \vee q$
T	**T**	**T**
T	**F**	**T**
F	**T**	**T**
F	**F**	**F**

This truth table indicates that given any two sentences p and q, their disjunction $p \vee q$ is false *only* when both p and q are false; otherwise it is true.

In everyday English, disjunctions are usually signalled by means of the terms "or" or "either-or" (as in this very sentence). But not always. For example, the inclusive disjunction "Either Hunt or Jessup spent over $5 million on their Senate campaigns" can also be expressed by saying "At least one of the two candidates, Hunt and Jessup, spent over $5 million on his campaign", a statement not containing the word "or".

As just stated, a sentence whose major connective is an inclusive "or" asserts that at least one of its disjuncts is true, leaving open the question whether or not *both* disjuncts are true. And a sentence whose major connective is an *exclusive* "or" asserts that (1) at least one of its disjuncts is true (as do disjunctions formed by the inclusive "or"); and (2) *at least one disjunct is false*. Thus, there is a sense in which the whole meaning of the inclusive "or" is only part of the meaning of the exclusive "or". So if we symbolize an exclusive use of the word "or" by "$\vee$", we lose part of its meaning. Surprisingly, in most arguments in which the exclusive "or" is used, no harm is done if we symbolize the "or" by "$\vee$". The validity of such arguments depends on the part of the meaning of the exclusive "$\vee$" that it shares with the inclusive "or", namely the part that asserts at least one disjunct is true.

But there are some arguments for which this is not the case. An example is the argument

1. Art took the makeup exam on Tuesday or on Wednesday (T or W).
2. Art took the makeup exam on Tuesday (T).

/∴ 3. Art did *not* take the makeup exam on Wednesday ($\sim W$).

If the inclusive "or" is used to symbolize the "or" in the first premise of this argument, then the resulting argument will be invalid, since it will state that

1. Art took the makeup exam on Tuesday, or Art took the makeup exam on Wednesday, or Art took the makeup exam on Tuesday and on Wednesday.
2. Art took the makeup exam on Tuesday.

/∴ 3. Art did *not* take the makeup exam on Wednesday.

But the original argument is valid. The trouble is that the "or" in the first premise of the original argument is the *exclusive* "or", and this time the additional claim made by the exclusive "or" cannot be omitted. We must not only assert that Art took the makeup exam on at least one of the two days, stated in symbols as $T \vee W$, but also *deny* that he took the exam on both days, stated in symbols as $\sim(T \cdot W)$. Thus, we should symbolize the first premise as $(T \vee W) \cdot \sim(T \cdot W)$.

In general, the whole meaning of a sentence of the form p or q in which the "or" is used in the exclusive sense can be symbolized as $(p \vee q) \cdot \sim(p \cdot q)$.

8 *Implications and the Material Conditional*

Consider the sentence "If Kennedy wins, then a Democrat wins". This compound sentence contains two atomic sentences, namely, "Kennedy wins" and "A Democrat wins", joined together by the sentence connective "If ______ then - - - - - ". A compound sentence of this kind is called a **conditional,** or **hypothetical.** The sentence between the "if" and the "then" is called its **antecedent,** and the sentence after the "then" its **consequent.** Thus, the general form of a conditional sentence is "if (antecedent) then (consequent)".

In English, there are many other ways to assert a conditional sentence. For instance, the above conditional could be stated as "Assuming that Kennedy wins, a Democrat wins", or as "A Democrat wins, if Kennedy wins", "So long as Kennedy wins, a Democrat wins", and so on.

Conditional sentences differ with respect to the kind of connection they express between antecedent and consequent. For example, the connection between antecedent and consequent in the sentence "If Art or Betsy will go, then Betsy or Art will go" is *logical,* but in the sentence "If Art goes, then Betsy will go" the connection is *factual*. (See Section 4 of the next chapter for more on this.)

But perhaps the most important way in which conditionals differ is with respect to *truth-functionality*. Although a few of the conditionals uttered in daily life are truth-functional, the vast majority are not.

Take the conditional sentence "If Art went to the show, then Betsy went also", partially symbolized as (1): "If *A* then *B*". Suppose Charles and Don wager on the truth value of this sentence, Charles betting that it is true, Don that it is false. Clearly, if Art did go but Betsy didn't, so that *A* is true and *B* false, then sentence (1) is false, and Don wins the bet. So the second line of the truth table for sentence (1) must contain an **F**.

But suppose neither Art nor Betsy went to the show, so that both *A* and *B* are false. Then it is not clear who should win the bet. Surely Charles would be foolish to agree that sentence (1) is false, and hence agree that Don wins the bet. For he could argue that although Betsy didn't go, sentence (1) doesn't assert that she did go, but only that she did *if Art did*. Since Art didn't go, sentence (1) is not false.

On the other hand, Don would be equally foolish to agree that sentence (1) is true, and hence that Charles wins the bet. For he could argue that sentence (1) asserts that Betsy went *if Art went,* but says nothing about what happened to Betsy if Art didn't go. Since Art didn't go, we can't say sentence (1) is true.

It would seem, then, that if both its antecedent and consequent are false, the truth value of the conditional sentence (1): "If *A* then *B*" is not determined by the truth values of its component sentences. Thus, sentence (1) contains a *non*-truth-functional use of the connective "If ______ then - - - - -". This causes little difficulty in ordinary betting situations (for example, Charles and Don could agree that if *A* turns out to be false, then the bet is off), but it won't do for logic.

This example illustrates the difficulty that arises when both antecedent and consequent of a conditional are false. Thus, it illustrates the difficulty presented by the fourth line of the truth table for "if ______ then - - - - -" sentences. But the same sort of problem arises with respect to the third line, and even the first.

Take the conditional sentence (2): "If Smith puts off his operation, then he'll be dead within six months", pronounced by a doctor about a particular cancer patient. Suppose Smith puts off the operation but is killed crossing the street two weeks later, so that both the antecedent "Smith puts off the operation" and the consequent "He'll be dead within six months" are true. (This is the case for the first line of the truth table for sentence (2).) Surely, the doctor is *not* justified in claiming that sentence (2) is true just because both its antecedent and consequent are true, for the consequent is true *accidentally,* and not because the antecedent is true. The doctor meant to assert not simply that Smith would be dead within six months if he were not operated on, but rather that if not operated on *his cancerous condition would cause his death* (if nothing else did first). So we are not justified in placing a **T** on the first line of the truth table for sentence (2). But we aren't justified in placing an **F** on the first line either, for Smith *might* have died of cancer within six months if he had not been killed in an auto accident. It seems then that the use of "If ______ then - - - - -" in sentence (2): "If Smith puts off his operation, then he'll be dead within six months" is not truth-functional.

However, our main concern here is not how conditionals differ but rather how they are alike, for we want to take the meaning common to all uses of the connective "If ______ then - - - - -" as the *entire* meaning of our implication sentence connective. It turns out that for a conditional sentence, truth-functional or not truth-functional, *if its antecedent is true and its consequent false, then the whole conditional sentence is false.* Therefore, part of what we do in asserting a sentence of the form "If p then q" is *deny* the conjunction of its antecedent with the negation of its consequent; that is, we deny $(p \cdot \sim q)$, and thus assert $\sim(p \cdot \sim q)$. We use this partial meaning shared by all conditional sentences as the *total* meaning of what is called a **material conditional,** or **material implication.**

To signify material implication, we introduce the sign "$\supset$", called **horseshoe.** (The arrow symbol "$\rightarrow$" also is common.) Thus, a sentence having the form $p \supset q$ is taken to mean the same thing as, and hence to be equivalent to, a sentence having the form $\sim(p \cdot \sim q)$. Consequently, the truth table for a sentence having the form $p \supset q$ must be the same as the truth table for an analogous sentence having the form $\sim(p \cdot \sim q)$.

The general method for determining the truth values of compound sentences is presented in Chapter Three. Let's anticipate a bit here and informally derive the truth table for sentences having the form $\sim(p \cdot \sim q)$.

Take the sentence "It is not the case both that Art went to the show and Betsy didn't", symbolized as $\sim(A \cdot \sim B)$. There are four possible combinations of truth values for A and B:

Case I: A is true and B is true (line 1 of the truth table for the sentence $\sim(A \cdot \sim B)$):

Since B is true, $\sim B$ is false. Hence $(A \cdot \sim B)$ is false, and $\sim(A \cdot \sim B)$ true. Therefore, line 1 of the truth table for $\sim(A \cdot \sim B)$ must contain a **T**.

Case II: A is true and B false (line 2 of the truth table for the sentence $\sim(A \cdot \sim B)$):

Since B is false, $\sim B$ is true. Hence $(A \cdot \sim B)$ is true, and $\sim(A \cdot \sim B)$ false. Therefore, line 2 of the truth table for $\sim(A \cdot \sim B)$ must contain an **F**.

Case III: A is false, B true (line 3 of the truth table):
Since A is false, $(A \cdot \sim B)$ is false. Hence $\sim(A \cdot \sim B)$ is true. Therefore, line 3 of the truth table for $\sim(A \cdot \sim B)$ must contain a **T**.

Case IV: A is false and B is false (line 4 of the truth table):
Since A is false, $(A \cdot \sim B)$ is false. Hence $\sim(A \cdot \sim B)$ is true. Therefore, line 4 of the truth table for $\sim(A \cdot \sim B)$ must contain a **T**.

Summing up, the truth table for $\sim(A \cdot \sim B)$, and therefore for $A \supset B$, is as follows:

A	B	$\sim(A \cdot \sim B)$	$A \supset B$
T	**T**	**T**	**T**
T	**F**	**F**	**F**
F	**T**	**T**	**T**
F	**F**	**T**	**T**

Once again, we can generalize, since the truth table for any two sentences connected by "$\supset$" will be the same as the one for $A \supset B$. Using the variables p and q, we indicate this in a truth table as follows:

p	q	$p \supset q$
T	**T**	**T**
T	**F**	**F**
F	**T**	**T**
F	**F**	**T**

We take this truth table to provide a definition or specification of meaning for the truth-functional horseshoe symbol.*

When symbolizing conditional sentences of ordinary English, it must be remembered that most ordinary conditionals are *not* truth-functional. Thus, when they are symbolized by "$\supset$", only part of their meaning is captured (namely the part they share with all conditionals), the other part being lost. In general, the part captured by material implication is all that

---

*Some other reasons for defining "$\supset$" as we have defined it are explained in Chapter Five, Section 7.

is needed to solve problems containing implications. But this is not always true, so that translating non-truth-functional implications by means of the truth-functional connective "⊃" sometimes involves complications and risks (to be discussed further in Chapter Eight, Section 8).

9 *Material Biconditionals*

Two sentences are said to be **materially equivalent** if they have the same truth value. We introduce the symbol "≡" to stand for material equivalence. (The symbols "iff" (if and only if) and "↔" also are used.) Thus, to assert that Art's having gone to the show (*A*) is materially equivalent to Betsy's having gone to the show (*B*), we can write "*A* is materially equivalent to *B*", or simply $A \equiv B$. (This sentence can also be expressed in English as "Art went to the show if, and only if, Betsy went to the show".) Obviously, the sentence $A \equiv B$ is true if and only if *A* and *B* have the same truth value, and in general a sentence $p \equiv q$ is true if and only if *p* and *q* have the same truth value. Hence, the truth table for material equivalence must be:

p	q	$p \equiv q$
T	T	T
T	F	F
F	T	F
F	F	T

We take this truth table to provide a definition or specification of meaning for the symbol "≡".

Compound statements formed by the symbol "≡" sometimes are called **material equivalences,** because if true they join together two smaller statements that have the same (equivalent) truth values. But these compounds are more frequently referred to as **material biconditionals,** or simply **biconditionals,** because they are themselves equivalent to two-directional material conditionals. For instance, the material biconditional "Art went to the show if and only if Betsy went to the show", in symbols $A \equiv B$, is equivalent to the two-directional conditional "If Art went to the show, then Betsy went to the show, and if Betsy went to the show, then Art went to the show", in symbols $(A \supset B) \cdot (B \supset A)$. This can be verified by proving that the truth table for $A \equiv B$ is the same as the truth table for $(A \supset B) \cdot (B \supset A)$.

The same problem concerning truth-functionality that arises for conditionals arises also for biconditionals.* In general, the question as to when equivalences can be symbolized by "≡" is answered in the same way that the similar question is answered concerning implications.

Exercise 2-2:

For each sentence on the left, determine the sentence forms on the right of which it is a substitution instance. (Remember that a sentence may be a substitution instance of several different sentence forms.)

1.	A	a.	p
2.	$A \supset B$	b.	q
3.	$(A \vee B) \supset C$	c.	$\sim p$
4.	$(\sim A \vee B) \supset C$	d.	$p \supset q$
5.	$\sim(A \vee B) \supset C$	e.	$\sim p \supset q$
6.	$\sim(\sim A \vee B) \supset C$	f.	$\sim(p \supset q)$
7.	$\sim[(A \vee B) \supset C]$	g.	$\sim(\sim p \supset q)$
8.	$\sim[\sim(A \vee B) \supset C]$	h.	$(p \vee q) \supset r$
9.	$\sim[\sim(\sim A \vee B) \supset C]$	i.	$(p \vee q) \supset \sim r$
10.	$\sim[(\sim A \vee B) \supset C]$	j.	$(\sim p \vee q) \supset r$
		k.	$\sim(\sim p \vee q) \supset r$
		l.	$\sim(p \vee q) \supset r$
		m.	$\sim[\sim(\sim p \vee q) \supset r]$
		n.	$\sim[(p \vee q) \supset r]$
		o.	$\sim[\sim(p \vee q) \supset r]$

Exercise 2-3:

Determine the sentence forms of which the following are substitution instances. *Example:* The sentence $A \supset \sim B$ is a substitution instance of p, $p \supset q$, and $p \supset \sim q$.

---

* Indeed, it arises for disjunctions also. Consider the disjunction "Either we operate or the patient dies". In this case, the truth of the left disjunct, "We operate", does not guarantee the truth of the whole compound sentence, "Either we operate or the patient dies", even if the patient does not die, because it may be that the patient wouldn't have died even if we had not operated. (The common claim that conjunction also is often non-truth-functional in everyday uses is not correct.)

1. $A \cdot \sim B$
2. $L \vee (M \cdot N)$
3. $\sim(H \vee K)$
4. $\sim[(A \equiv B) \supset C]$
5. $(A \cdot B) \equiv \sim B$
6. $\sim A \supset (B \supset A)$
7. $\sim[\sim(B \cdot D) \supset (R \vee D)]$

Exercise 2-4:

1. What's wrong with abbreviating the sentence "George Plimpton is a known public figure" by the letter *p*?
2. Can a sentence be a substitution instance of more than one sentence form? Explain, including an original example.
3. What are the two principal meanings of the term "or" when that term is used as a sentence connective? Include at least one original example of each.
4. What common words, other than *and,* are sometimes correctly translated by means of " · "?
5. According to the rule called *Double Negation* (to be introduced soon), *p* is equivalent to $\sim\sim p$. Does it follow that any substitution instance of *p* is also a substitution instance of $\sim\sim p$?
6. Is the sentence "Archie Leach and Cary Grant are well-known public figures" atomic or compound?
7. What about the sentence "Archie Leach is not a well-known public figure"?
8. And how about "Archie Leach and Cary Grant have been lifelong best friends"?
9. Or, "George Burns is not now, never has been, and never will be God"?

Key Terms Introduced in Chapter Two

Antecedent: The expression to the left of the "⊃" in a conditional sentence (or sentence form).

Atomic sentence: A sentence that contains no sentence connectives.

Biconditional: (See **Material biconditional.**)

Compound sentence: A sentence composed of one or more simple sentences plus one or more sentence connectives. *Example:* "Art is handsome *and* Betsy is smart".

Conditional: A compound sentence (or sentence form) having the structure "If ___ then ___" (or equivalent constructions).

Conjunct: The expression to the left of, or to the right of, the " · " in a conjunction.

Conjunction: A compound sentence (or sentence form) whose main connective is " · ", "and", "but", or a similar term.

Consequent: The expression to the right of the "⊃" in a conditional sentence (or sentence form).

Disjunct: The expression to the left of, or to the right of, the "or", or "∨", in a disjunction.

Disjunction: A compound sentence (or sentence form) whose main connective is an "or" or "∨".

Dot: Symbolized as " · ". The truth-functional sentence connective defined by the truth table

p	q	$p \cdot q$
T	**T**	**T**
T	**F**	**F**
F	**T**	**F**
F	**F**	**F**

Generally the best translation for the English connectives "and", "however", "but", and so on.

Exclusive disjunction: A compound sentence whose main connective is exclusive "or".

Exclusive "or": The truth-functional sentence connective defined by the truth table

p	q	p exclusive or q
T	**T**	**F**
T	**F**	**T**
F	**T**	**T**
F	**F**	**F**

No symbol was introduced for this sentence connective in this book, but p exclusive or q can be symbolized as $(p \vee q) \cdot \sim(p \cdot q)$. The English word "or" is often used in this sense. *Synonym:* **Exclusive disjunction.**

Horseshoe: The symbol "⊃", defined by the truth table

p	q	$p \supset q$
T	**T**	**T**
T	**F**	**F**
F	**T**	**T**
F	**F**	**T**

Hypothetical: (See **Conditional**.)

Iff: (See **Material biconditional**.)

Implication: (See **Conditional**.)

Inclusive disjunction: A compound sentence whose main connective is inclusive "or", or "∨".

Inclusive "or": Symbolized as "∨". The truth-functional statement connective defined by the truth table

p	q	$p \vee q$
T	**T**	**T**
T	**F**	**T**
F	**T**	**T**
F	**F**	**F**

Corresponds roughly to the English term "or", used in its inclusive sense, and also to the English term "and/or". *Synonyms:* **Vel, vee.**

Material biconditional: Statement whose main sentence connective is "≡". *Synonyms:* **Material equivalence, biconditional.**

Material conditional: A Compound statement whose main connective is "⊃". *Synonym:* **Material implication.**

Material equivalence: (1) Symbolized as "≡". The truth-functional sentence connective defined by the truth table

p	q	$p \equiv q$
T	**T**	**T**
T	**F**	**F**
F	**T**	**F**
F	**F**	**T**

Roughly equivalent to the English connective "if and only if". However, many English uses of "equivalence" and "if and only if" are not truth-functional. *Synonym:* **Iff.**

(2) Synonym for **Material biconditional.**

Material implication: (See **Material conditional.**)

Negation: A sentence whose main connective is "∼", "not", "no", or a similar term. (Also see **Tilde.**)

Propositional logic: (See **Sentential logic**.)

Sentence connective: A term or phrase used to make a larger sentence from two smaller ones. *Example:* "It's raining *and* it's cold". Also, the term "not" and its variations, when used to negate a sentence. *Example:* the word "not" in "Fred will *not* win at poker tonight".

Sentence constant: A capital letter abbreviating an English sentence, atomic or compound.

Sentence form: An expression containing sentence variables, such that if all of its sentence variables are replaced by sentence constants, the resulting expression is a sentence.

Sentence variable: A lowercase letter *p* through *z* used as a place holder in a sentence form (or other linguistic form) such that if all the sentence variables in a sentence form are replaced by capital letters (sentence constants), then the resulting expression is a sentence.

Sentential logic: The logic that deals with relationships holding between sentences, atomic or compound, without dealing with the interior structure of atomic sentences. The logic of truth functions. *Synonym:* **Propositional logic.**

Substitution instance: A sentence obtained from a sentence form by replacing all of the sentence variables in the sentence form by sentence constants, making sure that every occurrence of a given sentence variable is replaced by the same sentence constant.

Symbolic logic: The modern logic that includes sentential logic as a part (as well as the predicate logic to be discussed later).

Tilde: Symbolized as "~". The truth-functional sentence connective defined by the truth table

p	~*p*
T	F
F	T

Truth functional: A sentence connective is truth-functional if the truth values of the sentences formed by its use are determined by the truth values of the sentences it connects. Similarly, sentence *forms* constructed by means of truth-functional sentence connectives are such that the truth values of their *substitution instances* are determined by the truth values of their component sentences.

Truth table: A table giving the truth values of all possible substitution instances of a given sentence form, in terms of the possible truth values of the component sentences of these substitution instances. (Analogously, we can also speak of the truth table of a sentence.)

Truth value: There are two truth values, namely *true* and *false*.

Vee: (See **Inclusive "or"**.)

Vel: (See **Inclusive "or"**.)

Chapter Three

Sentential Logic—II

1 *Symbolizing Compound Sentences*

The grammatical structure of a sentence often mirrors its logical structure. So many sentences are correctly symbolized simply by following grammatical structure, replacing grammatical connectives such as "or" and "if—then" by their logical counterparts "$\vee$" and "$\supset$".

There is, however, an important rule to keep in mind: namely, to look first for the connective that connects the largest units of the sentence or, in other words, to *look for the connective with the greatest scope*—the main connective of the sentence. Take the sentence (1): "Either Art and Betsy will go to the show or else Art and Jane will go". Its correct symbolization is "$(A \cdot B) \vee (A \cdot J)$", because its main connective (the connective with the greatest scope) is "or". Compare that with the case for sentence (2): "Either Art or Betsy will go to the show, but Jane is not going to go". Its correct symbolization is "$(A \vee B) \cdot {\sim}J$", because its main connective is "but" (which means roughly "and, on the other hand").

In addition, *care must be taken to determine the correct scope of negations*. That is, care must be taken to determine how much of a sentence is negated by a negative term or expression. For instance, the scope of the negative expression in sentence (3): "Art will go, but it's not the case that Betsy will go" (colloquially, "Art will go but Betsy won't")* is just the atomic sentence "Betsy will go". So sentence (3) is correctly symbolized

---

* We don't want to be too fussy translating everyday talk into symbols. We don't want to require that all the sentences symbolized by a single letter be exactly alike. We'll count "Betsy won't go", "Betsy isn't going to go", and "She won't go" (when it's clear that the she referred to is Betsy) as enough alike to all be symbolized by the same letter. If we don't allow this shorthand, we're going to have to say that intuitively valid arguments like "If Reagan won, then Carter lost. Reagan was the winner. So Carter lost" are invalid.

as $A \cdot \sim B$, where "~" negates just B. But the negative expression in sentence (4): "It won't happen both that Art will go and Betsy will go" (colloquially, "Art and Betsy won't both go") is the whole remainder of that compound sentence. So sentence (4) is correctly symbolized as $\sim(A \cdot B)$, where "~" negates all of $(A \cdot B)$.

Examples:

Here are a few relatively simple symbolizations (letting A = "Art watched 'General Hospital'"; B = Betsy watched 'General Hospital'"; F = "Betsy flunked chemistry"; and M = "A miracle occurred").

	English sentence		Symbolization
1.	Art watched "General Hospital", but Betsy didn't.	1.	$A \cdot \sim B$
2.	If Art watched "General Hospital", then Betsy didn't.	2.	$A \supset \sim B$
3.	If Betsy watched "General Hospital", either she flunked her chemistry exam or a miracle occurred.	3.	$B \supset (F \vee M)$
4.	If Betsy watched "General Hospital" and no miracle occurred, then she flunked her chemistry exam.	4.	$(B \cdot \sim M) \supset F$
5.	Either Betsy watched "General Hospital" and a miracle occurred, or she flunked her chemistry exam.	5.	$(B \cdot M) \vee F$

Conditionals, or implications, are very important in daily life, and there are many different ways in which they can be expressed. Here are some examples, all correctly symbolized as $M \supset R$ (letting M = "Kingman breaks Maris's record" and R = "Kingman breaks Ruth's record").

1. If Dave Kingman breaks Roger Maris's home run record, then he'll break Babe Ruth's record also.
2. If Kingman breaks Maris's record, he'll break Ruth's record also.
3. Kingman will break Ruth's record, if he breaks Maris's.
4. In case Kingman breaks Maris's record, he'll have broken Ruth's also.
5. Kingman will break Ruth's record, should he break Maris's.
6. Kingman's breaking Maris's record means he'll also have broken Ruth's.

On the other hand, equivalences are fairly uncommon, and indeed there are only a few standard ways to express them (some quite stilted).

The two most common* are "just in case" and "if and only if", illustrated by the following:

1. Ronald Reagan kept warm at his inauguration if, and only if, he wore thermal underwear.
2. Ronald Reagan kept warm at his inauguration just in case he wore thermal underwear.

Examples:

Here are a few modestly complicated examples of correct symbolizations:

English sentence	Symbolization
1. If Betsy learned to read and write well, she got a good job and made lots of money. (L = "Betsy learned to read and write well"; J = "Betsy got a good job"; M = "Betsy made lots of money")	1. $L \supset (J \cdot M)$
2. If Betsy learned to read and write well, she got a good job and made lots of money—if she didn't have eight children. (E = "Betsy had eight children")	2. $(L \cdot {\sim}E) \supset (J \cdot M)$
3. If Betsy didn't make a lot of money, then either she didn't learn to read and write well, or she didn't get a good job, or she had eight kids.	3. ${\sim}M \supset [({\sim}L \vee {\sim}J) \vee E]$
4. Betsy didn't make lots of money or have eight kids, but she did learn to read and write well and she did get a good job.	4. $({\sim}M \cdot {\sim}E) \cdot (L \cdot J)$
5. If we don't control the money supply and break the power of OPEC, we won't control inflation. (M = "We control the money supply"; O = "We break the power of OPEC"; I = "We control inflation")	5. ${\sim}(M \cdot O) \supset {\sim}I$
6. Either we control the money supply and break the power of OPEC, or we won't control inflation and the economy will collapse. (E = "The economy will collapse")	6. $(M \cdot O) \vee ({\sim}I \cdot E)$
7. If the economy collapses, we'll know that we didn't break the power of OPEC, or perhaps didn't control the money supply—or maybe it'll be because of some international economic debacle. (D = "There is an economic debacle")	7. $E \supset [({\sim}O \vee {\sim}M) \vee D]$

---

*We are omitting, for a moment, the expressions "only if" and "unless", which sometimes express equivalence although usually they express just implication.

8. Neither controlling the money supply without breaking the power of OPEC, nor breaking the power of OPEC but not controlling the money supply will keep the economy from collapsing or avert an international economic debacle.

8. $[(M \cdot \sim O) \vee (O \cdot \sim M)] \supset (E \cdot D)$

Exercise 3-1:

Symbolize the following sentences, using the indicated abbreviations.

1. Neither the Russians nor Americans will reduce their nuclear arsenals. (R = "The Russians will reduce their nuclear arsenal"; A = "The Americans will reduce their nuclear arsenal")
2. Either the Russians and Americans both reduce their nuclear arsenals or neither will.
3. Either the Russians or Americans will reduce their nuclear arsenals or there'll be a nuclear catastrophe. (C = "There will be a nuclear catastrophe")
4. If America doesn't reduce its nuclear arsenal and the Russians don't either, then nuclear catastrophe is inevitable.
5. If the Americans or the Russians don't reduce their nuclear arsenals, then nuclear catastrophe is going to happen sometime.
6. Nuclear catastrophe is inevitable just in case Russia and America don't reduce their nuclear arsenals.
7. If the Russians reduce their nuclear stockpile, the United States will reduce theirs, but if America reduces its nuclear force, the Russians won't reduce theirs.
8. If the Russians don't reduce their nuclear arsenal, we won't, and if we don't, they won't, and so there'll be a nuclear catastrophe.
9. If flowers bloom in the spring but not in winter, then May is colorful but December is drab. (S = "Flowers bloom in spring"; W = "Flowers bloom in winter"; M = "May is colorful"; D = "December is drab")
10. Assuming flowers bloom in the spring but not in winter, May will be colorful, December drab.
11. If flowers bloom either in the spring or in the winter, the young will turn their thoughts to love. (L = "The young will turn their thoughts to love")
12. Flowers will bloom in the spring and May will be colorful just in case either the Americans or Russians reduce their nuclear force.
13. But if both countries reduce arsenals, it still won't be true that both May and December will be colorful (assume being colorful and being drab are opposites).
14. If the Russians and Americans don't reduce nuclear arsenals, May won't be colorful, and December will be drab, and so the young won't turn their thoughts to love.

Exercise 3-2:

Translate the following into more or less colloquial English sentences (trying not to mask logical structure). Let L = "Jerry watched the 'Late Late Flick'"; D = "Jerry watched 'Dallas'"; S = "Jerry says 'He don't'"; G = "Jerry speaks grammatically"; P = "Jerry always pays on dates"; M = "Jerry is a male chauvinist"; and F = "Freda will go out with Jerry".

1. $L \cdot {\sim}D$
2. ${\sim}L \vee D$
3. ${\sim}(L \cdot D)$
4. ${\sim}(L \vee D)$
5. ${\sim}(L \cdot {\sim}D)$
6. ${\sim}L \cdot {\sim}D$
7. ${\sim}(L \vee {\sim}D)$
8. ${\sim}L \vee {\sim}D$
9. $S \supset {\sim}G$
10. $G \supset {\sim}S$
11. ${\sim}P \supset {\sim}M$
12. ${\sim}M \supset {\sim}P$
13. $P \equiv M$
14. $P \supset (M \cdot F)$
15. $(M \cdot {\sim}P) \supset {\sim}F$
16. $({\sim}M \cdot {\sim}P) \supset ({\sim}F \cdot L)$
17. $F \supset ({\sim}P \vee G)$
18. $(P \cdot {\sim}F) \supset M$
19. ${\sim}F \supset ({\sim}G \vee M)$
20. $({\sim}G \vee {\sim}P) \supset {\sim}F$
21. $(S \vee P) \supset ({\sim}G \vee M)$
22. $(S \cdot {\sim}P) \supset ({\sim}G \cdot {\sim}M)$
23. ${\sim}(S \vee P) \supset {\sim}({\sim}G \cdot {\sim}M)$
24. $({\sim}S \cdot P) \supset [{\sim}({\sim}G \cdot M) \cdot F]$

Grammatical structure is often a good guide to logical structure. But sometimes it is misleading. An example is the sentence (1): "Bombing China is equivalent to an act of war against China". It is tempting to symbolize this sentence as $C \equiv W$ (where C = "We bomb China" and W = "We commit an act of war against China"), replacing the grammatical phrase "is equivalent to" by its apparent logical counterpart "$\equiv$". But that would be a mistake. Someone who asserts sentence (1) does not mean to assert an equivalence. He does not mean to assert both that if we bomb China then we commit an act of war against China *and* that if we commit an act of war against China then we bomb China. What he means to say is simply that if we bomb China then we commit an act of war against China. So he means to assert a conditional, namely $C \supset W$.

To avoid mistakes resulting from overly mechanical translation, we have to pay close attention to the meanings particular English sentences convey in specific contexts, realizing that natural languages are quite flexible both in grammatical construction and in their use of grammatical connectives. The same expressions can mean quite different things in different contexts. So in each case, we have to figure out what the sentence says and try to construct a symbolization that says the same (relevant) thing. And this takes a bit of practice. (Since we already know what these sentences mean, learning how to symbolize them correctly involves the odd-sounding but crucial knack of getting clear about what it is that we understand when we understand the meaning of a particular sentence in a natural language.)

In addition, several grammatical connectives—in particular, "only if" and "unless"—are sometimes troublesome. Take the sentence (5) "Geraldine Ferraro's smile is a political asset only if she brushes her teeth with Crest", partially symbolized as "P only if C". Clearly, anyone asserting statement (5) means to say *at least* that if Ferraro doesn't brush with Crest, $\sim C$, then her smile is not a political asset, $\sim P$, which amounts to $\sim C \supset \sim P$. In the next chapter, we'll prove that $\sim C \supset \sim P$ is equivalent to $P \supset C$. So at least part of the meaning of "P only if C" is captured by $P \supset C$.

But in some contexts, fairly uncommon, statement (5) may have additional meaning. For example, supposing Smith first has said that Ferraro's smile is definitely a political asset, Jones might reply by uttering (5) "Ferraro's smile is a political asset only if she brushes with Crest", and mean not only that if her smile is a political asset she brushes with Crest ($P \supset C$), but also that if she brushes with Crest her smile is a political asset ($C \supset P$), which amounts to saying $P \equiv C$. Although uncommon in everyday life, "only if" uses of this kind that translate into biconditionals instead of mere conditionals are occasionally uttered.

The term "unless" functions in much the same way as does "only if". Thus, in most contexts, the sentence (6) "Ferraro's smile is not a political asset unless she brushes with Crest" is correctly symbolized as the conditional $P \supset C$; but in a few contexts it is correctly symbolized as the biconditional $P \equiv C$.

There is no mechanical way to determine which of the two senses of "only if" is being used in a given case. We must determine what is intended in each case by an examination of its content given the *context* of its use, bringing to bear our general knowledge of English usage.

Exercise 3-3:

Symbolize the following sentences (assuming the most common context) using the indicated abbreviations. (Several of these are rather difficult and open to more than one interpretation.)

1. Harry will run (for class president) only if Janet runs also. (H = "Harry will run"; J = "Janet will run")
2. Harry won't run unless Janet runs.
3. Only if Janet runs will Harry run.
4. Unless Harry runs, Janet won't.
5. Pleasure will increase only if pain doesn't increase. (P = "Pleasure is increased"; N = "Pain is increased")
6. Pleasure will increase unless pain increases.

7. Pleasure will not increase only if pain is increased or we fail to reduce mental depression. (D = "We reduce mental depression")
8. Unless pleasure increases or pain decreases (doesn't increase), we'll fail to reduce mental depression.

2 *Truth Table Analysis*

In Chapter Two, truth table definitions were introduced for several truth-functional sentence connectives. This basic content of Chapter Two can be summarized in two truth tables, as follows.*

p	$\sim p$
T	**F**
F	**T**

p	q	$p \cdot q$	$p \vee q$	$p \supset q$	$p \equiv q$
T	**T**	**T**	**T**	**T**	**T**
T	**F**	**F**	**T**	**F**	**F**
F	**T**	**F**	**T**	**T**	**F**
F	**F**	**F**	**F**	**T**	**T**

We can determine the truth value of any compound sentence containing one of these truth-functional connectives, when provided with the truth values of the sentences they connect, simply by looking at the appropriate line in the truth tables and noting whether there is a **T** or an **F** at the appropriate spot.

Obviously, this method can be used to determine the truth values of more complicated sentences also. Suppose Art and Betsy are running for class president, and consider the sentence "It's not the case either that Art and Betsy will run or that Betsy won't run", symbolized as $\sim[(A \cdot B) \vee \sim B]$. Assume we are told that Art and Betsy both will run, so that A and B both are true. Then we can "figure out" the truth value of $\sim[(A \cdot B) \vee \sim B]$ as follows: Since A and B both are true, $(A \cdot B)$ must be true, by line 1 of the truth table for "$\cdot$". And since B is true, $\sim B$ must be false, by line 1 of the truth table for "$\sim$". Hence, $[(A \cdot B) \vee \sim B]$ must be true, by line 2 of the truth table for "$\vee$". And finally, since

* For handy reference, these truth tables are printed on the inside back cover.

$[(A \cdot B) \vee \sim B]$ is true, its negation $\sim[(A \cdot B) \vee \sim B]$ must be false, by line 1 of the truth table for "~".

The following diagram illustrates this process of truth table analysis as it was carried out on the sentence $\sim[(A \cdot B) \vee \sim B]$:

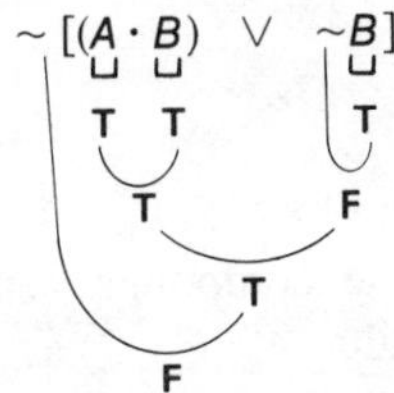

Notice that the process starts with the smallest units of the sentence and proceeds to larger and larger units, until the last loop determines the truth value of the sentence as a whole.

This method, called **truth table analysis,** can be used to determine the truth value of any compound sentence from the truth values of its component sentences.

The loop method just introduced is very graphic, and so many students find it to be the best method to use. But another way is, perhaps, more common, namely to place the truth values of the component sentences of a compound under the relevant sentence connectives. Using this *tabular* method, the truth table analysis for the sentence $\sim[(A \cdot B) \vee \sim B]$, assuming again that A and B both are true, will look like this:

$\sim[(A \cdot B) \vee \sim B]$
F TTT T FT

We construct this diagram by starting with the smallest units, noting first that since B is true, $\sim B$ must be false (justifying placing an F under the second tilde in the formula to indicate that $\sim B$ must be false). We then work with larger and larger component sentences, noting next that since A and B both are true, $A \cdot B$ must be true (justifying placing a T under the dot), then that since $(A \cdot B)$ is true, $(A \cdot B) \vee \sim B$ must be true (justifying placing a T under the vel), and finally that the whole statement must be false (justifying placing an F under the first tilde). Since this tilde at the beginning of the statement negates its whole remainder, the truth value placed under it is the truth value of the whole sentence $\sim[(A \cdot B) \vee \sim B]$.

When doing truth table analysis, either of the two methods just illustrated may be used, depending on which one seems more natural, or easier, to use.

Examples:

(In these examples, assume A, B, and C are true, D, E, and F false.)

Loop Method **Tabular Method**

1. 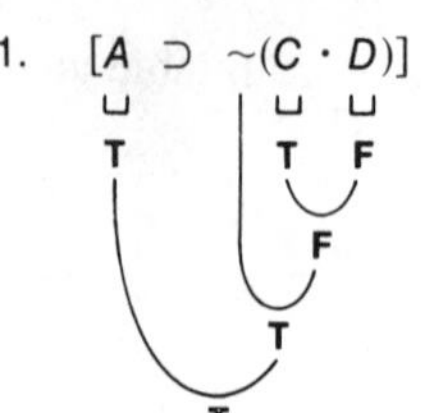

$[A \supset \sim(C \cdot D)]$
T T T T F F
↑
(So the whole sentence is true)

(Notice that the negation sign negates the whole compound sentence $(C \cdot D)$, and therefore is treated *after* the truth value of $(C \cdot D)$ is determined.)

2. $(D \vee \sim B) \equiv (C \cdot \sim D)$

F T F T F T T T F F

$(D \vee \sim B) \equiv (C \cdot \sim D)$
F F F T F T T T F
↑
(So the whole sentence is false)

3. 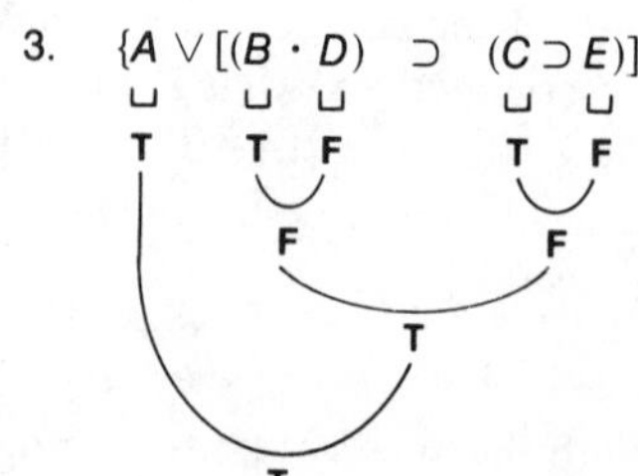

$A \vee [(B \cdot D) \supset (C \supset E)]$
T T T F F T T F F
↑
(So the whole sentence is true)

(Notice that the major connective in this sentence—that is, the connective that connects two component sentences to form sentence 3 as a whole—is "∨", and that therefore it is not really necessary to analyze the right-hand disjunct, because the left-hand disjunct—namely *A*—is true, and consequently the whole sentence is true.)

4. 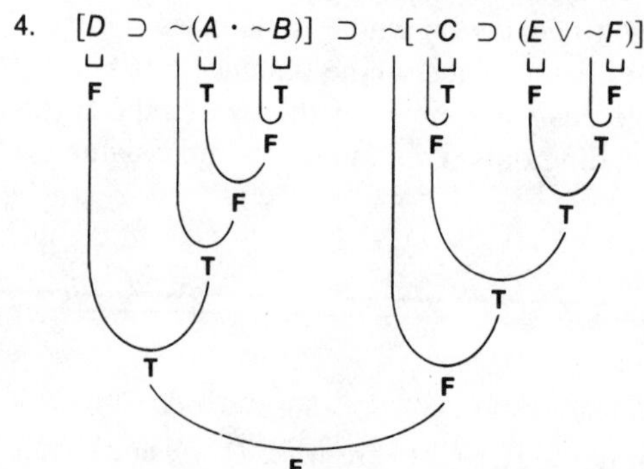

$[D \supset \sim(A \cdot \sim B)] \supset \sim[\sim C \supset (E \vee \sim F)]$

F T T T F F T F F F T T F T T F

5.

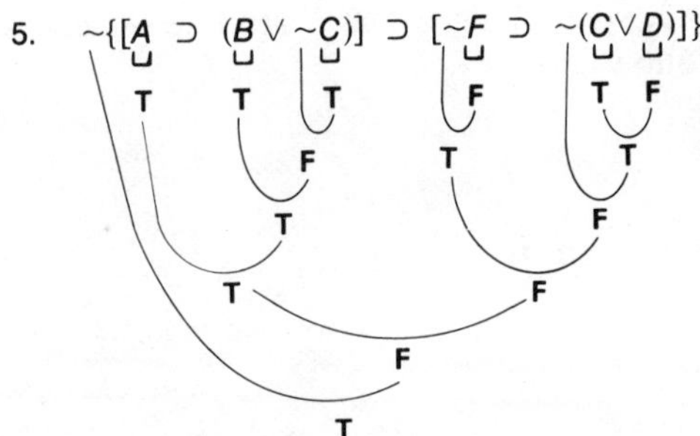

$\sim\{[A \supset (B \vee \sim C)] \supset [\sim F \supset \sim(C \vee D)]\}$

T T T T T F T F T F F F T T F

Exercise 3-4:

If *A* and *B* are true, and *C*, *D*, and *E* are false, what are the truth values of the following compound sentences?

1. $(A \vee D) \supset E$
2. $A \equiv (C \vee B)$
3. $B \supset (A \supset C)$
4. $\sim[(A \cdot \sim B) \supset (C \cdot \sim D)]$
5. $[(A \cdot B) \cdot C] \vee [(A \cdot C) \vee (A \cdot D)]$
6. $A \supset [(B \supset C) \supset (D \supset E)]$
7. $[(\sim A \cdot \sim B) \supset C] \vee (A \supset B)$
8. $[(A \supset \sim B) \vee (C \cdot \sim D)] \equiv [\sim(A \supset D) \vee (\sim C \vee E)]$
9. $[(E \vee \sim D) \cdot \sim A] \supset \{(\sim A \cdot \sim B) \cdot [(C \cdot D) \cdot E]\}$
10. $[A \supset (\sim A \vee A)] \cdot \sim[(A \cdot A) \supset (A \cdot A)]$

---

3 *Tautologies, Contradictions, and Contingent Sentences*

If all possible substitution instances of a sentence form are true, that sentence form is said to be a **tautologous sentence form** or simply a **tautology.** The sentence form $p \supset (q \supset p)$ is an example. It can be shown to be tautologous by examining all of its substitution instances, putting them into four categories as follows: first, substitution instances in which both p and q are replaced by true sentences (whether atomic or compound is not important); second, substitution instances in which p is replaced by a true sentence and q a false one; third, substitution instances in which p is replaced by a false sentence and q a true one; and finally, substitution instances in which both p and q are replaced by false sentences.

Let's begin by examining a substitution instance of the first kind, say the sentence $H \supset (K \supset H)$, where both H and K are true sentences. Its truth table analysis is as follows:

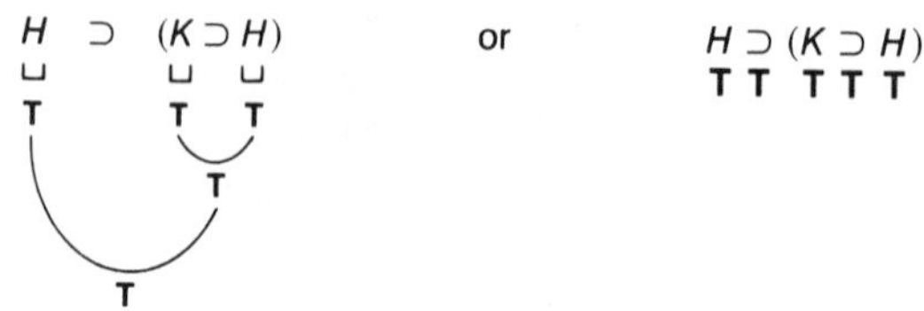

And of course, truth table analysis will yield a **T** for *every* substitution instance of $p \supset (q \supset p)$ in which both p and q are replaced by true sentences.

Now consider a substitution instance of the second kind, say $M \supset (N \supset M)$, in which p is replaced by the true sentence M, and q by the false sentence N. The truth table analysis for $M \supset (N \supset M)$ is:

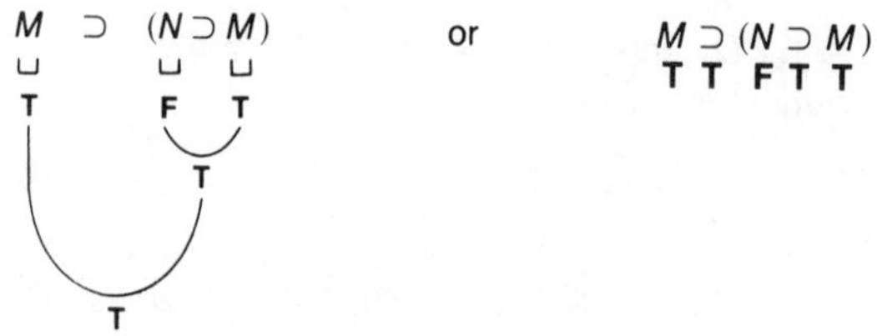

And once again truth table analysis will yield a **T** for *every* substitution instance of $p \supset (q \supset p)$ in which p is replaced by a true sentence and q by a false one.

Next, consider a substitution instance of the third kind, say the sentence $C \supset (D \supset C)$, in which p is replaced by the false sentence C, and q by the true sentence D. The truth table analysis for $C \supset (D \supset C)$ (and all substitution instances of the third kind) is:

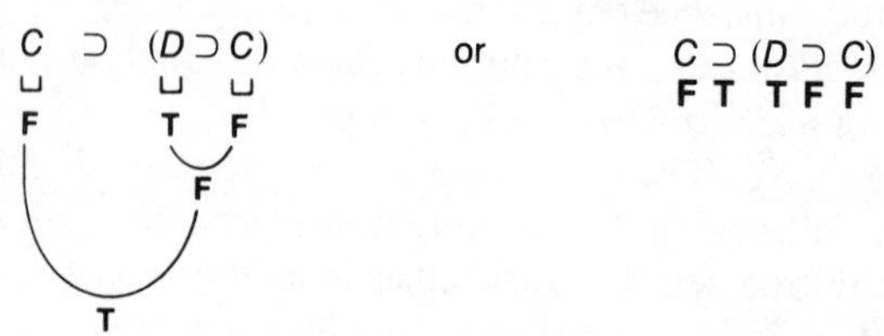

Finally, consider a substitution instance of the fourth kind, say the sentence $F \supset (G \supset F)$, in which p is replaced by the false sentence F, and q by the false sentence G. The truth table analysis for this sentence (and for all substitution instances of the fourth kind) is:

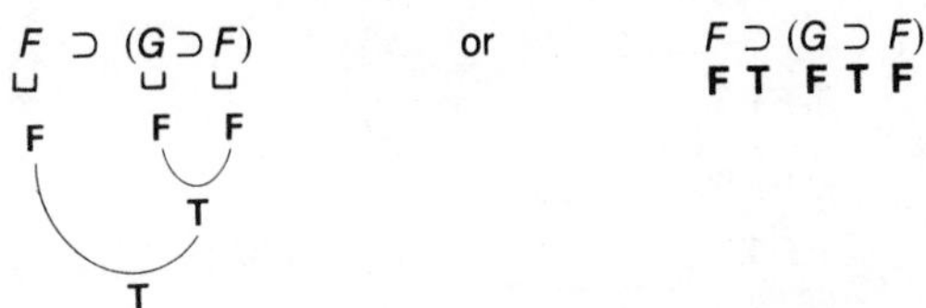

So *all substitution instances of* $p \supset (q \supset p)$ *are true sentences,* no matter what the truth values of their component sentences. The *form* or *structure* of these sentences* makes them true, not the truth values of their component sentences. The sentence form $p \supset (q \supset p)$ thus is a *tautologous sentence form*. Informally, substitution instances of tautologous sentence forms also can be called *tautologies,* although some logicians reserve that word for sentence forms only.

The above discussion of substitution instances of the sentence form $p \supset (q \supset p)$ makes it obvious that the truth table for it is as follows:

p	q	$p \supset (q \supset p)$
T	T	T
T	F	T
F	T	T
F	F	T

And it also makes obvious the general method for determining the truth table for any given sentence form, and thus for all of its substitution instances.

Now consider a second sentence form, namely the form $(p \cdot \sim p)$. What is its truth table? First, unlike the case for the sentence form $p \supset (q \supset p)$, the truth table for $p \cdot \sim p$ has only two lines, instead of

---

* Plus the meanings of their logical terms, such as "⊃".

four, since $p \cdot \sim p$ has only one variable, namely p, instead of two.* Second, its truth table has all **F**'s, instead of all **T**'s. This is proved by the following truth table analysis:

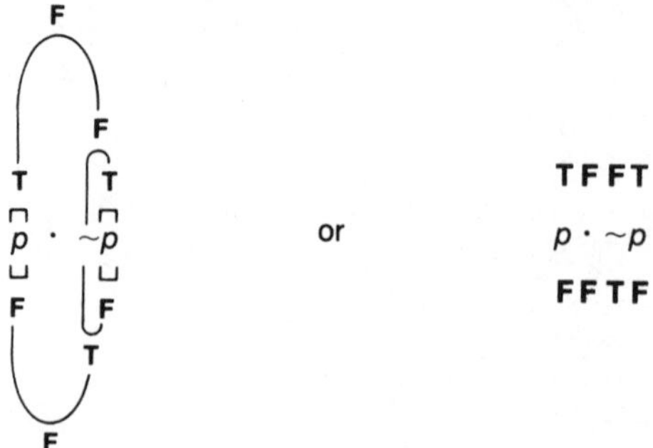

(The analysis above the sentence form $p \cdot \sim p$ is for the first case, in which p is replaced by a true sentence, and the analysis below $p \cdot \sim p$ is for the second case, in which p is replaced by a false sentence.)

Thus the truth table for $p \cdot \sim p$ is:

p	$p \cdot \sim p$
T	**F**
F	**F**

Since only **F**'s occur in its truth table, it follows that *all substitution instances of* $p \cdot \sim p$ *are false,* no matter what the truth values of the sentences that replace p. The *form,* or *structure,* of the substitution instances makes them false, not the truth values of their component sentences. A sentence form all of whose substitution instances are false is said to be a **contradictory sentence form,** or simply a **contradiction.** Informally, substitution instances of contradictory sentence forms also can be referred to as *contradictions,* although some logicians reserve this term for sentence forms only.

It is important to see that not all false sentences are contradictions. For instance, if Art goes to the show and Betsy does not, then the sentence "If Art goes then Betsy goes", in symbols $A \supset B$, is false. But it is not a contradiction, since it is *not* a substitution instance of a contradictory sentence form. Thus the notion of a contradictory sentence is different from that of a merely false sentence.

---

* The number of lines in the truth table of a given sentence form is equal to 2^n, where n is the number of variables in the sentence form. Thus a sentence form with one variable has $2^1 = 2$ lines in its truth table, one with two variables has $2^2 = 4$ lines, one with three variables has $2^3 = 8$ lines, and so on.

It is interesting to note that we cannot prove that a sentence is *not* contradictory by showing that it is a substitution instance of a noncontradictory sentence form. This is the case because all sentences, even contradictory sentences, are substitution instances of some noncontradictory sentence form or other. For instance, $S \cdot \sim S$ is a substitution instance of the form p, as well as the form $p \cdot q$, and both of these sentence forms are noncontradictory.

Finally, consider a third sentence form, namely $(p \supset q) \supset q$. We can determine its truth table by the following analysis:

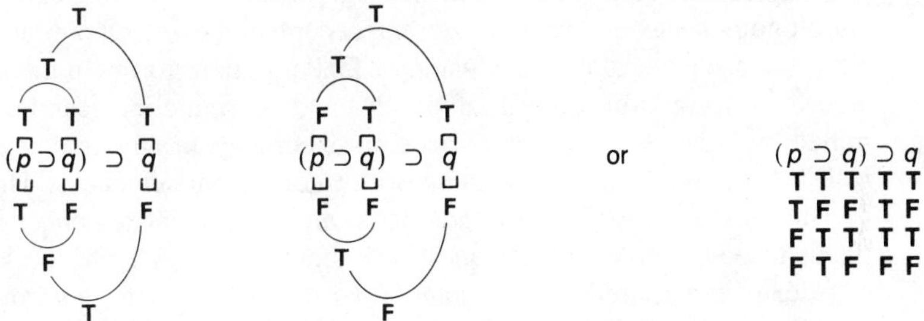

Thus its truth table will be:

p	q	$(p \supset q) \supset q$
T	T	T
T	F	T
F	T	T
F	F	F

Notice that there is at least one **T** and one **F** in this truth table. This means that we cannot determine the truth value of a substitution instance of this sentence form without knowing the truth value of its component sentences, since some substitution instances of $(p \supset q) \supset q$ are true and some false. A sentence form that has at least one **T** and one **F** in its truth table is said to be a **contingent sentence form.** Informally, substitution instances of contingent sentence forms that are *not* substitution instances of any tautologous or contradictory sentence forms can be referred to as **contingent sentences.**

Notice also that we cannot say that all substitution instances of contingent sentence forms are contingent sentences, since *all* sentences are substitution instances of some contingent sentence form or other. For instance, all sentences are substitution instances of the sentence form p, which is a contingent sentence form.

If the truth table analysis for a given sentence yields at least one **T** and one **F**, then it is not necessary to continue the analysis further to determine the nature of that sentence form, since it must be contingent. For example, if we start the truth table analysis of the sentence form $(p \supset q) \supset q$ with the first and last lines of its truth table, then it is not necessary to continue on to lines 2 and 3, since one **T** and one **F** have already been obtained and the sentence form must be contingent.

The division of sentences into tautologies, contradictions, and contingent sentences is of fundamental importance. In the first place, there is an important relationship between tautologies and valid argument forms. For to every deductively valid argument form there corresponds a conditional tautologous sentence form whose antecedent is the set of premises and whose consequent is the conclusion of that argument form. In the second place, the truth values of all tautologies and contradictions can be determined by logic alone, without appeal to experience or any kind of empirical test, although this is not the case for contingent sentences. Thus the division into tautologies, contradictions, and contingent sentences is pertinent to basic philosophical questions about the ways in which knowledge can be acquired. (For instance, it is pertinent to the controversies concerning the analytic-synthetic and *a priori-a posteriori* distinctions to be discussed in Appendix A.)

Exercise 3-5:

Determine which of the following sentence forms are tautologous, which contradictory, and which contingent.

1. $p \vee (q \supset {\sim}p)$
2. ${\sim}[p \supset (p \vee {\sim}p)]$
3. $(p \vee q) \supset [q \vee (p \supset p)]$
4. $p \supset [q \supset (p \supset r)]$
5. $[(p \cdot q) \cdot r] \vee [(p \cdot r) \vee (p \cdot q)]$
6. $\{(r \supset s) \supset [p \cdot (r \vee s)]\} \equiv [p \supset (s \supset r)]$
7. $\{[p \cdot (q \vee r)] \supset p\} \equiv q$
8. ${\sim}[p \supset ({\sim}p \supset {\sim}q)] \cdot ({\sim}p \cdot q)$
9. $[{\sim}({\sim}p \supset {\sim}q) \vee ({\sim}p \cdot {\sim}q)] \supset {\sim}({\sim}p \cdot {\sim}q)$
10. $\{p \supset [(q \vee r) \vee (s \vee {\sim}q)]\} \vee {\sim}p$

4 Logical Versus Material Equivalences and Conditionals

Having explained the differences between tautologous, contradictory, and contingent statements, we now can distinguish between two basic kinds of equivalences and conditional statements.

Take equivalences, and consider the statements $A \equiv B$ and $(A \vee B) \equiv (B \vee A)$ (where, say A = "Art is rich" and B = "Bonny is poor"). Using truth table analysis, we can show that the first is a *contingent* statement while the second is a *tautology*. The truth value of the first depends on the truth values of A and of B, and is simply a **material equivalence.** (A better term would have been *contingent* equivalence, since this term would indicate that the truth value of the first statement is contingent on the truth values of its parts.) But the truth value of the second, $(A \vee B) \equiv (B \vee A)$, is independent of the truth values of its parts (it is, in fact, a tautology) and is said to be a **logical equivalence,** because, being a tautology, its truth value is independent of the truth values of its parts and so can be determined by logic alone.

Similarly, the conditionals $A \supset B$ and $(A \cdot B) \supset (B \cdot A)$ are very different from each other. The first is a *contingent* conditional. Its truth value depends on the truth values of its components. But the second is *tautological*. Its truth value is independent of the truth values of its components. The first is said simply to be a **material conditional,** or **material implication,** while the second is said to be a **logical conditional, logical implication, logical entailment,** or **strict implication.**

Exercise 3-6:

Determine which of the following are just material equivalences or conditionals and which are logical equivalences or conditionals.

1. $A \supset (A \cdot C)$
2. $(F \vee G) \supset F$
3. $A \supset (A \vee \sim A)$
4. $(F \equiv G) \supset F$
5. $F \supset (G \equiv F)$
6. $(M \cdot \sim M) \supset (K \vee M)$
7. $(A \vee B) \equiv [A \vee (B \supset B)]$
8. $\sim[(M \supset \sim M) \supset (K \vee M)]$
9. $(L \supset \sim L) \equiv (L \cdot M)$
10. $[A \supset (B \supset A)] \equiv [B \supset (A \supset B)]$

Exercise 3-7:

1. What is the difference between contingent sentences and contingent sentence forms? (Include examples.)
2. Some substitution instances of contingent sentence forms are not themselves contingent sentences. Do any substitution instances of tautologous sentence forms exist that are not themselves tautologous sentences?
3. If a sentence form contains four variables, how many lines must its complete truth table analysis have?
4. What is wrong with the following truth table analysis?

$(p \vee q) \supset (\sim p \cdot \sim q)$

```
 T T T  F  T F F F T
 T T F  T  T F T T F
 F F F  F  F T F T F
```

Therefore, this is a contingent sentence form.

5. How about this one?

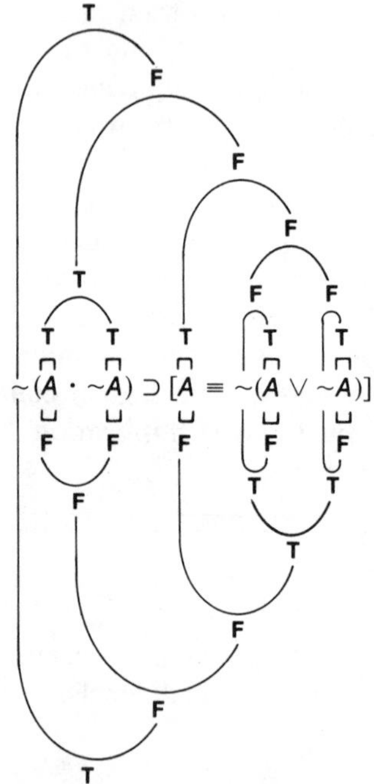

Therefore, this is a tautologous sentence form.

Key Terms Introduced in Chapter Three

Contingent sentence: A sentence that is *not* a substitution instance of any tautologous or contradictory sentence form.

Contingent sentence form: A sentence form that has at least one true and one false substitution instance.

Contradiction: (1) A sentence form all of whose substitution instances are false. (2) A substitution instance of a contradictory sentence form.

Contradictory sentence form: A sentence form all of whose substitution instances are false.

Logical conditional: (See **Logical implication.**)

Logical entailment: (See **Logical implication.**)

Logical equivalence: A tautology whose main connective is "≡". A tautological equivalence, probably true by means of logic alone.

Logical implication: A tautology whose main connective is "⊃". A tautological conditional probably true by means of logic alone.

Strict implication: (See **Logical implication.**)

Tautologous sentence form: A sentence form all of whose substitution instances are true.

Tautology: (1) A sentence form all of whose substitution instances are true. (2) A substitution instance of a tautologous sentence form.

Truth table analysis: A method for determining the truth value of a sentence from knowledge of the truth values of its component sentences. Similarly, a method for determining whether a sentence form is tautologous, contradictory, or contingent by considering the truth values of all possible substitution instances and for determining the validity of arguments in sentential logic (although we haven't yet demonstrated the latter).

Chapter Four

Sentential Logic—III

1 *Arguments and Argument Forms*

As stated in Chapter One, an *argument* consists of one or more sentences (called *premises* of the argument) offered in support of another sentence (called the argument's *conclusion*). An **argument form** is a group of sentence forms such that all of its substitution instances are arguments. For example, all substitution instances of the form

1. $p \supset q$
2. $p \quad /\therefore q$

are arguments, and hence that form is an argument form. (Of course in substituting into an argument form, every occurrence of a given sentence variable must be replaced by the same sentence wherever that variable occurs in the argument form.*)

Examples:

The following arguments are substitution instances of the argument form

1. $p \supset q$
2. $p \quad /\therefore q$

*But the *order* of the premises in an argument is irrelevant. Thus,

1. $A \supset B$	and	1. A
2. $A \quad /\therefore B$		2. $A \supset B \quad /\therefore B$

both are substitution instances of the argument form

1. $p \supset q$
2. $p \quad /\therefore q$

(1) 1. $A \supset B$
2. A $/ \therefore B$

(2) 1. $H \supset \sim K$
2. H $/ \therefore \sim K$

(3)* 1. $(A \vee B) \supset C$
2. $(A \vee B)$ $/ \therefore C$

(4) 1. $\sim(A \cdot B) \supset (C \vee D)$
2. $\sim(A \cdot B)$ $/ \therefore (C \vee D)$

A **valid argument form** is an argument form none of whose substitution instances have true premises and a false conclusion. All substitution instances of valid argument forms are **valid arguments.** An argument that is not a substitution instance of any valid argument form is an **invalid argument.** And an argument form with one or more substitution instances having true premises and a false conclusion is an **invalid argument form.** These facts are of crucial importance for logic, and almost everything else to be said in this chapter depends on them.

Perhaps the simplest way to determine the validity of an argument form is truth table analysis. If even a single line of the truth table for an argument form shows all of the premises to be true but the conclusion false, then the argument form in question is *in*valid (because its truth table shows it can have a substitution instance with true premises and a false conclusion). But if every line of a truth table that shows all of the premises to be true also shows the conclusion to be true, then the argument form is valid (because its truth table shows it cannot have a substitution instance with true premises and a false conclusion).

Take the argument form just mentioned.

(1) 1. $p \supset q$
2. p $/ \therefore q$

The truth table analysis for this argument form is as follows:

			First Premise	Second Premise	Conclusion
	p	q	$p \supset q$	p	q
1.	**T**	**T**	**T**	**T**	**T**
2.	**T**	**F**	**F**	**T**	**F**
3.	**F**	**T**	**T**	**F**	**T**
4.	**F**	**F**	**T**	**F**	**F**

*We obtain this argument as a substitution instance of the argument form in question by substituting $(A \vee B)$ for p in both premises, and C for q in premise 1 and in the conclusion.

Notice that there is a **T** for *both* premises only on line 1 of this truth table, and that there also is a **T** for the conclusion on that line. Hence, there is no substitution instance of this argument form having all of its premises true and its conclusion false. Therefore this argument form is a *valid* argument form.

An example of a valid argument having this form is:

1. If it's fall, then winter can't be far away.
2. It's fall.

/∴ 3. Winter can't be far away.

Or, in symbols:

1. $F \supset W$
2. F

/∴ 3. W

Now consider the *invalid* argument form:

1. $p \supset q$
2. $\sim p$ /∴ $\sim q$

Its truth table analysis is as follows:

			First Premise	Second Premise	Conclusion
	p	q	$p \supset q$	$\sim p$	$\sim q$
1.	**T**	**T**	**T**	**F**	**F**
2.	**T**	**F**	**F**	**F**	**T**
3.	**F**	**T**	**T**	**T**	**F**
4.	**F**	**F**	**T**	**T**	**T**

Both premises yield a **T** on the third and fourth lines of this truth table. But although the conclusion yields a **T** on the fourth line, it yields an **F** on the third. Thus, the third line of this truth table indicates that it is possible for a substitution instance of this argument form to have true premises and a false conclusion, and therefore proves that the argument form is not deductively valid.

Here is an example of an invalid argument having this form (with its symbolization to the right):

1. If it's spring, then the birds are chirping.		1. $S \supset B$
2. It isn't spring.		2. $\sim S$
/∴ 3. The birds aren't chirping.	/∴	3. $\sim B$

Clearly, this argument is invalid. (Since birds chirp in summer also, summer utterances of this argument may have true premises and a false conclusion.)

2 *Modus Ponens and Modus Tollens*

The argument form just proved valid, namely

$p \supset q$
$p \quad /\therefore q$

is called **Modus Ponens** (abbreviated **MP**). It is one of eighteen valid argument forms introduced in Part One of this book to be used in proving arguments valid; that is, it is one of eighteen valid argument forms to be used as rules of inference in constructing proofs of arguments.

Another of the eighteen valid argument forms is **Modus Tollens (MT):**

$p \supset q$
$\sim q \quad /\therefore \sim p$

We can prove that Modus Tollens is a valid argument form by truth table analysis, as follows:

			First Premise	Second Premise	Conclusion
	p	q	$p \supset q$	$\sim q$	$\sim p$
1.	T	T	T	F	F
2.	T	F	F	T	F
3.	F	T	T	F	T
4.	F	F	T	T	T

In this case, there is a **T** for both premises only on line 4 of the truth table. And there also is a **T** for the conclusion on that line. Hence, there is no substitution instance of the argument form Modus Tollens having both of its premises true but its conclusion false. Hence, Modus Tollens is a valid argument form.

Here is an example of a valid argument having this form (with its symbolization to the right):

	1.	If it's spring, then the birds are chirping.		1.	$S \supset B$
	2.	The birds aren't chirping.		2.	$\sim B$
$/\therefore$	3.	It isn't spring.	$/\therefore$	3.	$\sim S$

3 *Proofs Using Valid Argument Forms*

A **proof of an argument** is a list of sentences all of which are either premises of the argument or else follow from previous sentences on the list by valid argument forms (rules of inference), where the last sentence on the list is the conclusion of the argument.*

Here is a proof of a three-premise argument whose conclusion is line 5:

1.	$A \supset B$	p
2.	$B \supset C$	p
3.	$\sim C$	p /∴ $\sim A$

(The notation "p" to the right of lines 1, 2, and 3 indicates that these three lines are premises.)

4.	$\sim B$	2,3 **MT**
5.	$\sim A$	1,4 **MT**

(The notation to the right of line 4 indicates that line 4 "follows" from lines 2 and 3 by the valid argument form Modus Tollens **(MT),** introduced in the last section, and similarly for the notation to the right of line 5.)

Examples:

Here are two more examples of proofs using valid argument forms.

1.	$M \supset \sim N$	p
2.	M	p
3.	$H \supset N$	p /∴ $\sim H$
4.	$\sim N$	1,2 **MP**
5.	$\sim H$	3,4 **MT**

(Notice that in using **MP** to obtain line 4, we substituted $\sim N$ for the variable q. In using the eighteen valid argument forms, we may substitute *any* sentences, no matter how complex, provided we substitute *consistently*—that is, provided that whatever we substitute for one occurrence of a particular variable also is substituted for every occurrence of that variable in the given use of that argument form.)

1.	$(R \vee S) \supset (T \supset K)$	p
2.	$\sim K$	p
3.	$R \vee S$	p /∴ $\sim T$
4.	$T \supset K$	1,3 **MP**
5.	$\sim T$	2,4 **MT**

---

* Conditional and indirect proofs, introduced in the next chapter, are slightly different.

(Notice that in using **MP** to obtain line 4, the compound se
was substituted for *p* and the compound sentence $T \supset K$ was s
for *q*.)

4 *Disjunctive Syllogism and Hypothetical Syllogism*

Another of the eighteen valid argument forms is **Disjunctive Syllogism (DS),** which has two forms:

$p \vee q$ and $p \vee q$
$\sim p \quad /\therefore q$ $\quad \sim q \quad /\therefore p$

The truth table for the first version of **DS** is:

			First Premise	Second Premise	Conclusion
	p	q	$p \vee q$	$\sim p$	q
1.	**T**	**T**	**T**	**F**	**T**
2.	**T**	**F**	**T**	**F**	**F**
3.	**F**	**T**	**T**	**T**	**T**
4.	**F**	**F**	**F**	**T**	**F**

In this case, there is a **T** for both premises only on line 3, and there also is a **T** for the conclusion on that line. Hence, there is no substitution instance of this version of Disjunctive Syllogism having both of its premises true but its conclusion false. So this version of Disjunctive Syllogism is a valid argument form. (The reader should prove by truth table analysis that the other version of Disjunctive Syllogism is valid also.)

Now let's look at the valid argument form **Hypothetical Syllogism (HS):**

$p \supset q$
$q \supset r \quad /\therefore p \supset r$

The truth table for Hypothetical Syllogism contains eight lines, rather than four (as for **MP, MT,** and **DS**), because **HS** contains three variables, namely, *p*, *q*, and *r*.

				First Premise	**Second Premise**	**Conclusion**
				$p \supset q$	$q \supset r$	$p \supset r$
				T	**T**	**T**
				T	**F**	**F**
				F	**T**	**T**
				F	**T**	**F**
				T	**T**	**T**
6.	**F**	**T**	**F**	**T**	**F**	**T**
7.	**F**	**F**	**T**	**T**	**T**	**T**
8.	**F**	**F**	**F**	**T**	**T**	**T**

This truth table shows that both premises are true in lines 1, 5, 7, and 8, and in each of these lines the conclusion is true also. Hence, an argument of this form cannot have true premises and a false conclusion, and so must be valid. Therefore, Hypothetical Syllogism is a valid argument form.

Here is a proof using both Hypothetical Syllogism and Disjunctive Syllogism (as well as Modus Tollens):

1.	$A \vee B$	p
2.	$B \supset C$	p
3.	$A \supset B$	p
4.	$\sim C$	p $/\therefore B$
5.	$A \supset C$	2,3 **HS**
6.	$\sim A$	4,5 **MT**
7.	B	1,6 **DS**

Exercise 4-1:

For each line (other than premises) in the following proofs, state the line or lines from which it follows and the valid argument form (**MP, MT, DS,** or **HS**) used to obtain it. (The sample proof illustrates this procedure.)

Sample Proof

1.	$A \supset \sim B$	p
2.	$\sim\sim B$	p
3.	$\sim A$	1,2 **MT** (correct justification for line 3)

(1) 1. $A \supset B$ p
2. $A \vee C$ p
3. $\sim B$ p
4. $\sim A$
5. C

(2) 1. $D \vee E$ p
2. $D \supset \sim A$ p
3. $\sim E$ p
4. $A \vee B$ p
5. D
6. $\sim A$
7. B

(3) 1. $\sim R$ p
2. $\sim S \supset T$ p
3. $(A \supset B) \supset \sim S$ p
4. $\sim R \supset (A \supset B)$ p
5. $\sim R \supset \sim S$
6. $\sim R \supset T$
7. T

(4) 1. $A \supset (B \supset C)$ p
2. $\sim\sim F$ p
3. $\sim D \supset A$ p
4. $\sim C \vee \sim F$ p
5. $\sim D$ p
6. $\sim D \supset (B \supset C)$
7. $B \supset C$
8. $\sim C$
9. $\sim B$

(5) 1. $A \supset (B \supset C)$ p
2. $H \supset A$ p
3. $H \vee (A \vee B)$ p
4. $\sim(B \supset C)$ p
5. $\sim A$
6. $\sim H$
7. $A \vee B$
8. B

(6) 1. $(H \vee K) \supset R$ p
2. $A \supset (\sim M \supset \sim R)$ p
3. $\sim M$ p
4. $A \vee M$ p
5. A
6. $\sim M \supset \sim R$
7. $\sim R$
8. $\sim(H \vee K)$

Exercise 4-2:

Use **MP, MT, DS,** and **HS** to prove that the following arguments are valid.

(1) 1. $\sim R$ p
2. $S \supset R$ p /∴ $\sim S$

(2) 1. $R \supset S$ p
2. $T \supset R$ p
3. $\sim S$ p /∴ $\sim T$

(3) 1. $\sim M$ p
2. $N \supset G$ p
3. $N \vee M$ p /∴ G

(4) 1. $\sim G \supset (A \vee B)$ p
2. $\sim B$ p
3. $A \supset D$ p
4. $\sim G$ p /∴ D

(5) 1. $(A \supset B) \supset C$ p
2. $\sim D \vee A$ p

3. $\sim D \supset (A \supset B)$ p
4. $\sim A$ p $/\therefore C$

(6) 1. $A \supset (B \supset C)$ p
2. $\sim C$ p
3. $\sim D \supset A$ p
4. $C \vee \sim D$ p $/\therefore \sim B$

5 *Simplification and Conjunction*

Another of the eighteen valid argument forms is **Simplification (Simp),** which, like **DS,** has two forms:

$p \cdot q \;/\therefore p$ and $p \cdot q \;/\therefore q$

The truth table for the first version of Simplification is:

			Premise	Conclusion
	p	q	$p \cdot q$	p
1.	**T**	**T**	**T**	**T**
2.	**T**	**F**	**F**	**T**
3.	**F**	**T**	**F**	**F**
4.	**F**	**F**	**F**	**F**

In this case, there is a **T** for the premise only on line 1, and there also is a **T** for the conclusion on that line. So there is no substitution instance of this version of Simplification having a true premise and a false conclusion. Hence, this version of Simplification is a valid argument form. (The reader should prove by truth table analysis that the other version of Simplification is valid also.)

Now let's look at the valid argument form **Conjunction (Conj):**

p
$q \;/\therefore p \cdot q$

The truth table for Conjunction is:

			First Premise	Second Premise	Conclusion
	p	q	p	q	$p \cdot q$
1.	**T**	**T**	**T**	**T**	**T**
2.	**T**	**F**	**T**	**F**	**F**
3.	**F**	**T**	**F**	**T**	**F**
4.	**F**	**F**	**F**	**F**	**F**

In this case, there is a **T** for both premises only on line 1. There also is a **T** for the conclusion on that line. Hence, Conjunction is a valid argument form.

6 *Addition and Constructive Dilemma*

Another of the eighteen valid argument forms is **Addition (Add):**

$p \quad /\therefore p \vee q$

Its truth table is:

			Premise	Conclusion
	p	q	p	$p \vee q$
1.	T	T	T	T
2.	T	F	T	T
3.	F	T	F	T
4.	F	F	F	F

In this case, there is a **T** for the premise on lines 1 and 2, and there also is a **T** for the conclusion on each of these lines. So Addition is a valid argument form.

Now, let's look at the valid argument form **Constructive Dilemma (CD):**

$p \supset q$

$r \supset s$

$p \vee r \quad /\therefore q \vee s$

Since there are four letters (p, q, r, and s) in this form, its truth table has sixteen lines:

					First Premise	Second Premise	Third Premise	Conclusion
	p	q	r	s	$p \supset q$	$r \supset s$	$p \vee r$	$q \vee s$
1.	T	T	T	T	T	T	T	T
2.	T	T	T	F	T	F	T	T
3.	T	T	F	T	T	T	T	T
4.	T	T	F	F	T	T	T	T
5.	T	F	T	T	F	T	T	T
6.	T	F	T	F	F	F	T	F
7.	T	F	F	T	F	T	T	T
8.	T	F	F	F	F	T	T	F
9.	F	T	T	T	T	T	T	T
10.	F	T	T	F	T	F	T	T
11.	F	T	F	T	T	T	F	T
12.	F	T	F	F	T	T	F	T
13.	F	F	T	T	T	T	T	T
14.	F	F	T	F	T	F	T	F
15.	F	F	F	T	T	T	F	T
16.	F	F	F	F	T	T	F	F

In this case, there is an **F** for the conclusion only on lines 6, 8, 14, and 16. If there were a **T** for all three premises on any one of these lines, then Constructive Dilemma would be an invalid form. But in each of these four cases, there is an **F** for at least one of the premises. So none of the sixteen possible kinds of substitution instances of Constructive Dilemma has all true premises and a false conclusion. Therefore, Constructive Dilemma is a valid argument form.

Here is an example of an argument that has the form **CD:**

1. If a Democrat is elected, then taxes will go up.
2. But if a Republican is elected, then unemployment will go up.
3. A Democrat or a Republican will be elected.

/∴ 4. Either taxes will go up or unemployment will go up.

In symbols, this reads:

1. $D \supset T$
2. $R \supset U$
3. $D \vee R$

/∴ 4. $T \vee U$

The eight valid argument forms we have just introduced work in *one direction* only. They permit inference, for example, from $A \cdot B$ to A, by Simplification, but surely not from A to $A \cdot B$. (This is the chief difference between the eight valid argument forms just presented and the ten to be discussed next.) One-directional argument forms are said to be **implicational argument forms.**

Here is the complete list of eight valid implicational argument forms to be used as rules of inference in our system:*

Valid Implicational Argument Forms (Rules of Inference)

1. **Modus Ponens (MP):**

$p \supset q$
p /∴ q

2. **Modus Tollens (MT):**

$p \supset q$
$\sim q$ /∴ $\sim p$

3. **Disjunctive Syllogism (DS):**

$p \vee q$
$\sim p$ /∴ q

$p \vee q$
$\sim q$ /∴ p

4. **Simplification (Simp):**

$p \cdot q$ /∴ p
$p \cdot q$ /∴ q

*For handy reference, this list of valid argument forms and the one on page 68 are printed on the inside front cover.

5. **Conjunction (Conj):**

   p
   $q \quad /\therefore p \cdot q$

6. **Hypothetical Syllogism (HS):**

   $p \supset q$
   $q \supset r \quad /\therefore p \supset r$

7. **Addition (Add):**

   $p \quad /\therefore p \vee q$

8. **Constructive Dilemma (CD):**

   $p \supset q$
   $r \supset s$
   $p \vee r \quad /\therefore q \vee s$

Exercise 4-3:

For each line (other than premises) in the following proofs, state the line or lines from which it follows and the valid implicational argument form on the above list used to obtain that line.

(1)
1. $A \supset \sim B$ p
2. $A \vee C$ p
3. $\sim\sim B \cdot D$ p
4. $\sim\sim B$
5. $\sim A$
6. C

(2)
1. $A \supset B$ p
2. $A \cdot \sim D$ p
3. $B \supset C$ p
4. A
5. $A \supset C$
6. C
7. $\sim D$
8. $C \cdot \sim D$

(3)
1. C p
2. $A \supset B$ p
3. $C \supset D$ p
4. $D \supset E$ p
5. $C \supset E$
6. $C \vee A$
7. $E \vee B$

(4)
1. $(A \vee M) \supset R$ p
2. $(L \supset R) \cdot \sim R$ p
3. $\sim(C \cdot D) \vee (A \vee M)$ p
4. $\sim R$
5. $\sim(A \vee M)$
6. $\sim(C \cdot D)$

(5)
1. $(D \vee \sim H) \supset [R \cdot (S \vee T)]$ p
2. L p
3. $(L \vee M) \supset (D \cdot E)$ p
4. $L \vee M$
5. $D \cdot E$
6. D
7. $D \vee \sim H$
8. $R \cdot (S \vee T)$
9. $S \vee T$
10. $D \cdot (S \vee T)$

(6)
1. $(R \cdot S) \supset \sim(Q \vee T)$ p
2. $\sim B$ p
3. $(Q \vee T) \vee \sim(\sim B \cdot \sim A)$ p
4. $(\sim B \vee A) \supset (R \cdot S)$ p
5. $(\sim B \vee A) \supset \sim(Q \vee T)$
6. $\sim B \vee A$
7. $\sim(Q \vee T)$
8. $\sim(\sim B \cdot \sim A)$
9. $\sim(\sim B \cdot \sim A) \cdot \sim B$

Exercise 4-4:

Use the eight implicational argument forms to prove that the following arguments are valid.

(1) 1. $A \cdot B$
2. $B \supset C$ $/\therefore C$

(2) 1. $C \supset A$
2. $A \supset (B \cdot D)$
3. C $/\therefore B$

(3) 1. $A \supset B$
2. $C \cdot A$ $/\therefore B \vee D$

(4) 1. $(F \supset G) \vee H$
2. $\sim G$
3. $\sim H$ $/\therefore \sim F$

(5) 1. $(A \cdot D) \supset \sim C$
2. $(R \vee S) \supset (A \cdot D)$
3. $\sim C \supset \sim(A \cdot D)$
$/\therefore$ $(R \vee S) \supset \sim(A \cdot D)$

(6) 1. $(A \vee \sim C) \supset B$
2. A
3. $(A \vee \sim D) \supset (R \cdot S)$
$/\therefore$ $(R \cdot S) \vee B$

(7) 1. $(R \cdot A) \vee E$
2. $(R \cdot A) \supset D$
3. $\sim D$ $/\therefore E \cdot \sim D$

(8) 1. $\sim A$
2. $(C \vee A) \supset L$
3. $A \vee D$
4. $(D \vee U) \supset C$ $/\therefore L$

(9) 1. $R \supset (\sim P \vee \sim M)$
2. $\sim R \supset (\sim M \cdot \sim N)$
3. $\sim(\sim P \vee \sim M)$
4. $Z \vee R$ $/\therefore (\sim M \cdot \sim N) \cdot Z$

(10) 1. $[\sim A \cdot \sim(D \cdot E)] \supset (B \supset \sim D)$
2. $\sim(D \cdot E) \cdot \sim R$
3. $E \supset F$
4. $\sim A \vee (D \cdot E)$
5. $\sim(D \cdot E) \supset (B \vee E)$
$/\therefore \sim D \vee F$

7 *Double Negation and DeMorgan's Theorem*

We noted above that implicational argument forms are one-directional, and permit, for instance, inference from $A \cdot B$ to A, but not the reverse inference from A to $A \cdot B$. The sentence $A \cdot B$ *implies* the sentence A, but is *not equivalent* to it. (So the argument A $/\therefore A \cdot B$ is invalid.)

But now, consider the valid inference from A to $\sim\sim A$. In this case, we can reverse the process, that is, we can validly infer from $\sim\sim A$ to A. This reversibility is due to the fact that the sentence A not only implies the sentence $\sim\sim A$ but also is equivalent (indeed logically equivalent) to it, and equivalent sentences imply each other. It follows then that both of the following argument forms are valid:

1. p $/\therefore \sim\sim p$
2. $\sim\sim p$ $/\therefore p$

Since these two argument forms are just the reverse of each other, we can simplify matters by combining them into one "two-directional" argument form. Let's introduce the symbol "::" and use it to indicate that an argument form is two-directional. Then we can combine the above two one-directional (implicational) forms into one two-directional (equivalence) form as follows:

$p :: {\sim}{\sim}p$

This equivalence argument form is called **Double Negation (DN).** It permits inferences from any substitution instance of p to the analogous substitution instance of ${\sim}{\sim}p$, and from any substitution instance of ${\sim}{\sim}p$ to the analogous substitution instance of p. Thus, it permits all of the inferences permitted by the two implicational argument forms $p \quad /\therefore {\sim}{\sim}p$ and ${\sim}{\sim}p \quad /\therefore p$.

Argument forms, such as Double Negation, that permit inferences in both directions are called **equivalence argument forms** (because they permit inferences from given statements to statements with which they are logically equivalent).

Now let's consider the pair of valid equivalence argument forms called **DeMorgan's Theorem (DeM):**

${\sim}(p \cdot q) :: ({\sim}p \vee {\sim}q)$

${\sim}(p \vee q) :: ({\sim}p \cdot {\sim}q)$

The first of these forms permits inferences from any substitution instance of ${\sim}(p \cdot q)$ to the analogous substitution instance of ${\sim}p \vee {\sim}q$, and from ${\sim}p \vee {\sim}q$ to the analogous substitution instance of ${\sim}(p \cdot q)$; the second permits similar substitutions in both directions.

DeMorgan's Theorem is intuitively valid. For instance, it permits the intuitively valid inferences from

1. It's not true that Art and Betsy both will go to the show

in symbols ${\sim}(A \cdot B)$, to

2. Either Art won't go to the show or Betsy won't go to the show

in symbols ${\sim}A \vee {\sim}B$, and from

3. Art won't go and Betsy won't go

in symbols ${\sim}A \cdot {\sim}B$, to

4. It's not true that either Art will go or Betsy will go

in symbols ${\sim}(A \vee B)$.

One way to establish the validity of an equivalence argument form is to prove the validity of each of the two implicational forms of which it is composed. Another way is to prove that the sentence form to the left of the "::" sign is equivalent to the sentence form to the right. For instance, the truth table analysis:

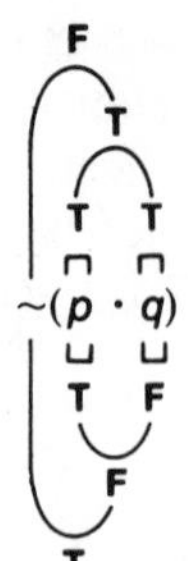

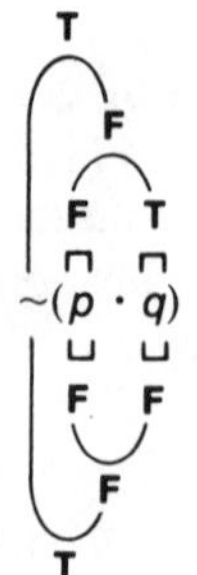

proves that the first version of DeMorgan's Theorem is valid, because it shows that the two sentence forms $\sim(p \cdot q)$ and $(\sim p \vee \sim q)$ are equivalent. In tabular form, this truth table reads:

				Left Side			Right Side
	p	q	$p \cdot q$	$\sim(p \cdot q)$	$\sim p$	$\sim q$	$\sim p \vee \sim q$
1.	T	T	T	F	F	F	F
2.	T	F	F	T	F	T	T
3.	F	T	F	T	T	F	T
4.	F	F	F	T	T	T	T

This shows that the left and right sides of the argument form $\sim(p \cdot q) :: (\sim p \vee \sim q)$ are equivalent (have the same truth values for any given assignment of truth values to p and q) and hence shows that this version of DeMorgan's Theorem is valid. (The reader should prove that the other version is valid also.)

8 *Commutation, Association, and Distribution*

Intuitively, the statement "Art will go or Betsy will go" ($A \vee B$) is equivalent to the statement "Betsy will go or Art will go", and the statement "Art will go and Betsy will go" is equivalent to the statement "Betsy will go and Art will go". These intuitions are captured by the two equivalence forms called **Commutation (Comm):**

$(p \vee q) :: (q \vee p)$

$(p \cdot q) :: (q \cdot p)$

The import of these two Commutation principles is that reversing the order of statements connected by "$\cdot$" or "$\vee$" does not change the truth values of the compound sentences they form. (The reader should prove by truth table analysis that both forms of Commutation are valid.)

Notice that Commutation does not hold for sentences connected by "$\supset$". For instance, the sentence "If Ronald Reagan is elected, then a

Californian is elected" $(R \supset C)$ is certainly not equivalent to the analogous statement "If a Californian is elected, then Ronald Reagan is elected" $(C \supset R)$.

Now consider the valid equivalence argument forms called **Association (Assoc):**

$[p \vee (q \vee r)] :: [(p \vee q) \vee r]$

$[p \cdot (q \cdot r)] :: [(p \cdot q) \cdot r]$

The point of these two argument forms is that the movement of parentheses in either of the ways specified does not change the truth values of compound sentences in which they occur. (The reader should prove by truth table analysis that both forms of Association are valid.)

Notice that Association holds only for compounds formed by two occurrences of " $\vee$ " or two occurrences of " $\cdot$ ". Thus, an inference from, say, $A \vee (B \cdot C)$ to $(A \vee B) \cdot C$ is *invalid*. Similarly, Association does not hold for compounds formed by two occurrences of "$\supset$". For instance, the inference from $A \supset (B \supset C)$ to $(A \supset B) \supset C$ is *invalid*.

Next, let's look at the two valid equivalence argument forms called **Distribution (Dist):**

$[p \cdot (q \vee r)] :: [(p \cdot q) \vee (p \cdot r)]$

$[p \vee (q \cdot r)] :: [(p \vee q) \cdot (p \vee r)]$

The truth table proofs of validity for Disribution are longer than those for the other equivalence rules discussed so far. Here is the proof for the second form of Distribution:

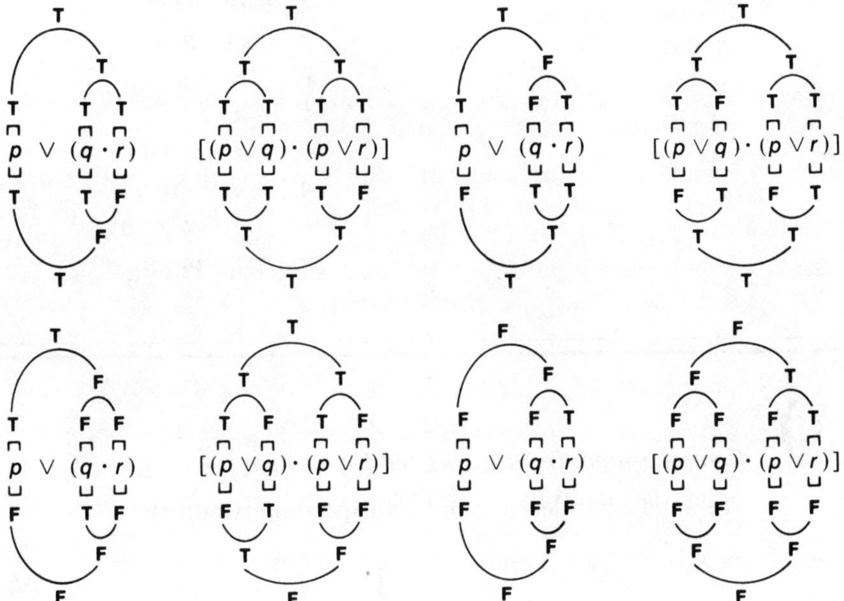

This proves that the second version of the equivalence argument form Distribution is valid, because it shows that the sentence forms $p \vee (q \cdot r)$ and $(p \vee q) \cdot (p \vee r)$ are equivalent. (The reader should prove the other version.)

Exercise 4-5:

For each line (other than premises) in the following proofs, state the line or lines from which it follows and the valid argument form used to obtain it.

(1)
1. $(B \cdot C) \vee D$ p
2. $\sim C$ p
3. $D \vee (B \cdot C)$
4. $(D \vee B) \cdot (D \vee C)$
5. $D \vee C$
6. D

(2)
1. R p
2. $(\sim C \vee \sim D) \vee S$ p
3. $\sim(D \cdot C) \supset \sim R$ p
4. $\sim\sim R$
5. $\sim(C \cdot D) \supset \sim R$
6. $\sim\sim(C \cdot D)$
7. $\sim(C \cdot D) \vee S$
8. S

(3)
1. $(A \cdot B) \vee C$ p
2. $\sim(A \vee \sim D)$ p
3. $C \vee (A \cdot B)$
4. $(C \vee A) \cdot (C \vee B)$
5. $C \vee A$
6. $\sim A \cdot \sim\sim D$
7. $\sim A$
8. C

(4)
1. $(A \vee B) \vee \sim C$ p
2. $(\sim A \cdot \sim C) \vee (\sim A \cdot D)$ p
3. $A \vee (B \vee \sim C)$
4. $\sim A \cdot (\sim C \vee D)$
5. $\sim A$
6. $\sim C \vee D$
7. $B \vee \sim C$
8. $\sim C \vee B$
9. $(\sim C \vee B) \cdot (\sim C \vee D)$
10. $\sim C \vee (B \cdot D)$

(5)
1. $\sim R \vee S$ p
2. $(A \vee B) \supset (R \cdot \sim S)$ p
3. $\sim R \vee \sim\sim S$
4. $\sim(R \cdot \sim S)$
5. $\sim(A \vee B)$
6. $\sim A \cdot \sim B$
7. $\sim A$
8. $\sim A \vee (\sim B \vee D)$
9. $(\sim A \vee \sim B) \vee D$
10. $D \vee (\sim A \vee \sim B)$
11. $D \vee \sim(A \cdot B)$

---

9 *Contraposition, Implication, and Exportation*

The valid equivalence form **Contraposition (Contra)**

$(p \supset q) :: (\sim q \supset \sim p)$

is useful when dealing with conditional sentences, in particular in some uses of the rule of conditional proof (to be introduced in Chapter Five).

The valid equivalence form **Implication (Impl)**

$(p \supset q) :: (\sim p \vee q)$

also is useful, in this case when we need to replace a conditional sentence by its disjunctive equivalent, or a disjunction by its conditional equivalent.

Contraposition is intuitively valid, and indeed holds for all kinds of implicational sentences, truth-functional or non-truth-functional.* But Implication holds only for truth-functional implications, that is, for *material implications* (hence the name "material implication" sometimes used for this valid equivalence form).

Next, let's look at the valid equivalence argument form called **Exportation (Exp):**

$[(p \cdot q) \supset r] :: [p \supset (q \supset r)]$

This rule captures the intuitive idea that if the conjunction of two sentences, $(p \cdot q)$, implies a third, then the first (p) implies that the second (q) implies the third (and vice versa). For instance, if it is true that if Frank is intelligent and works hard, then he'll get an A in his philosophy class (in symbols $(I \cdot H) \supset A$), then it follows that if he is intelligent, then if he works hard, he'll get an A (in symbols $I \supset (H \supset A)$).

The reader should prove by truth table analysis that Contraposition, Implication, and Exportation are valid argument forms.

10 *Tautology and Equivalence*

The two valid equivalence forms called **Tautology (Taut):**

$p :: (p \cdot p)$

$p :: (p \vee p)$

are used chiefly to get rid of redundant letters, as in the following proof:

1.	$A \supset \sim A$	p /∴ $\sim A$
2.	$\sim A \vee \sim A$	1, **Impl**
3.	$\sim A$	2, **Taut**

---

*This is certainly true for implications in the indicative mood. Whether it's true for implications in the subjunctive mood, such as the contrary to fact conditional "If Carter had been reelected in 1980, then Amy would have attended a private school in Washington", is another matter.

The two valid equivalence forms called **Equivalence (Equiv):**

$(p \equiv q) :: [(p \supset q) \cdot (q \supset p)]$

$(p \equiv q) :: [(p \cdot q) \vee (\sim p \cdot \sim q)]$

(the last of the eighteen valid forms to be introduced into our system), are needed to manipulate statements in which the symbol "≡" occurs, as in the following proof:

1.	$A \equiv B$	p
2.	B	p /∴ A
3.	$(A \supset B) \cdot (B \supset A)$	1, **Equiv**
4.	$B \supset A$	3, **Simp**
5.	A	2,4 **MP**

Here is a list of the ten valid equivalence argument forms to be used along with the eight valid implicational forms listed on pages 60–61 as rules of inference in our system:*

Valid Equivalence Argument Forms

9. **Double Negation (DN):**

$p :: \sim\sim p$

10. **DeMorgan's Theorem (DeM):**

$\sim(p \cdot q) :: (\sim p \vee \sim q)$

$\sim(p \vee q) :: (\sim p \cdot \sim q)$

11. **Commutation (Comm):**

$(p \vee q) :: (q \vee p)$

$(p \cdot q) :: (q \cdot p)$

12. **Association (Assoc):**

$[p \vee (q \vee r)] :: [(p \vee q) \vee r]$

$[p \cdot (q \cdot r)] :: [(p \cdot q) \cdot r]$

13. **Distribution (Dist):**

$[p \cdot (q \vee r)] :: [(p \cdot q) \vee (p \cdot r)]$

$[p \vee (q \cdot r)] :: [(p \vee q) \cdot (p \vee r)]$

14. **Contraposition (Contra):**

$(p \supset q) :: (\sim q \supset \sim p)$

15. **Implication (Impl):**

$(p \supset q) :: (\sim p \vee q)$

16. **Exportation (Exp):**

$[(p \cdot q) \supset r] :: [p \supset (q \supset r)]$

17. **Tautology (Taut):**

$p :: (p \cdot p)$

$p :: (p \vee p)$

18. **Equivalence (Equiv):**

$(p \equiv q) :: [(p \supset q) \cdot (q \supset p)]$

$(p \equiv q) :: [(p \cdot q) \vee (\sim p \cdot \sim q)]$

* Instead of using valid equivalence *argument* forms, many logic texts introduce about ten tautological equivalence *sentence* forms, such as $p \equiv \sim\sim p$ and $(p \supset q) \equiv (\sim p \vee q)$, plus a rule permitting infer-

It may be asked why we have chosen just these eighteen valid argument forms. In the first place, there are an infinite number of valid argument forms, so we could not prove and list every one. On the other hand, we don't want to list only the minimum number of argument forms required for a complete sentential logic, for such a short list would make proofs quite difficult to construct and much longer than is desirable. The usual procedure is to strike a happy medium, proving and listing about ten to twenty of the commonly used valid argument forms, making sure that the system is *complete* (that is, making sure that every valid argument of sentential logic can be proved using the listed valid argument forms). Our list of eighteen valid argument forms contains most of the commonly used forms and at the same time is complete (or, rather, will be complete when the rule of conditional proof is introduced in the next chapter).

One final reminder. When we use an equivalence argument form, we move from a given expression to one that is equivalent to it. Hence, we can use equivalence argument forms on parts of lines without fear of changing truth values, and thus without fear of inferring from true premises to a false conclusion. Thus, we can use Double Negation to infer validly from $A \vee B$ to $\sim\sim A \vee B$, because A is equivalent to $\sim\sim A$ and hence $A \vee B$ is equivalent to $\sim\sim A \vee B$. This is the important difference between equivalence and implicational argument forms: *Implicational argument forms must be used on whole lines only; equivalence forms may be used on parts of lines.*

Exercise 4-6:

For each line (other than premises) in the following proofs, state the line or lines from which it follows and the valid argument form used to obtain it.

(1)

1. $E \equiv F$ p
2. $\sim E \vee \sim F$ p
3. $(E \cdot F) \vee (\sim E \cdot \sim F)$
4. $\sim(E \cdot F)$
5. $\sim(E \cdot F) \vee E$
6. $(E \cdot F) \supset E$
7. $E \supset \sim F$
8. $(E \cdot F) \supset \sim F$
9. $E \supset (F \supset \sim F)$
10. $E \supset (\sim F \vee \sim F)$
11. $E \supset \sim F$

(2)

1. $A \supset (\sim B \supset C)$ p
2. $\sim B$ p
3. $\sim C$ p

---

ences from substitution instances of one side of these equivalences to analogous substitution instances of the other side. Proofs in such a system are just like proofs in our system. In fact, the differences between the two systems are entirely theoretical.

4. $\sim C \cdot \sim B$
5. $\sim(C \vee B)$
6. $A \supset (\sim B \supset \sim\sim C)$
7. $A \supset (\sim C \supset B)$
8. $A \supset (\sim\sim C \vee B)$
9. $A \supset (C \vee B)$
10. $\sim A$

(3)
1. $\sim H \supset \sim G$ p
2. $(R \vee \sim H) \vee K$ p
3. $(\sim H \vee R) \vee K$
4. $\sim H \vee (R \vee K)$
5. $H \supset (R \vee K)$
6. $G \supset H$
7. $G \supset (R \vee K)$
8. $\sim G \vee (R \vee K)$
9. $(\sim G \vee R) \vee K$
10. $K \vee (\sim G \vee R)$
11. $\sim\sim K \vee (\sim G \vee R)$
12. $\sim K \supset (\sim G \vee R)$
13. $\sim K \supset (G \supset R)$

(4)
1. $G \equiv (H \cdot K)$ p
2. $\sim G \supset H$ p
3. $K \vee G$ p
4. $[G \cdot (H \cdot K)] \vee [\sim G \cdot \sim(H \cdot K)]$
5. $\sim\sim G \vee H$
6. $G \vee H$
7. $G \vee K$
8. $(G \vee H) \cdot (G \vee K)$
9. $G \vee (H \cdot K)$
10. $\sim\sim G \vee (H \cdot K)$
11. $\sim\sim G \vee \sim\sim(H \cdot K)$
12. $\sim[\sim G \cdot \sim(H \cdot K)]$
13. $G \cdot (H \cdot K)$
14. G

(5)
1. $(R \equiv \sim S) \supset \sim R$ p
2. $\sim R \vee \sim S$ p
3. $[(R \supset \sim S) \cdot (\sim S \supset R)] \supset \sim R$
4. $\sim[(R \supset \sim S) \cdot (\sim S \supset R)] \vee \sim R$
5. $[\sim(R \supset \sim S) \vee \sim(\sim S \supset R)] \vee \sim R$
6. $[\sim(\sim R \vee \sim S) \vee \sim(\sim\sim S \vee R)] \vee \sim R$
7. $[\sim(\sim R \vee \sim S) \vee \sim(S \vee R)] \vee \sim R$
8. $[(\sim\sim R \cdot \sim\sim S) \vee (\sim S \cdot \sim R)] \vee \sim R$
9. $[(R \cdot S) \vee (\sim S \cdot \sim R)] \vee \sim R$
10. $(R \cdot S) \vee [(\sim S \cdot \sim R) \vee \sim R]$
11. $\sim(R \cdot S)$
12. $(\sim S \cdot \sim R) \vee \sim R$
13. $\sim R \vee (\sim S \cdot \sim R)$
14. $(\sim R \vee \sim S) \cdot (\sim R \vee \sim R)$
15. $\sim R \vee \sim R$
16. $\sim R$

11 *Principles of Strategy*

Books on chess and checkers often start out with a brief summary of the rules of the game, a list of rules indicating which kinds of moves are permitted. But the major part of a book of this kind discusses not permissive rules, but what might be called *principles of strategy*. The permissive rules usually allow more than one move (for instance, there are twenty permitted opening moves in a game of chess). But only a very few of these are likely to lead to winning positions. A good chess book helps the chess student to get the "feel" of good play, and to become familiar with principles of good strategy, principles that in general lead to strong positions. (For example, in chess, other things being equal, it is good strategy to develop a piece into the center of the board rather than to one side.) Of course, as every chess tyro soon learns, strict adherence to conventional strategy sometimes leads to disaster.

The analogy between the game of chess and the "game" of logic-problem-solving is very close. The eighteen valid argument forms (plus the rules to be added later) correspond to the rules of chess. They determine which steps (moves) are permitted in an argument or proof. But generally they permit many steps at any given point in a proof, only a very few of which are likely to lead to "winning the game", that is, to deriving the conclusion of the argument. A good logic player is one who develops a feel for good play, perhaps by becoming familiar with good strategy principles. Of course, principles useful to one person may not be useful to another, for psychological reasons. The few hints given below have proved useful to many students.

It should be remembered, however, that just as chess strategy principles are not part of the rules of chess, so logic strategy principles are not part of the rules of logic. In fact, logic strategy rules belong not to the context of justification, but rather to the context of discovery, since they do not justify moves in proofs, but rather help us to discover winning moves. The justification for the assertion of a line in a proof must always be a valid argument form or rule of inference.

Perhaps the most important strategy rule is to *look for forms that correspond to valid rules of inference*. Consider the following argument:

1. $[A \vee (\sim B \supset C)] \supset [\sim D \vee (C \cdot E)]$
2. $\sim[\sim D \vee (C \cdot E)]$ $\quad /\therefore \sim[A \vee (\sim B \supset C)]$

Beginners are likely to be overwhelmed by the large number of letters in this argument, or by the complexity of its premises, and thus be unable to discover a proof for it. But if they try to "see" the premises and conclusion in terms of their major forms, they will discover that the proof is quite simple. Notice that the major connective of the premise on line 1 is an implication, and that that premise has the form $p \supset q$. Now notice that the major connective of line 2 is negation, and that line 2 has the form $\sim q$, since what is negated on line 2 is the consequent (q) of line 1. (So the first two lines of the proof have the forms $p \supset q$ and $\sim q$.) Clearly here is an opportunity to use the argument form Modus Tollens, to obtain $\sim p$, which in this case is $\sim[A \vee \sim B \supset C]$, the desired conclusion. So we have "figured out" a simple proof:

1.	$[A \vee (\sim B \supset C)] \supset [\sim D \vee (C \cdot E)]$	p
2.	$\sim[\sim D \vee (C \cdot E)]$	p $\quad /\therefore \sim[A \vee (\sim B \supset C)]$
3.	$\sim[A \vee (\sim B \supset C)]$	1,2 **MT**

A simple proof indeed, once attention is paid to the general forms of the sentences that make up the proof.

Now consider another argument:

1. $\sim(A \vee B)$
2. $\sim A \supset C \quad /\therefore C$

Notice first that the letter *B* does not occur in the conclusion and that it occurs in the premises only once. Obviously, the information its presence adds to premise 1 is not necessary in deriving the conclusion. *A letter that occurs only once in the premises of an argument and not at all in the conclusion usually is excess baggage,* to be gotten rid of or (if possible) ignored. In this case, we can get rid of the superfluous letter *B* by separating the information it contains (which is not needed to derive the conclusion) from the other information contained in premise 1 (which *is* needed to derive the conclusion). We can do so by means of DeMorgan's Theorem, which should have suggested itself anyway because of the form of the first premise. So the start of our proof should be as follows:

1.	$\sim(A \vee B)$	p
2.	$\sim A \supset C$	p $/\therefore C$
3.	$\sim A \cdot \sim B$	1, **DeM**

The obvious next step is

4.	$\sim A$	3, **Simp**

thus getting rid of the unwanted letter *B*. And concluding with

5.	C	2,4 **MP**

Now consider the following proof:

1.	$C \supset A$	p
2.	$M \supset B$	p
3.	$B \supset C$	p
4.	M	p $/\therefore A$

Notice that the letter *A*, which occurs in the conclusion, is connected to the letter *C* in one of the premises, and *C* to *B*, and *B* to *M*. It is often useful to *trace the connections between the letters occurring in an argument, starting with the letter (or letters) occurring in the conclusion.* And then, having done so, it is often good strategy to *begin the proof with the letter (or letters) most distant from those in the conclusion,* which in this case means beginning with the letter *M*. So in this case, it is good strategy to begin the proof by using lines 2 and 4, which contain the letter *M*, to obtain a new line in the proof, namely:

5.	B	2,4 **MP**

The proof then continues

6.	C	3,5 **MP**
7.	A	1,6 **MP**

This proof also illustrates the fact that usually it is not fruitful to use the same line in a proof over and over again. *"Fresh information" (an untapped line in a proof) tends to be most useful.* Thus, after line 6 has been written down, every premise has been used in the proof except premise 1. At this point, the information in premise 1 is untapped, unused, and the information on line 6 is fresh, in the sense that it is *psychologically* new information. This is a strong clue that it is time to use line 6, in conjunction with premise 1, as in fact it is used to obtain line 7.

Let's reexamine one of the proofs considered on page 72, namely:

1.	$\sim(A \vee B)$	p
2.	$\sim A \supset C$	p /∴ C
3.	$\sim A \cdot \sim B$	1, **DeM**
4.	$\sim A$	3, **Simp**
5.	C	2,4 **MP**

As stated before, the key to the proof is line 3, obtained by using DeMorgan's Theorem. But line 4 is interesting also, since it illustrates the use of Simplification, and the power of breaking down large sentences into smaller ones. In general, *a letter (or negated letter) alone on a line is very useful in obtaining a desired conclusion.* And the most common method for obtaining a letter alone on a line is by Simplification.

It is often good strategy to *work backward from the conclusion* as well as forward from the premises. If we work backward from the conclusion and find a sentence that appears derivable from the premises, then we have discovered an intermediate target to aim at and have divided a relatively difficult task into two easier ones.

Consider the argument

1.	$A \supset B$	p
2.	$C \supset B$	p /∴ $(A \vee C) \supset B$

We can work backward from the conclusion, as follows:

i.	$(A \vee C) \supset B$	p (the conclusion)
ii.	$\sim(A \vee C) \vee B$	i, **Impl**
iii.	$(\sim A \cdot \sim C) \vee B$	ii, **DeM**
iv.	$B \vee (\sim A \cdot \sim C)$	iii, **Comm**
v.	$(B \vee \sim A) \cdot (B \vee \sim C)$	iv, **Dist**

At this point, we have learned that the conclusion $(A \vee C) \supset B$ is equivalent to $(B \vee \sim A) \cdot (B \vee \sim C)$. So by working backward from the conclusion, we have learned that the problem can be solved by working *forward* from the premises toward the intermediate sentence

$(B \vee \sim A) \cdot (B \vee \sim C)$. This turns out to be fairly easy to do, as the following illustrates:

1.	$A \supset B$	p
2.	$C \supset B$	p /∴ $(A \vee C) \supset B$
3.	$\sim A \vee B$	1, **Impl**
4.	$B \vee \sim A$	3, **Comm**
5.	$\sim C \vee B$	2, **Impl**
6.	$B \vee \sim C$	5, **Comm**
7.	$(B \vee \sim A) \cdot (B \vee \sim C)$	4,6 **Conj**

We are now ready to reverse the process of working backward from the conclusion, as follows:

8.	$B \vee (\sim A \cdot \sim C)$	7, **Dist**
9.	$(\sim A \cdot \sim C) \vee B$	8, **Comm**
10.	$\sim(A \vee C) \vee B$	9, **DeM**
11.	$(A \vee C) \supset B$	10, **Impl**

So by working backward from the conclusion as well as forward from the premises, we were able to construct a proof that might otherwise have eluded us.*

Finally, there is the desperation strategy rule of trial and error: *when completely stuck, try something—anything—you haven't tried yet.*

12 Common Errors in Problem Solving

There are several kinds of mistakes that beginners are likely to make in deriving proofs for arguments.

Using Implicational Forms on Parts of Lines

The valid implicational forms (numbers 1 through 8) can be used on *complete lines only*. For instance, we cannot go from

$(A \cdot B) \supset C$

---

*In the above example, we used only equivalence (two-directional) argument forms when working backward from the conclusion, because we wanted to be able to reverse the process. However, using a slightly different procedure, it's possible to also use any of the eight implication (one-directional) argument forms (for instance, *MP*, or *Conj*) and construct a proof working from the conclusion back up to the premises. But in doing so, beginners are apt to accidentally use the implication forms in the wrong direction, thus constructing invalid proofs. And anyway, in the vast majority of cases, it turns out to be easier and more intuitive to use more straightforward proof strategies. So beginners should avoid using implication argument forms when using the backward proof strategy; little will be lost and there will be no worry about using an argument form in one direction when it then cannot validly be reversed.

to

$(A \supset C)$ 5, **Simp**

dropping the letter *B* by Simplification. The reason is that the form of this process, namely $(p \cdot q) \supset r \;\; /\therefore\; (p \supset r)$, is *not* the form of Simplification, and, in fact, is an invalid argument form. (An example of an invalid argument that has this form is the following: If George drives an automobile 70 miles per hour and smashes into a reinforced concrete structure, then he will be killed. Therefore, if George drives an automobile 70 miles per hour, then he will be killed.)

Examples:

Here is a *correct* use of the implicational argument form Simplification:

1. $(A \vee \sim B) \cdot (C \vee \sim A)$ p $/\therefore (A \vee \sim B)$
2. $(A \vee \sim B)$ 1, **Simp**

In this case, the "$\cdot$" in line 1 is the major connective. Thus the whole of line 1 has the form $(p \cdot q)$ required for the use of the valid argument form Simplification.

Here is another example of the correct use of implicational forms:

1. $A \supset (B \cdot C)$ p
2. $(B \cdot C) \supset D$ p $/\therefore A \supset D$
3. $A \supset D$ 1,2 **HS**

This is a correct use of the implicational form Hypothetical Syllogism **(HS),** because **HS** requires that one whole line in a proof have the form $(p \supset q)$, and another whole line have the form $(q \supset r)$, and this proof does have two such lines, namely line 1, which has the form $(p \supset q)$, and line 2, which has the form $(q \supset r)$. Therefore **HS** permits the assertion of line 3, since that whole line has the required form $(p \supset r)$.

Remember that although the ten equivalence argument forms may be used on whole lines, just as the implicational forms, they also may be used on parts of lines, as in the following example:

1. $\sim(A \cdot B) \supset C$ p $/\therefore (\sim A \vee \sim B) \supset C$
2. $(\sim A \vee \sim B) \supset C$ 1, **DeM**

The use of equivalence argument forms on parts of lines is justified because their use always leads from a given sentence to an *equivalent* sentence.

Reluctance to Use Addition

Even after proving that Addition is a valid argument form, students are reluctant to use it, because they believe that somehow it is "cheating" to be able to "add" letters to a line simply at will. But a little thought about the matter should convince the hesitant that no cheating is involved in the use of Addition. Consider the example:

Art will go. Therefore either Art will go or Betsy will go.

symbolized as

1.	A	p /∴ $A \vee B$
2.	$A \vee B$	1, **Add**

If we accept the sentence "Art will go", then we must also accept the sentence "Either Art will go or Betsy will go", since Art's going alone makes that sentence true, whether Betsy goes or not.

This is sometimes overlooked because increasing the number of letters in a sentence often *adds to* or *strengthens* an assertion (as, for example, when someone says "Art will go", and then amends that to say "Art will go *and* Betsy will go"). But when the extra letter is added by Addition, the assertion is *weakened,* not strengthened. In a sense, the sentence "Art will go" is stronger than the sentence "Art will go or Betsy will go", since from the latter we can infer neither that Art will go nor that Betsy will go, but rather only the much weaker conclusion that one *or* the other (or both) will go.

The following extreme case nicely illustrates the weakening effect of the use of Addition:

1.	A	p /∴ $(A \vee \sim A)$
2.	$A \vee \sim A$	1, **Add**

In this extreme case, the use of Addition leads to the *weakest possible* kind of assertion, namely a tautology, which has no factual content whatever.

Reluctance to Use Distribution

In this case, the reluctance generally stems not from doubts as to its validity, but rather from inability to spot places where its application will be useful. The following proof contains a typical useful application of Distribution:

1.	$(A \vee B) \supset C$	p /∴ $A \supset C$
2.	$\sim(A \vee B) \vee C$	1, **Impl**

3. $(\sim A \cdot \sim B) \vee C$ — 2, **DeM**
4. $C \vee (\sim A \cdot \sim B)$ — 3, **Comm**
5. $(C \vee \sim A) \cdot (C \vee \sim B)$ — 4, **Dist** (the crucial use of **Dist**)
6. $(C \vee \sim A)$ — 5, **Simp**
7. $(\sim A \vee C)$ — 6, **Comm**
8. $(A \supset C)$ — 7, **Impl**

Notice that the use of Distribution is crucial in getting rid of the unwanted letter *B*, which occurs in the premise but not in the conclusion. Notice also that the *second* of the two distributive equivalence forms was used, and that it was used from *left to right* (that is, the move was from line 4, whose form $[p \vee (q \cdot r)]$ is that of the *left* side of the second distributive equivalence form, to line 5, whose form $[(p \vee q) \cdot (p \vee r)]$, is that of the *right* side). This is the most common use of Distribution, because the line obtained in this way always has a "·" as its major connective, and thus has the form $(p \cdot q)$ necessary for the use of Simplification.

Trying to Prove what Cannot be Proved

The number of mistakes of this kind is much too large to catalogue. We consider two such mistakes, committed perhaps because they are very similar to two valid procedures.

Consider the following four argument forms:

1. $(p \vee q) \supset r \quad /\therefore p \supset r$
2. $(p \cdot q) \supset r \quad /\therefore p \supset r$
3. $p \supset (q \vee r) \quad /\therefore p \supset r$
4. $p \supset (q \cdot r) \quad /\therefore p \supset r$

The first and fourth of these argument forms are valid. The second and third are *invalid,* as we can prove by truth table analysis.

The important point is not to waste time and effort trying to prove substitution instances of invalid forms. For example, in trying to prove the validity of the argument

1. $(A \cdot B) \supset C$
2. $\sim(\sim B \vee D)$
3. $(C \cdot \sim D) \supset E \quad /\therefore A \supset E$

it is useless to try to derive the sentence $A \supset C$ from line 1 alone since the form of such an inference, namely the form $[(p \cdot q) \supset r] /\therefore (p \supset r)$ is invalid. The sentence $A \supset C$ *can* be derived in this proof, but *not* from line 1 alone.

Similarly, it is useless to try to derive the sentence $A \supset B$ from the sentence $A \supset (B \vee C)$, since the form of such an inference, namely the form $p \supset (q \vee r)$ $/\therefore (p \supset q)$, is invalid.

Failure to Notice the Scope of a Negation Sign

A mistake of this kind is usually merely an oversight; however, it is quite common. In particular, negation signs that negate a whole sentence, or a large unit in a sentence, are misconstrued as negating only one letter. Thus, in a sentence such as $\sim(A \vee B)$ the negation sign sometimes is misconstrued as negating merely the letter A, instead of the whole unit $(A \vee B)$. The remedy for this kind of error is care, plus the realization that a negation sign before a unit set off by parentheses (or brackets) negates that entire unit.

Exercise 4-7:

Using the eighteen valid argument forms, prove that the following arguments are valid.

(1) 1. $(A \cdot B) \supset C$
2. A $/\therefore B \supset C$

(2) 1. $\sim R \vee \sim S$
2. $A \supset (R \cdot S)$ $/\therefore \sim A$

(3) 1. $\sim M \vee N$
2. $\sim R \supset \sim N$ $/\therefore M \supset R$

(4) 1. $A \supset B$
2. $\sim(B \cdot \sim C)$ $/\therefore A \supset C$

(5) 1. $\sim A \supset (B \cdot C)$
2. $\sim C$ $/\therefore A$

(6) 1. $F \supset G$
2. $\sim(H \cdot G)$
3. H $/\therefore \sim F$

(7) 1. $\sim(H \vee \sim K)$
2. $L \supset H$ $/\therefore L \supset M$

(8) 1. $M \equiv N$ $/\therefore \sim N \vee M$

(9) 1. $(A \cdot B) \vee (C \cdot D)$
2. $\sim A$ $/\therefore C$

(10) 1. $D \vee \sim A$
2. $\sim(A \cdot \sim B) \supset \sim C$
3. $\sim D$ $/\therefore \sim C$

(11) 1. $(A \cdot B) \supset C$
2. $A \cdot \sim C$ $/\therefore \sim B$

(12) 1. $\sim A$
2. $(A \vee B) \equiv C$
3. $\sim B$ $/\therefore \sim(C \cdot D)$

(13) 1. $S \vee (\sim R \cdot T)$
2. $R \supset \sim S$ $/\therefore \sim R$

(14) 1. $A \supset B$
2. $C \supset D$
3. $(B \vee D) \supset E$
4. $\sim E$ $/\therefore \sim(A \vee C)$

Exercise 4-8:

Prove valid using the eighteen valid argument forms. (Some of these are rather difficult.)

(1) 1. $R \supset (\sim A \cdot T)$
2. $B \vee \sim S$
3. $R \vee S$ /∴ $A \supset B$

(2) 1. $A \supset (B \supset C)$
/∴ $(\sim C \cdot D) \supset (B \supset \sim A)$

(3) 1. $\sim(A \cdot B) \equiv \sim C$
2. $(D \vee E) \supset C$ /∴ $E \supset A$

(4) 1. $D \supset B$
2. $D \supset (B \supset W)$
3. $B \supset (W \supset S)$ /∴ $D \supset S$

(5) 1. $P \supset [(Q \cdot R) \vee S]$
2. $(Q \cdot R) \supset \sim P$
3. $T \supset \sim S$ /∴ $P \supset \sim T$

(6) 1. $K \supset [(L \vee M) \supset R]$
2. $(R \vee S) \supset T$ /∴ $K \supset (M \supset T)$

(7) 1. $(P \vee R) \cdot (P \vee Q)$
2. $(Q \cdot R) \supset (V \supset W)$
3. $\sim[(P \supset S) \supset \sim(S \supset W)]$
4. $\sim W$ /∴ $V \supset S$

(8) 1. $A \supset B$
2. $C \supset D$
/∴ $(A \vee C) \supset (B \vee D)$

(9) 1. $A \equiv B$
2. $\sim(A \cdot \sim R) \supset (A \cdot S)$
/∴ $\sim(B \cdot S) \supset \sim(A \cdot R)$

(10) 1. $\sim[D \cdot \sim(E \vee B)]$
2. $\sim(E \vee F)$
3. $C \supset (E \vee A)$
/∴ $\sim(\sim A \cdot \sim B) \vee \sim(C \vee D)$

Exercise 4-9:

1. Why can't implicational argument forms be used on parts of lines in a proof? (Example)
2. Why *can* equivalence argument forms be so used? (Example)
3. Why are all substitution instances of a valid argument form valid arguments?
4. We said that all substitution instances of a valid argument form are thereby valid arguments. Why can't we say that all substitution instances of an invalid argument form are invalid arguments? (Example)
5. Prove that the following argument form is not a valid argument form, and so could not be added to our stock of 18 valid argument forms.

   $(p \supset q)$, $q \supset r$, $q \vee r$ /∴ $p \vee q$

Key Terms Introduced in Chapter Four

Addition (Add): The valid implicational argument form $p \quad /\therefore p \vee q$

Argument form: A group of sentence forms, all of whose substitution instances are arguments.

Association (Assoc): The valid equivalence argument forms

$$p \vee (q \vee r) :: (p \vee q) \vee r \qquad \text{and}$$
$$p \cdot (q \cdot r) :: (p \cdot q) \cdot r$$

Commutation (Comm): The valid equivalence argument forms

$$(p \vee q) :: (q \vee p) \qquad \text{and}$$
$$(p \cdot q) :: (q \cdot p)$$

Conjunction: (1) A compound sentence (or sentence form) whose main connective is "·". (2) The valid implicational argument form

p
$q \quad /\therefore p \cdot q$

(The abbreviation for this argument form is **Conj.**)

Constructive Dilemma (CD): The valid implicational argument form

$p \supset q$
$r \supset s$
$p \vee r \quad /\therefore q \vee s$

Contraposition (Contra): The valid equivalence argument form

$$(p \supset q) :: (\sim q \supset \sim p)$$

DeMorgan's Theorem (DeM): The valid equivalence argument forms

$$\sim(p \cdot q) :: (\sim p \vee \sim q) \qquad \text{and}$$
$$\sim(p \vee q) :: (\sim p \cdot \sim q)$$

Disjunctive Syllogism (DS): The valid implicational argument forms

$p \vee q \qquad\qquad\qquad p \vee q$
$\sim p \quad /\therefore q \qquad \text{and} \qquad \sim q \quad /\therefore p$

Distribution (Dist): The valid equivalence argument forms

$$p \cdot (q \vee r) :: (p \cdot q) \vee (p \cdot r) \qquad \text{and}$$
$$p \vee (q \cdot r) :: (p \vee q) \cdot (p \vee r)$$

Double Negation (DN): The valid equivalence argument form

$$p :: \sim\sim p$$

Equivalence (Equiv): The valid argument forms

$$(p \equiv q) :: (p \supset q) \cdot (q \supset p) \qquad \text{and}$$
$$(p \equiv q) :: (p \cdot q) \vee (\sim p \cdot \sim q)$$

Equivalence argument form: A two-directional argument form. *Double Negation* is a valid equivalence argument form.

Exportation (Exp): The valid equivalence argument form

$$[(p \cdot q) \supset r] :: [p \supset (q \supset r)]$$

Hypothetical Syllogism (HS): The valid implicational argument form

$p \supset q$
$q \supset r \quad /\therefore p \supset r$

Implication (Impl): The valid equivalence argument form

$$(p \supset q) :: (\sim p \vee q)$$

Implicational argument form: A one-directional argument form. *Modus Ponens* is a valid implicational argument form.

Modus Ponens (MP): The valid implicational argument form

$p \supset q$
$p \quad /\therefore q$

Modus Tollens (MT): The valid implicational argument form

$p \supset q$
$\sim q \quad /\therefore \sim p$

Proof of an argument: A series of sentences and/or sentence forms such that each member of the series is either a premise or else follows from a previous member of the series by a valid argument form, the last line being the argument's conclusion.

Simplification (Simp): The valid implicational argument forms

$p \cdot q \quad /\therefore p$ and $p \cdot q \quad /\therefore q$

Tautology (Taut): The valid equivalence argument forms

$p :: (p \cdot p)$ and $p :: (p \vee p)$

Valid argument form: An argument form all of whose substitution instances are valid arguments.

Chapter Five

Sentential Logic—IV

1 *Conditional Proofs*

Here is a very simple valid argument that so far cannot be proved valid in our system:

1. $A \supset B$ p $/\therefore A \supset (A \cdot B)$

To prove it valid, we can reason as follows: What would be the case *if* A were true? (We don't *know* that it is. It isn't given to us as a premise. But what *if* it were true?) If A were true, then clearly B also would be true, since by *Modus Ponens* we could move from $A \supset B$ (the given premise) and A (the *assumed* premise) to B. So if A were true, B also would be true, and thus $A \cdot B$ would be true (by Conjunction). We therefore have shown that *if* A, then $(A \cdot B)$,* or in symbols, $A \supset (A \cdot B)$, which is the conclusion of the argument in question. Thus we have proved that the argument

$A \supset B$ p $/\therefore A \supset (A \cdot B)$

is valid.

A proof of this kind is called a **conditional proof,** and the rule permitting the crucial step is therefore called **rule of conditional proof.** Once we add this rule, our proof procedure for sentential logic is *complete,* meaning that now every valid argument of a certain kind can be proved by means of its machinery.

Now let's put this proof into symbols:

1.	$A \supset B$	p $/\therefore A \supset (A \cdot B)$
2.	A	**Assumed Premise** (or simply **AP**)
3.	B	1,2 **MP**
4.	$(A \cdot B)$	2,3 **Conj**

* The references to truth are dispensable.

What we have proved so far is that *if A then* $(A \cdot B)$. Replacing the expression "if ______ then _ _ _ _ _ " by "⊃", we get

5. $A \supset (A \cdot B)$ 2–4, **Conditional Proof** (or **CP**)

The important point to notice is that the conclusion, line 5, depends only on the *original premise,* and not on the assumed premise stated on line 2. If premise 1 is true, then line 5 must be true, whether *A* (the assumed premise) is true or false. Line 5 does not assert that $(A \cdot B)$ is the case, but only that $(A \cdot B)$ is the case *on the condition* that A is the case. The notation to the right of line 5 indicates that the technique used is that of conditional proof **(CP)** using an **assumed premise** (an assumption—something not stated as a premise in the original problem); it lists the line of the assumed premise as well as the last line that depends on the assumed premise.

To keep track of assumed premises and the lines that depend on them, let's use arrows and lines so that the proof we have been discussing will look like this:

1.	$A \supset B$	p /∴ $A \supset (A \cdot B)$
→ 2.	A	**AP**
3.	B	1,2 **MP**
4.	$(A \cdot B)$	2,3 **Conj**
5.	$A \supset (A \cdot B)$	2–4, **CP**

The arrow pointing at line 2 indicates that line 2 contains an assumed premise not given as part of the original problem. The line drawn down from line 2 to below line 4 indicates that lines 2, 3, and 4 *depend on* line 2 (in addition perhaps to the original premise). And the horizontal line drawn between lines 4 and 5 indicates that the lines to follow *do not* depend on line 2; that is, it indicates that the scope of the assumed premise ends with line 4.

Using the arrow and line notation just introduced, we can express the structure of the rule of conditional proof (or argument form) as follows:

This indicates that a premise is assumed, other lines are derived from it, and then the assumed premise is *discharged* as a premise, being retained as the antecedent of the line $p \supset q$.

Another way to consider conditional proofs is this. In a sense, *every* valid argument is conditional, since the truth of the conclusion is conditional upon the truth of the premises on which the conclusion depends. What is different about a so-called *conditional* proof is simply that some lines in a conditional proof depend on a line (the assumed premise) on which the conclusion does not depend, a line that was not given as a premise in the original problem. It is as though a line is introduced as a premise, a conclusion is drawn from it (in conjunction with the other premises), and then that premise is discharged as a premise (or "taken back" as a premise), being retained rather as a *condition* on the acceptance of the conclusion, that is, retained as the antecedent of a new conditional conclusion.*

For instance, suppose we know that if Art went to the show, then Betsy went also ($A \supset B$), and then are told that Art definitely did go (A). On the basis of this information we can conclude (validly) that Art and Betsy both went to the show ($A \cdot B$). But suppose we then are told that the information that Art went to the show is not reliable; perhaps he went, perhaps not. In that case, we no longer can conclude (validly) that Art and Betsy both went to the show. However, we can reason that since the assumption that Art went to the show (in conjunction with the premise $A \supset B$) led to the conclusion that Art and Betsy both went to the show, it still is the case that *if* Art went to the show, *then* Art and Betsy both went; that is, it still is the case that $A \supset (A \cdot B)$. A proof of this kind is a *conditional proof* because it involves temporary use of a premise that is later discharged *as a premise* but retained as the antecedent of a conditional conclusion.

In the above example, only one assumed premise was used. But *any number* of assumptions can be introduced into a proof, provided that every one is eventually discharged, so that the conclusion of the argument depends only on the given premises. And an assumption need not be the antecedent of the conclusion. *Any* assumption may be made, again provided that it is eventually discharged. Of course it is good strategy to use certain assumed premises and not others, but the *rules of logic* permit the use of any assumed premise later discharged. The following is a typical example:

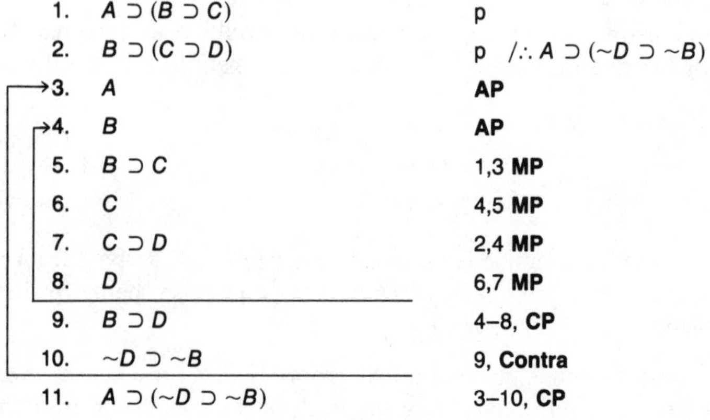

1.	$A \supset (B \supset C)$	p
2.	$B \supset (C \supset D)$	p /∴ $A \supset (\sim D \supset \sim B)$
→3.	A	**AP**
→4.	B	**AP**
5.	$B \supset C$	1,3 **MP**
6.	C	4,5 **MP**
7.	$C \supset D$	2,4 **MP**
8.	D	6,7 **MP**
9.	$B \supset D$	4–8, **CP**
10.	$\sim D \supset \sim B$	9, **Contra**
11.	$A \supset (\sim D \supset \sim B)$	3–10, **CP**

*Obviously, once an assumed premise is discharged, we no longer can use it, or any line that depends on it, to derive additional lines. For instance, in the previous example, we cannot assert as line 6 the sentence $\sim\sim(A \cdot B)$, following from line 4 by **DN**, since we have already discharged line 2 as a premise.

In this example, there are *two* assumed premises, A and B. One, A, is the antecedent of the conclusion, but the other obviously is not. And it is not the antecedent of the (complex) consequent either. Rather it is the antecedent of the *contrapositive** of the consequent. This illustrates two fine points of strategy: first, if the consequent of the conclusion is itself a conditional statement, then it may be useful to have more than one assumed premise; and second, it sometimes is useful to assume the antecedent of the *contrapositive* of a conditional rather than the antecedent of the conditional itself. (The second becomes quite important in the predicate logic to be discussed in the next three chapters.)

Examples:

The following proofs contain correct uses of the rule of conditional proof:

(1)

1.	$A \supset B$	p
2.	$C \vee \sim A$	p /∴ $A \supset (B \cdot C)$
→3.	A	**AP**
4.	B	1,3 **MP**
5.	$\sim\sim A$	3, **DN**
6.	C	2,5 **DS**
7.	$B \cdot C$	4,6 **Conj**
8.	$A \supset (B \cdot C)$	3–7, **CP**

(2)

1.	$(A \vee B) \supset (C \cdot D)$	p
2.	$(D \vee E) \supset F$	p /∴ $A \supset F$
→3.	A	**AP**
4.	$A \vee B$	3, **Add**
5.	$C \cdot D$	1,4 **MP**
6.	D	5, **Simp**
7.	$D \vee E$	6, **Add**
8.	F	2,7 **MP**
9.	$A \supset F$	3–8, **CP**

(3)

1.	$(Z \supset Y) \supset X$	p
2.	$T \vee S$	p
3.	$\sim(Z \cdot T)$	p
4.	$\sim Y \supset \sim S$	p /∴ X
→5.	Z	**AP**

---

*The *contrapositive* of a given sentence is the sentence obtained from the given sentence by Contraposition.

	6.	$\sim Z \vee \sim T$	3, **DeM**
	7.	$\sim\sim Z$	5, **DN**
	8.	$\sim T$	6,7 **DS**
	9.	S	2,8 **DS**
	10.	$S \supset Y$	4, **Contr**
	11.	Y	9,10 **MP**
	12.	$Z \supset Y$	5–11, **CP**
	13.	X	1,12 **MP**
(4)	1.	$(M \vee N) \supset P$	p /∴ $[(P \vee Q) \supset R] \supset (M \supset R)$
	→2.	$(P \vee Q) \supset R$	**AP**
	→3.	M	**AP**
	4.	$M \vee N$	3, **Add**
	5.	P	1,4 **MP**
	6.	$P \vee Q$	5, **Add**
	7.	R	2,6 **MP**
	8.	$M \supset R$	3–7, **CP**
	9.	$[(P \vee Q) \supset R] \supset (M \supset R)$	2–8, **CP**
(5)	→1.	$A \cdot B$	**AP** /∴ $(A \cdot B) \supset [(B \supset A) \cdot (B \supset B)]$
	2.	A	1, **Simp**
	3.	$A \vee \sim B$	2, **Add**
	4.	$\sim B \vee A$	3, **Comm**
	5.	$B \supset A$	4, **Impl**
	6.	B	1, **Simp**
	7.	A	5,6 **MP**
	8.	$B \vee \sim B$	6, **Add**
	9.	$\sim B \vee B$	8, **Comm**
	10.	$B \supset B$	9, **Impl**
	11.	$(B \supset A) \cdot (B \supset B)$	5,10 **Conj**
	12.	$(A \cdot B) \supset [(B \supset A) \cdot (B \supset B)]$	1–11 **CP**

(Note that the conclusion of this valid proof depends on no premises whatever, since the assumed premise on line 1 was discharged at the end of the proof. This conclusion is, therefore, a tautology, and thus a *logical implication,* or, as will be explained in Chapter Eight, Section 4, a *theorem of logic.*)

Exercise 5-1:

Prove valid using **CP** (and the eighteen valid argument forms).

(1) 1. B /∴ $A \supset (A \cdot B)$

(2) 1. $A \supset (B \cdot C)$ /∴ $A \supset C$

(3) 1. $B \supset C$ /∴ $(A \supset B) \supset (A \supset C)$

(4) 1. $A \supset (B \supset C)$
2. $\sim C$ /∴ $A \supset \sim B$

(5) 1. C /∴ $A \supset (B \supset C)$

(6) 1. $A \supset (B \supset C)$
2. $A \supset B$ /∴ $A \supset C$

(7) 1. $A \supset B$
2. $A \supset C$ /∴ $A \supset (B \cdot C)$

(8) 1. $(A \cdot B) \supset C$
2. $(B \cdot C) \supset D$ /∴ $(A \cdot B) \supset D$

(9) 1. $A \vee \sim(B \cdot C)$ /∴ $B \supset (C \supset A)$

(10) 1. $A \supset (B \supset C)$
2. $C \supset D$ /∴ $A \supset (B \supset D)$

Exercise 5-2:

Use **CP** to prove arguments (1)–(6) and (8)–(10) in Exercise 4-8. (Notice that use of **CP** tends to make proofs shorter and easier.)

2 *Indirect Proofs*

A contradictory sentence is a necessarily false sentence. And a false sentence cannot be inferred validly from true premises. So if we infer validly to a contradictory sentence, we know that at least one of our premises must be false.

Now consider, say, a four-premise argument, and assume we know that three of its four premises are true. If we derive a contradiction from that set of four premises, we have proved that the fourth premise in the set is false (since at least one member of the set is false, and we assume that the other three are true). So we also have proved that the negation of the fourth premise is true (since the negation of a false sentence is true). We have here the main ideas behind the **rule of indirect proof (IP).** (Indirect proofs also are known as **reductio ad absurdum proofs.**)

Take the argument:

1. $A \supset B$ p
2. $B \supset C$ p
3. A p /∴ C

First, let's add the negation of the conclusion, namely $\sim C$, to the above set of premises, to obtain the following set:

1. $A \supset B$ p

2. $B \supset C$ p
3. A p
4. $\sim C$ **AP**

Then we can obtain a contradiction as follows:

5. $\sim B$ 2,4 **MT**
6. $\sim A$ 1,5 **MT**
7. $A \cdot \sim A$ 3,6 **Conj**

Obviously, if premises 1, 2, and 3 are true, then the added premise 4, $\sim C$, is false. And if $\sim C$ is false, then C must be true. Hence, we have shown that the argument

1. $A \supset B$
2. $B \supset C$
3. A $/\therefore C$

is valid, because we have shown that if its premises are true, then its conclusion, C, must be true (because $\sim C$ must be false).

The general method employed in an indirect proof, then, is to add the negation of the conclusion* of an argument to its set of premises and derive a contradiction. The derivation of the contradiction proves that if the original premises are true, then the added premise must be false, and consequently proves that if the original premises are true then the *negation* of the added premise must be *true*. Since the negation of the added premise is the conclusion of the argument in question, derivation of the contradiction proves that if the original premises are true then the conclusion must be true, and hence proves that the argument is valid.

Here is another example of an indirect proof (using arrows and lines as in conditional proofs to keep track of assumed premises and the lines that depend on them):

1. $A \supset X$ p
2. $(C \vee \sim X) \supset A$ p $/\therefore X$
→3. $\sim X$ **AP** (the negation of the conclusion)
4. $\sim A$ 1,3 **MT**
5. $\sim(C \vee \sim X)$ 2,4 **MT**
6. $\sim C \cdot \sim\sim X$ 5, **DeM**
7. $\sim C \cdot X$ 6, **DN**
8. X 7, **Simp**
9. $X \cdot \sim X$ 3,8 **Conj**
10. X 3–9, **IP**

---

*Let's be generous and allow C to be the negation of some conclusion $\sim C$, so that we don't have to use double negation on $\sim\sim C$.

Notice that the contradiction obtained is simply the conjunction of the assumed premise and the conclusion. This is perfectly permissible; the derivation of any explicit contradiction is all that is required. (An *explicit* contradiction is a contradiction having the form $p \cdot \sim p$.) Notice also that the proof does not stop with line 8. The proof must continue because line 8 depends on the assumed premise $\sim X$, so all that has been proved up to that point is $\sim X \supset X$. But once the explicit contradiction is obtained, the rule of indirect proof permits the assertion of the conclusion independently of the assumed premise.

Another way to see that the rule of indirect proof is valid involves noticing that an indirect proof is just a special kind of conditional proof.*
Consider the following proof:

1. $A \vee B$ — p
2. $A \supset B$ — p /∴ B
→3. $\sim B$ — **AP**
4. $\sim A$ — 2,3 **MT**
5. A — 1,3 **DS**
6. $A \cdot \sim A$ — 4,5 **Conj**

At this point, the rule of indirect proof permits the assertion of *B:*

7. B — 3–6 **IP** (indirect proof)

Line 7 is permitted in an indirect proof because the premise assumed (in line 3) is the negation of the conclusion, *B;* and use of that assumed premise (plus the original premises) led to a contradiction.

Step 7 can be shown to be valid by making two things clear:

(1) A contradictory sentence implies any and every sentence. This is illustrated by the following argument:

1. $A \cdot \sim A$ — p /∴ X
2. A — 1, **Simp**
3. $A \vee X$ — 2, **Add**
4. $\sim A$ — 1, **Simp**
5. X — 3,4 **DS**

Obviously, the conclusion *X* might have been *any* sentence whatever. Therefore, from the contradiction $A \cdot \sim A$, indeed from any contradiction, it is clear that *any* sentence whatever can be obtained.

---

* Since this is the case, it follows that our system is complete without the rule of indirect proof. We include the rule anyway, because it helps to shorten many proofs and because it has been customary to do so throughout most of the long history of logic, as the name *reductio ad absurdum* suggests.

(2) Once a contradiction is obtained, the desired conclusion can be obtained by a conditional proof.

Consider the indirect proof again, but this time without the last line:

1.	$A \vee B$	p
2.	$A \supset B$	p /∴ B
→3.	$\sim B$	**AP**
4.	$\sim A$	2,3 **MT**
5.	A	1,3 **DS**
6.	$A \cdot \sim A$	4,5 **Conj**

Suppose now that we treat the proof as an ordinary conditional proof. Then the conclusion *B* can be derived within the scope of the assumed premise:

7.	B	2,5 **MP**

However, the proof is not complete at this point. We have not derived line 7 by means of the original premises alone, because line 7 lies within the scope of the assumed premise $\sim B$. What has been proved is that:

8.	$\sim B \supset B$	3,7 **CP**

But from this point it is a simple matter to obtain *B*:

9.	$\sim\sim B \vee B$	8, **Impl**
10.	$B \vee B$	9, **DN**
11.	B	10, **Taut**

This example illustrates the fact that whenever the negation of the conclusion of an argument is taken as an assumed premise in a conditional proof and a contradiction is derived, then it must be possible to obtain the conclusion of the argument by the procedure just illustrated (so that the conclusion depends on the original premises, but not on the assumed premise). But since this always can be done, there is little point in actually doing so in every case. Instead, we permit the use of the rule of indirect proof, which we now see is simply a shortened form of conditional proof. In general then, once a contradiction is obtained, the conclusion of an argument can be asserted.

Exercise 5-3:

Prove the following arguments valid, using **IP**.

(1) 1. $A \vee B$
2. $A \vee \sim B$ /∴ A

(2) 1. $\sim A \supset B$
2. $\sim(\sim A \cdot B)$ /∴ A

(3) 1. $A \supset (B \cdot C)$
2. $\sim B$ /∴ $\sim A$

(4) 1. $A \vee (\sim B \cdot C)$
2. $B \supset \sim A$ /∴ $\sim B$

(5) 1. $A \supset \sim B$
2. $B \vee C$
3. $A \vee C$ /∴ C

(6) 1. $(A \cdot B) \supset C$
2. $\sim A \supset C$
3. B /∴ C

(7) 1. $A \supset B$
2. $C \supset D$
3. $(B \vee D) \supset E$
4. $\sim E$ /∴ $\sim(A \vee C)$

(8) 1. $A \supset (B \supset C)$
2. $A \supset B$
3. $\sim C \supset (A \vee D)$ /∴ $C \vee D$

(9) 1. $\sim A$
2. $(A \vee B) \equiv C$
3. $\sim B$ /∴ $\sim(C \cdot D)$

(10) 1. $C \supset [D \vee \sim(A \vee B)]$
2. $\sim A \supset B$ /∴ $\sim D \supset \sim C$

Exercise 5-4:

Prove valid, first without using **IP** or **CP**, and then using **IP**, and compare the lengths and difficulty of the corresponding proofs.

(1) 1. $A \supset B$
2. $C \supset A$
3. $C \vee (B \cdot D)$ /∴ B

(2) 1. $H \supset (A \supset B)$
2. $\sim C \supset (H \vee B)$
3. $H \supset A$ /∴ $C \vee B$

(3) 1. $P \vee Q$
2. $Q \supset (R \cdot S)$
3. $(R \vee P) \supset T$ /∴ T

(4) 1. $(A \vee B) \supset (C \supset \sim D)$
2. $(D \vee E) \supset (A \cdot C)$ /∴ $\sim D$

(5) 1. $A \supset \sim(B \vee C)$
2. $\sim D \supset (\sim A \supset \sim E)$
3. $\sim(\sim E \vee F)$
4. $\sim F \supset (A \supset B)$ /∴ D

(6) 1. $(L \vee N) \supset (F \cdot P)$
2. $F \supset (H \cdot K)$
3. $H \supset (\sim L \cdot M)$ /∴ $\sim L$

3 *Proving Invalidity*

If an argument form is invalid, then it is not possible to construct a valid proof for it. But failure to construct a valid proof does not show that an argument form is invalid. It may be that such a proof exists, but we were not ingenious enough to find it. Instead, we can prove an argument form invalid by presenting a substitution instance of that form which has true premises and a false conclusion, for no substitution instance of a *valid* argument form can have true premises and a false conclusion.

Example:

Argument Form

1. $p \supset q$
2. $q \supset r$ $/ \therefore r \supset p$

Substitution Instance (where we substitute a false sentence, say the sentence **F,** for both occurrences of p, and a true sentence, say the sentence **T,** for both occurrences of q and both occurrences of r)

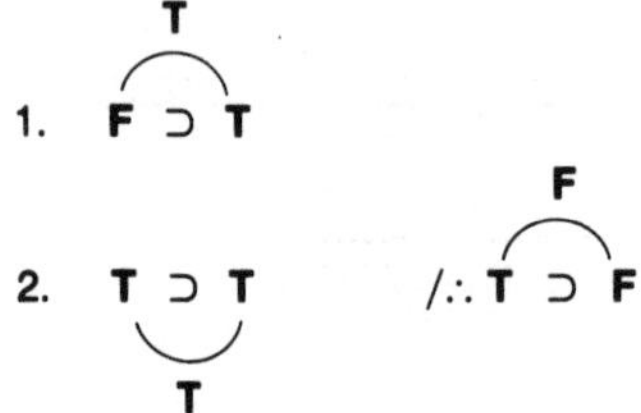

This shows that the substitution instance has true premises and a false conclusion, and hence is invalid. So it follows that the argument form of which it is a substitution instance also is invalid.

It might be thought that an invalid *argument* can be proved invalid by showing that it is a substitution instance of an invalid argument form, just as a valid argument can be proved valid by showing that it is a substitution instance of a valid argument form. But this is not the case, because *every* argument, valid or invalid, is a substitution instance of some invalid argument form or other. For instance, the valid two-premise argument

$A \supset B$
A $/ \therefore B$

is a substitution instance of the invalid argument form

p
q $/ \therefore r$

Instead, arguments can be proved invalid by a slightly different method. Take the invalid argument:

1. $A \supset B$
2. $B \supset C$ $/ \therefore C \supset A$

Its invalidity is not due to the fact that it is a substitution instance of an invalid argument form (since all arguments are), but rather to the fact that it is *not* a substitution instance of *any valid* argument form.* If it were a substitution instance of even one valid argument form, then it would be valid. Therefore, to prove that it is an invalid argument, we must prove that it is not a substitution instance of *any* valid argument form. We can do this by showing that it *is* a substitution instance of a particular invalid argument form, called its propositional form. The **propositional form** of an argument is the argument form obtained from that argument by replacing each capital letter (sentence constant) in the argument by a small letter (sentence variable), taking care to observe the rule that all occurrences of a given capital letter (sentence constant) are replaced by occurrences of the *same* small letter (sentence variable), where, of course, that small letter is *not* used to replace occurrences of any other capital letter in the argument.

Examples:

The propositional form of the argument

1. $A \supset B$
2. $B \supset C \quad /\therefore C \supset A$

is

1. $p \supset q$
2. $q \supset r \quad /\therefore r \supset p$

And the propositional form of the argument

1. $(M \cdot N) \supset P$
2. $\sim P \quad /\therefore P \supset \sim Q$

is

1. $(p \cdot q) \supset r$
2. $\sim r \quad /\therefore r \supset \sim s$

---

* More precisely, it isn't a substitution instance of any valid form expressible in the notation of sentential logic. When we get to Part Two of this text and develop a *predicate* logic, some arguments that can be proved invalid using the notation of sentential logic will be shown to be valid, using the broader notation and machinery of predicate logic. (A classic example is mentioned on page 107.) When we speak of invalidity in this section, we mean invalid using just the machinery of sentential logic, which does not delve into the interior structure of sentences symbolized by single capital letters.

It can be proved that if the propositional form of a given argument is invalid, then *all* argument forms of which that argument is a substitution instance are invalid,* and consequently the argument itself is invalid. Therefore, to prove that an argument is invalid, prove that its propositional form is invalid. And to prove that its propositional form is invalid, prove by truth table analysis that at least one of its substitution instances has true premises and a false conclusion.

Example:

The propositional form of the argument

1. $A \supset B$
2. B $/\therefore A$

is

1. $p \supset q$
2. q $/\therefore p$

Replace q with some true sentence **T** and p by some false sentence **F**, and we can prove quite easily that the resulting substitution instance

1. **F** $\supset$ **T**
2. **T** $/\therefore$ **F**

has true premises and a false conclusion. Hence the original argument is invalid.

Of course in practice we can simplify this procedure by omitting the middle step involving argument forms. Thus, we can prove the above argument invalid as follows:

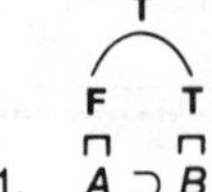

---

* Indeed, this method constitutes a mechanical procedure for determining validity (as well as invalidity) in propositional logic. For if we prove that there is no way to assign truth values so as to make the conclusion of an argument false and all of its premises true, then we have proved the argument is valid. Unfortunately, this truth table method of proving validity will not work in all cases in the predicate logic to be introduced in the next chapter.

T F

2. B /∴ A

This shows that it is *possible* for the argument in question to have true premises and a false conclusion, and therefore demonstrates that it is invalid.

It is interesting to notice what happens when we try to prove a *valid* argument invalid by this method. Consider the valid argument

1. $[(A \cdot B) \supset \sim C]$
2. A
3. C $/\therefore \sim B$

In this example, we must assign a **T** to *B*, in order to falsify the conclusion, and a **T** to *A*, as well as to *C*, in order to render the second and third premises true. But notice that if we do so, then we falsify the first premise, as the following indicates:

F

T F

T T T

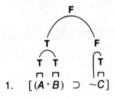

1. $[(A \cdot B) \supset \sim C]$

T

2. C

T

3. A

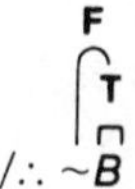

/∴ ~B

So there is no way to falsify the conclusion and at the same time render *all* of the premises true. The argument is valid.*

Exercise 5-5:

Prove that the following arguments are invalid.

---

* Because the propositional form of an argument captures the most structural detail of that argument of any of its several argument forms.

(1) 1. $H \supset K$
2. $\sim H$ /∴ $\sim K$

(2) 1. $R \vee N$
2. $L \supset N$
3. R /∴ $\sim N$

(3) 1. $(\sim R \vee M) \supset N$
2. $\sim N$ /∴ $\sim R$

(4) 1. $A \supset B$
2. $(C \cdot B) \vee D$ /∴ A

(5) 1. $A \supset \sim B$
2. $(B \cdot C) \vee A$ /∴ $\sim B$

(6) 1. $P \supset Q$
2. $R \supset S$
3. $R \vee Q$ /∴ $P \vee S$

(7) 1. $(A \cdot B) \supset (C \vee D)$
2. $C \supset A$
3. $\sim C \vee \sim D$
4. B /∴ $A \supset D$

(8) 1. $A \supset (B \supset C)$
2. $C \supset (D \supset E)$
3. $A \supset B$
4. $E \supset A$ /∴ $D \supset E$

(9) 1. $A \supset (B \cdot C)$
2. $\sim D \vee \sim E$
3. $D \supset (A \vee F)$
4. $F \supset (C \supset E)$ /∴ $F \vee \sim D$

(10) 1. $Q \supset W$
2. $\sim P \supset \sim W$
3. $\sim N$
4. $W \supset (P \vee Q)$
5. $R \supset (S \vee T)$
6. $S \supset (Q \vee N)$
/∴ $R \supset (\sim Q \supset W)$

4 *Proving Premises Inconsistent*

In general, logic alone cannot determine the truth values of premises. But if the premises of an argument (taken as a unit) are **contradictory,** that is, **inconsistent,** then at least one of them must be false, and this fact can be proved by logic alone. To prove that an argument has inconsistent (contradictory) premises, use the eighteen valid argument forms to derive a contradiction from the premises. (And, of course, to prove *any* set of statements inconsistent, use the same method.)

For example, consider an argument whose premises are

1. $A \supset B$ p
2. $A \supset \sim B$ p
3. A p

From these premises we can derive a contradiction, as follows:

4. B 1,3 **MP**
5. $\sim B$ 2,3 **MP**
6. $B \cdot \sim B$ 4,5 **Conj**

Since line 6 is a contradiction, it must be false. And if it is false, then at least one premise must be false, since line 6 follows validly from the premises. Thus, taken together, the premises form a false conjunction. But that conjunction is not contingently false, since its falsehood was proved by logic alone. So it must be false because it is *contradictory,* that is, inconsistent.

We also can prove that a set of premises is inconsistent by truth table analysis. For instance, we can do so for the above argument, as follows:

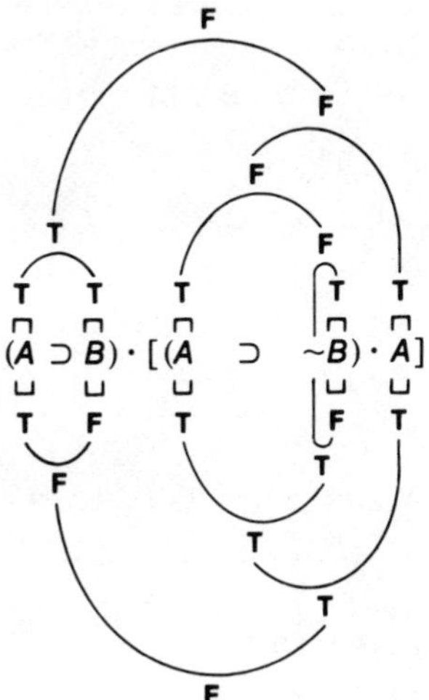

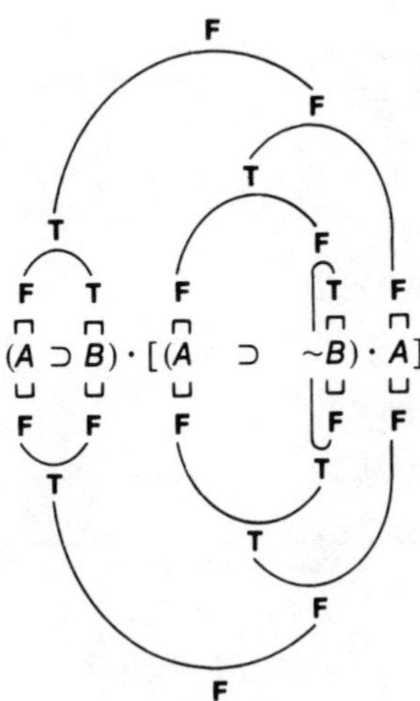

However, the method of truth table analysis often is quite tedious, and cannot be used in the predicate logic to be introduced in the next chapter.

Example:

1.	$(A \vee B) \supset C$	p
2.	$B \cdot D$	p
3.	$\sim C$	p
4.	$\sim(A \vee B)$	1,3 **MT**
5.	$\sim A \cdot \sim B$	4, **DeM**
6.	B	2, **Simp**
7.	$\sim B$	5, **Simp**
8.	$B \cdot \sim B$	6,7 **Conj**

(Therefore, the premises are inconsistent.)

Exercise 5-6:

A. Prove that the following arguments all have inconsistent premises.

(1)
1. B ⊃ (~C · ~D)
2. C ∨ D
3. B /∴ ~D ⊃ C

(2)
1. ~A ∨ B
2. ~B ∨ ~A
3. A /∴ B

(3)
1. A · ~B
2. B ⊃ A
3. A ⊃ B /∴ B

(4)
1. ~R · ~S
2. S ∨ (~S · T)
3. ~(R ∨ S) ⊃ ~(S ∨ T) /∴ R

(5)
1. A ⊃ (B ∨ C)
2. ~(~A ∨ C)
3. ~B /∴ C

(6)
1. A ⊃ (C ⊃ B)
2. (B · C) ∨ A
3. C ∨ (B · A)
4. B ⊃ ~C
5. D ∨ B
6. B · ~A /∴ B ∨ (A ⊃ D)

(7)
1. A ⊃ (C ⊃ D)
2. ~A ⊃ (D ⊃ C)
3. (A ∨ ~A) ⊃ ~D
4. (A · D) ∨ (~A · ~D)
5. (C · D) ∨ (~C · ~D)
6. A /∴ D

(8)
1. A ⊃ (B ⊃ C)
2. ~[~C ∨ (A ∨ ~D)]
3. ~{~A ∨ [C ⊃ (B · D)]}
/∴ (A ∨ C) ⊃ D

B. You can know all of these arguments are valid without proving any of them. Why? How?

5 Proving Premises Consistent

The premises of an argument form are said to be **consistent** if at least one substitution instance of that argument form has all true premises. Consequently, to prove that an argument form has consistent premises, find and present one such substitution instance. (And, of course, to prove *any* set of statements consistent, use the same method.)

Example:

Suppose the premises of an argument form are:

1. p ⊃ q   p
2. p ⊃ ~q   ~p

Then we can prove that these premises are consistent by presenting the following substitution instance, where **F** is a false sentence:

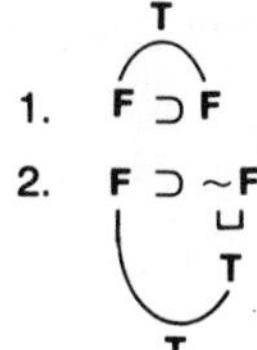

Since both premises of this substitution instance are true, its premises, as well as the premises of the argument form of which it is a substitution instance, are consistent. (Notice that it's perfectly all right to substitute the same sentence for occurrences of *p* as for *q*.)

To prove that an *argument* has consistent premises, we need only show that its *propositional form* has consistent premises.

Example:

Consider the premises of the following argument.

1. $A \supset B$
2. $A \supset \sim B$ /∴ $\sim A$

The propositional form of this argument is:

1. $p \supset q$
2. $p \supset \sim q$ /∴ $\sim p$

But we already know that there is a substitution instance of this form with true premises, namely

1. **F** ⊃ **F**
2. **F** ⊃ ~**F** /∴ ~**F**

where **F** is some false sentence. Consequently, the premises of the original argument are consistent.

Of course, in practice we can simplify this procedure by omitting the step involving propositional forms.

Example:

Using the simplified method, we can prove that the premises

1. $A \supset B$
2. $A \supset \sim B$

of an argument are consistent as follows:

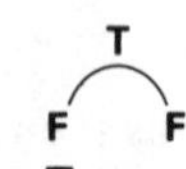

1. $A \supset B$
2. $A \supset \sim B$

F F T T

Exercise 5-7:

Prove that the sets of premises in each of the following arguments are consistent.

(1)
1. $B \supset A$
2. $C \supset B$
3. $\sim C \cdot A \quad /\therefore A \supset C$

(2)
1. $A \cdot \sim B$
2. $B \vee \sim C$
3. $\sim(\sim C \cdot B) \quad /\therefore \sim(A \cdot B)$

(3)
1. $(A \vee B) \supset \sim C$
2. $C \supset A$
3. $D \supset C \quad /\therefore (C \vee A) \supset D$

(4)
1. $(D \supset E) \vee (D \supset C)$
2. $D \cdot A$
3. $A \supset (C \supset D) \quad /\therefore C$

(5)
1. $A \supset (B \cdot \sim C)$
2. $D \supset E$
3. $\sim(\sim D \vee F)$
4. $D \supset (A \vee C)$
5. $C \supset (\sim F \supset \sim C) \quad /\therefore A$

(6)
1. $P \supset (\sim D \supset Q)$
2. $\sim[(Q \vee \sim R) \cdot (\sim P \vee D)]$
3. $\sim P \vee [\sim D \supset (Q \supset R)] \quad /\therefore B$

(7)
1. $[M \equiv (N \supset P)] \supset \sim N$
2. $P \supset N$
3. $\sim M \quad /\therefore N$

(8)
1. $(A \equiv A) \equiv (\sim A \equiv \sim A)$
2. $(B \supset A) \equiv (\sim B \supset \sim A) \quad /\therefore B \supset A$

It is important to note that failure to derive a contradiction from a set of premises does not prove that the premises are consistent, for we may have overlooked a way to derive a contradiction. Hence, to prove that premises are consistent, we must use a method like the one presented in this section.

6 *Adding Valid Argument Forms*

Once we have become familiar with the eighteen valid argument forms, once we have become *practiced* in their use, once all systematic errors in their use have been eliminated, it becomes convenient to simplify proofs by combining two or more rules into one step. Logical candidates are rules that are frequently used together; for example, **DeM** and **DN, DN** and **Impl,** and two uses of **DN.**

Here is a proof using the first two of these shortcuts:

1.	$A \vee B$	p
2.	$\sim(B \cdot \sim C)$	p $/\therefore \sim A \supset C$
3.	$\sim A \supset B$	1, **DN, Impl**
4.	$\sim B \vee C$	2, **DeM, DN**
5.	$B \supset C$	4, **Impl**
6.	$\sim A \supset C$	3,5 **HS**

And here is one using double negation twice on one line:

1.	$(F \cdot G) \supset H$	p
2.	$\sim(\sim F \vee \sim G)$	p $/\therefore H$
3.	$\sim\sim F \cdot \sim\sim G$	2, **DeM**
4.	$F \cdot G$	3, **DN** (twice)
5.	H	1,4 **MP**

We could, of course, accomplish the same proof simplification by introducing new rules analogous to these rule combinations. For example, we could introduce a new rule allowing inferences of the form $p \vee q \quad /\therefore \sim p \supset q$, and use it in going from line 1 to line 3 in the first proof above.

In fact, there is no reason why we could not add any reasonable number of valid rules to our list of eighteen (plus **CP** and **IP**), *provided* that any new rule added is proved to be valid, say by truth table analysis. Here are a few candidates that may be useful in shortening proofs:

$p \equiv q$ $p \quad /\therefore q$	$(p \equiv q) :: (q \supset p)$
$p \equiv q$ $\sim p \quad /\therefore \sim q$	$\sim(p \cdot \sim q) :: p \supset q$
	$\sim(p \supset q) :: p \cdot \sim q$

Exercise 5-8:

Determine which of the following can and which cannot be added to our set of valid argument forms.

1. $p \vee (q \vee r) :: r \vee (q \vee p)$
2. $p \cdot (q \cdot r) :: r \cdot (p \cdot q)$
3. $p \supset (q \supset r) :: r \supset (q \supset p)$
4. $p \vee \sim q :: p \supset \sim q$
5. $p \supset q \quad /\therefore \sim(\sim q \supset p)$
6. $p \supset q, p \supset \sim q \quad /\therefore \sim p$

7 *Material Implication and Valid Argument Forms*

In the discussion of material implication in Chapter Two, we pointed out that most implications used in daily life are not truth functional. Nevertheless, we introduced the truth-functional implication, *material implication,* and gave reasons for defining it as we did.

Now we are able to provide another reason for translating implications by means of material implication, and for using the particular truth table definition of material implication given in Chapter Two. The reason is that we want intuitively valid arguments and argument forms to remain valid when translated into our notation, and we want intuitively invalid arguments and argument forms to remain invalid. If we use any other truth table definition for implication, then we will be unable to attain this goal.

To illustrate this fact, we shall consider the following four argument forms:

(1)
1. If p then q*
2. $p \quad /\therefore \sim q$

(2)
1. If p then q
2. $p \quad /\therefore q$

(3)
1. If p then q
2. $\sim p \quad /\therefore \sim q$

(4)
1. If p then q
2. $\sim p \quad /\therefore q$

The first of these argument forms is obviously invalid. Symbolizing its

* Or "p implies q", and so on.

first premise by means of material implication (defined as in Chapter Two), we can prove that argument form (1) is invalid by truth table analysis, as follows:

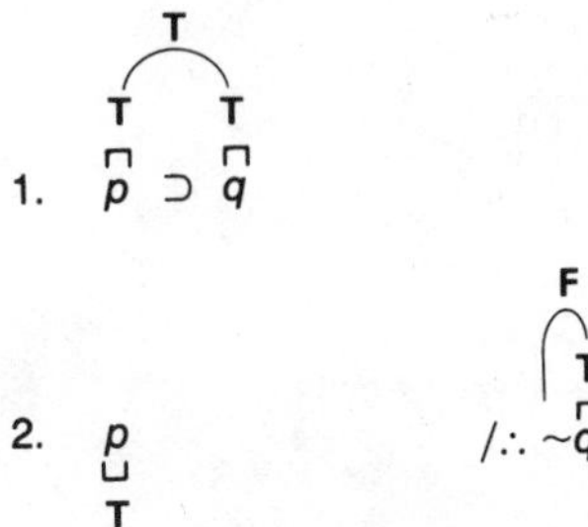

Notice however, that if there were an **F** on the first line of the truth table for material implication, instead of a **T**, then we could not prove that argument form (1) is invalid. On the contrary, we could prove it valid as follows:

		First Premise	Second Premise	Conclusion
p	q	$p \supset q$	p	$\sim q$
T	T	F	T	F
T	F	F	T	T
F	T	T	F	F
F	F	T	F	T

(This truth table would prove that argument form (1) is valid because it would indicate that none of its substitution instances could have true premises and a false conclusion, for *both* premises of such a substitution instance could never be true simultaneously.)

So we cannot place an **F** on the first line of the truth table for material implication. Instead, we must place a **T** on that line, to preserve the invalidity of certain intuitively invalid argument forms.*

Now consider argument form (2) above. This argument form, Modus Ponens, obviously is valid. Indeed, if we allow symbolization of its first

---

*Note that we can't prove the invalidity of the argument form in question by changing any of the other three truth values in the truth table for material implication. For example, changing line three from **T** to **F** could not possibly yield a case with all true premises and a false conclusion. So to be able to prove this argument form invalid, we must place a **T** on line one of the truth table for "⊃". (Similar remarks apply to the three argument forms about to be considered.)

premise by means of material implication, then we have already proved that it is valid by truth table analysis. Of course, if there were a **T** on the second line of the truth table for material implication, instead of an **F**, then we could not prove Modus Ponens valid. Indeed, we could prove it *invalid* by truth table analysis, as follows:

```
        T
      ⌒
    T   F
    ⌐   ⌐
1.  p ⊃ q

    T                   F
    ⌐                   ⌐
2.  p               /∴ q
```

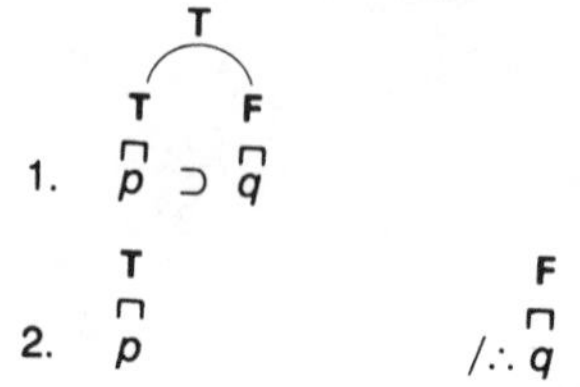

So it is clear that we cannot allow a **T** on the second line of the truth table for material implication. Instead, we must place an **F** on that line, to preserve the validity of valid argument forms such as Modus Ponens.

Next, consider argument form (3) above. This form obviously is not valid. In fact, its invalidity has been so infamous in the history of philosophy that reasoning having this form has acquired a special title, namely "fallacy of denying the antecedent". Symbolizing the first premise of (3) by material implication, defined as in Chapter Two, we can prove that (3) is invalid by truth table analysis, as follows:

```
        T
      ⌒
    F   T
    ⌐   ⌐
1.  p ⊃ q
                        F
                        ⌒T
                        ⌐
2.  ~p              /∴ ~q
     ⌙
     F
    T
```

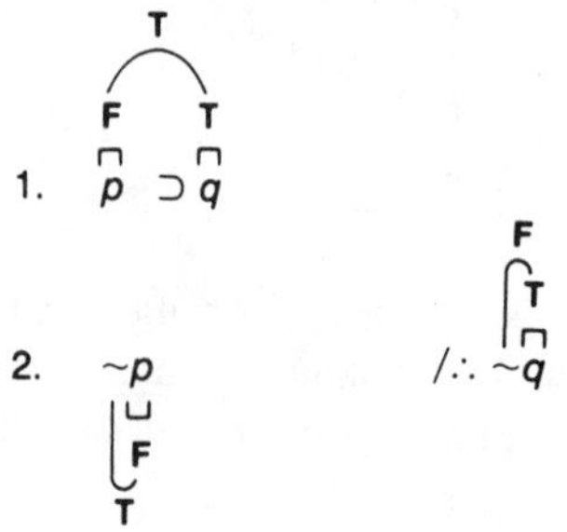

But if there were an **F** on the third line of the truth table for material implication, instead of a **T**, then we could not prove that (3) is invalid. On the contrary, we could prove it valid, as follows:

		First Premise	Second Premise	Conclusion
p	q	$p \supset q$	$\sim p$	$\sim q$
T	T	T	F	F
T	F	F	F	T
F	T	F	T	F
F	F	T	T	T

(This truth table would prove the argument form in question valid, because it would indicate that none of its substitution instances could have true premises and a false conclusion.)

So it is clear that we cannot allow an **F** on the third line of the truth table for material implication. Instead, we must place a **T** on that line, to preserve the invalidity of certain intuitively invalid argument forms.

Finally, consider argument form (4) above. Clearly, this form also is not valid. Symbolizing its first premise using material implication defined as in Chapter Two, we can prove that (4) is invalid by truth table analysis, as follows:

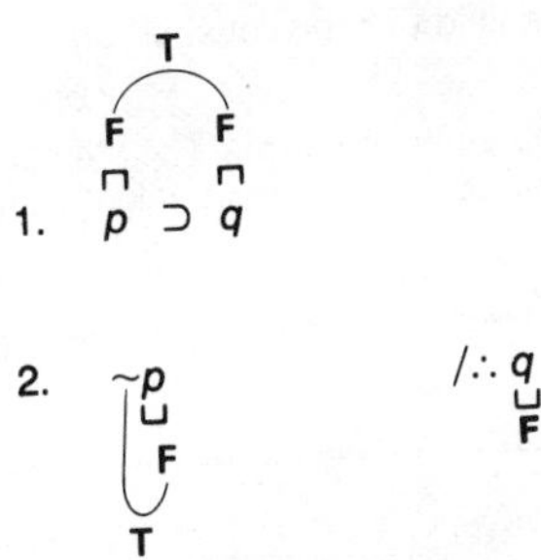

But, if there were an **F** on the fourth line of the truth table for material implication, instead of a **T**, then we could not prove (4) invalid. On the contrary, we could prove it valid, as follows:

		First Premise	**Second Premise**	**Conclusion**
p	q	$p \supset q$	$\sim p$	q
T	**T**	**T**	**F**	**T**
T	**F**	**F**	**F**	**F**
F	**T**	**T**	**T**	**T**
F	**F**	**F**	**T**	**F**

It follows that we cannot allow an **F** on the fourth line of the truth table for material implication. We must place a **T** on that line to preserve the invalidity of certain intuitively invalid argument forms.

The general conclusion to be drawn from the four examples above is that we must use material implication, as it was defined in Chapter Two, to assure that our translations of certain valid arguments and argument forms will be valid, and to assure that our translations of certain invalid arguments and argument forms will be invalid.*

* This justification of the truth table for material implication was suggested to me by Alan Hausman and by Richard Cole.

Exercise 5-9:

1. Every argument must be either valid or invalid. So shouldn't failure to prove an argument is valid indirectly prove that it is invalid?
2. Why bother to find out whether the premises of an argument are consistent or inconsistent? (Example)
3. If the premises of a valid argument are consistent, is its conclusion necessarily true? (Example)
4. Suppose you know that a particular argument is deductively valid and has a false conclusion. What, if anything, can you tell from this about its premises?
5. Carefully explain in what sense an indirect proof is just a kind of conditional proof. (Example)
6. Suppose you are told that all substitution instances of the sentence form $\sim(p \vee A)$ are false, but aren't told whether *A* is true or false. Can you figure out *A's* truth value? How?

Key Terms Introduced in Chapter Five

Assumed premise: An assumption added to the given premises in an argument.

Conditional proof, rule of (CP): The rule that permits inference from a sentence *q* to a sentence $p \supset q$, if the assumption of *p* permitted the derivation of *q*.

Consistent: Noncontradictory.

Inconsistent: Contradictory.

Indirect proof, rule of (IP): The rule that permits inference to the negation of a sentence from which a contradiction has been derived. *Synonym:* **Reductio ad absurdum proof.**

Propositional form: The form of a symbolized sentence (or argument) obtained by replacing each sentence constant in the symbolized sentence (or argument) by a sentence variable (taking care to replace a given capital letter by the same sentence variable throughout and making sure not to replace two different capital letters by the same sentence variable). *Example:* The propositional form of

$$\sim[A \supset (\sim B \vee C)] \supset \sim C$$

is

$$\sim[p \supset (\sim q \vee r)] \supset \sim r$$

Reductio ad absurdum proof: (See **Indirect proof.**)

Part Two

Chapter Six

Predicate Logic

Predicate Logic—I

The sentential or propositional logic presented in the first five chapters deals with the internal structure of compound sentences, but not with the internal structure of atomic sentences. Let's now examine what is called **predicate logic,** or **quantifier logic,** a logic concerned with the interior structure of both atomic and compound sentences.

Predicate logic gives us a way to prove the validity of many valid arguments which are invalid when symbolized in the notation of sentential logic. For example, the standard and ancient syllogism

1. All humans are mortal.
2. All Greeks are human. /∴ All Greeks are mortal.

must be symbolized in sentential logic in a way that makes it invalid, for instance as

1. *A*
2. *B* /∴ *C*

Yet surely this syllogism is valid. Once we have introduced the machinery of predicate logic, we'll be able to prove it is valid quite easily.

1 *Individuals and Properties*

Consider the sentence "Art is happy". This sentence asserts that some particular object or entity, Art, has a certain property, namely the property of being happy. If we let the capital letter *H* denote the property of being happy, and the lowercase letter *a* name the individual, Art, we can symbolize this sentence as *Ha*. Similarly, the sentence "Betsy is happy" can be symbolized as *Hb*, the sentence "Art is friendly" as *Fa*, and the sentence "Betsy is friendly" as *Fb*. The sentences, *Fa*, *Fb*, *Ha*, and *Hb* are alike in that they have the same general structure. In each of these sentences a *property* is ascribed to some *individual entity*. This is one of the basic patterns of atomic sentences.

Another basic pattern is illustrated by the sentence "Art is taller than Betsy". This sentence asserts that there is a particular property (______ being taller than _ _ _ _ _) that holds *between* the two individual objects Art and Betsy. If we let *a* denote Art, *b* Betsy, and *T* the property of one thing being taller than another, we can symbolize the sentence "Art is taller than Betsy" as *Tab*. Similarly, we can symbolize the sentence "Betsy is taller than Art" as *Tba*. And if we let *F* denote the property of one thing being a friend of another (______ is a friend of _ _ _ _ _), then we can symbolize the sentence "Art is a friend of Betsy" as *Fab*, and so on.

Properties such as *taller than* and *is a friend of*, which hold between two or more entities, are called **relational properties.** The particular properties in question are *two-place* related properties, since they hold between two entities. But we can also have three or four (or more) place properties. For instance the property of being between two other objects (______ is between _ _ _ _ _ and _ _ _ _ _ _ _) is a *three-place* relational property.

In some respects, the above analysis of the structure of atomic sentences is very much like those given in traditional grammar texts. For instance, a traditional grammar text would analyze the sentence "Art is human" as containing a *subject,* "Art", and a *predicate,* "is human". (Indeed, the term "predicate" is often used by logicians instead of the term "property". Hence the name "predicate logic".) However, traditional grammars generally analyze all atomic sentences into this subject-predicate form. For instance, they construe the sentence "Art is taller than Besty" as ascribing a predicate, being taller than Betsy, to a subject, Art. This is quite different from our analysis, for our analysis construes the sentence "Art is taller than Betsy" as concerning two subjects (or individual objects or entities), namely Art and Betsy, and construes this sentence as stating that a relational property holds between them. (Of course, we also can construe the sentence "Art is taller than Betsy" as ascribing the nonrelational property of being-taller-than-Betsy to Art, in which case that sentence will be symbolized as *Ta,* but to do so is to mask part of the structure of that sentence.)

Let's now be more specific about the two notational conventions introduced above. First, *capital letters* are used to denote properties, whether relational or nonrelational. And second, *small letters* (up to and including the letter *t*) are used to denote individual objects, things, and entities, that is, any things that can have properties ascribed to them about which we wish to speak.*

---

* Except properties themselves. Systems that permit ascription of properties to properties encounter serious technical difficulties. (See, for instance, Chapter Nine, Section 7.)

Capital letters used to denote properties are called **property constants,** and small letters (up to and including *t*) used to denote things, objects, and individual entities are called **individual constants.**

In addition, the small letters *u* through *z* are used as **individual variables,** replaceable by individual constants. (Their use is explained further on the next page.)

These notational conventions are to be used in addition to those previously introduced. We still allow the use of capital letters as sentence abbreviations, and the use of the small letters from *p* through *z* as sentence variables, just as in propositional logic.

Examples:

Let *P* denote the property of being president, *C* the property of being charismatic, *r* Reagan, and *m* Mondale. Then the expressions on the left translate the sentences on the right into the notation of predicate logic:

1.	*Pr*	Reagan is president.
2.	~*Pm*	Mondale is not president.
3.	*Pr* ∨ *Pm*	Reagan is president or Mondale is president.
4.	*Pm* ∨ *Cr*	Mondale is president or Reagan is charismatic.
5.	*Pr* · *Cr*	Reagan is president and Reagan is charismatic.
6.	*Pr* ⊃ ~*Pm*	If Reagan is president, then Mondale is not president.
7.	~(*Pm* · *Cm*)	It's not the case that Mondale is both president and charismatic.
8.	*Pr* ⊃ ~(*Cm* · *Cr*)	If Reagan is president, then it's not true that Mondale and Reagan are both charismatic.

Now let *Dxy* denote the relational property of *x* having defeated *y*, *f* denote Joe Frazier, *a* Muhammad Ali, and *s* Sonny Liston:

9.	*Dfa*	Joe Frazier defeated Muhammad Ali.
10.	*Dfa* ∨ *Dfs*	Frazier defeated either Ali or Sonny Liston.
11.	*Dfs* ⊃ *Dfa*	If Frazier defeated Liston, then he defeated Ali.
12.	~*Dfs* · *Dfa*	Frazier didn't defeat Liston, but he did defeat Ali.
13.	*Dfa* · *Daf*	Frazier defeated Ali, but Ali also defeated Frazier.
14.	~(*Dfa* · *Dfs*)	It's not true that Frazier defeated both Ali and Sonny Liston.
15.	(*Das* · *Daf*) · ~(*Dsa* · *Dfa*)	Ali defeated Liston and Frazier, but Liston and Frazier didn't both defeat Ali.

Exercise 6-1:

Symbolize the following sentences, using the indicated letters.

1. Geraldine Ferraro is married. (f = "Geraldine Ferraro"; Mx = "x is married")
2. Walter Mondale is married. (m = "Walter Mondale")
3. In fact, Geraldine Ferraro and Walter Mondale both are married.
4. But Ferraro isn't married to Mondale. (Mxy = "x is married to y")
5. So, obviously, Mondale isn't married to Ferraro.
6. Nevertheless, if Ferraro is married, so is Mondale.
7. But if Ferraro is married, it's to John Zaccaro. (c = "John Zaccaro")
8. Anyway, Ferraro is married either to Mondale or Zaccaro.
9. Of course, she isn't married to both of them.
10. And surely Zaccaro isn't married to both Ferraro and Jane Fonda. (j = "Jane Fonda")

In developing a predicate logic, we do not abandon propositional logic. Instead we include it within predicate logic. So mixed sentences are possible. An example is the sentence "Art is handsome and Betsy is beautiful" symbolized as $A \cdot Bb$. Of course, we also can symbolize that sentence as $Ha \cdot Bb$ (so as to reveal the structure of the two atomic sentences "Art is handsome" and "Betsy is beautiful"). And we also can symbolize it as $Ha \cdot B$. Thus, letters may serve more than one function. For instance, the letter B in this example serves in one place as a sentence constant and in another as a property constant. This ambiguity is harmless because it is clear in every case which function a letter serves. A property constant always occurs with a small letter next to it, while a sentence constant never does.

The expression formed by combining a property constant and an individual constant is a sentence. The sentence Pr referred to above is an example. It has a truth value, namely the value **T** if Reagan is indeed president, and **F** if he is not. But what about an expression formed by combining a property constant with an *individual variable,* say the form Hx? First, this form is not a sentence, since x is a variable. (Writing Hx is like writing H____, where the solid line serves as a place holder, to be filled in by an individual constant.) So the form Hx is neither true nor false. And second, since we can obtain a sentence from Hx by replacing the variable x with a small letter denoting some object or entity, Hx is a *sentence form*. For instance, we can obtain the sentence Ha from Hx by replacing the variable x with the small letter a.

Examples:

The following are examples of sentence forms and some of their substitution instances which are sentences.

	Sentence Form		Substitution Instances
1.	Hy	1.	$Ha, Hb, Hc, \ldots$
2.	$Bx \supset Hy$	2.	$Bb \supset Ha, Bb \supset Hb, Ba \supset Hb, Ba \supset Ha, \ldots$
3.	$(Hx \cdot Bx) \supset Hy$	3.	$(Hb \cdot Bb) \supset Ha, (Ha \cdot Ba) \supset Hc, \ldots$

2 *Universal Quantifiers*

In sentential logic, to obtain a sentence from a sentence form, we have to replace all of the sentence variables in the sentence form by sentence constants. Thus from the sentence form $p \supset q$ we obtain the sentence $A \supset B$, as well as many others. In predicate logic this also can be done, as was explained above. Thus from the sentence form *Hx* we obtain the sentences *Ha*, *Hb*, and so on. However, it is a fact of fundamental importance that in predicate logic a sentence can be obtained from a sentence form *without* replacing its individual variables by individual constants. For example, we can obtain a sentence from the sentence form *Hx* without specifying some particular entity that has the property *H*, by specifying instead *how many* entities have that property. This idea is familiar from its use in everyday English. For instance, in English we can form a sentence by ascribing the property of honesty to a particular man. The sentence "Art is honest" is an example. But we can also form a sentence by saying *how many* men are honest. The sentences "All men are honest" and "Some men are honest" are examples.

In predicate logic two symbols, called **quantifiers,** are used to state how many. The first is the **universal quantifier,** used to assert that *all* entities have some property or properties. The symbols (x), (y), and so on, that is, individual variables placed between parentheses, are used for this purpose. Thus to symbolize the sentence "Everything moves", or "All things move", start with the sentence form *Mx* and prefix the universal quantifier (x) to obtain the sentence $(x)(Mx)$, read as "For all *x*, *x* moves", or "For all *x*, *Mx*", or "Given any *x*, *Mx*", and so on.

Just how many *x*'s constitute *all* depends on how many things we want our language to be able to deal with. For instance, in some systems for arithmetic, we want the individual constants to denote numbers, so in such a system the number of *x*'s will be infinite. The **domain of discourse** for a system for arithmetic is (so to speak) the "world of numbers". Usually, the domain of discourse is not explicitly specified, but assumed to be "everything", or perhaps all concrete (as opposed to abstract) things.

In sentential logic, parentheses are used to remove ambiguity. For instance, the parentheses in the sentence $\sim(A \cdot B)$ indicate that the negation sign negates the whole compound sentence, and not just the atomic sentence A. The parentheses indicate the *scope* of the negation sign, that is, how much of the sentence the negation sign negates.

In predicate logic parentheses serve a similar function. Take the sentence "Everything has mass and is extended". It is correctly symbolized as $(x)(Mx \cdot Ex)$ (where Mx = "x has mass" and Ex = "x is extended"), and is read "For all x, x has mass and x is extended", or "Given any x, that x has mass and is extended". The parentheses around the expression $(Mx \cdot Ex)$ indicate that the **scope** of the (x) quantifier is the entire remaining part of the sentence, namely $(Mx \cdot Ex)$, which is said to be *within the scope* of the (x) quantifier. Similarly, the brackets in $(x)[(Mx \cdot Ex) \supset Cx]$ indicate that the scope of this (x) quantifier is the entire remainder of that sentence.

However, when the scope of a quantifier extends just over the next minimal unit, parentheses may be omitted for the sake of simplicity. Thus, we may symbolize the sentence "Everything is heavy" either as $(x)(Hx)$ or as $(x)Hx$ (omitting parentheses of scope).

This expression $(x)(Mx \cdot Ex)$ is a sentence, but $(Mx \cdot Ex)$ is a sentence *form,* not a sentence. Is the expression $(x)(Mx) \cdot Ex$ a sentence? The answer is that it is not, because it contains an individual variable that is not quantified, namely the x in Ex. Unquantified variables are called **free variables.** Quantified variables, such as the middle x in $(x)(Mx) \cdot Ex$, are said to be **bound variables.** An expression that contains one or more free variables is a sentence *form,* not a sentence.

Finally, it should be noted that merely being within the scope of a quantifier is not sufficient to make a variable a bound variable. To be bound, a variable must be within the scope of a quantifier using the same letter. Thus the y in $(x)(Fy \supset Gx)$ is within the scope of the (x) quantifier but is not bound by it, whereas the x in $(x)(Fy \supset Gx)$ is both within the scope of the (x) quantifier and bound by it.

Exercise 6-2:

For each expression below, indicate (1) which variables are *free* and which *bound;* (2) which letters serve as *individual constants* and which as *property constants;* (3) which free variables are within the scope of some quantifier or other and which individual constants are *not* within the scope of any quantifier.

1. $(x)(Fx \supset Ga)$
2. $(x)(Fa \supset Gx)$
3. $(x)[Fx \supset (Gy \vee Hx)]$
4. $(x)Fx \supset (y)(Gyx)$
5. $Fa \vee (x)[Gax \supset (\sim Kxy \cdot Hb)]$
6. $(x)Fax \supset (y)[Fyx \supset (\sim Gxa \vee Fxy)]$

Now consider the sentence "All humans are mortal". It is correctly symbolized as $(x)(Hx \supset Mx)$ (where H = "human", and M = "mortal"), and is read "For all x, if x is human, then x is mortal", or "Given any x, if x is human then x is mortal", which is roughly what the sentence "All humans are mortal" asserts.

Notice that "All humans are mortal" is *not* symbolized as $(x)(Hx \cdot Mx)$, for that says that given any x, it is *both* human *and* mortal, or, what amounts to the same thing, that all things are both human and mortal, and this is not what the sentence "All humans are mortal" means. (Note that "All humans are mortal" is true, while "All things are both human and mortal" is false.)

Examples:

Here are some English sentences and their correct symbolization in predicate logic notation (using obvious abbreviations).

English Sentence	Symbolization
1. Everything is movable.	1. $(x)Mx$
2. Not everything is movable.	2. $\sim(x)Mx$
3. Nothing is movable.	3. $(x)\sim Mx$
4. Everything is immovable.	4. $(x)\sim Mx$

(Notice that 3 and 4 are equivalent.)

5. It's not true that everything is immovable.	5. $\sim(x)\sim Mx$
6. (All)* sugar tastes sweet.	6. $(x)(Sx \supset Tx)$
7. If something is a piece of sugar, then it tastes sweet.	7. $(x)(Sx \supset Tx)$

(Notice that 6 and 7 are equivalent.)

8. Everything is either sweet or bitter.	8. $(x)(Sx \vee Bx)$
9. Either everything is sweet or else everything is bitter.	9. $(x)Sx \vee (x)Bx$

* In English, the quantifiers "all" and "some" often are omitted when context makes it clear what is intended.

(Notice that 8 and 9 are *not* equivalent.)

10.	Each person fears death.	10.	$(x)(Px \supset Fx)$
11.	Everyone fears death.	11.	$(x)(Px \supset Fx)$

(Notice that 10 and 11 are equivalent.)

12.	No one fears death.	12.	$(x)(Px \supset \sim Fx)$
13.	Not everyone fears death.	13.	$\sim(x)(Px \supset Fx)$
14.	All honest people fear death.	14.	$(x)[(Px \cdot Hx) \supset Fx]$
15.	No one who is honest fears death.	15.	$(x)[(Px \cdot Hx) \supset \sim Fx]$
16.	Not all honest people fear death.	16.	$\sim(x)[(Px \cdot Hx) \supset Fx]$
17.	Anyone who doesn't fear death isn't honest.	17.	$(x)[(Px \cdot \sim Fx) \supset \sim Hx)]$
18.	Although all honest people fear death, Jane doesn't.	18.	$(x)[(Px \cdot Hx) \supset Fx] \cdot \sim Fj$
19.	Everyone either is honest or fears death.	19.	$(x)[Px \supset (Hx \vee Fx)]$
20.	It's false that no honest people fear death.	20.	$\sim(x)[Px \cdot Hx) \supset \sim Fx]$

Of course, there is nothing sacred about the variable x. For instance, the sentence "Sugar tastes sweet" can be symbolized as $(y)(Sy \supset Ty)$ or $(z)(Sz \supset Tz)$, just as well as $(x)(Sx \supset Tx)$. All three of these sentences say the same thing. (In math we can write $(y + z) = (z + y)$ just as well as $(x + y) = (y + x)$; both of these formulas say the same thing.)

Exercise 6-3:

Symbolize the following sentences, using the indicated letters.

1. All events have causes. (Ex = "x is an event"; Cx = "x has a cause")
2. Every event has a cause.
3. Not all events have causes.
4. No events have causes.
5. All natural events have causes. (Nx = "x is natural")
6. All events that have causes are natural.
7. No unnatural events have causes.
8. Anything that is caused is a natural event.
9. No natural events are uncaused.
10. Events are either natural or uncaused.

Exercise 6-4:

Symbolize the following sentences, letting Sx = "x is a logic student"; Lx = "x is logical"; Px = "x is popular"; and j = "Jane".

1. Logic students are logical.
2. No. Logic students definitely are not logical.
3. Well, not all logic students are logical.
4. Anyway, it's true that those who are logical are not popular.
5. So if all logic students are logical, none of them is popular.
6. But if not all of them are logical, then not all of them are unpopular.
7. Nor is it true that those who are unpopular all are illogical.
8. Now if those who are popular haven't studied logic, then if Jane is illogical, she must have studied logic.
9. And if she is illogical, it's false either that logic students universally are logical or that the unpopular universally are logical.
10. Supposing Jane is both unpopular and illogical, then logic students are neither all popular nor all logical.

3 *Existential Quantifiers*

We now introduce a second quantifier, the **existential quantifier,** used to assert that *some* entities, or at least one entity, have a given property. The symbol $(\exists x)$ is used for this purpose. Thus to symbolize the sentence "Something is heavy", or the sentence "At least one thing is heavy", start with the sentence form Hx and prefix an existential quantifier to it. The result is the sentence $(\exists x)Hx$, read "For some x, x is heavy", or "There is an x such that x is heavy", or just "Some x is heavy".

The sentence $(\exists x)Hx$ is as simple as an existentially quantified sentence can be. Other equally simple sentences are "Something is tall" $(\exists x)Tx$, "Something is important" $(\exists x)Ix$, and so on. Adding negation increases complexity. For example, the expression $(\exists x){\sim}Hx$ symbolizes the sentence "Something is not heavy", and the expression ${\sim}(\exists x)Hx$ the sentence "It's false that something is heavy".

More complicated symbolizations are obtained in other ways. Thus, to symbolize the sentence "Something is both heavy *and* expensive", conjoin Hx (for "x is heavy") with Ex (for "x is expensive") to get $(Hx \cdot Ex)$, and then add an existential quantifier to get $(\exists x)(Hx \cdot Ex)$. Similarly, to symbolize "Something is both round and green" conjoin Rx (for "x is round") with Gx (for "x is green") to get $(Rx \cdot Gx)$, and then add an existential quantifier to get $(\exists x)(Rx \cdot Gx)$.

Examples:

Here are some other English sentences and their symbolizations using existential quantifiers (letting Px = "x is a person" and using other obvious abbreviations).

	English Sentence		Symbolization
1.	Some people are honest.	1.	$(\exists x)(Px \cdot Hx)$
2.	Some people are not honest.	2.	$(\exists x)(Px \cdot {\sim}Hx)$
3.	Some honest people are mistreated.	3.	$(\exists x)[(Px \cdot Hx) \cdot Mx]$
4.	Some people are liars or thieves.	4.	$(\exists x)[Px \cdot (Lx \vee Tx)]$
5.	It's not true that some people are honest.	5.	${\sim}(\exists x)(Px \cdot Hx)$
6.	Some people are neither honest nor truthful.	6.	$(\exists x)[Px \cdot {\sim}(Hx \vee Tx)]$, or $(\exists x)[Px \cdot ({\sim}Hx \cdot {\sim}Tx)]$
7.	Some things are neither expensive nor worthwhile.	7.	$(\exists x){\sim}(Ex \vee Wx)$, or $(\exists x)({\sim}Ex \cdot {\sim}Wx]$

Exercise 6-5:

Symbolize the following sentences, letting Ax = "x is an athlete"; Ox = "x is overpaid"; Ex = "x is an entertainer"; and Mx = "x is an employee".

1. Some athletes are overpaid.
2. Some athletes are not overpaid.
3. It's not true that some athletes are overpaid.
4. But it is true that some overpaid employees are not athletes.
5. And there are employees who are neither athletes nor overpaid.
6. Some employees are overpaid entertainers, but some are merely overpaid.
7. Some nonathlete entertainers are neither overpaid nor employees.
8. Some employees are not athletes, nor are they entertainers or overpaid.
9. There are overpaid entertainers who are neither employees nor athletes.
10. It's false that if some athletes are overpaid, then some are not entertainers.

In the explanation above, we construed quantifiers as stating *how many*. But there is another way to construe them, perhaps more revealing, which interprets quantified sentences as shorthand versions of much longer sentences of a certain kind.

Imagine a limited universe containing, say, only four individual entities. What would quantified sentences assert in such a universe? For instance, what would the sentence $(x)Fx$ assert? The answer (roughly) is that it would assert that *Fa and Fb and Fc and Fd*.* In other words, it would assert that $(Fa \cdot Fb) \cdot (Fc \cdot Fd)$. Thus in this limited universe, the symbolization $(x)Fx$ would be shorthand for the expression $(Fa \cdot Fb) \cdot (Fc \cdot Fd)$, called the **expansion** of $(x)Fx$ with respect to that limited universe.

Of course our logic is applicable to the real universe, which contains many more than four individual entities. Can we construe quantified sentences in a universally applicable logic as a shorthand way of writing very long conjunctions? The answer is that we *could* construe them in this way *if* (1) there were only a finite number of entities in the real universe, and (2) we had a name in our language for every entity. But unfortunately we do not have a name for every entity in the real universe of discourse, and the number of entities we want to talk about is not finite. For instance, in arithmetic, we want to be able to assert the sentence "Every even number is divisible by 2", that is, assert that 2 is divisible by 2, *and* 4 is divisible by 2, *and* 6 is divisible by 2, and so on. But since the number of numbers is infinite, we cannot actually write down a conjunction equivalent to the sentence "Every even number is divisible by 2". Instead we must use a universal quantifier to symbolize that sentence. For instance, using obvious abbreviations, we can symbolize it as $(x)[(Nx \cdot Ex) \supset Dx]$. So we cannot say that a universally quantified sentence is *equivalent* to any very long conjunction that we might construct. Nevertheless, it is intuitively helpful to think of sentences such as $(x)Fx$ and $(x)(Hx \supset Mx)$ as shorthand for very long conjunctions.

Now consider a sentence containing an *existential* quantifier, say, the sentence $(\exists x)Fx$. In a limited universe containing only three objects, this sentence asserts *not* that *Fa and Fb and Fc*, since that is what is asserted by $(x)Fx$, but rather that *Fa or Fb or Fc*. So its expansion in this limited universe is $[(Fa \vee Fb) \vee Fc]$.

Examples:

The following are expansions for a language containing three individual constants, *a*, *b*, and *c*.

---

*This is only roughly true because universally quantified sentences also assert that the items listed are all the items there are (in the universe of discourse), and merely listing the items, even though all in fact are listed, does not *say* that all are listed.

1. **Symbolization:** $(\exists x)\sim Fx$
Expansion: $\sim Fa \vee (\sim Fb \vee \sim Fc)$
2. **Symbolization:** $\sim(\exists x)Fx$
Expansion: $\sim[Fa \vee (Fb \vee Fc)]$
3. **Symbolization:** $(x)(Fx \supset Gx)$
Expansion: $(Fa \supset Ga) \cdot [(Fb \supset Gb) \cdot (Fc \supset Gc)]$
4. **Symbolization:** $(\exists x)\sim(Fx \cdot Gx)$
Expansion: $\sim(Fa \cdot Ga) \vee [\sim(Fb \cdot Gb) \vee \sim(Fc \cdot Gc)]$
5. **Symbolization:** $(x)[(Fx \cdot Gx) \supset Hx]$
Expansion: $[(Fa \cdot Ga) \supset Ha] \cdot \{[(Fb \cdot Gb) \supset Hb] \cdot [(Fc \cdot Gc) \supset Hc]\}$
6. **Symbolization:** $(\exists x)[(Fx \cdot Gx) \vee Hx]$
Expansion: $[(Fa \cdot Ga) \vee Ha] \vee \{[(Fb \cdot Gb) \vee Hb] \vee [(Fc \cdot Gc) \vee Hc]\}$

Exercise 6-6:

Construct expansions in a two-individual universe of discourse for the following sentences.

1. $(x)(Fx \cdot Gx)$
2. $(\exists x)(Fx \vee Gx)$
3. $(x)[Fx \supset (Gx \vee Hx)]$
4. $(\exists x)[Fx \cdot (Gx \vee Hx)]$
5. $(x)\sim(Fx \supset Gx)$
6. $(\exists x)\sim(Fx \cdot Gx)$
7. $\sim(x)(Fx \supset Gx)$
8. $\sim(\exists x)(Fx \vee Gx)$
9. $(x)[Fx \supset (Gx \supset Hx)]$
10. $(x)[Fx \supset \sim(Gx \cdot Hx)]$

Sentences of the form "Some ______ are _ _ _ _ _", such as the sentence "Some humans are mortal", are often symbolized incorrectly by beginners. The correct symbolization for the sentence "Some humans are mortal" is $(\exists x)(Hx \cdot Mx)$, because this sentence asserts that there is something, x, which is both human and mortal. The temptation is to symbolize it as $(\exists x)(Hx \supset Mx)$, by analogy with the symbolization of the sentence "All humans are mortal", which is correctly symbolized as $(x)(Hx \supset Mx)$. But in this case the similar grammatical structure of the two English sentences is misleading. (Sentences having the same form as $(\exists x)(Hx \supset Mx)$ are rarely spoken in everyday life.)

To see the difference between the sentence $(\exists x)(Hx \cdot Mx)$ and the sentence $(\exists x)(Hx \supset Mx)$, examine their expansions, namely $[(Ha \cdot Ma) \vee (Hb \cdot Mb)] \vee \ldots$ and $[(Ha \supset Ma) \vee (Hb \supset Mb)] \vee \ldots$. (The dots are used in the sense of "and so on" or "etc.", since we cannot completely write down an infinitely long conjunction or disjunction.) The expansion $[(Ha \cdot Ma) \vee (Hb \cdot Mb)] \vee \ldots$ is true because there are some things that are both human and mortal, but the expansion $[(Ha \supset Ma) \vee$

$(Hb \supset Mb)] \vee \ldots$ would be true even if there were no humans at all, mortal or immortal. The reason it would be true is this: Suppose *a* denotes some item that is not human. Then the disjunct $Ha \supset Ma$ is true, because its antecedent *Ha* is false. Therefore, because one of its disjuncts is true, the whole long disjunction $[(Ha \supset Ma) \vee (Hb \supset Mb)] \vee \ldots$ is true. Its truth has nothing to do with human mortality; it would be true even if there were no human beings. But the expansion $[(Ha \cdot Ma) \vee (Hb \cdot Mb)] \vee \ldots$ would *not* be true if there were no human beings, since if that were the case, then all of its disjuncts would be false. (If there were no human beings in the universe, then $(Ha \cdot Ma)$ would be false, $(Hb \cdot Mb)$ would be false, $(Hc \cdot Mc)$ would be false, and indeed every disjunct of the infinitely long disjunction in question would be false, so that the infinitely long disjunction itself would be false.) So the correct symbolization for "Some humans are mortal" is $(\exists x)(Hx \cdot Mx)$ and not $(\exists x)(Hx \supset Mx)$.

Exercise 6-7:

Translate the following into English, being as colloquial as possible. Let Tx = "x is a TV newscaster"; Px = "x has a pleasant personality"; Ex = "x is a political expert"; b = "Barbara Walters"; c = "Walter Cronkite"; h = "Howard Cosell".

1. $(\exists x)(Tx \cdot Px)$
2. $(\exists x)(Tx \cdot \sim Ex)$
3. $\sim(\exists x)(Tx \cdot Ex)$
4. $(x)(Tx \supset \sim Ex)$
5. $\sim(x)(Tx \supset Ex)$
6. $(x)[(Ex \cdot \sim Px) \supset \sim Tx]$
7. $(\exists x)[Tx \cdot \sim(Px \cdot Ex)]$
8. $(\exists x)[Tx \cdot (Px \vee Ex)]$
9. $(x)(Tx \supset Ex) \supset \sim Tb$
10. $Tc \supset (y)[(Ty \cdot Py) \supset \sim Ey]$
11. $(x)(Tx \supset Px) \supset \sim Th$
12. $(x)[Tx \supset (Px \cdot Ex)] \supset \sim(Tc \vee Th)$

Exercise 6-8:

Symbolize the following sentences, using the indicated symbols as abbreviations.

1. Some people are rich but unhappy (not happy). (Px = "x is a person"; Rx = "x is rich"; Hx = "x is happy")
2. All rich people are unhappy.
3. Not all rich people are unhappy.
4. No rich people are unhappy.

5. Some people who aren't rich are happy.
6. But some poor (nonrich) people are unhappy.
7. It's not true that all happy people are poor.
8. But it is true that all poor people who are unhappy want to be rich. (Wx = "x wants to be rich")
9. Further, some happy poor people want to be rich.
10. If all happy people are poor, then some rich people are unhappy.
11. And if all who are unhappy aren't rich, then some who are rich are happy.
12. But if all unhappy people are rich, then it isn't true that all rich people are happy.

Symbolizations Containing Overlapping Quantifiers

Symbolizations may contain quantifiers having overlapping scopes. An example is the sentence "Everything is different from everything", which in symbols becomes $(x)(y)(Dxy)$ or, omitting the parentheses of scope, $(x)(y)Dxy$. This sentence is false, of course, since nothing can be different from itself. But it is meaningful, and so we want to have a way to symbolize it. (Notice that the sentence "Everything is different from everything" is not the same as the sentence "Everything is different from everything *else*". To symbolize the latter, we need a symbol for identity, which is introduced in Chapter Nine.)

Examples:

Here are some examples of multiply quantified sentences with overlapping quantifier scopes, along with their correct symbolizations (letting Lxy = "x loves y", and—to simplify matters—restricting the domain of discourse to human beings).

	Sentence		Symbolization
1.	Everyone loves everyone.	1.	$(x)(y)Lxy$
2.	Someone loves someone.	2.	$(\exists x)(\exists y)Lxy$
3.	Not everyone loves everyone.	3.	$\sim(x)(y)Lxy$
4.	No one loves anyone.	4.	$(x)(y)\sim Lxy$

The examples just considered all contain overlapping quantifiers of the same type. For instance, in sentence 1 above, both quantifiers are universal quantifiers; in sentence 2 both are existential quantifiers. In such cases, the order in which the quantifiers occur is not relevant to the meanings of the sentences. Thus, $(x)(y)Lxy$ says the same thing as $(y)(x)Lxy$.*

But when an existential and a universal quantifier are involved, order becomes crucial. Compare, for instance, the order of quantifiers in the two expressions $(x)(\exists y)Lxy$ and $(\exists y)(x)Lxy$. (In the former, the existential quantifier is within the scope of the universal quantifier, while in the latter it is the other way around.) If we let Lxy = "x loves y" and restrict the domain of discourse to human beings, then $(x)(\exists y)Lxy$ says that every x (every person) loves some person or other, while $(\exists y)(x)Lxy$ says that some y (some person) is such that everyone loves that person. In other words, $(x)(\exists y)Lxy$ says that everyone loves someone or other, while $(\exists y)(x)Lxy$ says that there is someone who is loved by everyone, and these clearly are different.

One way to better understand sentences of this kind is to become familiar with the *expansions* of various multiply quantified sentences. Take the sentence "Everyone loves everyone", in symbols $(x)(y)Lxy$, and consider its expansion in a universe containing just two individuals, a and b. To say that everyone loves everyone is to say that every x loves every y. Since there are exactly two x's in this universe, this says that the first x, namely a, loves every y (in symbols $(y)Lay$), and the second x, namely b, loves every y (in symbols $(y)Lby$). So a partial expansion of $(x)(y)Lxy$ is just the conjunction of $(y)Lay$ and $(y)Lby$, or $(y)Lay \cdot (y)Lby$. To obtain the complete expansion of $(x)(y)Lxy$, we also have to expand for the (y) quantifier. First, the left conjunct, $(y)Lay$, says that a loves every y, which in this two-individual universe means that $Laa \cdot Lab$. And second, the right conjunct, $(y)Lby$, says that b loves every y, which in this two-individual universe means that $Lba \cdot Lbb$. So the complete expansion of $(x)(y)Lxy$ is the conjunction $(Laa \cdot Lab) \cdot (Lba \cdot Lbb)$.

Now consider the sentence "Someone loves someone (or other)", in symbols $(\exists x)(\exists y)Lxy$. To say that someone loves someone is to say that there is some x that loves some y. Since there are exactly two individuals in the universe in question, this is to say that either a loves some y (in symbols $(\exists y)Lay$) or b loves some y (in symbols $(\exists y)Lby$), in other words that $(\exists y)Lay \vee (\exists y)Lby$. The left disjunct, $(\exists y)Lay$, says that a loves either a or b, or in symbols that $Laa \vee Lab$. And the right disjunct, $(\exists y)Lby$, says that b loves either a or b, or in symbols that $Lba \vee Lbb$. So the complete expansion for $(\exists x)(\exists y)Lxy$ is the disjunction $(Laa \vee Lab) \vee (Lba \vee Lbb)$. (Compare this with the expansion for $(x)(y)Lxy$.)

---

*Of course, order is important when quantifiers have different scopes. For example, we can't reverse the positions of the universal quantifiers in $(x)[Fx \supset (y)Gxy]$ to get $(y)[Fx \supset (x)Gxy]$, because these two symbolizations clearly have different meanings (the second is not even a sentence, since the first x occurring in it is a free variable).

Examples:

Here are more examples of multiply quantified sentences (including a few with mixed quantifiers), their correct symbolizations, and their expansions in a two-individual universe of discourse.

1. **Sentence:** No one loves anyone.
Symbolization: $(x)(y){\sim}Lxy$
Expansion: $({\sim}Laa \cdot {\sim}Lab) \cdot ({\sim}Lba \cdot {\sim}Lbb)$

2. **Sentence:** It's not true that someone loves some person (or other).
Symbolization: ${\sim}(\exists x)(\exists y)Lxy$
Expansion: ${\sim}[(Laa \vee Lab) \vee (Lba \vee Lbb)]$

Notice that this is just the expansion of the sentence "Someone loves someone (or other)" *negated*. (Notice also that the expansions of sentences 1 and 2 are logically equivalent.)

3. **Sentence:** There is somebody who doesn't love someone (or other).
Symbolization: $(\exists x)(\exists y){\sim}Lxy$
Expansion: $({\sim}Laa \vee {\sim}Lab) \vee ({\sim}Lba \vee {\sim}Lbb)$

4. **Sentence:** Not everyone loves everyone.
Symbolization: ${\sim}(x)(y)Lxy$
Expansion: ${\sim}[(Laa \cdot Lab) \cdot (Lba \cdot Lbb)]$

Notice that number 4 is just the expansion of the sentence, "Everyone loves everyone", *negated*. (Notice also that the expansions of sentences 3 and 4 are logically equivalent by DeMorgan's Theorem).

5. **Sentence:** Everyone loves someone (or other).
Symbolization: $(x)(\exists y)Lxy$
Expansion: $(Laa \vee Lab) \cdot (Lba \vee Lbb)$

(We arrive at this expansion by expanding first with respect to the universal quantifier to obtain the semi-expansion $(\exists y)Lay \cdot (\exists y)Lby$, then expanding the left conjunct to obtain $(Laa \vee Lab) \cdot (\exists y)Lby$, and finally the right conjunct to obtain $(Laa \vee Lab) \cdot (Lba \vee Lbb)$.)

6. **Sentence:** Someone is such that everyone loves that person. (Or, more colloquially, someone is loved by everyone.)
Symbolization: $(\exists y)(x)Lxy$
Expansion: $(Laa \cdot Lba) \vee (Lab \cdot Lbb)$

(To arrive at this expansion, we can expand first with respect to the existential quantifier, to obtain the semi-expansion $(x)Lxa \vee (x)Lxb$, then expanding the left disjunct to obtain $(Laa \cdot Lba) \vee (x)Lxb$, and finally the right disjunct to obtain $(Laa \cdot Lba) \vee (Lab \cdot Lbb)$.)

(Sentences 5 and 6 are important because their expansions show that the order of mixed quantifiers *does* make a difference.)

7. **Sentence:** There is someone whom no one loves.
Symbolization: $(\exists x)(y){\sim}Lyx$
Expansion: $({\sim}Laa \cdot {\sim}Lba) \vee ({\sim}Lab \cdot {\sim}Lbb)$

8. **Sentence:** Everyone is such that someone (or other) does not love him. (Or, more colloquially, everyone is unloved by someone (or other).)
Symbolization: $(x)(\exists y)\sim Lyx$
Expansion: $(\sim Laa \vee \sim Lba) \cdot (\sim Lab \vee \sim Lbb)$

Exercise 6-9:

Symbolize the following sentences (letting Sxy = "x is smaller than y"), and construct their expansions in a two-individual universe of discourse.

1. Everything is smaller than everything.
2. Something is smaller than something (or other).
3. There is something smaller than everything.
4. Everything is smaller than something (or other).
5. Not all things are smaller than something (or other).
6. There isn't anything that is smaller than everything.
7. Nothing is smaller than anything.
8. There is something such that everything is smaller than that thing.

5 *Proving Validity*

The eighteen valid argument forms plus **CP** and **IP**, which constitute the proof machinery of sentential logic, are incorporated intact into predicate logic. Here is a proof that illustrates their use in predicate logic:

1.	$\overset{p}{\overbrace{Fa}} \supset \overset{q}{\overbrace{Ga}}$	p
2.	$\overset{p}{\overbrace{Fa}}$	p /∴ Ga
3.	$\overset{q}{\overbrace{Ga}}$	1,2 **MP**

Notice that in this use of Modus Ponens the expressions *Fa* and *Ga* are treated as units, just as we treated the capital letters, *A*, *B*, and so on, in propositional logic. Thus, the expression on line 1 is taken to be a substitution instance of the sentence form $p \supset q$, where the unit *Fa* is substituted for *p* and the unit *Ga* is substituted for *q*.

Here is another example:

$\quad\quad\;\; p \quad\;\; q$
1. $(x) \sim (Fx \cdot Gx)$ p $/\therefore (x)(\sim Fx \lor \sim Gx)$

$\quad\quad\;\; p \quad\;\; q$
2. $(x)(\sim Fx \lor \sim Gx)$ 1, **DeM**

In this case, the application of DeMorgan's Theorem to line 1 does not involve the whole of line 1. This is permissible because, as stated in Chapter Four, the ten equivalence forms among the eighteen valid argument forms can be used on parts as well as wholes of sentences and sentence forms.

But the eight implicational forms cannot be used on parts of sentences (or sentence forms). Their use is restricted to whole sentences, as in the previous example containing a valid use of Modus Ponens. Here is a "proof" that is invalid because an implicational argument form (Modus Ponens) is used on part of a line:

1. $(x)(Fx \supset Gx)$ p
2. Fx p $/\therefore Gx$
3. Gx 1,2 **MP**

This "proof" is invalid because the whole of line 1 has the form $(x)(p \supset q)$, and not the form $(p \supset q)$ necessary for the application of Modus Ponens.

We introduce five valid argument forms (inference rules) to be used in predicate logic proofs in addition to the valid argument forms of propositional logic. The first four are implicational (one-directional), and are used to drop or add quantifiers. (The fifth is discussed in the next chapter.)

Universal Instantiation (UI): Consider the argument

1. $(x)(Fx \supset Gx)$ p
2. Fa p $/\therefore Ga$

Suppose Fx = "x is friendly" and Gx = "x is gentle". Then line 1 asserts that for all x, if x is friendly, then x is gentle, or that everything that is friendly is gentle. Surely it follows from this that if a particular x, say the person a, is friendly, then he's also gentle, because whatever is true of *everything* must be true of any *particular* thing. Hence it is legitimate to write as the next line in the proof

3. $Fa \supset Ga$ 1, **UI** (Universal Instantiation)

Then we can assert the conclusion

4. Ga 2,3 **MP**

We call the rule of inference that permits the leap from line 1 to line 3

Universal Instantiation, because it yields an *instance,* $(Fa \supset Ga)$, of the *universal* generalization $(x)(Fx \supset Gx)$.

It is important to note that a universal quantifier must quantify a *whole line* in a proof to be dropped by **UI.** Thus **UI** cannot be applied to the line

1. $(x)Fx \supset (\exists y)Gy$

to obtain

2. $Fa \supset (\exists y)Gy$

because the (x) quantifier in line 1 does not quantify the whole of that line.

Similarly, **UI** cannot be applied to the line

1. $\sim(x)(Fx \supset Gx)$

to obtain

2. $\sim(Fa \supset Ga)$

because the (x) quantifier in line 1 does not quantify the negation sign, and thus does not quantify the entire line.

Perhaps a better intuitive understanding of the nature and general validity of **UI** can be obtained by again thinking of symbolizations containing quantifiers as a kind of shorthand for expanded expressions. Take the quantified expression $(x)(Fx \supset Gx)$. Its expansion is $[(Fa \supset Ga) \cdot (Fb \supset Gb)] \cdot \ldots$ If we take this *expansion* as a premise, rather than the expression itself, then we can infer to $Fa \supset Ga$ by Simplification (plus Association), without appealing to a new inference rule at all. Using rule **UI** to move from $(x)(Fx \supset Gx)$ to $Fa \supset Ga$ is like using Simplification to move from $[(Fa \supset Ga) \cdot (Fb \supset Gb)] \cdot \ldots$ to $Fa \supset Ga$.

Strictly speaking, Universal Instantiation should be permitted only if the variables freed by dropping the universal quantifier are replaced by individual *constants*. But it is useful to permit their replacement by individual variables also. For instance, we permit inferences by **UI** from $(x)(Fx \supset Gx)$ to $Fx \supset Gx$ and $Fy \supset Gy$, and to $Fa \supset Ga$ and $Fb \supset Gb$. (More will be said about the technical aspects of this in Chapter Seven.)

Examples:

The following are examples of correct uses of **UI.**

(1)
1. $(x)[(Fx \cdot Gx) \supset Hx)]$ p
2. $(Fy \cdot Gy) \supset Hy$ 1, **UI**

	3.	$(Fa \cdot Ga) \supset Ha$	1, **UI**
	4.	$(Fx \cdot Gx) \supset Hx$	1, **UI**
(2)	1.	$(x)(y)[(Fx \cdot Gy) \supset Hxy]$	p
	2.	$(y)[(Fx \cdot Gy) \supset Hxy]$	1, **UI**
	3.	$(Fx \cdot Gz) \supset Hxz$	2, **UI**
	4.	$(Fx \cdot Gx) \supset Hxx$	2, **UI**
	5.	$(Fx \cdot Gy) \supset Hxy$	2, **UI**
(3)	1.	$(x)[(Fx \cdot Gx) \supset Hax]$	p
	2.	$(Fx \cdot Gx) \supset Hax$	1, **UI**
	3.	$(Fy \cdot Gy) \supset Hay$	1, **UI**
	4.	$(Fa \cdot Ga) \supset Haa$	1, **UI**

Universal Generalization (UG): Now consider the proof

1.	$(x)(Fx \supset Gx)$	p
2.	$(x)(Gx \supset Hx)$	p $/\therefore (x)(Fx \supset Hx)$
3.	$Fy \supset Gy$	1, **UI**
4.	$Gy \supset Hy$	2, **UI**
5.	$Fy \supset Hy$	3,4 **HS**

The derivation of line 5 illustrates an important reason for introducing the four quantifier rules, namely to provide a way to use the eight implicational forms of propositional logic in predicate logic proofs. If we were not allowed to drop quantifiers, the eight implicational forms could not be used on lines containing quantified sentences, because they must be used on whole sentences or sentence forms only.

Now, having dropped the quantifiers and derived line 5, we need to add a quantifier to obtain the conclusion:

6.	$(x)(Fx \supset Hx)$	5, **UG** (Universal Generalization)

We introduce the rule called **Universal Generalization (UG)** to permit valid steps like the one from line 5 to line 6. Subject to certain important restrictions to be discussed later, rule **UG** permits the addition of universal quantifiers *that quantify whole sentences*.

In the example just given, the addition of the universal quantifier clearly is legitimate, since the validity of all previous steps did not require that the letter y be used. *Any* letter could have been used, or *every* letter, taken one at a time. Hence, the step to $(x)(Fx \supset Hx)$ is legitimate.

The use of **UG** should be familiar to students of geometry. In geometry, a proof that a given triangle has a particular property is considered proof that *all* triangles have that property, provided that the given triangle is *arbitrarily selected*. Similarly, **UG** is a valid step (with the exceptions to be noted in the next chapter) provided that it is applied in cases where the actual letters employed (in the above example the letter y) are arbitrarily selected, and any other letters could have been selected just as well.

Examples:

The following proof contains correct uses of **UG**.

1.	$(x)(y)(Fxy \supset Gyx)$	p
2.	$(y)(Fxy \supset Gyx)$	1, **UI**
3.	$(Fxy \supset Gyx)$	2, **UI**
4.	$(x)(Fxy \supset Gyx)$	3, **UG**
5.	$(z)(Fxz \supset Gzx)$	3, **UG**
6.	$(z)(Fzy \supset Gyz)$	3, **UG**
7.	$(x)(z)(Fzx \supset Gxz)$	6, **UG**
8.	$(y)(x)(Fxy \supset Gyx)$	4, **UG**

Existential Instantiation (EI): Next, consider the proof

1.	$(x)(Hx \supset Kx)$	p
2.	$(\exists x)Hx$	p /∴ $(\exists x)Kx$
3.	Hy	2, **EI** (Existential Instantiation)

In this proof, line 3 follows from line 2 by the inference rule called **Existential Instantiation (EI).**

Technically, we should not permit this step from line 2 to line 3, because y is a variable. Instead, we should introduce a new set of terms, construed not as *variables,* but rather as *unknowns,* or *ambiguous names.* The difference between a variable and an unknown is illustrated by an example from algebra. In the algebraic theorem

$$(x)(y)[(x + y) = (y + x)]$$

x and y function as variables, since the theorem is true of all numbers. (The expansion of this theorem is $[(1 + 1 = 1 + 1)$ and $(1 + 2 = 2 + 1)]$ and $[(2 + 1 = 1 + 2)$ and $(1 + 3 = 3 + 1)]$ and . . . running through all combinations of two numbers.) But in the algebraic problem

1. $x + 1 = 3$
2. $x = 2$

the x on line 1 functions not as a variable but as an *unknown value,* to be discovered, as it is on line 2, where it turns out to be the number two. So also, in the step from

2. $(\exists x)Hx$

to

3. Hy

the letter y serves not as a variable but as an unknown, in the sense that if $(\exists x)Hx$ is true, then there is some value of x (exactly which value is unknown), which has the property H. In line 3 we call that unknown value y.

This use of the term y also is familiar from its use in the law. For example, if we don't know who has committed a particular crime, although we know that someone (at least one person) committed it, we can refer to that person as "John Doe". We could adopt the John Doe notation if we wanted to, so that from line 2

2. $(\exists x)Hx$

we would go to

3. Hd

(where d = "John Doe"). But it turns out that there is no need for such a precise notation. So for the sake of simplicity, we permit the letters x, y, z, and so on, to serve not only as variables, but also as unknowns, or ambiguous names (such as "John Doe"), just as is done in algebra.

Let's digress a moment to note the following improper procedure involving **EI** and **UG**. We said before that **UG** is valid only from *arbitrarily selected* letters. It follows, then, that this use of **UG** is invalid:

1.	$(\exists x)Fx$	p
2.	Fx	1, **EI**
3.	$(x)Fx$	2, **UG** (invalid)

Let Fx = "x is a fool", and restrict the universe of discourse to human beings. Then this argument moves from the truth "Someone is a fool" to the falsehood "Everyone is a fool", and is clearly invalid. (The x on line 2 is not arbitrarily selected, since some x's are fools, but some are not, so that we cannot select *any* (random) x.)

Similarly, letting a = "Adam", we cannot validly infer from, say, Fa to $(x)Fx$, for that would be to infer from the truth that Adam was a fool (anyone who gets himself evicted from the Garden of Eden has to qualify for "Dunce of the Year" award) to the falsehood that everyone is a fool.

Existential Generalization (EG): So far, the proof in question reads as follows:

1.	$(x)(Hx \supset Kx)$	p
2.	$(\exists x)Hx$	p /∴ $(\exists x)Kx$
3.	Hy	2, **EI**

Continuing,

4.	$Hy \supset Ky$	1, **UI***
5.	Ky	3,4 **MP**
6.	$(\exists x)Kx$	5, **EG** (Existential Generalization)

The step from line 5 to line 6 is justified by the inference rule **Existential Generalization (EG).** This use of **EG** obviously is valid, since if some John Doe or other has the property *K*, then there is something that has that property.

Subject to certain restrictions to be discussed later, we are permitted to drop and add existential quantifiers at will using the rules **EI** and **EG** respectively, *provided they are dropped from or added to whole lines of proofs*.

Examples:

The following proofs contain examples of correct uses of **EI** and **EG**.

(1)	1.	$(\exists x)(\exists y)(Fx \cdot Gxy)$	p
	2.	$(\exists y)(Fx \cdot Gxy)$	1, **EI**
	3.	$(\exists y)(Fz \cdot Gzy)$	1, **EI**
	4.	$(Fz \cdot Gzy)$	3, **EI**
	5.	$(Fx \cdot Gxy)$	2, **EI**
	6.	$(\exists z)(Fz \cdot Gzy)$	5, **EG** (or 4, **EG**)
	7.	$(\exists x)(Fx \cdot Gxy)$	5, **EG** (or 4, **EG**)
	8.	$(\exists y)(\exists x)(Fx \cdot Gxy)$	7, **EG**
	9.	$(\exists z)(\exists x)(Fx \cdot Gxz)$	7, **EG**
	10.	$(\exists x)(\exists z)(Fz \cdot Gzx)$	6, **EG**
(2)	1.	$(\exists x)[Fx \cdot (y)Gxy]$	p
	2.	$Fx \cdot (y)Gxy$	1, **EI**
	3.	$Fz \cdot (y)Gzy$	1, **EI**
	4.	$(y)Gxy$	2, **Simp**
	5.	Gxy	4, **UI**

---

* Just as in line 3, the letter *y* serves as an unknown, or ambiguous name, and not as a variable, even though we informally refer to it as a variable.

6.	$(\exists y)Gxy$	5, **EG**
7.	$(\exists x)(\exists y)Gxy$	6, **EG**
8.	$(\exists z)(\exists y)Gzy$	6, **EG**
9.	Fz	3, **Simp**
10.	$Fz \cdot (\exists z)(\exists y)Gzy$	8,9 **Conj**
11.	$(\exists x)[Fx \cdot (\exists z)(\exists y)Gzy]$	10, **EG**

Exercise 6-10:

Which lines in the following are *not* valid? Explain why in each case.

(1)	1.	$(x)[(Hx \cdot Kx) \supset Mx]$	p
	2.	$(\exists x)(Hx \cdot Kx)$	p
	3.	$Hx \cdot Kx$	2, **EI**
	4.	Mx	1,3 **MP**
	5.	$(\exists x)Mx$	4, **EG**
(2)	1.	$(x)(Fx \supset Gx) \supset Ma$	p
	2.	$(x)(\sim Gx \supset \sim Mx)$	p
	3.	$\sim Gx \supset \sim Mx$	2, **UI**
	4.	$(x)(\sim Gx \supset \sim Fx) \supset Ma$	1, **Contra**
	5.	$(\sim Gx \supset \sim Fx) \supset Ma$	4, **UI**
	6.	Ma	3,5 **MP**
	7.	$(x)Mx$	6, **UG**
(3)	1.	$(\exists x)(Fx \cdot \sim Mx)$	p
	2.	$(x)[(Gx \vee Hx) \supset Mx]$	p
	3.	$Fy \cdot \sim My$	1, **EI**
	4.	$(Gy \vee Hy) \supset My$	2, **UI**
	5.	$\sim My$	3, **Simp**
	6.	$\sim(Gy \vee Hy)$	4,5 **MT**
	7.	$(\exists x)\sim(Gx \vee Hx)$	6, **EG**
(4)	1.	$(\exists x)(Px \cdot Qx)$	p
	2.	$Py \cdot Qy$	1, **EI**
	3.	Qy	2, **Simp**
	4.	$Qy \vee \sim Ry$	3, **Add**
	5.	$(x)(Qx \vee \sim Rx)$	4, **UG**
	6.	$(x)(\sim Rx \vee Qx)$	5, **Comm**
	7.	$(x)(Rx \supset Qx)$	6, **Impl**

(5)	1.	$(\exists x)[(Px \cdot Qx) \vee Rx]$	p
	2.	$(x)\sim Rx$	p
	3.	$(\exists x)(Px \vee Rx)$	1, **Simp**
	4.	$Px \vee Rx$	3, **EI**
	5.	$\sim Px$	2,4 **DS**
	6.	$(x)\sim Px$	5, **UG**
	7.	$\sim Py$	6, **UI**
	8.	$(z)\sim Pz$	7, **UG**

Exercise 6-11:

1. What is wrong with symbolizing the sentence "Wilt Chamberlain was a tall basketball player" as $Tc \cdot Bc$, where Tx = "x is tall" and Bx = "x is a basketball player"?
2. Explain why the sentence "All atomic wars will be lost" is not correctly symbolized as $(x)(Wx \cdot Lx)$.
3. Give an original example (not mentioned in the text) of a two-place, a three-place, and a four-place relational predicate.
4. Explain why the sentence "Some atomic wars will be lost" is not correctly symbolized as $(\exists x)(Wx \supset Lx)$.
5. What is wrong with the following expansion of the formula $(x[Fx \supset (\exists y)(Gxy)]$ for a universe of two individuals?
   $[(Fa \supset Gaa) \vee Gab] \cdot [Fb \supset (Gab \vee Gbb)]$

Key Terms Introduced in Chapter Six

Bound variable: A variable within the scope of a relevant quantifier. For example, in the expression $(x)Fxy$, the variable x, but not the variable y, is bound by the (x) quantifier.

Domain of discourse: The items we want our statements to deal with. For instance, in arithmetic, the domain of discourse is the "world of numbers". In daily life, the usual domain of discourse is implicitly taken to be everything.

Existential Generalization (EG): The inference rule permitting the addition of an existential quantifier to certain expressions (also permitting certain other changes in the expression); for example, the inferences from $Fx \cdot Gxy$ to $(\exists x)(Fx \cdot Gxy)$, or $(\exists z)(Fz \cdot Gzy)$.

Existential Instantiation (EI): The rule permitting inferences from existentially quantified expressions to certain of their instances; for example, the inferences from $(\exists x)(Fx \cdot Gxy)$ to $Fx \cdot Gxy$ or $Fz \cdot Gzy$.

Existential quantifier: The symbols $(\exists x)$, $(\exists y)$, and so on, as used in sentences such as $(\exists x)Fx \cdot Gx)$ and $(\exists x)(\exists y)Fxy$.

Expansion (of a quantified sentence): A quantified sentence "spelled out" for a particular domain of individuals; for example, the expansion of the sentence $(x)(Fx \vee Gx)$ for a domain of two individuals, a and b, is $(Fa \vee Ga) \cdot (Fb \vee Gb)$, and the expansion of the sentence $(\exists x)(Fx \cdot Gx)$ for the same domain is $(Fa \cdot Ga) \vee (Fb \cdot Gb)$.

Free variable: An unbound variable. A variable not within the scope of a relevant quantifier. For example, in the expression $(x)Fxy \supset Gxy$, the second x variable and both y variables are free.

Individual constants: The small letters *a* through *t* used to denote particular *individuals,* as opposed to *properties;* for example, *a* used to designate the person Art.

Individual variables: The small letters *u* through *z* used as variables replaceable by individual constants.

Predicate logic: The recently developed logic that deals with the interior structure of atomic as well as compound sentences. *Synonym:* **Quantifier logic.**

Property constants: Capital letters used to denote particular *properties,* as opposed to *individuals;* for example, *F*________ used to denote "________ is friendly".

Quantifier: A symbol used (roughly) to state how many items (all or some) in the universe of discourse are being referred to. See also **Universal quantifier** and **Existential quantifier.**

Quantifier logic: (See **Predicate logic.**)

Relational property: A property that holds between two (or more) individual entities, for example, the property "________ is next to - - - - - ".

Scope (of a quantifier): The extent of an expression quantified by a quantifier.

Universal Generalization (UG): The inference rule permitting the addition of a universal quantifier to certain expressions (also permitting certain other changes in the expression); for example, the inferences from $Fx \supset Gx$ to $(x)(Fx \supset Gx)$ or $(y)(Fy \supset Gy)$.

Universal Instantiation (UI): The inference rule permitting inferences from universally quantified sentences (or sentence forms) to certain of their instances; for example, the inferences from $(x)(Fx \supset Gx)$ to $Fa \supset Ga$ or $Fx \supset Gx$, and from $(x)Fxy$ to Fzy.

Universal quantifier: The expressions (x), (y), and so on, as used in sentences such as $(x)(Hx \supset Mx)$ and $(y)Fy$.

Chapter Seven

Predicate Logic—II

1 Precise Formulation of the Quantifier Rules

Although the general idea behind the use of the four quantifier rules is fairly simple (and intuitive), their precise formulation turns out to be quite complicated (and in a few cases, nonintuitive).

To state the quantifier rules precisely and economically, we need a way to refer to a great many expressions at once. For example, we want our precise statement of rule **UI** somehow to refer to, and permit, all of the following inferences:

1. $(x)Fx \quad /\therefore Fy$
2. $(x)Fx \quad /\therefore Fx$
3. $(z)(Fz \supset Gz) \quad /\therefore Fy \supset Gy$
4. $(x)(Fx \supset Gx) \quad /\therefore Fx \supset Gx$
5. $(x)(y)Fxy \quad /\therefore (y)Fxy$
6. $(y)(z)Fyz \quad /\therefore (z)Fxz$
7. $(x)[Fx \supset (\exists y)Gy] \quad /\therefore Fx \supset (\exists y)Gy$
8. $(x)Fx \quad /\therefore Fa$
9. $(x)Fxy \quad /\therefore Fyy$
10. $(x)[(Fx \cdot Gx) \supset (\exists x)Hx] \quad /\therefore [(Fy \cdot Gy) \supset (\exists x)Hx]$

In each of these inferences the premise is a universal quantifier plus a formula quantified by it. Suppose we refer to the variables so quantified as *u*.* Then we can say that in each of the above inferences the premise has

---

* Technically, this use of the letter *u* violates a convention set down earlier, since *u* is not being used here as the same kind of variable as, say, *x* and *y*. (The same is true of the use of *w* on the next few pages.)

the form

$(u)(\ldots u \ldots)$

We thus can use this scheme to represent any expression in which the initial quantifier, whether (x), (y), (z), or whatever, quantifies the whole remainder of the expression.

In each of the above examples, the conclusion is obtained by dropping the initial universal quantifier and replacing all occurrences of the variable bound only by that quantifier either by occurrences of itself, or by occurrences of some other variable, or by a constant. For example, in 3, the (z) quantifier was dropped and each z variable bound in the assumption was replaced by a y variable free in the conclusion, and in 4, the (x) quantifier was dropped, and each bound x variable was replaced by itself. In general, we can say that in each of the above uses of **UI** we moved from an expression of the form

$(u)(\ldots u \ldots)$

to an expression of the form

$(\ldots w \ldots)$

where the expression $(\ldots w \ldots)$ resulted from replacing all occurrences of u free in $(\ldots u \ldots)$ by occurrences of w free in $(\ldots w \ldots)$.

There are two things to notice. First, the phrase "occurrence of u free in $(\ldots u \ldots)$" refers to occurrences of u which, although bound in the *entire* expression $(u)(\ldots u \ldots)$, are *free* once the (u) quantifier is dropped, and thus are not bound by a quantifier that occurs within the expression $(\ldots u \ldots)$ itself. For example, the inference in 10, above, can be said to have the form

$(u)(\ldots u \ldots)$
$/\therefore (\ldots w \ldots)$

where we let (u) be (x), $(\ldots u \ldots)$ be $[(Fx \cdot Gx) \supset (\exists x)Hx]$, and $(\ldots w \ldots)$ be $[(Fy \cdot Gy) \supset (\exists x)Hx]$. In this inference, when the universal quantifier (x) is dropped, the first two x variables in $[(Fx \cdot Gx) \supset (\exists x)Hx]$ become free, but the third x does not, because it is still bound by an existential quantifier, namely $(\exists x)$. So we require that the first two variables be replaced by variables free in $(\ldots w \ldots)$, or by a constant, but do *not* require that the third x variable be free in $(\ldots w \ldots)$, because that x is bound in $(\ldots u \ldots)$, and so must remain bound in $(\ldots w \ldots)$.

The second thing to notice is that we must replace all occurrences of u free in $(\ldots u \ldots)$ by *free* occurrences of w in $(\ldots w \ldots)$.

The schematic notation just introduced also is used in the formulation of **EI**, **UG**, and (with a slight modification) **EG**. For instance, we shall characterize **UG** as a process in which we move from an expression $(\ldots u \ldots)$ to an expression $(w)(\ldots w \ldots)$, by replacing all free occurrences of u in $(\ldots u \ldots)$ by occurrences of w free in $(\ldots w \ldots)$. (Of course, such occurrences of w will be bound in the whole expression $(w)(\ldots w \ldots)$. The point is that they not be bound by a w quantifier occurring within $(\ldots w \ldots)$.

We now are ready to state our precise version of the quantifier rules.*

First, let u and w be any variables or constants† (unless otherwise specified). Second, in using the rules **UI**, **EI**, or **UG**, let the expression $(\ldots w \ldots)$ denote any sentence or sentence form that results from replacing all occurrences of u free in the sentence or sentence form $(\ldots u \ldots)$ by occurrences of w free in $(\ldots w \ldots)$. Finally, in using rule **EG**, let the expression $(\ldots w \ldots)$ denote any sentence form that results from replacing *one or more* (but not necessarily all) occurrences of u free in $(\ldots u \ldots)$ by occurrences of some variable w free in $(\ldots w \ldots)$.

Rule UI: $(u)(\ldots u \ldots)$ $/ \therefore (\ldots w \ldots)$

Rule EI: $(\exists u)(\ldots u \ldots)$ $/ \therefore (\ldots w \ldots)$

Provided:
1. w is not a constant.
2. w does not occur free previously in the proof.

Rule UG: $(\ldots u \ldots)$ $/ \therefore (w)(\ldots w \ldots)$

Provided:
1. u is not a constant.
2. u is not free in a line obtained by **EI**.
3. u is not free in an assumed premise within whose scope $(\ldots u \ldots)$ occurs.
4. To each w free in $(\ldots w \ldots)$ there corresponds a u free in $(\ldots u \ldots)$.

Rule EG: $(\ldots u \ldots)$ $/ \therefore (\exists w)(\ldots w \ldots)$

Provided:
1. To each w free in $(\ldots w \ldots)$ there corresponds a u free in $(\ldots u \ldots)$

One final point. With one exception, the rules as stated can handle expressions containing vacuous quantifications such as $(x)(x)Fx$, $(x)(y)Fy$, and so on. It is not absolutely necessary that we consider such expressions to be meaningful sentences; a complete system for predicate logic can be constructed without them. But it is useful to allow such sentences, and customary to do so. The one case of this kind not handled by the quantifier rules presented here concerns rule **EG**. As we have stated it, rule **EG** forbids inferences such as the one from $(x)Fx$ to $(\exists y)(x)Fx$. But we can easily extend the rules to include such cases if we wish, by adding the condition that vacuous quantifiers can be added (or, indeed, dropped) at any time.

---

* See Chapter Eighteen for an explanation of why the quantifier rules must be so complicated.

† Of course u cannot be a constant in the cases of **UI** and **EI**, and w cannot be a constant in the cases of **EG** and **UG**.

Since the four quantifier rules (precisely stated) are quite complex and not entirely intuitive, a fair amount of study and practice is required to master them. The following examples are included as an aid in their mastery.

Examples:

The following proofs contain examples of both valid and invalid uses of the four quantifier rules.

(1)	1.	$(\exists x)(\exists y)(Fx \supset Gy)$	p
	2.	$(\exists y)(Fx \supset Gy)$	1, **EI**
	3.	$Fx \supset Gy$	2, **EI**
	4.	$Fx \supset Gx$	2, **EI** (invalid, because x occurs free previously in the proof, namely on line 2)
	5.	$Fx \supset Ga$	2, **EI** (invalid, because a is a constant)
	6.	$(\exists x)Fx \supset Gy$	3, **EG** (invalid, because $(\exists x)$ does not quantify the whole of line 6)
	7.	$(\exists x)(Fx \supset Gy)$	3, **EG**
	8.	$(z)(\exists x)(Fx \supset Gz)$	7, **UG** (invalid, because y was already introduced into the proof free by **EI**)
(2)	1.	$(\exists x)(y)[Fxy \supset (\exists z)(Gxz \supset Hy)]$	p
	2.	$(y)[Fxy \supset (\exists z)(Gxz \supset Hy)]$	1, **EI**
	3.	$(y)[Fzy \supset (\exists z)(Gzz \supset Hy)]$	1, **EI** (invalid, because every x free in $(y)[Fxy \supset (\exists z)(Gxz \supset Hy)]$ is not replaced by a z free in line 3)
	4.	$Fxx \supset (\exists z)(Gxz \supset Hx)$	2, **UI**
	5.	$Fxx \supset (Gxz \supset Hx)$	4, **EI** (invalid, because $(\exists z)$ does not quantify the whole of line 4)
	→ 6.	Fxx	**AP**
	7.	$(\exists z)(Gxz \supset Hx)$	4,6 **MP**
	8.	$Gxu \supset Hx$	7, **EI**
	9.	$(\exists y)(Gyu \supset Hx)$	8, **EG** (valid)
	10.	$(\exists z)(\exists y)(Gyz \supset Hz)$	9, **EG** (invalid, because to each z free in $(\exists y)(Gyz \supset Hz)$ there does *not* correspond an x free in $(\exists y)(Gyu \supset Hx)$)
	11.	$(\exists y)(Gyu \supset Hy)$	8, **EG**
	12.	$(\exists z)(\exists y)(Gyz \supset Hy)$	11, **EG**
	13.	$Fxx \supset (\exists z)(\exists y)(Gyz \supset Hy)$	6–12, **CP**
	14.	$(x)[Fxx \supset (\exists z)(\exists y)(Gyz \supset Hy)]$	13, **UG** (invalid, because x was already introduced into the proof free by **EI**)
	15.	$(\exists x)[Fxx \supset (\exists z)(\exists y)(Gyz \supset Hy)]$	13, **EG**

---

2 *Mastering the Four Quantifier Rules*

The task of mastering the four quantifier rules can be lightened a bit by concentration on their *nonintuitive* elements.

Take rule **UG**. This rule contains four restrictions, and hence appears quite formidable at first glance. But in actual applications of **UG**, even beginners are unlikely to violate the first or fourth restrictions. For instance, they would not be tempted to violate the first restruction on **UG** and infer from *Fa* to *(x)Fx*. So beginners should concentrate on the second and third restrictions. In particular, they should be on the lookout for invalid inferences such as the one from 3 to 4 in the proof

1.	$(x)(\exists y)(Fx \cdot Gyx)$	p
2.	$(\exists y)(Fx \cdot Gyx)$	1, **UI**
3.	$Fx \cdot Gyx$	2, **EI**
4.	$(x)(Fx \cdot Gyx)$	3, **UG** (invalid)

for this inference violates the second restriction on **UG**. Similarly, they should look out for invalid inferences like the one from 1 to 2 in the proof

→1.	$Fy \supset (x)Gx$	**AP**
2.	$(z)[Fz \supset (x)Gx]$	1, **UG** (invalid)

for this inference violates the third restriction on **UG**.

Now consider rule **UI.** Since there are no restrictions placed on this rule, about the only thing to bear in mind in its use is that rule **UI** *permits* inferences such as the one from 2 to 3 in the proof

1.	$(\exists x)(y)(Fxy \supset Gx)$	p
2.	$(y)(Fxy \supset Gx)$	1, **EI**
3.	$Fxx \supset Gx$	2, **UI** (valid)

Next, consider rule **EI**. Although it contains two restrictions, few will be tempted to violate the first one, and infer, say, from $(\exists x)Fx$ to *Fa*. Nor will many be tempted to violate the second one, and infer, say, from 2 to 4 in the proof

1.	$(\exists x)Fx$	p
2.	$(\exists x)Gx$	p
3.	Fx	1, **EI**
4.	Gx	2, **EI** (invalid)*

---

* See Chapter Eighteen for more on the invalidity of this move from $(\exists x)Gx$ to *Gx*.

5. $Fx \cdot Gx$ 3,4 **Conj**

6. $\exists x(Fx \cdot Gx)$ 5, **EG**

So there should be no great difficulty in mastering rule **EI**.

Finally, consider rule **EG**. This rule contains one restriction, but even beginners are unlikely to violate it. Instead, the problem with **EG** is that it *permits* inferences that seem at best nonintuitive. For instance, it permits the inference from 2 to 3 in the proof

1. $(x)(Fx \supset Ga)$ p
2. $Fa \supset Ga$ 1, **UI**
3. $(\exists x)(Fa \supset Gx)$ 2, **EG** (valid)

This inference is valid because the instructions for the application of rule **EG** specify that in using **EG**, the expression (. . . *w* . . .) results from the replacement of *one or more* (but not necessarily all) occurrences of *u* free in (. . . *u* . . .) by occurrences of some variable *w* in (. . . *w* . . .).

To sum up, in using the four quantifier rules, students should pay special attention to the second and third restrictions on **UG**, the second restriction on **EI**, and the fact that certain somewhat nonintuitive inferences are permitted by **UI** and **EG**. And, of course, it must be remembered that these rules are to be applied to whole lines of proofs only. Inferences such as the one from 1 to 2 in the proof

1. $\sim(x)Fx$ p
2. $\sim Fx$ 1, **UI** (invalid)

are *never* valid. If they were valid, then in this case we could move to

3. $(x)\sim Fx$ 2, **UG**

thus inferring from, say, "It's not true that everything is friendly" to "Everything is not friendly", a clearly invalid inference.

Exercise 7-1:

Indicate which (if any) of the inferences in the following proofs are invalid, and state *why* they are invalid.

(1)
1. $(\exists x)(y)Fxy$ p
2. $(y)Fxy$ 1, **EI**
3. Fxx 2, **UI**
4. $(\exists x)Fxx$ 3, **EG**

(2)
1. $(\exists x)Fx$ p

	2.	$(\exists x)Gx$	p
	3.	Fy	1, **EI**
	4.	Gy	2, **EI**
	5.	$Fy \cdot Gy$	3, 4, **Conj**
	6.	$(\exists y)(Fy \cdot Gx)$	5, **EG**
	7.	$(\exists z)(\exists y)(Fy \cdot Gz)$	6, **EG**

(3)	1.	$(x)(\exists y)(Fx \supset Gy)$	p
	2.	$(\exists y)(Fx \supset Gy)$	1, **UI**
	3.	$Fx \supset Gy$	2, **EI**
	4.	$(x)(Fx \supset Gy)$	3, **UG**
	5.	$(\exists y)(x)(Fx \supset Gy)$	4, **EG**

(4)	1.	$(x)(\exists y)(Fx \supset Gy)$	p
	→ 2.	Fx	**AP**
	3.	$(\exists y)(Fy \supset Gy)$	1, **UI**
	4.	$Fy \supset Gy$	3, **EI**
	5.	Gy	2,4 **MP**
	6.	$(\exists w)(Fw \supset Gy)$	4, **EG**
	7.	$Fw \supset Gy$	6, **EI**
	8.	$(\exists w)(Fw \supset Gw)$	7, **EG**
	9.	$(\exists w)[(Fw \supset Gw) \cdot Gy]$	5,8 **Conj**
	10.	$Fx \supset (\exists w)[(Fw \supset Gw) \cdot Gy]$	2–9, **CP**
	11.	$(x)\{Fx \supset (\exists w)[(Fw \supset Gw) \cdot Gy]\}$	10, **UG**

(5)	1.	$(x)(y)[(z)Fzx \cdot (Gy \cdot Hd)]$	p
	2.	$(y)[(z)Fza \supset (Gy \cdot Hd)]$	1, **UI**
	3.	$(z)Fza \supset (Ga \cdot Hd)$	2, **UI**
	4.	$Fba \supset (Ga \cdot Hd)$	3, **UI**
	5.	$(\exists y)[Fby \supset (Gy \cdot Hd)]$	4, **EG**
	→ 6.	Fby	**AP**
	7.	$Gy \cdot Hd$	5,6 **MP**
	8.	Hd	7, **Simp**
	9.	$(\exists x)Hx$	8, **EG**
	10.	Gy	7, **Simp**
	11.	$(x)Gx$	10, **UG**
	12.	$Fby \supset (x)Gx$	6–11, **CP**
	13.	$(y)Fby \supset (x)Gx$	12, **UG**

Exercise 7-2:

Prove valid:

(1) 1. $(x)(Rx \supset Bx)$
2. $(\exists x){\sim}Bx$ $/\therefore (\exists x){\sim}Rx$

(2) 1. $(x)(Fx \supset Gx)$
2. $(x)(Ax \supset Fx)$
3. $(\exists x){\sim}Gx$ $/\therefore (\exists x){\sim}Ax$

(3) 1. $(x)(Mx \supset Sx)$
2. $(x)({\sim}Bx \lor Mx)$
$/\therefore (x)({\sim}Sx \supset {\sim}Bx)$

(4) 1. Ka
2. $(x)[Kx \supset (y)Hy]$ $/\therefore (x)Hx$

(5) 1. $(\exists x)Rx$
2. $(x)({\sim}Gx \supset {\sim}Rx)$
3. $(x)Mx$ $/\therefore (\exists x)Gx \cdot (\exists x)Mx$

(6) 1. $(\exists x)(Ax \cdot Bx)$
2. $(y)(Ay \supset Cy)$ $/\therefore (\exists x)(Bx \cdot Cx)$

(7) 1. $(z)[Az \supset ({\sim}Bz \supset Cz)]$
2. ${\sim}Ba$ $/\therefore Aa \supset Ca$

(8) 1. $(x)[(Fx \lor Rx) \supset {\sim}Gx]$
2. $(\exists x){\sim}({\sim}Fx \cdot {\sim}Rx)$
$/\therefore (\exists y){\sim}Gy$

(9) 1. $(x)(Kx \supset {\sim}Lx)$
2. $(\exists x)(Mx \cdot Lx)$ $/\therefore (\exists x)(Mx \cdot {\sim}Kx)$

(10) 1. $(x)[(Rx \cdot Ax) \supset Tx]$
2. Ab
3. $(x)Rx$ $/\therefore Tb \cdot Rb$

3 *Rule QN*

We now add four related equivalence rules (applying the name **QN** for **Quantifier Negation** indiscriminately to all of them):

1. $(u)(\ldots u \ldots) :: {\sim}(\exists u){\sim}(\ldots u \ldots)$
2. $(\exists u)(\ldots u \ldots) :: {\sim}(u){\sim}(\ldots u \ldots)$
3. $(u){\sim}(\ldots u \ldots) :: {\sim}(\exists u)(\ldots u \ldots)$
4. $(\exists u){\sim}(\ldots u \ldots) :: {\sim}(u)(\ldots u \ldots)$

where the expression $(\ldots u \ldots)$ is some sentence or sentence form, generally (but not necessarily) containing at least one occurrence of u free in $(\ldots u \ldots)$.*

Rule **QN** permits the assertion of one side of these equivalence argument forms once the other side has been obtained in a proof.

---

* Our predicate logic system is complete without rule **QN**, but custom and especially utility dictate its inclusion.

Example:

The following proof illustrates the correct use (as well as usefulness) of rule **QN**:

1.	$(\exists x)(Fx \cdot Gx) \supset (x){\sim}(Hx \supset Kx)$	p
2.	$(\exists x)(Hx \supset Kx)$	p $/\therefore (x)(Fx \supset {\sim}Gx)$
3.	$(\exists x)(Fx \cdot Gx) \supset {\sim}(\exists x)(Hx \supset Kx)$	1, **QN**
4.	${\sim}{\sim}(\exists x)(Hx \supset Kx)$	2, **DN**
5.	${\sim}(\exists x)(Fx \cdot Gx)$	3,4 **MT**
6.	$(x){\sim}(Fx \cdot Gx)$	5, **QN**
7.	$(x)({\sim}Fx \vee {\sim}Gx)$	6, **DeM**
8.	$(x)(Fx \supset {\sim}Gx)$	7, **Impl**

Notice that rule **QN** may be applied on parts of lines, because it is an equivalence argument form, unlike the four rules for dropping and adding quantifiers. The derivation of line 3 in the above proof is an example.

It is fairly easy to provide an intuitive justification for rule **QN**. Take its first formulation, namely

$$(u)(\ldots u \ldots) :: {\sim}(\exists u){\sim}(\ldots u \ldots)$$

Clearly, all substitution instances of the left-hand side of this expression are equivalent to the analogous substitution instances of its right-hand side. An example is the left-hand substitution instance "Everything is movable" (in symbols $(x)Mx$), which is equivalent to the analogous right-hand substitution instance, "It is not the case that something is not movable" (in symbols ${\sim}(\exists x){\sim}Mx$).

In like manner, it is fairly easy to become convinced that all four versions of rule **QN** are intuitively acceptable.

In addition, we can provide proofs for the four versions of rule **QN**, in that we can prove that corresponding equivalences are theorems of logic (discussed further in Chapter Eight). For instance, we can prove that the sentence $(\exists x)Fx \equiv {\sim}(x){\sim}Fx$, an equivalence corresponding to a substitution instance of the **QN** form $(\exists u)(\ldots u \ldots) :: {\sim}(u){\sim}(\ldots u \ldots)$, is a theorem of logic.

Exercise 7-3:

Prove valid:

(1) 1. $(\exists x)Fx \lor (\exists x)Gx$
2. $(x){\sim}Fx$ $/\therefore (\exists x)Gx$

(2) 1. $(x)(Hx \supset {\sim}Kx)$
$/\therefore {\sim}(\exists y)(Hy \cdot Ky)$

(3) 1. ${\sim}(x)Ax$ $/\therefore (\exists x)(Ax \supset Bx)$

(4) 1. ${\sim}(\exists x)Fx$ $/\therefore Fa \supset Ga$

(5) 1. $(x)[(Fx \lor Hx) \supset (Gx \cdot Ax)]$
2. ${\sim}(x)(Ax \cdot Gx)$ $/\therefore (\exists x){\sim}Hx$

(6) 1. ${\sim}(x)(Hx \lor Kx)$
2. $(y)[({\sim}Ky \lor Ly) \supset My]$
$/\therefore (\exists z)Mz$

(7) 1. $(x)[(Ax \lor Bx) \supset Cx]$
2. ${\sim}(\exists y)(Cy \lor Dy)$ $/\therefore {\sim}(\exists x)Ax$

(8) 1. $(x)(Gx \supset Hx)$
2. $(\exists x)(Ix \cdot {\sim}Hx)$
3. $(x)({\sim}Fx \lor Gx)$ $/\therefore (\exists x)(Ix \cdot {\sim}Fx)$

(9) 1. $(x)[(Ax \cdot Bx) \supset Cx]$
2. $Aa \cdot Ba$
3. ${\sim}Cb$ $/\therefore {\sim}(Ab \cdot Bb)$

(10) 1. $(x)[(Rx \lor Qx) \supset Sx]$
2. $(\exists y)({\sim}Qy \lor {\sim}Ry)$
3. $(\exists z){\sim}(Pz \lor {\sim}Qz)$ $/\therefore (\exists w)Sw$

(11) 1. $(x)[(Bx \cdot Ax) \supset Dx]$
2. $(\exists x)(Qx \cdot Ax)$
3. $(x)({\sim}Bx \supset {\sim}Qx)$ $/\therefore (\exists x)(Dx \cdot Qx)$

(12) 1. $(x)[Px \supset (Ax \lor Bx)]$
2. $(x)[(Bx \lor Cx) \supset Qx]$
$/\therefore (x)[(Px \cdot {\sim}Ax) \supset Qx]$

(13) 1. $(x)[Px \supset (Qx \lor Rx)]$
2. $(x)[(Sx \cdot Px) \supset {\sim}Qx]$
$/\therefore (x)(Sx \supset Px) \supset (x)(Sx \supset Rx)$

Exercise 7-4:

Prove valid (some of these are rather difficult):

(1) 1. $(\exists x)[Ax \cdot (y)(Qy \supset Lxy)]$
2. $(x)[Ax \supset (y)(Iy \supset {\sim}Lxy)]$ $/\therefore (x)(Qx \supset {\sim}Ix)$

(2) 1. $(\exists x)[Fx \cdot (y)(Gy \supset Hxy)]$ $/\therefore (\exists x)[Fx \cdot (Ga \supset Hxa)]$

(3) 1. ${\sim}(\exists x)(Axa \cdot {\sim}Bxb)$
2. ${\sim}(\exists x)(Cxc \cdot Cbx)$
3. $(x)(Bex \supset Cxf)$ $/\therefore {\sim}(Aea \cdot Cfc)$

(4) 1. $(x)(Ax \supset Hx)$
2. $(\exists x)Ax \supset {\sim}(\exists y)Gy$ $/\therefore (x)[(\exists y)Ay \supset {\sim}Gx]$

(5) 1. $(x)[(Fx \lor Gx) \supset (Hx \cdot Kx)]$
2. $(x)\{(Hx \lor Lx) \supset [(Hx \cdot Nx) \supset Px]\}$ $/\therefore (x)[Fx \supset (Nx \supset Px)]$

(6) 1. $(x)[Ax \supset (Bx \supset {\sim}Cx)]$
2. ${\sim}(\exists x)(Cx \cdot Dx) \supset (x)(Dx \supset Ex)$
$/\therefore {\sim}(\exists x)[Dx \cdot ({\sim}Ax \lor {\sim}Bx)] \supset (x)(Dx \supset Ex)$

(7) 1. $(x)(Ex \vee Gx)$
2. $(x)(y)[(\sim Lx \vee Mx) \supset Nyx]$
$/\therefore (x)[\sim(\exists y)(Gy \vee Lx) \supset (\exists z)(Ez \cdot Nzx)]$

(8) 1. $(x)[(\exists y)(Ay \cdot Bxy) \supset Cx]$
2. $(\exists y)\{Dy \cdot (\exists x)[(Ex \cdot Fx) \cdot Byx]\}$
3. $(x)(Fx \supset Ax)$ $/\therefore (\exists x)(Cx \cdot Dx)$

(9) 1. $(x)(Ax \supset Bx)$ $/\therefore (x)[(\exists y)(Ay \cdot Cxy) \supset (\exists z)(Bz \cdot Cxz)]$

(10) 1. $(\exists x)Fx \supset (x)[Px \supset (\exists y)Qxy]$
2. $(x)(y)(Qxy \supset Gx)$ $/\therefore (x)[(Fx \cdot Px) \supset (\exists y)Gy]$

---

4 *A Simpler Set of Quantifier Rules*

The quantifier rules **UI**, **EI**, **UG**, **EG**, and **QN** discussed in Chapter Seven (together with the eighteen valid argument forms—plus **CP** and **IP**) form a complete set of rules for quantifier logic. Sets of this kind have become standard because they allow inferences that fairly closely resemble those of certain technical fields (such as mathematics), and also because they permit relatively short proofs.

But there are simpler sets of quantifier rules. We now present a very simple set indeed, almost as simple as any set can be and still be complete. (However, we pay a price for this simplicity of rules, namely complexity of proofs—as well as an inability to parallel certain standard ways of reasoning.)

First, let's adopt two of the four **QN** rules. Where *u* is any individual variable,

$(u)\sim(\ldots u \ldots) :: \sim(\exists u)(\ldots u \ldots)$

$(\exists u)\sim(\ldots u \ldots) :: \sim(u)(\ldots u \ldots)$

And now, let's restate and adopt rules **UI** and **EI**:

1. Let *u* be any individual variable and *w* any individual variable or, in the case of **UI**, any individual constant.
2. Let the expression $(\ldots w \ldots)$ result from the replacement of all occurrences of *u* free in the expression $(\ldots u \ldots)$ by occurrences of *w* free in the expression $(\ldots w \ldots)$. Then

Rule UI: $(u)(\ldots u \ldots)$ $/\therefore (\ldots w \ldots)$

Rule EI: $(\exists u)(\ldots u \ldots)$ $/\therefore (\ldots w \ldots)$

Provided: *w* does not occur free previously in the proof.

It should be obvious from this formulation that every inference permitted by the simpler rules also is permitted by the standard rules, although the reverse is not true. So the alternative rules permit a subset of the inferences permitted by the standard rules. It follows that the standard rules contain features that are *logically superfluous*, although they are certainly not superfluous in other ways (chiefly in permitting proofs that more faithfully mirror informal reasoning in mathematics and logic).

The key to use of the simpler quantifier rules is that in most cases we must use **IP**.* Here is a simple example:

1.	$(x)(Fx \supset Gx)$	
2.	$(\exists x)Fx$	$/\therefore (\exists x)Gx$
→3.	$\sim(\exists x)Gx$	**AP**
4.	$(x)\sim Gx$	3, **QN**
5.	Fx	2, **EI**
6.	$Fx \supset Gx$	1, **UI**
7.	Gx	5,6 **MP**
8.	$\sim Gx$	4, **UI**
9.	$Gx \cdot \sim Gx$	7,8 **Conj**
10.	$(\exists x)Gx$	3–9, **IP**

And here is a more complicated example:

1.	$(\exists y)(x)(Fx \supset Gy)$	$/\therefore (\exists x)Fx \supset (\exists x)Gx$
→2.	$\sim[(\exists x)Fx \supset (\exists x)Gx]$	**AP**
3.	$(x)(Fx \supset Gy)$	1, **EI**
4.	$\sim[\sim(\exists x)Fx \vee (\exists x)Gx]$	2, **Impl**
5.	$\sim\sim(\exists x)Fx \cdot \sim(\exists x)Gx$	4, **DeM**
6.	$\sim\sim(\exists x)Fx$	5, **Simp**
7.	$(\exists x)Fx$	6, **DN**
8.	Fx	7, **EI**
9.	$Fx \supset Gy$	3, **UI**
10.	Gy	8,9 **MP**
11.	$\sim(\exists x)Gx$	5, **Simp**
12.	$(x)\sim Gx$	11, **QN**
13.	$\sim Gy$	12, **UI**
14.	$Gy \cdot \sim Gy$	10,13 **Conj**
15.	$(\exists x)Fx \supset (\exists x)Gx$	2–14, **IP**

---

* The reason is that we have no **UG** or **EG** at our disposal, and hence have no way of deriving a conclusion that is either a universal or an existential generalization.

Exercise 7-5:

Using the simpler set of quantifier rules, prove that each of the following is valid.

(1) 1. $(\exists x)(Fx \cdot Gx)$ $/\therefore (\exists x)Fx$

(2) 1. $\sim(\exists x)Fx$ $/\therefore Fa \supset Ga$

(3) 1. $(x)(Hx \supset \sim Kx)$
$/\therefore \sim(\exists y)(Hy \cdot Ky)$

(4) 1. $(y)[Fy \vee (\exists x)Gx]$
2. $(x)\sim Fx$ $/\therefore (\exists x)Gx$

(5) 1. $(x)[(Rx \cdot Ax) \supset Tx]$
2. Ab
3. $(x)Rx$ $/\therefore Tb \cdot Rb$

(6) 1. Ka
2. $(x)[Kx \supset (y)Hy]$ $/\therefore (x)Hx$

(7) 1. $(x)(Fx \supset Gx)$
2. $(\exists x)\sim Gx$ $/\therefore (\exists x)\sim Fx$

(8) 1. $\sim(\exists x)Ax$ $/\therefore (\exists x)(Ax \supset Gx)$

(9) 1. $(x)(Mx \supset Sx)$
2. $(x)(\sim Bx \vee Mx)$
$/\therefore (x)(\sim Sx \supset \sim Bx)$

(10) 1. $(\exists x)Rx$
2. $(x)(\sim Gx \supset \sim Rx)$
3. $(\exists x)Mx$ $/\therefore (\exists x)Gx \cdot (\exists x)Mx$

Exercise 7-6:

Using the simpler set of quantifier rules, prove that each of the following is valid (the last two are rather difficult).

(1) 1. $(x)(y)(Fxy \supset Gx)$
2. $(\exists x)(\exists y)Fxy$ $/\therefore (\exists x)Gx$

(2) 1. $(\exists y)(x)Fxy$ $/\therefore (x)(\exists y)Fxy$

(3) 1. $(\exists x)[Fx \cdot (y)Hxy]$ $/\therefore (\exists x)(Fx \cdot Hxa)$

(4) 1. $(x)[Fx \supset (\exists y)Gxy]$
2. $(\exists x)Fx$ $/\therefore (\exists x)(\exists y)Gxy$

(5) 1. $(\exists x)[Ax \cdot (y)(By \supset Cxy)]$
$/\therefore (y)[By \supset (\exists x)(Ax \cdot Cxy)]$

(6) 1. $(\exists x)Ax \supset \sim(\exists y)Gy$
$/\therefore (x)[(\exists y)Ay \supset \sim Gx]$

(7) 1. $(\exists x)Fx \supset (\exists x)Gx$
$/\therefore (\exists y)(x)(Fx \supset Gy)$

Key Term Introduced in Chapter Seven

Quantifier Negation (QN): The rule permitting inference from a given universally (existentially) quantified expression to an equivalent existentially (universally) quantified expression. For example, QN permits us to infer from $(x)Fx$ to $\sim(\exists x)\sim Fx$, and from $\sim(\exists x)Fx$ to $(x)\sim Fx$.

(See also the list of key terms at the end of Chapter Six.)

Chapter Eight

Predicate Logic—III

1 *Proving Invalidity*

As we pointed out when discussing sentential logic, failure to find a valid proof for an argument does not justify concluding that the argument is invalid (because we may lack sufficient ingenuity or simply have overlooked the proof). Nor can we prove an argument is not valid by deriving the negation of its conclusion from its premises (because if its premises are *inconsistent,* then we can validly infer both to the conclusion and its negation). Instead, we can use a method very similar to the one used in sentential logic: to prove an argument invalid, find an argument having the same form* that we're sure has true premises and a false conclusion.

Take the argument

1. $(x)(Ax \supset Bx)$
2. $(x)(Cx \supset Bx)$ $\quad /\therefore (x)(Ax \supset Cx)$

We can prove that this argument is invalid by constructing an argument of the same form which we already know is invalid. For instance, if Hx = "x is human", Mx = "x is mortal", and Dx = "x is a dog", then we already know that the argument

1. $(x)(Hx \supset Mx)$
2. $(x)(Dx \supset Mx)$ $\quad /\therefore (x)(Hx \supset Dx)$

is invalid (since we know that all humans are mortal and all dogs are mortal but all humans are *not* dogs). Hence our original argument must also be invalid, since it has the same form.

We can also prove invalidity by considering limited domains, or limited universes, of discourse. For example, restrict the domain of dis-

---

*To make this precise, we have to extend the notion of a propositional form so as to cover the internal structure of sentences.

course to human beings and consider the argument

$(x)(\exists y)Fyx \quad /\therefore (\exists y)(x)Fyx$

We can prove this argument invalid by showing that the argument

$(x)(\exists y)Myx \quad /\therefore (\exists y)(x)Myx$

(where Myx = "y is the mother of x"), an argument with the same form as the original argument, has a true premise and a false conclusion. (The premise translates to say the truth that *everyone has a mother*, the conclusion to say the falsehood that *someone is mothered by everyone*.)

A particularly useful limited domain of discourse is the universe of numbers. Restricting the universe of discourse to numbers, we can prove that the argument

1. $(x)(Fx \supset Gx)$
2. $(x)(Hx \supset Gx) \quad /\therefore (x)(Fx \supset Hx)$

is invalid by showing that the argument

1. $(x)(Sx \supset Ox)$
2. $(x)(Tx \supset Ox) \quad /\therefore (x)(Sx \supset Tx)$

(where Sx = "x is greater than six", Ox = "x is greater than one", and Tx = "x is greater than ten"), is an argument with the same form as the original argument, and has true premises and a false conclusion.* We can be sure both of the premises of this argument are true because we know that all numbers greater than 6 are greater than 1 (which is what its first premise asserts) and that all numbers greater than 10 are greater than 1 (what its second premise asserts). And we can be sure the conclusion of this argument is false because we know that *not* all numbers greater than 6 also are greater than 10 (contrary to the conclusion, which states that all numbers greater than 6 *are* greater than 10). So this argument is invalid and hence the original argument, having the same form, also must be invalid.

Example:

We can prove the argument

1. $(\exists x)(Fx \cdot Gx)$
2. $(\exists x)(Gx \cdot Hx) \quad /\therefore (\exists x)(Fx \cdot Hx)$

---

* Another way to write this argument would be

1. $(x)[(x > 6) \supset (x > 1)]$
2. $(x)[(x > 10) \supset (x > 1)] \quad /\therefore (x)[(x > 6) \supset (x > 10)]$

invalid by constructing the following invalid mathematical argument having the same form:

1. $(\exists x)[(x \text{ is odd}) \cdot (x > 10)]$
2. $(\exists x)[(x > 10) \cdot (x \text{ is even})]$ /∴ $(\exists x)[(x \text{ is odd}) \cdot (x \text{ is even})]$

Clearly, premise 1 is true (for example, the number 11 is odd and greater than 10), and premise 2 is true (for example, the number 12 is even and greater than 10), while the conclusion is false (since no number is both odd and even).

Sometimes, when we want to prove a given argument invalid, we may have a bit of trouble finding another argument with the same form that has obviously true premises and a clearly false conclusion. In such cases, we can use another, related, method for proving invalidity, a method that works because the validity or invalidity of an argument doesn't depend on the actual truth or falsity of its premises and conclusion. If an argument *could have* true premises and a false conclusion (whether it does or not is irrelevant), then it is invalid. So this second method for proving the invalidity of an invalid argument is to show that it *could have* true premises and a false conclusion.

Perhaps the most intuitive way to do this is to invent an imaginary world having very few items in it, and show that in this imaginary universe an argument having the same form as our original argument could have true premises and a false conclusion. For example, imagine a world with just two items in it, namely the two people John Jones and Mary Brown. Now consider some argument about the real world, say, the argument:

1. $(\exists x)(Fx \cdot Gx)$ p
2. $(\exists x)(Gx \cdot Hx)$ p /∴ $(\exists x)(Fx \cdot Hx)$

Using the imaginary world method for proving invalidity, we can prove this argument invalid by showing that an argument with the same form that happens to be about the imaginary people Jones and Brown could have true premises and a false conclusion. For example, if we make Fx = "x is friendly", Gx = "x is gigantic", and Hx = "x is happy" (whatever these terms meant in the original argument), then we can prove the resulting argument, and so the original one, both are invalid, as follows: First, construct the expansion of the argument about our two-person imaginary world, letting j = "Jones" and b = "Brown":

1. $(Fj \cdot Gj) \vee (Fb \cdot Gb)$
2. $(Gj \cdot Hj) \vee (Gb \cdot Hb)$ /∴ $(Fj \cdot Hj) \vee (Fb \cdot Hb)$

Next, show that this is an invalid argument by inventing truth values for the units in this expansion so that its premises turn out to be true while its conclusion is false. Since Jones and Brown inhabit an imaginary world, one that we've invented ourselves, we can assign any truth values we wish to its components, provided only that we do so *consistently*. (We wouldn't want to assign, say, **T** to the occurrence of *Fj* in the first premise and then assign **F** to the *Fj* occurring in the conclusion, since that would make our imaginary world not only imaginary but also *impossible*. We want our imaginary world to be possible—meaning that it is a *consistent* world, not a contradictory one.)*

Here's one way to invent truth values for our imaginary world so that the argument we've constructed about it has true premises and a false conclusion, and thus is invalid:

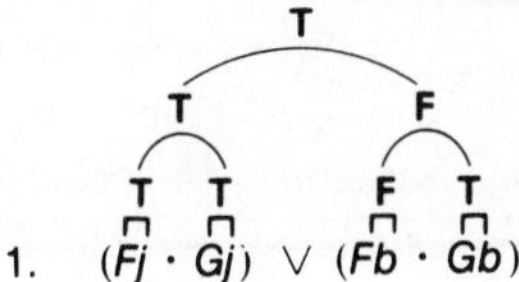

2. $(Gj \cdot Hj) \vee (Gb \cdot Hb)$ $\quad$ $/\therefore (Fj \cdot Hj) \vee (Fb \cdot Hb)$

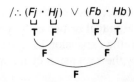

This proves that in a universe of discourse containing exactly two entities, *j* and *b*, the premises $(\exists x)(Fx \cdot Gx)$ and $(\exists x)(Gx \cdot Hx)$ both could be true while the conclusion $(\exists x)(Fx \cdot Hx)$ is false, or, in other words, that it is logically possible for the premises to be true and the conclusion false. Therefore, the argument is invalid, and the original argument, with the same form, also is invalid.

Example:

Argument

1. $(x)(\exists y)Gyx \quad /\therefore (\exists y)(x)Gyx$

---

* This sense of possibility and impossibility is said to be *logical*, as opposed to *physical* possibility and impossibility. To see the difference in these, consider the two statements, "Sugar makes coffee taste salty" and "This lump is sugar, but it isn't sugar". The first is physically impossible, because it violates what experience tells us can happen. But it isn't logically impossible, because there is no contradiction in the idea that sugar *might* make coffee taste salty; we can *imagine* that sugar tastes salty. But the second of these two statements is both physically and logically impossible, because it is contradictory to think of something being both sugar and not sugar—we can't even *imagine* something that is sugar not being sugar (at the same time that it is sugar).

Proof of Invalidity

Assume a universe of discourse containing exactly two individuals, *a* and *b*. In this universe, the argument in question is equivalent to the expansion

1. $(Gaa \vee Gba) \cdot (Gab \vee Gbb)$ $/ \therefore (Gaa \cdot Gab) \vee (Gba \cdot Gbb)$

which is proved invalid by assigning truth values as follows:

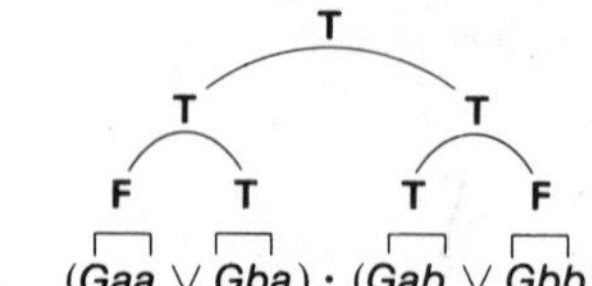

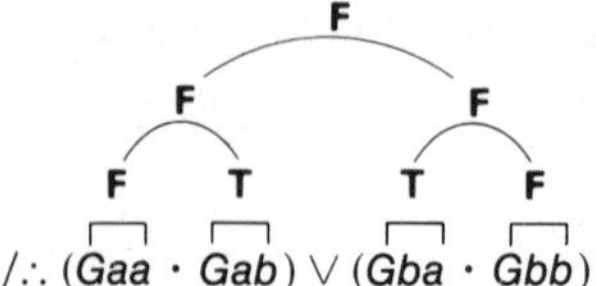

1. $(Gaa \vee Gba) \cdot (Gab \vee Gbb)$ $/ \therefore (Gaa \cdot Gab) \vee (Gba \cdot Gbb)$

However, we must remember that the expansion of an argument for a one-individual or two-individual universe of discourse may be valid even though the expansion for a larger universe of discourse is invalid. For instance, the expansion of the argument

1. $(\exists x)(Fx \cdot Gx)$
2. $(\exists x)(Gx \cdot Hx)$ $/ \therefore (\exists x)(Fx \cdot Hx)$

for a one-individual universe of discourse, namely

1. $Fa \cdot Ga$
2. $Ga \cdot Ha$ $/ \therefore Fa \cdot Ha$

is valid, but its expansion in a two-individual universe of discourse is invalid, as we have just demonstrated.

Exercise 8-1:

Prove that the following arguments are *in*valid.

(1) 1. $(\exists x)(Ax \cdot \sim Bx)$
2. $(\exists x)(Ax \cdot \sim Cx)$
3. $(\exists x)(\sim Bx \cdot Dx)$
$/ \therefore$ $(\exists x)[Ax \cdot (\sim Bx \cdot Dx)]$

(2) 1. $(x)(Fx \supset Gx)$
2. $(x)(\sim Fx \supset Ex)$
$/ \therefore$ $(x)(\sim Gx \supset \sim Ex)$

(3) 1. $(\exists x)(Px \cdot \sim Qx)$
2. $(x)(Rx \supset Px)$
$/ \therefore$ $(\exists x)(Rx \cdot \sim Qx)$

(4) 1. $(x)[(Px \cdot Qx) \supset Rx]$
2. $(\exists x)(Qx \cdot \sim Rx)$
3. $(\exists x)(Px \cdot \sim Rx)$
$/ \therefore$ $(\exists x)(\sim Px \cdot \sim Qx)$

(5) 1. $(x)(Px \supset Qx)$
2. $(x)(Qx \supset Rx)$
/∴ $(\exists x)(Px \cdot Rx)$

(6) 1. $(x)[Mx \supset (Nx \supset Px)]$
2. $(x)(\sim Qx \supset \sim Px)$
/∴ $(x)[\sim Qx \supset (Mx \vee Nx)]$

(7) 1. $(\exists x)(Ax \cdot Bx)$
2. $(x)(\sim Bx \vee \sim Cx)$
/∴ $(x)(\sim Ax \vee \sim Cx)$

(8) 1. $(\exists x)(Ax \vee \sim Bx)$
2. $(x)[(Ax \cdot \sim Bx) \supset Cx]$
/∴ $(\exists x)Cx$

(9) 1. $(x)[Fx \supset (\exists y)Gxy]$
/∴ $(\exists x)(y)(Fx \supset Gxy)$

(10) 1. $(x)[Fx \supset (\exists y)Gxy]$
2. $(\exists x)Fx$
3. $(\exists x)(\exists y)Gxy$
/∴ $(x)(\exists y)Gxy$

(11) 1. $(x)(\exists y)Fxy$
2. $(\exists x)(\exists y)\sim Fxy$
/∴ $(\exists x)(y)Fxy$

(12) 1. $(x)(y)(Fxy \supset Gxy)$
2. $(\exists x)[Fx \cdot (\exists y)Gyx]$
/∴ $(x)(y)[Fxy \supset (Gxy \cdot Gyx)]$

2 *Consistency and Inconsistency of Premises*

Just as in propositional logic so also in predicate logic, the whole method for proving the consistency of premises is *part* of the method for proving the invalidity of an argument with those premises.

Example:

We can prove that the argument

1. $(x)(Fx \supset Gx)$
2. $(x)(Gx \supset Hx)$
3. $(\exists x)Fx$ /∴ $(\exists x)Hx$

has consistent premises by finding an argument having the same form that contains all true premises. (The truth value of the conclusion is irrelevant to the consistency of the premises.) For instance, if the universe of discourse is restricted to numbers, then the argument

1. $(x)[(x > 10) \supset (x > 5)]$
2. $(x)[(x > 5) \supset (x > 0)]$
3. $(\exists x)(x > 10)$ /∴ $(\exists x)(x > 0)$

which has the same form as the original argument, contains only true premises, and hence the premises of the original argument must be consistent.

To prove that the premises of an argument are *inconsistent,* we use the same method as in sentential logic, namely the derivation of a contradiction.

Example:

The premises of the argument

1. $(x)(Fx \supset Gx)$ — p
2. $(x)(Fx \supset \sim Gx)$ — p
3. $(\exists x)Fx$ — p $/\therefore (x)Hx$

are proved inconsistent by deriving an explicit contradiction, as follows:

4. Fx — 3, **EI**
5. $Fx \supset Gx$ — 1, **UI**
6. $Fx \supset \sim Gx$ — 2, **UI**
7. Gx — 4,5 **MP**
8. $\sim Gx$ — 4,6 **MP**
9. $Gx \cdot \sim Gx$ — 7,8 **Conj**

Incidentally, this proves that this argument is *valid,* since from a contradiction any and all conclusions validly follow. But it is also *unsound;* for at least one member of an inconsistent set of premises must be false.

Exercise 8-2:

Determine which of the following sets of premises are consistent and which are inconsistent.

(1)
1. $(x)[Ax \supset (Bx \cdot Cx)]$
2. $(\exists x)(Ax \cdot \sim Cx)$ $/\therefore (\exists x)(Ax \cdot \sim Bx)$

(2)
1. $(\exists x)(Rx \vee Mx)$
2. $(x)(Mx \supset \sim Rx)$ $/\therefore (\exists x)Mx$

(3)
1. $(x)[(Lx \cdot \sim Mx) \supset Nx]$
2. $(x)[(Lx \cdot Mx) \supset \sim Nx]$
3. $(\exists x)Mx$
4. $(\exists x)\sim Mx$ $/\therefore (\exists x)(Lx \cdot \sim Nx)$

(4) 1. $(\exists x) \sim Bx$

2. $(\exists x)Bx$

3. $\sim(\exists x)Kx$

4. $(x)(\sim Kx \supset \sim Bx)$ $/\therefore (x)Kx$

(5) 1. $(x)[Rx \supset \sim(Tx \cdot \sim Sx)]$

2. $(\exists x)[(Rx \cdot Tx) \cdot Sx]$

3. $(\exists x)(\sim Rx \cdot \sim Sx)$ $/\therefore (\exists x)(Rx \cdot \sim Sx)$

(6) 1. $\sim(x)[Dx \supset (\sim Fx \vee Gx)]$

2. $\sim(\exists x)[Fx \cdot (Dx \vee \sim Fx)]$ $/\therefore (\exists x)(Dx \cdot \sim Fx)$

(7) 1. $(\exists x)(\exists y)Fxy$

2. $(x)(y)\sim(Fxy \vee Fyx)$ $/\therefore \sim(\exists x)(\exists y)Fxy$

(8) 1. $(x)(\exists y)(Fxy \supset Gx)$

2. $\sim(x)[(y)Fxy \supset Gx]$ $/\therefore (\exists x)(\exists y)(Fxy \cdot Gx)$

3 *More Difficult Symbolizations*

A good deal of care is needed in symbolizing sentences containing words or phrases such as "only", "none but", and "unless".

Consider sentence (1): "Only men are strong". Restricting the universe of discourse to human beings, this sentence is correctly symbolized as $(x)(Sx \supset Mx)$. It is tempting to symbolize it incorrectly as $(x)(Mx \supset Sx)$, thus interpreting it to mean that all men are strong. But to say that *only* men are strong is not to say that *all* men are strong. Suppose it is true that some men are strong and some not, but no women (or children) are strong. Then the sentence "All men are strong" will be false (since some men are not strong), whereas the sentence "Only men are strong" will be true. Hence, the symbolization $(x)(Mx \supset Sx)$ cannot be a correct symbolization of sentence (1).

Another way to look at the problem is this. To say that only men are strong is to say that anyone who is not a man is not strong or, what amounts to the same thing, that all nonmen are nonstrong. Since the sentence "All nonmen are nonstrong" is correctly symbolized as $(x)(\sim Mx \supset \sim Sx)$, the equivalent sentence (1): "Only men are strong" also is correctly symbolized in this way. And since $(x)(\sim Mx \supset \sim Sx)$ is equivalent to $(x)(Sx \supset Mx)$, it follows that sentence (1) is correctly symbolized as $(x)(Sx \supset Mx)$.

Sentences containing the phrase "none but" are handled in a similar fashion. For instance, sentence (2): "None but men are strong" is correctly symbolized as $(x)(Sx \supset Mx)$. (Thus sentences (1) and (2) are equivalent.)

The phrase "none but" in a sentence of this kind means roughly the same thing as the phrase "none except". For instance, the sentence "None but the ignorant are happy" means the same thing as the sentence "None, except the ignorant, are happy". Therefore both of these sentences are symbolized as $(x)(Hx \supset Ix)$. (Similarly, the phrase "nothing less than" usually means the same as "only", as in the sentence "Nothing less than a million dollars will satisfy those spoiled rich kids".)

English usage also permits the word "unless" to be used in place of the words "only", "none but", or "none except". For instance, instead of saying (1): "Only men are strong" or (2): "None but men are strong", we can say (3): "No one is strong unless he is a man". All of these sentences say roughly the same thing, and hence for our purposes can be symbolized in the same way.

Examples:

Here are some sentences (hopefully false) containing the expressions "only", "none but", and "unless", along with their correct symbolizations.

1. Only celebrities can be elected president.
   $(x)(Ex \supset Cx)$
2. No one can be elected president unless he or she is a celebrity.
   $(x)(Ex \supset Cx)$
3. None but celebrities can be elected president.
   $(x)(Ex \supset Cx)$
4. Only glib politicians can be elected president.
   $(x)[Ex \supset (Gx \cdot Px)]$
5. None but glib politicians can be elected president.
   $(x)[Ex \supset (Gx \cdot Px)]$
6. No one can be elected president unless he is a glib politician.
   $(x)[Ex \supset (Gx \cdot Px)]$

Most other frequently occurring sentence patterns are fairly easy to symbolize. But a few are tricky. For instance, sentence (4): "All women *and* children are exempt from the draft" is correctly symbolized as $(x)[(Wx \vee Cx) \supset Ex]$, *not* as $(x)[(Wx \cdot Cx) \supset Ex]$. For the latter asserts that all things that are *both* women *and* children are exempt, whereas the implication of (4) is that all things that are *either* women *or* children are exempt.

In this case, the "and" in the antecedent of sentence (4) misleads us into using the symbol "$\cdot$" instead of "$\vee$". However, there is a fairly straightforward symbolization of (4) containing the symbol "$\cdot$", namely $(x)(Wx \supset Ex) \cdot (x)(Cx \supset Ex)$. For to say that all women are exempt from the draft and all children are exempt from the draft is to say exactly that all women and children are exempt from the draft. And, indeed, $(x)(Wx \supset Ex) \cdot (x)(Cx \supset Ex)$ and $(x)[(Wx \vee Cx) \supset Ex]$ are logically equivalent (as the reader can easily prove).

Examples:

The following are examples of English sentences with correct symbolizations (using obvious abbreviations).

1. All students who attend college are well educated.
$(x)[(Sx \cdot Cx) \supset Ex]$
2. All men and women are adults.
$(x)[(Mx \vee Wx) \supset Ax]$
3. All lawyers are intelligent *and* shifty.
$(x)[Lx \supset (Ix \cdot Sx)]$
4. All doctors are intelligent *or* high-priced.
$(x)[Dx \supset (Ix \vee Hx)]$
5. Not all doctors are moneygrubbers.
$\sim(x)(Dx \supset Mx)$, or $(\exists x)(Dx \cdot \sim Mx)$
6. No doctors are moneygrubbers.
$(x)(Dx \supset \sim Mx)$, or $\sim(\exists x)(Dx \cdot Mx)$
7. No men who attend college are ignorant.
$(x)[(Mx \cdot Ax) \supset \sim Ix]$, or $\sim(\exists x)[(Mx \cdot Ax) \cdot Ix]$
8. There are no ignorant men who have attended college.
$(x)[(Ix \cdot Mx) \supset \sim Ax]$ or $\sim(\exists x)[(Ix \cdot Mx) \cdot Ax]$

(Since sentences 7 and 8 are logically equivalent, their correct symbolizations are logically equivalent.)

Each of the above symbolizations contains only one quantifier. Those containing two or more quantifiers sometimes are much more difficult.

Consider sentence (5): "If someone is too noisy then everyone in the room will be annoyed". Restricting the universe of discourse to human beings, we can partially symbolize (5) as

If $(\exists x)(Nx)$ then $(y)(Ry \supset Ay)$

and then complete the symbolization as

$(\exists x)(Nx) \supset (y)(Ry \supset Ay)$

But the grammatically similar sentence (6): "If someone is too noisy, then everyone in the room will be annoyed *with him*" must be symbolized somewhat differently. We cannot partially symbolize (6) as

If $(\exists x)(Nx)$ then $(y)(Ry \supset Ayx)$

and then complete the symbolization as

$(\exists x)(Nx) \supset (y)(Ry \supset Ayx)$

because the last x variable in this expression is a *free variable,* so that this expression is not a sentence.

And we cannot rectify this error simply by extending the scope of the existential quantifier; that is, we cannot correctly symbolize sentence (6) as

(7) $(\exists x)[Nx \supset (y)(Ry \supset Ayx)]$

Although (7) is a sentence, it is not equivalent to (6). Sentence (7) asserts that there is at least one person such that if that person is too noisy then everyone in the room will be annoyed with him. This would be true if everyone became annoyed when one person, say Smith, was too noisy, but not when some other person, say Jones, was too noisy. But the implication of sentence (6) is that if *anyone* is too noisy then everyone will be annoyed with that person. So (6) cannot be correctly symbolized by (7). Instead, we can symbolize sentence (6) as

$(x)[Nx \supset (y)(Ry \supset Ayx)]$

using a *universal* x quantifier.

In this case, it is the word "someone" that is misleading. It sometimes functions as an existential quantifier and sometimes as a universal quantifier. The words "something", "somewhere", "sometime", and so on, are misleading in the same way. Hence it is wise to pay close attention to the precise meaning of a sentence in which any of these terms occurs before deciding whether its correct symbolization requires an existential or a universal quantifier.

Even so, it still may seem strange that sentence (5) is correctly symbolized as $(\exists x)(Nx) \supset (y)(Ry \supset Ay)$, using an existential quantifier whose scope is restricted to the antecedent of the symbolization, while sentence (6) is correctly symbolized as $(x)[Nx \supset (y)(Ry \supset Ayx)]$, using a universal quantifier whose scope is the entire symbolization. But perhaps this strangeness can be dispelled to some extent by pointing out that $(\exists x)(Nx) \supset (y)(Ry \supset Ay)$ is *equivalent* to $(x)[Nx \supset (y)(Ry \supset Ay)]$. In other words, there is a sense in which the term "something" functions as a universal quantifier in sentence (5) just as it does in sentence (6). (The significance of all of this will become clearer after logical truths are discussed in Section 4 of this chapter.)

Now consider sentence (8): "If someone is too noisy, then if everyone in the room is annoyed, someone will complain". Restricting the universe of discourse to human beings, we can partially symbolize this sentence as

If $(\exists x)(Nx)$ then [if $(y)(Ry \supset Ay)$ then $(\exists z)(Cz)$]

and complete the symbolization as

$$(\exists x)(Nx) \supset [(y)(Ry \supset Ay) \supset (\exists z)(Cz)]$$

But the grammatically similar sentence (9): "If someone is too noisy, then if all of the people in the room are annoyed, they all will dislike *him*" must be symbolized somewhat differently. We cannot partially symbolize it as

If $(\exists x)(Nx)$ then [if $(y)(Ry \supset Ay)$ then (Dyx)]

and complete the symbolization as

$$(\exists x)(Nx) \supset [(y)(Ry \supset Ay) \supset (Dyx)]$$

because the last x and y variables in this symbolization are *free variables*, so that this expression is not a sentence. Instead, the correct symbolization of (9) is

$$(x)\{Nx \supset (y)[(Ry \supset Ay) \supset (Ry \supset Dyx)]\}$$

Examples:

The following are examples of English sentences with correct symbolizations. (Px = "x is a person"; the other abbreviations are obvious.)

1. Everyone knows someone (or other).
   $(x)[Px \supset (\exists y)(Py \cdot Kxy)]$
2. Everyone knows everyone.
   $(x)[(Px \supset (y)(Py \supset Kxy)]$ or $\sim(\exists x)[Px \cdot (\exists y)(Py \cdot \sim Kxy)]$
3. Someone knows everyone.
   $(\exists x)[Px \cdot (y)(Py \supset Kxy)]$ or $(\exists x)[Px \cdot \sim(\exists y)(Py \cdot \sim Kxy)]$
4. Someone knows someone (or other).
   $(\exists x)[Px \cdot (\exists y)(Py \cdot Kxy)]$
5. No one knows everyone.
   $(x)[Px \supset (\exists y)(Py \cdot \sim Kxy)]$ or $\sim(\exists x)[Px \cdot (y)(Py \supset Kxy)]$
6. No one knows anyone.
   $(x)[Px \supset \sim(\exists y)(Py \cdot Kxy)]$ or $\sim(\exists x)[Px \cdot (\exists y)(Py \cdot Kxy)]$
7. Not everyone knows everyone.
   $\sim(x)[Px \supset (y)(Py \supset Kxy)]$ or $(\exists x)[Px \cdot (\exists y)(Py \cdot \sim Kxy)]$
8. Not everyone knows someone (or other).
   $\sim(x)[Px \supset (\exists y)(Py \cdot Kxy)]$ or $(\exists x)[Px \cdot (y)(Py \supset \sim Kxy)]$
9. Honest candidates always get defeated by dishonest ones.
   $(x)\{(Cx \cdot Hx) \supset (\exists y)[(Cy \cdot \sim Hy) \cdot Dyx]\}$
10. Some honest candidates get defeated by dishonest ones.
    $(\exists x)\{(Cx \cdot Hx) \cdot (\exists y)[(Cy \cdot \sim Hy) \cdot Dyx]\}$

11. No honest candidates get defeated by dishonest ones.
$\sim(\exists x)\{(Cx \cdot Hx) \cdot (\exists y)[(Cy \cdot \sim Hy) \cdot Dyx]\}$

12. All candidates who get defeated by honest candidates are themselves dishonest.
$(x)\{\{Cx \cdot (\exists y)[(Cy \cdot Hy) \cdot Dyx]\} \supset \sim Hx\}$

13. All barbers who don't shave themselves don't shave any barbers.
$(x)[(Bx \cdot \sim Sxx) \supset \sim(\exists y)(By \cdot Sxy)]$

14. Barbers who don't shave themselves are shaved by someone who is a barber.
$(x)[(Bx \cdot \sim Sxx) \supset (\exists y)(By \cdot Syx)]$

15. Barbers shave all and only those who are barbers.
$(x)[Bx \supset (y)(Sxy \equiv By)]$

16. If someone is a barber who does not shave himself, then someone does not get shaved by any barber.
$(\exists x)(Bx \cdot \sim Sxx) \supset (\exists y)[Py \cdot (z)(Bz \supset \sim Szy)]$

17. If there is anyone who does not shave himself, then if no one is shaved by any barber, he (who does not shave himself) will not be shaved by any barber.
$(x)\{(Px \cdot \sim Sxx) \supset \{(y)[Py \supset \sim(\exists z)(Bz \cdot Szy)] \supset \sim(\exists v)(Bv \cdot Svx)\}\}$

18. If there is someone who does not shave himself, then if no barber shaves anyone, there is someone who is not shaved by anyone.
$(\exists x)(Px \cdot \sim Sxx) \supset \{(y)[By \supset (z)(Pz \supset \sim Syz)] \supset (\exists u)[Pu \cdot (w)(Pw \supset \sim Swu)]\}$

Exercise 8-3:

Symbolize the following sentences (using the indicated predicate letters), so as to reveal as much of the internal structure of each sentence as possible.

1. Women are fickle. (Wx = "x is a woman"; Fx = "x is fickle")
2. A barking dog never bites. (Bx = "x barks"; Dx = "x is a dog"; Nx = "x never bites")
3. There are gray dogs. (Dx = "x is a dog"; Gx = "x is gray")
4. Not all women are fickle. (Wx = "x is a woman"; Fx = "x is fickle")
5. Some barking dogs are annoying. (Dx = "x is a dog"; Bx = "x barks"; Ax = "x is annoying")
6. Nothing logical is difficult. (Lx = "x is logical"; Dx = "x is difficult")
7. Some coeds are both beautiful and intelligent. (Cx = "x is a coed"; Bx = "x is beautiful"; Ix = "x is intelligent")
8. Only the rich deserve the fair. (Rx = "x is rich"; Fx = "x is fair"; Dxy = "x deserves y")
9. None but the rich deserve the fair.
10. No one deserves the fair unless he is rich.
11. Seniors and football players are excused. (Sx = "x is a senior"; Fx = "x is a football player"; Ex = "x is excused")
12. But junior women are not excused. (Jx = "x is a junior"; Wx = "x is a woman"; Ex = "x is excused")
13. Some people are happy only when drunk. (Px = "x is a person"; Hx = "x is happy"; Dx = "x is drunk")

14. Among dogs, mongrels, and only mongrels, are intelligent. (*Dx* = "*x* is a dog"; *Ix* = "*x* is intelligent"; *Mx* = "*x* is a mongrel")

15. Art won't get an A unless he studies with Jane. (*a* = "Art"; *j* = "Jane"; *Ax* = "*x* gets an A"; *Sxy* = "*x* studies with *y*")

16. Anyone who consults a psychiatrist ought to have his head examined. (*Px* = "*x* is a person"; *Cxy* = "*x* consults *y*"; *Sx* = "*x* is a psychiatrist"; *Ex* = "*x* ought to have his head examined")

17. No one learns anything unless he teaches it to himself. (*Px* = "*x* is a person"; *Lxy* = "*x* learns *y*"; *Txyz* = "*x* teaches *y* to *z*")

18. Everyone owes something to someone. (*Px* = "*x* is a person"; *Oxyz* = "*x* owes *y* to *z*")

19. Someone owes something to someone.

20. Someone owes something to everyone.

21. Someone owes everything to someone.

22. Everyone owes something to everyone.

Exercise 8-4:

Follow the instructions for *Exercise 8-3*. (Some of these are rather difficult.)

1. If any sophomore fails, then he deserves to fail. (*Sx* = "*x* is a sophomore"; *Fx* = "*x* fails"; *Dx* = "*x* deserves to fail")

2. If any senior fails, then some junior ought to tutor him. (*Sx* = "*x* is a senior"; *Fx* = "*x* fails"; *jx* = "*x* is a junior"; *Txy* = "*x* ought to tutor *y*")

3. If any sophomore fails, then every sophomore will fail. (*Sx* = "*x* is a sophomore"; *Fx* = "*x* fails")

4. If every senior fails, then if some seniors are intelligent, some seniors ought to be ashamed of themselves. (*Sx* = "*x* is a senior"; *Fx* = "*x* fails"; *Ix* = "*x* is intelligent"; *Ox* = "*x* ought to be ashamed of himself")

5. If any seniors fail, then if they are intelligent, some intelligent junior ought to tutor them. (*Sx* = "*x* is a senior"; *Fx* = "*x* fails"; *Ix* = "*x* is intelligent"; *Jx* = "*x* is a junior"; *Oxy* = "*x* ought to tutor *y*")

6. God only helps those who help themselves. (*g* = "God"; *Hxy* = "*x* helps *y*"; *Px* = "*x* is a person")

7. Only someone who hasn't sinned is permitted to cast stones at those who have. (*Px* = "*x* is a person"; *Sx* = "*x* has sinned"; *Cxy* = "*x* is permitted to cast stones at *y*")

8. Someone who sometimes sins against some people always sins against God. (*Px* = "*x* is a person"; *Sxyz* = "*x* sins against *y* at *z*"; *Tx* = "*x* is a time"; *g* = "God")

9. You can fool some of the people all of the time, and all of the people some of the time, but you can't fool all of the people all of the time. (*Px* = "*x* is a person"; *Tx* = "*x* is a time"; *Fxy* = "*x* can be fooled at *y*")

Exercise 8-5:

Translate the following into English, giving the predicate letters and individual constants their indicated meanings, making sure your translations are as close to colloquial English as you can make them.

Bxy = "x believes in y"	Px = "x is a person"
Dx = "x is disenfranchised"	Rx = "x is a redeeming feature"
Hxy = "x has y"	Vx = "x votes"
Mxy = "x is the master of y"	a = "Art"; g = "God"

1. $(x)(Px \supset Bxg)$
2. $(\exists x)(Px \cdot Bxg)$
3. $(x)(Px \supset \sim Bxg)$
4. $\sim(x)(Px \supset Bxg)$
5. $\sim(\exists x)(Px \cdot Bxg)$
6. $(x)[(Px \cdot \sim Vx) \supset Dx]$
7. $(x)[(Px \cdot Dx) \supset \sim Mxx]$
8. $\sim(x)[(Px \cdot \sim Vx) \supset Dx]$
9. $(x)[Px \supset (\exists y)(Ry \cdot Hxy)]$
10. $(\exists x)[Px \cdot (y)(Ry \supset \sim Hxy)]$
11. $(\exists x)[Rx \cdot (y)(Py \supset Hyx)]$
12. $(x)[Rx \supset (\exists y)(Py \cdot \sim Hyx)]$
13. $\sim(\exists x)(\exists y)[(Px \cdot Ry) \cdot Hxy]$
14. $(x)[Px \supset (y)(Ry \supset \sim Hxy)]$
15. $(x)\{Px \supset [(y)(Ry \supset Hxy) \supset Bxg]\}$
16. $\sim Va \supset \{(x)[(Px \cdot \sim Vx) \supset Dx] \supset Da\}$
17. $(x)\{(Px \cdot Vx) \supset (y)[(Py \cdot \sim Vy) \supset Mxy]\}$
18. $(x)\{(Px \cdot Vx) \supset (\exists y)[(Py \cdot \sim Vy) \cdot Mxy]\}$

4 *Theorems of Logic*

The conclusion of a valid deduction in which there are no given premises is said to be a **theorem of logic.** It is something that can be proved by *logic* alone. All of the tautologies of sentential logic are theorems of logic by this definition, because they can be proved without using contingent premises.

But the tautologies of sentential logic also can be proved by truth table analysis. In this respect, they differ from most theorems of predicate logic, for we can prove by truth table analysis only those theorems of predicate logic that are substitution instances of tautologous sentence forms of sentential logic. The sentence $(x)Fx \vee \sim(x)Fx$ is an examit is a substitution instance of the tautology $p \vee \sim p$, and is a theorem of predicate logic provable by truth table analysis.

But most theorems of predicate logic must be proved by the standard predicate logic proof method. (Since they cannot be proved by truth table analysis, they are not tautologies, at least not in the sense in which we are using that term.*)

* However, some philosophers use the word "tautology" as a synonym for "theorem of logic", and others in even broader senses.

1. $(x)(y)Fxy \equiv (y)(x)Fxy$
2. $(x)Gy \equiv Gy$
3. $(\exists x)Gy \equiv Gy$
4. $(\exists x)(y)Fxy \supset (y)(\exists x)Fxy$ (but *not* vice versa)
5. $(x)(Fx \cdot Gx) \equiv [(x)Fx \cdot (x)Gx]$
6. $[(x)Fx \vee (x)Gx] \supset (x)(Fx \vee Gx)$ (but *not* vice versa)
7. $(x)(Fx \supset Gx) \supset [(\exists x)Fx \supset (\exists x)Gx]$ (but *not* vice versa)
8. $(\exists x)(Fx \cdot Gx) \supset [(\exists x)Fx \cdot (\exists x)Gx]$ (but *not* vice versa)
9. $(\exists x)(Fx \vee Gx) \equiv [(\exists x)Fx \vee (\exists x)Gx]$

In the following theorems, the letter P denotes any sentence or sentence form that does *not* contain a free occurrence of the variable x. Thus in number 10, P might be Fa, Fy, $(y)(Fy \supset Gy)$, and so on.

10. $[(x)Fx \cdot P] \equiv (x)(Fx \cdot P)$
11. $(x)(Fx \vee P) \equiv [(x)Fx \vee P]$
12. $(x)(P \supset Fx) \equiv [P \supset (x)Fx]$
13. $(x)(Fx \supset P) \equiv [(\exists x)Fx \supset P]$
14. $(\exists x)(P \cdot Fx) \equiv [P \cdot (\exists x)Fx]$
15. $(\exists x)(P \vee Fx) \equiv [P \vee (\exists x)Fx]$
16. $(\exists x)(Fx \supset P) \equiv [(x)Fx \supset P]$
17. $(\exists x)(P \supset Fx) \equiv [P \supset (\exists x)Fx]$

Exercise 8-7:

1. Why can't we prove an argument invalid by deriving the negation of its conclusion from its premises? (Example)
2. Explain why "Only television programs reach a mass audience" is not correctly symbolized as $(x)(Tx \supset Rx)$, where Rx = "x reaches a mass audience".
3. Determine whether the formula $(x)(y)Fxy \supset (x)(\exists y)Fxy$ is a theorem of logic or not.
4. *True or false:* Truth table analysis can never be used on quantified sentences to prove they are theorems of logic. (Explain)
5. *True or false:* Some theorems of predicate logic can be proved to be theorems only by using **CP** or **IP.** (Explain)
6. Translate the following back into as close to everyday English as you can (letting g = "Wayne Gretsky"; Bxy = "x is a better hockey player than y", and restricting the domain of discourse to persons):

   (1) $(x)(\exists y)Bxy$ (2) $\sim(\exists x)Bxg$ (3) $(\exists x)(y)Bxy \supset Bgg$

schema exactly parallels the proof of its substitution instance. And second, these theorem schemas are very important in deriving what are known as *normal forms* of formulas (not discussed in this text, but useful when doing higher-level work in logic). In addition, it's useful to notice which of these are only one-way, or implicational, theorems so that we don't waste time trying to prove substitution instances of their reversals.

Key Terms Introduced in Chapter Eight

Logical contradictions: Sentences that are the negations of logical truths. Sentences that can be proved false by logic alone. For example, $\sim(x)(Fx \supset Fx)$ is a logical contradiction.

Logical truths: Theorems of logic that also are sentences, and hence true; for example, $A \vee \sim A$ and $(x)(Fx \vee \sim Fx)$. Theorems of logic that also are *sentence forms* are not logical truths, because they have no truth values. *Synonym:* **Truths of Logic.**

Theorem of logic: The conclusion of a deductively valid argument that has no given (as opposed to assumed) premises. *Examples:* $A \vee \sim A$, $\sim(p \cdot \sim p)$, $(x)Fx \supset (\exists x)Fx$.

Truths of logic: (See **Logical truths.**)

Chapter Nine

Predicate Logic—IV

1 Identity

The verb "to be", in all its variations ("is", "was", and so on), is ambiguous. Take the following sentences:

John is tall.

Mark Twain is Samuel Clemens.

In the first sentence, the word "is" indicates that the property of being tall is a property of John. This is sometimes called the *predicating function* of the word "is". But in the second sentence, no property is predicated of Mark Twain. Instead, the word "is" indicates an *identity* between the person who is Mark Twain and the person who is Samuel Clemens. It would be correct to symbolize the first sentence as Tj, but *in*correct to symbolize the second sentence as Ct (where t = "Mark Twain" and C = "Samuel Clemens").

We introduce a new symbol, the **identity symbol** "=", to indicate identity. Using this new symbol, we can symbolize the sentence "Mark Twain is Samuel Clemens" as $t = c$. Similarly, we can symbolize the sentence "United Brands is United Fruit" as $b = f$, the sentence "Archie Leach is Cary Grant" as $l = g$, and so on.

Now let's look at the following argument, in which the identity sign is used:

1.	Wtf	(Mark Twain wrote *Huck Finn.*)
2.	$t = c$	(Mark Twain is Samuel Clemens.)
/∴	Wcf	(Samuel Clemens wrote *Huck Finn.*)

Clearly, this argument is valid. But so far, our system provides no justification for the conclusion. Let's now introduce such a justification, namely the **rule of identity (ID),** which states, in effect, that we may substitute identicals for identicals. The rule can be schematized as follows:

1. $(\ldots u \ldots)$
2. $u = w$ $/\therefore (\ldots w \ldots)$

Where u and w are any individual constants or individual variables, and where $(\ldots w \ldots)$ results from replacing one or more occurrences of u free in $(\ldots u \ldots)$ by occurrences of w free in $(\ldots w \ldots)$.

Examples:

The following examples illustrate the use of the identity sign and also the rule of identity **(ID)** in proofs.

(1)	1.	$Fa \supset Ga$	p
	2.	$\sim Ga$	p
	3.	$a = b$	p $/\therefore \sim Fb$
	4.	$\sim Fa$	1,2 **MT**
	5.	$\sim Fb$	3,4 **ID** (rule of identity)
(2)	1.	$(x)[(x = b) \supset Fx]$	p
	2.	$a = b$	p
	3.	$a = c$	p $/\therefore Fc$
	4.	$(a = b) \supset Fa$	1, **UI**
	5.	Fa	2,4 **MP**
	6.	Fc	3,5 **ID**

Expressions such as $\sim(a = b)$ also can be written as $a \neq b$. Here is a proof using this notation:

(3)	1.	$(x)[(x \neq b) \supset Fx]$	p
	2.	$a \neq b$	p $/\therefore Fa$
	3.	$(a \neq b) \supset Fa$	1, **UI**
	4.	Fa	2,3 **MP**

To make our system complete, we introduce a rule, let's call it **Identity Reflexivity,** or **IR,** allowing introduction of the formula $(x)(x = x)$ into a proof at any time.* Most valid arguments containing uses of the identity symbol can be proved without resorting to **IR,** but a few cannot. Here is an example:

---

*In the history of logic, the idea that any given thing is identical with itself, called the *law of identity* (one of the basic principles believed in times past to be *the* fundamental laws of thought), has usually been expressed as "*a* is *a*." But the meaning of this formula is better expressed in our notation by $(x)(x = x)$. Why we have named this principle *Identity Reflexivity* will become apparent from the discussion of the property of reflexivity later in this chapter.

1.	$(x)[(x = a) \supset Fx]$	$/\therefore Fa$
2.	$(a = a) \supset Fa$	1, **UI**
3.	$(x)(x = x)$	**IR**
4.	$a = a$	3, **UI**
5.	Fa	2,4 **MP**

Exercise 9-1:

Prove valid:

(1) 1. $Fa \cdot (x)[Fx \supset (x = a)]$

2. $(\exists x)(Fx \cdot Gx)$ $/\therefore Ga$

(2) 1. $(x)(Px \supset Qx)$

2. $(x)(Qx \supset Rx)$

3. $Pa \cdot {\sim}Rb$ $/\therefore {\sim}(a = b)$

(3) 1. $(\exists x)\{\{Px \cdot (y)[Py \supset (y = x)]\} \cdot Qx\}$

2. ${\sim}Qa$ $/\therefore {\sim}Pa$

(4) 1. $(\exists x)(y)\{[{\sim}Fxy \supset (x = y)] \cdot Gx\}$
$/\therefore (x)\{{\sim}Gx \supset (\exists y)[{\sim}(y = x) \cdot Fyx]\}$

(5) 1. $(\exists x)\{Px \cdot \{(y)[Py \supset (y = x)] \cdot Qx\}\}$

2. $(\exists x){\sim}({\sim}Px \vee {\sim}Ex)$
$/\therefore (\exists x)(Ex \cdot Qx)$

(6) 1. $(x)[Fx \supset (x = a)]$

2. $(x)[Mx \supset (x = b)]$

3. $(\exists x)(Fx \cdot Mx)$ $/\therefore a = b$

(7) 1. $(x)[Gx \supset (a = x)]$

2. $(x)(Gx \supset Fx)$

3. $(x)(y)[(Fx \vee Fy) \supset (x = y)]$

4. Gb $/\therefore a = c$

Once the identity sign is added to predicate logic, we can symbolize sentences stating quantities other than all, some, and none.

At Least

We already know how to symbolize sentences containing the expression "at least one", namely by means of the existential quantifier. Thus the sentence "There is at least one student" can be symbolized as $(\exists x)Sx$.

But we cannot symbolize the sentence "There are at least *two* students" as $(\exists x)(\exists y)(Sx \cdot Sy)$, because the x and y referred to might be the same entity. However, using the identity sign, we can correctly symbolize it as

$$(\exists x)(\exists y)[(Sx \cdot Sy) \cdot (x \neq y)]$$

This expression says that there is an x that is a student, and a y that is a student, *and x is not identical with y*, which is what the sentence "There are at least two students" states.

Similarly, we can symbolize the sentence "There are at least three students" as

$$(\exists x)(\exists y)(\exists z)\{[(Sx \cdot Sy) \cdot Sz] \cdot \{[(x \neq y) \cdot (x \neq z)] \cdot (y \neq z)\}\}$$

And in the same way, we can handle the phrases "at least four", "at least five", and so on.

At Most

Next take the sentence "There is at most one student". It is correctly symbolized as

$$(x)\{Sx \supset (y)[Sy \supset (x = y)]\}$$

The reason for the universal quantifier is that this sentence asserts not that there are any students, but rather that *there is not more than one* student. It would be true if there were no students at all, as well as if there were exactly one.

Similarly, we can symbolize the sentence "There are at most *two* students" as

$$(x)(y)\{[(Sx \cdot Sy) \cdot (x \neq y)] \supset (z)\{Sz \supset [(z = x) \vee (z = y)]\}\}$$

And in the same way we can handle sentences containing the phrases "at most three", "at most four", and so on.

Exactly

Now consider the sentence "There is *exactly one* student". First, if there is exactly one student, then there *is at least one*. So part of the meaning of "exactly one" is captured by the phrase "at least one", and hence part of the meaning of the sentence "There is exactly one student" can be symbolized as $(\exists x)Sx$. And second, if there is exactly one student then there is *at most* one student. So the rest of the meaning of "exactly one" is captured by the phrase "at most one". Thus, "There is exactly one student" is correctly symbolized as

$$(\exists x)\{Sx \cdot (y)[Sy \supset (x = y)]\}$$

This asserts that there is at least one student, x, and given any allegedly other student, y, y is identical with x. That is, it asserts that there is at least one student and at most one student, which is what is said by "There is exactly one student".

Similarly, we can symbolize the sentence "There are exactly two students" as

$$(\exists x)(\exists y)\{[(Sx \cdot Sy) \cdot (x \neq y)] \cdot (z)\{Sz \supset [(z = x) \vee (z = y)]\}\}$$

And obviously, the same method can be applied in symbolizing the phrases "exactly three", "exactly four", and so on.

Addition of the identity sign to our vocabulary also enables us to symbolize several other kinds of statements we couldn't handle before, including the following two:

Only

Take the statement "Only George didn't pass the exam." We can't symbolize that statement simply as $\sim Pg$, because that says just that George didn't pass the exam, but not that *only* George didn't pass. Instead, we can symbolize it as

$$\sim Pg \cdot (x)\{[Sx \cdot (x \neq g)] \supset Px\}$$

This statement says that George didn't pass the exam but that all the other students did, which is what the original statement asserts.

Everyone But

Now consider the statement "Every student in this class but George passed the exam". Another way to say the same thing is to say that George didn't pass the exam, but every student in the class *not identical with George* passed, easily symbolized using identity (and obvious abbreviations) as

$$\sim Pg \cdot (x)\{[Sx \cdot (x \neq g)] \supset Px\}$$

Similarly, all sorts of other expressions can be captured once the identity sign is introduced. Perhaps the most important of these expressions are the definite descriptions discussed in the next section.

Examples:

Here are a few more examples of symbolizations using the identity sign (restricting the universe of discourse to human beings).

1. Everyone loves exactly one person.
   $(x)(\exists y)\{Lxy \cdot (z)[Lxz \supset (z = y)]\}$
2. Everyone loves exactly one *other* person.
   $(x)(\exists y)\{[(x \neq y) \cdot Lxy] \cdot (z)[Lxz \supset (z = y)]\}$
3. Everyone loves only himself (interpreted to mean that everyone loves himself and no one else).
   $(x)\{Lxx \cdot (y)[(y \neq x) \supset \sim Lxy]\}$

4. At most, everyone loves only himself.
$(x)(y)[Lxy \supset (x = y)]$

5. Someone loves someone.
$(\exists x)(\exists y)Lxy$

6. Someone loves someone else.
$(\exists x)(\exists y)[Lxy \cdot (x \neq y)]$

7. Some people love only other people.
$(\exists x)(y)[Lxy \supset (x \neq y)]$

8. Some people love no one else.
$(\exists x)(y)[(x \neq y) \supset \sim Lxy]$

9. Only Art loves Betsy (interpreted to imply that Art does love Betsy).
$Lab \cdot (x)[Lxb \supset (x = a)]$

10. Every planet except the Earth is uninhabitable.
$(x)\{[Px \cdot (x \neq e)] \supset \sim Ix\}$

Exercise 9-2:

Symbolize the following, using the indicated letters.

1. Only George Washington was the first president of the United States. (g = "George Washington; Fx = "x is the first U.S. president.")
2. Only Ronald Reagan was president of the Screen Actors' Guild and also U.S. president. (r = "Ronald Reagan"; Px = "x is president of the United States"; Sx = "x is president of the Screen Actors' Guild")
3. At least one famous Hollywood actor was elected governor of California. (Fx = "x is a famous Hollywood actor"; Gx = "x was elected governor of California")
4. At most, two famous Hollywood actors ran for governor of California. (Rx = "x ran for governor of California")
5. Exactly three famous Hollywood actors have been president of the Screen Actors' Guild.
6. No president of the United States has also been president of the Screen Actors' Guild, except for Ronald Reagan.

2 *Definite Descriptions*

We can refer to a person or entity by *name,* for example, "Samuel Clemens", "Mt. Everest", or by *description,* for example, "the author of *Huck Finn*", "the tallest mountain in the world". A description of this kind is called a **definite description,** because it picks out or describes one definite entity. The identity sign is needed in order to symbolize sentences containing definite descriptions.

Take the sentence "The president of the United States is religious". A person who utters this sentence asserts (in part) that there is one and only one person who is president of the United States, since it would be inappropriate to talk about *the* president of the United States if there were more than one such person. Therefore, this sentence can be symbolized by first symbolizing "There is exactly one president of the United States", and then adding that he is religious. So the sentence "The president of the United States is religious" is symbolized as

$$(\exists x)\{\{Px \cdot (y)[Py \supset (x = y)]\} \cdot Rx\}$$

The first conjunct asserts that some (at least one) entity is president of the United States, the second that at most one is, and the third that that entity is religious.*

Examples:

Here are a few more sentences containing definite descriptions and their correct symbolizations (again restricting the universe of discourse to human beings).

1. Everyone admires the most intelligent person in the world.
   $(\exists x)\{(y)[(x \neq y) \supset Ixy] \cdot (z)Azx\}$
   (Ixy = "x is more intelligent than y"; Axy = "x admires y")
2. The most intelligent person in the world is also the most admired.
   $(\exists x)(\exists y)\{\{(z)[(x \neq z) \supset Ixz] \cdot (w)[(y \neq w) \supset Ayw]\} \cdot (x = y)\}$
   (Axy = "x is more admired than y")
3. The most intelligent person in the world admires only intelligent people.
   $(\exists x)\{(y)[y \neq x) \supset Ixy] \cdot (z)(Axz \supset Iz)\}$
4. The person most admired by Art is also admired by Betsy.
   $(\exists x)\{(y)[(x \neq y) \supset Aaxy] \cdot Abx\}$
   ($Axyz$ = "x admires y more than z"; Axy = "x admires y"; a = "Art"; b = "Betsy")
5. Art's father admires him.
   $(\exists x)\{\{Fxa \cdot (y)[Fya \supset (x = y)]\} \cdot Axa\}$
6. Art's father admires the most intelligent person in the world.
   $(\exists x)\{(y)[(x \neq y) \supset Ixy] \cdot (\exists z)\{Fza \cdot (w)[Fwa \supset (w = z)] \cdot Azx\}\}$
7. Every man admires the most beautiful woman.
   $(\exists x)\{Wx \cdot (y)\{[Wy \cdot (y \neq x)] \supset Bxy\} \cdot (z)(Mz \supset Azx)\}$
   (Bxy = "x is more beautiful than y"; Mx = "x is a man")

The same caution is necessary in symbolizing sentences containing phrases like "the Chairman" and "the tallest man in the world" as is

---

*This analysis was first proposed by Bertrand Russell. See his "On Denoting", *Mind,* n.s., vol. 14 (1905), reprinted in Robert C. Marsh, ed., *Logic and Knowledge* (New York: Macmillan, 1956).

necessary in symbolizing other complicated sentences. In particular, sentences of this kind frequently are *ambiguous;* before symbolizing them we must get clear as to which meaning we intend our symbolization to capture.

Take the sentence "The present king of France is *not* bald", which can mean either that there is one and only one present king of France and he is not bald, or that it is not the case that there is one (and only one) present king of France (bald or otherwise). If the former is intended, then the sentence in question is correctly symbolized as

$$(\exists x)\{\{Px \cdot (y)[Py \supset (x = y)]\} \cdot {\sim}Bx\}$$

(where Px = "x is, at present, king of France" and Bx = "x is bald"). If the latter is intended, then it is correctly symbolized as

$${\sim}(\exists x)\{\{Px \cdot (y)[Py \supset (x = y)]\} \cdot Bx\}$$

Caution also is necessary because phrases that usually function as definite descriptions occasionally do not. An example is the sentence "The next person who moves will get shot", snarled by a gunman during a holdup. Clearly, the gunman does not intend to assert that there is one and only one person who will get shot if he moves. Instead, he intends to say that *anyone* who moves will get shot. So his threat is correctly symbolized as

$$(x)[(Px \cdot Mx) \supset Sx]$$

Another example is the sentence "The female of the species is vain", which means something like "All females are vain" or "Most females are vain", but surely does not say anything about *the* one and only female.

On the other hand, some uses of the phrase "the so and so" that may appear *not* to function as definite descriptions really do. For instance, when the presiding officer of the U.S. Senate recognizes "the senator from California", it may appear that that phrase cannot be functioning as a definite description, since there are *two* California senators. However, in this context the phrase "the senator from California" means the one who has requested the floor. But if, say, both California senators request the floor at the same time (and they're standing right next to each other), the presiding officer would use a phrase like "the *junior* senator from California" or "the *senior* senator from California", thus unambiguously selecting one definite person to have the floor.

Exercise 9-3:

Symbolize the following sentences, using the indicated letters.

1. Every student is more intelligent than some student (or other). (Sx = "x is a student"; Ixy = "x is more intelligent than y")

2. Some student is more intelligent than every other student.
3. Not every student is more intelligent than all other students.
4. Bonny is the most intelligent student of all. (b = "Bonny")
5. Harry is more intelligent than any other student, except Bonny. (h = "Harry")
6. Of all the intelligent students, Bonny is the most beautiful. (Ix = "x is intelligent"; Bxy = "x is more beautiful than y")
7. The two California senators like each other. (Cx = "x is a California senator"; Lxy = "x likes y")
8. The two California senators represent California in the U.S. Senate. ($Rxyz$ = "x represents y in z"; c = "California"; s = "the U.S. Senate")
9. If Harry isn't the most intelligent student, then there is only one student who is more intelligent than he is.
10. The most intelligent student in the United States will receive the "most intelligent student" award from the president of the United States. ($Rxyz$ = "x will receive y from z"; n = "the president of the United States"; m = "the most intelligent student award")

3 *Properties of Relations*

There are several interesting properties which relational properties themselves may possess.

Symmetry

All two-place relations (relations of the general form Fxy) are either **symmetrical, asymmetrical,** or **nonsymmetrical.** A relation is **symmetrical** *iff** when one thing bears that relation to a second, the second must† bear it to the first. So a relation designated by Fxy is a symmetrical relation *iff* it must be the case that

$$(x)(y)(Fxy \supset Fyx)$$

The relation "__________ is married to - - - - -" is an example of a symmetrical relation. For given any x and y, if x is married to y, then y must be married to x.

An asymmetrical relation is just the opposite of a symmetrical relation. Thus a relation is **asymmetrical** *iff* when one thing bears that relation to a second, the second thing *cannot* bear it to the first. So a relation desig-

* That is, "if and only if".

† The sense of "must" involved here, indeed even the use of that term in characterizing relations of this kind, is in dispute. The same is true of the related term "cannot" used as a synonym for "it is not possible that".

nated by Fxy is asymmetrical *iff* it must be the case that

$(x)(y)(Fxy \supset \sim Fyx)$

The relation "__________ is the father of - - - - - - -" is an example of an asymmetrical relation. For given any x and y, if x is the father of y, then it must be false that y is the father of x.

All relations which are neither symmetrical nor asymmetrical are **nonsymmetrical.** For example, the relation "__________ loves - - - - - - -" is nonsymmetrical, since loving someone entails neither being loved by that person nor not being loved by that person.

Transitivity

All two-place relations are either **transitive, intransitive,** or **nontransitive.** A relation is **transitive** *iff* when one thing bears that relation to a second, and the second to a third, then the first must bear it to the third. Thus a relation designated by Fxy is transitive *iff* it must be the case that

$(x)(y)(z)[(Fxy \cdot Fyz) \supset Fxz]$

The relation "__________ is taller than - - - - - - -" is an example. For if a given person is taller than a second, and the second is taller than a third, then the first must be taller than the third.

It is interesting to note that the statement of a property of a relation often is required in order to present a valid proof for an otherwise invalid argument. For instance, the argument

1. *Tab* (Art is taller than Betsy.)
2. *Tbc* (Betsy is taller than Charles.)

/∴ *Tac* (Art is taller than Charles.)

is invalid *as it stands* (using the machinery of predicate logic), but can be made valid by the introduction of a premise concerning the transitivity of the relation "taller than", as follows:

1.	Tab	p
2.	Tbc	p
3.	$(x)(y)(z)[(Txy \cdot Tyz) \supset Txz]$	p /∴ Tac
4.	$(y)(z)[(Tay \cdot Tyz) \supset Taz]$	3, **UI**
5.	$(z)[(Tab \cdot Tbz) \supset Taz]$	4, **UI**
6.	$(Tab \cdot Tbc) \supset Tac$	5, **UI**
7.	$(Tab \cdot Tbc)$	1,2 **Conj**
8.	Tac	6,7 **MP**

A relation is **intransitive** *iff*, when one thing bears that relation to a second, and the second to a third, then the first *cannot* bear it to the third.

Thus, a relation designated by Fxy is intransitive *iff* it must be the case that

$$(x)(y)(z)[(Fxy \cdot Fyz) \supset {\sim}Fxz]$$

The relation "__________ is the father of _ _ _ _ _ _ _" is an example. For if one person is the father of a second, and the second of a third, then the first cannot be the father of the third.

All relations which are neither transitive nor intransitive are **nontransitive.** For example, the relation "__________ loves _ _ _ _ _ _ _" is nontransitive, since if one person loves a second, and the second loves a third, it follows neither that the first person loves the third nor that the first person doesn't love the third.

Reflexivity

The situation with respect to reflexivity is more complex.

A relation is **totally reflexive** *iff* everything must bear that relation to itself. So a relation designated by Fxy is totally reflexive *iff* it must be the case that

$$(x)Fxx$$

The relation "__________ is identical with _ _ _ _ _ _ _" is an example. For everything must be identical with itself.

Almost all interesting relations are *not* totally reflexive. There is no name in common use for relations which are not totally reflexive, but we can say that a relation designated by Fxy is not totally reflexive *iff* it is **not** necessarily the case that

$$(x)Fxx$$

The relation "__________ loves _ _ _ _ _ _ _" (restricting the domain of discourse to human beings) is an example. For it is not necessarily true that all human beings love themselves.

A relation is said to be **reflexive** *iff* everything which bears that relation to anything must bear it to itself. That is, a relation designated by Fxy is reflexive *iff* it must be the case that

$$(x)(y)[Fxy \supset (Fxx \cdot Fyy)]$$

An example is the relation "__________ belongs to the same political party as _ _ _ _ _ _ _", since if a given entity, say Art, belongs to the same political party as anyone else, say Betsy, then Art must belong to the same political party as himself, and so must Betsy.

Notice that "__________ belongs to the same political party as _ _ _ _ _ _ _" is *not* totally reflexive, since *everything* does *not* belong to the same political party as itself. For example, a piece of chalk doesn't belong to any political party at all. So some reflexive relations are not totally reflexive. But all totally reflexive relations are reflexive.

A relation is **irreflexive** *iff* nothing can bear that relation to itself. Thus, a relation designated by *Fxy* is irreflexive *iff* it must be the case that

$(x){\sim}Fxx$

The relation "__________ is taller than - - - - - - -" is an example. For nothing can be taller than itself.

Finally, all relations which are neither reflexive nor irreflexive are **nonreflexive.** For example, the relation "__________ loves - - - - - - -" is nonreflexive because (1) it is not reflexive (a person can love someone else, but not love himself), and (2) it is not irreflexive (a person can love someone else *and* also love himself).

Exercise 9-4:

(A) Determine the status of the following relations with respect to symmetry, transitivity, and reflexivity:

1. __________ loves - - - - - - -.
2. __________ is the father of - - - - - - -.
3. __________ is ≧ - - - - - - -.
(concerning numbers only)
4. __________ is north of - - - - - - -.
5. __________ is at least one year younger than - - - - - - -.
6. __________ is identical with - - - - - - -.
7. __________ is the brother of - - - - - - -.
8. __________ sees - - - - - - -.

(B) Prove that all asymmetrical relations are irreflexive.

---

4 Higher Order Logics

The predicate logic discussed so far expressly forbids sentences which ascribe properties to properties themselves, and restricts quantification to *individual* variables. A predicate logic restricted in this way is said to be a **first order predicate logic.** We now will consider the bare bones of a higher order predicate logic.

Quantifying Over Property Variables

Just as we can have individual variables, so we can have **property variables.** Let's use the capital letters F, G, H, and K as property variables, for the time being forbidding their use as property constants. The expression Fa will then be a sentence *form,* and not a sentence. But obviously, we can obtain a sentence from this expression by replacing the property variables F by a property constant. Thus, we can obtain the sentence Sa (where Sx = "x is smart") from the sentence form Fa. (Hence Sa is a *substitution instance* of Fa.)

But we also can obtain a sentence from the sentence form Fa by *quantifying* the property variable F. Thus we can obtain the sentences $(F)(Fa)$, read "Art has every property", or "Given any property, F, Art has F", and $(\exists F)(Fa)$, read "Art has some property (or other)", or "There is some property F such that Art has F".

We also can have sentences which quantify both property variables and individual variables. An example would be the sentence "Everything has some property (or other)", symbolized as $(x)(\exists F)Fx$.

Examples:

Some other examples of symbolizations containing quantified property variables are:

1.	$(x)(F)Fx$	(Everything has every property.)
2.	$(\exists x)(F)Fx$	(Something has every property.)
3.	$(\exists x)(\exists F)Fx$	(Something has some property [or other].)
4.	$(F)(\exists x)Fx$	(Every property belongs to something [or other].)
5.	$(\exists F)(x)Fx$	(Some property belongs to everything.)
6.	$\sim(\exists x)(F)Fx$	(Nothing has all properties.)
7.	$(F)\{Fa \supset \sim(\exists x)[(Px \cdot Fx) \cdot (x \neq a)]\}$	(No one else has any property which Art has.)
8.	$(\exists F)\{Fa \cdot (y)\{[Py \cdot (y \neq a)] \supset \sim Fy\}\}$	(Art has some property no one else has.)

Now that we have introduced property variables and the quantification of property variables, we can give a more precise definition of the identity symbol, for we can say that the expression $x = y$ means that *necessarily* $(F)(Fx \equiv Fy)$. It follows then that $(x)(y)[(x = y) \equiv (F)(Fx \equiv Fy)]$, from which we can prove that the identity relation is transitive, symmetrical, and reflexive. (Recall that we labeled one of the identity rules of inference *Identity Reflexivity*.)

Higher Order Properties

So far, we have considered only properties of *individuals*. But *properties* themselves can have properties. For instance, *honesty* is a *rare* property, while (unfortunately) dishonesty is quite common. Similarly, courage is an honorable property, cowardice dishonorable.

Let's use the symbols A_1, B_1, C_1, etc., to refer to properties of properties. Then we can symbolize the sentence "Honesty is a rare property" as $R_1 H$, and the sentence "Courage is a useful property" as $U_1 C$. Similarly, we can symbolize the sentence "We all have useful properties" as $(x)[Px \supset (\exists F)(Fx \cdot U_1 F)]$, and so on.

Examples:

Some other examples of symbolizations containing properties of properties are:

1. $(F)U_1 F$ — (All properties are useful.)
2. $(\exists F)(U_1 F \cdot R_1 F)$ — (Some useful properties are rare.)
3. $(\exists F)(G_1 F \cdot Fa)$ — (Art has some good properties [qualities].)
4. $(\exists F)[(G_1 F \cdot Fa) \cdot Fb]$ — (Art and Betsy share some good qualities.)
5. $(F)[(Fb \cdot G_1 F) \supset Fa]$ — (Art has all of Betsy's good qualities.)
6. $(x)\{(\exists F)\{Fx \cdot (G)[Gx \supset (F = G)]\} \supset \sim(\exists H)(Hx \cdot G_1 H)\}$ — (Nothing which has only one property has any good properties.)

Unfortunately, higher order logics involving properties of properties have encountered important difficulties, which have as yet not been satisfactorily worked out. Some of these problems are discussed briefly in the last section of this chapter.

5 *Limitations of Predicate Logic*

At the beginning of the discussion of predicate logic, we pointed out that certain kinds of valid arguments are invalid when symbolized in the notation of sentential logic. We then proceeded to develop predicate logic, which provides a method for symbolizing these arguments and for proving them valid.

The question naturally arises whether there are other arguments which, although invalid using the notation and proof technique of predicate logic, are valid in some wider (perhaps ideal) deductive system. The answer is that there may be such arguments.

Consider the argument

1. Art knows that he'll go either to the show or to the concert (but not to both).
2. Art knows that he won't go to the show.

/∴ Art knows that he'll go to the concert.

Clearly this argument is valid in some sense or other. But there is no way to symbolize it in the standard predicate logic notation so that we can prove it is valid. For instance, if we symbolize the argument as

1. *Kaf*
2. *Kag*

/∴ *Kah*

where K = "knows that", f = "he'll go either to the show or the concert", g = "he won't go to the show", and h = "he'll go to the concert", then clearly we cannot prove that it is valid.

This is an example of an argument involving what are sometimes called **indirect contexts.** In this case, the clue that we are dealing with an indirect context is the phrase "knows that". Some other phrases that usually indicate indirect contexts are "believes that", "is looking for", "prays to", and "is necessary that".

So far, the logic of indirect contexts has not been worked out, at least not to the satisfaction of most philosophers. The whole area is one of extreme disagreement, and the predicate logic presented in this and other textbooks is not able to deal adequately with it.

There are other cases where it is claimed that the predicate logic presented here is inadequate. We present two which are the centers of interesting disputes.

The first is illustrated by the argument:

1. Art sang the Hamilton school song beautifully.

/∴ Art sang the Hamilton school song.

Again, the argument is valid, and again it is claimed that we cannot prove that it is valid using the notation and proof technique of predicate logic.

Several solutions have been proposed for this problem. One is simply that there is a "missing premise". According to this solution, the argument in question is invalid *as it stands,* but can be made valid by supplying an obvious "missing premise", namely the premise that if someone sang a particular song beautifully, then he sang that song. Once we add this missing premise, the argument can be proved quite easily in predicate logic.

Another dispute involves what we might call "semantically valid arguments". Suppose for the moment that the term "bachelor" means exactly the same thing as "unmarried adult male". Then it is clear that the argument

1. All bachelors are handsome.
/∴ All unmarried adult males are handsome.

is valid in some sense or other. But again, it appears to be invalid in the predicate logic system developed in this text.

Several ways have been proposed to handle so-called semantically valid arguments. One is to introduce a rule permitting the substitution of terms *synonymous* with any terms occurring in an argument as stated.

Another way is to claim that these arguments are enthymematic—that they have "missing premises". In the example in question, the missing premise is that all bachelors are unmarried adult males.

And a third way is to *deny that the argument in question is valid,* on the grounds that *truly synonymous* expressions do not exist, at least not in natural languages. (The underlying issue here is the validity of the so-called analytic-synthetic distinction, discussed in Appendix A.)

Finally, note that predicate logic has trouble dealing with statements about *dispositional* properties and with *subjective* statements, in particular *counterfactual conditionals*.

Dispositional properties are powers, potentials, or dispositions of objects. An example is the dispositional property of being *flammable*. Although dispositional properties cannot be experienced through the five senses, in some cases their observable "mates" can be. For instance, we can't see that a piece of dry wood is flammable (dispositional term), but when it is lighted, we can see it *burn* (observational property). Since dispositional properties can't be experienced directly, we must *infer* to their existence. So they are a kind of *theoretical* entity (see Chapter Fourteen for more on theoretical entities).

Obviously, dispositional properties such as being flammable or flexible are closely connected to their observational mates. Being flexible, for instance, is connected to the observational property of *bending,* for to say that something is flexible is to say that it has the *power, potential,* or *disposition* to bend, under certain conditions. Similarly, to say that something is flammable is to say that it has the power, disposition, or potential to burn. And so on for other dispositional properties.

The problem for logic has to do with the correct symbolization of statements about dispositional properties. What does it *mean* to say, for instance, that sugar is *soluble* (dispositional property) in water? What is a disposition, power, or potential?

The problem is easy to overlook in everyday life because an easy answer seems readily available. It seems natural to suppose, for instance, that when we say a particular lump of sugar has the dispositional property of being soluble in water, we mean simply that *if* we place the lump in water (under suitable conditions of temperature, water saturation, and so on) *then* it will dissolve. Similarly, if we say that a plastic tube is flexible, we mean that *if* suitable pressure is applied to it, *then* it will bend. And so on.

Therefore, it seems initially plausible to say that given a sentence containing a dispositional term, we can replace it by an "If ______ then _ _ _ _ _ " sentence containing not the dispositional term but rather its observational mate. For instance, we seem able to replace the dispositional sentence "Lump of sugar *s* is soluble" by the statement "If *s* is placed in water under suitable conditions, then *s* will dissolve", and replace the dispositional sentence "Piece of wood *w* is flammable" by the sentence "If oxygen and heat are applied to *w* under suitable conditions, then *w* will burn".

All of this seems reasonable until we try to put these sentences into the symbolic notation of predicate logic or into some other equally precise notation. Take the dispositional sentence "Lump of sugar *s* is soluble". It seems plausible to translate that sentence into the nondispositional sentence "If *s* is placed in water, then it will dissolve", symbolized as $Ws \supset Ds$ (omitting the qualification about suitable conditions for the moment). But does the sentence $Ws \supset Ds$ really mean the same thing as the dispositional sentence "Lump of sugar *s* is soluble"? Unfortunately, it does not.

To see that it does not, consider the *false* dispositional sentence "Piece of copper *c* is soluble" and its analogous translation to "If *c* is placed in water, then *c* will dissolve", symbolized as $Wc \supset Dc$. Suppose we never place *c* in water, so that the antecedent Wc is false. If so, then the whole sentence $Wc \supset Dc$ will be true, because all conditional statements with false antecedents are true. But if the sentence $Wc \supset Dc$ is true, it cannot possibly be a correct translation of the *false* sentence "Piece of copper *c* is soluble", since a sentence and its correct translation cannot have different truth values.

Analogously, the translation of the sentence "Lump of sugar *s* is soluble" into $Ws \supset Ds$ also must be incorrect, even though in this case, luckily, both the sentence translated and the sentence it is translated into have the same truth value. That this is a matter of luck becomes obvious when we realize that the analogous translation of the sentence "Lump of sugar *s* is not soluble", into "If *s* is placed in water then it will not dissolve", also is true if *s* is never placed in water. But surely, the two statements "*s* is soluble" and "*s* is not soluble" cannot both be true.

To put the difficulty another way, if we translate all dispositional sentences into nondispositional conditional sentences in the above way, then all of these conditionals with false antecedents will have to be judged to be true, even though many of the dispositional sentences they are intended to translate (for example, "Piece of copper *c* is soluble", "Lump of sugar *s* is not soluble") are false.

The conclusion we must draw is that dispositional sentences cannot be replaced by nondispositional material conditional sentences, or at least not in this simple way. The so-called problem of dispositionals is to find a satisfactory way to translate sentences of this type.

It has been suggested that the correct analysis of dispositional sentences is not into *indicative* conditionals but rather into **subjunctive** or **contrary-to-fact conditionals.** For instance, according to this view, the correct translation of "*s* is soluble" is not into the indicative conditional "If *s* is placed in water, then it will dissolve" but rather into the subjunctive conditional "If *s were* placed in water, then it *would* dissolve", or into the *contrary-to-fact* conditional "If *s had been* placed in water, then it *would have* dissolved".

The trouble with this analysis of dispositional sentences into subjunctive or contrary-to-fact (counterfactual) conditionals is that subjunctive and counterfactual sentences present a translation problem just as baffling as the one presented by dispositional sentences.

Take the counterfactual "If *s* had been placed in water, then it would have dissolved". Suppose we try to translate that sentence into the truth-functional notation of propositional or predicate logic.

The obvious starting point in such a translation procedure is to replace the "If ______ then _ _ _ _ _ " of the counterfactual by the " $\supset$ " of truth-functional logic. If we do so, then the counterfactual in question translates into "(*s* had been placed in water) $\supset$ (*s* would have dissolved)". The trouble with this translation is that its antecedent and consequent are not sentences, and so the whole conditional is not a sentence. To make it a sentence, we must replace the subjunctive antecedent and consequent with their corresponding "mates" in the indicative mood. For instance, we must replace the antecedent "*s* had been placed in water" by the indicative sentence "*s* is placed in water" (or by "*s* was placed in water"), and replace the consequent "*s* would have dissolved" by the indicative sentence "*s* dissolves" (or by "*s* dissolved"). The result is the translation of the counterfactual "If *s* had been placed in water, then *s* would have dissolved" into the indicative conditional "If *s* is placed in water, then *s* will dissolve" (or "If *s* was placed in water, then *s* dissolved"), which in symbols is $Ps \supset Ds$. In a similar way, we can translate all other counterfactuals.

But once we actually translate in this way, it becomes obvious that such translations are unsatisfactory, because the end product of this translation procedure for counterfactual sentences is exactly the same, and just as inadequate, as the end product of the translation procedure for dispositional sentences discussed in the last section. So the suggested method of translating counterfactual sentences cannot be correct. Similar remarks apply to other kinds of subjunctive conditionals. The so-called problem of counterfactuals, really a problem concerning all kinds of subjunctive conditionals, is to find a way to symbolize subjunctives so that they can be handled by some sort of appropriate logical machinery. Until it is solved, the formal logic we have developed so far will not be able to handle all arguments about dispositions or arguments in the subjunctive mood (e.g., contrary-to-fact conditionals).

6 *Philosophical Difficulties*

In addition to the problems discussed in the previous section, there are serious philosophical problems underlying the whole of sentential or of predicate logic. Let's now briefly discuss a few of these problems.

Propositions versus Sentences

One basic issue is whether logic deals with *sentences* or *propositions*. For instance, in using the argument form

If *p* then *q*
If *q* then *r*
/∴ If *p* then *r*

the English equivalent of Hypothetical Syllogism, whatever is substituted for one *p* must be substituted for the other, and similarly for *q* and *r*. We must substitute the *very same thing* for both occurrences of *p*. But what is this same thing we must substitute? Some philosophers say we must substitute the same *sentence,* while others say that we must substitute sentences that express the same *proposition*.

We can think of a *sentence* as a series of ink marks on paper (or sounds in the air). Thus, as you read the sentence that precedes this one, you look at particular ink marks on a particular sheet of paper, and those ink marks may be said to *be* a particular sentence. But we would ordinarily say that someone else reading another copy of this book might read the *same* sentence. Thus, the everyday meaning of the word "sentence" is ambiguous. So let's resolve the ambiguity by saying that both of you looked at different **sentence tokens** of the same **sentence type.** Here is another sentence token of that sentence type:

We can think of a sentence as a series of ink marks on paper (or sounds in the air).

During the rest of this discussion, when we use the word "sentence", let's mean *sentence type,* because no one would argue that the same sentence token has to be substituted in two different places in an argument form (since that is impossible). Thus no one would argue that the principal unit dealt with in logic is sentence tokens.

As for **propositions,** recall our earlier example. The expressions "Snow is white" and "Der Schnee ist weiss" are tokens of two different sentence types, and thus of two different sentences. But they seem to have something in common, they seem to "express the same idea", or "say the same thing", or "have the same meaning". Whatever they have in common, whether meaning or something else like it, we shall call a *proposition*. Then we can say that these two expressions, although different sentences, express the same proposition.

Of course, two sentences don't have to be in different languages to express the same proposition. For instance, the two different sentences "Snow is white" and "White is the snow" express the same proposition, as do "John loves Mary" and "Mary is loved by John".

Now the principal objection to saying that logic deals with propositions rather than sentences is simply that the very existence of propositions can be doubted. Sentences, or at least sentence tokens, can be *looked at* or *heard;* they are perceivable. But you can't perceive a proposition. (Nor is it exactly clear what a proposition is supposed to be.)

Well, if propositions are such doubtful entities, can we make sense of logic without them? There seem to be good reasons to answer *no* to that question.

In the first place, if logic deals with sentences and not propositions, then the rules of logic are at best much more restricted than is normally supposed. Take Simplification. We ordinarily suppose that the following argument is valid because it is an instance of Simplification:

(1) 1. Art will get elected, and he'll serve well.
/∴ He's going to get elected.

But if logic deals with sentences, this argument is not a valid instance of Simplification (or any other standard rule of inference). For Simplification has the form

p and *q*
/∴ *p*

and if we substitute the sentence "Art will get elected" for the first p, we must substitute the same sentence for the second p. We cannot substitute the sentence "He's going to get elected" for the second p, because that is a different *sentence* from "Art will get elected" (although it expresses the same proposition).

The obvious thought is that in this case "Art will get elected" and "He's going to get elected" are *synonymous* (have the same meaning), and that all we have to do is allow synonymous sentences to replace one another whenever it is convenient to do so. The trouble is that those who reject propositions cannot appeal to sameness of meaning, for in the last analysis that amounts to a tacit appeal to propositions (or at least to abstract entities just as mysterious to those who reject propositions as propositions themselves).

In addition, when propositions are rejected, problems arise because terms and sentences in natural languages tend to be *ambiguous*. For ambiguity also leads to trouble when substituting sentences into valid argument forms. Take the argument:

	1.	Whales are fish.	p
	2.	If whales are fish, then whales are cold-blooded.	p
/∴	3.	Whales are cold-blooded.	1,2 **MP**

Premise 1 of this argument is true if we construe the word "fish" in its everyday sense, and premise 2 is true if we construe that word in its scientific sense. And yet the conclusion clearly is false. So it seems that **MP** has let us down.

The usual explanation, of course, is that the trouble arises because the word "fish" is being used ambiguously. If the word "fish" is used unambiguously throughout the proof, then the argument is valid, but one or the other of its premises is false (depending on what sense of that word we use). But if we use the word "fish" *equivocally,* meaning one thing in one premise and another thing in the other, then the argument is *invalid*. In either case, we have not validly proceeded from true premises to a false conclusion.

But this explanation is not open to those who claim that logic deals with sentences and not propositions. For them, the form of **MP** is satisfied whenever the letters p and q are replaced respectively in each of their occurrences by the same *sentences*. And in the above example, each use of p is replaced by the same sentence, namely "Whales are fish". Of course, that sentence is used ambiguously, but that is another matter.

Another way to put the problem facing those who advocate sentences over propositions is just that those who reject propositions have a hard time separating uses of a sentence that have one meaning from those that have another. (For instance, they won't be able to say that in the above argument the sentence "Whales are fish" expresses one proposition when said truly and another proposition when said falsely.) Their problem, in other words, is to find some way to distinguish ambiguous uses of terms and sentences without appealing to propositions, a problem some of their opponents (including most definitely this writer) feel confident they cannot solve.

A Third Truth Value?

Sentential logic is a two-valued truth-functional logic. But are most natural language sentences two valued? It has been argued that they are not.

Recall our discussion of definite descriptions (in Section 6 of this chapter), and consider the sentence "The present king of France is bald". According to the analysis in Section 6, asserting this sentence amounts to saying that (1) there is a present king of France; (2) there is only one present king of France; and (3) that person is bald.

But it has been argued that this analysis is incorrect, because it confuses *referring* to something with asserting that it exists. In saying that the present king of France is bald, according to this view, a speaker does not assert that a present king of France exists. Instead, *he presupposes* that the thing referred to, the present king of France, exists. But to presuppose that there is a present king of France is not to *assert* that there is a present king of France (nor—according to this view—does that presupposition *logically imply* the existence of a present king of France).

Now as a matter of fact there is no present king of France. So a person uttering the sentence "The present king of France is bald" will fail in his attempt to refer. Hence, it is claimed, that sentence, although meaningful, is neither true nor false, and thus literally has no truth value. It follows then that it is incorrect to say that all sentences are either true or false.*

If correct, this is a very serious matter for logic, for we would have to change all of the truth table definitions of the sentence connectives, and even have to give up the law of the excluded middle (that p or $\sim p$).

But the presupposition theory is not the only argument in favor of giving up two-valued logic. Another takes its cue from paradox-generating sentences such as "This very sentence is false".† Someone uttering this sentence intends to refer to that very sentence; and since the sentence does exist, there is no failure of reference. Nevertheless, it has been argued that, though meaningful, this sentence has no truth value. For if it is true, then it is false, and if it is false, then it is true. Hence we must regard it as neither true nor false, even though meaningful, and therefore we must give up two-valued logic.††

The Status of Sentence Connectives in Predicate Logic

In sentential logic we explained the meaning of the logical connectives "$\supset$", "$\cdot$", "$\vee$", "$\equiv$", and "$\sim$", by means of truth tables, thus making them *truth-functional* connectives. But now consider their occurrences in quantified sentences, for instance in the sentence $(x)(Fx \supset Gx)$. The ex-

---

*This is roughly the view argued by P. F. Strawson. (More precisely, he argues that assertion of the sentence "The present king of France is bald" fails to make a true or false *statement*. But what it is to utter a statement other than asserting a proposition is not clear.) See Strawson's "On Referring", *Mind*, n.s., vol. 59 (1950), and Bertrand Russell's reply, "Mr. Strawson on Referring", in Russell, *My Philosophical Development* (London: Allen & Unwin, 1959), pp. 238–45.

†Discussed further in the last section of this chapter.

††This is essentially the argument proposed in Frederick B. Fitch, *Symbolic Logic* (New York: The Ronald Press, 1952), p. 8.

pressions Fx and Gx are *sentence forms,* and hence cannot have truth values. Thus, there is no truth value for the expression $Fx \supset Gx$, and so the use of the horseshoe symbol "$\supset$" in $(x)(Fx \supset Gx)$ does not appear to be truth functional. But if it isn't truth functional, how is it defined?

This problem is frequently overlooked, perhaps because an easy solution seems readily at hand. Recall that when we first discussed quantifiers, we said (in Chapter Six, Section 3) that it was convenient to regard quantified sentences as very long conjunctions (in the case of universally quantified sentences) or disjunctions (in the case of existentially quantified sentences). For instance, in a two-individual universe of discourse, $(x)(Fx \supset Gx)$ amounts to the expansion $(Fa \supset Ga) \cdot (Fb \supset Gb)$, and $(\exists x)(Fx \supset Gx)$ amounts to the expansion $(Fa \supset Ga) \vee (Fb \supset Gb)$. Now clearly, the horseshoe symbols occurring in these expansions are truth functional. Hence, we can regard those occurring in the related quantified sentences as truth functional.

The trouble with this, alluded to before, is that in some cases the domain of discourse is infinitely large (an example is the domain of positive integers), or even nondenumerably large (an example is the domain of real numbers). When dealing with domains of this size, we cannot replace quantified sentences with their expansions.

Nevertheless, some philosophers* regard quantified sentences as very long conjunctions or disjunctions, even though they cannot actually be written down, and thus feel justified in believing that the connectives occurring in quantified sentences are truth functional. Perhaps, then, the issue is whether it makes a difference that we cannot actually write down an infinitely long conjunction or disjunction. If so, this dispute may be related to the dispute about propositions and sentences. For there are no infinitely long sentences, but assuming there are any propositions at all, there may be propositions that could be expressed by infinitely long conjunctions or disjunctions, if only we were able to write them down.

Whatever the solution to the above may be, there is another objection to the view that quantified sentences are shorthand for very long conjunctions or disjunctions. When we say, for instance, that $(x)Fx$, we seem to say more than that $(Fa \cdot Fb) \cdot \ldots$. The sentence $(x)Fx$ seems to do more than merely list all the items $a, b, c, \ldots$ and say they have the property F. It also says that the items $a, b, c, \ldots$ in the expansion of $(x)Fx$ are in fact *all the items there are* (or all the items in the domain of discourse). The expansion doesn't say this, while the quantified sentence does. Hence, it can be argued that a quantified sentence and its expansion are not equivalent. If this argument is a good one, then the question of how

---

* See, for instance, Richard L. Purtill, *Logic for Philosophers* (New York: Harper & Row, 1971), pp. 226–27.

to interpret the occurrences of connectives in quantified sentences remains unsolved.

Difficulties with Truth-Functional Translations

When we introduced the sentence connective "$\supset$", we pointed out that it is a truth-functional connective and is to be used in translating everyday "If ______ then - - - - - " sentences, even though most such sentences are not truth functional. We justified this on several grounds, one of which was that such translations render valid arguments into valid arguments and invalid arguments into invalid arguments.

We saw in the previous section how this translation procedure failed when applied to subjunctive sentences. But some philosophers claim that it fails also for indicative sentences. Consider the following argument.*

(1) If this is gold, then it is *not* soluble in water.
/∴ It's not the case that if this is gold, then it *is* soluble in water.

If we mechanically translate this argument as

(2) $G \supset \sim S$
$/\therefore \sim(G \supset S)$

we get into trouble, because (2) is *invalid,* whereas (1) is valid. And yet (2) seems to be the straightforward truth-functional translation of (1).

One way to solve this problem is to deny that the conclusion of (1) is correctly symbolized as $\sim(G \supset S)$. It might be claimed, for instance, that the placement of the negating expression in the conclusion deceives us into thinking that the whole remainder of the sentence is being negated, whereas only the consequent is being negated.

We already have precedent for the assumption that the placement of a negating expression doesn't always reflect its logical scope. Recall our discussion of the sentence "The present king of France is *not* bald", which in some contexts may mean that it is not the case that there is a present king of France, bald or otherwise. In examples of this kind, the negating term, although toward the end of the sentence, actually negates all the rest of the sentence. So in the gold example, the negating term, although at the beginning of the sentence, may negate just the second half of the sentence.

However, it isn't at all clear that this proposed solution to the problem is adequate.† And if it isn't, then we are faced with an extremely serious

---

* Taken from Charles L. Stevenson, "If-iculties", *Philosophy of Science,* vol. 41 (1970), pp. 27–49.

† Most objections to it tend to be quite complicated. But one is fairly simple: In the gold example, if we symbolize as suggested, the argument becomes totally trivial, namely $G \supset \sim S \quad /\therefore G \supset \sim S$; yet the original argument seems to have more to it than that.

translation problem, standing in the way of the acceptance of any truth-functional logic as a device useful in dealing with real life arguments.

7 *Logical Paradoxes*

In addition to the problems just discussed that trouble first-order predicate logic, higher order logics are plagued by the so-called **logical paradoxes,** some of which date back to the time of the early Greeks.

Syntactic Paradoxes

In a first-order predicate logic there is no straightforward way to express the predication of properties to other properties. The usual way to express such predications is via the symbolism of a *second-order* (or higher) predicate logic. In Section 4 of this chapter, we very briefly discussed higher order logics and in particular the predication of properties to other properties. (An example is the property of *honesty,* which seems itself to have the property of being *rare*—in that its extension is rather small.) But if we allow the predication of properties to properties, then certain alleged paradoxes called **syntactic paradoxes** can be generated.

If we can predicate properties of other properties, it seems reasonable to suppose that we can predicate properties of *themselves*. For example, it seems reasonable to suppose that the property of being *comprehensible* itself is comprehensible (in contrast to the property of being *incomprehensible,* which itself is not incomprehensible), and reasonable to suppose that the property of being *common* (as opposed to rare) is itself common. But sometimes the predication of a property to itself yields trouble. The most famous example is the so-called **impredicable paradox.**

Let's call any property that can be truly predicated of itself a *predicable property,* and any property that cannot be truly predicated of itself an *impredicable property*. Using this notation we can say that the property of being *common* is a predicable property, since being common is a common property, and that the property of being *rare* is an *im*predicable property, since being rare is *not* a rare property (because there are many kinds of rare things).

But what about the property of being *impredicable?* Can this property be truly predicated of itself? The unfortunate answer seems to be that if the property of being impredicable *is* predicated of itself, then it *is not* predicated of itself, and if it *is not* predicated of itself, then it *is* predicated of itself. Hence, the paradox.

To make this clear, let's symbolize the property of being predicable as P, and the property of being impredicable as $\overline{P}$. Thus, to say a given property F is P is to say that FF, and to say that a given property F is $\overline{P}$ is to say that $\sim FF$.

To start with, either $\overline{P}$ is itself $\overline{P}$ or else $\overline{P}$ is P. Suppose $\overline{P}$ is $\overline{P}$. If $\overline{P}$ is $\overline{P}$, then $\overline{P}$ *is* predicated of itself, and hence $\overline{P}$ is P. So if $\overline{P}$ is $\overline{P}$, then $\overline{P}$ is P.

Now suppose $\overline{P}$ is P. If $\overline{P}$ is P, then $\overline{P}$ is *not* predicated of itself, and hence $\overline{P}$ is $\overline{P}$. So if $\overline{P}$ is P, then $\overline{P}$ is $\overline{P}$.

It follows that if $\overline{P}$ is $\overline{P}$, then it is P, and if $\overline{P}$ is P, *then it is* $\overline{P}$. Translating this back into plain English, what we have shown is that if the property of being impredicable is *impredicable,* then it is predicated of itself, and hence is *predicable*. And if the property of being impredicable is *predicable,* then it is not predicated of itself (impredicable would have to be *im*predicable to be predicated of itself), and hence is *impredicable*.

This contradictory result can be made even more explicit by writing down the definition of $\overline{P}$, and then constructing a simple argument, as follows:

1. $\overline{P}F = df \sim FF$

That is, to say that a property, F, is impredicable is to say that it is not the case that F is F. From which it follows that given any property F, F is $\overline{P}$ if and only if it is not the case that F is F. In other words,

2. $(F)(\overline{P}F \equiv \sim FF)$

Hence, substituting $\overline{P}$ for F, we get (by **UI**)

3. $\overline{P}\,\overline{P} \equiv \sim \overline{P}\,\overline{P}$

from which an explicit contradiction can be derived.

Several solutions to paradoxes of this kind have been proposed. One of them is the **simple theory of types.*** According to this theory, all entities divide into a hierarchy of types, starting with individual entities, moving to properties of individual entities, then to properties of properties of individual entities, and so on. For instance, Art is an individual entity; the property of being honest is a property Art may possess (hence honesty is a property of individuals); and the property of being rare is a property possessed by the property of being honest (hence rarity is a property of properties).

Having arranged entities in this way, the simple theory of types requires that the type of a property be higher than any property of which it can be predicated. For instance, if being old is predicated of Art, then it cannot be predicated either of itself or any other property.

It is customary to mark the distinction between properties of individu-

---

*Proposed by Bertrand Russell. See *Principles of Mathematics* (Cambridge: Cambridge University Press, 1903), Appendix B.

als and properties of properties by some notational device, such as the use of standard type to denote properties of individuals and boldface type to denote properties of properties of individuals.

Using a notation of this kind, a sentence such as "Art is not old" will be symbolized as $\sim Oa$, and a sentence such as "Honesty is rare" will be symbolized as $\boldsymbol{RH}$.

Notice that the sentence "Honesty is rare" is correctly symbolized as $\boldsymbol{R}H$, and *not* as RH, for according to the theory of types, the property of being rare, which is predicable of properties, is of a type one level higher than properties that are predicable of individuals.

To summarize, the simple theory of types requires, first, that we arrange entities into a hierarchy of categories or types, starting with individuals, moving to properties of individuals, and then to properties of properties, properties of properties of properties, and so on; and second, that the type of a property be one type higher than any property or entity of which it can be predicated.

An obvious consequence of the simple theory of types is that no property can be predicated of itself. And it is this consequence that solves the impredicable paradox, for if no property can be predicated of itself, then it becomes senseless to ask if the property of being impredicable is *itself* impredicable.

The simple theory of types has been objected to as both *ad hoc* and *counter-intuitive*. For example, according to the simple theory of types, the rareness we can predicate of, say, a postage stamp is different from the rareness we can predicate of the property of being honest. But it seems intuitively clear that it is the very same property of rareness which is predicable of postage stamps and of honesty.

The counter-intuitive nature of the simple theory of types is further illustrated by the fact that it forbids assertion of sentences such as "Some members of every type (in the hierarchy of types) are rare", a sentence that seems not only *meaningful,* but also *true*.

Indeed, it has been argued that the very statement of the simple theory of types presupposes a violation of the theory itself. For instance, the simple theory of types presupposes that all individuals, properties of individuals, properties of properties, and so on, have the property of being *type classifiable* (that is, have the property of belonging to exactly one category in the hierarchy of types). But the property of being type classifiable is not permitted by the simple theory of types. Hence the theory presupposes what it will not permit.

Semantic Paradoxes

While adoption of the simple theory of types has its difficulties, it does solve syntactic paradoxes like the impredicable paradox. But unfortunately, it fails to solve the paradoxes usually referred to as **semantic paradoxes.**

The most famous semantic paradox is the so-called "paradox of the liar", which was first posed by the ancient Greeks. Put into more modern dress, the paradox is this: It seems reasonable to suppose that every declarative sentence is either *true* or *false*. But consider the sentence

(1) Sentence (1) is false.

Is sentence (1) true, or is it false? The unfortunate answer seems to be that if sentence (1) is true, then it is false, and if it is false, then it is true.

Take the first possibility, namely that sentence (1) is true. If (1) is true, and (1) asserts that (1) is false, then it follows that (1) is false. So if (1) is true, then (1) is false.

Now suppose (1) is false. If (1) is false, and (1) asserts that (1) is false, then it follows that it is false that (1) is false, and therefore follows that (1) is true. So if (1) is false, then (1) is true. Either way, we have a contradiction, and hence a paradox.

An obvious thought is to solve the liar paradox by ruling out (as meaningless) any sentence that refers to itself. (Indeed the liar paradox often is conceived of—erroneously—as a paradox of self-reference.) But unfortunately, the liar paradox can be generated without self-reference. For example, consider the following two sentences:

(2) Sentence (3) is false.

(3) Sentence (2) is true.

Sentence (2) refers to sentence (3), and sentence (3) refers to sentence (2), but neither (2) nor (3) refers to itself. So both of these sentences satisfy the requirement that sentences not be self-referential, and they seem to have the form required of legitimate declarative sentences.

But is sentence (2) true, or is it false? Again, the unfortunate answer seems to be that if it is true, then it is false, and if it is false, then it is true.

Take the first possibility, namely that sentence (2) is true. If (2) is true, and (2) asserts that (3) is false, it follows that (3) is false. But if (3) is false, and (3) asserts that (2) is true, it follows that it is *false* that (2) is true, and hence that (2) is false. So if (2) is true, then (2) is false.

Now suppose sentence (2) is false. If (2) is false, and (2) asserts that (3) is false, it follows that it is false that (3) is false, and hence that (3) is true. But if (3) is true, and (3) asserts that (2) is true, it follows that (2) is true. So if (2) is false, then (2) is true. Again we have a contradiction, and hence again we have a paradox.

One way to solve the semantic paradoxes is to distinguish between **levels of language,** that is, between languages that are used to talk about nonlinguistic things and those used to talk about other languages. A language used to talk about some other language is considered to be on a higher level than the language talked about,* so that sentences asserting the truth or falsity of a given sentence must be placed in a language at least one level higher than the given sentence. For instance, the sentence "The sentence 'Art is tall' is true" must be placed in a language one level higher than the language in which the sentence "Art is tall" occurs.†

It is clear that adoption of the above machinery solves the liar paradox. In the first place, all self-referential sentences, such as sentence (1), will be rejected as meaningless. And in the second place, at least one of every pair of sentences like sentences (2) and (3) will be rejected as meaningless. (For instance, if (2) occurs in a given language, and (3) in a language one level higher, then (2) will be rejected as meaningless—whatever the fate of (3)—because no sentence can be permitted to assert the truth or falsity of a sentence in the same or a higher level language.)

But not all philosophers accept the levels of language solution.†† Perhaps the main reason is that it seems to be much too strong, eliminating as meaningless not only the troublesome sentence (1), but also many apparently meaningful sentences. For instance, it eliminates the sentence "Every language (including this one) permits the expression of at least one true sentence", which may be false, but does seem to be meaningful.

Exercise 9-5:

Here are versions of several well-known logical paradoxes. Show how in each case a solution offered for one of the paradoxes in this chapter might plausibly be said to solve these puzzles.

1. **Bonny:** My teacher said in class today that all generalities are false. Do you think that's true?
Charlie: Who knows? Maybe yes, maybe no.
Bonny: *I* know. It's false. Look. Suppose it were true. Then the statement (A) "All generalities are false" would be true. But (A) itself is a generality. So if (A) is true, it's true that *all* generalities are false, so (A) must be false. So if (A) is true, then it's false. Well then, (A) must be false. Right?
Charlie: Wrong! But I don't know why.

---

* This division into higher and lower language levels is discussed in greater detail in Appendix B, Section 4.

† This solution was first proposed by Bertrand Russell in his "Introduction" to Ludwig Wittgenstein's *Tractatus Logico-Philosophicus* (New York: Harcourt Brace, 1922), p. 23. See also Alfred Tarski, "Semantic Conception of Truth", *Philosophy and Phenomenological Research,* vol. 4 (1944), pp. 341–75.

†† For example, see Frederick B. Fitch, *Symbolic Logic* (New York: Ronald Press, 1952), p. 111 and Appendix C.

2. **Charlie:** What we need is a bibliography listing all bibliographies.
Bonny: That would be nice. But how about a bibliography that lists all and only those bibliographies that do not list themselves?
Charlie: Not terribly useful. But why not?
Bonny: Here's why not. Such a bibliography either lists itself or it doesn't. Right? If it does list itself, then it violates the condition that it list *only* those bibliographies that don't list themselves. So it can't list itself. But if it doesn't list itself, then it violates the condition that it list *all* those bibliographies that do not list themselves. So either way the conditions of such a bibliography are violated. So there cannot be such a bibliography.
Charlie: That's what's wrong with you philosophy majors—you think too much for your own good.

3. **Bonny:** Ready for another one?
Charlie: No. But you'll go ahead anyway.
Bonny: O.K. Let's call a number *interesting* if we can say something special about that number that we can't say about any other number (not counting things such as being identical with themselves, or one greater than the next number, and things like that.) Every low number clearly is interesting: one is the lowest number; two is the lowest even number; three is the number of logic books on my shelf; four is the number of offensive backs in football, and so on. But when we get to extremely large numbers, the situation would seem to be different; for instance, there seems to be nothing interesting about $(10^{61} + 33)$. So some numbers are *not* interesting. Right?
Charlie: Right, . . . on your definition of interestingness.
Bonny: Wrong! I'm going to prove to you that there are no *un*interesting numbers. Imagine two huge bags, A and B, A containing all the interesting numbers, B the uninteresting ones. If there are no uninteresting numbers, bag B will be empty. So you think B will not be empty, because you think some numbers are uninteresting. But if there are *any* numbers in bag B, there must be a lowest one, right?
Charlie: Right.
Bonny: Well, if that's true, then we can say something about that number that we can't say about any other number, namely that it is the lowest uninteresting number. Right?
Charlie: Right.
Bonny: Well, *isn't that interesting!*
Charlie: What?!?
Bonny: So there can't be a lowest uninteresting number, because that would be interesting. But if there is no lowest uninteresting number, then there aren't *any. Q.E.D.*

4. **Bonny:** Now I'm going to show you that your intuitions about classes are all wet. For instance, you believe that *any items can form a class,* don't you, and also that *there is a universal class* that *contains everything?*
Charlie: Sure, why not?
Bonny: Well, here's why not. If any items can form a class, then classes themselves can be items that form a class. So we can construct a class containing other classes as members (for example, the class of all classes containing exactly 10 members), and even construct a class containing itself as a member (for example, the class consisting of itself and the class of states in the Union).
Charlie: That last is a weird class, but why not?
Bonny: Here's why not. Divide all classes into those that are a member of themselves (for example, the class containing all classes that are members of themselves) and those that are not (for example, the class containing all football players and nothing else). Then the class containing all classes that are a member of themselves would seem to contain itself. But what about the class containing all classes that do *not* contain themselves? Is it a member of itself? Clearly not, since it is the class of all classes that are *not* members of themselves. Well, then, is it *not* a member of itself? Again, clearly not, for if it were not, then it would be a class that is not a member of itself, and hence would be a member of itself. So, if it is a member of itself, it isn't a member of itself, and if it isn't, it is. Clearly, there is no class containing just those classes that are not members of themselves. Hence, every bunch of items does not form a class, and, incidentally, it therefore can't be true that there is a universal class containing everything.
Charlie: Very clever, but I'll figure out what's wrong . . . later.

Exercise 9-6:

1. Which of the following require an identity sign if we are to symbolize them so as to reveal the most possible internal structure?

(1) The horse is an intelligent animal.

(2) The horse that wins the derby wins a lot of money.

(3) W. A. Mozart is the greatest composer in history.

(4) Mozart is a better composer than anyone else.

(5) No one had a higher grade-point average than Stu.

(6) The graceful winner also is a graceful loser.

(7) Stu had the highest grade-point average.

2. Explain the difference between the properties of being *symmetrical, asymetrical,* and *nonsymmetrical*. (Include at least one original example of each.)

3. In Part One, we defined "⊃" *truth functionally*. What objection is there to the use of this truth-functional definition of "⊃" in predicate logic when dealing with indicative sentences?

4. When using, say, **Modus Ponens,** $p \supset q, p \quad /\therefore q$, whatever is substituted for the first p must be substituted for the second. What is it that we must substitute? Is it sentence tokens, sentence types, propositions, or what? (Defend your answer.) If you don't know, explain what's troubling about each of the three alternatives mentioned.

5. True or false? Defend your answers.

(1) To say that food has the disposition or power to nourish is to say that *if* we eat food, *then* we'll be nourished.

(2) We can't solve the problem of dispositionals just by translating them into related counterfactuals, because the problems in symbolizing counterfactuals are pretty much the same as those encountered in symbolizing dispositionals.

(3) The subjunctive conditional "If we were to make cigarettes illegal, then more people would smoke" is correctly symbolized as $C \supset S$, where C = "we make cigarettes illegal" and S = "more people will smoke".

6. Which of the following underlined words are used as dispositionals, and which are not? Explain.

(1) The sugar was observed to dissolve.

(2) But no one has ever observed the solubility of sugar.

(3) Since I was wearing sunglasses, I assumed the leaves were not as green as they looked.

(4) None of her teachers *teach* Betsy, but she is teachable.

(5) Tobacco is a more dangerous drug than marijuana.

(6) Bonny is a very dependable person.

(7) In fact, she has a sterling character.

Key Terms Introduced in Chapter Nine

Asymmetrical relation: A relation *Fxy* such that it must be the case that $(x)(y)(Fxy \supset \sim Fyx)$. The relation "________ is the mother of _ _ _ _ _ " is asymmetrical.

Contrary-to-fact conditional (counterfactual): A subjunctive conditional whose antecedent is contrary to fact. The sentence "If Art *had* studied hard, then he *would have* become a great logician" is contrary-to-fact conditional.

Definite description: A descriptive phrase used to select or refer to a particular individual entity; for example, "*The tallest man in the world* is over eight feet tall", "Mark Twain is *the author of Huck Finn*", and "*The chairman of the club* is late tonight".

Dispositional property: An unobservable power or potential of an item. *Example:* the power of being soluble.

First-order predicate logic: The predicate logic that forbids sentences ascribing properties to properties themselves, but restricts quantification to individual variables. The logic presented in Part Two, prior to Section 4 of this chapter, is a first-order predicate logic.

Identity, Rule of (ID): The inference rule permitting the substitution of identicals. *Example:* the inference from *Ta* and $a = b$ to *Tb*.

Identity Reflexivity, Rule of (IR): The inference rule permitting introduction of the obviously true formula $(x)(x = x)$ into a proof at any time.

Identity symbol: The symbol " = ", used to indicate identity between entities. For instance, we can symbolize the sentence "Mark Twain is Samuel Clemens" as $t = s$.

Impredicable paradox: The paradox concerning the predicate *impredicable,* namely that if impredicable is itself impredicable, then it is predicable, and if impredicable is not impredicable, then it is impredicable.

Indirect context: Context involving believing, knowing, seeking, necessity, possibility, and so on. Sentences containing indirect contexts generally contain phrases such as "believes that", "is looking for", or "it is necessary that", which introduce the indirect context. (Some typical sentences containing indirect contexts are "Art is looking for Betsy", "Art believes that Betsy is tall", "It is possible that it will rain tomorrow".)

Intransitive relation: A relation *Fxy* such that it must be the case that when one thing bears that relation to a second, and the second to a third, then the first cannot bear it to the third. The relation "________ is a mother of _ _ _ _ _ " is an example.

Irreflexive relation: A relation *Fxy* such that it must be the case that $(x)\sim Fxx$. The relation "________ is lighter than _ _ _ _ _ " is an example.

Levels of language theory: The theory that certain parts of the semantic apparatus of a language, in particular the truth conditions of a language, must be contained not in the language itself but in the *metalanguage,* in order to get around the difficulties illustrated by paradoxes such as the liar paradox.

Logical paradoxes: Paradoxes generated or clarified by the use of logic, for example, the syntactic and semantic paradoxes.

Nonsymmetrical relation: A relation that is neither symmetrical nor asymmetrical. The relation "________ loves _ _ _ _ _ " is nonsymmetrical.

Nontransitive relation: A relation that is neither transitive nor intransitive. The relation "________ loves _ _ _ _ _ " is an example.

Property variable: A variable ranging over properties. (Property variables are admissible only in higher order logics.) An example is the property *F* in the statement, "Art has some property, *F*, or other."

Reflexive relation: A relation *Fxy* such that it must be the case that $(x)(y)[Fxy \supset (Fxx \cdot Fyy)]$. The relation "________ belongs to the same church as _ _ _ _ _ " is a reflexive relation.

Semantic paradox: A paradox such that most philosophers would accept only a *semantic* solution to it. For example, the liar paradox is a semantic paradox. Most philosophers accept a semantic theory, the so-called levels of language theory, as a solution to this paradox.

Sentence token: A series of marks on paper, or sounds in the air, used to make a sentence.

Sentence type: The class of sentence tokens of the same sentence; for example, the two sentence tokens "Snow is white" and "Snow is white" are tokens of the same sentence type.

Simple theory of types: The syntactic theory according to which all properties are categorized in a hierarchy of categories, starting with properties of things, properties of properties, properties of properties of properties, and so on. The theory was proposed as a solution to syntactic paradoxes such as the impredicable paradox.

Subjunctive conditional: A conditional sentence in the subjunctive mood. The sentence "If Art were to study hard, then he would be a great logician" is a subjunctive conditional.

Symmetrical relation: A relation *Fxy* such that it must be the case that $(x)(y)(Fxy \supset Fxy)$. The relation "________ is divorced from _ _ _ _ _ " is an example.

Syntactic paradox: A paradox such that most philosophers would accept only a *syntactic* solution to it. For instance, the impredicable paradox is a syntactic paradox.

Totally reflexive relation: A relation *Fxy* such that it must be the case that $(x)Fxx$. (Hardly any interesting relations are totally reflexive.) The relation "_____ is identical with _ _ _ _ _" is totally reflexive.

Transitive relation: A relation *Fxy* such that it must be the case that $(x)(y)(z)[(Fxy \cdot Fyz) \supset Fxz]$. The relation "_____ is shorter than _ _ _ _ _" is an example.

Part Three

Traditional Logic

Chapter Ten

Syllogistic Logic–I

The logic discussed in Parts One and Two was first developed in the late nineteenth and early twentieth century. But it did not arise in a vacuum. The discipline of logic has existed for over two thousand years, since the first system was developed by Aristotle. It has become customary to apply the term "symbolic" to systems like sentential and predicate logic, and the terms **traditional, Aristotelian,** and **syllogistic** to the earlier systems.*

Predicate logic is much more powerful than syllogistic logic—for instance, every argument provable in syllogistic logic is provable in predicate logic, but *not* vice versa. Nevertheless, within its limits, syllogistic logic constitutes a useful and (for some) fascinating logical tool.

In this part of the text, we present a fairly brief version of the material contained in recent traditional logic texts (for instance, we include Venn diagrams, which are a product of the nineteenth century), starting with an account of syllogistic logic.

1 *Categorical Propositions*

Syllogistic logic is primarily concerned with *categorical propositions.* **Categorical propositions** assert or deny relationships between terms or classes. For instance, the sentence "All humans are mortal" is a categorical proposition, and asserts (roughly) that all members of the class of humans are members of the class of mortals.

The term "humans", which designates the class of human beings, is said to be the **subject,** or **subject term,** and the term "mortal", which

---

*The term "symbolic logic" is not used to refer to traditional logic, although it too employs special symbols.

designates the class of mortals, is said to be the **predicate,** or **predicate term,** of the categorical proposition "All humans are mortal". Similarly, all categorical propositions contain a subject and a predicate, as well as some form of the verb "to be" ("is", "are", and so on) relating the subject and predicate.

There are four kinds of categorical propositions: (1) **universal affirmative,** having the general form "All *S* are *P*" (where *S* denotes some subject class and *P* some predicate class); (2) **universal negative,** having the general form "No *S* are *P*"; (3) **particular affirmative,** having the general form "Some *S* are *P*"; and (4) **particular negative,** having the general form "Some *S* are not *P*".

It is customary to use the capital letter *A* in symbolizing universal affirmative propositions. Thus, the universal affirmative "All humans are mortal" is symbolized as *HAM* (where *H* = "human" and *M* = "mortal"). Similarly, it is customary to use *E* for universal negatives, *I* for particular affirmatives, and *O* for particular negatives. Thus, the universal negative "No humans are mortal" is symbolized as *HEM*, the particular affirmative "Some humans are mortal" as *HIM*, and the particular negative "Some humans are not mortal" as *HOM*. It also is customary to refer to universal affirmative propositions as *A* propositions, universal negative propositions as *E* propositions, and so on.

Notice that *A*, *E*, *I*, and *O* propositions differ with respect to two kinds of properties; namely, **quality** (being either affirmative or negative) and **quantity** (being either universal or particular). Thus, all *I* propositions are both *affirmative* (quality) and *particular* (quantity). For example, the *I* proposition "Some humans are mortal" is *affirmative* (quality), because it *affirms* that some humans are mortal, and *particular* (quantity), because it affirms that *some* (not necessarily all) humans are mortal. On the other hand, all *E* propositions are both *negative* (quality) and *universal* (quantity). For example, the *E* proposition "No humans are mortal" is *negative* (quality), because it *denies* that humans are mortal, and *universal* (quantity), because it denies of *all* humans that they are mortal.

The English language, like all natural languages, permits a great deal of variety in the expression of propositions. Take St. Augustine's interesting thesis that all sin is a kind of lying, which can be put into *A* form as "All sins are lies". We can also express this thesis in English as "Sins are lies", "He who sins, lies", "Sinning is lying", "To sin is to lie", "Anyone who sins, lies", "Whoever sins, lies", and so on. All of these therefore translate into *A* propositions.

Examples:

Here are a few more sentences that translate into *A* propositions.

Men are naturally selfish.	(All men are naturally selfish.) (MAS)
Anyone who is a woman is maternal.	(All women are maternal.) (WAM)
Copper conducts electricity.	(All copper things are electrical conductors.) (CAE)
Sugar tastes sweet.	(All things composed of sugar are sweet tasting.) (SAT)
Vanity is a universal condition.	(All humans are vain.) (HAV)
Those who live by the pen are called liars.	(All professional writers are liars.) (WAL)
Whoever smokes grass is immoral.	(All grass smokers are immoral.) (GAI)
The gods have mercy.	(All gods are merciful.) (GAM)
Show me an officer and I'll show you a dandy.	(All officers are dandies.) (OAD)

And here are a few sentences that translate into *E* propositions.

Men are not selfish by nature.	(No men are naturally selfish.) (MES)
Women aren't maternal.	(No women are maternal.) (WEM)
Copper doesn't conduct electricity.	(No copper things are electrical conductors.) (CEE)
Sugar doesn't taste sweet.	(No things made from sugar are sweet tasting.) (SET)
Vanity is unheard of among humans.	(No humans are vain.) (HEV)
There has never been a professional writer who lies.	(No professional writers are liars.) (WEL)
Among the immoral of the world, none are listed as smoking grass.	(No grass smokers are immoral.) (GEI)
The gods have no mercy.	(No gods are merciful.) (GEM)
No one who is an officer also is a dandy.	(No officers are dandies.) (OED)

Here are some sentences that translate into *I* propositions.

There are honest men.	(Some men are honest.) (MIH)
There exist some elements that are inert.	(Some elements are inert.) (EII)
There are active paraplegics.	(Some paraplegics are active.) (PIA)
Lots of rivers have wide mouths.	(Some rivers are wide-mouthed.) (RIW)
Musicians occasionally have tin ears.	(Some musicians are tin-eared.) (MIT)
Killers frequently are paranoid.	(Some killers are paranoid.) (KIP)
A few senators are against big business.	(Some senators are against big business.) (SIA)
An occasional *Playboy* interview is with a presidential candidate.	(Some *Playboy* interviews are interviews with presidential candidates.) (PIC)
Policemen have been known to take bribes.	(Some policemen are bribable.) (PIB)

And here are some sentences that translate into *O* propositions.

There are dishonest men.	(Some men are not honest.) (SOH)

Most elements are not inert.	(Some elements are not inert.) (EOI)
There are inactive paraplegics.	(Some paraplegics are not active.) (POA)
Many rivers don't have wide mouths.	(Some rivers are not wide-mouthed.)(ROW)
Most musicians don't have a tin ear.	(Some musicians are not tin-eared.) (MOT)
A few killers are not paranoid.	(Some killers are not paranoid.) (KOP)
The majority of senators are not against big business.	(Some senators are not against big business.) (SOB)
Most *Playboy* interviews are not with presidential candidates.	(Some *Playboy* interviews are not with presidential candidates.) (POC)
Policemen have been known who will not take bribes.	(Some policemen are not bribable.) (POB)

Exercise 10-1:

Translate the following sentences into equivalent *A*, *E*, *I*, or *O* propositions, underlining subject and predicate terms, and then symbolize.

1. Whoever is rich is a sinner.
2. The poor are lazy.
3. Most children aren't naughty.
4. Porno flicks aren't erotic.
5. Albino crows are known to exist.
6. Amateurs aren't professionals.
7. There are plenty of immodest failures.
8. Most prescription drugs are harmful.
9. Human beings are omnivorous.
10. Children are available to play the part.
11. Omnivores occasionally are vegetarians.
12. None who have dry wits drink.
13. Some drinkers have wet whistles.
14. Those who forget the past suffer from amnesia.
15. Most movie stars aren't happy.
16. Omnivores usually are not vegetarians.

2 *Existential Import*

A proposition is said to have **existential import** if its subject and predicate are taken to refer to classes that are not empty. For instance, if we assume existential import for the *A* proposition "All angels are without moral blemish", then we are assuming that there are angels, and also that there are things without moral blemish.

Syllogistic logic traditionally rested on the assumption that all the propositions to be dealt with do have existential import. In other words, syllogistic logic traditionally was restricted to categorical propositions whose terms all were taken to refer to nonempty classes.

Such a restriction severely limits the scope of syllogistic logic, since it often is quite important to reason about nonexistent entities—for one thing to make sure that they remain nonexistent. (We want to reason about World War III precisely to prevent such a disaster from occurring.) Yet if we are to retain several of its interesting and important features (and have them be *valid*), we must restrict the use of traditional logic to propositions that have existential import.

So let's assume for the moment that all of the categorical propositions to be dealt with do have existential import.

3 *The Square of Opposition*

The **square of opposition** illustrates some of the more interesting features of traditional logic:

(1) *Corresponding A and O propositions are contradictories*. Two propositions are **contradictory propositions** if *both cannot be true, and both cannot be false*. (So one must be true, the other false). For instance, the *A* proposition "All humans are mortal" is true, while its contradictory "Some humans are not mortal", an *O* proposition, is false.

(2) *Corresponding E and I propositions also are contradictories*. Hence, both cannot be true, and both cannot be false. For example, the *I* proposition "Some humans are mortal" is true, and its contradictory "No humans are mortal", an *E* proposition, is false.

(3) *Corresponding A and E propositions are contraries*. Two propositions are **contrary propositions** if *both cannot be true, but both can be false*. For instance, the *A* proposition "All scientists are philosophers" is false, and its contrary "No scientists are philosophers", an *E* proposition, also is false (since some scientists are philosophers and some aren't). This is an example of contraries both of which are false. And the *A* proposition "All humans are mortal" is true, while its contrary "No humans are mortal", an *E* proposition, is false. This is an example of contraries one of which is true, one false. (But we cannot give an example of contrary propositions both of which are true, because this case cannot occur.)

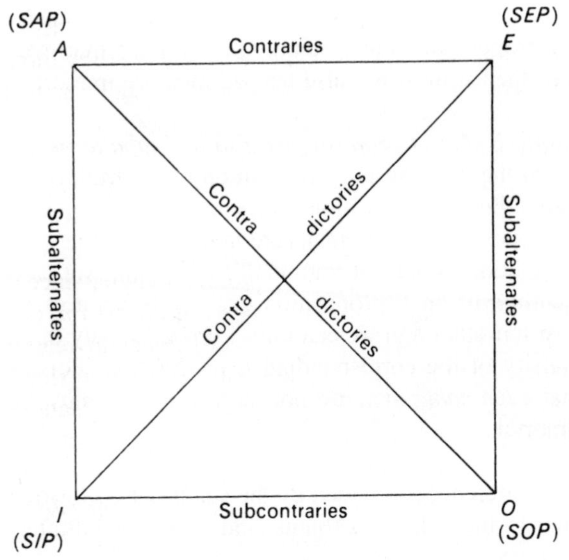

(4) *Corresponding I and O propositions are subcontraries.* Two propositions are **subcontrary propositions** if *both cannot be false, but both can be true.* For instance, the *I* proposition "Some scientists are philosophers" is true, and its subcontrary "Some scientists are not philosophers", an *O* proposition, also is true. This proposition is an example of subcontraries both of which are true. And the *I* proposition "Some humans are mortal" is true, while its subcontrary "Some humans are not mortal", an *O* proposition, is false. This proposition is an example of subcontraries one of which is true, one false. (But we cannot give an example of subcontraries both of which are false, because this case cannot occur.)

(5) *Corresponding A and I propositions are subalternates.* **Subalternate propositions** are such that *if the universal member of the pair* (for instance, an *A* proposition) *is true, then so is the particular member of the pair* (for instance, the corresponding *I* proposition). The propositions "All humans are mortal", a true *A* proposition, and "Some humans are mortal", a true *I* proposition, are subalternates.

Notice that if a particular *A* proposition is *false*, nothing can be inferred as to the truth value of its subalternate; it may be true or it may be false. For instance, the false *A* proposition "All scientists are philosophers" has as its subalternate the *true I* proposition "Some scientists are philosophers", while the false *A* proposition "All humans are immortal" has as its subalternate the *false I* proposition "Some humans are immortal". Thus subalternation, conceived as a rule of inference, is *one-directional;* we can infer from the truth of an *A* proposition to the truth of its corresponding *I* proposition, but we cannot infer from the truth of an *I* proposition to the truth of its corresponding *A* proposition.

However, we can infer from the falsity of an *I* proposition to the falsity of the corresponding *A* proposition. For instance, if it is false that even *some* men are immortal, then it must be false that *all* men are immortal.

(6) Finally, *corresponding E and O propositions also are subalternates.* Hence, we can infer from the truth of an *E* proposition to the truth of its subalternate, the corresponding *O* proposition. For example, we can infer from the truth of the *E* proposition "No humans are immortal" to the truth of its subalternate "Some humans are not immortal". But again, we cannot infer from the *falsehood* of an *E* proposition to the falsehood of its corresponding *O* proposition, although we can infer from the falsity of an *O* proposition to the falsity of the corresponding *E* proposition. For instance, if it is false that even *some* men are not mortal, then it must be false that *no* men are mortal.

The information about inferences provided by the square of opposition can also be put in tabular form, as follows (blanks indicate no valid inference possible).

***A* true:**	*E* false	*I* true	*O* false
***A* false:**	*E* ______	*I* ______	*O* true
***E* true:**	*A* false	*I* false	*O* true
***E* false:**	*A* ______	*I* true	*O* ______
***I* true:**	*A* ______	*E* false	*O* ______
***I* false:**	*A* false	*E* true	*O* true
***O* true:**	*A* false	*E* ______	*I* ______
***O* false:**	*A* true	*E* false	*I* true

Examples:

(1) On the assumption that the *A* proposition "All college students are intelligent", in symbols *CAN*, is true (whether in fact it is or not), we can infer that

1. *CIN* is true (by subalternation).
2. *CON* is false (because *CAN* and *CON* are contradictories).
3. *CEN* is false (because *CAN* and *CEN* are contraries).

(2) On the assumption that the *I* proposition "Some college students cheat on exams", in symbols *CIX*, is false, we can infer that

1. *CEX* is true (because *CIX* and *CEX* are contradictories).
2. *COX* is true (because *CIX* and *COX* are subcontraries).
3. *CAX* is false (because *CEX* and *CAX* are contraries).

(3) On the assumption that the *E* proposition "No college students cheat on exams", in symbols *CEX*, is true, we can infer that

1. *CIX* is false (because *CEX* and *CIX* are contradictories).
2. *CAX* is false (because *CEX* and *CAX* are contraries).
3. *COX* is true (by subalternation).

(4) On the assumption that the *O* proposition "Some college students do not cheat on exams", in symbols *COX*, is true, we can infer only that *CAX* is false.

Exercise 10-2:

(1) Suppose the categorical proposition "All U.S. presidents are male" in symbols *PAM*, is true. Using the machinery provided by the square of opposition, what can be inferred about the truth values of the following?

1. *PIM*
2. *PEM*
3. *POM*

(2) Suppose *PAM* is false. Then what can be inferred about the truth values of the following?

1. *PIM*
2. *PEM*
3. *POM*

(3) Suppose "Some congressmen are sexual gluttons", in symbols *CIS*, is true. Then what can be inferred about the truth values of the following?

1. *CES*
2. *COS*
3. *CAS*

(4) Suppose *CIS* is false. Then what can be inferred about the truth values of the following?

1. *CES*
2. *COS*
3. *CAS*

4 *Conversion, Obversion, Contraposition*

(1) *Conversion*. In the process of **conversion,** we replace the subject of a

proposition with its predicate and its predicate with its subject. For instance, *SAP* converts to *PAS*, *SEP* converts to *PES*, *SOP* to *POS*, and so on.

But conversion is a *valid* process only if used on *E* or *I* propositions. We can validly infer from *SEP* to *PES*, and from *SIP* to *PIS*, but not from *SAP* to *PAS*, and not from *SOP* to *POS*. For example, we can validly infer from "No scientists are philosophers" to "No philosophers are scientists", but not from "All scientists are philosophers" to "All philosophers are scientists".

(2) *Conversion by limitation*. In the process of **conversion by limitation** we replace the subject term of an *A* proposition with its predicate term and its predicate term with its subject term, and then change the quantity of the proposition from *A* to *I*. For instance, we can infer by conversion by limitation from the *A* proposition "All humans are mortal" (in symbols *HAM*) to the *I* proposition "Some mortals are human" (in symbols *MIH*). Conversion by limitation is always a valid process.

(3) *Obversion*. In the process of **obversion,** we change the quality of a proposition (from affirmative to negative or from negative to affirmative), and then replace its predicate with the negation or **complement** of the predicate. Using the bar symbol "–" placed over a term to symbolize the complement (negation) of that term (so that the complement of the term *P* is symbolized as $\overline{P}$), we can obvert, say, the *E* proposition *SEP* ("No scientists are philosophers") by first changing the quality of that proposition from negative to affirmative, obtaining the proposition *SAP*, and then replacing the predicate with its complement, obtaining the proposition $SA\overline{P}$ ("All scientists are nonphilosophers"). Thus, *SEP* obverts to $SA\overline{P}$. Similarly, *SAP* obverts to $SE\overline{P}$, *SIP* obverts to $SO\overline{P}$, and *SOP* obverts to $SI\overline{P}$. Obversion is *always* valid.

(4) *Contraposition*. In the process of **contraposition,** we replace the subject of a proposition with the complement of its predicate and replace its predicate with the complement of its subject. Thus, the contrapositive of *SAP* is $\overline{P}A\overline{S}$, and the contrapositive of *SOP* is $\overline{P}O\overline{S}$. Contraposition is valid for *A* and *O* propositions, but not for *E* and *I* propositions. Hence, we can validly infer from, say, $SA\overline{P}$ to $PA\overline{S}$, and from $\overline{P}O\overline{S}$ to *SOP*, but not from *SEP* to $\overline{P}E\overline{S}$, and not from *SIP* to $\overline{P}I\overline{S}$.*

(5) *Contraposition by limitation*. Finally, we can validly infer from a

---

* Note that the contraposition of syllogistic logic is different from what we called contraposition in our exposition of symbolic logic. The former has the structure $(x)(Fx \supset Gx) :: (x)(\sim Gx \supset \sim Fx)$, while the structure of the latter is $(p \supset q) :: (\sim q \supset \sim p)$. Contraposition in syllogistic logic is thus like a quantified version of the contraposition introduced into symbolic (sentential) logic.

given *E* proposition to a particular related *O* proposition by the process called **contraposition by limitation.** For instance, we can validly infer from the *E* proposition "No humans are immortal", in symbols *HEI*, to the *O* proposition "Some mortals (nonimmortals) are not nonhuman", in symbols $\overline{I}O\overline{H}$, by contraposition by limitation.

Contraposition by limitation obviously is valid, since it is simply the combination of subalternation (of an *E* proposition) and contraposition (of the resulting *O* proposition).

Notice that conversion, obversion, and contraposition are, in effect, *equivalence inference rules;* that is, they work in both directions. For instance, we can infer from *SAP* to $\overline{P}A\overline{S}$ by contraposition *and* also from $\overline{P}A\overline{S}$ to *SAP*. But conversion by limitation and contraposition by limitation are just *implicational inference rules;* that is, they work in only one direction. For instance, we can infer from *SAP* to *PIS* by conversion by limitation, but *not* from *PIS* to *SAP*.

Examples:

On the assumption that the *A* proposition "All college students are intelligent", in symbols *CAN*, is true, we can infer that

1. $CE\overline{N}$ is true (by obversion).
2. $\overline{N}A\overline{C}$ is true (by contraposition).
3. $\overline{N}EC$ is true (by obversion of $\overline{N}A\overline{C}$).
4. $\overline{N}IC$ is true (by conversion by limitation).
5. *CIN* is true (by conversion of *NIC*).
6. $NO\overline{C}$ is true (by obversion of *NIC*).
7. $CO\overline{N}$ is true (by contraposition of $NO\overline{C}$).

Making use of the processes illustrated by the square of opposition, we also can infer from the truth of *CAI* that

8. *CON* is false (because *CAN* and *CON* are contradictories).
9. $\overline{N}O\overline{C}$ is false (by contraposition of *CON*).
10. $CI\overline{N}$ is false (by obversion of *COI*).
11. $\overline{N}IC$ is false (by obversion of $\overline{N}O\overline{C}$).
12. *NEC* is false (because *NIC* and *NEC* are contradictories).
13. *CEN* is false (by conversion of *NEC*).
14. $CA\overline{N}$ is false (by obversion of *CEN*).
15. $NA\overline{C}$ is false (by contraposition of $CA\overline{N}$).

Exercise 10-3:

What can be said about the truth values of the sentences in the following sets, assuming that the first sentence in each set is true?

(1)
1. No Watusis are Eskimos.
2. All Eskimos are non-Watusis.
3. Some Watusis are not Eskimos.
4. Some Eskimos are Watusis.
5. Some Eskimos are non-Watusis.

(2)
1. All great lovers are highly sexed.
2. Some great lovers are highly sexed.
3. No great lovers are highly sexed.
4. Some highly sexed people are great lovers.
5. No highly sexed people are great lovers.

(3)
1. No women are submissive individuals.
2. Some submissive individuals are not women.
3. No submissive individuals are nonwomen.
4. All women are submissive individuals.
5. Some women are submissive individuals.

(4)
1. Some blacks are not subject to racial discrimination.
2. Some subject to racial discrimination are blacks.
3. No blacks are subject to racial discrimination.
4. All blacks are subject to racial discrimination.
5. Some not subject to racial discrimination are blacks.

5 *Syllogistic Logic—Not Assuming Existential Import*

The logic developed so far rests on a blanket assumption of existential import. But no such assumption is made in everyday life. For instance, someone uttering the proposition "Let him who is without sin cast the first stone" does not necessarily assume that there are any men free from sin. Similarly, a scientist who says "All objects cooled down to absolute zero will conduct electricity" does not intend to imply that anything ever will be cooled down to absolute zero.

How much of the traditional logic just described is *invalid* if we do *not* make a blanket assumption of existential import?

Subalternation is invalid. For instance, if there are no Martians, then the *A* proposition, "All Martians are immortal", in symbols *MAI*, is true (vacuously, because all of the zero number of Martians are immortal), while its subalternate "Some Martians are immortal", in symbols *MII*, is false because nothing is both a Martian and immortal. So we cannot allow subalternation from an *A* to an *I* proposition. The same is true of subalternation from an *E* to an *O* proposition.

Conversion by limitation and contraposition by limitation both are invalid. For instance, if there are no Martians, then the *A* proposition "All Martians are immortal", in symbols *MAI*, is true, while the *I* proposition obtained from it by conversion by limitation, namely the proposition "Some immortals are Martians", in symbols *IIM*, is false.

A and E propositions are not contraries. We said before that two propositions are contraries if both cannot be true, but both can be false, and that *A* and *E* propositions are contraries. However, if we allow the use of empty classes, then corresponding *A* and *E* propositions both can be true, and *A* and *E* propositions will not be contraries. For instance, if there are no Martians, then the *A* proposition "All Martians are immortal" (*MAI*) and the *E* proposition "No Martians are immortal" (*MEI*) both are true (vacuously). Hence, they are not contraries in the traditional sense.*

I and O propositions are not subcontraries. We said before that two propositions are subcontraries if both cannot be false, but both can be true, and that *I* and *O* propositions are subcontraries. However, if we allow the use of empty classes, then both of two corresponding *I* and *O* propositions can be false, and so some *I* and *O* propositions will not be subcontraries. For example, if there are no Martians, then the *I* proposition "Some Martians are immortal" (*MII*) and the *O* proposition "Some Martians are not immortal" (*MOI*) both are false. Hence they are not subcontraries in the traditional sense.†

To sum up, if we allow the subject or predicate terms of propositions to refer to empty classes, then subalternation, conversion by limitation, and contraposition by limitation are all invalid, some corresponding *A* and *E* propositions are not contraries, and some corresponding *I* and *O* propositions are not subcontraries.

---

*However, some texts define contraries as pairs of universal propositions that differ only in quality. According to this definition corresponding *A* and *E* propositions automatically become contraries.

†However, some texts define subcontraries as pairs of particular propositions that differ only in quality. According to this definition, corresponding *I* and *O* propositions automatically become subcontraries.

But corresponding A and O propositions remain contradictories, as do corresponding E and I propositions. And conversion of E and I propositions, obversion, and contraposition of A and O propositions all remain valid.

Exercise 10-4:

In this exercise, do *not* assume existential import.

(1) If it is false that all existentialists are theists, that is, false that EAT, then what can be said about the truth values of the following?

1. EET
2. TEE
3. $\overline{T}IE$
4. $\overline{T}A\overline{E}$
5. EOT
6. TIE

(2) If it is true that no existentialists are theists, then what can be said about the truth values of the above six propositions?

(3) If the proposition "All senators are promiscuous", in symbols SAP, is true, what can be inferred about the truth values of the following?

1. $\overline{P}IS$
2. $SE\overline{P}$
3. $\overline{P}E\overline{S}$
4. $SI\overline{P}$
5. $\overline{P}ES$
6. $\overline{S}AP$
7. $\overline{P}O\overline{S}$
8. $\overline{S}OP$
9. $\overline{P}A\overline{S}$

(4) If $\overline{S}E\overline{P}$ is false, what can be inferred about the truth values of the above nine positions?

(5) Suppose you know that the classes S, P, $\overline{S}$, and $\overline{P}$ all are nonempty. And suppose you know that "No non-S are P". What else can you infer? (Justify your answer.)

---

6 Diagramming Categorical Propositions

In this section, let's continue to permit the subject and predicate terms of propositions to refer both to empty classes and to classes that have members. In other words, let's continue to do without any blanket assumption of existential import.

Alternate Terminology

Let's represent the null class, that is, the empty class, the class having no members, by O. Then $S = O$ will symbolize "The class S is empty", and $S \neq O$ will symbolize "The class S is not empty". Let SP designate the class of things (if any) that are members of both S and P. And let $S\bar{P}$ designate the class of things (if any) that are members of both S and $\bar{P}$. We now are ready to introduce another and quite revealing method for symbolizing categorical propositions.

(1) Consider the A proposition "All Martians are pink", in symbols MAP. This proposition asserts that anything that is a Martian also is pink. So it *denies* that anything is both a Martian and *nonpink*. Thus, it denies that the class of things that are both Martians and nonpink has any members. Hence, it can be correctly symbolized as $M\bar{P} = O$, which asserts that the class of things that are both Martians and nonpink is empty.

(2) Now consider the E proposition "No Martians are pink", in symbols MEP. This proposition denies that anything is both a Martian and pink. So it *asserts* that the class of things that are both Martians and pink is empty. Hence, it can be correctly symbolized as $MP = O$.

(3) Next, consider the I proposition "Some Martians are pink", in symbols MIP. This proposition asserts that there are some things that are both Martians and pink and thus that the class of things that are both Martians and pink is not empty. Hence, it can be symbolized as $MP \neq O$.

(4) Finally, consider the O proposition "Some Martians are not pink", in symbols MOP. This proposition asserts that there are some things that are both Martians and *not* pink; that is, it asserts that the class of things that are both Martians and *nonpink* is not empty. So it can be correctly symbolized as $M\bar{P} \neq O$.

To sum up: In general, letting S and P represent the subject and predicate terms respectively of categorical propositions, we can symbolize A propositions as SAP or as $S\bar{P} = O$, E propositions as SEP or as $SP = O$, I propositions as SIP or as $SP \neq O$, and O propositions as SOP or as $S\bar{P} \neq O$.

Notice that this new way to symbolize categorical propositions clearly reveals that corresponding A and O propositions, and corresponding E and I propositions, are *contradictories*. (For instance, the E proposition $SP = O$ clearly contradicts the I proposition $SP \neq O$.) Notice also that this notation clearly reveals that A and E propositions do not assert the existence of anything, while I and O propositions do assert the existence of things, namely members of particular classes.

Exercise 10-5:

Symbolize the following propositions, using both of the notations introduced in this chapter.

Example: All scientists are philosophers.

a. *SAP*

b. $S\bar{P} = O$

1. Some scientists are impractical. (S = "scientists"; P = "practical")
2. No philosophers are millionaires. (P = "philosopher"; M = "millionaire")
3. All nonmathematicians are spendthrifts. (M = "mathematician"; S = "spendthrift")
4. Some mathematicians are not able to multiply. (M = "mathematician"; A = "able to multiply")
5. No nonscientists are able to repair flush toilets. (S = "scientist"; R = "able to repair flush toilets")
6. All philosophers are Michael Jackson fans. (P = "philosopher"; J = "Michael Jackson fans")
7. Some who believe in God are existentialists. (E = "existentialist"; B = "believer in God")
8. Some lawyers are drunks who have managed to pass a bar exam. (L = "lawyers"; D = "drunks who have managed to pass a bar exam")
9. All professors who forget useless trivia are failures on TV quiz shows. (P = "professors who forget useless trivia"; F = "failures on TV quiz shows")

Venn Diagrams

It is both useful and informative to use **Venn diagrams** to picture categorical propositions. First, let's represent the class S and P by overlapping circles, as follows:

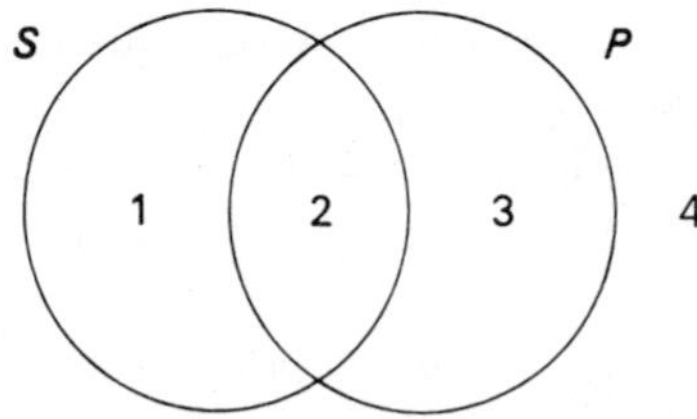

In this diagram, area 1 represents the class of things that are S but not P (that is, the class $S\bar{P}$), area 2 the class of things that are both S and P (that is, the class SP), area 3 the class of things that are P but not S (that is, the class $\bar{S}P$), and area 4 the class of things that are neither S nor P (that is, the class $\bar{S}\bar{P}$).

Now consider the A proposition $S\bar{P} = O$, which asserts that the class $S\bar{P}$ is empty. We can diagram $S\bar{P} = O$ by *shading out the $S\bar{P}$ area,* that is, by shading out area 1 (to indicate that the class $S\bar{P}$ is empty), as follows:

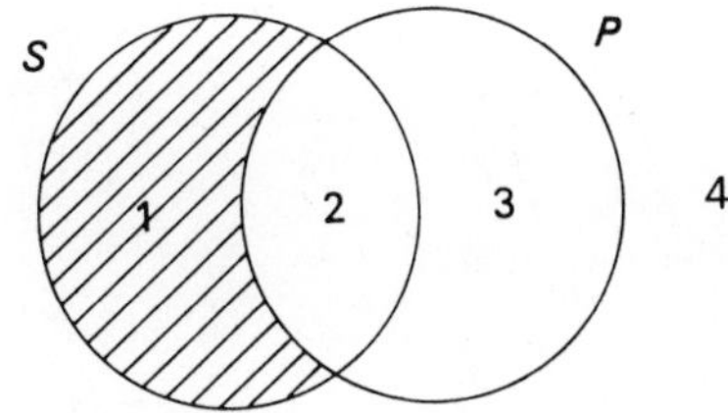

Next, consider the *E* proposition $SP = O$, which asserts that the class SP is empty. We can diagram $SP = O$ by *shading out the SP area,* that is, by shading out area 2 (to indicate that the class SP is empty), as follows:

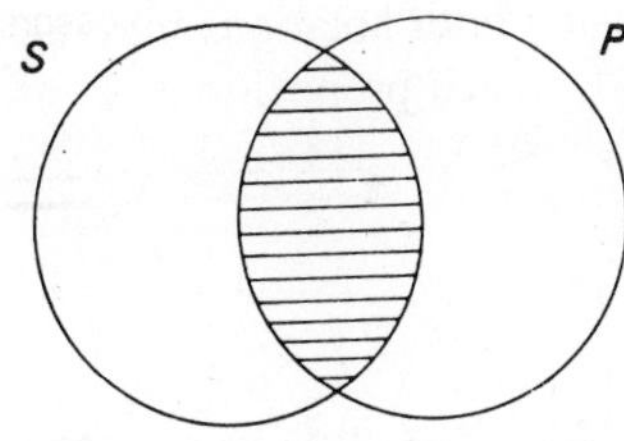

Now, consider the *I* proposition $SP \neq O$, which asserts that the class SP is *not* empty, but has at least one member. We can diagram $SP \neq O$ by *placing a mark (say the letter X) in the SP area,* that is, in area 2 (to indicate that the class SP is *not* empty), as follows:

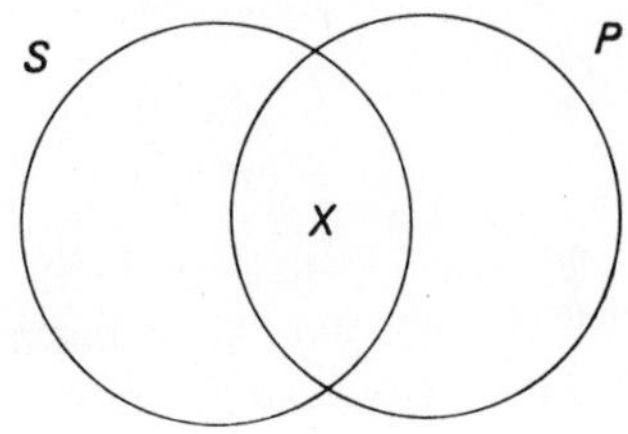

Finally, consider the *O* proposition $S\bar{P} \neq O$, which asserts that the class $S\bar{P}$ is not empty, but has at least one member. We can diagram $S\bar{P} \neq O$ by placing an *X* in the $S\bar{P}$ area, that is, in area 1 (to indicate that the class $S\bar{P}$ is not empty), as follows:

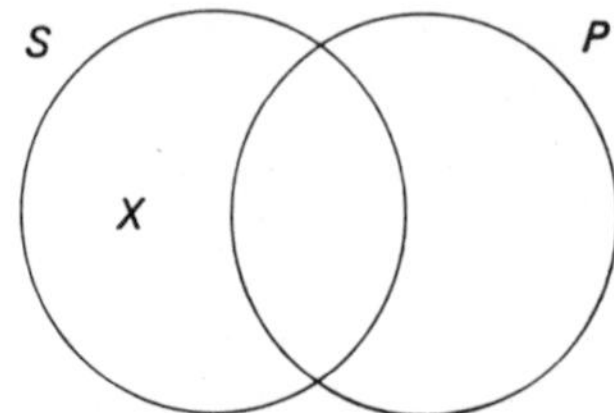

In the next chapter, when syllogistic arguments are discussed, this method of portraying categorical propositions will be used in determining syllogistic validity-invalidity.

Exercise 10-6:

Symbolize the following propositions, using both notations introduced in this chapter; then draw a Venn diagram for each proposition.

Example: All millionaires are crooks.

a. MAC

b. $M\overline{C} = O$

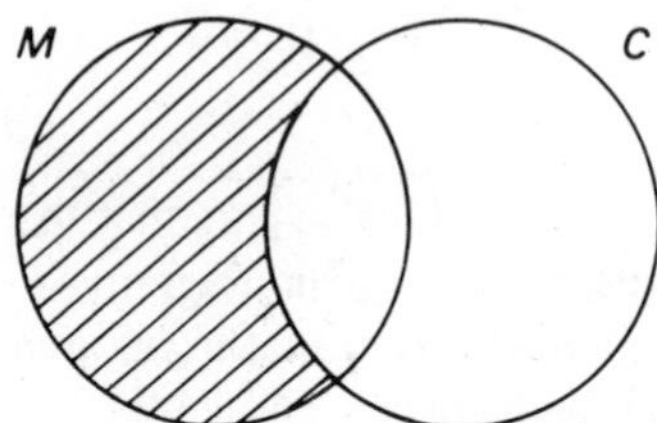

1. Some millionaires are crooks.
2. No crooks are millionaires.
3. Some crooks are not millionaires.
4. No millionaires are noncrooks.
5. All environmentalists are a bit overzealous.
6. No environmentalists who tell the truth are taken seriously.
7. Some overzealous environmentalists are pretty unpopular.
8. Some college alumni are still panty raid fans.
9. No panty raid fans are still in college.
10. Some panty raid fans are not nonmatriculating students.
11. All non-football fans are pretty lonely in the fall.
12. Some who broadcast the news on TV are non-high school graduates.

Exercise 10-7:

1. What is lost, if anything, by restricting syllogistic logic so that it deals only with propositions having existential import? (Explain, including examples.)

2. Which of the following are *equivalence* inference rules? (Defend your answers.)

(1). Conversion
(2). Contraposition by limitation
(3). Obversion
(4). Subalternation

3. Which of the following become invalid or, in the case of (5) and (6), false once we remove the restriction to propositions that have existential import? (Defend your answers.)

(1). Contraposition
(2). Conversion by limitation
(3). Subalternation
(4). Obversion
(5). *A* and *O* propositions are contradictories
(6). *A* and *E* propositions are contraries

Key Terms Introduced in Chapter Ten

***A* Proposition:** (See **Universal affirmative proposition.**)

Aristotelian logic: (See **Syllogistic logic.**)

Categorical proposition: A subject-predicate proposition that asserts, or denies, a relationship between two classes.

Complement: The negation of a term. The *complement class* of a given class is the class of all things that are *not* members of the given class.

Contradictory propositions: Two propositions such that if one of them is true, the other must be false, and vice versa. Corresponding *A* and *O* propositions, and *E* and *I* propositions, are contradictories.

Contraposition: The rule permitting inference from a given proposition to a corresponding proposition in which the subject term has been replaced by the complement of the predicate term and the predicate term has been replaced by the complement of the subject term. For example, we can infer by contraposition from *SAP* to $\overline{P}A\overline{S}$. Contraposition is valid only for *A* and *O* propositions.

Contraposition by limitation: The rule permitting subalternation and contraposition (of the resulting proposition) to be performed on an *E* proposition, resulting in a particular *O* proposition. For example, using contraposition by limitation we can infer from the *E* proposition *SEP* to the *O* proposition $\overline{P}O\overline{S}$. Contraposition by limitation is valid only on the assumption of existential import.

Contrary propositions: Two propositions such that it is not possible for both of them to be true, although it is possible for both of them to be false. Assuming existential import, corresponding *A* and *E* propositions are contraries.

Conversion: The rule permitting inference from a given proposition to another proposition just like the first one, except that its subject and predicate terms have been reversed. For example, the proposition *SEP* converts to *PES*. Conversion is valid only for *E* and *I* propositions.

Conversion by limitation: The rule permitting inference from an *A* proposition to the converse of a corresponding *I* proposition. For example, we can infer from *SAP* to *PIS* by conversion by limitation. However, conversion by limitation is valid only on the assumption of existential import.

***E* Proposition:** (See **Universal negative proposition.**)

Existential import: A categorical proposition has existential import if it is assumed that its subject term and predicate term, as well as their complements, do not refer to empty classes.

***I* Proposition:** (See **Particular affirmative proposition.**)

***O* Proposition:** (See **Particular negative proposition.**)

Obversion: The rule permitting inference from a given proposition to a corresponding proposition in which the quality has been changed and the predicate term replaced with its complement. For example, we can infer from *SAP* to $SE\bar{P}$ by obversion. Obversion *always* is valid.

Particular affirmative proposition: A categorical proposition having the form "Some *S* are *P*", where *S* and *P* denote classes. *Synonym:* ***I* Proposition.**

Particular negative proposition: A categorical proposition having the form "Some *S* are not *P*", where *S* and *P* denote classes. *Synonym:* ***O* Proposition.**

Predicate (of a categorical proposition): The term after the verb *to be,* for instance, the word "hairsplitters" in "All logicians are hairsplitters".

Quality (of a proposition): Every categorical proposition must have the quality either of being *affirmative* or of being *negative*.

Quantity (of a proposition): Every categorical proposition must be either *universal* or *particular.*

Square of opposition: A diagram used to illustrate several of the inferential relationships (such as contradictoriness and contrariety) holding between categorical propositions.

Subalternation: The rule permitting inference from an *A* proposition to a corresponding *I* proposition, or from an *E* proposition to a corresponding *O* proposition. Subalternation is valid only on the assumption of existential import.

Subcontrary propositions: Two propositions such that it is not possible for both of them to be false, although it is possible for both of them to be true. Assuming existential import, corresponding *I* and *O* propositions are subcontraries.

Subject (of a categorical proposition): The term before the verb *to be* and after the term "all", "some", or "no"; for instance, the word "logician" in "All logicians are hairsplitters". (See also **Predicate.**)

Syllogistic logic: The traditional logic centering on and developed from the syllogistic theory of Aristotle. The term now is often used to distinguish the traditional logic from modern symbolic logic. *Synonyms:* **Aristotelian logic, Traditional logic.**

Traditional logic: (See **Syllogistic logic.**)

Universal affirmative proposition: A categorical proposition having the form "All *S* are *P*", where *S* and *P* denote classes. *Synonym:* ***A* Proposition.**

Universal negative proposition: A categorical proposition having the form "No *S* are *P*", where *S* and *P* denote classes. *Synonym:* ***E* Proposition.**

Venn diagrams: Overlapping circles, used to diagram categorical propositions and categorical syllogisms.

Chapter Eleven

Syllogistic Logic—II

1 Syllogisms

A **syllogism** is a particular kind of argument containing three categorical propositions, two of them premises, one a conclusion. One of the earliest syllogisms is the following:

All humans are mortal.
All Greeks are humans.
∴ All Greeks are mortal.

which can be symbolized as:

MAP
SAM
∴ *SAP*

The term *P*, the predicate of the conclusion, is said to be the **major term** of the syllogism; the term *S*, the subject of the conclusion, is said to be the **minor term;** and the term *M*, which occurs once in each premise but not in the conclusion, is said to be the **middle term.** Every syllogism has exactly three terms, each one repeated twice (but none repeated twice in the same proposition).

The **mood** of a syllogism is determined by the kind of propositions it contains. For instance, the above syllogism contains three *A* propositions, and so its mood is *AAA*. Similarly, the mood for the syllogism

All mathematicians are philosophers.
Some scientists are mathematicians.
∴ Some scientists are philosophers.

which is symbolized as

MAP
SIM
∴ *SIP*

is *AII*.

The **figure** of a syllogism is determined by the positions of its major, minor, and middle terms in its premises. There are four figures, namely:

I.	II.	III.	IV.
M_P	*P_M*	*M_P*	*P_M*
S_M	*S_M*	*M_S*	*M_S*
∴ *S_P*	∴ *S_P*	∴ *S_P*	∴ *S_P*

Notice that the order of premises is important in determining the mood or the figure of a syllogism. The rule is that the predicate of the conclusion, the major term, must occur in the first premise. A syllogism with its premises in the proper order (and, of course, containing only three terms, each one appearing twice) is said to be in **standard form.**

The **form** of a syllogism is simply the combination of mood and figure. For instance, the two syllogisms discussed above have the forms *AAA*-I and *AII*-I respectively, and the syllogism

MAP
MES
∴ *SEP*

has form *AEE*-III. (This syllogism happens to be invalid, but invalid syllogisms are still syllogisms.)

Examples:

Here are more examples of syllogisms and their forms:

1. *IAO*-III:
   MIP
   MAS
   ∴ *SOP*
2. *AEE*-IV:
   PAM
   MES
   ∴ SEP
3. *EOO*-II
   PEM
   SOM
   ∴ *SOP*
4. *AIE*-I
   MAP
   SIM
   ∴ *SEP*
5. *EEE*-III
   MEP
   MES
   ∴ *SEP*
6. *EIO*-I
   MEP
   SIM
   ∴ *SOP*

Exercise 11-1:

Using the *A*, *E*, *I*, *O* notation, symbolize the following arguments, put them into standard syllogistic form, and determine their mood and figure (and thus their form).

1. Some beatles are musicians.
   All musicians are rhythmic.
   ∴ Some beatles are rhythmic.
2. All things made out of grass are green.
   Some things made out of grass are cigarettes.
   ∴ Some cigarettes are green.
3. All homosexuals are gay.
   Some homosexuals are not happy people.
   ∴ Some happy people are not gay.
4. No Republicans are donkeys.
   Some politicians are not Republicans.
   ∴ Some politicians are donkeys.
5. All Democrats are donkeys.
   Some politicians are Democrats.
   ∴ Some donkeys are politicians.
6. No men not named after their fathers are juniors.
   Some college students are not men not named after their fathers.
   ∴ Some college students are not juniors.
7. All men whose sons are named after them are seniors.
   No coeds are men whose sons are named after them.
   ∴ No coeds are seniors.
8. No skiers are bathing lions.
   All bathing lions are cool cats.
   ∴ No cool cats are skiers.

2 *Determining Syllogism Validity*

A syllogism is said to be **valid,** or **deductively valid,** if its form makes it impossible for the syllogism to have both premises true and its conclusion false. All other syllogisms are said to be **invalid,** or **deductively invalid.** A valid syllogism *guarantees* the truth of its conclusion *provided* both of its premises are true. An invalid syllogism *may* have a false conclusion even though both of its premises are true. So an invalid syllogism obviously does not guarantee anything about its conclusion, which is why we say it is invalid.

If a syllogism having a given form is a *valid* syllogism, then all syllogisms having that form are valid, and if a syllogism having a given form is *invalid,* then all syllogisms having that form are invalid.*

3 Venn Diagram Proofs of Validity or Invalidity

Perhaps the most common way to determine the validity or invalidity of syllogisms and of what we might call "syllogism forms" is by using Venn diagrams.

To diagram a syllogism, three overlapping circles are required, one for each term. In overlapping the three circles, seven areas are formed (plus an eighth outside the circles, representing the class $\overline{S}\overline{M}\overline{P}$):

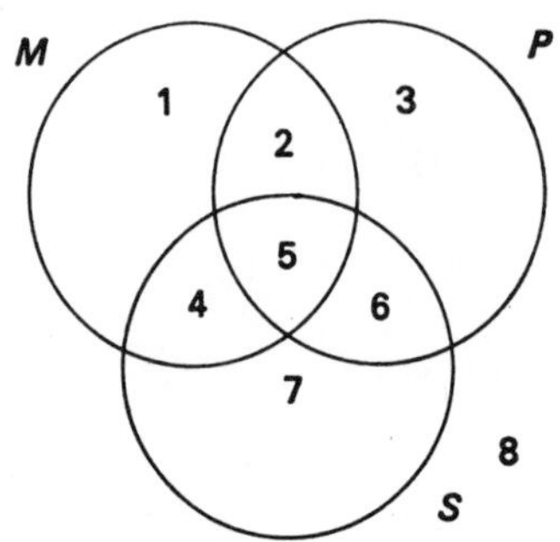

Area 1 represents the class $M\overline{P}\overline{S}$, 2 the class $MP\overline{S}$, 3 the class $\overline{M}P\overline{S}$, 4 the class $M\overline{P}S$, and so on. The *pair* of areas 1 and 4, taken together, represent the class $M\overline{P}$; the pair 3 and 6, the class $\overline{M}P$; the pair 6 and 7, the class $\overline{M}S$; and so on. (We need *two* areas to represent these classes because in drawing a third overlapping circle we divide each of the areas $M\overline{P}$, $\overline{M}P$, $\overline{M}S$, and so on, in half.) If we write in class names, instead of numbers, then the three-circle diagram looks like this:

---

*Except for the cases considered in Section 9 of this chapter.

In the Middle Ages, students determined the validity of a syllogistic form by reciting a chant containing a name for each of the valid moods in each figure. For instance, the name "bArbArA" occurs in the chant for the first figure, indicating that the form *AAA*-I is valid.

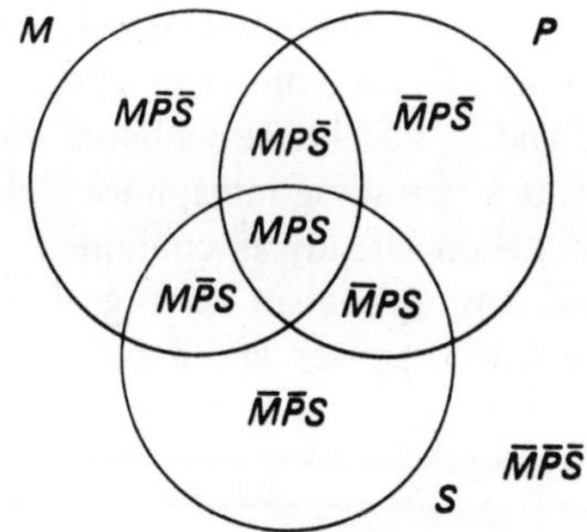

Now consider the syllogism

MAP		$M\overline{P} = O$
SAM	alternately symbolized as	$S\overline{M} = O$
∴ *SAP*		∴ $S\overline{P} = O$

To diagram its first premise, *MAP*, we shade out the two $M\overline{P}$ areas, namely 1 and 4, to indicate that they are empty:

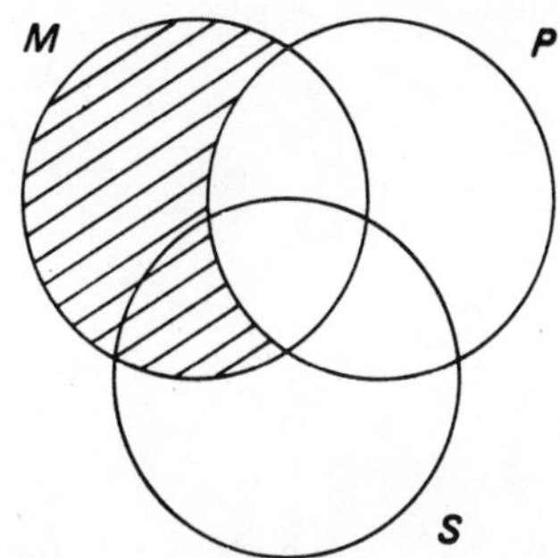

And to diagram its second premise, *SAM*, we shade out the two $S\overline{M}$ areas, namely 6 and 7:

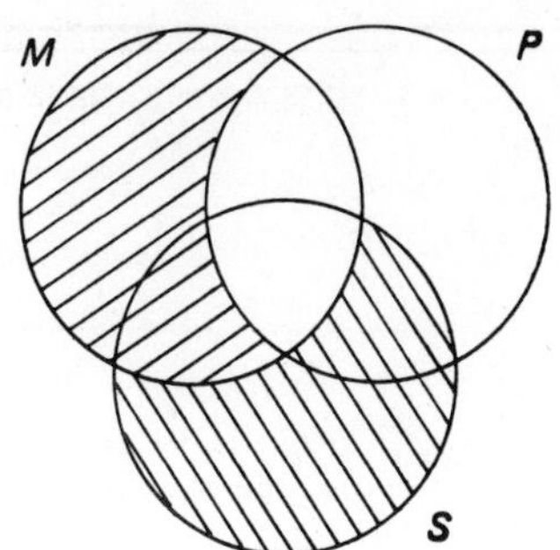

Were we now to diagram its conclusion, *SAP*, we would shade out the two $S\bar{P}$ areas, 4 and 7. But in diagramming the two premises of this argument, we have already shaded out 4 and 7, and hence *we have already diagrammed its conclusion*. This indicates (speaking metaphorically) that the information contained in the conclusion already is contained in the premises. Hence, the syllogism, and any syllogism having the form *AAA*-I, is valid, since it cannot have true premises and a false conclusion.

Now consider the syllogism

	MAP		$M\bar{P} = O$
	SEM	alternately symbolized as	$SM = O$
∴	SEP	∴	$SP = O$

To diagram its first premise, we shade out areas 1 and 4, and to diagram its second premise, we shade out 4 and 5, to get:

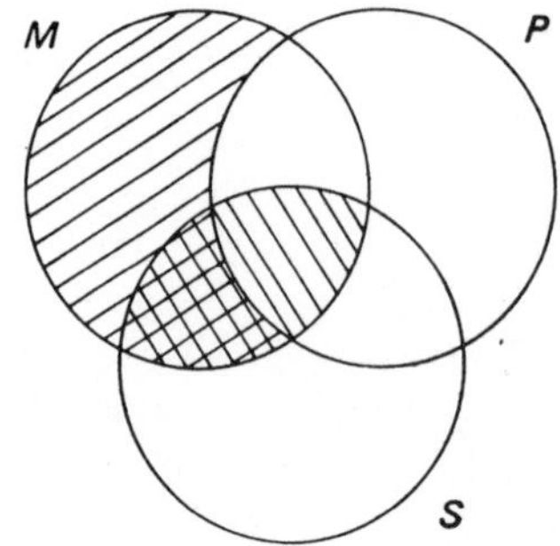

But to diagram its conclusion, we would have to shade out 5 and 6. It happens that we have shaded out 5, but we have *not* shaded out 6. So in diagramming the premises of this syllogism, we have *not* also diagrammed its conclusion. Hence, it is *possible* for its premises to be true and its conclusion false, and so the syllogism in question is invalid.

Examples:

1. We can diagram the premises of the syllogism

All philosophers are Martians.
No Martians are stupid.
∴ No philosophers are stupid.

in symbols

	PAM			$P\bar{M} = O$
	MES	or		$MS = O$
∴	*PES*		∴	$PS = O$

as follows:

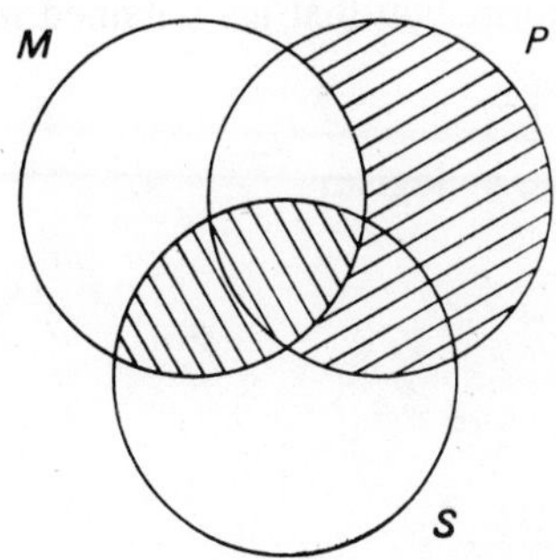

This proves that the syllogism is valid since in diagramming its premises we have shaded out areas 5 and 6 and, hence, also diagrammed its conclusion.

2. We can diagram the premises of the syllogism

No politicians are honest.
Some Americans are politicians.
∴ Some Americans are not honest.

in symbols

	PEH			$PH = O$
	AIP	or		$AP \neq O$
∴	*AOH*		∴	$A\bar{H} \neq O$

by shading out the *PH* areas, then placing an *X* in area 4 to indicate that the class *AP* is not empty:

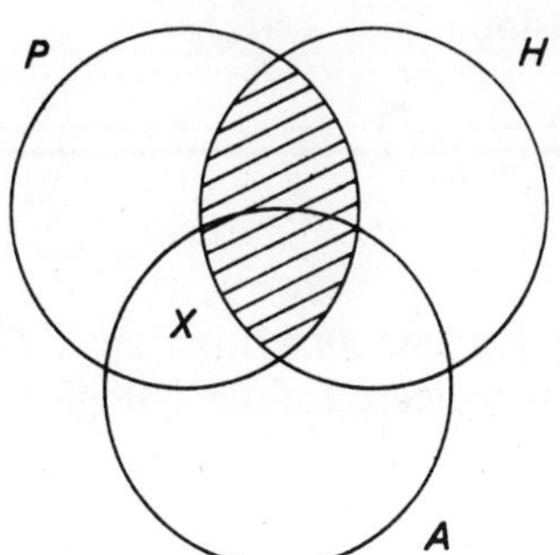

Although in diagramming the premises of this syllogism we have not quite diagrammed its conclusion (as will become evident in the next few paragraphs), we still have proved that the syllogism is valid. The reason for this is that the conclusion, $A\overline{H} \neq O$, asserts that areas 4 and 7 are not *both* empty (that is, it asserts that either 4 or 7 has something in it), and in diagramming the premises we have placed an X in 4. So the premises of this argument already contain the information that is contained in the conclusion.

3. We can diagram the premises of the syllogism

No doctors are cigarette smokers.
Some doctors are philosophers.
∴ Some philosophers are cigarette smokers.

in symbols

	DEC		$DC = O$
	DIP	or	$DP \neq O$
∴	*PIC*	∴	$PC \neq O$

as follows:

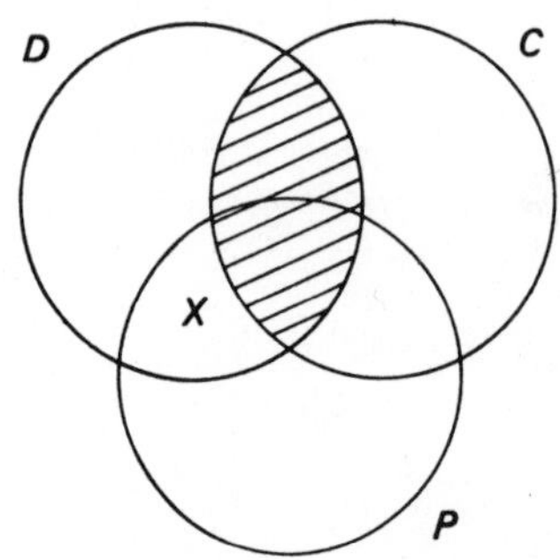

This proves that the syllogism is not valid, because in diagramming its premises we did *not* place an X in either 5 or 6, which (roughly) is what would be required to diagram its conclusion.

In diagramming the premises of a syllogism, sometimes an X can be placed in either one of two areas. This is the case for the syllogism

	MAP		$M\overline{P} = O$
	SIP	alternately symbolized as	$SP \neq O$
∴	*SIM*	∴	$SM \neq O$

We diagram the first premise as follows:

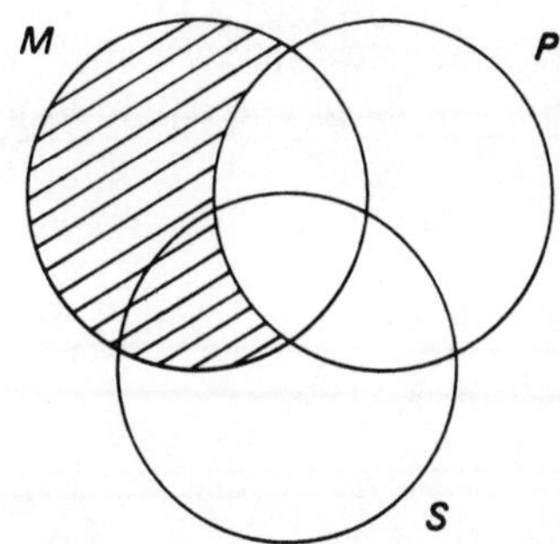

But in diagramming the second premise, the question arises as to whether to place an *X* in area 5 or in area 6. The answer is that we should not place an *X* in either area, since the premises assert only that one or the other (or perhaps both) of the classes represented by these areas has members, without indicating definitely either that the class *SMP* (5) has members or that the class $S\overline{M}P$ (6) has members. To indicate that the premises merely tell us that either *SMP* or $S\overline{M}P$ has members, without telling us which one, we can place an *X on the line* between 5 and 6. And then, the diagram will look like this:

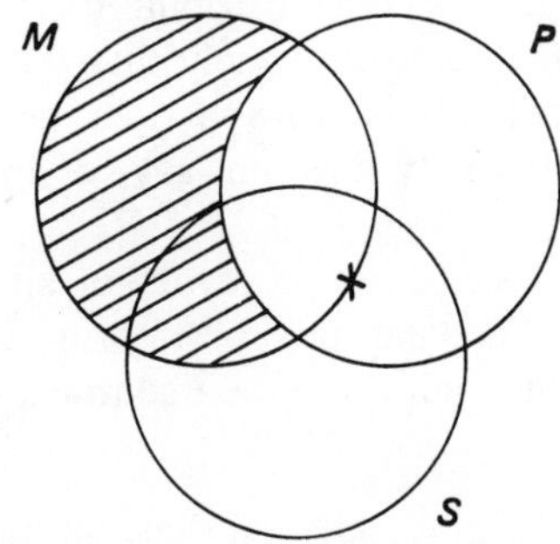

Is this syllogism valid? If it were, then in diagramming its premises, we would have placed an *X* either in 4 or in 5. Now clearly no *X* has been placed in 4, for that area is shaded out. But no *X* has been placed in 5 either, for the *X* was placed *on the line* between 5 and 6. So we cannot guarantee the truth of the conclusion *SIM* on the basis of the evidence afforded by its premises, and hence the syllogism is *invalid*. (This is the *only* even mildly difficult case that can arise in proving validity or invalidity using Venn diagrams, so it is worthwhile to expend a little extra effort to understand it.)

In any event, cases of this kind present no problem in practice, since all syllogisms diagrammed by placing an *X* on a line are invalid. (Similarly, all syllogisms diagrammed by *doubly shading out an area* are invalid.)

Exercise 11-2:

Test the syllogisms in Exercise 11-1 for validity, using Venn diagrams as just discussed.

4 *Five Rules for Determining Validity or Invalidity*

An alternative (and much older) method for determining the validity or invalidity of syllogisms and syllogism forms is to use rules stating properties that all valid syllogisms must possess.

But before introducing a particular set of five rules of this kind, chosen from among several modestly similar sets, we must discuss the concept of **distribution.** In traditional logic texts, it is usually stated that a term in a proposition is *distributed* if (roughly) it says something about *all* members of the class designated by that term. For instance, the *A* proposition "All scientists are mathematicians" is said to distribute its subject term, since it says something about *all* scientists (namely that they are mathematicians), but not its predicate term, because it does not say something about *all* mathematicians. (It surely does not say, or imply, that all mathematicians are scientists.)

Traditional logic texts work out the distribution properties of all four kinds of categorical propositions. Letting *S* stand for subject terms and *P* for predicate terms, we can summarize the findings of the traditional logician as follows:

Table of Distribution

1. *A* propositions distribute *S*.
2. *E* propositions distribute *S* and *P*.
3. *I* propositions distribute neither *S* nor *P*.
4. *O* propositions distribute *P*.

Most students readily accept the results summarized in the first three lines of this table. But they find the idea expressed on the fourth line, that *O* propositions distribute their predicate terms, rather counter-intuitive. And yet there is a certain plausibility to this idea. For instance, it seems plausible to say that the *O* proposition "Some scientists are not philosophers" distributes its predicate term, because it says of *all* philosophers that they are not some scientists (that is, that they are excluded from part of the class of scientists). In any event, we must say that *O* propositions distribute their predicates, or the five rules about to be presented will not function properly.*

According to these five rules for determining the validity/invalidity of syllogisms, all valid syllogisms must have:

1. A middle term that is distributed at least once.
2. No term distributed in the conclusion that is not distributed in a premise.
3. At least one affirmative (nonnegative) premise.
4. A negative conclusion if one of its premises is negative, and a negative premise if the conclusion is negative.
5. At least one particular premise if the conclusion is particular (that is, at least one *I* or *O* premise if the conclusion is an *I* or *O* proposition).

Any syllogism that does not have all five of these properties is invalid. (The fifth rule is required only if we allow propositions to refer to empty classes.)†

Examples:

1. The syllogism

	Some mathematicians are scientists.		*MIS*
	All philosophers are mathematicians.		*PAM*
∴	Some scientists are philosophers.	∴	*SIP*

violates the rule requiring that the middle term be distributed at least once, and hence is invalid.

* Unfortunately, the traditional characterization of the concept of distribution is not satisfactory even for *A*, *E*, and *I* propositions. Take the *A* proposition "All bachelors are unmarried adult males" (let's assume that "bachelor" *means* "unmarried adult male"). Clearly, if this proposition "refers to" all bachelors, thus distributing its subject term, then it also "refers to" all unmarried adult males, thus distributing its predicate term. Hence, the traditional account of distribution is inadequate. There are ways of getting around this difficulty, but they require decisions on philosophical problems beyond the scope of this text, and hence are omitted.

† A sixth rule, requiring that there be exactly three terms in a valid syllogism, often is added to these five. But this rule is unnecessary, since an argument that does not have exactly three terms, each one repeated twice, is not a syllogism according to the generally accepted definition of that term.

2. The syllogism

	All mathematicians are scientists.		*MAS*
	All philosophers are mathematicians.		*PAM*
∴	All scientists are philosophers.	∴	*SAP*

violates the rule requiring that no term be distributed in the conclusion which is not distributed in a premise, and hence is invalid.

3. The syllogism

	Some scientists are not mathematicians.		*SOM*
	No mathematicians are philosophers.		*MEP*
∴	Some scientists are not philosophers.	∴	*SOP*

violates the rule requiring at least one affirmative premise, and hence is invalid.

4. The syllogism

	Some scientists are not mathematicians.		*SOM*
	All mathematicians are philosophers.		*MAP*
∴	Some scientists are philosophers.	∴	*SIP*

violates the rule requiring that the conclusion be negative, if a premise is negative, and hence is invalid. (This rule also requires that a premise be negative if the conclusion is negative.)

5. And the syllogism

	No scientists are mathematicians.		*SEM*
	All mathematicians are philosophers.		*MAP*
∴	Some scientists are not philosophers.	∴	*SOP*

violates the rule requiring that at least one premise be particular, if the conclusion is particular, and hence is invalid.

Exercise 11-3:

Put the following arguments into standard syllogistic form, and test for validity, using either the five rules of valid syllogisms or Venn diagrams.

1. HER
   $NI\overline{H}$
   ∴ NOR

2. $BO\overline{M}$
   $BE\overline{R}$
   ∴ RIM

3. $PI\bar{N}$
$NA\bar{R}$
∴ $RI\bar{P}$

4. $PA\bar{N}$
$NA\bar{G}$
∴ $GE\bar{P}$

5. $\bar{S}AP$
$\bar{P}EM$
∴ $\bar{S}E\bar{M}$

6. HAP
$\bar{T}EP$
∴ $HE\bar{T}$

7. $HI\bar{G}$
NIH
∴ NIG

8. $HO\bar{T}$
$TE\bar{M}$
∴ $HO\bar{M}$

9. $\bar{M}AP$
$\bar{S}AM$
∴ $SA\bar{P}$

10. $ME\bar{P}$
$\bar{S}O\bar{M}$
∴ $\bar{S}OP$

5 *The Antilogism*

Although methods like the two just discussed are perhaps the most popular, there are other, quite ingenious methods for determining the validity/invalidity of syllogisms, which the reader may find preferable. An elegant example is the "antilogism" test invented in 1883 by Christine Ladd-Franklin.*

The antilogism method is related to the principle of *indirect proof,* or *reductio ad absurdum,* introduced in Part One of this text. Here is how it works:

A. Translate the syllogism to be tested into the alternate notation involving classes that we introduced in the last chapter. For example, translate the syllogism

All famous rock singers are youngsters.
All youngsters are wet behind the ears.
∴ All famous rock singers are wet behind the ears.

into the notation:

$F\bar{Y} = O$
$Y\bar{W} = O$
∴ $F\bar{W} = O$

* This proof procedure was pointed out to me by Professor Eva H. Cadwallader, Westminster College (New Wilmington, Pa.). See her article, "Christine Ladd-Franklin's Antilogism", *Newsletter on the Teaching of Philosophy,* Fall 1980, pp. 13–15.

(The order of premises has no significance whatever.)

B. Now replace the conclusion with its negation, resulting in an **antilogism.** Doing this for the example above, we get:

$F\overline{Y} = O$

$Y\overline{W} = O$

$\therefore$ $F\overline{W} \neq O$

C. The syllogism being tested is *valid* if it meets all three of the following conditions, and is *invalid* otherwise:

1. Exactly one of the three statements making up its antilogism is an *inequality*. (The conclusion, $FW \neq O$, of the above antilogism is an example of an inequality.)

2. One of the two equalities (the two premises $F\overline{Y} = O$ and $Y\overline{W} = O$, in the above antilogism are examples of equalities) has a term *negated* in the other equality. (In our sample antilogism, the term Y in the second premise is negated in the first.)

3. Each of the two terms in the inequality is either negated in both its appearances in the antilogism or else not negated in either. (In our example, both occurrences of F are *un*negated, both occurrences of W are negated.) So the sample antilogism satisfies the third condition as well as the other two, and therefore the original syllogism from which the antilogism is derived is valid.*

Here are four syllogisms that fail to satisfy one or another of the three criteria of the antilogism method, and so are invalid:

1. | | *Syllogism* | | *Antilogism* |
|---|---|---|---|
| | $P\overline{M} \neq O$ | | $P\overline{M} \neq O$ |
| | $S\overline{M} = O$ | | $S\overline{M} = O$ |
| $\therefore$ | $S\overline{P} = O$ | $\therefore$ | $S\overline{P} \neq O$ |

This syllogism fails the first condition of validity because its antilogism contains two inequalities ($PM \neq O$ and $SP \neq O$).

2. | | *Syllogism* | | *Antilogism* |
|---|---|---|---|
| | $M\overline{P} = O$ | | $M\overline{P} = O$ |
| | $M\overline{S} = O$ | | $M\overline{S} = O$ |
| $\therefore$ | $SP \neq O$ | $\therefore$ | $SP = O$ |

* Professor Cadwallader points out two interesting advantages of the antilogism method over the use of Venn diagrams. First, we don't have to eliminate complements of terms so as to reduce to exactly three terms. And second, since almost 2/3 of the invalid syllogism forms fail the first antilogism criterion, we can often save time and effort by mentally negating a syllogism's conclusion and "seeing" that it is invalid, without translating into the class notation ($SP = O$, and so on).

This syllogism fails the first condition of validity because its antilogism contains no inequalities.

3. *Syllogism* / *Antilogism*

	Syllogism		Antilogism
	$P\bar{M} = O$		$P\bar{M} = O$
	$S\bar{M} = O$		$S\bar{M} = O$
∴	$S\bar{P} = O$	∴	$S\bar{P} \neq O$

This syllogism fails the second condition of validity because there is no term in one of its antilogism's two equalities that is negated in the other. (The letter *M* is negated in both equalities.)

4. *Syllogism* / *Antilogism*

	Syllogism		Antilogism
	$MP = O$		$MP = O$
	$S\bar{M} = O$		$S\bar{M} = O$
∴	$S\bar{P} = O$	∴	$S\bar{P} \neq O$

This syllogism violates the third condition because *P* occurs negated in its antilogism's conclusion but *un*negated in its first premise.*

Exercise 11-4:

Test the syllogisms in Exercise 11-1 for validity/invalidity using the antilogism method. (Which of the three methods presented in this chapter for determining validity or invalidity of syllogisms do you prefer? Why?)

Exercise 11-5:

Symbolize the following arguments, put them into standard syllogistic form, and test for validity using one or another of the methods introduced in this chapter.

1. Some doctors are unethical. For all rich tax evaders are unethical, and some doctors are rich tax evaders.

---

* Another neat method for determining syllogism validity/invalidity is Harry Gensler's "star test". (See his article in *Notre Dame Journal of Formal Logic*, vol. 14 (1973), pp. 457–66.) If we asterisk all of the *distributed* occurrences of terms in the premises of a syllogism and all of the *undistributed* occurrences of terms in its conclusion, then the syllogism is valid if every term is asterisked exactly once and there is exactly one occurrence of a predicate term (Gensler calls them "right hand letters") that is asterisked.

2. All doctors are unethical. For all rich tax evaders are unethical, and all rich tax evaders are doctors.
3. No pot smokers are heroin addicts, and no heroin addicts are well adjusted. Therefore no pot smokers are well adjusted.
4. No pot smokers are heroin addicts. So some pot smokers are not well adjusted, because all heroin addicts are well adjusted.
5. Some draft evaders are not conscientious objectors, and some conscientious objectors are not Quakers. So some draft evaders are not Quakers.
6. No Quakers are draft evaders. Thus, some conscientious objectors are not draft evaders, since some conscientious objectors are Quakers.
7. Since some taxes are designed to benefit rich stock-and-bond holders, and all taxes are burdens borne by the average taxpayer, it follows that some burdens borne by the average taxpayer are designed to benefit rich stock-and-bond holders.
8. No taxes are designed to benefit rich stock-and-bond holders. So some burdens borne by the average taxpayer are not designed to benefit rich stock-and-bond holders, since some taxes are not burdens borne by the average taxpayer.
9. Some Americans are members of minority groups. And all members of minority groups are ardently courted by cynical politicians. So it follows that some Americans are ardently courted by cynical politicians.
10. Some Americans are members of minority groups. And some members of minority groups are ardently courted by realistic politicians. Therefore, some Americans are ardently courted by realistic politicians.

6 *Syllogistics Extended*

Several ways have been invented to extend the scope of syllogistic logic beyond the simple cases we have so far discussed. Let's now consider some of these methods.

(1) Many arguments containing four, five, and even six terms can be reduced to three terms, and thus to syllogistic form, by eliminating negation signs or by replacing terms with their synonyms. For instance, we eliminate a negation sign, and reduce the number of terms in the nonsyllogistic argument*

	All scientists are philosophers.		SAP
	No mathematicians are nonscientists.		$ME\bar{S}$
∴	All mathematicians are philosophers.	∴	MAP

from four to three, by using *obversion* to replace its second premise with the equivalent proposition

* Sometimes it is said that an argument of this kind *is* a syllogism, but not a *standard form* syllogism, thus taking any set of three categorical propositions to constitute a syllogism, no matter how many terms it contains.

All mathematicians are scientists. *MAS*

thus obtaining the valid syllogism

All scientists are philosophers. *SAP*
All mathematicians are scientists. *MAS*
∴ All mathematicians are philosophers. ∴ *MAP*

Similarly, we can reduce the number of terms in the nonsyllogistic argument

Some enclosed figures are squares. *FIS*
All triangles are enclosed figures. *TAF*
∴ Some three-sided enclosed figures are squares. ∴ *EIS*

from four to three by replacing the phrase "three-sided enclosed figures" with its synonym "triangles", thus obtaining the syllogism

Some enclosed figures are squares. *FIS*
All triangles are enclosed figures. *TAF*
∴ Some triangles are squares. ∴ *TIS*

Of course, this syllogism is *invalid,* but it is a syllogism.

(2) Many arguments that are not in syllogistic form because they contain propositions that are not *categorical* propositions can be translated into syllogistic form by translating the propositions they contain into categorical propositions. Sometimes, this can be accomplished by a simple change in word order. For instance, the proposition "Gamblers are all broke" may be translated into categorical form as "All gamblers are broke".

Sometimes, simply adding a suppressed quantifier will suffice to translate a proposition into categorical form. Thus, an argument containing the proposition "Women are fickle" may be translated into categorical form as "All women are fickle". And, clearly, "Every man is mortal" can be translated into the categorical proposition "All men are mortal" and "Many gamblers are broke" into "Some gamblers are broke".

(3) In addition, many other minor grammatical changes can be made. For instance, we can translate the argument

All boy scouts do good deeds.
Some girl scouts do good deeds.
∴ Some girl scouts are boy scouts.

into syllogistic form by replacing its first and second premises by the equivalent propositions "All boy scouts are doers of good deeds" and "Some girl scouts are doers of good deeds", respectively, thus obtaining the (invalid) syllogism

All boy scouts are doers of good deeds.
Some girl scouts are doers of good deeds.
∴ Some girl scouts are boy scouts.

(4) All *categorical* propositions say something about *classes*. Thus, technically, no *singular* proposition is a categorical proposition. Hence no syllogism can contain a singular proposition. (A **singular proposition** is a proposition one of whose terms refers to an *individual* rather than to a class. Thus, "Socrates is mortal", "Art is tall", and "This man is short", all are singular propositions.)

But there are several standard ways to translate singular propositions into categorical propositions. One is simply to replace the singular term in such a proposition by a class term naming a class that can contain only one member (namely the individual referred to by the singular term). Thus, "Art is tall" can be translated into "All members of the class whose sole member is Art are tall". (We can also translate "Art is tall" into "All things identical with Art are tall", since only one thing, Art, is identical with Art.)

Using this method, we can translate the famous argument

All men are mortal
Socrates is a man.
∴ Socrates is mortal.

into syllogistic form as follows:

	All men are mortal.		*HAM*
	All members of the class whose sole member is Socrates are men.		*SAH*
∴	All members of the class whose sole member is Socrates are mortal.	∴	*SAM*

Indeed, since we can always replace singular statements with categorical equivalents, it has become customary to treat singular propositions as categorical propositions, considering *affirmative* singular propositions, such as "Socrates *is* a man" as *A* propositions, and *negative* singular propositions, such as "Socrates is *not* mortal" as *E* propositions, without bothering to translate as we have done above. Thus the argument

	All men are mortal.		*HAM*
	Socrates is a man.		*SAH*
∴	Socrates is mortal.	∴	*SAM*

is customarily treated as a syllogism, and in fact, a valid one.

(5) Sometimes a more radical translation procedure is required to translate propositions into categorical form, a procedure that involves the introduction of new classes. Take the proposition "We always have death

and taxes". We can translate this sentence into categorical form by using the class of *times* (suggested by the temporal term "always"), to obtain the categorical proposition "All times are times in which we have death and taxes". (Notice that the subject class in this case is the class of times, and the predicate class is a *subclass* of the class of times, namely the class of times at which we have death and taxes.)

But, as usual, care must be used in translating. For instance, we don't want to translate the invalid argument

Every time Art gets an A on a logic exam he is happy.
Art always gets A's on logic exams.
———
∴ Art always is happy.

as

	All times at which Art gets A's on logic exams are times at which Art is happy.		*LAH*
	All times are times at which Art gets A's on logic exams.		*TAL*
∴	All times are times at which Art is happy.	∴	*TAH*

since the latter is a *valid* argument, and we don't want to translate invalid arguments into valid ones. The mistake was to translate the second premise, "Art always gets A's on logic exams", so as to have Art taking logic exams at *all* times. Clearly, what we mean when we say "Art always gets A's on logic exams" is more accurately rendered as "All times *at which Art takes logic exams* are times at which he gets A's". And if we correctly symbolize this premise, then the resulting argument will not even be a syllogism, much less a valid one.

Exercise 11-6:

Translate each of the following arguments into standard form, and test for validity, using one or another of the methods introduced in this chapter.

1. All sinners are punished in the next life. And all nonsinners are nonmurderers. So it follows that all murderers are punished in the next life.
2. Most sinners are not murderers, since most people punished in the next life are nonmurderers, and sinners are punished in the next life.
3. Eighteen-year-olds are permitted to vote. But not all who are permitted to vote in fact do vote. So there must be some eighteen-year-olds who don't exercise their right to vote.
4. Those who ignore relevant facts are likely to be mistaken. So the wise man is not likely to be mistaken, because he takes all known relevant facts into account.
5. Only the rich deserve the fair. So it follows that some handsome men aren't nonrich, since some who deserve the fair aren't nonhandsome.

6. All logic classes are extremely interesting. So some classes that are harder than average are extremely interesting, since some logic classes are harder than average.
7. No logic classes are dreadfully boring, because no classes about good reasoning are boring, and all logic classes are about good reasoning.
8. All classes that are either interesting or difficult are uncrowded, due to the fact that all uncrowded classes are unexciting, and all interesting or difficult ones are exciting.
9. Salesmen will do whatever is most likely to sell their product. So salesmen often will tell lies, because telling the truth often is not the best way to sell a product.
10. Because Harry enjoys himself only when he has lots of money and because Harry always enjoys going out with Jane, it follows that Harry only goes out with Jane when he has lots of money.
11. He who lives by the sword dies by the sword. So all officers die with their boots on, since officers surely do live by the sword.
12. Some who live by the pen are called liars, and some are called sages. So there are people said to have great sagacity who have been referred to as frequent stretchers of the truth.
13. If to be human is to be vain, then everyone must be regularly looking in mirrors; everyone knows vanity tends to seek its own reflection.
14. We'll always have death and taxes. Right? And nobody ever gave in to either without a fight. Right? So that's why we're always fighting, fighting, fighting. Right!
15. Wet-whistled drunks all tend to be loud and shrill, which no doubt accounts for all the attention they get. Moral: Quiet people get ignored.

7 *Enthymemes*

Arguments in daily life often omit premises that everyone can be expected to know. For instance, someone might argue that Texas is larger than France, and hence, that some state in the United States is larger than France, omitting as understood the fact that Texas is a state in the United States.

Sometimes the *conclusion* of an argument is omitted as obvious. And sometimes a premise *and* the conclusion are omitted. An example would be a mother who says, "Now son, it's eight o'clock, and all little boys have to go to bed at eight o'clock", thus omitting the premise that the son is a little boy, as well as the conclusion that the son has to go to bed.

An argument that omits a premise (or a conclusion) as "understood" is said to be an **enthymemic argument,** or simply an **enthymeme.**

Obviously, there is no point in declaring an argument in everyday life invalid when the addition of premises accepted by all concerned will render the argument valid. Life is short and we have neither the time nor the inclination to be precise and complete about everything. So in determining the validity of arguments from everyday life, we should add any premises it is reasonable to assume all would concede, when such additions will make an argument in question valid.

Exercise 11-7:

The following arguments are invalid as they stand. Supply a missing premise for each one that (perhaps with some arranging and synonym substitution) will turn it into a valid syllogism, and prove that the resulting syllogism is indeed valid.

1. No honest men are crooks. It follows then that no businessmen are honest.
2. Abortion takes the life of a fetus. So abortion takes the life of a human being.
3. Most adults are drug users, since caffeine and nicotine are drugs.
4. Smith must be in pretty good shape. After all, he eats plenty of brown rice.
5. Most American history textbooks conceal our theft of the American continent from the Indians. So most American history textbooks tell lies.
6. Anyone who listens to television news programs listens to very superficial accounts of the news. So you waste your time if you watch TV news programs.
7. Anyone whose primary interest is prestige or an easy life can't be a very good minister. So there must be some bishops who are pretty poor ministers.
8. Plenty of high school dropouts are smarter than lots of college graduates. So there must be an awful lot of people who never finished high school who are not incapable of holding high-level management positions.
9. Our Iranian policy was based on the judgment of some of America's best-known political scientists. So it wasn't a foolish policy.
10. No one with a scrambled brain is likely to do much good in this world. So a lot of people who have taken LSD have had it so far as being part of an effective force for good is concerned.

8 *Sorites*

Consider the argument

MAP
SAM
RAS
∴ *RAP*

As it stands, it cannot count as a valid syllogism, since it contains four terms and three premises, and hence is not even a syllogism, much less a valid one. But clearly, it is a valid argument of some sort. In order to bring it into the syllogistic framework, we can consider it to be an *enthymematic version* of a chain of two valid syllogisms. For instance, we can take the first two propositions as the premises of the valid syllogism:

MAP
SAM
∴ *SAP*

and then use the conclusion *SAP* and the third proposition *RAS* as premises of the valid syllogism:

SAP
RAS
∴ *RAP*

Let us refer to any argument of the kind just considered which can be treated as a chain of enthymematic syllogisms as a **sorites.***

Sorites can have as many premises as you wish. Here is one with four premises:

MAP
SAM
RIS
NEP
∴ *RON*

This sorites breaks down into the following chain of valid syllogisms:

NEP
MAP
∴ *MEN*

MEN
SAM
∴ *SEN*

SEN
RIS
∴ *RON*

Since all three of these syllogisms are valid (which is left to the reader to prove), the sorites as a whole is valid.

Exercise 11-8:

Translate the following sorites into standard form and determine whether they are valid or invalid.

1. Men are fickle.
   No one is disliked who is good at logic.
   Fickle people are disliked.
   ∴ No men are good at logic.

2. No skiers are nonathletic.
   Some nutritionists are skiers.
   Athletes are not brawny.
   ∴ Some nutritionists are nonbrawny.

---

* Originally, the term "sorites" referred only to a special kind of enthymematic syllogism chain. But in recent years it has come to refer indiscriminately to all kinds.

3. Barbers are extroverts.

   No good barbers are nonbarbers.

   Some good barbers are high-strung.

∴ Some high-strung people are not extroverts.

4. No scientists are nonmathematicians.

   Geologists are friendly.

   No mathematicians are friendly.

∴ No geologists are scientists.

5. Occasionally one finds a genius in graduate school.

   No one can be admitted to grad school who isn't a college graduate.

   People in graduate school are not college graduates.

∴ Some geniuses cannot be admitted to graduate school.

6. No one whose soul is not sensitive can be a Don Juan.

   There are no profound scholars who are not great lovers of music.

   Only profound scholars can be dons at Oxford.

   No insensitive souls are great lovers of music.

∴ All Oxford dons are Don Juans.*

9 *Technical Restrictions and Limitations*

In Chapter Eight, we pointed out that there are intuitively valid arguments that are not provable using predicate logic. One of the examples given there was the valid argument

Art knows that he'll go either to the show or to the concert (but not to both).

Art knows that he won't go to the show.

∴ Art knows that he'll go to the concert.

Unfortunately, traditional logic is even less complete than predicate logic; that is, there are arguments provable using predicate logic that are not provable using traditional logic, even as we have extended it in Section 5 above. Here is a famous example.†

All horses are animals.

∴ All heads of horses are heads of animals.

In recent years, much work has been done in an effort to extend the scope of syllogistic logic to make it equal to that of predicate logic. There seems to be no reason why this effort should not succeed, but so far it has not.

---

*Taken from C. L. Dodgson (Lewis Carroll), *Symbolic Logic* (1896), a book that, as one would expect, contains lots of very humorous and interesting examples.

†Given by Bertrand Russell, an inventor of predicate logic.

In addition to being less complete than predicate logic, traditional logic has other difficulties. In particular, it breaks down when applied to certain odd kinds of arguments.* A typical example is the following:

	All scientists are mathematicians.		SAM
	Some brilliant scientists are not mathematicians.		BOM
∴	No scientists are brilliant scientists.	∴	SEB

According to the five rules for valid syllogisms, this syllogism is invalid, since it contains a term *(B)* that is distributed in the conclusion but not in a premise. And according to the Venn diagram technique, the syllogism is invalid:

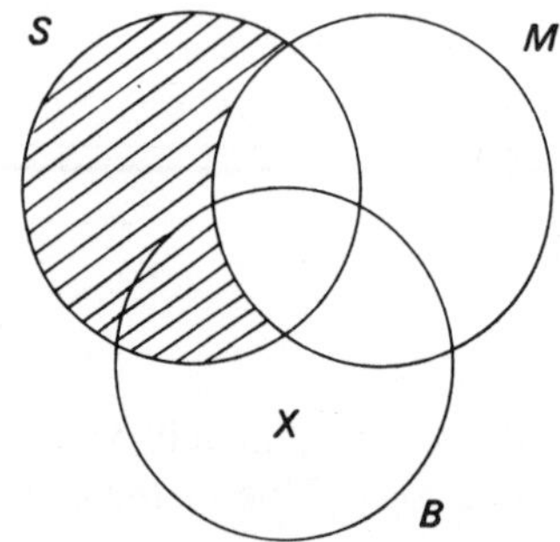

Nevertheless, this argument is valid, because *its premises are contradictory.*†

Here is another argument that is not handled correctly either by the five rules of valid syllogisms or by Venn diagrams:

---

*See James W. Oliver, "Formal Fallacies and Other Invalid Arguments", *Mind,* n.s., vol. LXXVI (1967), pp. 463–78, for an excellent account of these difficulties.

†We can prove its validity using predicate logic machinery as follows:

1.	$(x)(Sx \supset Mx)$	p
2.	$(\exists x)[(Bx \cdot Sx) \cdot \sim Mx]$	p $/\therefore (x)[Sx \supset \sim(Sx \cdot Bx)]$
3.	$(Bx \cdot Sx) \cdot \sim Mx$	2, **EI**
4.	$\sim Mx$	3, **Simp**
5.	$Bx \cdot Sx$	3, **Simp**
6.	Sx	5, **Simp**
7.	$Sx \supset Mx$	1, **UI**
8.	Mx	6,7 **MP**
9.	$Mx \vee (x)[Sx \supset \sim(Sx \cdot Bx)]$	8, **Add**
10.	$(x)[Sx \supset \sim(Sx \cdot Bx)]$	4,9 **DS**

(Notice that lines 4 and 8 explicitly contradict each other, so that *any* conclusion whatsoever could have been derived.)

	All philosophers are tall or nontall.	*PAT*
	All philosophers are short or nonshort.	*PAS*
∴	Some tall-or-nontall things are short or nonshort.	*TIS*

Again, using either Venn diagrams or the five rules of valid syllogism, we arrive at the incorrect conclusion that this syllogism is invalid. Nevertheless, the argument is valid, this time because *its conclusion is logically true*.*

Obviously, something must be done to remedy the defects in syllogistic logic illustrated by these two examples. Two remedies come to mind. One is to say simply that *as syllogistic arguments* they are invalid, although they are valid in some *wider* system not yet worked out. Another way is to require that the premises of a syllogism, taken together, be consistent (that is, noncontradictory), and that its conclusion not be logically true.†

But remedies of this kind are not entirely satisfactory. More work must be done on these problems before the traditional syllogistic logic will be entirely acceptable.

---

* We can prove its validity using predicate logic as follows:

1.	$(x)[Px \supset (Tx \vee {\sim}Tx)]$	p
2.	$(x)[Px \supset (Sx \vee {\sim}Sx)]$	p /∴ $(\exists x)[(Tx \vee {\sim}Tx) \cdot (Sx \vee {\sim}Sx)]$
→ 3.	${\sim}Tx$	**AP**
4.	${\sim}Tx \vee {\sim}Tx$	3, **Add**
5.	${\sim}Tx$	4, **Taut**
6.	${\sim}Tx \supset {\sim}Tx$	3–5, **CP**
7.	$Tx \vee {\sim}Tx$	6, **Impl, DN**
→ 8.	${\sim}Sx$	**AP**
9.	${\sim}Sx \vee {\sim}Sx$	8, **Add**
10.	${\sim}Sx$	9, **Taut**
11.	${\sim}Sx \supset {\sim}Sx$	8–10, **CP**
12.	$Sx \vee {\sim}Sx$	11, **Impl, DN**
13.	$(Tx \vee {\sim}Tx) \cdot (Sx \vee {\sim}Sx)$	7,12 **Conj**
14.	$(\exists x)[(Tx \vee {\sim}Tx) \cdot (Sx \vee {\sim}Sx)]$	13, **EG**

(Notice that the two given premises were not used in deriving the conclusion. We didn't have to use them because the conclusion [being logically true] follows from the null set of premises.)

† The problem for traditional logic posed by logically true and logically false categorical propositions is, in fact, even broader than we have indicated. For instance, it also occurs for the notions of contraries, subcontraries, and so on. Thus, logically true *A* propositions, such as "All bachelors are unmarried", cannot have contraries, even assuming existential import. And logically false *I* propositions cannot have subcontraries. For more on these difficulties, see David Sanford, "Contraries and Subcontraries", *Noûs*, vol. 2 (1968), pp. 95–96.

Exercise 11-9:

1. *True or False:* Since the order of premises in part determines the figure of a syllogism, changing the order of its premises may change its validity. (Defend your answer.)
2. *True or False:* If in diagramming the premises of a syllogism using Venn diagrams we also have diagrammed its conclusion, then the syllogism is valid. (Defend your answer.)
3. When diagramming a syllogism to determine its validity, we sometimes have to place an x on the line between two slots. Carefully explain why. (Example)
4. Carefully explain why *E* propositions distribute both their subject and predicate terms, and why *I* propositions distribute neither. (Examples)
5. Are singular propositions such as "Ronald Reagan is an actor" also categorical propositions? (Explain, with examples.)
6. Figure out an *original* example (genuinely different from the one in the text) of a valid argument, provable using the machinery of predicate logic but not of syllogistic logic; prove the argument is valid; and explain why syllogistic machinery doesn't permit proof.
7. Figure out an *original* example of a valid argument that is invalid according to the five rules of valid syllogism and Venn diagram proof procedures; prove the argument valid; and then explain why syllogistic rules go wrong. (Hard question)

Key Terms Introduced in Chapter Eleven

Antilogism: The result of negating the conclusion of a syllogism. Example:

	Syllogism		*Antilogism*
	$M\bar{P} = O$		$M\bar{P} = O$
	$S\bar{M} = O$		$S\bar{M} = O$
∴	$S\bar{P} = O$	∴	$S\bar{P} \neq O$

Distribution: A term in a syllogism is distributed if the proposition refers to *all* members of the class designated by that term.

Enthymeme: An argument in which a premise, or premises, is omitted as understood. (Sometimes it is the *conclusion* that is omitted as understood.)

Figure: The property of a syllogism determined by the positions of its major, minor, and middle terms in its premises.

Form: The property of a syllogism determined by its mood and figure.

Major term: The predicate term of the conclusion of a syllogism.

Middle term: The term in a syllogism that occurs once in each premise but not in the conclusion.

Minor term: The subject term of the conclusion of a syllogism.

Mood: The property of a syllogism determined by the quality of its three propositions. For example, the syllogism *HAP, PEG, /∴ GEH* has the mood *AEE*.

Singular proposition: A proposition one of whose terms refers to an individual entity rather than a class. For example, "Socrates is human" is a singular proposition.

Sorites: An enthymemic version of a chain of syllogisms.

Standard form (of a syllogism): The form of a syllogism in which the premise placed first contains the predicate of the syllogism's conclusion.

Syllogism: An argument containing three categorical propositions, two of which are premises and one a conclusion, such that the three propositions taken as a group contain exactly three terms, each of which occurs twice (none occurring twice in a given proposition). Example:

HAM
GAH
∴ *GAM*

Chapter Twelve

Fallacies

First, the bad news about fallacy theory. Although traditional syllogistic logic is incomplete, still it provides a correct account as far as it goes (with only minor changes—as noted in the previous chapter). On the other hand, traditional theories of fallacy contain serious defects that render all of the various accounts unsatisfactory. Worse, there is no modern fallacy theory that is entirely correct.

Now for the good news. Even the defective traditional accounts are useful tools for avoiding bad arguments or reasoning in everyday life. Further, there are one or two modern fallacy theories that come reasonably close to being correct, and they're even more useful in everyday life.

The following account is taken from one recent attempt to improve our understanding of the nature of fallacious argument and reasoning.*

The theory of fallacious argument or reasoning constitutes an important part of logical theory, because (it turns out) in everyday life the rejection of bad arguments is often the key to being in a position to accept the good.†

1 *The Nature of Fallacy*

We can divide arguments into those that are *cogent*—and thus should be

* See the author's "The Nature and Classification of Fallacies", in *Informal Logic: The First International Symposium*, ed. J. Anthony Blair and Ralph H. Johnson (Inverness, Calif.: Edgepress, 1980). And for more on the use of fallacy theory in everyday reasoning, and in particular for more examples from everyday life, see the author's *Logic and Contemporary Rhetoric*, 4th ed. (Belmont, Calif.: Wadsworth Publishing Co., 1984).

† Roughly speaking, the reason is that acceptance or rejection of an argument in everyday life depends on our judgment of whether it is *sound,* which depends on our *background beliefs,* or *world views,* which in turn depends on the acceptance or rejection of previously encountered arguments. Thus, acceptance of a fallacious argument may poison all of our reasoning on a given topic.

persuasive—and those that are *fallacious*—and therefore should not be persuasive. A **cogent argument** must satisfy three conditions: (1) its premises must provide good grounds for its conclusion;* (2) it must have warranted (acceptable) premises; and (3) its premises must contain all available relevant information (known to the reasoner in question). A **fallacious argument** is simply an argument that is not cogent, which means an argument that either (1) does not provide good grounds for its conclusion; (2) contains an unwarranted premise; or (3) ignores relevant information.

Examples:

The following argument is fallacious because its premises don't provide good grounds for its conclusion:

1. Anyone who gets a billion votes will win a U.S. presidential election.
2. Ronald Reagan won a U.S. presidential election.

/∴ 3. Ronald Reagan got over a billion votes.

Here is an argument that is fallacious because it contains unwarranted premises:

1. Anyone who shakes hands with a chimney sweep will have good luck.
2. Dick Van Dyke shook hands with a chimney sweep.

/∴ 3. Dick Van Dyke will have good luck.

And here is an argument with warranted premises that is fallacious because it fails to use all relevant information:

1. Fred Gordon prayed for a cancer remission and overcame his allegedly incurable cancer.
2. So did Harold Hyatt, Arthur Sneed, and George Klinks.

/∴ 3. Anyone who prays for a cancer remission will be cured.

(The omitted relevant information is that many have prayed for cancer remissions and died of cancer.)

It is important to notice that cogency and fallaciousness are sometimes relative to particular arguers or reasoners. What persuades one person may be fallacious for another because people in different places, times,

---

*That is, the argument must be either deductively valid or inductively correct (bringing to mind the distinction discussed in Chapter One, Section 2).

or circumstances, have different sorts of information and theories at their disposal. Given what twelve-year-olds know, they may be justified in holding simplistic views, say about how society functions, that most adults should reject as contrary to what experience has taught them. So long as we're thinking just of argument validity/invalidity, or inductive correctness/incorrectness, this difference in **background information,** or **world view,** is irrelevant. But once we move to the twin notions of cogency and fallaciousness, this difference becomes very relevant indeed, because of the second and third requirements of cogent reasoning just mentioned.

It is also very important to notice that reasoning from false premises is not necessarily fallacious. Cogent reasoning requires **warranted** (justified) premises, not necessarily true ones. In the first place, we don't have to know everything about a topic to reason cogently about it (a very fortunate thing indeed, given that we're all at least partly ignorant about almost everything). We don't want to say, for instance, that an ancient scientist who classified whales as fish, rather than mammals, reasoned fallaciously in expecting them to have gills instead of lungs. All that we should require is that scientists take account of what they, in their time, place, and circumstance, could be expected to know. Whales, after all, do greatly resemble fish, so that in the absence of direct evidence to the contrary, it was reasonable to classify them as fish and to expect, therefore, that they would turn out to have gills. The point is that in those days, having the information they had, the theory that whales are fish and have gills was a warranted theory, even though a false one.

Further, even when we reason well, and from *true* premises, we may reason fallaciously. Suppose it turns out that astronauts from outer space visited the Earth in ancient times. Nevertheless, Erich von Daniken's theory that they landed at a particular spot in South America would still be fallacious, even if that's exactly where they landed, because von Daniken suppressed evidence contrary to his theory (which wasn't well supported by the evidence he did appeal to anyway). That guesses turn out to be correct doesn't make them cogent; it just makes the guesser lucky. Of course experience shows that warranted beliefs are more often true (or at least more often *accurate**) than unwarranted ones, which is the most important reason for insisting on reasoning from warranted premises.†

---

* Newtonian mechanics, like most scientific theories, turns out to be false, although an extremely close approximation to the truth. It is, however, extremely *accurate* for most real-life cases (sending space ships to the moon as well as firing ballistic missiles).

† The fallacy theory just presented is much different from most (and for good reason). Take what is said in three other popular texts. Irving Copi, in his *Introduction to Logic,* 5th ed. (New York: Macmillan), characterizes a fallacy as a kind of invalid argument, which clearly is unsatisfactory, since (to mention just one reason) the standard fallacy called *begging the question* generally is committed via valid arguments. Stephen Barker, in his text *The Elements of Logic,* 4th ed. (New York: McGraw-Hill, 1985), Chapter Six, says in effect that arguments are fallacious if they are invalid, have inconsistent premises,

2 *Fallacy Classification*

Fallacies can be classified according to what makes an argument fallacious (logical factors) or according to what leads us to commit fallacies (psychological factors). (As we shall see later, however, the standard and useful fallacy species cross-cut this difference.) If we classify according to *logical** factors (ultimately the crux of the matter, since the reason an argument is fallacious is always that it violates a logical criterion), we get three broad fallacy classes, corresponding to the three ways in which reasoning can go wrong. Let's call them **invalid inference, unwarranted premise,** and **suppressed** (or ignored) **evidence.** (Notice that these categories overlap—an argument may be invalid, contain unwarranted premises, *and* suppress evidence.)

The other interesting way to divide fallacies is according to the psychological factors that lead us to accept bad arguments. Unfortunately, psychology has not yet had its Aristotle, much less its Russell, Pierce, or Frege, so that any psychological division must be quite tentative. Even so, there appear to be three main psychological factors leading us astray, namely (1) strong emotions (in particular conflicting emotions); (2) strong desires to believe certain ideas (leading to self-deception and wishful thinking); and (3) limitations on our reasoning ability. The fallacy categories that correspond to these three psychological factors might be called **emotional confusion; powerful desire** or **wishful thinking;** and **rational limitation.**

The first two of these psychological classes break down into so many species that there is no point in trying to catalogue them. But the third one, *rational limitation,* can profitably be divided further into three species, namely **complexity,** where the mind is unable to handle a mass of information or to bring to bear relevant information†; **similarity,** where

---

or are question begging, which fails (to mention just one reason) because it neglects the standard fallacy called *false dilemma* (which is typically committed via uncritical acceptance of a questionable disjunction—the point being that Barker has no criterion for deductive reasoning requiring that premises be *warranted*). And Robert Baum, in his text *Logic,* 2nd ed. (New York: Holt, Rinehart, and Winston, 1981), p. 124, defines good arguments as arguments that are valid, contain well-established and true premises, and are not question begging, and then says that all other arguments are fallacious, which is unsatisfactory (to mention just one reason) because it makes all scientists who happen to reason from false, but well-confirmed theories, guilty of fallacy.

* Thinking of the logical in the broad sense is often referred to as *epistemological.*

† The ability to bring relevant information to bear on an issue is generally held to be one of the key components of intelligence—brilliant people are much better at this than the rest of us. What this means is that the theory of fallacious reasoning is connected to what is sometimes called the *logic of discovery* (as opposed to the logic discussed in most of this book, which is a logic of *justification*). (Of

we become confused by the similarity of a fallacious reasoning process to a legitimate one; and **false principle,** where we accept as genuine a fallacious principle of reasoning (an example being the gambler's fallacy, which says that short streaks, say a streak of six 7s in a row at craps, change the short-term probabilities, so that after six 7s the odds on seven are less than usual.)

We're now going to look into several of the more important standard fallacy species, none of which were devised with the above fallacy classification in mind, and in fact cross-cut that classification. As we shall see, knowing the broader fallacy theory is of some value when using the standard fallacy divisions. In any event, it is important to remember that the ultimate reason for rejecting an argument *always* must be the belief that the argument is either invalid or contains unwarranted premises or fails to utilize available relevant information. Paying attention to psychological (or other) considerations is just a way to avoid accepting arguments that are fallacious for one or more of the three logical reasons just mentioned.

3 *Inconsistency*

One of the most important fallacies is that of **inconsistency.** We argue *inconsistently* if we argue from contradictory premises, or if we argue for contradictory conclusions.

But in daily life, it usually is hard to classify statements as premises or conclusions. So we are justified in pinning the *inconsistency* label on anyone who asserts contradictory statements.

The fallacy of *inconsistency* is important, first because it is committed so frequently, and second because it is the most definitely fallacious of all fallacies. A person may try to wriggle out of the fallacy of, say, *provincialism,* by arguing that *provincialism* is not always fallacious, but it is pretty hard to argue that *inconsistency* ever is anything but fallacious. (Of course, politicians are pretty adept at *reinterpreting* themselves out of the fallacy of *inconsistency,* but that's another matter.)

It should be clear that *inconsistency* is a species of the logical genus

---

course, many deny that there can be such a thing as a logic of discovery.) To see the connection, consider the standard fallacy category *false dilemma* (to be discussed soon). We often fall for a *false dilemma* simply because we don't know the information that would tell us it is false. But sometimes we fall for a false dilemma because we fail to think of the relevant information, even though we know it very well. The point is that the more intelligent we are, the more likely we are to bring such information to bear at the right moment. The ability to avoid fallacious reasoning is, after all, a kind of intelligence, and a logic of discovery, if we ever devise one, will help all of us do what only geniuses now can do with even modest consistency.

*unwarranted premise,** since at least one of a set of inconsistent premises must be false; so that once we notice they are inconsistent, they should be considered unwarranted.

An interesting way to rate political candidates is to see how inconsistent they are.

(1) A candidate may contradict himself within a single speech or news conference. Of course, he rarely will do so explicitly—that would be too obvious. Instead, he'll try to conceal his inconsistency as much as possible. Typical is the candidate who in the same speech favors large increases in government service (to attract voters who will benefit from them) and also favors important tax reductions (to attract voters burdened by heavy taxes). Since government services cost money, a package of increased services/decreased taxes can be regarded as inconsistent in the absence of a plausible explanation as to how it can be done. Requiring that a candidate's figures "add up" is a way of requiring a candidate to be consistent.

(2) A candidate may be consistent within a given speech or news conference but contradict what he has said on other occasions *without explaining the switch* (or without indicating there has been a switch). The goal of a candidate is to get elected. In most cases, he knows that to win he has to appeal to voters with conflicting interests; he thus has to get voters on different sides of campaign issues to believe he is on *their* side. So he says one thing before one group and the opposite before another.

In any event, most recent candidates have tended to be wildly inconsistent over time, although it generally has taken them longer than it did Ronald Reagan in one 1980 campaign effort:†

1/7/80:

"I just don't believe the farmer should be made to pay a special price for our diplomacy, and I'm opposed to [the U.S. embargo on Soviet Union grain purchases]". (*Washington Post*, 1/7/80)

1/8/80:

"If we are going to do such a thing to the Soviet Union as a full grain embargo, which I support, first we have to be sure our own allies would join us on this". (*Claremont* [New Hampshire] *Eagle Times*, 1/9/80)

(3) A candidate may be inconsistent by supporting a general policy while opposing specific instances of that policy (or while supporting specific instances of competing general policies). Thus, during his first term in office, President Reagan supported the general policy of lower

---

* Except perhaps on rare occasion when, fallible human beings that we are, we may not have discovered a quite devious contradiction in our system of beliefs.

† President Reagan's inconsistency was noted in the excellent little book *There He Goes Again: Ronald Reagan's Reign of Error,* by Mark Green and Gail MacColl (New York: Pantheon Books, 1983), which contains hundreds of Reagan gaffs.

taxes, increased spending for defense, balanced budgets and a reduced federal bureaucracy while at the same time proposing budgets to Congress that in the aggregate would (and did) result in ever larger budget deficits and a larger federal bureaucracy.*

(4) Finally, a candidate may be inconsistent between his words (his political rhetoric) and his actions (how he uses his political power). Richard Nixon was a sworn enemy of wage and price controls—but he instituted such controls in 1971.† Similarly, one Jimmy Carter campaign theme was that when elected he would bring new faces into government, but when he announced his cabinet and chief advisors, we heard mostly familiar names of "in" people like Cyrus Vance (Secretary of State), Zbigniew Brzezinski (head of the National Security Council), Harold Brown (Secretary of Defense), and Charles Schultz (chairman of the Council of Economic Advisors).

Of course, politicians aren't the only ones who are inconsistent. Political writers also frequently talk out of both sides of the mouth. For example, in the early 1980s, *New York Times* columnist Anthony Lewis and many other liberal pundits attacked Catholic priests and bishops who politicked against abortion and birth control measures on the grounds that the church and the clergy should stay out of politics; yet in the 1960s and 1970s these same writers were loudest in their praise of Catholic and other clergy who worked hard and risked their necks championing civil rights.

However, someone who utters inconsistent statements, or says one thing but does another, is not automatically guilty of the fallacy of *inconsistency*. After all, only a fool never changes his mind. Thus, the mere fact that then Senator Edmond Muskie first supported and later opposed the Vietnam war does not convict him of *inconsistency,* for when he changed his position he admitted his prior belief had been an error, and explained why he had changed his mind. The Nixon and Reagan examples above catch these men in the fallacy of *inconsistency* because neither of them admitted previous errors; they just started talking on the other side of the issue.

In most cases, what a person says is inconsistent only when other facts, perhaps even a whole world view, are brought to bear. Here, for

---

* The increase was partly hidden; for instance, by increasing the practice of hiring private consultants to do what government bureaucrats previously did.

† We are stretching the notion of fallacy just a bit here to fit the realities of daily life. Someone, especially someone in public life, who acts in a serious situation without later admitting his action was wrong (we assume appropriate occasions to make such an admission, and also assume no event has taken place rendering the situation relevantly different) implies by his silence that his action was right. A person's failure to admit he has acted incorrectly, given an appropriate opportunity to do so, amounts to a statement that his action was correct. Silence often speaks as loudly as words.

example, is a statement by U.S. Supreme Court Justice William Rehnquist: " . . . law and order will be preserved at whatever cost to individual liberties and rights".* Now, taken alone, this statement is not inconsistent. It becomes inconsistent only when it is added that the foundation of U.S. law is the U.S. Constitution, part of which (the Bill of Rights) guarantees certain individual liberties and rights. So a Supreme Court judge cannot *preserve* law and order at the expense of those liberties and rights, since in the United States they are part of the definition of law and order. Mr. Rehnquist was indeed guilty of the fallacy of *inconsistency*.

4 *Suppressed Evidence*

Those who conceal evidence unfavorable to their own positions are guilty of the fallacy of **suppressed evidence.** And those who accept the conclusions of such arguments when they should have known or suspected that evidence was being suppressed commit the fallacy of *suppressed evidence*. An example is the man who says, "Don't tell me about that; I don't want to know about it". He may well use all of the relevant information he knows, but clearly he is irrational in deliberately overlooking likely adverse evidence.

An ad stating that a health food butter is made of "pasteurized cream taken from tuberculin-tested herds" committed this fallacy, since it failed to point out that almost all butter sold in the United States meets those specifications. So the ad failed to furnish a good reason for paying more for this particular health food butter. (Those who were taken in by the ad committed the fallacy of *suppressed evidence* only if they had reason, or should have had reason, to suspect that this kind of evidence was being suppressed.)

Henry W. Block of H & R Block, the largest income tax preparation company, argued fallaciously in a statement against a proposal to simplify federal income tax laws (for example, to eliminate deductions):[†]

> There's nothing simple about taxes and never will be. Behind the seductive rhetoric of one tax structure for all are pitfalls that would literally destroy the basic principle of everyone paying a fair share.

Block knew very well, as every taxpayer should, that the principle of everyone paying a fair share of taxes had long since been violated, if it ever was adhered to. He suppressed this information because a simplified tax law would be a disaster for his business. (Again, those with little relevant background information are fair game.)

---

*Quoted in *I. F. Stone's Bi-Weekly*, 1 November 1971, p. 3.

[†] Quoted by Nicholas von Hoffman in *The Progressive*, 22 June 1976, p. 23.

5 *Unwarranted Statement*

If we accept statements at face value that we should doubt (given our background information), then we commit the fallacy of accepting an **unwarranted statement,** or **unwarranted premise.** (Sometimes it is premises that are unwarranted, sometimes an unsupported or poorly supported conclusion. But in everyday life, as usual, it's often hard to tell which.)

Recall the misplaced faith many Americans had, almost to the end, that Richard Nixon did not take part in the Watergate cover-up. Acceptance of his claim of innocence became less and less credible as the evidence mounted against him. Yet many continued to accept his unwarranted claims of innocence, primarily out of loyalty. Of course, loyalty is a wonderful trait, but it's out of place when trying to make sound judgments.

One way to avoid accepting questionable statements is to *add up the figures,* or *read between the lines*. For example, an article on Ann Landers (of advice column fame) stated that she personally reads every one of the more than a thousand letters she receives every day, considering it a sacred trust. The article states that this conscientious practice has paid off for her not just with fame and a high salary but also with income from about a hundred speeches she delivers every year. But even if she spent eight hours every day reading those letters, that would mean reading about two letters every minute (no time off for coffee breaks), a task even Ann Landers isn't likely to be up to. And when would she get time to write her column or prepare and deliver a hundred speeches? So the claim that she actually reads every one of the over a thousand letters she receives every day is questionable indeed.

6 *Equivocation*

A term or expression is used *ambiguously,* or *equivocally,* in an argument when used in one sense in one place and in another sense in another place. Clearly, an argument containing such an ambiguous use of language is invalid.* If you are convinced of the conclusion of such an argument because you fail to notice the equivocal use of language, then you are guilty of the fallacy of **equivocation,** also called the fallacy of **ambiguity.**

You also commit this fallacy if you accept the conclusion of an argument having failed to notice that the argument is cogent only if a key ex-

---

* Thus, fallacies of ambiguity typically fall into the broader category of *invalid inference*.

pression is construed one way while its premises are true only if that expression is construed in some other way.

An example is a letter to the editor that defended our involvement in the Vietnam war on grounds that the South Vietnamese "were guaranteed self-determination by the 1954 Geneva Accords". Now if this is taken to mean that the Geneva Accords guaranteed South Vietnam *self-determination free from North Vietnam* if they so chose, then this does constitute a good (although certainly not conclusive) argument for our involvement in Vietnam—namely to uphold the Geneva Accords.

But taken that way, it is false, for the Geneva agreements guaranteed a single, free election *throughout* Vietnam, North and South alike, in order to *unite* the whole country, not separate it into two parts.

On the other hand, if the quote is taken to mean that the South Vietnamese were guaranteed self-determination in the sense that (as part of Vietnam) they would be participants in a Vietnam-wide election to determine the makeup of a government to rule the whole of Vietnam, then it is true. But, of course, then it isn't as good an argument for our involvement in Vietnam.

Another example of the fallacy of *equivocation* was contained in an ad touting sugar consumption, which stated that "sugar is an essential component of the body . . . a key material in all sorts of metabolic processes." The ambiguity centers on the word "sugar". If taken to mean *glucose* (blood sugar), the statement is true. But if taken to mean *ordinary table sugar* (and the average reader could be expected to construe it that way), then it is false. The advertiser thus can claim the ad tells the truth by construing the word "sugar" to mean glucose, knowing that most of the readers will construe it to mean ordinary table sugar, and thus (believing, perhaps, that they are protected by "truth in advertising" regulations) erroneously conclude that table sugar is an essential food.

7 *Two Wrongs Make a Right*

A person is guilty of the fallacy **two wrongs make a right** (also called the *tu quoque* fallacy) when he or she answers a charge of wrongdoing, not by showing that no wrong was committed, but rather by a similar countercharge. The erroneous rationale behind this fallacy is that if "they" do it, so can we (or perhaps that they, being guilty, are wrong to blame us).*

---

* It should be noted that *two wrongs* is not always fallacious. It isn't, for instance, when we "fight fire with fire". The extreme example of this is killing enemy soldiers in a justified war.

Thus, in wartime (declared or otherwise), charges that our side commits atrocities are often answered by the countercharge that the enemy engages in similar or even worse atrocities, as though this somehow absolves us from moral responsibility for our acts.

In the 1976 campaign, vice-presidential candidate Robert Dole played the role of "hatchet man" for President Ford. But he went too far with a remark that the four wars we have engaged in during the twentieth century were "Democrat wars".* So he backtracked a bit by arguing that if the Democrats kept bringing up Watergate, it was fair for him to raise questions about wars that had occurred during Democratic administrations. This was an especially poor use of *two wrongs* because only one of the alleged wrongs (Watergate) really was; to blame Democrats for U.S. entrance into World War II, given the fact of Pearl Harbor, is ridiculous.

Most political examples of *two wrongs make a right* are of the fuzzy variety, as is the case with most fallacies. Jerry Brown, a presidential candidate in 1976, used a fuzzy version of *two wrongs* when asked about press coverage of alleged CIA and FBI illegal activities (*Playboy* magazine, April 1976): "A vigorous free press is essential, but the constant harping on things that have gone on in this government—*I really wonder if they're that different from what's gone on in other governments*". Brown didn't quite say that evils committed by other governments justify this government's evil deeds, but he did strongly suggest it.

It should be noted that *two wrongs make a right* is a variation of the fallacy *many wrongs make a right,* or *common practice,* where an action is defended against attack by pointing out that that action is common practice.

8 *Appeal to Authority*

The fallacy of **appeal to authority** (Latin name: *argumentum ad verecundiam*) is committed when we accept a statement *because* an authority, expert, or famous person accepts it or claims to accept it. For instance, it is committed by anyone who is persuaded that our foreign policy is correct because the president and his cabinet members support it.

But appealing to an authority is not always fallacious. For instance, we do not reason fallaciously when we conclude that we have a particular illness because a doctor says that we do.

Sometimes it is quite difficult to decide whether an appeal to authority constitutes a fallacy. This is especially true for topics on which even the

---

* The use of "Democrat" where "Democrat*ic*" would have been correct was deliberate; Dole almost always used this emotively negative name for his opponents' party. (In uttering this remark, Dole also committed the fallacy of *questionable cause,* to be discussed soon.)

"experts" disagree, such as religion, ethics, art, and politics. It has been argued that this disagreement among experts places a burden on each of us to do some of our own thinking in these fields. If this is true, then appeal to authority in these fields in place of a certain amount of study and hard thought constitutes a fallacy. (This does not mean we ought never consult "experts" in these fields, but only that we must do some of the reasoning on these topics ourselves.)

The members of Congress who tend to respond to controversies over Defense Department budgets by accepting the word of the experts on the matter (Defense Department military personnel) commit this fallacy. After all, it is precisely the Defense Department's opinions that are being challenged. The job of a member of Congress in such a situation is to examine the evidence and reasoning of the military (and others) and arrive at an independent conclusion.

In assessing appeals to authority in a given field, it is important to bear in mind the "state of the art". Is that the sort of thing on which expert testimony would be reliable? It's also important to know whether alleged or apparent experts really are knowledgeable in their fields. Many people naively expect elected representatives and high government officials to know what they're talking about, in spite of the violent disagreements between such experts on many topics, and in spite of the failures of many of their programs (for example, the failures of several recent national administrations to control inflation, the national debt, balance of payments, and so on).

Here is one "knowledgeable" government official in action (from a 1980 *San Francisco Chronicle* item):

> U.S. Ambassador [to Singapore] Richard Kneip didn't know there were two Koreas or that India and Pakistan had fought a war in 1971, says a career diplomat dismissed by Kneip after eight months as his chief deputy. One day, during a discussion of the resurgence of Islam, . . . Kneip had asked him, "What's Islam?" He said Kneip, shortly after his arrival had asked senior staff members: "Did you say there are two separate Korean governments? How come? You mean there has been a war between India and Pakistan? What was that all about?"

Those who know how U.S. ambassadors are picked would not find this abysmal ignorance surprising.

Exercise 12-1:

Determine which fallacies (if any) discussed so far occur in each of the following passages, and state your reasons for thinking so. For example, if you think the fallacy is *inconsistency,* show what the contradiction is, and if *equivocation,* show the different senses of terms used and how they lead to confusion. (Remember that fallacies in daily life often are not clear-cut, and reasonable people may disagree about them.)

1. **Ad against smoking:**

   100,000 doctors have quit smoking cigarettes
   (Maybe they know something you don't)

2. Food seems to have a mysterious fascination for homosexuals. Many of the world's greatest chefs have been homosexuals . . . the more potent a man becomes in his bedroom, the more potent he is in business. . . . Orgasm among nymphomaniacs is just as rare as among prostitutes . . . blind girls particularly become adept at secret masturbation. (David Reuben, M.D., *Everything You Always Wanted To Know about Sex . . . But Were Afraid to Ask* (New York: David McKay, 1970)

3. **Question:** Is the Republican Party a permanent minority party or is it a dying party?
   Senator John Sparkman: Well, I suppose it could be both. (Reported by Alexander Cockburn, *Village Voice,* 22 March 1976)

4. **Jane:** The medical industry in this country delivers such a poor product. Who needs it? Oh, there are a few successes, like penicillin, the elimination of smallpox, and appendix operations, but usually when you get better after seeing a doctor, you'd have gotten better anyway.
   McBird: You're so right. Another thing is how the poor are generally shut out from modern medical care in this country today.
   Jane: Yes, that's true, too. We need to change this. Why should the middle and upper classes, but not the poor, share in the important benefits of modern medicine?

5. From the side panel of a *Cap'n Crunch* cereal box:
   A serving of *Cap'n Crunch* contains 12 grams of sugar. That's about two rounded teaspoonsful, enough to make *Cap'n Crunch's* wholesome blend of corn and oats taste great . . . Yet a serving of *Cap'n Crunch* contains no more sugar than many other everyday foods.

6. Kids, Parents Told Pot Is Only the Beginning: New York narcotics detective Victor Juliano insists he has never "arrested an addict who was on the hard stuff who had not started by smoking pot". . . . The marijuana, he said, generally leads to a psychological inducement to take stronger drugs.

7. William Safire, *New York Times,* 16 September 1976, p. 39, discussing Daniel Schorr's leak of the Pike Report on the CIA to the *Village Voice:*
   Too many editorialists at first missed the significance of all that was at stake, and the Congressmen sensed that weakness and moved in. "If Schorr didn't do anything wrong," one of the committee members asked me, "why did CBS suspend him?"

8. Salad dressing is the only thing we put our name on.

   (Ad for *Wishbone* brand salad dressing, manufactured by Thomas J. Lipton, Inc., distributors of the famous Lipton tea products)

9. From Bob Woodward and Carl Bernstein's *The Final Days:*
   Nixon said that he knew that surreptitious entries and wiretaps—after all, that was what Watergate was all about, wasn't it?—were a way of life in the Kennedy and Johnson administrations. "I know this has been going on for twenty years. It is the worst kind of hypocrisy for the Democrats to make so much of it". . . . There had to be a way to make the other side pay the price, Nixon said . . . what he did should be measured against the record of prior administrations. Get a comprehensive list of all the national security wiretaps conducted by the Kennedy and Johnson administrations, Nixon ordered. . . . The President knew, the staff knew, and the other side knew that what *his* people had done was nothing—literally nothing—compared to what had gone on before. They were all innocent.

10. Senator James Buckley, New York, quoted in the *Village Voice,* 13 September 1976:
    Any serious discussion of marijuana must begin by acknowledging that marijuana is a dangerous drug. It is at least as dangerous, and probably a good deal more dangerous, than either alcohol or tobacco, of which drugs society now seems prepared to control by every means short of criminal penalties, and the abuse of drugs should not be invoked to justify the legalization and potential abuse of marijuana. "While the nature and extent of marijuana's effect on one's health has been neither conclusively established nor entirely eliminated, the fact that this question remains open argues in my view for restraint of the impulse to legalize marijuana".

11. Advertisement in *Psychology Today* (February 1981):
Buy a 14K Gold Heart for $5 Until May 25. As part of an advertising program we will send a solid 14K gold floating heart pendant charm to every reader of *Psychology Today* who reads and responds to this printed notice before Midnight, May 25, for the sum of $5 plus $1 shipping and handling. . . . There is a limit of one (1) heart per address, but if your request is made before May 16, you may request a second heart by enclosing an additional $5 plus $1 shipping and handling. No request will be accepted past the dates noted above; your uncashed check will be returned if postmarked later than those dates.

12. *Bufferin* advertisement:
No regular aspirin product reduces fever better.

13. *Crest* commercial on TV:
Announcer: Hey, some smile. . . . Brushing with Crest?
Person: A smile's gotta last a lifetime; can't afford cavities.
Announcer: Figured you for an exciting stripe or gel.
Person: Toothpastes don't excite me. Beautiful checkups, *that* excites me. . . . Crest works. Has more evidence . . . In my lifetime alone, Crest fluoristan has prevented more cavities than all other toothpastes combined. . . . Brush up on the evidence—you end up with Crest on your brush.
Voice: More evidence—great checkups.
Person: *That's* exciting.

14. From the side of a *Cap'n Crunch* cereal box:
It makes sense to include vitamin-fortified *Cap'n Crunch* as part of a nutritious breakfast. Served with 1/2 cup milk, one ounce of *Cap'n Crunch* provides 25% of the U.S. Recommended Daily Allowances of eight essential vitamins and minerals.

9 Begging the Question

When arguing, it is impossible to provide reasons for every claim. Some of what we say or do must go unjustified, at least for the moment. But if, in the course of a discussion or debate, we endorse without proof some form or other of the very question at issue, we are guilty of the fallacy often called **begging the question,** or **circular reasoning,*** a species of the broad category *unwarranted premise*.

A person commits the fallacy of *begging the question* when trying to prove to a nonbeliever that God exists because it says so in the Bible, since acceptance of what is said in the Bible itself rests on belief that the Bible is inspired by God. (Notice that the fallacy *begging the question* is

*The fallacy *begging the question* is hard to state precisely so as not to beg several philosophical questions. For instance, as we've defined it here, anyone who is (otherwise) justified in accepting the conclusion of a deductively valid argument is guilty of this fallacy *if* the "containment" theory of valid deduction—mentioned on page 5—is correct, since on that view such a conclusion merely repeats explicitly what the premises say implicitly. In such a case, no question is begged if the explicit information in the conclusion is *psychologically* new, even though logically equivalent to what is questioned, or at issue. For more on underlying issues related to the "spelling out" theory, see Richard Cole and Howard Kahane, "Hard and Soft Intensionalism", *Review of Metaphysics,* vol. XXIII (1970), pp. 399–416.

not automatically committed by just any reference to Biblical statements that God exists. Such a reference at, say, a revival meeting would probably not be question begging, since God's existence would probably not be *questioned*, or *at issue*, in such a setting.)

Political arguments frequently beg the question. For instance, a person testifying during the 1972 controversy over abortion laws in Massachusetts argued that abortion is wrong since a baby shouldn't have to suffer because of the selfish desires or the illness of the mother. But by calling the fetus a *baby*, the arguer implicitly claimed it is a human being, which is an important point at issue in the abortion dispute.

10 *False Dilemma*

Another fallacy in the category *unwarranted premise* is that of **false dilemma.** This fallacy occurs when the number of possible positions or alternatives to some question is erroneously reduced. Usually the improper reduction is to just two alternatives (which accounts for the name *black and white* often given to this fallacy).

The man who divides all other nations in the world into those that are communist and hence anti-United States, and those that are anti-communist and hence pro-United States, commits this fallacy, because he fails to consider the possibility that some nations might be neutral or perhaps against both the United States and the communist nations. Similarly, the person who argues for capitalism on the grounds that its alternative, socialism, is unacceptable, is guilty of this fallacy because he overlooks the possibility of various *combinations* of socialism and capitalism as well as other economic systems.

Of course, the invitation to fall for the fallacy of *false dilemma* isn't going to carry a label on it. Here is part of an advertisement for the "Warren–Barnhart Debate" held at North Texas State University in 1980:

> The arena has been set. The contestants are preparing themselves. The event—the Warren–Barnhart debate. On the timely question of ethics and morality. Dr. Barnhart's position is that if an act brings pleasure, then it is right. If an act is unpleasant, then it is wrong. But if two actions bring pleasure, then the one with the greatest amount of pleasure should be adopted. Dr. Warren's position is that an act is right or wrong based upon God's word—the New Testament. The stances have been made. The time is drawing nigh for the confrontation. The only thing lacking now are the spectators. And their judgment of which position is right.

Notice how the last line invites us to suppose that one or the other of the two views presented is correct, thus leading us to ignore the many other possibilities and accept the debate winner's position as correct.

11 *Straw Man*

A person who misinterprets an opponent's position so that it will be easier to attack, or attacks weaker opponents while ignoring the arguments of stronger opponents, commits the fallacy of the **straw man.** This fallacy is the stock in trade of most politicians. For instance, when running for office (which is usually), they are fond of characterizing the positions of their opponents in the poorest possible way, making it all the easier to knock them down.

Throughout his career, Richard Nixon was a master at the *straw man* game. Here is a rather mild example from a 1970 speech:*

> There are those who protest that if the verdict of democracy goes against them, democracy itself is at fault, the system is at fault; who say that if they don't get their own way, the answer is to burn or bomb a building.

He then was able to easily demolish this very weak position. Nixon was referring to "radical liberals", one small and very vulnerable group within the liberal opposition to his policies. By attacking them, while ignoring liberals with more plausible objections and less extreme behavior, he made it appear that his typical opponent, or at least a large number of his opponents, held such views. (Had he also attacked the more important of his opponents, the matter would have been different. But he didn't.) Thus, his comment constitutes an attack on a relatively straw man.

This attack also contained another element of the fallacy of the *straw man*. For not only did he select his weakest political opponents to attack, but he also misrepresented their position. For in 1970 the Far Left did not argue that if they didn't get their own way, the answer is to burn or bomb; rather they argued that when *justice* cannot be obtained in any other way, when the government won't respond to peaceful demands for justice, *then* violence is required.

Political uses of *straw man* tend to be versions of the broader category *unwarranted premise*. In Nixon's case, he wanted us to accept the conclusion that he was better than his opponents by presenting us with unwarranted versions of his opponents' positions, which he expected (usually correctly) most people would not question. (The fallacy *straw man* also illustrates how easy it is to fleece the ignorant. A person absolutely ignorant about the political arena would have no reason to doubt Nixon's pronouncements.)

Straw man is often used in denying an allegation. The trick is to deny a straw allegation instead of the real one. (Your denial may then even have the virtue of being true.) Of course, you haven't denied the actual charge leveled against you, but if you're lucky, or ingenious, that may not be noticed.

Congressman Wayne Hays, accused of putting his mistress, Elizabeth Ray, on his congressional payroll as a typist (true) denied he ever put her

---

* Delivered at Kansas State University, September 16, 1970. For other Nixon examples of *straw man*, see his 1972 Republican convention acceptance speech, in which he outrageously distorted the positions of his Democratic party opponents before replying to them.

on his payroll "as a mistress". Of course not. That was the problem; supposedly she was being paid for typing. (This trick gave Hays a slight respite, but timing was against him; the Ray–Hays scandal followed on the heels of the more serious Wilbur Mills–Fanny Foxe scandal.)

12 *Provincialism*

The fallacy of **provincialism** is committed when someone accepts (or rejects) a statement or argument (in particular on a controversial topic) *because* he identifies with a particular group. For instance, this fallacy is committed by Americans who reject claims that U.S. Army men in Vietnam committed atrocities, or that U.S. airmen bombed civilians, because "our boys" couldn't do such a thing.

Provincialism is often believed to be a fallacy committed almost exclusively by the uneducated or the unscientific. But that is not true. As an example, Dr. Andrew Patterson, advisor to the New York Knicks basketball team and presumably a scientifically trained person, rejected the use of acupuncture on Knicks players, stating, "as far as I'm concerned, there is simply not enough demonstrable evidence at the present time to prove it has any scientific merit".* What the good doctor meant, of course, was *Western* evidence; the Chinese had plenty of evidence on the merits of acupuncture, which few Western doctors had bothered to examine.

13 *Ad Hominem Argument*

The fallacy of **ad hominem** argument consists of an attack on the person who argued against, rather than his argument. For instance, the person who replied to the arguments of a draft evader against our involvement in Vietnam by calling the draft evader a coward committed this fallacy.

Indeed, *ad hominem* argument is quite common in politics, where it frequently is sufficient to brand an opponent as a communist, socialist, or anarchist to dispose of his arguments. Thus Richard Nixon's opponents in his early California campaigns were defeated not by attacks against their arguments or positions, but rather by being branded as "pinkos".

But *ad hominem* arguments are not always fallacious. For instance, a lawyer who attacks the testimony of a witness by questioning his or her moral character argues *ad hominem* but may not commit a fallacy.

The question of when an *ad hominem* argument is fallacious, and when not, is quite complex. In general, it can be said that such an argument is

---

* *New York Daily News*, 28 March 1972, p. 85.

not fallacious when the person argued against is or claims to be an *expert* on the question at issue. Courtroom witnesses, doctors, auto mechanics, lawyers, and others often present arguments against which we, as nonexperts, may be unable to argue directly. So information about the character of an expert may well be an important kind of evidence in deciding whether to accept or reject an expert's opinion.

But in these cases, we certainly do not prove by *ad hominem* argument that the expert testimony or advice is incorrect. At best, an *ad hominem* argument only provides grounds for canceling or disregarding the testimony or advice of an expert. It does not provide good grounds for assuming that the expert's opinion is incorrect. For instance, if a doctor who advises operating on a particular patient turns out to be a charlatan, it is rash to conclude that no operation is necessary.

In general, fallacious *ad hominems* are examples of the broader category *invalid inference,* since such attacks do not justify the intended conclusion that the person attacked is not to be believed.

14 *Hasty Conclusion*

The fallacy of **hasty conclusion** is committed when a conclusion is accepted on the basis of relevant but insufficient evidence.

The most common variety of hasty conclusion is the fallacy of the **questionable cause** (traditionally referred to by its Latin name *post hoc, ergo propter hoc*—after this, therefore because of this). In this variation, the conclusion hastily arrived at is that something is the *cause* of something else. Robert Dole was guilty of this fallacy during his 1976 run for vice-president when he blamed all four wars we have engaged in in this century on the Democrats on grounds that the Democrats were in power in Washington when we entered each of them.

A church message that argued against current criticisms of the "proven worthy traditions of patriotism, permanent family ties, the Church and the Protestant concept that working to succeed is a good thing" gave as evidence the following:

> Last weekend Australia played the USA in World Cup Tennis. Interviews with Australian players indicated that they were keyed up to win for the honor of their country. Interviews with Americans indicated they didn't even understand this patriotic motivation; that they were playing for personal success and mostly for the money. RESULT—Australia won six matches; the USA one.

But the conclusion was a bit hasty. Isn't it possible, even likely, that Australia won because on that day they were represented by more talented tennis players? Before accepting the conclusion that lack of patriotism did us in, we ought to check other cases to determine the motivating power of patriotism versus that of personal glory and money.

15 *Statistical Fallacies*

Statistical fallacies are primarily just statistical variations of standard fallacies. But because all of us are subject to a flood of statistics these days, perhaps a separate discussion of a few statistical fallacies is in order.

Small Sample

The fallacy of the **small sample** is the statistical analogue of the fallacy of *hasty conclusion*. For instance, this fallacy is committed when we project the results of a poll of two or three hundred students around the nation onto the entire U.S. college student population.

An interesting variation on this fallacy concerns statistical trends involving small populations. For instance, a newspaper headline stated that crimes of violence increased 25 percent in a certain locality over the previous year; but it turned out that the increase was from four crimes of this type last year to five this year.

Faulty Comparison

Statistics have such an authoritative ring that it seems possible to do just about anything with them and get away with it. One trick is to compare statistics in a way that *seems* to yield significant results but in fact does not, because the statistics are not of comparable types or quality, or because a more important statistical comparison has been overlooked or suppressed. Let's call this the fallacy of **faulty comparison.**

Gerald Ford was guilty of this fallacy several times during the 1976 presidential campaign debates, as well as in his 60-second radio and TV spot commercials. He argued that his record on unemployment was good on grounds that more Americans had jobs in 1976 during his administration than ever before in our history. But in doing so, he appealed to statistics that were irrelevant to the claim they were intended to support. His trick becomes clear when we look at statistics he suppressed that show that more Americans also were *un*employed during his administration than ever before in our history—the higher employment and unemployment both resulting from the fact that there were more Americans alive during his administration than ever before in our history. He should have compared the *percentage* of the work force unemployed during his time in office with those of recent administrations, but this comparison would have shown Ford's record to be one of the worst in recent history, so Ford chose to ignore it. (Incidentally, Ronald Reagan was guilty of pretty much the same ploy in the 1984 campaign.)

Here is an example of an interesting variety of *faulty comparison*. Suppose it is discovered that 0.05 percent of all women who use a particular kind of birth control pill get a blood clot of a certain kind. If we conclude that there is a significant statistical connection between taking birth control pills and getting blood clots, then we reason fallaciously; for we must determine how many women get blood clots of this kind who do *not* use this birth control pill. The statistic 0.05 percent indicates a causal correlation only if it varies significantly from the statistic concerning women who do not use the pill. In other words, the correct comparison is between 0.05 percent and the percentage, whatever it is, of those women not using the pill who get blood clots.

Statistical trends also can be misleading if based on information of differing quality. One of the best examples is the current claim made by many police officials around the country that there is much more crime today than there was 50 or 100 years ago. These officials cite statistics on complaints, arrests, and so on, which seem to uphold their claims that crime is increasing. But we have good reason to believe that the collection of crime information has greatly improved over the years, and that some localities keep better records than others. Hence, we cannot make quick comparisons based on statistics that differ so greatly in quality.

Biased Statistics

The fallacy of **biased statistics** is committed when we use statistics drawn from a sample that we know (or should know) is not likely to be *representative* of the population being sampled.

During the 1936 presidential election, the *Literary Digest* conducted a pre-election poll, obtaining the names of those polled primarily from telephone directories and lists of automobile registrations, and predicted that Alf Landon would defeat Franklin Roosevelt. (The actual election, of course, resulted in a tremendous landslide victory for Roosevelt.) The magazine's mistake consisted in failing to realize that the persons polled were very unlikely to be representative of the voting population as a whole. The average income of those polled was bound to be much higher than the national average, since in those days many more people than now were poor, and most of the poor could not afford telephones or automobiles. Since economic status tends to influence voting preferences, a representative political poll must reflect all economic levels in a society. A poll that doesn't do so will be relatively useless.

The fallacy of *biased statistics* (a species of *suppressed evidence*) is extremely common, in particular because of wishful thinking and self-deception. One of the great truths about human nature is that in certain circumstances, especially when their own important interests are at stake, people will tend to find reasons for believing what they want to believe, if at all possible. Sixteenth-century Italian historian, Guicciardini, noted this truth in the following remark concerning the persistence of belief in astrology in the face of overwhelming negative evidence: "How happy are the astrologers, who are believed if they tell one truth to a hundred lies, while other people lose all credit if they tell one lie to a hundred truths".

Unknowable Statistics

Statistics often are made up or guessed at on the basis of little or no evidence, or stated so that their approximate nature is masked in precision. When statistics of this kind are used as though they were the genuine article, the result is the fallacy of the **unknowable statistic.** A marvelous example of this fallacy is contained in a request for funds to prevent war, which began:

> Dear Friend: In the past 5,000 years men have fought in 14,523 wars. One out of four persons living during this time have been war casualties. A nuclear war would add 1,245,000,000 men, women, and children to this tragic list.

Precise figures, such as 14,523, give the impression that historians have compiled a vast list of all wars fought in the last 5,000 years, whereas in fact no such list has been (or will be) compiled. The best we can do is estimate roughly how many wars have occurred, based on our limited knowledge of a very small sample of known wars. (Thus, after great study, someone might be able to estimate that roughly 10,000 to 25,000 wars have occurred in the past 5,000 years, without committing the fallacy.) But we cannot even make a rough estimate of the number of human beings who would be killed in a nuclear war. There is no generally accepted method for arriving at such an estimate, and even the "experts" who are willing to venture a guess do so hesitantly, often making estimates that differ widely from those of other "experts". For human beings today, this kind of statistic is essentially unknowable.

Accidental Correlation

The fallacy of **accidental correlation** consists in erroneously assuming that a correlation observed between two or more factors represents a *causal* correlation. (This is a variety of the fallacy *questionable cause.*) For example, when black servicemen scored lower than whites on U.S. Army IQ tests during World Wars I and II, many whites took this to be proof that whites have higher average native intelligence than blacks. But, passing over the question whether some single thing exists, called *intelligence,* and that IQ tests accurately measure it, background information leads us to suspect that environmental differences between U.S. blacks and whites may very well account for differences in test scores.

Taking the statistical correlation as a *causal* connection thus makes one guilty of the fallacy *accidental correlation*. (Interestingly, whites who argued that the Army test scores proved whites more intelligent on an average than blacks passed over test results showing northern whites *and blacks* did better on World War I tests than did southern *whites;* they didn't conclude that northern blacks are more intelligent on an average than southern whites. Similarly, although U.S. Jews, and now Asians, average higher on IQ tests than most other U.S. groups, few theorists argue that these groups have higher average native intelligence.)

16 Some Other (Traditional) Fallacies

Let's end our account of fallacies with a brief discussion of a few other fallacies usually disussed in traditional texts.

Amphiboly

The fallacy of **amphiboly** is a variation of the fallacy of *ambiguity*. Someone commits this fallacy when he or she is deceived or confused by an ambiguous *grammatical construction* rather than by ambiguous words.

Since serious current examples occur so rarely, textbook writers* generally resort to ancient examples (Oracle at Delphi: "If Croesus went to war with Cyrus, he would destroy a mighty kingdom"), or to amusing but trivial ones (World War II poster: "Save soap and waste paper").†

Composition and Division

The fallacy of **composition** is committed when we reason that some property possessed by every member of a class (or every part of a whole) also is possessed by the class (or whole). The fallacy of **division** is just the opposite. It is committed when we infer that some property of a class (or whole) is a property of each of its members (or parts).

Textbook examples of the fallacies of *composition* and *division* tend to be contrived or trivial. Thus one textbook gives as an example of the fallacy of *composition* the argument that " . . . since every part of a certain machine is light in weight, the machine as a whole is light in weight", and of *division* the argument that " . . . a girl must have a large room because she lives in a large dormitory".

---

* Including, it must be admitted, this one when writing the first edition of this text.

† Both of these examples (and one to follow soon) are taken from Irving M. Copi, *Introduction to Logic*, 4th ed. (New York: Macmillan, 1972), pp. 93–94.

A more serious example of the fallacy of *composition* is the "salesman's fallacy".* Salesmen often state the price of an item in terms of monthly, weekly, or even daily payments ("Just put two quarters in the slot every day . . . "), thus hiding an item's true (high) price in the small amount of each installment. Some auto salesmen, for instance, answer questions about auto prices by providing monthly payment figures, expecting (correctly) that some buyers will not add up the total to find the real cost of an automobile.

Appeal to Force

The fallacy of **appeal to force** (Latin name: *argumentum ad baculum*) is said to be committed when an attempt is made to persuade someone to accept a conclusion by applying pressure of some kind or other.

But *appeal to force* is not a fallacy, even according to the definitions of fallacy given in traditional texts. For instance, a senator who votes for a certain bill because of pressure applied by a lobbyist is not necessarily convinced that the bill is a good one. (This is a standard textbook example.) Rather he is convinced of the quite different conclusion that it is in his best interests to *vote* for the bill, and that conclusion, unfortunately for democracy, frequently is not fallacious.

Appeal to Pity

The fallacy of **appeal to pity** (Latin name: *argumentum ad misericordiam*) is committed when one is persuaded to accept a conclusion because of pity or sympathy. For instance, it is committed by a juror who votes for acquittal out of sympathy for the accused.

Many cases generally considered to be instances of this fallacy very likely are not. For instance, when a juror votes for acquittal out of pity, it is not at all clear that pity has persuaded him of the *innocence* of the accused. The vote for acquittal may indicate simply that the juror has been persuaded that the accused should not be punished, whether guilty or not.

Formal and Informal Fallacies

Traditional textbooks generally divide all fallacies into two kinds: *formal* and *informal*. The term **formal fallacy** is generally applied to invalid arguments that *resemble* valid deductive arguments. They are said to be fallacies of *structure* or *form* as opposed to *content*. The standard examples are syllogisms that violate any of the rules of valid syllogism discussed in the previous chapter, and the fallacies of *affirming the*

---

* Thanks to Nelson Pole for pointing out this variety of *composition*, and for giving it the appropriate name.

consequent and *denying the antecedent*. *Affirming the consequent* has the form "If p then q, q, $/\therefore p$", while *denying the antecedent* has the form "If p then q, not p, $/\therefore$ not q".

In contrast, an **informal fallacy** is said to be a fallacy of *content* rather than *structure* or *form*. Most of the fallacies we have discussed above are generally classified as informal.

But this division of fallacies into formal and informal suffers from two major defects. First, the fallacies usually placed in the category *formal fallacy* hardly ever occur in serious technical writing or even in daily life (because everyday arguments just aren't that "tight"). Thus, this category has little practical use. And second, many instances of the so-called informal fallacies are invalid, and thus just as fallacious because of their form as instances of, say, *affirming the consequent*.

Exercise 12-2:

Determine which fallacies (if any) occur in each of the following items, and state your reasons for thinking so. For example, if you think the fallacy is straw man, show how the straw position distorts the real one, and if false dilemma, how there are other alternatives. (Remember that fallacies in daily life are often not clear-cut.)

1. Bumper sticker:

   America. Love It or Leave It.

2. Academy Award Winner Louise Fletcher Falls Victim to Oscar's Marital Jinx

   (Headline on article in *Midnight,* 15 November 1976—in the article that follows we learned that she had become the sixth female Oscar winner in the last twelve years to experience marital difficulties.)

3. The astonishing strength of President Ford in the middle-income retirement village of Leisureville here raises the possibility of a Florida primary win Tuesday decisive enough to crush Ronald Reagan's hopes for the presidential nomination. . . . We interviewed registered Republicans with the help of [Patrick] Caddell's polltakers and found these results: 37 for Ford; 13 for Reagan; 6 undecided. (Evans and Novak, *New York Post,* 5 March 1976)

4. . . . Capitalism is the economic system in which the means of production and distribution are privately owned and operated for profit. The alternative system is called socialism, the theory of the ownership and operation of the means of production by society, with all members sharing in the work and the products. (John S. Knight, *Detroit Free Press,* 3 July 1970)

5. Dear Former Subscriber:
   By 1750, humanity's fund of knowledge had doubled from what it was at the birth of Christ. It doubled again by 1900. And again by 1950. And again by 1960. And yet again by 1968. Mankind is gaining knowledge at an astonishing accelerating rate. Which means that it becomes increasingly difficult for any one individual to keep pace. And keep from becoming intellectually obsolete. (Subscription letter from *Intellectual Digest*)

6. It's a known fact that people who brush their teeth regularly have less tooth decay and fewer gum problems. And what you're doing when you brush your teeth is remove the film of *plaque*, which forms on teeth and gums. When you brush, scientists have therefore concluded, you stop tooth decay by removing the plaque. So you can forget fluorides, calcium, and all the rest; brush your teeth carefully and say goodbye to cavities. . . . It was also learned recently that people in low income areas have six times as many cavities as people in higher income areas. So dental hygienists now feel we have to get children in poorer areas to brush their teeth as well as do children in other neighborhoods.

7. *Quaker Oats box top:*

   Free Cookie Tin with two proofs of purchase and 75¢
   See back

8. After presenting statistics showing that National League batters were hitting more home runs, getting more base hits, and so on, than American League batters, and concluding that National League batters were just better, a Hartford *Courant* sports writer (Terry Price, 29 August 1972) presented the following corroborating evidence: Many staunch AL fans will argue that the pitching in the junior loop (AL) is superior to that in the senior circuit and perhaps they are right—but not by much. Twenty-eight pitchers in the AL have earned run averages under 3.00 while twenty-four moundsmen in the NL are under that mark.

9. The question has been whether (a) you permit migrant workers, many of whom come in from Mexico, to continue to work at a price that is acceptable to employer and employees; or (b) you simply forbid said workers to come in to work at wages we consider too low. (William F. Buckley, Jr., in a 1970 political column)

10. An American Auto Association ad for new members pointed out that over 23,000,000 Americans had joined, and said,

    Over 23,000,000 can't be wrong! You owe it to yourself to investigate!

11. Letter to the Editor:
    Wondering if perhaps all the complaining about the poor old Post Office might not be a bit wide of the mark, I arranged to have friends in Chicago and Boston mail letters to me in Philadelphia. Both letters were mailed at about 4:30 P.M. on June 21, the Boston letter arriving in my box at 11:45 A.M. the next day and the Chicago letter the following morning. Was service any better in the "good old days"? Enough with knocking the Post Office. Mail service is just about as fast as could reasonably be expected, and I proved it!

12. John Stuart Mill furnishes us another example in support of the theory. For he had an extremely intellectual and intelligent father, James Mill, and was taught most academic subjects at an extremely early age. The result, just as our theory would predict: an IQ of 185 for John Stuart Mill. (Article on human intelligence and environment, making reference to the nineteenth-century philosopher and his father.)

13. **Exam question:** What is the best complete moral theory (that is, best complete set of rules to decide which actions people ought to do) that you know of?
    Student answer: I believe that every person is free to do what they want to do, so long as they do not infringe on the rights of others—the crux of my moral theory is that no person has a right to infringe on the rights of others.

14. From a student term paper: Capital punishment is sometimes O.K. A mass murderer who is freed may kill again. So we are justified in taking his life, because the public would suffer terror and fear if we set him free.

15. Jay Gourley, reporter for the *National Enquirer*, responding to the charge that he invaded Henry Kissinger's privacy in reporting on the contents of garbage taken from Kissinger's house (reported in *Washington Monthly*, October 1975):

    Of all the printed commentary . . . only a few editorial writers thought to express the obvious point that when it comes to invasion of privacy, the man who as National Security Advisor helped bug the home phones of his own staff members is one of our nation's leading practitioners.

16. **Jane:** Abortion is murder. So it's wrong.
McBird: It isn't murder, because a fetus isn't a human being.
Jane: Listen. Let's look it up in the new medical dictionary you got for Christmas. I'm sure it'll have whether a fetus is a person or not.
McBird: Of course; that'll settle the argument.

17. **Jane:** White women are more irresistible than black women.
McBird: What makes you think so?
Jane: They get raped ten times as often.
McBird: How do you know a thing like that?
Jane: I've been keeping track in several Connecticut newspapers, and ten times as many rapes of white women are reported as of black women.

18. Article in *Washington Star* (26 September 1980):
Detroit—Republican presidents tend to have an erratic effect on car production, which generally is more stable under Democratic administrations. If Ronald Reagan becomes our next president, the odds are 2-to-1 that the assembly lines will turn more slowly in 1981 than in 1980. If Jimmy Carter is re-elected, auto output is sure to climb. This is the indication from the auto-making trend of the post-World War II administrations of Presidents Harry Truman, Dwight Eisenhower, John Kennedy, Lyndon Johnson, Richard Nixon, Gerald Ford, and Jimmy Carter.
Current events in Detroit favor Reagan. When auto production goes up in an election year, history says a Democrat is twice as likely to win the presidency as a Republican. But when output goes down, as it has this year, Democrats have never won. Adlai Stevenson was twice victimized by that political peculiarity at the hands of Eisenhower.

19. **McBird:** I can prove to you that five is both odd and even. Wanna bet?
Jane: Sure, I'll bet. I'm too smart to fall for stupid reasoning.
McBird: Well, three and two are odd and even. Right?
Jane: Yes, of course.
McBird: And five is three and two?
Jane: Yes, yes.
McBird: Well, if three and two are odd and even, and five is three and two, then it follows by logic that five is odd and even. Gotcha!
Jane: Hmmm. You are a sneaky one, McBird.

20. Pope Pius XII (in 1944):
If the exclusive aim of nature [for sexual intercourse] or at least its primary intent had been the mutual giving and possessing of husband and wife in pleasure and delight; if nature had arranged that act only to make their personal experience joyous in the highest degree, and not as an incentive in the service of life; then the Creator would have made use of another plan in the formation of the marital act.

21. Skydivers are sometimes considered flaky—people with a death wish. Not so, says [George] Kreiger [leader of U.S. parachute team competing in Rome for World Championship]. "That's a distorted image. We know what we are doing. There are very few injuries, even sprained ankles. The fatality rate is less than 1/2 of 1 percent". (*Baltimore Evening Sun,* 24 August 1976).

22. From review of James Michener's book *Iberia:* "Some things haven't changed. Michener leads off his chapter on bullfights with an argument between [an] American and Spaniard about brutal sports—which the Spaniard wins by pointing out that more young men get killed playing American football than in the bullring".

23. Letter from the National Association of Female Executives, Inc.:
Dear Career Woman:
Does [belonging to] NAFE really help?
Only 9.7% of American working women earn over $15,000 a year—but *75% of NAFE members do.* Only 0.8% of American working women earn over $25,000 a year—*but 25% of NAFE members do.* We can't guarantee that NAFE membership will automatically double or triple your salary, but most of our members do credit us with helping them advance in their careers farther, faster, and easier than they otherwise would have.

24. Article in *The Nation* on the Three Mile Island nuclear leak and shutdown, 25 April 1981: Dr. George Tokuhata, director of the Pennsylvania Bureau of Epidemological Research, announced, according to a March 20 story by United Press International, that "final figures now indicate that there had been no rise in the infant mortality rate in the ten-mile radius of the plant".

 . . . A key support for his conclusion was his finding that the infant mortality rate within a ten-mile radius of the plant was the same—19.3 deaths per thousand live births—in the three-month period after the accident on March 28, 1979, as it was in the January–March period just before it.

25. Monsanto Chemical Company advertisement:

 Mother Nature is lucky her products don't need labels. All foods, even natural ones, are made up of chemicals. But natural foods don't have to list their ingredients. So it's often assumed they're chemical-free. In fact, the ordinary orange is a miniature chemical factory. . . . This doesn't mean natural foods are dangerous. If they were, they wouldn't be on the market. The same is true of man-made foods. All man-made foods are tested for safety. And they often provide more nutrition, at a lower cost, than natural foods. They even use many of the same chemical ingredients. So you see, there really isn't much difference between foods made by Mother Nature and those made by man. What's artificial is the line drawn between them. **Monsanto:** Without chemicals, life itself would be impossible.

26. Item from the Cato Institute *Policy Report:* Postmaster General William Bolger Thursday defended his decision to lease a private jet—at $47,000 a month—as a way to save "executive time". . . .

 Bolger acknowledged he can't justify the lease "on the basis of cost" but said, "pure economic justification is not the measure by which the true value of efficient transportation should be judged" (*U.S.A. Today,* 16 December 1983).

Key Terms Introduced in Chapter Twelve

Accidental correlation: The fallacy of erroneously assuming that an observed correlation represents a *causal* correlation.

Ad hominem argument: The fallacy of attacking the person who argues rather than his or her argument.

Ambiguity: The fallacy resulting from ambiguous use of terms. An ambiguous term is one that has more than one meaning. *Synonym:* **Equivocation.**

Amphiboly: The fallacy resulting from ambiguity of grammatical construction rather than of terms.

Appeal to authority: Incorrect acceptance of a conclusion solely or primarily on the word of an authority. *Synonym:* **Argumentum ad verecundiam.**

Appeal to force: The attempt to persuade by means of force or threats. *Synonym:* **Argumentum ad baculum.**

Appeal to pity: The attempt to persuade by appeal to pity. *Synonym:* **Argumentum ad misericordiam.**

Argumentum ad baculum: (See **Appeal to force.**)

Argumentum ad misericordiam: (See **Appeal to pity.**)

Argumentum ad verecundiam: (See **Appeal to authority.**)

Begging the question: An argument that is viciously circular. (See also **Circular reasoning.**)

Biased statistics: The fallacy of reasoning from statistics or evidence known to be nonrepresentative of the population as a whole.

Circular reasoning: Fallaciously using an intended conclusion, usually expressed in different words, to support that conclusion. (See also **Begging the question.**)

Cogent argument: An argument that is valid, has warranted premises, and uses all relevant information available or known to the arguer. *Antonym:* **Fallacious argument.**

Commission of a fallacy: Fallacious reasoning or arguing.

Composition: The fallacy of reasoning from the fact that every member of a class (or every part of a whole) has a certain property to the conclusion that the class itself (or the whole itself) has that property.

Division: The fallacy of reasoning from the fact that a certain class (or whole) has a given property to the conclusion that every member of the class (or every part of the whole) has that property.

Equivocation: (See **Ambiguity.**)

Fallacious argument: An argument that is not cogent, because it is invalid, has unwarranted premises, or fails to take account of available relevant information. *Antonym:* **Cogent argument.**

False dilemma: The erroneous reduction of the number of possible positions or alternatives in order to argue for one of the stated alternatives.

Faulty comparison: The fallacy of incorrectly comparing data that differ in quality or are of incomparable types.

Formal fallacy: A fallacy that closely resembles a valid argument form of some deductive system.

Hasty conclusion: The fallacy of too quickly generalizing from one or a few instances.

Inconsistency: The fallacy of arguing from inconsistent premises, or inconsistent conclusions. Also committed by an inconsistency between words and actions.

Informal fallacy: A fallacy of *content,* rather than structure.

Provincialism: Acceptance or rejection of a statement or argument *because* of identification with a particular group.

Questionable cause: The variety of the fallacy *hasty conclusion* in which we conclude (hastily) that one thing is the cause of something else.

Small sample: The fallacy of reasoning from too small a sample. This fallacy is the statistical analogue of the fallacy of hasty conclusion.

Straw man: Arguing against a proposition similar to the position of one's opponent but different in ways that make it easier to attack, or being convinced by such an argument.

Suppressed evidence: Arguing so as to conceal evidence unfavorable to one's conclusion. Anyone convinced by such an argument who should have realized that evidence was being suppressed also commits this fallacy.

Two wrongs make a right: The fallacy in which a charge is answered by a similar countercharge. The defense "Well, you did the same thing yourself" generally commits this fallacy.

Unknowable statistic: The fallacy committed when statistics are made up, or guessed at, on insufficient evidence, or when the approximate nature of the statistics is masked in precision.

Unwarranted premise: Arguing from, or being convinced by, an argument containing a premise one ought to doubt.

Unwarranted statement: Arguing from, or being convinced by, a statement one ought to doubt.

Chapter Thirteen

Definitions

Traditional logic texts, and many modern ones, contain material on definitions. Given the importance of keeping straight the meanings of terms and phrases, and the ease with which ambiguity creeps into and ruins otherwise good reasoning, inclusion of this material in a logic text is not surprising.

A **definition** is an explanation of the meaning of a word (or phrase). In this sense, definitions are about *words,* and not about the things words are used to talk about. For instance, the dictionary definition

automobile: a self-propelled vehicle suitable for use on a street or roadway

does not say anything about automobiles, but rather explains the meaning of the *word* "automobile". To be precise, then, we should place the term "automobile" and the phrase used to define it in quotes, to indicate that we are speaking about words, and not about things referred to by those words. Thus, we should write the above definition as follows:

"Automobile" means the same as "self-propelled vehicle suitable for use on a street or roadway".

We introduce the symbol $= df$ to abbreviate the phrase "means the same as". Thus the above definition can be written "automobile" $= df$ "self-propelled vehicle suitable for use on a street or roadway".

When we define a word by furnishing other words that have the same meaning, the word so defined is said to be the **definiendum** and the words that define it the **definiens.** In the example just given, "automobile" is the definiendum and "self-propelled vehicle suitable for use on a street or roadway" is the definiens.

1 *Lexical and Stipulative Definitions*

There are many different kinds of definitions. Two important kinds are *lexical* and *stipulative*. A **lexical definition** is one that attempts to report usage. Thus, all good dictionary definitions are lexical, since they tell how the words of a particular language actually are used by the speakers of that language.

Sometimes it is quite difficult to provide good lexical definitions. One reason for this is that words often are **ambiguous,** that is, have more than one meaning. An example is the word "mouth", which sometimes is used to refer to a portion of the human anatomy and sometimes to the place where a river enters a larger body of water.

It often is difficult to keep the different meanings of a term separate. One dictionary distinguishes thirty-one different meanings for the word "good". Clearly, some of these meanings must differ from others in very subtle ways that could easily be confused. (This is the chief psychological reason for the ease with which the fallacy of equivocation, discussed in the previous chapter, is committed.)

Another reason for the difficulty in providing good lexical definitions is that it often is quite difficult to find a set of properties such that all and only those things denoted by the term to be defined have that set of properties. Take the word "automobile". What set of properties do all automobiles have that no other objects have? The definition cited above does not list such a set, since motorcycles, motor scooters, go-carts, even tractors and tanks have the properties of being self-propelled and suitable for use on streets or roadways.

Finally, a major reason for the difficulty in providing good lexical definitions is that most words in natural languages are **vague,** that is, do not have a precise meaning. Is a three-wheeled motor vehicle an automobile? Is a station wagon? A bus? A truck? How small can an automobile be before it becomes a *toy* automobile? Ordinary usage does not provide answers to questions of this kind; the word "automobile" is vague. Another example is the word "tall". At what height does an adult human being cease being of medium height and become tall? Ordinary usage does not provide a precise answer to this question.

Notice also that vagueness is not always a bad quality. Often, terms are vague because they are more useful that way. For instance, the word "tall" is useful precisely because it is vague, since "tall" is a term we often use when we don't choose to (or can't) state the exact height of someone. If we always had to be absolutely precise in what we say, most of us would have to remain silent most of the time.

Of course, one important use of vague (as well as ambiguous) language is to obfuscate or bamboozle. Where, for instance, would political rhetoric be if no terms were vague or ambiguous?

A **stipulative definition** is one which, instead of reporting actual usage, *specifies* or *stipulates* the meaning of a word or phrase. For instance, a state legislature may stipulate that for purposes of a particular statute the term "automobile" shall mean "self-propelled vehicle having more than three wheels whose primary purpose is to convey human beings from place to place". Or a college catalogue may define the term "college" as meaning "four-year accredited institution of higher learning".

Stipulative definitions can be divided into two main kinds, namely those that introduce brand-new terms and those that stipulate new meanings for old terms ("reforming" definitions). For instance, we could stipulate that the brand-new term "multimarried" mean "person married more than twice", and the brand-new term "aunticle" mean "aunt or uncle". Or we might stipulate that the old term "valid argument" mean "argument for which there is a proof in predicate logic".

Stipulative definitions that specify new meanings for old terms also can be broken down into two kinds, namely those that *add to the meaning* of an old term, by reducing its vagueness, and those that *change the meaning* of an old term in areas in which they are already clear. For instance, we reduce the vagueness of the already existing term "skyscraper" by defining it to mean "building over 500 feet tall". And we change the meaning of an old term in an area in which it is already clear when we define the term "democracy" to mean "dictatorship of the proletariat".

Reforming definitions play a particularly important role in the law and in science. In the law they are important because the answer to the question whether a statute applies in a particular case often hinges on the meaning of a term that is vague in everyday use. For example, if a statute levying a tax on automobiles fails to provide a stipulative definition for the term "automobile", there will be no way to know whether to levy the tax on motorcycles, motor scooters, three-wheeled vehicles, taxis, or station wagons.

But it is not possible to remove the vagueness of a term completely. Borderline cases always can arise. In several states there has been litigation over the question whether certain vehicles, such as go-carts, are automobiles under the statutory definitions. Suppose a definition of "automobile" expressly excludes motorcycles from that category. Problems still might arise about when something ceases to be a motorcycle and becomes an automobile. For given something that is clearly a motorcycle, we can continually modify it in relevant ways until finally, no matter how precisely we define terms, it will not be clear whether the modified vehicle is a motorcycle or an automobile.

Reforming definitions also are very important in science. In classifying plants and animals, scientists may take a term with an established meaning, and give it a different and (for their purposes) more useful meaning. For example, they have redefined the term "fish" to exclude whales and porpoises, which they classify as mammals along with many land animals that (superficially) they do not resemble. They have done so because they find it useful to classify animals by their ancestry, and because whales and porpoises are structurally more similar to mammals than to other sea animals.

Reforming definitions in science often are called *theoretical definitions,* because they draw on scientific theory. Thus the definition of "Morning Star" as "Venus when seen in the morning eastern sky" draws on the astronomical theory that relates the Morning Star and the planet Venus.

There is a tendency for scientific hypotheses or theories to become embedded in definitions. For example, at one time it was not known that copper conducts electricity; so at that time conductivity was not a defining characteristic of copper. But when it became well known that copper does conduct electricity, the *meaning* of the term "copper" began to change, so that now a scientist might hesitate before calling a nonconducting material "copper", even if it had all the other qualities of copper.

2 *Intensional, Extensional, and Ostensive Definitions*

An **extensional definition** of a term is simply a list of all the things to which the term applies. For instance, the term "Scandinavian country" can be defined extensionally to mean "Sweden or Norway or Denmark or Iceland". In most cases, it is very hard, if not impossible, to furnish an extensional definition of a term. For example, it would be impossible to define the term "human being" extensionally, since to do so we would have to list the name of every human being who ever has lived, or will live.

An **intensional definition** of a term lists a set of properties such that the term applies to all things having that set of properties, and to nothing else. For instance, the definition "male human being over 21 years of age who is as yet unmarried" might be given as an intensional definition of the term "bachelor", since it lists a set of properties something must possess to be a bachelor.

Notice that intensional definitions need not, and usually do not, list all of the properties common to everything named by the term defined. For instance, it may well be the case that all bachelors weigh more than 50 pounds, but if so this is an accidental fact, and not a defining property of bachelorhood. Even if there happens to be no bachelor who weighs less than 50 pounds, there *could be* one, in the sense that *if* something *were* to be male, human, over 21, and as yet unmarried, then that thing *would be* a bachelor according to our definition, even though that thing weighed less than 50 pounds.

An extensional definition can be said to provide the *extensional meaning,* or the *extension,* of a term, and an intensional definition the *intensional meaning,* or the *intension,* of a term. It is important to notice that terms can have different intensional meanings and yet have the same extensional meaning. For example, the phrases "most populous city in the

United States" and "city in which the U.N. Building is located" have different intensional meanings but the same extensional meaning, since it just happens that New York is both the most populous city in the United States *and* the city in which the U.N. Building is located.

Finally, an **ostensive definition** of a term is one that indicates the meaning of that term by providing a *sample* of the things denoted. For instance, we can define "automobile" as "anything like Chevrolets, Fords, Volkswagens, Cadillacs, and Plymouths". Or we can define "automobile" by *pointing to examples* of automobiles.

Good ostensive definitions often also indicate things *not* denoted by the term being defined. For example, in defining "automobile" by pointing to typical examples of automobiles, we might also point to motorcycles and motor scooters, and indicate that they are not automobiles.

Obviously, ostensive definitions are risky, in a way that extensional definitions are not. An extensional definition gives the *complete* extension of a term, and thus leaves little margin for error, while an ostensive definition furnishes only *part* of the extension of a term. Suppose we define "ball" ostensively by pointing to several typical examples, which just happen to be red. Then a child might easily get the idea that "ball" denotes the color red. Or suppose we define "university" ostensively by reference to Harvard, Penn, U.C.L.A., Kansas, C.U.N.Y., Maryland, and Oxford. Then someone might conclude that Swarthmore, Oberlin, Reed, and Whitman are universities, although in fact they are colleges, not universities.

These examples show that ostensive definitions are inherently ambiguous. A striking example is furnished by J. H. Weeks in his book *Among Congo Cannibals*.* Weeks wanted to know the synonym for "table" in a Congo language, and asked several boys by tapping on a table with his finger, asking "What is this?" He was rewarded with five different words, which he later learned referred to the material from which the table was made, to hardness, to the table covering, to the act of tapping, and (luckily) to tables.

One way to reduce ambiguity is by careful selection of examples, both positive and negative. If we suspect that a child may interpret the term "ball" as a color term, then we include balls of several different colors in our ostensive sample. In the university example, we might include several colleges, say Wellesley, Bryn Mawr, and Smith, as examples of nonuniversities. But we can never preclude the possibility of error. For instance, one might conclude that Wellesley, Bryn Mawr, and Smith are not universities because they are primarily *women's* institutions, and thus be misled about the meaning of the term "university".

---

* This example is quoted in Lionel Ruby, *The Art of Making Sense*, 2nd ed. (Philadelphia: J. B. Lippincott, 1954).

3 Two Kinds of Intensional Definitions

A good intensional definition of a word provides us with another word or words having the same meaning as the defined word. A definition that provides us with just one word is said to be a definition by **synonym.** Words in foreign languages are often learned in this way. For instance, we might teach someone the meanings of the German words "Hund", "Zeitung", and "Feuer" by presenting the English synonyms "dog", "newspaper", and "fire".

But if the word we wish to define has no close synonym (or if all of its close synonyms themselves require definitions) some other method must be used.

One of the oldest methods is definition by **genus** and **difference.** A definition of this kind specifies a particular class (the genus) and then divides that class by means of some characteristic (the difference). The subclass of the genus selected by that characteristic is said to be a **species** of the genus. For example, if we define "child" as "immature person", *person* is the genus, *child* is the species of that genus, and *immaturity* is the difference. Or if we define "murder" as "immoral killing", *killing* is the genus, *murder* is the species, and *immoral* is the difference.*

4 Criteria for Good Intensional Definitions

There is a great deal of controversy concerning criteria for good intensional definitions. We restrict the discussion to several of the standard criteria of this kind. The first four are traditional criteria of an informal nature, the remainder are those that all good definitions in formal systems (of the type discussed in Appendix D) must satisfy.

A good definition must not be too wide or too narrow. A definition is *too wide* if it applies to things we don't want the term in question to apply to. For example, "wheeled self-propelled vehicle" is too wide to be a good definition of the term "automobile", because it applies to airplanes, trains, and motorcycles. And "rational animal", an ancient definition of "man", is too wide to be a good definition of that term if, as may be the case, chimpanzees, gorillas, or porpoises are rational.

A definition is *too narrow* if it does not apply to all the things that we want the term in question to apply to. For instance, "wheeled vehicle propelled by an internal combustion engine and primarily intended for land travel" does not properly define the term "automobile" because it

---

* But note that from the point of view of logic, if not of history, genus and difference can be reversed. Thus we can construe *murder* as a subclass of the genus *immoral act*, the difference being *killing;* or construe *child* as a subclass of immature entities, *person* being the difference.

does not apply to automobiles powered by steam or electricity. And "rational animal" does not properly define "man" because (unfortunately) lots of human animals are not rational.

A good definition ought to avoid unnecessarily vague, ambiguous, obscure, or metaphorical language. Consider the expression "a certain type of self-propelled land vehicle" as a definition of the term "automobile". Clearly, an automobile *is* a certain type of self-propelled land vehicle. But *which* type? The definition does not say, and to that extent is unnecessarily vague. Or consider the expression "ship of the desert" as a definition of the term "camel". While this metaphorical description does indicate the main use to which camels are put in dry areas, it hardly is an adequate definition of the term "camel".

A good definition must not be circular. One standard way to state this criterion is to say that a definition is circular if it uses either the very word being defined or a grammatical variation of that word. Thus, the expression "one who engages in gardening" would be a circular definition of the term "gardener".

Unfortunately, this standard version of the circularity criterion is not satisfactory. For one thing, in certain contexts it is perfectly proper, even desirable, to define a word by using a grammatical variation of itself. For instance, the definition of "gardener" as "one who engages in gardening" is perfectly acceptable, *provided* a noncircular definition of "gardening" is furnished.*

We can salvage the circularity criterion by rephrasing it to state that a good definition must not be *viciously* circular. Consider a definition of "teacher" as "one who engages in teaching", and a definition of "teaching" as "that activity engaged in by a teacher". Taken alone, these definitions are not viciously circular, but taken together, they are. In effect, they tell us that the word "teacher" means the same as "one who engages in that which is engaged in by a teacher", so that someone who does not already know the meaning of the word "teacher" still would not know to which things that term applies.

A good definition of a term states the essential properites of the things named by that term. There is a great deal of controversy concerning this criterion, primarily because it uses the distinction between *essential* and *accidental* properties, which many philosophers reject.

But whether in the final analysis one accepts or rejects this distinction, there is a certain amount of plausibility to it. Take the term "bachelor".

---

* Another reason that this standard version of the circularity criterion is not satisfactory is that circular definitions of the kind called "recursive definitions" are perfectly acceptable. An example of a recursive definition is the definition of "WFF" in Appendix B. Since this definition uses the very term "WFF" that it defines, it is circular according to the above criterion.

As stated before, it may well be that all bachelors have the property of weighing more than 50 pounds, as well as of being unmarried. But we would not refuse to call someone a bachelor *simply* because he weighed less than 50 pounds. We would be inclined to say that if it is a fact that all bachelors weigh more than 50 pounds, then it is an *accidental,* or *contingent,* fact. On the other hand, being unmarried is an *essential* property of being a bachelor. In other words, it is not just an accidental, or contingent, fact that all bachelors are unmarried; unmarriedness is an essential property of bachelorhood. The essential property criterion requires that a good definition list all of the essential properties that something must have to be the kind of thing named by the term being defined.

One important dispute over this criterion concerns the question of whether *definitions themselves* determine which attributes are essential and which accidental or whether the nature of the world does so. Put in other terms, the question is whether the defining attributes can be selected arbitrarily or whether the world itself "naturally" divides into kinds of things, each kind having its own "essences" or essential properties, so that a good definition merely states the essences of the various natural kinds. (The latter position is often called the doctrine of "natural kinds".)

If one accepts the view that definitions themselves arbitrarily determine which properties are essential, then the essential property requirement will, in general, be fulfilled automatically, and the criterion itself will be trivial. But if one accepts the doctrine of natural kinds, then the criterion will be of great importance.

The essential property criterion has been criticized on the grounds that it applies only to terms that serve as *names*. For instance, it is hard to see what is named by the logical connectives "or" and "and", and hard to imagine what it would mean to speak of the essential properties of "or-ness" and "and-ness".

It also has been objected to on the grounds that it is not appropriate for definitions of *relational* properties or *functions*. Terms for relational properties usually are best defined by what are called **contextual definitions,** that is, by definitions that define a term in the context in which it occurs, not in isolation. Consider the following contextual definition of "average density", which might be introduced into a scientific theory:

$$\text{Average density of } x =_{df} \frac{\text{mass of } x \text{ (in grams)}}{\text{volume of } x \text{ (in cc)}}$$

It is hard to see what could be meant by speaking of accidental or essential properties in a case such as this one, yet this is perhaps the most common type of definition in both science and mathematics. So it can be argued that the essential property criterion does not apply to definitions in science and mathematics. If correct, this charge constitutes an important objection to that criterion (and also to the widely accepted idea that the best definitions are those by genus and difference).

Finally, it may be argued that in many (perhaps most) cases there is no satisfactory way to determine whether a given property is essential or accidental. Suppose we find something that in all other respects seems to be copper, but fails to conduct electricity. Does that thing merit the title "copper"? The answer is not clear-cut. And even in cases where a clear-cut answer is possible, it may change from time to time. (Several hundred years ago conductivity surely would have been considered an accidental property of copper, if a property at all.) Consequently, many philosophers have become convinced that, at best, *definitions themselves* determine which properties are essential and which accidental and not the nature of the world, or any essences possessed by all of the things named by a term. They have become convinced that the essential attributes theory amounts simply to the trivial statement that a property is essential if it is listed in a definition. Thus, if we choose to define "copper" in a certain way, then conductivity will be an essential property of copper. But if we choose to define "copper" in another way, then conductivity will not be an essential property of copper. (Of course, how we choose to define that term depends in large part on what we cannot choose. No one would choose to alter the definition of *copper* to require nonconductivity of electricity as a defining property because then the term *copper* would not apply to anything whatever—the definition would be useless—and we would still need a term to apply to the electrical conductor we use in electric wires, Lincoln pennies, etc.)

We now turn to the criteria for good definitions in formal systems of the type to be discussed in Appendix B.

A defined term must be eliminable from a system into which it is introduced. A term is said to be *eliminable* from a system if every sentence in the system in which it occurs can be replaced by an equivalent sentence in which that term does not occur. Suppose we construct a formal system suitable for use in anthropology, in which the terms "male" and "married" are primitive terms (that is, terms not defined in the system). Then we can introduce the term "bachelor" into the system as a defined term, letting it mean the same as "not-married male". Clearly, the term "bachelor" so defined is eliminable in the sense just stated. For instance, if the sentence "All bachelors are handsome" is a sentence in the system, then it can be replaced by the equivalent sentence "All not-married males are handsome", a sentence that does not contain the defined term "bachelor". Similarly, the term "bachelor" will be eliminable from all other sentences in the system.*

---

*Notice that the truth table definitions of the sentence connectives given in Part One of this text do not satisfy this criterion. That is true because the sentential logic presented in Part One is not a formal system in the sense in question here. But in Appendix B, where a strictly formal system for sentential logic is presented, all of the criteria discussed here for good definitions in formal systems are satisfied.

A good definition must not permit the proof of something that cannot be proved without it. (This is often called the "nonconstructibility" criterion.) A famous example of the violation of this criterion concerns the so-called pseudo-operator, symbolized by "★". Suppose that in a system for arithmetic we stipulate that $[(x \star y) = z] = df\,[(x < z)\ \&\ (y < z)]$.*
Then, using the other (valid) principles of arithmetic, we construct the following proof:

1. $1 \star 2 = 3$ (because $(1 < 3) \cdot (2 < 3)$)
2. $1 \star 2 = 4$ (because $(1 < 4) \cdot (2 < 4)$)

/∴ $3 = 4$ (because quantities equal to the same quantity are equal to each other)

which contradicts the truth of arithmetic that $3 \neq 4$, and obviously cannot be proved in an arithmetic system without the pseudo-operator definition. This proves that the pseudo-operator definition violates the criterion of nonconstructibility, and must be rejected.

Finally, *a good definition makes clear the form of the contexts in which the term defined is to be used.* (While it is not necessary to consider this criterion separately, pedagogically it is very useful to do so.) Take the word "father". There are two different ways in which this term can be used, namely as a one-place and as a two-place property term. For example, in the sentence "John is a father" it functions as a one-place property term, while in the sentence "John is the father of Harry" it functions as a two-place property term. Consequently, we must provide two separate definitions for the term "father", indicating the kind of contexts (one place or two place) in which it can occur. For instance, we can stipulate that "*x* is the father" = *df* "*x* is male, and *x* is a parent of some *y* or other", and "*x* is the father of *y*" = *df* "*x* is male, and *x* is a parent of *y*".†

Exercise 13-1:

Which of the following might serve reasonably well as definitions? Explain why the others might be inadequate.

1. An obligation is what one is obliged to do.
2. Human beings are featherless bipeds.
3. A hexagon is an enclosed plane figure having six equal sides and six equal angles.
4. Architecture is frozen music.

---

* "$x \star y$" is read as "*x* star *y*". This example is mentioned in Patrick Suppess, *Introduction to Logic* (Princeton, N.J.: Van Nostrand, 1957), pp. 151–52.

† In the notation of predicate logic these definitions read $Fx = df\,[Mx \cdot (\exists y)Pxy]$ and $Fxy = df\,(Mx \cdot Pxy)$, respectively.

5. A contract is an agreement to perform an action.
6. You have faith in something when you believe it without having a reason or justification.
7. The impractical is what is not practical.
8. "Ocean" refers to the Atlantic, Indian, Arctic, and Pacific bodies of water, but not to the Baltic, Mediterranean, or bodies of water of that sort.
9. Murder is the deliberate killing of a human being.
10. Philosophy is part of that which is written or talked about among those generally regarded as philosophers.

Exercise 13-2:

1. Give an original example (that is, one not occurring in the text) of an intensional lexical definition, and explain why it is an example.
2. Give an original example of an extensional or ostensive lexical definition, and explain why it is an example.
3. In the text, we introduced the new term "aunticle" and stipulated that it means "aunt or uncle". Introduce a new term of your own that you think might have some usefulness, and provide a stipulative definition for it.
4. List several ordinary English words (not mentioned in the text) that are *vague,* and explain their vagueness.
5. List several ordinary English words that are *ambiguous,* and provide reasonably accurate definitions for at least two senses of each.

Exercise 13-3:

Which of the following might serve as definitions by genus and difference? Explain why the others could not. (Do you think some of the others would be adequate as definitions anyway?)

1. A *sister* is a female sibling.
2. A *porpoise* is a dolphin.
3. Someone is *polygamous* if multimarried.
4. A *freshman* is a college undergraduate in the first year of study.
5. A *broom* is an object for sweeping.
6. A *queen* is a female ruler.
7. A *satellite* is a body that revolves around a celestial body.
8. A *sibling* is a brother or sister.

---

5 *Cognitive and Emotive Meaning*

If a sentence is to be informative, or as grammarians would say, if it is to state a fact, and thus be a declarative sentence, some of its words must refer to things, events, or properties. Some of its words thus must have what we shall call **cognitive meaning.***

But words also have **emotive meaning;** that is, they also may have positive or negative overtones. The emotive charge of some words is obvious. Think of the terms used in expressing prejudices against members of certain groups, words like "nigger", "wop", "kike", "queer", and "fag". Or think of the "four-letter words" for certain sexual or eliminative bodily functions.

The emotively charged words just listed have negative emotive meanings. But lots of words have positive emotive overtones. Examples are "freedom", "love", "springtime", and "peace".

On the other hand, many words have either neutral or mixed emotive meanings. "Pencil", "hydrogen", "run", and "river" tend to be neutral words. "Socialism", "automobile", "politician", and "whiskey" tend to have mixed emotive meanings.

In fact, almost any word that is emotively positive (or negative) to some may be just the opposite to others, perhaps because one person's meat often is another's poison. "God" has quite different emotive overtones for a sincere believer and for an atheist; "dictatorship", a negative word for most Americans, in some contexts has positive overtones in the Soviet Union, and "black" is beautiful to some but not to others.

Terms that on first glance appear neutral often turn out to be emotively charged, although the charge may be fairly small. In fact, sometimes we fail to notice quite large emotive charges, perhaps because of prejudice or provincialism, or because the everyday often gets overlooked. The words "bureaucrat", "government official", and "public servant" all refer to roughly the same class of people, and thus have roughly the same cognitive meaning, but their emotive meanings, frequently overlooked, are quite different. Of the three, only "government official" is close to being neutral.

Propagandists, politicians, and writers for TV, newspapers, and other media frequently take advantage of the fact that words have emotive as well as cognitive meanings. For instance, in the decade or so after World War II, when the word "communism" had extremely negative overtones in the United States, political fortunes were made through reckless charges that so-and-so was a communist, or "pinko", or "fellow trav-

* Sometimes this is called "literal" meaning. But that term is ambiguous, often being contrasted with metaphorical meaning, whereas we want cognitive meaning to contrast with emotive meaning.

eler", and many bills were defeated in Congress by being labeled "socialistic".

But these cases of manipulation are obvious. The more subtle cases may well be more insidious in the long run, because they are harder to guard against and are more pervasive. It would take a very perceptive grade school or even high school student to notice, for example, that history textbooks typically refer to American Indians as "savages", "ferocious", "cruel", and "cunning", while referring to the white settlers who killed them and took away their land as "civilized", "brave", "defending their cabins and farms", and so on. Few students notice that Indian victories tend to be called "massacres", but white victories "battles", or that an Indian chief may be referred to as a "dreaded Indian leader", but no U.S. president *ever* is referred to in American textbooks as a "dreaded American leader".*

And yet the perspectives we bring to bear on political and social issues—our "world views"—are molded in part by our school textbooks, and also in part by what we read in magazines and newspapers and hear on television and radio. To the extent that these media use the emotive meanings of words and phrases to imprint their points of view on us, *we* are being manipulated. Perhaps the best defense against this is to understand the nature of emotive meaning and its tremendous propaganda potential. A rose by any other name might *not* smell just as sweet, and it's important that we recognize this fact.

Exercise 13-4:

Here is a list of more or less emotively neutral words or phrases. For each item, find an emotively positive or emotively negative word or phrase having roughly the same factual or cognitive meaning.

1. young woman
2. horse
3. unmarried woman
4. janitor
5. interest (on a loan)
6. collector of solid waste
7. United States
8. military force
9. officer seeker
10. exception to revenue statute
11. job
12. Caucasian
13. tool
14. cemetery
15. one who very much likes to eat
16. bar

* For details, see the author's *Logic and Contemporary Rhetoric*, 4th ed. (Belmont, Calif.: Wadsworth Publishing Co., 1984), or *Textbooks and the American Indian* (San Francisco: Indian Historical Press, 1970).

17. clever
18. toilet paper
19. law income
20. fighter
21. alcoholic
22. deceased relative

Exercise 13-5:

Appropriately fill in as many of the blanks below as you can, taking care that all the words or phrases on a given line have the same general cognitive meaning (as do all of the words on sample line 0):

	Emotively Negative	Emotively Neutral	Emotively Positive
0.	fuzz, cop, pig, flatfoot	policeman	peace officer, officer
1.	big cheese, big shot	________	________
2.	grab	________	________
3.	________	________	investigative journalist
4.	________	jail, prison	________
5.	________	very intelligent (person)	________
6.	smell	________	________
7.	________	elderly person	________
8.	conquer, subdue, subjugate	________	________
9.	________	underdeveloped (nation)	________
10.	________	________	fastidious, painstaking

Key Terms Introduced in Chapter Thirteen

Ambiguous: Having more than one meaning. For instance, the word "sock" is ambiguous, since in some contexts it means "to strike or hit", and in others it refers to an item of apparel.

Cognitive meaning: That part of the meaning of a word that concerns its reference, or its nonemotive meaning.

Contextual definition: A definition of a word or phrase in the kind of context in which it occurs. For example, the definition "*x* is the father of *y*" = *df* "*x* is a parent of *y*, and *x* is male" is a contextual definition, while the definition "father" = *df* "male parent" is not.

Definiendum: Latin word meaning "word being defined".

Definiens: Latin word meaning "words used to define some other word".

Definition: An explanation of the meaning of a word or phrase.

Difference: A criterion for dividing a genus into two groups. Thus, the difference *industrial* can be used to divide nations into the species *industrial nation* and *nonindustrial nation.*

Emotive meaning: The positive or negative emotive overtones of words.

Extensional definition: A definition that lists all of the things to which the word or phrase being defined applies.

Genus: A larger class divided into smaller ones called *species.*

Intensional definition: A definition that lists a set of properties such that the term being defined applies to all things having that set of properties, and to nothing else.

Lexical definition: A definition that attempts to report the actual usage of a word or phrase.

Ostensive definition: A definition that indicates the meaning of a word or phrase by pointing out a sample of the things denoted by the term.

Species: Subclass of a larger class called a *genus.*

Stipulative definition: A definition that specifies, or stipulates, the meaning of a word or phrase.

Synonym (for a given term): A word having the same meaning as the given term.

Vague: Not having a precise meaning. For example, the term "tall" is vague, since there is no precise point at which something achieves the status of tallness. Most words and phrases, perhaps all words and phrases, are vague in some way or other.

Part Four

Induction, Probability, and Scientific Method

Chapter Fourteen

Induction

In Chapter One, we divided correct arguments into two kinds, *deductively valid* arguments and *inductively correct,* or *inductively strong,* arguments. We now turn to an examination of inductively correct and incorrect arguments and their role in the logic or methodology of science.

However, a note of caution again is in order. Although it is true that literally *nothing* in philosophy is accepted by all philosophers, the material on symbolic logic presented in the first two parts of this text comes as close as anything to being generally accepted and noncontroversial. But almost all of the material to be presented now on induction and science is highly controversial, and the viewpoint expressed is just one of many.

1 *The Difference Between Induction and Deduction*

In Chapter One we defined a *deductively valid argument* as one whose premises (if true) guarantee the truth of its conclusion. Speaking metaphorically, we said that the reason such a guarantee can be made is that the content of the conclusion of a deductively valid argument is already contained in its premises (either explicitly or implicitly). And we said that the premises of a deductively valid argument, taken together with the negation of its conclusion, imply a contradiction.

We also said that an *inductively correct argument* is an argument whose premises (if true) provide good, but not conclusive, grounds for accepting its conclusion. Its premises make the conclusion more probable, but do not guarantee its truth. It is logically possible for the conclusion of an inductively correct argument to be false even though all of its premises are true. The premises of such an argument, taken together with the negation of its conclusion, do *not* imply a contradiction.

For instance, a hundred years ago a scientist might validly have concluded that all things made of asbestos do not conduct electricity, on the evidence that all *tested* things made of asbestos failed to conduct electricity. The conclusion of this argument happens to be false, since (as we now know) asbestos conducts electricity at temperatures close to absolute zero. But the conclusion of the original argument, based on less evidence, does follow from its premises. We are justified in accepting the conclusion of this argument if the information contained in its premises constitutes all that we know about the conductivity of asbestos.

Thus, there is a "gap" between the premises and the conclusion of an inductively correct argument. This gap is the characteristic mark of all inductive arguments. It is both their *weakness* and their great *strength*. It is their weakness because false conclusions can follow from true premises. It is their strength because it enables us to reason from what we have observed to what we have as yet not observed. Without induction, science would be impossible, except as a mere description of what has been observed. Similarly, no expectations in everyday life—say that bread will nourish or strychnine kill—would ever be justified.

According to a common misconception about the distinction between deduction and induction, deductively valid reasoning involves inference from the general to the specific (particular) or from the more general to the less general, whereas inductively correct reasoning involves inference from the specific (particular) to the general, or from the less general to the more general. For example, the deductively valid argument

1. All intelligent students will get A's in logic.

/∴ 2. If Art is an intelligent student, then Art will get A's in logic.

proceeds from the general to the specific, and the inductively correct argument

1. So far, every intelligent student has done A work in logic.

/∴ 2. All intelligent students (past, present, and future) do A work in logic.

proceeds from the less general to the more general.

But only a moment's reflection is needed to see that this view of deductive and inductive reasoning is erroneous. First, deductively valid arguments do not always proceed from the general to the specific. For instance, they often proceed from the general to the equally general. An example is the argument

1. All men are mortal.

/∴ 2. All who aren't mortal aren't men.

And they often proceed from the specific to the specific. An example is the argument

1. In 1984, Ronald Reagan was more popular but less intelligent than Walter Mondale.

/∴ 2. In 1984, Ronald Reagan was more popular than Walter Mondale.

And they sometimes even proceed from the specific to the general (or the less general to the more general), although cases of this kind tend to be a bit contrived. Here are two examples:

1. John is mortal.

/∴ 2. All who know John know someone who is mortal.

1. John is mortal.
2. John is not mortal or all men are mortal.

/∴ 3. All men are mortal.*

Further, inductively correct arguments do not always proceed from the specific to the general. For instance, they often proceed from the specific to the specific. An example is the analogical argument

1. The 1984 election resulted in a Republican landslide.

/∴ 2. The 1988 election will result in a Republican landslide.

And they often proceed from the general to the equally general.

1. All NFL teams made tons of money this year.

/∴ 2. All NFL teams will make tons of money next year.

Finally, here is one that moves from the more general to the less general.

1. All NFL teams made money this year.

/∴ 2. The San Francisco 49ers NFL team will make money next year.

It should be clear then that there is no truth to the view that deductively valid reasoning proceeds from the general to the specific, or from the more general to the less general, and inductively correct reasoning from the specific to the general, or the more specific to the less specific.

2 *Kinds of Inductive Arguments*

The basic idea in inductive reasoning is that of *pattern,* or *resemblance.* We want our ideas about what this or that will be like in future to fit a pattern gleaned from what this or that was like in the past. (The problem, of course, is to find patterns or resemblances that fit, or take account of, everything we've experienced of the past.)

Inductive arguments can be divided into several different kinds.

---

*This example is from Nelson Pole, "A Deductive Argument with a Specific Premise and a General Conclusion", *Notre Dame Journal of Formal Logic,* vol. XVI (1975), pp. 543–44. Pole points out that those who don't feel this argument moves from the less general to the more general (on grounds that premise 2 is as general as the conclusion) should consider the following deductively valid argument:

1. John is not mortal.

/∴ 2. John is not mortal or all men are mortal.

See also Chapter One of Brian Skyrms, *Choice and Chance,* 3rd ed. (Belmont, Calif.: Wadsworth, 1985).

Inductive Generalization, Categorical Form

When we reason or argue from a premise or premises concerning particular instances, or from all examined cases of a certain kind, to a conclusion that is universal, or concerning all cases (examined or unexamined) of a certain kind, our reasoning has the form of a **categorical inductive generalization,** or **universal inductive generalization,** or simple **inductive generalization.** (These terms also apply to the conclusions of inductive generalizations.) An example is the argument

1. All examined copper things conduct electricity.

/∴ 2. All copper things (examined or as yet unexamined) conduct electricity.*

Categorical inductive generalizations all have the same general form, which can be put in either one of two ways. The first way is:

1. $Fa \cdot Ga$†
2. $Fb \cdot Gb$
3. $Fc \cdot Gc$

⋮

N. No *F* is known not to have *G*.

∴ *N* + 1. All *F*'s are *G*'s.

And the second (equivalent) way is:

1. All examined *F*'s are *G*'s.

/∴ 2. All *F*'s are *G*'s.

Translated into the notation of predicate logic, and letting Ex = "x is examined for the presence or absence of G", this reads:

1. $(x)[(Fx \cdot Ex) \supset Gx]$

/∴ 2. $(x)(Fx \supset Gx)$

While there is much controversy over how to weigh the strength of a categorical inductive generalization, it is widely believed that the *probability,* or *degree of confirmation,* of a hypothesis, or the *evidential support* for a hypothesis, increases with each new confirming instance of it.

---

* In this case, the premise of our inductive generalization is true. But the generalization would be just as inductively correct if its premise were false. The goodness of inductive reasoning depends on the connection between premises and conclusion, not on the truth of the premise. What makes an argument inductively strong is that if its premises *were* true, they *would* support acceptance of its conclusion.

† Because we are dealing with the *form* of categorical inductive generalizations, "*F*", "*G*", "*a*", "*b*", and "*c*" are being used as variables.

For example, each newly examined instance of the hypothesis "All copper conducts electricity" increases the probability of that hypothesis. However, as the number of confirming instances mounts up, each new confirming instance counts less than the preceding instance. (Exactly how much less it counts is one of those things on which there is no general agreement.)

Even more controversial is the idea that the more important confirming cases are those that also disconfirm competing hypotheses. Looking out the window and finding yet another crow that's black doesn't do much, if anything, for the theory that all crows are black, given that we've already seen plenty of crows in similar circumstances. But hearing about black crows in some tropical area where crows had not previously been observed does count as good confirmation of the theory that all crows are black because, in this view, it disconfirms the competing theory that bird species in general, and thus crows in particular, vary in color from one sort of environment to another. (This idea is discussed further in Chapter Sixteen, Section 2.)

And some hold that the important confirmations of a theory are those that confirm consequences of the theory of a kind that hadn't been confirmed before. For example, successfully applying Newton's laws to determine the moon's gravitational force (as encountered by astronauts), tests a different consequence of Newton's laws than the usual ones about the moon's orbit or the trajectory of bullets on Earth.

Finally, some people say that there is no such thing as confirmation of an hypothesis, strictly speaking. What is often called *confirmation* on this view is better seen as the attempt to *falsify* an hypothesis; we speak (but shouldn't) about confirmation when attempts to falsify fail. (This is the view of Karl Popper, whose ideas on falsification and what he calls *corroboration* are discussed in Chapter Sixteen, Section 6.)

Many scientific hypotheses have the form of categorical inductive generalizations; for example, "All copper conducts electricity". But it is frequently held that the typical and important scientific hypotheses are not categorical inductive generalizations. The claim is that such categorical generalizations are characteristic of the early stages of a science, giving way fairly quickly to something more advanced and sophisticated. For example, some claim that even Galileo constructed more advanced hypotheses than the one above, since he constructed *quantitative* hypotheses. An example is the hypothesis (slightly simplified here) that the distance an object falls in free flight equals 16 times the square of the time it falls, or in symbols $S = 16t^2$. Their claim is that the *mathematical equation* is the standard or at least most important form of scientific hypothesis.

There can be no doubt that many scientific hypotheses are constructed in the form of mathematical equations. But this fact does not constitute evidence against the importance of categorical inductive generalizations in science, since mathematical equations themselves can be stated as categorical generalizations. For example, we can translate the equation $S = 16t^2$ into the categorical generalization "All freely falling bodies are such that if S is the distance they fall, and t is the time it takes them to fall that distance, then $S = 16t^2$".

Inductive Generalization, Statistical Form

When we reason or argue from a premise or premises concerning groups of instances to a conclusion that is *statistical* in form, our reasoning has the form of a **statistical inductive generalization.** An example is the argument

1. Half of the tosses of this coin observed so far landed heads up.

/∴ 2. Half of all tosses of this coin (observed or otherwise) will land heads up.

The general form of statistical generalizations can be stated as:

1. *N* percent of all *F*'s tested for *G* have *G*.

/∴ 2. *N* percent of all *F*'s (tested or otherwise) have *G*.

Statistical generalizations play an important role in science. A great many of the hypotheses in the social sciences (economics, sociology, and others) are statistical, and many basic hypotheses of physics itself are statistical. Two important examples are the Second Law of Thermodynamics (the law of increasing entropy) and the gas laws. For example, the gas laws say nothing about the pressure of a gas at any given point on the surface of an enclosed container, but rather what the *average,* or *statistical,* pressure will be, calculated on the basis of the temperature and volume of the enclosed gas.

But a statistical generalization is generally not as informative or useful as the corresponding universal generalization would be. Take the statistical generalization "One-fifth of all adult Americans who smoke an average of one or more packs of cigarettes per day will die of lung cancer within 25 years". Obviously, if true, this constitutes very valuable information, for it warns those who fall into the stated category (adult Americans who smoke at least one pack per day) of their "chances" of getting lung cancer if they persist in smoking so heavily.* But it doesn't tell anyone that *he* will get lung cancer merely because he is an adult American who smokes at least one pack of cigarettes per day.

However, suppose we discover that heavy cigarette smoking is only

---

* That their chances are one in five is significant because we know that hardly any people who don't smoke tobacco get lung cancer.

one of two factors leading to lung cancer, the other factor being, say, a particular abnormality in the surface tissue of the lung (let's call it "abnormality *A*"); that is, suppose we discover that *every investigated* case of heavy smoking in which abnormality *A* is present also is a case of lung cancer death. Then we could construct the following inductively strong argument:

1. All heavy smokers who have been found to have abnormality *A* have died of lung cancer.

/∴ 2. All heavy smokers who have abnormality *A* die of lung cancer.

The conclusion of this argument is a categorical inductive generalization concerning the connection between smoking and death by lung cancer and would be much more informative and useful than the statistical generalization cited above. For if some person, say Art, were found on examination to have abnormality *A*, then we could present him with an argument such as

1. All heavy smokers who have abnormality *A* die of lung cancer.
2. Art has abnormality *A*.

/∴ 3. If Art is (or becomes) a heavy smoker, then Art will die of lung cancer.

Surely this argument is more relevant to Art's decision about whether to smoke than the previous *statistical* argument linking heavy smoking and lung cancer. A corresponding *statistical* generalization, such as "One-fifth of all heavy smokers will die of lung cancer", which when combined with the information that Art is a heavy smoker, leads to the conclusion that *the chance is one in five* that Art will die of lung cancer, certainly is not so informative or useful as the conclusion that Art *definitely* will die of lung cancer if he becomes a heavy smoker.

In view of the above, the question naturally arises whether with sufficient knowledge we could not (at least theoretically) replace all statistical generalizations with categorical ones. It seems plausible to assume that this always can be accomplished by taking account of more and more relevant factors. For instance, knowledge that a given coin is symmetrical permits the conclusion that half of all random tosses with that coin will land heads up. But it seems plausible to assume that with *better knowledge,* that is with knowledge of more relevant factors (such as the force of each toss, its starting position, wind velocity, and so on), we could conclude that *all* tosses of a certain kind (tossed with a certain force or tossed from a certain starting position) will land heads up.

However, we cannot say ahead of time that all statistical generalizations are replaceable by categorical generalizations. In each case, we must examine the world to determine whether more relevant factors exist. (Of course, simply failing to find relevant factors does not prove that none exist. We may not have been sufficiently ingenious to discover them.) So the question of whether a given statistical generalization can be replaced by a corresponding categorical generalization can be answered only by accumulating more empirical evidence, to the extent that it can be answered at all.*

On the other hand, it is clear that we can regard a categorical inductive generalization as a special kind of statistical generalization, namely the kind in which the percentage of F's tested that turn out to be G's happens to be 100 percent. In other words, we can take the basic pattern of categorical inductive generalizations to be

1. 100 percent of all F's tested for G have G.

/∴ 2. 100 percent of all F's (tested or otherwise) have G.

which clearly is just a special case of the general pattern for statistical generalization.

Analogies

When we infer from a premise or premises concerning particular instances (or all known instances) of a certain kind to a conclusion concerning some other particular instance of that kind, we infer **analogically,** or by **analogy.** For example, we infer *analogically* when we reason from the premise that a course given last year by a particular teacher was interesting to the conclusion that the course the teacher is giving this year will be interesting.

Some analogies are *stronger* than others. Analogies differ in the *degree* to which they support their conclusions. For one thing, the greater the number of instances mentioned in the premises, the stronger the analogy. Thus, if we reason from the fact that both of two courses taken from a particular teacher were interesting to the conclusion that the next course we take from that teacher will be interesting, our analogy is better than if we reason on the basis of only one course taken from that instructor.

Analogies also are stronger if the instances they concern are alike in more relevant ways. Thus, if we reason from the fact that the two interesting courses taken previously from a particular teacher both were logic courses to the conclusion that the next logic course we take from him will be interesting, our analogy is better than if the next course we take from him happens to be ethics.

However, only *relevant* ways in which the instances are alike count. For example, it might be irrelevant if the classes both happened to meet in the same room, or at the same time of day. But it is quite difficult to know in general, or even in a particular case, exactly which things are

---

* Some claim that evidence discovered by twentieth-century physicists, in particular evidence supporting the Heisenberg Indeterminacy Principle, provides empirical reason for believing that at least some, and perhaps all, of the ultimate laws of physics are *statistical* and not categorical. See, for instance, Hans Reichenbach, *Rise of Scientific Philosophy* (Berkeley and Los Angeles: University of California Press, 1953), Chap. 10.

relevant and which are not. The room in which a course is to be taught *may* be relevant to how interesting it will be. (For example, it will be relevant if the teacher in question dislikes large, poorly lit rooms, and the next course that teacher teaches happens to be in such a room.)

It follows from what has just been said that what is a strong analogy for one person, given what that person knows, may be quite weak for a second, given what that second person knows. For instance, film fans who assumed the Woody Allen comedy *What's Up, Tiger Lily* would be a funny movie because other Allen comedies were funny reasoned correctly (even though their conclusion was false). But fans who knew the flick was just a tenth-rate Japanese thriller with Western voice-over were justified in drawing just the opposite conclusion.

Analogies conveniently divide into two kinds, namely **categorical analogies** and **statistical analogies.**

Valid categorical analogies have the general form

1. All *F*'s tested or observed for *G* have *G*.

/∴ 2. This particular *F*, untested as yet for *G*, has *G*.

The argument discussed above, about taking a class from a particular teacher, is an example of a categorical analogy.

Valid statistical analogies have the general form

1. *N* percent (or most, or almost all) of the *F*'s tested for *G* have *G*.

/∴ 2. The probability is *N* percent (or the probability is high) that this particular *F*, as yet untested for *G*, has *G*.

Most analogies made in everyday life are statistical analogies. In daily life, we rarely encounter cases in which all of the known cases of a certain kind have some particular relevant property. For instance, even the best teacher is likely to teach an uninteresting class at least once, thus falsifying the premise of any *categorical* analogy whose conclusion is that his next course will be interesting, but not falsifying the premise of some statistical analogy whose conclusion is that his next course *probably* will be interesting.

It is sometimes held that analogical reasoning is not *fundamental,* in that any given analogy can be shown to be an enthymemic version of a categorical or statistical generalization. Take the analogy whose conclusion is that the next class taught by a particular teacher probably will be interesting. In this case, it is said, the complete form of our reasoning would be

1. Almost all classes taught so far by the teacher in question have been interesting.

/∴ 2. Almost all of the classes that teacher teaches are interesting.

3. This particular class will be taught by the teacher in question.

/∴ 4. This particular class will probably be interesting.

Exercise 14-1:

Here are three analogical arguments, each one followed by a set of five additional premises. Some of these extra premises, if added to the original analogy, increase its strength; others decrease it. State which of the extra premises increase, and which decrease the strength of the original analogy, and explain why you think so.

1. The Carnegie Hall Cinema is playing Ingmar Bergman's flick *Scenes from a Marriage* tonight. This is a serious foreign film, and the last five foreign movies I saw seemed to me to be quite good. So I expect to like *Scenes from a Marriage.*
   a. Three of the other five were also Bergman films.
   b. All five were comedies.
   c. Liv Ullman stars in *Scenes,* but wasn't in any of the other five.
   d. I saw all five on a Wednesday evening. Today is Tuesday.
   e. All five were in black and white. *Scenes* is in color.

2. **Jane:** I'm thinking of taking another lover.
   McBird: Oh, no! I realize we have an agreement about open marriage and all that, but I'm afraid if you do, this time you'll break up our marriage.
   Jane: When I had that affair with Paul, did it break up our marriage?
   McBird: No, it didn't. But why should I support you if you have affairs?
   Jane: Or after the one with Coop? Or Herb? Or Hal?
   McBird: I guess not.
   Jane: Well, what are you worrying about?
   McBird: Oh, I suppose you're right, as usual.
   a. Jane's prospective lover is McBird's best friend.
   b. The affairs with Paul, Coop, Herb, and Hal all occurred several years ago, before Jane's children grew up and left the nest.
   c. Jane just inherited a small fortune from her parents.
   d. Jane's affairs with Coop, Herb, Paul, and Hal all occurred right after McBird had had severe depressions following traumatic dreams about his greatly lamented deceased first wife, but McBird hasn't had such a dream, or any depression, in a long time.
   e. Jane was just granted tenure at Podunk College.

3. They say that heart attacks run in families because of like habits and similar genes. Boy that makes me worried! My father died of a heart attack at age 55, my mother at 31, my grandfather (father's side) at 62, his wife at 58, my other grandmother at 63, and three aunts before age 65. I should be worried—all signs point to an early heart attack.
   a. I don't smoke cigarettes; my father and his father smoked over a pack a day for many years.
   b. All my close relatives ate the same sort of Central European diet—lots of animal fats, pastries, highly seasoned foods; I'm a vegetarian and health nut.
   c. I'm a college graduate; my father dropped out after the eighth grade and my mother finished high school, but my grandparents never even started kindergarten.
   d. My father stood on his feet in a retail store for 55 to 60 hours per week for 25 years; my grandfather sat at a sewing machine. In contrast, I jog 2–5 miles every other day; I'm not sedentary as they were.
   e. I remember that everyone in my family was always worried about money; we all ate well, but money for extras was very scarce. Looking back, they were all "type A" people—nervous, always in a hurry, late, tense. Now *I'm* a cool cat with the world's best occupation (for me)—good pay, job security, fun things to do, flexible hours, and lots of free time.

Exercise 14-2:

Here are some arguments containing analogical reasoning. In each case state how strong you believe the analogy to be, given your background information, and explain your conclusion.

1. The Christians say, "Creatures are not bound with desires unless satisfaction for those desires exists." A baby feels hunger: well, there is such a thing as food. A duckling wants to swim: well, there is such a thing as water. Men feel sexual desire: well, there is such a thing as sex. If I find in myself a desire which no experience in this world can satisfy, the most probable explanation is that I was made for another world. (C. S. Lewis, *Mere Christianity*)

2. That the aggressor, who puts himself into the state of war with another, and unjustly invades another man's right, can, by such an unjust war, never come to have a right over the conquered, will be easily agreed by all men, who will not think that robbers and pirates have a right of empire over whomsoever they have force enough to master, or that men are bound by promises which unlawful force extorts from them. Should a robber break into my house, and with a dagger at my throat, make me seal deed to convey my estate to him, would this give him any title? Just such a title by his sword has an unjust conqueror who forces me into submission. (John Locke, *Of Civil Government*)

3. If a single cell, under appropriate conditions, becomes a man in the space of a few years, there can surely be no difficulty in understanding how, under appropriate conditions, a cell may, in the course of untold millions of years, give origin to the human race. (Herbert Spencer, *Principles of Biology*)

4. "Do you think," said Candide, "that men have always massacred each other, as they do today, that they have always been false, cozening, faithless, ungrateful, thieving, weak, inconstant, mean-spirited, envious, greedy, drunken, miserly, ambitious, bloody, slanderous, debauched, fanatic, hypocritical, and stupid?"

   "Do you think," said Martin, "that hawks have always eaten pigeons when they could find them?"

   "Of course I do," said Candide.

   "Well," said Martin, "if hawks have always had the same character, why should you suppose that men have changed theirs?" (Voltaire, *Candide*)

5. We may observe a very great similitude between this earth which we inhabit and the other planets. . . . They all revolve around the sun as the earth does. . . . They borrow all their light from the sun, as the earth does. Several of them are known to revolve round their axis like the earth, and by that means, must have a like succession of night and day. . . . From all this similitude, it is not unreasonable to think that those planets may, like our earth, be the habitation of various orders of living creatures. (Thomas Reid, *Essays on the Intellectual Powers of Man*)

6. I am the father of two daughters. When I hear . . . that we can't protect freedom in Europe, in Asia, or in our own hemisphere, and still meet our domestic problems, I think it is a phony argument. It is just like saying that I can't take care of Luci because I have Lynda Bird. (President Lyndon B. Johnson, February 1968)

7. The philosopher Epicurus argued that the gods have bodies, because the gods are intelligent and all known intelligent entities (human beings) have bodies.

8. Suppose someone tells me that he has had a tooth extracted without an anesthetic, and I express my sympathy, and suppose I am then asked, "How do you know it hurt him?" I might reasonably reply, "Well, I know that it would hurt me. I have been to the dentist and know how painful it is to have a toothache stopped without an anesthetic, let alone taken out. And he has the same sort of nervous system as I have. I infer, therefore, that in these conditions he felt considerable pain, just as I should myself". (A. J. Ayer, "One's Knowledge of Other Minds", *Theorea*, 1953)

Inference from Observed to Unobservable

We have divided inductively correct inferences into three kinds, namely categorical, statistical, and analogical. But there are other useful ways to divide them.

In particular, it is important to distinguish between reasoning from what is observed to what is as yet unobserved *but can be observed,* and reasoning from what is observed to what *even in principle cannot be observed.*

For instance, we reason from the observed to the *observable* when we infer from the fact that most autos of a certain kind have lasted a long time to the conclusion that a particular auto of this kind will last a long time. That an auto lasts a long time is something we can directly observe. But we reason or infer from the observed to that which even in principle *cannot be observed* when we infer from the fact that Smith's finger was pricked by a pin, followed by the rapid withdrawal of his hand, facial grimaces, exclamations of "ouch", and so on, to the conclusion that Smith is in pain. In this case, we cannot directly observe the thing inferred, namely Smith's pain, for it is impossible to experience or observe directly someone else's mental activity. In this case we must infer the unobservable pain from what we take to be causally related to the pain, namely the withdrawal of Smith's hand, his facial expression, his utterances, and so on.

Those things, like mental states, that cannot be observed directly are often called **theoretical entities,** to distinguish them from things that can be observed directly, called **observable entities.** But there is a great deal of controversy about which things are, in fact, directly observable.

In addition, it is useful to divide the entities commonly classed as theoretical into four kinds.

(1) *Physical particles,* such as electrons, which many scientists claim cannot be directly observed even in principle, constitute a kind of theoretical entity, for we must *infer* their existence.*

(2) **Dispositional properties** (discussed briefly in Chapter Nine) constitute another kind of theoretical entity. An example is the property of being *flammable*. We can observe that something *burns,* but not that it is *flammable*. Similarly, we can observe that something *bends,* but not that it is *flexible*. Burning and bending are *observable* properties; flammability and flexibility are *dispositional* properties. Since disposi-

---

*Roughly, electrons are claimed to be unobservable because observing (in the sense of "seeing") requires the use of entities (like light rays) that cannot interact appropriately with something so small as an electron.

tional properties are not directly observable, we must *infer* their existence. They constitute a kind of theoretical entity.*

(3) *Mental events* or *mental experiences* constitute still another kind of theoretical entity. However, this kind of theoretical entity is different from all others in that every given entity of this kind can be experienced by someone or other (namely the person who "has" the mental experience), although it cannot be observed by anyone else. For instance, my pain can be (and is) experienced by me, but not by anyone else. And your pain can be (and is) experienced by you, but not by anyone else. From *your* point of view, *my* pain is theoretical, while from *my* point of view, *your* pain is theoretical. This is different from the case with respect to say, electrons, because (according to many scientists) no one can directly observe electrons. (It should be noted that according to one philosophical theory called the *neural identity* theory, consciousness is a brain process, and therefore *is* observable.)

(4) Finally, many philosophers consider all *physical objects, material objects,* or material substance, to be theoretical entities. They believe that it is what they call *sense data* that we experience directly, and not the physical objects that may be causally related to them.† If we believe in the existence of physical objects in addition to the existence of sense data, and perhaps causally related to sense data, then this belief (if rationally founded) will be based on *inductive inferences* from what we experience, namely sense data, to their cause, namely physical objects.

We characterized theoretical entities as things that we cannot observe. But words such as "cannot", called *modal terms,* are notoriously tricky. In particular, the word "cannot" itself is *ambiguous*. When we say that electrons cannot be observed, we mean that it is impossible to observe them. Similarly, when we say that we cannot observe someone else's mental experiences, we mean that it is impossible for us to observe them.

---

* We omit discussion of entities like electro-magnetic fields, in particular the question whether they can be analyzed as dispositional properties of particles or constitute a separate and different sort of theoretical entity.

† We cannot go into a detailed discussion concerning sense data at this point. But we can understand roughly what the philosopher who postulates the existence of sense data is talking about by thinking of a very vivid dream or hallucination concerning, say, seeing one's father, and comparing that experience with the experience of *really* seeing one's father. Taken alone, the dream or hallucination may be identical with the experience of really seeing one's father. Now in the dream, the *experience of* seeing one's father surely is mental. So when really seeing one's father, the *experience* (as opposed perhaps to its cause) must also be mental, since taken alone (out of context) it is identical with the mental dream experience of seeing one's father. Roughly speaking, the sense data philosopher merely attaches the label *sense data* to the content of an experience, whether of the dream-hallucination kind, or the "real" vision kind. And, of course, he attaches that label to auditory experience, olfactory experience, and others, as well as to visual experience.

However, the senses of "impossible" are different in each case. In the first case, we mean that it is *physically impossible* to observe electrons directly; that is, we mean that the laws of nature (the way the world happens to be) precludes our observing electrons. Or, to put it another way, we mean that it is a *contingent fact* that we cannot observe electrons. But in the second case, we mean that it is *logically impossible* to observe someone else's experiences directly. We can have experiences that are just like someone else's experiences, but we cannot literally share the same experience.

So before we can say what kinds of things are theoretical entities (and thus cannot be observed), we must know what kind of impossibility is appropriate. It will come as no surprise that philosophers disagree on the matter.

Exercise 14-3:

In your opinion, which of the following underlined terms refer to theoretical entities and which to observable ones (or both)? Explain.

1. George picked up the book on the table, and observed that it had an odd red cover.
2. Opening the book, he noticed that the first sentence was about Newton's law concerning gravitational force.
3. It was, strangely, the very same sentence that started the physics text he used last year, when he first took Physics I.
4. His attention wandered from Newton to what he knew would come sooner or later, twentieth-century physics, field theories, neutrinos, and all that sort of thing.
5. Vague thoughts of dropping out of school crossed his mind, especially when he realized he also was enrolled in Chemistry I this semester.
6. He walked into the next room and picked up his chemistry text—its cover looked red, but the light was poor, so he wasn't sure.

---

3 *Cause and Effect*

Inductive reasoning is used to discover the **causes** of different kinds of events. For instance, we can infer inductively from the premise that everyone observed to eat a certain kind of food gets food poisoning to the conclusion that everyone who eats that kind of food will get food poisoning, and then be justified in saying that eating that particular kind of food is a *cause* of food poisoning. (Contracting the food poisoning will then be considered the *effect* of the cause, that is, the effect of eating that kind of food.)

But what does it mean to say that one thing is the cause of another, or that two things are causally related? One of the simplest of the many answers given to this question is that when we say something like "A causes B", the most we are justified in asserting is that *whenever A occurs, B occurs.** Or to be more precise, what we mean by "A causes B" is that whenever an A-like event occurs, a B-like event occurs (since events A and B are "singular", and cannot occur more than once). For instance, to say that eating food of type F causes food poisoning of type P is to say that whenever anyone eats F he contracts P, or in symbols $(x)(Fx \supset Px)$, where Fx = "x is a person who eats food of type F", and Px = "x contracts food poisoning of type P".

But we cannot say that A is the cause of B if B occurs *before* A occurs, even if it happens to be true that whenever A-like events occur, B-like events occur. For example, suppose the only way one can get type P food poisoning is to eat type F food. In other words, suppose it is true not only that $(x)(Fx \supset Px)$, but also that $(x)(Px \supset Fx)$. Even so, we cannot say that contracting P causes the eating of F, because the eating of F occurs before the onset of P. (But we can say that P and F are *causally connected,* or *causally related*. In general, to say that a given thing, A, is the cause of some other thing, B, is to say more than that A and B are causally related.)

Whatever the merits of Hume's philosophical analysis of cause, in everyday life we tend to think of the cause of a thing as whatever we would need to do or change so as to bring about a certain effect. To take a simplified example, we know inductively that any well-made match heated sufficiently in the presence of oxygen will light. In symbols $(x)\{[(Mx \cdot Hx) \cdot Px] \supset Lx\}$ (where Mx = "x is a well-made match", Hx = "x is heated to a sufficiently high temperature", Px = "x is in the presence of oxygen", and Lx = "x lights"). If asked why a given match lit, we can say either that it did so because it was struck (heated) in the presence of oxygen, or simply that it do so because it was struck (heated), omitting reference to the presence of oxygen as understood. In other words, we can furnish an instance of the antecedent (or part of the antecedent) of the inductive generalization $(x)\{[(Mx \cdot Hx) \cdot Px] \supset Lx\}$ as the *cause* of the analogous instance of its consequent.

However, we cannot do this in every case. For instance, the inductive generalization just referred to, namely $(x)\{[(Mx \cdot Hx) \cdot Px] \supset Lx\}$, is equivalent to the inductive generalization $(x)\{[(Mx \cdot Hx) \cdot \sim Lx] \supset \sim Px\}$. But usage does not permit us to say that in a given case oxygen was not present *because* the match didn't light when heated; that is, usage does not permit us to refer to an instance of the antecedent of the inductive generalization $(x)\{[(Mx \cdot Hx) \cdot \sim Lx] \supset \sim Px\}$ as the *cause* of

---

*This answer originated with David Hume. See his *An Inquiry Concerning Human Understanding*, Sections IV and VII, and *A Treatise of Human Nature*, Book I, Part III, Section XIV.

the analogous instance of its consequent. This is true in spite of the fact that *if* the inductive generalization is true, and an instance of its antecedent is true, then the analogous instance of its consequent must be true.

There must be a difference between the case where we say (correctly) that the match lit *because* it was heated in the presence of oxygen, and the case where we say (incorrectly) that the match was not in the presence of oxygen *because* it was heated when it didn't light. And the difference in this case primarily concerns human agency. For we can *make* a match light by striking it (heating it) in the presence of oxygen, but we cannot make a match be not in the presence of oxygen by striking it (heating it) and having it not light. (Indeed, human agency is the primary reason we refuse to say that an event *A* that occurs after some other event *B* is the cause of that event. Obviously, we cannot influence the past, and hence cannot cause *B* to have occurred by producing *A*.)

Science has taken its notion of **causal connection,** or **causal relationship,** from the everyday notion of cause, or *cause and effect*. For example, Gallileo discovered a causal connection between the distance a thing falls on Earth and the time it falls. (Note that it doesn't sound right to say that dropping a ball, say, 64 feet *caused* it to fall for two seconds.)

Just as many other concepts, the notion of cause is really a cluster of related concepts, not just one crisp concept. Thus, we often speak of the cause of something as what would be needed to be changed in order to produce that thing, even though we mere mortals aren't able to bring it about. For example, a scientist may speak of how we could cause human beings to live indefinitely long lives by effecting certain changes in body chemistry, even though there is no conceivable chance in the forseeable future that we could in fact make these bodily changes.

This use of the concept of cause is legitimate because if we *were* able to make the requisite chemical changes in our bodies, we *could* cause human beings to live indefinitely. Similarly, we say that night is *not* the cause of day, even though night is always followed by day, because we know what to do to cause night not to be followed by day, even though we can't do it (for instance, we can't set off atom bombs of sufficient force to stop Earth from turning on its axis, but if we could do so, then we could cause night not to be followed by day).

We also should be aware of the fact that there are other common ideas about the nature of causation. For instance, some writers speak of the cause of a thing or event as simply the **sufficient condition** for bringing it about. They would say that the cause of Marie Antoinette's death was being guillotined, because having one's head cut off is a sufficient condition of death.

In addition, some writers refer to a **necessary condition** of a thing as either the cause or (more usually) as a part of the cause of that thing. Thus, the presence of oxygen, while it can't be said to be the complete cause of the lighting of a match, can be thought of as part of the cause, a necessary condition of the effect, since in the absence of oxygen, a match will not light.

Further, it also seems to make sense to speak of causing something by doing something else even though that other thing is neither a necessary nor a sufficient condition for bringing the first thing about. For example, we said before that we can cause a match to light by striking it, even though that is neither a necessary condition of its lighting (because we can heat the match in other ways) nor a sufficient condition (because the match won't light in the presence of oxygen if it's wet, or isn't heated).

Finally, we often speak of causation in statistical or probability cases, where it isn't true that producing the cause necessarily produces the effect, but only that it will probably produce it. Thus, we speak of the cause of Smith's lung cancer being his having smoked two packs of cigarettes a day for twenty years, even though lots of similarly heavy smokers don't get lung cancer. The reason we can say so is, again, *agency*. For example, one way to *cause* someone to get lung cancer (even if it won't work in every case) is to bring about that person's smoking of two packs of cigarettes a day for twenty years.

4 *Mill's Methods*

As stated above, *inductive generalization* is a way to justify conclusions about causal relationships among events or phenomena. Thus, if every observed instance in which we put sugar in unsweetened coffee is an instance in which the coffee is sweetened, we conclude that sugar will sweeten coffee, and that putting the sugar in the coffee caused it to be sweet.

The method of justifying causes and the method of statistical generalization are closely related to a set of procedures called **Mill's Methods,*** proposed as ways to *discover* causal relationships, as well as to *justify* beliefs in causal relationships. Our interest in the methods concerns their use to justify beliefs, since (obviously) discovery of beliefs is not part of the context of justification.

We present three of the five methods, omitting two as essentially similar to the others.

---

* After John Stuart Mill (1806–1873), who is chiefly responsible for their popularization, though not their initial formulation (for which much is owed to John Herschel). For more on Mill's view of Mill's Methods, see his *System of Logic*.

The Method of Agreement

The method of **agreement** is very much like inductive generalization. According to the method of agreement, if we find two or more instances in which a given phenomenon, *P*, occurs, and only one other phenomenon, *Q*, is present in each instance, then we can conclude that *P* and *Q* are causally connected (that is, that *P* is the cause of *Q*, or *Q* of *P*).

Mill's example of a scientific use of the method of agreement is that all objects observed to have a crystalline structure have been found to have one and only one other factor in common, namely that they have solidified from a fluid state. Using the method of agreement, he concluded that having solidified from a fluid state is the *cause* of their crystalline nature. (It can't be the effect because their fluid state precedes their crystalline state.)

Another example is furnished by the food poisoning case previously mentioned. If eating food of type *F* is the only common factor among cases of food poisoning of type *P*, then we can conclude by the method of agreement that it is the cause of the food poisoning.

The structure of the method of agreement becomes more apparent when put into tabular form. Suppose in the food poisoning case that we suspect one of four factors caused the food poisoning, namely day-old chicken salad, a dirty dish used to serve bread and pastry, an infected cut on the thumb of the cook who prepared the spaghetti, and an old gallon carton of chocolate milk left out of the refrigerator. When using the method of agreement, we want to check every case in which the effect occurred to see if there is some one factor common to all of these cases. If, say, five out of eight people contracted the food poisoning, then the table illustrating our use of the method of agreement might look like this (letting "*P*" = "factor present" and "*A*" = "factor absent"):

Cases	Ate Chicken Salad	Ate Pastry	Ate Spaghetti	Drank Milk	Got Food Poisoning
Smith	P	P	A	A	P
Jones	A	P	A	A	A
Chan	A	A	P	P	A
Brown	P	P	P	A	P
Sanchez	A	P	A	A	A
Gordon	P	P	P	P	P
Green	P	P	P	A	P
Cohen	P	A	A	A	P

This table shows that the only suspected factor present in all five cases of food poisoning was the eating of chicken salad. So we should tentatively conclude that this common factor is the cause of the food poisoning (the food poisoning couldn't have been the cause of the eating of chicken salad).

In both of the cases just discussed, use of the method of agreement revealed something *present* that caused the effect. In the crystal case the factor present was the process of solidifying from a fluid state; in the food poisoning case it was the consumption of type F food. But the cause of an event may be the *absence* of some factor (in most cases a factor usually present), and we can extend the use of the method of agreement to cover such cases.

An example is the discovery that rickets, a crippling bone disease once common especially among children in northern Europe, is caused by an absence of sunlight.* Rickets first became a matter of concern in England in the late 1600s, and was then observed to spread throughout northern Europe as this part of the world became highly industrialized. Most of the victims were poor children, so it was natural to assume that malnutrition was the cause, since poor people often suffer from diseases caused by malnutrition. But it turned out that English city children, rich and poor, developed rickets more often than did rural children whose diets were not as healthy. Similarly, it was discovered that rickets does not occur among the poor in Japan and other Eastern countries. So it was clear that rickets was not associated in every case with the absence of healthy food—it therefore would have been fallacious to continue believing that poor diet is the cause of rickets.

It was also discovered that well-fed London zoo animals often developed rickets, although wild animals never do, and that young women and children among high-caste Hindus and upper-class Moslems in India also developed the disease, although poor Hindus and Moslems seldom did so. This suggested that *confinement* is the cause of rickets, since zoo animals are more confined than wild animals, and the upper-class women and children in India were confined to darkened indoor quarters most of the time by ancient custom. But the city children of London (and other industrial cities of northern Europe) were not confined and yet they too developed rickets. So the theory that confinement is the cause of rickets had to be given up, since the presence of rickets was not always associated with the presence of confinement.

Finally, it was realized that absence of sunlight is the cause of rickets. The Industrial Revolution brought with it a tremendous increase in the use of coal, and coal dust in the air reduced the amount of sunlight (already relatively low in northern Europe because of generally cloudy winters), especially in large cities, where the incidence of rickets was highest; in India, upper-class women and children confined indoors also received much less sunlight than other Indians. When this connection be-

---

* Strictly speaking, lack of sunlight is said to be a *remote*, not a *proximate* cause of rickets, for it has subsequently been discovered that ultraviolet radiation in sunlight enables the body to synthesize the hormone calciferol, needed for proper bone growth; lack of calciferol is a more proximate cause of rickets than lack of sunlight. See "Rickets", *Scientific American*, December, 1970.

tween reduced sunlight and rickets was noticed, it was assumed, in accordance with Mill's method of agreement, that lack of sunlight is the cause of rickets. (It couldn't be the other way around; that is, the presence of rickets could not be the cause of lack of sunlight.)

The main difficulty with the method of agreement (and indeed with all of Mill's methods) is that all examined instances of a phenomenon *never* have only one other factor in common. Take the rickets example. It may well be that all of the women and children who were observed to have contracted rickets were under 5′10″ tall and weighed less than 190 pounds. None may have been completely bald, or suffering from skin cancer or sleeping sickness. To assign the blame for rickets to lack of sunlight, according to Mill's methods, we must eliminate *all* other common factors, yet clearly it is impossible to do this since there are indefinitely many factors (such as those just mentioned) to eliminate. Mill's method of difference (and the slightly different joint method of agreement and difference) often can be used to eliminate some of these other factors, but unfortunately cannot ever eliminate all of them (at least not when used by finite beings such as we humans are).

The Method of Difference

According to the method of **difference,** if an instance in which a certain phenomenon, *P*, occurs and an instance in which *P* does not occur are alike in every respect except one, say *Q*, and if *Q* is present only in the instance in which *P* is present, then *P* is the cause (or part of the cause) of *Q*, or *Q* is the cause (or part of the cause) of *P*. In other words, if there is some factor, *Q*, present in an instance when *P* is present, and absent in an instance when *P* is absent, and the two instances are alike in every other respect, then *P* is the cause of *Q*, or *Q* is the cause of *P*.

Again consider the rickets case. Having noticed that the absence of sunlight is associated with the presence of rickets, we can increase the likelihood that lack of sunlight causes rickets by noticing that in those times and places where rickets is totally absent, lots of sunlight is always present. The form of such reasoning is this: We find cases where a lack of sunlight *(P)* and presence of rickets *(Q)* are present together and then find a case where there is no lack of sunlight (absence of *P*) and rickets is absent (absence of *Q*), thus increasing the likelihood that lack of sunlight is the cause of rickets.

You may have noticed that when we put the food poisoning case into tabular form to illustrate the method of agreement, we included cases where food poisoning was not contracted as well as those in which it was. We didn't have to include them to illustrate this method, but in everyday life, when we don't know ahead of time which will be positive and which negative cases, we would likely include both kinds of cases. In any event, counting just the negative cases where food poisoning was absent, the table could be used to illustrate the method of difference:

Cases	Ate Chicken Salad	Ate Pastry	Ate Spaghetti	Drank Milk	Got Food Poisoning
Jones	A	P	A	A	A
Sanchez	A	P	A	A	A
Chan	A	A	P	P	A

This table shows that only one of the suspected factors (eating chicken salad) was absent in every case in which there was no food poisoning, indicating that that factor might have been the cause of the food poisoning. After all, if eating pastry was the cause, everyone who ate pastry should have come down with the food poisoning; but two who did eat it didn't get poisoned. Similarly, eating spaghetti or milk doesn't seem to have been the cause of the food poisoning, so that eating chicken salad was probably the cause.

Obviously, using the methods of agreement and difference *together* should yield better, more highly confirmed conclusions than using either method separately. Our original food poisoning table illustrated this *joint method of agreement and difference,* showing as it did that (1) all cases in which food poisoning was present were cases in which chicken salad was eaten, and (2) all cases where there was no food poisoning were cases in which no chicken salad was eaten:

Cases	Ate Chicken Salad	Ate Pastry	Ate Spaghetti	Drank Milk	Got Food Poisoning
Smith	P	P	A	A	P
Jones	A	P	A	A	A
Chan	A	A	P	P	A
Brown	P	P	P	A	P
Sanchez	A	P	A	A	A
Gordon	P	P	P	P	P
Green	P	P	P	A	P
Cohen	P	A	A	A	P

The above were *positive* uses of Mill's methods; that is, uses designed to show that two factors are causally related. But these methods may also be used negatively, to show that two factors are not causally related. In the rickets case, it was proved that malnutrition is not the cause of rickets by observing cases where malnourishment was present and rickets absent, even though in some cases the two occur together. In other words, we take the failure of our observations to conform to Mill's methods as evidence that there is no causal connection between rickets and malnourishment.

Similarly, to check whether the observed connection between rickets and relatively short height (being under 5′10″ tall) is causal, we try to find cases where rickets is absent, yet short height is present; finding many such cases, we can conclude that being shorter than 5′10″ is not the cause of rickets.

The Method of Concomitant Variation

According to the method of **concomitant variation,** if a given phenomenon varies in amount or degree in some regular way with the amount or degree of some other phenomenon, then the two factors are causally related.

Take the relationship between cigarette smoking and lung cancer. Surveys show that there is a *direct* relationship between smoking cigarettes and dying from lung cancer—those who smoke more cigarettes get lung cancer more often. Hence we conclude that cigarette smoking is causally related to death by lung cancer. (Notice that we cannot say that cigarette smoking is *the* cause of death from lung cancer, since some men who do not smoke at all die of lung cancer, indicating that there must be other causes of that disease.)

Or take the causal relationship between air pressure and the height of a column of mercury in a barometer. In this case, there is a direct quantitative relationship between the two that is so close that we use the effect (the height of the column of mercury) to *measure* the cause (the amount of air pressure).

Many objections have been raised against the use of Mill's Methods. The most frequent is that Mill's Methods, even when correctly applied, may lead to erroneous, even absurd, consequences. One famous example concerns the drinker who drinks scotch and soda one night, bourbon and soda the next night, gin and soda the next, and Irish whiskey and soda on the last night, each drinking bout being followed by a severe hangover. Using Mill's Methods, the drinker concludes that *soda,* the one common factor present on each of the four occasions, must be the cause of the hangovers.

But objections of this kind are spurious. In the drinking example, either the drinker did know that another factor, namely alcohol, was present in each case, or he did not. If he knew this, then he did not apply Mill's Methods correctly, since he knew that soda was not the only common factor. And if he did not know that alcohol was present in each case, then he was justified in applying Mill's Methods in spite of the fact that his conclusion is false and even appears ridiculous. The falsity of the conclusion is not evidence against Mill's Methods because these methods are inductive, and it is the mark of inductive methods that they sometimes yield false conclusions.

In addition, the fact that the conclusion appears ridiculous to us also is not a mark against Mill's Methods, because *we* know that bourbon, scotch, gin, and Irish whiskey all contain alcohol, and we know that hangovers are caused by excessive intake of alcohol. But if we did not know this (and we assume the drinker did not), then the conclusion that hangovers are caused by soda consumption would appear to be quite reasonable. (Incidentally, once the drinker realizes that there is another common factor, alcohol, in every case in which he had a hangover, then he can use Mill's Methods to determine which of these factors causes hangovers, simply by trying a case in which soda is present, but not alcohol, and then a case in which alcohol is present, but not soda.)

There also is the difficulty (mentioned in the discussion of the method of agreement) that the first of Mill's Methods requires all examined instances of a given phenomenon, *P*, to have only *one* factor in common, a requirement that is never satisfied. Some of the factors common to all observed *P*'s can be eliminated by using the method of difference. But all such factors cannot be eliminated in this way. (For one thing, the number of common factors is simply too large to eliminate, even in wholesale batches.)

One way to get around this difficulty is to restate the *method of agreement* as follows: If we find two or more instances in which a given phenomenon, *P*, occurs, such that only one other *known relevant* phenomenon, *Q*, is present in each instance, then we can assume that *P* and *Q* are causally connected.*

Of course, this constitutes more a rephrasing of the problem than a solution to it, for it raises the question of how we are to determine that a given phenomenon is relevant. Unfortunately, no completely satisfactory answer to this question has been provided.[†]

Exercise 14-4:

Show for each of the following whether it contains a correct use of Mill's Methods, and if so which one(s).

---

* We also have to add that the more instances in which *P* and *Q* are known to be present, the more probable the conclusion. For if we conclude with a *high* degree of confidence that *P* causes *Q* when the known instances linking *P* and *Q* are very few, then we commit the fallacy of *hasty conclusion*.

[†] However, the answer must lie in the direction of so-called background information. We know whether or not a given phenomenon is relevant because of information *other* than that the two phenomena in question have always appeared together. For instance, we know from background information that the color of a pair of dice is not relevant to its performance, while its center of gravity and precise shape are very relevant indeed. So anyone looking for the cause of the poor performance of loaded dice will ignore their color and concentrate on their center of gravity and precise shape.

1. If you heat a normally combustible item in a vacuum, or in water, or in any medium that lacks air, combustion will not take place. But if you heat such an object with air present, it will take place. So there is no question but that heating in the presence of air is the cause of combustion.
2. According to some economists, very large increases in an already huge national debt should fairly quickly lead to increases in the rate of inflation, because there should be a corresponding increase in the money supply. So the Reagan administration ran the biggest budget deficits in U.S. peacetime history. By 1985 the national debt was out of sight, and yet inflation was down several percentage points.
3. Smith reasoned that if strong labor unions demanding and getting high salaries are the primary cause of inflation, then less well-organized industries should have little or no price inflation. But on checking, he discovered that the industries studied did suffer from price inflation, although their prices rose more slowly than did those of industries having strong, well-organized unions.
4. Being told by a health enthusiast that my extreme lethargy might be caused by low blood sugar, I took his advice and stopped eating snacks high in carbohydrates and low in protein and almost immediately felt better.
5. Prison experience unquestionably boosts the chance that an offender will break the law again. In one experiment, conducted by The California Youth Authority, a group of convicted juvenile delinquents were given immediate parole and returned to their homes or foster homes, where they got intensive care from community parole officers. After five years, only 28 percent of this experimental group have had their paroles revoked, compared to 52 percent of a comparable group that was locked up after conviction. (*Time*, 24 March 1967, p. 21)
6. I'm satisfied that smoking marijuana does not by itself lead one to try heroin. For one thing, I know quite a few people who have been smoking the stuff for years, but have never tried heroin.
7. Louis Pasteur's theory that vaccination with anthrax virus produces immunity to anthrax disease was confirmed by an interesting experiment. Over twenty farm animals were vaccinated with the virus, and then these animals, plus a like number not so vaccinated, were given a normally fatal dose of anthrax germs. None of the vaccinated animals contracted the disease; all those not vaccinated contracted it.
8. Mr. Joule of Manchester conclusively proved that friction is the cause of heat by expending exact quantities of force by rubbing one substance against another, and showed that the heat produced was exactly greater or less in proportion as the force was greater or less. (W. S. Jevons)
9. If a man's destiny is caused by the star under which he is born, then all men born under that star should have the same fortune. However, masters and slaves and kings and beggars are born under the same star. (Pliny the Elder, *Natural History*)
10. It once was assumed that large brains (relative to body weight) are the cause of great intelligence, because the brains of several known geniuses had, after their deaths, turned out to be much larger than average. But when the brain of Anatole France was examined after his death, it was discovered to be quite small relative to his overall body size. However, his brain contained an unusually large number of deep furrows (resulting in a much larger than usual outer surface), as did the brains of several other geniuses when examined after their deaths. So rather than brain size, it would appear that it is the amount of outer brain surface that leads to genius in human beings.
11. **McBird:** I wouldn't run for president in 1980 for all the tea in Safeway.
    Mary: Well, even the Prohibition Party won't nominate you, so it's academic. But why wouldn't you run?
    McBird: Because the person elected every twenty years, starting with 1840, died in office. There's a curse on those elected every twenty years, and I'm too young to die so soon.
12. I placed two silver dimes next to this bar, and they moved toward it. I then tried a few paper clips, a teaspoon, some nails, and a small pair of scissors, and they all moved toward it. So I tried a one-ounce liquor glass, a couple of envelopes, a half-gallon carton of milk,

and a spool of thread; none moved toward the bar. Obviously, this wonderful bar attracts all metals, but nothing else.

13. All children up to fifth grade in a certain California elementary school were given a standard IQ test which teachers were told was a test designed to predict which students would have the largest intellectual growth in the following two years. After the test was administered, teachers were given the names of students selected at random (some had scored high and some low), but were told that these students had scored high on the test and therefore could be expected to "spurt" ahead academically in the following year. During the next two years, students were given follow-up IQ tests, and it was found that in some grades—especially the first and second—those designated as likely fast learners improved more than did those not so designated. Since the "spurters" were chosen at random, it was concluded that a teacher's expectations are a causal factor in improving student IQ. (From Robert Rosenthal and Lenore F. Jacobson, "Teacher Expectations for the Disadvantaged", *Scientific American,* April 1968)

14. A researcher noticed that several victims of keratitis (a kind of blindness) were deficient in riboflavin. So he examined others suffering from the disease, and they too were low on that nutrient. Finding no other likely cause for the disease, the researcher theorized that keratitis is caused by a lack of riboflavin and confirmed his hunch by giving keratitis victims large doses of riboflavin and observing that the keratitis was cured.

Exercise 14-5:

True or False? Explain your answer.

1. An inductively strong argument can have true premises and a false conclusion.
2. Although false that induction goes from the particular to the general while deduction goes the other way, still it's true that induction goes from the less general to the more general, while deduction goes just the other way.
3. There is no such thing as a correct *statistical* inductive generalization.
4. We can regard a categorical inductive generalization as a special kind of statistical generalization in which the ratio of examined *F*'s that are *G*'s is 100 percent.
5. The same hypothesis may be highly probable (highly confirmed) given one set of evidence, while disconfirmed by another.
6. One way to state the pattern or form of correct categorical inductive generalizations is this:

    1. All examined *F*'s are *G*'s.

    /∴ 2. All *F*'s are *G*'s.

7. The greater the number of instances mentioned in the premises of an analogical argument, the higher their degree of support for its conclusion.
8. The greater the difference between items mentioned in the premises of an analogical argument, the lower their degree of support for the conclusion.
9. It has been claimed that analogies are just enthymematic versions of categorical or statistical inductions.
10. *Theoretical entities* are entities referred to in as yet unsupported scientific theories. After such a theory receives sufficient confirmation, its formerly theoretical entities are then considered to be *existent,* not theoretical, entities.

11. The property of being water soluble is a dispositional property, hence also a theoretical one.
12. The physically impossible violates at least one law of nature, while the logically impossible violates at least one law of logic.
13. What Mill's method of agreement requires is that we find at least two occurrences of some phenomenon, *P*, that are also occurrences of some phenomenon, *Q*; finding them, we're entitled to assert that *P* is (probably) the cause of *Q*.
14. The main problem with Mill's method of agreement is that all examined instances of a phenomenon never have only one other factor in common.
15. Mill's methods can be used negatively to discover that one phenomenon, *P*, is *not* the cause of another, *Q*, by finding an instance of *P* that is not an instance of *Q*.

Key Terms Introduced in Chapter Fourteen

Analogical inference: An inductive inference from particular instances to a conclusion concerning some other particular instance. An example is the inference from the evidence that three English suits wore well to the conclusion that some other English suit will wear well.

Categorical analogy: Inductive inference from the evidence that all tested *F*'s are *G*'s to the conclusion that some as yet untested *F* is a *G*.

Categorical inductive generalization: An inductive inference from particular instances to a universal conclusion. An example is the inference from the evidence that all *observed* ravens are black to the categorical generalization that all ravens are black.

Causal connection (or relationship): A certain kind of constant conjunction between two sorts of things (for instance, between putting sugar in coffee and having the coffee taste sweet).

Cause and effect: A kind of causal connection in which the earlier of a pair of causally connected items is said to be the *cause* and the later the *effect*.

Dispositional property: An unobservable property or power. An example is the property of being flexible.

Method of agreement: One of Mill's Methods, namely the method of inferring that if *P* is the only factor present in every observed occurrence of *Q*, then *P* and *Q* are causally related.

Method of concomitant variation: One of Mill's Methods, namely the method of inferring that if a given phenomenon varies in some regular way with some other phenomenon, then the two phenomena are causally related.

Method of difference: One of Mill's Methods, namely the method of inferring that whatever is present when *Q* is present, and absent when *Q* is absent, is causally related to *Q*.

Mill's Methods: Methods for finding (or confirming) causal relationships, championed by the nineteenth-century philosopher, John Stuart Mill.

Observable entity: That which can be experienced or observed directly. *Antonym:* **Theoretical entity.**

Statistical analogy: Inductive inference from the evidence that *N* percent of the tested *F*'s are *G*'s to the conclusion that the probability is *N* percent that some as yet untested *F* is a *G*.

Statistical inductive generalization: An inductive inference from particular instances to a statistical conclusion. An example is the inference from the evidence that half of all tosses with this coin so far landed heads up, to the statistical conclusion that half of all tosses with this coin will land heads up.

Theoretical entity: Postulated entity that cannot be experienced or observed directly. *Antonym:* **Observable entity.**

Chapter Fifteen

Probability

Probabilities and sentences about probabilities play an important role both in everyday life and in science, as the following examples illustrate:

1. The probability of getting a seven with an honest pair of dice is 1/6.
2. Art will probably beat Charles at squash this afternoon.
3. We'll probably have rain tomorrow.
4. The probability that a given American male will die of lung cancer in the next year is 0.0008.
5. The theory of relativity is more probable on today's evidence than on the evidence available in 1919.
6. The probability that a given birth will be a male birth equals 0.51.

But philosophers differ radically in their analyses of the concept of probability. The following exposition construes probabilities as primarily of two different kinds, namely the *subjective* and the *contingent*.

1 *Contingent Probabilities*

Statements about **contingent probabilities,** sometimes called **objective probabilities,** or **ontological probabilities,** make claims about the nature of the world, or some portion of it. For example, someone who says that the probability is 1/6 of getting 7 with an honest (symmetrical) pair of dice may mean that in a reasonably long series of tosses with honest dice seven will turn up about one-sixth (1/6) of the time, or, in other words, that the **relative frequency** with which 7's turn up when we use honest dice equals 1/6 of all tosses.

The dice example concerns a game of chance, and is noteworthy because the first full-blown mathematical theories about probabilities were worked out concerning games of chance. But the calculation of contingent probabilities is useful in virtually every aspect of life. For example, airlines typically overbook popular flights based on their knowledge of the contingent probability that customers holding reservations will actually show up. They have no way of telling in advance whether a given reservation holder will show up, but they have learned from experience what the approximate relative frequency of no-shows will be.

In fact, if we did away with calculations of contingent probabilities, an extremely large part of science would be lost. For example, in physics, the gas laws, entropy law, and theories about the half-lives of radioactive substances, among others, would bite the dust.

2 *Subjective Probabilities*

Statements about **subjective probabilities,** sometimes called **epistemic probabilities,** make claims about *strengths of belief* about the world, not about the world itself. For instance, Maryland state legislators who enacted a state lottery were very confident that their state would make a great deal of money from the lottery in the long run, even though it was logically possible that the state would lose money on the venture. (Their confidence was based in part on the fact that the odds against each lottery player would be about two to one—sucker odds). One legislator expressed this confidence by saying that "it is extremely probable—I have complete confidence—that the state will gross approximately 50 percent of all the money bet." His statement expressed a subjective probability, not a contingent one, because it made a claim about his strength of belief in the profitability of the lottery.

In the lottery example, the legislator asserted his very strongly held belief that Maryland's lottery would return handsome profits to the state (it has). But he didn't mean simply to express his personal belief. After all, people have believed all sorts of foolish things—on the basis of flimsy evidence, or because of wishful thinking or poor reasoning. He meant to say that his belief was *rational,* or *reasonable;* the kind of belief sane, unbiased people should accept. When theorists talk about subjective probabilities, they generally have in mind, as we do now, not just any old strengths of belief but rather *rational* strengths of belief, justified by good reasons or evidence.

What makes a statement about *contingent* probabilities true always is the way the world happens to be compared to how the statement in question claims it to be. For example, the contingent probability statement about the probability equaling 1/6 of getting 7's with honest pairs of dice is true just in case the relative frequency of 7 with honest dice does in fact equal 1/6. Similarly, what makes the contingent probability claim that over 95 percent of all heart bypass operations are successful false is that the actual frequency of success has been much lower than 95 percent.

But what makes subjective probability statements true or false* is quite different. For they always concern *beliefs* about the world, not the world "out there" itself. For example, most experts believed fairly strongly, and for very good reasons, that the 1985 Superbowl game between Miami and San Francisco would be fairly close, although in fact San Francisco won handily; but their claims of a high subjective probability for the game being close were true, because justified by very good arguments, even though the game in fact was not close. (Recall that perfectly good inductive arguments, even those based on a great deal of evidence, may turn out to have false conclusions.)

In general, what makes rational subjective probability statements true is that they are *justified* by good deductive or inductive reasoning; what makes them false is that they are not so justified. But what makes contingent probability statements true or false never has to do with the quality of our justification for such a claim. For instance, political polls often are flawed by being based on biased samples, so that acceptance of their results is unjustified. But such polls sometimes produce accurate predictions anyway (by luck). If one of these biased polls predicts that a certain candidate will win 56 percent of the votes and he or she does win that percentage, the prediction is true. That it was based on a biased sample is irrelevant to its truth. But a strong *belief* based on a poll known to be biased is an unjustified belief, and a statement that it is rational to strongly hold such a belief is false. That such a belief turns out to be true is irrelevant to the fact that it was irrational to hold it. Fools sometimes luckily are right in their claims although wrong to have held them; geniuses sometimes are wrong in their beliefs, even though right to have held them.

3 *Single-Case Probabilities*

Theorists sometimes object to the relative frequency interpretation of contingent probabilities because (among other reasons) it doesn't seem able to handle a particular very common type of contingent probability—the so-called **single-case** probability.

Consider a typical weather prediction, say, that the probability of rain tomorrow is 90 percent. It seems wrong to construe such a prediction as concerned with the relative frequency of rain tomorrow, since it makes no sense to say that the relative frequency of rain tomorrow will equal 90 percent. After all, it either will or won't rain tomorrow, so that the rela-

---

* Some theorists prefer to think of subjective probabilities that express *rational* strengths of belief and not just anyone's actual state of mind as not either true or false but rather as *justified* or *unjustified*. On this view, if the evidence or reasons supporting a subjective probability claim are good, it is justified; otherwise it isn't. But this is just a terminological difference.

tive frequency of rain will be one if it does, and zero if it doesn't. Therefore, 90 percent is an impossible relative frequency.

Some theorists therefore construe apparent single-case probabilities statements as disguised statements about long-run relative frequencies.* Take the statement that the probability of rain tomorrow equals 90 percent. They would construe that statement as really about the relative frequency of rain a day after days on which the weather conditions are like those existing today.

But this analysis seems to be wrong. To see that it is, consider the single-case statement that the probability of getting killed in one play of Russian roulette with a six-shooter equals 1/6. The theory in question would have to construe such a statement as an assertion that the relative frequency with which players get killed playing Russian roulette equals 1/6. However, although this statistical claim happens to be true, it doesn't accurately interpret the single-case probability statement in question. Those who play Russian roulette just once care little about long-term statistics (in the long run, all Russian roulette players die). What they care dearly about is what will happen when they, at a particular moment, spin the chamber and pull the trigger, or, since they can't know that, what their *chances* are of being killed when they pull the trigger, which is what the single-case probability of 1/6 tells them.

Some writers take another tack and say that single-case probability statements are not about relative frequencies, indeed aren't about contingent probabilities at all, but rather are about subjective probabilities. They would construe the statement about the probability of rain tomorrow being 90 percent as an assertion that a rational person should believe with reasonably strong conviction that it will rain (so that a rational person would *expect* rain, but not be certain of it).

But this too seems wrong. Take the Russian roulette case. On the theory now being considered, the statement about the probability of losing at Russian roulette being 1/6 has to be interpreted to mean it is rational for the player in question to believe five times more strongly that he will survive than that he won't. This, however, simply is false. It isn't rational for a Russian roulette player to believe either that he will survive or that he won't (no matter with what strength of belief), since all that is known is that 5/6 of such fools survive while 1/6 don't. Will a particular player be lucky and survive? That is precisely what a Russian roulette player doesn't know and has no reason to believe. A significant feature of the game of Russian roulette is, after all, that no player has reason to believe either in his own survival or in his own death.

---

*For instance, see Ronald Gierre, *Understanding Scientific Reasoning,* 2nd ed., (New York: Holt, Rinehart and Winston, 1984), p. 203. Gierre seems to equate relative frequencies with what he calls *tendencies,* but gives no justification for doing so.

When talking about single cases in everyday life, we often speak of the *likelihood,* or the *chances,* or *tendencies*. For example, we say, "The *chances* are that Reagan will win the election", or "It's *likely* that this time the CIA will conceal embarrassing evidence", and so on. If these kinds of cases can't be handled as either contingent probabilities expressing relative frequencies or as subjective probabilities, is there some other kind of probability, contingent or otherwise, concerned with likelihoods, chances, or tendencies? And if so, just what are these strange creatures? (In any case, as we shall see, we often know fairly well how to *calculate* single-case probabilities even if we don't quite understand what they are.)

4 *Principle of Indifference*

Classical theorists often appealed to a principle for calculating probabilities called the **principle of indifference,** or **principle of nonsufficient reason.** According to this principle, alternative outcomes supported by matched, or equally good,* evidence are to be considered equally probable.

Suppose we want to bet on a football game about which we know only that both teams have good quarterbacks and wide receivers (fanciful example). Since what we know about one team is matched by what we know about the other, it seems reasonable to conclude that the probability of one team winning equals that of the other. So the principle of indifference has a certain plausibility to it.

However, when we stray from its strictest version, the principle becomes less plausible. This is true in particular when applied to cases of "equal ignorance", where we have no reasons for preferring one alternative over another. (In such cases, the "weight of the evidence" can be thought of as matched (namely zero) for every possible outcome.)

One problem is simply how to calculate the number of possible outcomes. In games of chance, we can arbitrarily choose their number, for example, as we do in roulette (the ordinary kind), where, for instance, a play in which the ball landed between numbers would be declared a nonplay. In other areas of life, options tend to be less structured.

But even with respect to games of chance, the principle sometimes is ambiguous concerning the number of possible outcomes. Suppose we want to calculate the probability of getting one heads and one tails in two tosses of a symmetrical coin. How do we decide how many outcomes there are? Counting one way, there are three: (1) no heads, two tails; (2) one heads, one tails; and (3) two heads, no tails. Counting another way,

---

* Advocates differ in their precise interpretation of the principle.

there are four: (1) tails, tails; (2) tails, heads; (3) heads, tails; and (4) heads, heads. The first way yields a probability of 1/3 for getting one heads and one tails in two tosses, the second way a probability of 1/4. Most of us would choose the latter value of 1/4, but the principle of indifference is itself indifferent between the two.*

Another frequently raised objection to the principle of indifference is that it applies only in a very few cases, chiefly to symmetrical games of chance such as dice, because in everyday life it's unusual to have matching evidence concerning the various possible outcomes. In our made-up football example, we did have that kind of evidence, but in real life, even in the case of football games, we rarely do.

And finally, the principle has been objected to on the grounds that it yields *contradictory* probability values in certain kinds of cases.

To illustrate this charge, let's use the formula relating the distance, D, a thing travels with the time, T, and the rate of speed, R, that it travels. If something travels a distance of exactly one mile, then $R = 1/T$, and $T = 1/R$. (This follows from the general formula that $D = R \times T$, by substituting 1 for D and transposing.)

Now let's assume that an auto travels a distance of exactly one mile at a constant rate of speed somewhere between 40 and 60 miles per hour. According to the classical theory, the probability equals 1/2 that the auto travels at a rate of speed between 40 and 50 miles per hour, because the number of *possible* rates of speed between 40 and 50 miles per hour is exactly half the number of possible rates of speed between 40 and 60 miles per hour.†

Now let's calculate the probability that the *time* it takes to travel the one mile is between 1/40th and 1/50th of an hour. According to the formula that $T = 1/R$, if the auto travels at 40 miles per hour, then it takes 1/40th of an hour to travel the one mile, and if it travels at 60 miles per hour, it takes 1/60th of an hour. So it must take between 1/40th and 1/60th of an hour to travel the mile at a rate of speed between 40 and 60 miles per hour. Hence, according to the classical theory of probability, the probability is *greater* than 1/2 that the time it takes the auto to travel the mile is between 1/40th and 1/50th of an hour. This follows from the

---

* At least one recent writer opted for the former, namely Rudolf Carnap. See his "On the Application of Inductive Logic", *Philosophy and Phenomenological Research,* vol. 8 (1947), pp. 133–48.

† Actually, this isn't quite true. The number of possible rates of speed between 40 and 50 miles per hour *exactly equals* the number of possible rates of speed between 40 and 60 miles per hour, since the number in each case is infinite (in fact, non-denumerably infinite). To make the classical theory work at all in this case, we have to assume either that only a finite number of different rates of speed are possible, or that some way can be found to distinguish between infinities of the same level. The point of the above example is that on either assumption contradictory probability values result from use of the principle of indifference, and hence from use of the classical theory.

fact that the interval between 1/40 and 1/50 is larger than the interval between 1/50 and 1/60, so that more than half of the possible times between 1/40th and 1/60th of an hour are between 1/40th and 1/50th of an hour.

But now trouble arises. We first calculated that the probability is 1/2 that the rate of speed of the auto is between 40 and 50 miles per hour. We then calculated that the probability is greater than 1/2 that the time it takes the auto to travel the mile is between 1/40th and 1/50th of an hour. But if the auto travels the mile at a rate of speed between 40 and 50 miles per hour, it follows that it must travel the mile in a time between 1/40th and 1/50th of an hour (because $T = 1/R$). Hence, the probability that it travels the mile in a time between 1/40th and 1/50th of an hour must equal the probability that it travels at a rate of speed between 40 and 50 miles per hour. In other words both probabilities must equal 1/2, which contradicts the previous result that the probability is greater than 1/2 that the auto takes between 1/40th and 1/50th of an hour to travel the mile.

Clearly, a principle that yields contradictory probability values is seriously defective. At least one attempt has been made to remove this defect,* but further examination of the problem is beyond the scope of this text.

5 *Calculating Relative Frequencies*

Whatever the merits of the principle of indifference when applied to the calculation of subjective probabilities, most frequency probability theorists reject it out of hand as a way to calculate relative frequencies when the matched "evidence" is equal ignorance of the outcomes. The reason is that they (just as this writer) believe ignorance cannot ever justify beliefs, even probability beliefs, about the nature of the world. Instead, in the simplest (and perhaps most common) cases, they calculate (initial) probabilities by means of statistical inductive generalizations of the kind discussed in the previous chapter. For instance, in calculating the probability that a given American male will die of lung cancer in a given year, they might use statistical evidence of the relative frequency of death by lung cancer in American males in previous years, and assume that the relative frequency will remain the same this year.

---

* By Rudolf Carnap. Carnap's theory requires that we eliminate defined terms and reduce to our primitive vocabulary before calculating probabilities. There will be only one way to do this for any given choice of language base. The trouble with Carnap's solution is that there are apparently equally good language bases that yield different probability values. See Carnap's *Logical Foundations of Probability,* 2nd ed. (Chicago: Univ. of Chicago Press, 1962); and *The Continuum of Inductive Methods* (Chicago: Univ. of Chicago Press, 1952).

Of course, when relevant *background evidence* or *background theories* are available, they should be used to correct direct statistical inductions. Consider, for instance, the calculation of the probability that a given birth will be a male birth. It may happen that the relative frequency of male births to total number of births in a given nation remains relatively stable over a long period of time at, say, 0.51. If we have no additional information, then the frequency theory requires that we calculate the probability that a given birth in that nation will be a male birth as 0.51.

But we may well have additional information. For example, we may know that a war is about to begin and have statistical evidence that in the past the relative frequency of male births has increased in wartime (because the average age of parents decreases, and younger parents tend to have a greater percentage of male offspring). Obviously, we ought not predict that the relative frequency of male births will continue to be 0.51. Instead, we ought to raise that value to take into account the expected increase in early marriages, with its expected increase in male births.

In like manner, many probability hypotheses can be corrected by means of background information or background hypotheses.

Exercise 15-1:

Which of the following sentences are best construed as being about contingent probabilities (relative frequencies) and which about subjective probabilities (rational strengths of belief) or something else? Explain and defend your answers.

1. The probability that a president of the United States will be over six feet tall is greater than 1/2.
2. There probably is no life on any planet of Alpha Centauri.
3. It's always more likely that the richer of two candidates for public office will win.
4. The odds are one to ten that Dave Kingman will hit a home run on any given time at bat.
5. It was much more likely that there would be good rather than bad weather when the tall ships sailed into New York harbor on July 4, 1976.
6. The evidence gets stronger all the time in support of the theory that increases in salt intake lead to analogous increases in blood pressure—so you better believe it.
7. The San Francisco 49ers will probably play in the 1986 Superbowl (author's prediction made in July 1985).
8. The probability that Harold Gordon will ever be elected president of the United States is even lower than the probability that Jane McBird ever will be elected.
9. Jimmy the Greek's last odds on the 1976 election were six to five in favor of Ford; even J. G. misses on occasion.
10. No one can calculate the probability of his own survival in the event of a nuclear war.

Exercise 15-2:

1. Explain in your own words what the chief differences are between probabilities construed as relative frequencies and as rational strengths of belief.
2. What is the principle of indifference, and how is it used? In your opinion, is its use justified? Defend your answer.
3. No U.S. president so far elected has been Jewish. Should we therefore be committed to the view that no Jewish person will ever be president of the United States? Explain.
4. **Jane McBird:** Harold Gordon just had an incredible run of luck; bucking odds of thousands to one, he picked every NFL football winner on Sunday. So he's not likely to pick a winner on tonight's Monday evening game, because the odds have to even out and they're tremendously against anyone picking so many winners—he's due to lose, and I'm betting against him.
   Comment on this remark.
5. Do you think there are such things as likelihoods (chances, tendencies)? If so, how are they to be interpreted? If not, what are people talking about when they refer, say, to the chances that the Democrats will capture the White House in the next election?

6 *The Probability Calculus*

So far we have considered how what are called *initial* probabilities are to be calculated. Let's now consider how, given certain probabilities (initial or otherwise), other probabilities can be calculated from them. The **probability calculus** has been constructed to answer this question.

Some pairs of events are such that the occurrence of one of them has an *effect* on the occurrence of the other. For example, drawing an ace from a deck of cards (without putting it back into the deck) has an effect on the chances of getting an ace on the next draw.

But other pairs of events are such that the occurrence of one has no effect on the other. For example, drawing an ace from a deck of cards has *no* effect on the chances of getting an ace on the next draw *if* the ace has been put back into the deck before the second draw. (The cards don't "know" that an ace was picked on the first draw.) If two events are such that the occurrence of one has no effect on the occurrence of the second, they are said to be **independent events.**

In addition, some pairs of events are such that it is *logically possible* for both of them to occur. For example, it is logically possible for a die to land with face six up on its first throw and also to land with face six up on its second throw.

But other pairs of events are such that it is not logically possible for both to occur. For example, it is not logically possible for face five *and* face six to turn up on a single throw of a die. If two events are such that it is not logically possible for both to occur, they are said to be **mutually exclusive events.**

Let's use the symbol P as an abbreviation for the term "probability". And let's use p and q as variables, ranging over events. Then we can write the basic rules of the probability calculus, as follows:

1. **Restricted Conjunction Rule**

If p and q are independents events, then $P(p \cdot q) = P(p) \times P(q)$.

For instance, if the probability of getting a six on a given throw $(p) = 1/6$, and the probability of getting a six on some other throw $(q) = 1/6$, then since p and q are independent of each other, the probability of getting sixes on both throws equals the probability of getting a six on the first throw *times* the probability of getting a six on the second throw. Thus, the probability of getting sixes on both throws equals $1/6 \times 1/6$, or $1/36$.

2. **General Conjunction Rule**

$P(p \cdot q) = P(p) \times P(q, \text{given } p)$.

For instance, if the probability of picking a spade on a second draw, *given that a spade was picked on the first draw* (and not replaced) = 12/51,* then the probability that spades will be drawn on both the first and second draws $= 1/4 \times 12/51 = 1/17$.

Notice that if $P(q, \text{given } p) = P(q)$, then the two conjunction rules both yield the same result. In fact, this is the case in which p and q are independent of each other.

3. **Restricted Disjunction Rule**

If p and q are *mutually exclusive* events, then $P(p \vee q) = P(p) + P(q)$.

For example, if the probability of getting a five on a given throw of a die = 1/6, and the probability of getting a six on a given throw of that die = 1/6, then the probability of getting a five *or* a six on a given throw of the die $= 1/6 + 1/6 = 2/6 = 1/3$.

4. **General Disjunction Rule**

$P(p \vee q) = P(p) + P(q) - P(p \cdot q)$.

For instance, if the probability of getting a six on any given throw of a die = 1/6, then the probability of getting at least one six out of two throws (that is, a six on the first throw or a six on the second) = $1/6 + 1/6 - (1/6 \times 1/6) = 2/6 - 1/36 = 11/36$.

Notice that if p and q are mutually exclusive then $P(p \cdot q) = 0$, and then the two disjunction rules yield the same result.

---

* Because twelve spades remain out of 51 cards.

In addition, it is customary to assume that the probability of a *contradiction* = 0, and the probability of a *logical truth* = 1. In symbols, this reads

5. $P(p \cdot \sim p) = 0.$
6. $P(p \vee \sim p) = 1.$

It follows from this that the probability of $\sim p = 1 - P(p)$; that is,

7. $P(\sim p) = 1 - P(p).$

We have now, in effect, provided seven rules for calculating complicated probabilities from simpler ones. But one further kind of complicated probability needs mentioning, namely what is sometimes called an **inverse probability.**

Suppose we know that 90 percent of the families in a certain city own a television set, and that among these, 10 percent also own a computer. Suppose we also know that among the 10 percent who don't own a TV set, 20 percent do own a computer. What is the probability that a family owning a computer also owns a TV set?

To deal with this problem, let $P(p)$ = the probability that a given family owns a TV set. Then in our example,

$P(q) = 0.9$ $\qquad$ $P(p, \text{given } q) = 0.1$

$P(\sim q) = 0.1$ $\qquad$ $P(p, \text{given } \sim q) = 0.2$

(The probabilities on the left are sometimes called *prior probabilities* and those on the right *conditional probabilities,* or *forward probabilities.*) We want to calculate the probability that a given computer owning family also owns a TV set, in symbols $P(q, \text{given } p)$, and for this purpose we can use a simplified version of **Bayes' Theorem,** namely,*

$$P(q, \text{given } p) = \frac{P(q) \times P(p, \text{given } q)}{[P(q) \times P(p, \text{given } q)] + [P(\sim q) \times P(p, \text{given } \sim q)]}$$

Plugging in values from the case at hand, we get,

$$P(q, \text{given } p) = \frac{0.9 \times 0.1}{(0.9 \times 0.1) + (0.1 \times 0.2)} = \frac{0.09}{0.11} = \frac{9}{11}$$

Bayes' Theorem is intuitively plausible. In our example, common sense says the probability that a computer family also is a television set family should depend on, first, the prior probability that a family owns a television set and, second, the conditional probability that a family own-

* The general form of Bayes' Theorem is

$$P(q_1, \text{given } p) = \frac{P(q_1) \times P(p, \text{given } q_1)}{[P(q_1) \times P(p, \text{given } q_1)] + \cdots + [P(q_n) \times P(p, \text{given } q_n)]}$$

We use the general formula when there are more than two values for q to consider.

ing a television set also owns a computer. And this is what Bayes' Theorem calculates.*

Bayes' Theorem is clearly legitimate in cases, like the above, where the relevant prior probabilities are known (in our example, presumably known by statistical inductions from samples). But objections have been raised against the use of Bayes' Theorem when prior probabilities are not known (a common kind of case). Those who accept the principle of indifference can, of course, answer such objections by saying that in the absence of reasons for preferring one value over another, all prior probabilities will be considered equal. But for those who reject the principle of indifference, this line is not open.

In addition to questions about the applicability of Bayes' Theorem when prior probabilities are not known, questions have been raised as to the applicability of the probability calculus in general. Does it apply to all kinds of probabilities?

It seems clear that it does apply to probabilities construed as relative frequencies. For instance, given that the relative frequency of 7's is 1/6 and that of 11's is 1/18, the relative frequency of 7's *or* 11's will in fact approach 2/9 (in the long run), the value calculated according to the restricted disjunction rule. But do they apply to subjective probabilities, that is, to probabilities construed as rational strengths of beliefs? Most writers say *yes,* because using any other calculation rules leads to clearly unacceptable results, in particular making possible what is called a "Dutch Book".

The term comes from gambling. Gamblers who are sufficiently careless or ignorant in placing a series of bets may find that no matter what happens, the bookie must win. When this happens, they're said to have a **Dutch Book** made against them. Obviously, any system of rules for calculating odds that might lead gamblers to allow a Dutch Book to be made against them is not an acceptable system.

It turns out that any system that deviates from the standard probability calculus is susceptible to a Dutch Book (can have a Dutch Book made

---

* We can prove Bayes' Theorem, in the sense that it can be derived from a few of the other rules for calculating probabilities. Here is a proof of the simplified version of Bayes' Theorem:

1. $P(q, \text{given } p) = \dfrac{P(p \cdot q)}{P(p)}$ From General Conjunction Rule

2. $P(q, \text{given } p) = \dfrac{P(p \cdot q)}{P[(p \cdot q) \vee (p \cdot \sim q)]}$ Because p is logically equivalent to $(p \cdot q) \vee (p \cdot \sim q)$

3. $P(q, \text{given } p) = \dfrac{P(p \cdot q)}{P(p \cdot q) + P(p \cdot \sim q)}$ From Restricted Disjunction Rule

4. $P(q, \text{given } p) = \dfrac{P(q) \times P(p, \text{given } q)}{[P(q) \times P(p, \text{given } q)] + [p(\sim q) \times P(p, \text{given } \sim q)]}$ General Conjunction Rule

against it). So most writers would say that only the standard calculus is acceptable as a measure of fair odds, and of rational strengths of beliefs. (More will be said about this when we discuss the justification of induction in Section 7 of the next chapter.)

The above line of reasoning certainly has merit, at least with respect to single-case probabilities construed as likelihoods, chances, odds, and the like. After all, a system of rules can't calculate fair odds if it is susceptible to a Dutch Book.

But when we consider, say, the probabilities of theories, construed as rational strengths of beliefs in those theories, the going gets more problematic. Suppose we have quite good evidence confirming three independent scientific theories, one in physics, another in, say, geology, and a third in biology. Suppose that the evidence is sufficiently confirming to make the rational strength of belief in the first theory equal 0.8, in the second 0.8, and the third 0.75. Then if we apply the restricted conjunction rule, we must conclude that the rational strength of belief in all three theories (that all three are true) equals 0.48, just below the halfway point, 0.5, that marks the division between belief and disbelief, meaning that we should be a bit more skeptical than believing concerning the combined truth of all three theories, even though we should be modestly believing of each one taken alone. Yet why not believe, even if hesitantly, that all three are true, given our evidence supporting much stronger belief in each theory individually?

Similarly, applying the general disjunction rule, we must conclude that the rational strength of belief that at least one of the three theories will turn out to be true, given probabilities of 0.8, 0.8, and 0.75 respectively, equals 0.99, close to certitude. But why should this be the correct value? Not being very certain of any one taken alone, why be so certain of at least one of the three? (Notice that professional gamblers may believe the correct *odds* on a particular horse in the Derby are, say, 3 to 2, or even money, or 2 to 3, without having a belief (of whatever strength) that the horse in question will win.)*

Exercise 15-3:

Use the probability calculus to determine the following probabilities, showing enough work to justify your answers.

---

*The classic article on the other side is Frank Ramsey, *The Foundation of Mathematics* (London: Routledge and Kegan Paul, 1931), pp. 166–68; see also John Kemeny, "Fair Bets and Inductive Probabilities", *Journal of Symbolic Logic,* vol. 20 (1955), pp. 263–73; and Brian Skyrms, *Choice and Chance,* 3rd ed. (Belmont, Calif.: Wadsworth, 1985).

1. What is the probability of getting (a) an even number face up on a given throw of a symmetrical die; (b) an odd number?
2. What is the probability of getting (a) two heads in a row with a symmetrical coin; (b) three heads in a row?
3. Suppose it's as likely that a person be born on one day as on another. Then what is the probability that two people chosen at random both were born on April 19? (Forget about leap year.)
4. What is the probability of getting an even number or a number less than 3 (or both) with a standard six-sided die on a single toss?
5. Using a pair of symmetrical dice, what is the probability of getting (a) two sevens on the first two tosses; (b) any combination of sevens and elevens on the first two tosses?
6. Alpha Alpha Alpha fraternity has a blind date affair each month with Phi Phi Phi sorority. The custom is to randomly pair ten members of each group with ten of the other. What is the probability that Babs, a member of Phi Phi Phi, will be paired with the same guy on the next two dates?
7. What is the probability of getting *at least* two heads out of three with a symmetrical coin?
8. What is the probability of getting *exactly* two heads out of three with a symmetrical coin?
9. Suppose you draw two cards from a standard deck, replacing the first one before drawing the second. What is the probability that you'll get (a) two aces; (b) at least one ace; (c) two spades; (d) at least one spade?
10. Suppose you draw two cards from a standard deck, *not* replacing the first one before drawing the second. What is the probability that you'll get (a) two aces; (b) at least one ace; (c) two spades; (d) two black aces?

Key Terms Introduced in Chapter Fifteen

Bayes' Theorem: The simplified version is

$$P(q, \text{given } p) = \frac{P(q) \times P(p, \text{given } q)}{[P(q) \times P(p, \text{given } q)] + [P(\sim q) \times P(p, \text{given } \sim q)]}$$

The completely general version is

$$P(q_1, \text{given } p) = \frac{P(q_1) \times P(p, \text{given } q_1)}{[P(q_1) \times P(p, \text{given } q_1)] + \cdots + [P(q_n) \times P(p, \text{given } q_n)]}$$

Chances: See **Single-case probabilities.**

Contingent probabilities: Probabilities construed to be about the nature of the world, or some particular portion of it. Statements about relative frequencies are correctly construed as stating contingent probabilities.

Dutch Book: A series of bets placed so that a gambler must lose, no matter what the outcomes of the individual bets.

Epistemic probabilities: See **Subjective probabilities.**

General conjunction rule: The rule that

$$P(p \cdot q) = P(p) \times P(q, \text{given } p)$$

General disjunction rule: The rule that

$$P(p \vee q) = P(p) + P(q) - P(p \cdot q)$$

Independent events: Events that are not logically or causally related. An example is the event of drawing an ace from a deck and the event of again drawing an ace from the deck when the first ace has been put back into the deck.

Inverse probabilities: Backward probabilities. *Example:* The inverse probability of p, given q is $P(q$, given $p)$.

Likelihoods: See **Single-case probabilities.**

Mutually exclusive events: Events such that it is logically impossible for both to occur. An example is the event of picking an ace on a given draw and picking a deuce on the same draw.

Objective probabilities: See **Contingent probabilities.**

Ontological probabilities: See **Contingent probabilities.**

Principle of indifference: The principle that two events are to be considered equally probable if there is no reason to prefer one to the other.

Principle of non-sufficient reason: See **Principle of indifference.**

Probability calculus: A set of rules for calculating probabilities from initial probabilities. For instance, the restricted disjunction rule is a member of this set, and allows us to calculate, say, that the probability of getting a red jack or black queen with an ordinary card deck is $1/26 + 1/26 = 2/26 = 1/13$.

Relative frequency (of an outcome): The number of favorable outcomes in a series of outcomes compared to the number of all outcomes, favorable or unfavorable. *Example:* The relative frequency with which 7's occur with honest dice equals $1/6$.

Restricted conjunction rule: The rule that if p and q are independent events, then

$$P(p \cdot q) = P(p) \times P(q)$$

Restricted disjunction rule: The rule that if p and q are mutually exclusive events, then

$$P(p \vee q) = P(p) + P(q)$$

Single-case probabilities: Probabilities for single events. (These do not seem construable as relative frequencies.) *Example:* The probability of heads on the next toss of this coin equals $1/2$.

Subjective probabilities: Probabilities construed as strengths of beliefs about reality (in contrast to beliefs about reality itself). The most interesting kinds are *rational* strengths of beliefs. *Example:* The rational strength of belief in the Big Bang Theory of the universe is greater today, given today's evidence, than ever before.

Chapter Sixteen

Scientific Method

Let's step back for a moment and view the scientific forest before taking a closer look at the trees. Scientific method is just common sense writ large, sharpened, fine tuned, and applied (in the best cases) with creative persistence and patience. There is nothing mysterious or impenetrable about how scientists go about justifying their hypotheses (in principle, even if only in the better cases in practice).

In outline, common sense requires that beliefs about the nature of the world be justified, more or less, by cogent arguments.* Recall that in Chapter Twelve we characterized an argument as cogent if it is either deductively valid or inductively correct (strong), has warranted premises, and does not suppress known relevant information. Scientific method has no other way, no magical formula, for coming to justified beliefs about the nature of the world. Its "secret" lies in the persistent accumulation of knowledge by thousands (now literally millions) of practitioners who have required of each other the elimination so far as is possible of the shoddy, wishful thinking that peppers everyday reasoning.

Of course, none of us like to believe that *we* act on supersition.† Yet millions of people play the slots at Las Vegas and Atlantic City (typical winner's comment: "I *knew* I was going to hit the big jackpot this time"), enter their state lotteries (a form of voluntary tax that is currently a superstitious fad), and read the daily newspaper horoscope columns.

---

* The cautious wording is due to the fact that in everyday life, as in everyday scientific practice, complete and precise arguments frequently are dispensed with in favor of less formal arguments, in particular when there is reason to be confident that greater precision could be obtained if necessary.

† The author of this text has been taking vitamin C religiously for years in the belief it protects against colds, even though mounting evidence indicates it doesn't (a typical case of superstitious behavior, much like baseball players hooked on a particular glove).

Science has eliminated such foolishness and restricts its reasoning to the sort that characterizes our best everyday practices. In particular, the rules of the scientific game force scientists to reject unjustified theories* and to give up their most cherished theories when experience shows that they are false (or unsupported by good evidence).

Typical scientific theories, even when a science just begins to get off the ground, are a complicated mixture of deductive and inductive arguments, but the key arguments are inductive. Good scientists try to find *patterns* in what we have experienced so far, in particular in their scientific experiments†, and project these patterns via induction to larger slices of reality. They take the patterns gleaned in "samples" of the world to be the patterns of larger parts of it. (Patterns suitably projected, of course. No scientists, for instance, would reason that because heavy elements are abundant on Earth they will be abundant on the Sun, or in the Universe as a whole.) In everyday life, common sense reasons from past experiences via induction that sugar sweetens, vinegar sours, bread nourishes, and drought kills crops. Scientists, using the same common sense, but much more persistently and stringently, conclude in the same way that copper conducts electricity, cigarette smoking causes cancer, the Earth's path around the Sun is an ellipse, and radioactive substances have half-lives.

Having now taken a brief look at the scientific forest, let's take a closer look at some of the trees. But remember that our concern here is with scientific method in the context of justification, with how scientists justify their theories. How they come to discover them is a topic better left to psychologists (who are beginning to make some progress in understanding that knotty topic).

1 *Confirmation of Categorical Hypotheses*

In Chapter Fourteen, we stated that in general the probability of a categorical or universal generalization is increased by each *instance* of it that we observe. Thus, the probability of the hypothesis "All copper conducts

---

* Scientists use the terms "theory" and "hypothesis" ambiguously. In one sense, both of these terms refer to untested speculations, or insufficiently confirmed patterns. In another, they refer to well-established, well-confirmed and accepted patterns. The second sense is synonymous with the expressions "scientific law" and "law of nature". (In still another sense, the term "theory" is used in contrast to "law," as in "theory of evolution" as compared to "Newton's gravitation law.")

† A scientific experiment is just a kind of deliberately arranged experience, unlikely to be otherwise encountered in everyday life, or likely to be encountered only at some distant time and place. An example is mixing chemicals to see the result—such a mixture may never be encountered in everyday life, or only on rare isolated occasions a scientist can't wait to run across. But whether an event is found "in nature" or arranged in a laboratory is irrelevant to scientific procedure.

electricity" is increased by each new instance we observe of something copper that conducts electricity.

But if the *probability* (in whatever sense of that term is appropriate here) of a hypothesis is increased by its instances, so also is its *degree of confirmation*. Indeed, most philosophers link the concept of degree of confirmation with one or another of the kinds of probabilities discussed in Chapter Fifteen, in particular with rational degrees of belief.

The **degree of confirmation** of a hypothesis is the *degree of evidential support* for that hypothesis—the degree to which what we have observed of the world supports a given hypothesis about the world.

Recall that one way to state the general form of categorical generalization is:

1. $Fa \cdot Ga$
2. $Fb \cdot Gb$
3. $Fc \cdot Gc$

⋮

N. No *F* is known not to have *G*.

∴ *N* + 1. All *F*'s are *G*'s (that is, $(x)(Fx \supset Gx)$).

From the point of view of *confirmation*, it is clear that each of the premises, $Fa \cdot Ga$, $Fb \cdot Gb$, and so on, is a **confirming instance** of $(x)(Fx \supset Gx)$. So let's introduce a slightly different pattern, to show more explicitly that it is those things that are *instances of*, or *follow from*, a universal generalization that *confirm* it. This basic pattern is

1. $(H \cdot A) \supset O$
2. O

∴ 3. H

where *H* is the hypothesis being confirmed, *A* is some **antecedent condition** observed or confirmed to be the case, and *O* is the confirming observation.

Take a very simple hypothesis, such as (H_1): "All metals, when heated, expand", in symbols $(x)[(Mx \cdot Hx) \supset Ex]$. This hypothesis, when coupled with the antecedent condition that *a* is a metal that is heated, implies the consequence that *a* expands. Hence, if we find that *a* does in fact expand when heated, this constitutes a confirming instance for (H_1). Putting this example into the general pattern, we get:

1. $\{(x)[(Mx \cdot Hx) \supset Ex] \cdot (Ma \cdot Ha)\} \supset Ea$
2. Ea

∴ 3. $(x)[(Mx \cdot Hx) \supset Ex]$

In actual practice, we rarely encounter examples in which the observational or experimental result (on line 2) follows from a single categorical generalization (plus antecedent conditions). Instead, we find that the observational results follow from the hypothesis being confirmed plus one or more other hypotheses, generally called **auxiliary hypotheses,** where the auxiliary hypotheses already are well confirmed and accepted as part of the body of scientific knowledge.

In addition, in actual practice we generally find that we cannot state the exact pattern of inference in the precise notation of predicate logic, partly because actual theories tend to contain *loose ends* or *imprecise uses of language*. But this does not mean that *in principle* they could not be put into a basic pattern of this kind (and this *does* mean that it would be a mark against a theory if we were sure that it could not be so put).

The "sea of air" hypothesis,* proposed to account for the fact that suction pumps will not raise water beyond a certain height (about 34 feet at sea level), is a hypothesis of this "messy" kind. According to this theory, there is a sea of air surrounding the surface of the Earth which presses down on it, just as water presses down on something at the bottom of the sea. This theory explains the ability of a pump to raise water from the ground as being due to the *pressure* of the sea of air, that is, to *air pressure,* and explains the fact that there is a limit to the height that water can be pumped as being due to the limit of the air pressure. But if this limit is 34 feet, and if mercury is about 14 times heavier than water, then if the sea of air theory is correct, it follows that air pressure will hold up a column of mercury only 1/14 as high as a column of water. Hence, when we test, and discover that a column of mercury is held up about 1/14 times as high as 34 feet (about 30 inches), this constitutes a *confirming instance* for the sea of air hypothesis.

Letting H_1 refer to the sea of air hypothesis, H_2 to the hypothesis that the sea of air can hold up a column of water about 34 feet high, H_3 to the hypothesis that mercury is 14 times heavier than water, A_1 to the antecedent condition that a tube of mercury closed at one end is placed into a dish of mercury open-end down, and O_1 to the observational result that the column of mercury is held up in the tube to a height of about 30 inches, we can schematically illustrate this confirmation process as follows:

1. $\{[H_1 \cdot (H_2 \cdot H_3)] \cdot A_1\} \supset O_1$
2. O_1

/∴ 3. $H_1 \cdot (H_2 \cdot H_3)$

/∴ 4. H_1†

---

* Formulated by Torricelli, a follower of Galileo.

† (Since H_2 and H_3 are already well confirmed, the important confirmation is of H_1, which follows from $H_1 \cdot (H_2 \cdot H_3)$ by Simplification.

Translating this back into English, we get roughly:

1. If the Earth is surrounded by a sea of air pressing down on it, and if this air pressure holds up a column of water 34 feet high, and if mercury is 14 times heavier than water, and finally, if there is a tube full of mercury closed at one end with its open end inserted into a dish of mercury, then the height of the mercury in this tube is about 30 inches.
2. The height of the mercury in this tube *is* about 30 inches.

/∴ 3. The Earth is surrounded by a sea of air pressing down on it, and this air pressure holds up a column of water 34 feet high, and mercury is 14 times heavier than water.

/∴ 4. The Earth is surrounded by a sea of air pressing down on it.

Of course, even in this form, the example is somewhat simplified.

Generalizing on the above example, we can say that the basic pattern of confirmation is:

1. $\{[H_1 \cdot (H_2 \cdot \ldots)] \cdot (A_1 \cdot \ldots)\} \supset O$
2 O

/∴ 3. $[H_1 \cdot (H_2 \cdot \ldots)]$

/∴ 4. H_1

The basic pattern of *disconfirmation* is similar to the one for confirmation:

1. $\{[H_1 \cdot (H_2 \cdot \ldots)] \cdot (A_1 \cdot \ldots)\} \supset O$
2. $\sim O$

/∴ 3. $\sim\{[H_1 \cdot (H_2 \cdot \ldots)] \cdot (A_1 \cdot \ldots)\}$

/∴ 4. $\sim H_1$*

An example is the disconfirmation of the hypothesis, H_1, that the Earth is flat, where H_2 is a theory of light that says (among other things) that light travels in straight lines, and A_1 is the antecedent condition that a particular ship comes into view over the horizon. If the hypothesis H_1 is correct (in addition to the already well-confirmed hypothesis H_2), then the observational result will be that the whole ship, from top to waterline,

---

* Omitting several steps. The entire pattern is

1. $\{[H_1 \cdot (H_2 \cdot \ldots)] \cdot (A_1 \cdot \ldots)\} \supset O$
2. $\sim O$
3. $\sim\{[H_1 \cdot (H_2 \cdot \ldots)] \cdot (A_1 \cdot \ldots)\}$
4. $\sim[H_1 \cdot (H_2 \cdot \ldots)] \vee \sim(A_1 \cdot \ldots)$
5. $\sim\sim(A_1 \cdot \ldots)$
6. $\sim[H_1 \cdot (H_2 \cdot \ldots)]$
7. $\sim H_1 \vee \sim(H_2 \cdot \ldots)$
8. $\sim\sim(H_2 \cdot \ldots)$

/∴ 9. $\sim H_1$

will first be observed as a rather small object on the horizon which grows larger and larger as it approaches the shore. But in fact, when the ship comes over the horizon, the *top* is observed first. So it is not the case that the whole ship, from top to waterline, is observed when the ship first comes into sight. Hence, one or another of the hypotheses that yield this false observational consequence is disconfirmed. Since H_2 already is very well *confirmed,* we assign the *dis*confirmation to H_1, the hypothesis that the Earth is flat.

2 *Criteria for Confirmation Instances*

When discussing categorical inductive generalizations in Chapter Fourteen, we noted that their *degree* of probability or confirmation depends on several criteria, such as the number of confirming instances. We also noted that these criteria are quite controversial. Let's again discuss such criteria, thinking of them as determining *degrees* of confirmation. The following six criteria are frequently discussed in the literature (although there certainly is no general agreement about their validity).

(1) It is generally held that each confirming instance increases the degree of confirmation of a hypothesis, and similarly that each disconfirming instance decreases the degree of confirmation of a hypothesis.* In many cases, disconfirming instances also are falsifying instances. But this is not true in every case. For example, disconfirming instances of the hypothesis "Every substance is soluble in some solvent or other", in symbols $(x)(\exists y)Sxy$, do not falsify that hypothesis. An example would be the (slightly) disconfirming instance of a substance that is not soluble in a particular solvent.

(2) Some claim that the larger the class of (physically) possible confirming instances, the smaller the degree of confirmation afforded by any given number of actual confirming instances. For example, they would claim that if there are only about 100 million crows in the world, then 100,000 observations of black crows constitute better confirmation of the hypothesis "All crows are black" than if there are, say, 10 billion crows.

But others claim that at best this criterion only applies to cases where the number of possible confirming instances is small, and it is feasible to

---

* Some alleged counterexamples turn out to be cases in which lower level disconfirming (confirming) cases are confirming (disconfirming) on a higher level. So they aren't really counterexamples, but rather show a minor complexity of our theory, namely that higher level theories may overturn lower-level ones. Some other alleged counterexamples turn out to involve surreptitious and questionable uses of the principle of indifference.

examine all, or almost all, possible confirming cases. For instance, they might be willing to accept this criterion with respect to a hypothesis such as "All American males over seven feet tall have flat feet", since so few American males are over seven feet tall, but they would deny it with respect to hypotheses such as "All crows are black", since there are so many crows that it is not feasible to examine all or even most of them for color.

(3) Another widely accepted criterion concerns what is called **instance variety.** According to this criterion, the more that confirming instances of a given hypothesis *differ* from each other (in relevant ways*), the better the resulting confirmation. For example, having already confirmed the sea of air hypothesis by a test concerning a column of mercury, we now get better confirmation by testing some other substance, or by performing the mercury test on a mountain top (where the air pressure ought to be lower), than by simply repeating the same kind of experiment with mercury at roughly the same elevation.

It is easy to see why instance variety is so important, for each new kind of instance is a test of a different *consequence* of a hypothesis. Suppose we examine 1,000 crows for color, and they all happen to be *male*. Then, in effect, although we have 1,000 confirming cases for the hypothesis "All crows are black", we have not tested an important consequence of that hypothesis, namely the subhypothesis "All *female* crows are black". Since sex is likely to be relevant to color, we obtain far better confirmation of the hypothesis "All crows are black" by examining, say, 500 male and 500 female crows, than by examining 1,000 male crows.

(4) Some philosophers hold to an **eliminative theory of confirmation,** according to which a hypothesis is confirmed only by those of its instances that also *disconfirm competing hypotheses.*†

Take the example discussed in Chapter Fourteen concerning the hypothesis (H_1): "All people who contract food poisoning have eaten chicken salad", and assume that all confirming cases up to a given time happen to be cases in which pastry also was eaten. Then, if we find a case of food poisoning in which chicken salad but *not* pastry was eaten, we have a case in which the hypothesis (H_2): "All people who contracted

---

* The vital question of how we are to distinguish relevant from irrelevant differences has not as yet received a satisfactory answer.

† See G. H. von Wright, *Logical Problems of Induction,* 2nd rev. ed. (New York: Barnes and Noble, 1965), Chap. VI. Also see the author's "Baumer on the Confirmation Paradoxes", *British Journal for the Philosophy of Science,* vol. 18 (1967), pp. 52–56, and "Eliminative Confirmation and Paradoxes", vol. 20 (1969), pp. 160–62, in which it is argued that the eliminative theory of confirmation fails to solve the confirmation paradoxes.

food poisoning ate pastry", a competitor of the hypothesis (H_1), is eliminated. Hence, an instance of this kind is confirming for (H_1).

But if we merely find another case in which P and F are present, but no competitor of the hypothesis (H_1) is eliminated, then that case does not count as a confirming case for (H_1) even though it is an instance of it.

(5) Some philosophers require that confirming instances be observations or tests performed *after* a hypothesis has been proposed, on the grounds that we can always construct theories that can account for the data observed up to a given point. According to this view, the trick is to construct hypotheses that not only account for what has been observed but also predict new phenomena.

However, there are at least two major difficulties with this view. First, although it always is theoretically possible to construct hypotheses that account for the observed data, we often *in fact* are unable to find such a hypothesis. At least we often are unable to construct simple theories of this kind.

And second, upon closer inspection the criterion turns out to be not so intuitively plausible as it seemed at first glance. For example, if Brown thinks of a hypothesis before a confirming instance is found for it, but Jones doesn't think of it until after the confirming instance, it follows from the criterion in question that the hypothesis is better confirmed for Brown than for Jones, even though Brown and Jones have identical evidence for it. And this seems unreasonable.

(6) Finally, there are several confirmation criteria of a more technical nature. An example is the requirement that a hypothesis be *genuinely relevant* to the derivation of its confirming instances. If an instance follows from the auxiliary hypotheses plus antecedent conditions alone, without the need of a given hypothesis, then the hypothesis is not confirmed by that instance.

The need for this requirement stems from the fact that if a given hypothesis P entails some instance Q, then $P \cdot R$ (where R is any hypothesis whatever) also entails Q. But we don't want Q to confirm R, because Q is not a genuine consequence of R.*

3 *Nonevidential Criteria*

In addition to criteria for the acceptability of confirmation instances, there are so-called nonevidential criteria for the acceptability of well-confirmed hypotheses. We need such criteria because not all well-

---

* See also the material on Karl Popper and Nelson Goodman in Section 7 at the end of this chapter.

confirmed hypotheses can be accepted into the body of scientific knowledge. In particular we need criteria in order to select between competing well-confirmed hypotheses.

Perhaps the most important nonevidential criterion is **simplicity.** It is generally supposed, even by many scientists, that simplicity is a mere matter of convenience or elegance. But nothing could be further from the truth. Of course, in determining between *equivalent* hypotheses, we choose the simpler hypothesis for the sake of convenience. But when we choose the simpler of two nonequivalent hypotheses, and choose it because it is simpler, something much more than convenience or elegance is involved.

Suppose the points on the following graph represent the results of experiments relating two factors, *x* and *y*. We ordinarily would draw the "smooth curve" (A) through the test points to represent our hypothesis explaining how the two factors, *x* and *y*, relate to each other. We surely would not draw the irregular curve (B). And yet both curves pass through all of the points representing the experimental results. Hence, the theories represented by these two curves are equally well confirmed by the evidence. We choose the hypothesis represented by curve (A) over the one represented by curve (B) because it is the simpler of the two hypotheses.

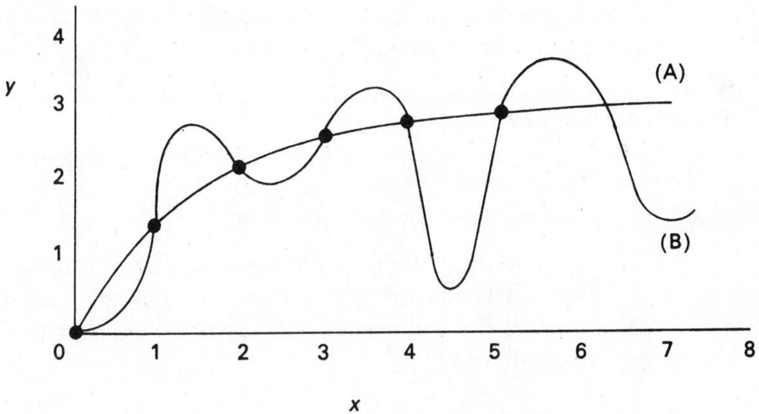

Or consider the two nonequivalent equations, (E_1): $x = y + 1$, and (E_2): $x = y^3 - 3y^2 + 3y + 1$, and suppose we observe that whenever $x = 1$, $y = 0$, whenever $x = 2$, $y = 1$, and whenever $x = 3$, $y = 2$. Since these values are exactly the ones entailed by (E_1) and (E_2), both of these hypotheses are confirmed, and indeed *equally* confirmed, by them. But surely we would reject (E_2) in favor of (E_1), because (E_1) is simpler than (E_2).

Notice again that our choice of the simpler hypothesis is not a mere matter of convenience or elegance. (E_2) and (E_2) are different hypotheses.

They predict different results for values of y greater than 2. (For instance, for $y = 3$, (E_1) predicts that $x = 4$, while (E_2) predicts that $x = 10$.) Consequently, it makes a great deal of difference which one of these two hypotheses we choose. To some extent, simplicity determines our beliefs about the world.*

4 *Statistical (Probability) Pattern of Confirmation*

In Chapter Fourteen, we characterized the general form of statistical inference as

1. *N* percent of all *F*'s tested have *G*.
2. *N* percent of all *F*'s (tested or otherwise) have *G*.

Let's now introduce a slightly different pattern, to illustrate more clearly how statistical hypotheses are confirmed:

1. If *N* percent of all *F*'s have *G*, then in a random sample of sufficient size,† about *N* percent of all *F*'s will probably have *G*.
2. In a particular random sample of sufficiently large size, about *N* percent of all *F*'s have *G*.

/∴ 3. *N* percent of all *F*'s have *G*.

Analogously, let's introduce a slightly different basic pattern of *dis*confirmation for statistical hypotheses:

1. If *N* percent of all *F*'s have *G*, then in a random sample of sufficiently large size, about *N* percent of all *F*'s will probably have *G*.
2. Concerning a particular observed random sample of sufficiently large size, it is *not* the case that about *N* percent of all *F*'s have *G*.

/∴ 3. It is not the case that *N* percent of all *F*'s have *G*.

(Bear in mind that a disconfirming case for a statistical hypothesis in general does not falsify that hypothesis. This follows from the fact that *N* percent of *all F*'s still may have *G*, even though *N* percent of the *F*'s in the sample do not.)

In addition to the general kinds of criteria of confirmation for categorical hypotheses discussed above, there are special criteria for statistical hypotheses, concerned in particular with the evaluation of evidence sam-

---

*The suggestion that we get around this appeal to simplicity by conducting more tests is not satisfactory. For it is always possible to construct more than one formula that conforms to the observed results, *no matter how many tests we have conducted*. Hence, at some point we must stop testing (even if only for the moment) and appeal to simplicity. Otherwise, no scientific hypothesis will ever attain a sufficiently high degree of confirmation to be accepted as a warranted belief.

†The question of what constitutes a sufficiently large random sample is a quite difficult one.

ples. An example of this sort of criterion is *standard deviation,* based on the idea that a group of samples having similar relative frequencies confirms a hypothesis better than a group of samples that does not.

5 *Scientific Explanation*

Explanation, confirmation, and *prediction* all are closely related. A hypothesis is *confirmed* by what it *predicts,* and it also *explains* what it predicts.*

This close relationship often is masked by the elliptical nature of most explanations in daily life. For example, if a child asks why a match lit, the answer "because it was struck (heated)" is an acceptable explanation. But a more complete explanation would be that the match lit because it was heated in the presence of oxygen, and all well-made matches light when heated in the presence of oxygen.

The more complete explanation makes reference, first, to a *general hypothesis* (that all well-made matches heated in the presence of oxygen light), and second, to *antecedent conditions* (that the match in question was well made and was heated in the presence of oxygen).

Deductive Nomological Explanation

If what is explained *deductively* follows from the general hypotheses and antecedent conditions, then the explanation is said to be a **deductive nomological explanation.**† An explanation of this kind is satisfactory if (1) the general hypotheses appealed to are well confirmed and have satisfied the nonevidential criteria for acceptable hypotheses, such as simplicity; (2) the antecedent conditions are true, or at least well confirmed; and (3) the thing explained follows from the general hypotheses plus antecedent conditions. The pattern of deductive nomological explanation is this:

1. $H_1, H_2, \ldots$
2. $A_1, A_2, \ldots$

/∴ 3. E

---

*Note, however, that some philosophers deny that low level empirical hypotheses explain anything. For example, they would deny that we explain why a particular pump (at sea level) pumps water only a maximum of about 34 feet by appeal to the low level empirical generalization that all pumps at sea level pump water a maximum of 34 feet. For more on this, see the discussion in Section 7 of this chapter.

†Using the terminology of Hans Reichenbach and Carl Hempel, whose "explanation of explanation" is being followed here. See Reichenbach's *Nomological Statements and Admissible Operations* (Amsterdam: North Holland Publishing, 1954); and Hempel's *Philosophy of Natural Science* (Englewood Cliffs, N.J.: Prentice-Hall, 1966), Chaps. 5 and 6.

(where H_1, H_2, . . . are general hypotheses, A_1, A_2, . . . are antecedent conditions, and E is the event being explained).

The match explanation mentioned above is an example of a deductive nomological explanation, since the lighting of the match follows deductively from the general hypothesis plus antecedent conditions.

Nondeductive (Probabilistic) Explanation

Many explanations are not deductive. According to one standard account, **probabilistic explanations** have the general pattern:

1. The probability of *E*, given *A*, = *n*.
2. *a* is a case of *A*.

/∴ 3. The probability of *a* being an event of type *E* = *n*.

For example, if the probability of death in any given year (E) given that one has Hodgkin's disease (A) = 0.95, and if Jones has Hodgkin's disease, then the probability that Jones will die in any given year equals 0.95, which explains why Jones died.* (Ordinarily, we would furnish only the elliptical explanation that Jones died because he had Hodgkin's disease.)

Unfortunately, nondeductive explanations are not quite that simple. For instance, we do not believe that Jones died of Hodgkin's disease *simply* because the probability = 0.95 that anyone with that disease won't live out the year. Our acceptance of Hodgkin's disease as the explanation of death is based also on our knowledge that the probability of death in any given year for those who *don't* have that disease (but otherwise are similar) is a great deal lower. So at the very least, we must amend the basic pattern of probabilistic (nondeductive) explanation to read:

1. The probability of *E*, given *A*, = *n*.
2. The probability of *E*, given ~*A*, = *m* (where *n* is significantly greater than *m*).
3. *a* is a case of *A*.

/∴ 4. Probably, *a* is a case of *E*.

Spurious Explanations

Many supposedly scientific explanations fail to conform to the above model of explanation, and many acceptable scientific theories often are used in spurious explanations.

The theory of evolution is a good example of a legitimate scientific

* Perhaps it would be better to say that it *probably* explains why Jones died. Often, when more than one cause for an event is possible, we can determine only a probable cause for that event.

theory that is sometimes used in an illegitimate way in spurious explanations.

For instance, the explanation that a given species of rabbit failed to survive because rabbits of that species were not "fit" to survive is spurious if the only evidence of unfitness provided is that the species in fact failed to survive. For then to say that the rabbits died because they were unfit to survive comes close to saying that they failed to survive because they failed to survive, which is *logically true,* and hence has no empirical content.

Similarly, the economist who says that the price of wheat rose because *demand* was greater than *supply* provides a spurious explanation if his only evidence is that the price of wheat rose, for then he is saying little more than that the price rose because the price rose.

Of course, many explanations in terms of supply and demand are not spurious. If the economist who explains that the price of certain stocks went down because supply exceeded demand then goes on to state that the increase in supply resulted from the sale of large blocks of stocks by institutions and mutual funds caused by lack of confidence in the economy, then the explanation may be legitimate.

The structure of an acceptable scientific explanation must be such that the event explained could have been *predicted* from the general hypotheses employed plus antecedent conditions.* The explanation that a particular piece of metal expanded because it was heated, and all metals expand when heated, illustrates this connection between legitimate explanations and predictions. If we had known ahead of time that the piece of metal would be heated, then we could have predicted that it would expand, since metals expand when heated. Any explanation that fails this "prediction test" must be regarded as spurious.

Take the so-called vitalistic explanation that a particular organism regenerated a lost limb because of nonphysical teleological agencies, called "entelechies", which direct organic processes within a range left open by the principles of physics and chemistry.

This vitalistic explanation is spurious because it does not imply, and hence does not *predict,* when or under what conditions the given organism will regenerate a limb. And it fails to predict because the general theory that it uses about entelechies, even taken in conjunction with antecedent conditions, *implies nothing specific*.

---

* At least this is true for deductive explanations. Whether it is true for probabilistic explanations is a very difficult question.

6 *Challenges to Our Account of Scientific Method*

Proponents of other views concerning scientific method have presented several different kinds of objections to it.

Theoretical Hypotheses Are Alleged to Be Different

Many philosophers argue that the account of scientific method we have given so far is correct as an account of what they would call **empirical hypotheses,** but not as an account of what they call **theoretical hypotheses.**

The difference between empirical and theoretical hypotheses is illustrated by the sea of air theory. When a farmer notices that his pump will raise water only to a height of about 34 feet, and notices that the same is true for his neighbors' pump, his conclusion that all pumps will raise water only to a height of about 34 feet is an empirical hypothesis. Roughly, his observation is said to be an empirical hypothesis because (1) it is a mere inductive generalization of the observational instances that constitute his evidence, and (2) his hypothesis is about the very same kinds of entities that his observational instances are about (namely pumps and water raised by pumps). In addition, his hypothesis is not theoretical because it makes no reference to **theoretical** (unobservable) **entities** as opposed to **empirical** (observable) **entities.**

But now consider the sea of air hypothesis, which explains *why* pumps raise water a maximum of about 34 feet. In this case, the theory is about some entity, *air pressure,* which is not directly observable, and which the evidence concerning pumps and water is not about. Hence, the sea of air hypothesis is a *theoretical hypothesis,* or simply a *theory,* whereas the pump hypothesis is merely an *empirical* hypothesis.

In general, the charge against what we have said about scientific method is that (1) theories have a different logic (play a different role in science) than do empirical hypotheses, and (2) our account of inductive inference, confirmation, and explanation applies only to empirical hypotheses. If correct, this charge is certainly of major significance, for most important hypotheses of science resemble the sea of air hypothesis much more than they resemble the water pump hypothesis.

But is the charge correct? It can be argued that it is not, chiefly because it is doubtful whether the distinction between empirical and theoretical hypotheses can be drawn even roughly in a way that supports the claim that our account of confirmation, explanation, and so on, does not apply to theoretical hypotheses.

In particular, it seems questionable to make the distinction between empirical and theoretical hypotheses rest on the *observability* of the entities the hypotheses are about, since many, perhaps even most, alleged theoretical hypotheses are not about unobservables. For instance, the hypothesis that certain kinds of food decay are caused by bacteria, which is often taken to be a theoretical hypothesis, concerns *bacteria,* which can be observed through a microscope.*

Another criterion frequently used to distinguish empirical from theoretical hypotheses is that theoretical hypotheses say things about entities not mentioned in their evidence, whereas empirical hypotheses are mere generalizations of their instances, saying nothing about entities not mentioned in their evidence.

For example, the hypothesis that all ravens are black, claimed to be an empirical hypothesis, is confirmed by recognizable instances (such as "*a* is a raven and is black", "*b* is a raven and is black") of that hypothesis. But Newton's law of gravitation, claimed to be a theoretical hypothesis, does not seem to have any recognizable instances in isolation from the other universal generalizations of Newtonian mechanics (such as the laws of motion). For example, the motion of the Earth around the Sun at any given time does not seem to constitute an instance of Newton's gravitation law *alone,* but rather of the whole of Newtonian mechanics (given a great many antecedent conditions, such as the masses of the Earth, Sun, and Moon, and their velocities at a particular time).

There are two important things to be said about this claim. First, the claim that Newton's law of gravitation has no recognizable instances seems flatly false. For example, it seems plausible to say that the motion of the Earth around the Sun at a given time is an instance of this law, since it is a case in which two bodies (the Earth and Sun) are attracted to each other with a force that is proportional to the product of their masses and inversely proportional to the square of the distance between them, as Newton's law of gravitation requires. Of course, we cannot directly *observe* this attractive force, and we must use other hypotheses of Newtonian mechanics to infer from what we actually observe (plus antecedent conditions) to the conclusion that this *is* an instance of Newton's law of gravitation. But we have already argued that observability is not a pertinent criterion, and even in the case of the hypothesis that all ravens are black we must use other hypotheses to infer from what we actually observe (plus antecedent conditions) to the conclusion that a given case is an instance of that hypothesis. (For example, we must use a theory of

---

* Some claim that entities such as bacteria are not observable in that they cannot be observed by the unaided use of one or more of the five senses. But surely the restriction of observability to what can be observed through the unaided use of the five senses is much too strong. For instance, the person who wears glasses is generally taken to perceive the observable world when he looks through glasses. (Similar remarks apply to someone who uses a hearing aid.) There seems to be no essential difference between looking at the world through eyeglasses and looking at the world through a microscope. Hence, if what is observed through eyeglasses is considered to be observable, then what is observed through a microscope must be also. Bacteria, then, must be counted as observable entities.

light according to which *looking* black—even with a purple tinge—in certain light constitutes evidence that something *is* black, and that black-looking birds of a certain kind are in fact ravens.)

Second, even supposing that empirical hypotheses could be distinguished from theoretical ones in the way just described, it does not follow that what we have said about science and inductive generalization does not apply to both theoretical and empirical hypotheses.

In addition, what we have said about *confirmation* and *explanation* surely does apply to both theoretical and empirical hypotheses. For instance, from Newton's law of gravitation (H_1), plus other laws of Newtonian mechanics ($H_2 \cdot \ldots$), plus antecedent conditions ($A_1 \cdot \ldots$), we can infer to the motion of the Earth around the Sun at a particular time (O), so that the occurrence of O constitutes a *confirming instance* for H_1, and the occurrence of O is *explained* by $H_1 \cdot (H_2 \cdot \ldots)$ plus the antecedent conditions.

Hence, we are justified in concluding that what we have said is a *general,* and not merely a restricted, account of the role of generalization, confirmation, and explanation in science.

Induction Is Unjustified—The Old Riddle of Induction

Recall that the characteristic mark of all inductive (nondeductive) reasoning is a "gap" between premises and conclusion. As soon as this gap was realized,* the question of *how any inductive argument can be justified* was raised; that is, the question was raised about the *rationality* of the acceptance of hypotheses on inductive grounds.

Unfortunately, a good answer to this question has been hard to come by. A great many solutions to the problem of induction have been proposed, most of which can be classified into four categories.

(1) The most obvious thought is that we are justified in using induction because it "works". All of science is based on inductive conclusions of some sort or other, and everyone knows how successful science is. Everyone knows that scientific method, which uses induction, *works.*

Unfortunately, this obvious solution to the problem is not satisfactory. It simply isn't true that we know that induction works, or is successful. At best, what we know is that it *has worked,* or *has been successful.* But will it be successful in the future? We don't know. Indeed, the problem

---

* The philosopher David Hume was the first person to perceive it clearly, and to try to bridge it. See *A Treatise of Human Nature,* Book I, Part IV, Section 1; and *An Enquiry Concerning Human Understanding,* Section V.

seems to be that we haven't the slightest reason to think induction will be successful in the future.

It often is claimed that in fact we do have a very good reason for thinking that induction will be successful in the future, namely its success in the past. But only a little thought is needed to see that this reason will not do. For to argue that induction *will* be successful because it *has* been successful is to argue *inductively*. (The premise of such an argument is "Induction has been successful [on the whole] up to now", and its conclusion is "Induction always will be successful [on the whole]". Clearly, this argument itself is an inductive argument.) So when we argue this way, we use induction to justify itself, which means that we argue circularly, and hence fallaciously.

(2) Perhaps the most popular solutions to the problem of induction are those that use some principle concerning the *uniformity of nature,* such as the principle that *every event has a cause*.

For instance, if we assume that nature is uniform, then we can reason inductively from the fact that all examined pieces of copper are uniform with respect to conductivity to the conclusion that all pieces of copper (examined or as yet unexamined) are uniform with respect to the conducting of electricity.

But solutions of this kind are unsatisfactory. First, even if nature is uniform, there is no guarantee that the particular uniformities we have observed up to a given time will hold in the future; the true uniformities of nature may be more complex or subtle. And second, the assumption that every event has a cause, or that nature is uniform, itself can be challenged. *Why* assume that nature is uniform? Again, there seems to be no answer. (Remember that we cannot argue that the assumption that nature is uniform has been fruitful in the past, and hence is likely to be fruitful in the future, for such an argument would be an inductive argument, and we cannot use induction to justify a principle of uniformity and then use that principle to justify the use of induction.)

(3) Some philosophers have proposed justifications based on the so-called self-corrective nature of induction.* For example, suppose we conclude that half of 10,000 tosses of a coin will land heads up, on the basis of the evidence that half of the first 100 tosses of this coin landed heads up. Suppose this conclusion is false. Then we can "correct" it simply by observing larger and larger coin tossing samples, basing our con-

---

* See, for instance, Charles Peirce, "Induction as Experimental and Self-correcting", *Collected Papers of Charles Sanders Peirce,* vol. VI, ed. Charles Hartshorne and Paul Weiss (Cambridge, Mass.: Harvard University Press, 1935). Reprinted in Edward H. Madden, *The Structure of Scientific Thought* (Boston: Houghton-Mifflin, 1960), pp. 296–98.

clusion about the relative frequency of heads in the total series of 10,000 tosses on the relative frequency of heads in the largest sample we have at any given time. If we continue the process long enough, at some point we must reach the correct value. Hence, it is claimed, we are justified in using inductive reasoning in such cases because the process is self-correcting; repeated applications must get us closer and closer to the truth.

Suppose, for instance, that one half of 10,000 tosses of a coin in fact will land heads up. If we get heads on exactly half of the first 5,000 tosses, then we know with deductive certainty that the relative frequency of heads compared to total tosses in the entire series of 10,000 tosses must be somewhere between 1/4 and 3/4.* Hence our prediction that half of the 10,000 tosses will be heads cannot be off by more than ± 1/4.

Now suppose that after 8,000 tosses the observed relative frequency of heads is still 1/2. Then we know at this point that the relative frequency of heads in the total series of 10,000 tosses must be somewhere between 2/5 and 3/5.† Hence, at this point our prediction that half of the 10,000 tosses will be heads cannot be off by more than ± 1/10. So we are getting closer and closer to the correct value (no matter what that value happens to be), since the *largest possible error* in our predictions keeps getting smaller and smaller.

The trouble is that our predictions get closer and closer to the correct value because larger and larger portions of the series concern *past tosses* and are incorporated into our *evidence,* while smaller and smaller portions of the series concern *future tosses*. At no point do we have any guarantee that we are getting any closer to the actual relative frequency of heads among *future* (unexamined) tosses of the coin. But if the self-corrective claim is to have any force, it must apply to predictions about the future (or the as yet unexamined past).

The situation is even worse for infinitely long series, since the relative frequency of any given finite portion of an infinite series is compatible with any relative frequency whatever in the infinite series. For instance, even if every one of millions of tosses of a coin lands heads up, the *limit* of such an infinite series of tosses (assuming an infinite series of tosses is possible) still might equal zero. Hence, for an infinite series, inductive practices embody no self-corrective feature whatever.

We must conclude, then, that we cannot justify the use of induction on the grounds that it is self-correcting.

(4) Finally, there are the so-called dissolutions of the problem of in-

---

* If the 5,000 remaining tosses all are tails, then the relative frequency will be 1/4, and if they all are heads, then the relative frequency will be 3/4.

† If the 2,000 remaining tosses all are tails, then the relative frequency will be 2/5, and if they all are heads, then the relative frequency will be 3/5.

duction, according to which the very problem itself is a pseudoproblem.* We shall consider two of the many solutions of this kind. In the first, it is claimed that it is not rational to doubt the principles of inductive reasoning because these principles themselves *determine* (in part) what it means to be rational. In other words, if we doubt the rationality (the reasonableness) of the use of induction, then we simply don't know what it means to be rational.

Unfortunately, this argument is defective. Were we to find ourselves in a community in which it is considered rational to believe everything said by the oldest member of the community, it would be reasonable to inquire if it *really* is rational to do so. And if the reply were that what it *means* to be rational is to believe the oldest member of the community, then it would be perfectly proper to ask *why* we should be rational. Put into this context, the problem of induction is that we seem to have no answer to the question "Why be rational?" either for the peculiar concept of rationality in the imaginary community just described or for the concept of rationality in the real community.

According to the second kind of "dissolution" of the problem, there is no problem of justifying the use of inductive principles because *no justification is possible,* and if none is possible, then none can be required. Two kinds of arguments have been presented in support of this claim.

First, it has been argued that such a justification would have to be either *inductive* or *deductive*. An inductive justification would be circular, since it would use the very principles of reasoning we are trying to justify. And we could never construct a valid deductive justification, because it is impossible to prove deductively that nature is uniform, or that every event has a cause, or that the future will resemble the past.†

But this argument is defective. It is true that metaphysical assumptions, such as the uniformity of nature, cannot be proved deductively. But a deductive justification does not necessarily require that any such principle be proved. Perhaps other kinds of assumptions can be proved that will justify the use of induction.††

---

*See, for instance, A. J. Ayer, *Language, Truth and Logic* (New York: Dover Publications), pp. 49–50.

† What is often meant by such an argument is that metaphysical principles of this kind are not *theorems of logic,* or *deductively obtainable from the null set of premises,* or *knowable prior to any particular empirical observations.*

†† For instance, the pragmatic justification presented by Hans Reichenbach in *The Theory of Probability* (Berkeley: University of California Press, 1949), pp. 469–82, is based on an attempt to prove deductively that if any method of predicting the future is successful, then the use of induction will be successful. Unfortunately, his justification is fallacious (for rather complicated reasons). But it has never been proved that a justification *like* it might not be successful.

Second, it has been argued that just as the theorems in an axiom system cannot all be proved (without circularity or infinite regress), so also all principles of *reasoning* or *inferring* cannot be justified (without circularity or infinite regress). Hence, we should not be surprised that no justification of induction is possible.

Clearly, there is something to this last argument. It is true that we cannot justify every principle of reasoning any more than we can prove every theorem. And it may well be that the basic inductive principle will be among those that remain forever unjustified and hence remain forever as a kind of primitive inference rule. But the argument in question does not prove this. All that it proves is that some principle or other will remain unjustified. It does not prove induction is that principle.

On the other hand, recognition of the important fact* that some principle or other must remain unjustified may make it more tolerable that as yet no one seems to have been able to justify the basic principle of induction.

Not All Instances of Theories Confirm Them—The New Riddle of Induction

Perhaps the most curious of the objections raised against our account of scientific method is the one posed by Nelson Goodman's so-called *new riddle of induction.*

The old riddle, you will recall, has to do with justifying induction and inductive inferences in general, and in particular with justifying the belief that generalizations are confirmed by their instances (as, say, the generalization "All dogs have tails" is confirmed by finding an instance of it—namely a dog with a tail). The new riddle, according to Goodmanites, has to do with distinguishing those generalizations that *are* confirmed by their instances from those that are not.

To see the difference between these two kinds of cases, consider the following example. Suppose one hundred emeralds, all of them green, are observed for color. This would usually be considered good evidence for the hypothesis or generalization (H-1) "All emeralds are green". But now let's introduce a new color term, "grue", referring to all things examined for color before a particular time *t*, say January 1, 1990, that are green, and to other things just in case they are blue. Then emeralds, for instance, will be "grue" just in case they either are green and the time in question is before time *t* or are blue and the time in question is at *t* or after. An emerald examined now and found to be green would thus be "grue", but one examined in the twenty-first century and found to be

* An instance of what this writer considers to be one of the few truly profound philosophical truths: to prove *anything*, something or other must be assumed without proof. (Philosophers of old spoke of starting from indubitable or *self-evident* truths.)

green would not be "grue" (it would, however, be *bleen,* that is, it would be either examined before time *t* and blue, or not so examined and green).

All of the one hundred green emeralds observed in our hypothetical example are "grue", as well as green, since they're green and the time is prior to time *t.* So according to what has been said so far about confirmation, it would seem that the one hundred observed "grue" emeralds constitute confirming instances of the hypothesis (H-2): "All emeralds are grue", just as these same emeralds, being green, confirm (H-1): "All emeralds are green". But (H-1) and (H-2) *conflict* with each other, because according to (H-1) emeralds observed after time *t* will be green while according to (H-2) they will be blue. In fact, of course, no one would accept (H-2) no matter how many confirming cases we find in its favor. Goodman's problem is to find some way to distinguish "grue-like" illegitimate predicates and hypotheses from legitimate green-like ones, so that hypotheses like (H-1) will be confirmed by their instances while those like (H-2) will not.

Most of the proposed solutions to this problem are seriously defective. Rudolf Carnap, for example, argued that terms like "grue" are what he called "positional", meaning that they are terms whose definitions in part refer to individual objects, or to individual places or times. But Carnap's solution is unsatisfactory, in particular because lots of "good" predicates are positional and in fact are used in acceptable generalizations all the time. Some examples given by Goodman are "Ming", "Arctic", and "Pleistocene". Generalizations like "All Ming vases are expensive" would usually be held to be confirmed by their instances (in this case, by particular Ming vases that are expensive).

The interesting thing about Goodman's riddle is that an obvious answer lies right at hand, and was proposed soon after Goodman formulated the problem; indeed it must have occurred independently to countless readers of the literature since then. Take our two competing hypotheses (H-1) "All emeralds are green", and (H-2) "All emeralds are "grue". The first contains the "good" term "green", the second the "bad" term "grue". What is good about the former but bad about the latter? The first thought many of us have is that all green things *resemble* each other in a certain way, namely by being green in color, while there is no such color resemblance uniting all grue things, since items that are grue prior to time *t* are green, while those that are grue after time *t* are blue. What the term "green" *means* requires all items referred to by that predicate to resemble each other in color—share a common color—namely green. But what the term "grue" means does not require this; prior to time *t* grue things are green, after time *t* they are blue. By simply saying that only those generalizations containing terms like "green" are confirmed by their instances, the problem would seem to be solved. That is, it seems as though we can quite easily solve the problem by rejecting all generalizations containing terms, like "grue", which select classes of items that do not necessarily all resemble each other in some relevant way. One idea behind inductive reasoning is, after all, to find items that resemble each other in some specified way that also share some other common property. In the case of (H-1): "All emeralds are green", we find stones that resemble each other in being beryl silicates (and thus emeralds)* and discover that they also share the common property of being green. In the case of (H-2) "All emeralds are grue", there also is a shared common property, namely that of being grue, but that is not a *resembling* property—all grue things do not resemble each other in the appropriate way.

Perhaps the main reason why this obvious solution to the grue problem has not settled the matter is that Goodman provided what most writers on the subject have accepted as a conclusive objection to it. Goodman argued that given *any* two things, however different they may seem, we can always invent a property they both share, as we did in fact in inventing the property of being grue. That is, he argued that all grue things do in fact share a common property, namely that of being grue, and thus do in fact resemble each other (since they all are grue). We've noticed that all emeralds have resembled each other by being green, perhaps, because "green" is a term we've become familiar with through long use—it has become well *entrenched* in our language. But we've failed to notice that all emeralds so far encountered have resembled each other by being grue, perhaps because we're not familiar with and haven't used the term "grue"—it hasn't become entrenched in our language.

Underlying Goodman's view on the grue question is an extreme version of a very old philosophical position, called *nominalism* (something some of the nonnominalistic writers on the subject seem to have overlooked). In its extreme form, nominalism says that "there is nothing common to a class of particulars called by the same name other than that they *are* called by the same name."† That is why Goodman says that just as green things resemble each other in being green so also grue things equally resemble each other in being grue.††

But suppose we reject the nominalist's view and accept the commonsense, everyday idea of resemblance that makes it wrong to speak of

---

* Goodman's choice of example was unfortunate in that according to one common definition of *emerald* a nongreen beryl silicate would not be an emerald.

† A. D. Woozley in his article "Universals", in the *Encyclopedia of Philosophy*, edited by Paul Edwards (New York: Collier MacMillan, 1967). Woozley's article also contains an excellent rebuttal of this extreme form of nominalism (in the opinion of this writer).

†† Goodman's basic nominalistic principle is that there are individual things in the world, and sums of individual things, but no general properties. (See his article "A World of Individuals" in *The Problem of Universals*, Notre Dame, Ind.: Notre Dame Univ. Press, 1956.) But he is quickly led to the version of nominalism Woozley discussed, and without doubt believes that any two things (for example, any two emeralds) may resemble each other just as much as any other two things (for example, any two green emeralds).

"grue" things as resembling each other just as much as do green things. (This is in fact what the vast majority of philosophers have done over the ages.) Then the Goodman problem fails to get off the ground,* and our account of the philosophy of science remains intact.

Falsification Versus Confirmation

Another challenge to this texts's view of the nature of nondeductive reasoning comes from Karl Popper and the Popperians, who argue roughly that there is no such thing as confirmation, or that confirmation is not a legitimate, justified process. On this view, trying to *falsify* a theory or hypothesis makes sense, because the process of falsification is deductively valid; but trying to confirm a theory does not make sense, because the process of confirmation, being an inductive procedure, is not deductively valid.

To see what Popperians are up to, consider the simplest basic pattern of falsification as compared to the simplest pattern of confirmation:

	Falsification			**Confirmation**
	1. $(H \cdot A) \supset O$		1.	$Fa \cdot Ga$
	2. $\sim O$		2.	$Fb \cdot Gb$
	3. $\sim(H \cdot A)$			⋮
	4. A		N.	No F's are known to be $\sim G$'s
∴	5. $\sim H$	∴	N + 1.	$(x)(Fx \supset Gx)$

The important thing to notice, say Popperians, is that in the falsification pattern the inferences to lines 3 and 5 are deductively valid (lines 1, 2, and 4 are premises), so that every line in the proof is justified. But in the confirmation pattern, the crucial step from lines 1, 2, . . . N (all of which are premises) to line N + 1 is not deductively valid. And, since David Hume has shown that no inductive leaps whatsoever are justified, this particular inductive leap is not justified, and hence is not legitimate.

Take a simple (and false) version of astrology, say one stating that a person's fate is determined by the positions of the stars in the sky at the time of birth. If this theory were true, beggars and kings born at the same time would have similar fates; but as we (not to mention Pliny, the Elder) pointed out some time ago, they don't, and so this version of astrology is *falsified* by the evidence:

---

*There are, of course, some wrinkles to take care of. For example, Goodman argues that lots of acceptable terms, such as "electrical conductor", are not resembling terms in the everyday sense; we therefore have to show what the resemblances might be like in these cases. See my *Pathological Predicates and Projections (American Philosophical Quarterly*, vol. 8 (1971), pp. 171–78), for more on this, and also for some other thoughts on the grue problem and how to solve it, as well as for a bibliography on the subject (up to 1971).

		Argument		Pattern
	1.	If the stars determine one's fate, and beggar Jones and King Smith are born under the same stars, then Jones and Smith will have the same fates.	1.	$(H \cdot A) \supset O$
	2.	But Jones and Smith don't have the same fates.	2.	$\sim O$
/∴	3.	It's false both that the stars determine one's fate and that Jones and Smith were born under the same stars.	3.	$\sim(H \cdot A)$
	4.	But Jones and Smith were born under the same stars.	4.	A
/∴	5.	It's false that the stars determine one's fate.	5.	$\sim H$

Notice that the crucial step, 3, is derived from steps 1 and 2 by the *deductively valid* process Modus Tollens. According to Popperians, the legitimacy of this process makes the process of falsification legitimate; and it is the deductive *in*validity of the key step in confirmation (coupled with a Hume-style proof that inductive steps in general are not justifiable) that makes such a process *il*legitimate.

Now take the confirmation of the "sea of air" hypothesis, discussed earlier. According to our view, that theory was confirmed because it (plus already well-confirmed theories and specific auxiliary facts) implied results that in fact were observed. (The column of mercury in the tube in fact was about 30 inches high at sea level.) Popperians are, of course, willing to admit that the sea of air hypothesis (plus auxiliary facts and theories) does deductively imply what is observed, but they point out that the reverse is not true; what is observed (plus auxiliary facts and theories) does not imply the sea of air hypothesis, and therefore the step in which we did this is deductively invalid. Since Hume has shown that no other kind of justification is possible for this step, Popperians reject it as illegitimate.

Of course, Popperians don't want us to be going around falsifying true theories. Attempts to falsify don't and shouldn't succeed every time. In fact, Popperians say, when it comes time to act, we do so according to those theories that we have *tried but failed to falsify*. These theories are said to be **corroborated,** but not confirmed.

The trouble with the Popperian view is that the process of corroboration is just as deductively invalid as is confirmation, and indeed is simply a kind of confirmation under an assumed name.* So Popper's theory collapses into one very much like the confirmation theories he tried to get rid of, and thus is not a serious challenge to the view presented in this text.

Of course, Popperians can escape from this criticism by denying that

---

*Popper's method for calculating *degrees* of corroboration, say as he presented it in his book *The Logic of Scientific Discovery* (New York Basic Books, 1959) is seriously defective either as a measure of confirmation or, assuming they're different, of corroboration. But that is another matter.

theories can be corroborated and accepting just the key element in Popper theory stating that only falsification is a legitimate process. But then their theory fails to conform to common sense, or to actual practice, in that theories are in fact *accepted* (witness their being *acted on*), not merely falsified. Failure to be falsified is in fact taken to count in favor of an hypothesis (in the usual cases), and it is this that we have called *confirmation*. A person who accepts only the process of falsification cannot justify ever *acting* on the basis of a theory, however simple and obvious—for instance, that bread nourishes or that copper conducts electricity. But in fact, every sane person does so countless times every day.

The Raven Paradox

Earlier, we said that generalizations are confirmed by their *instances*. Let's now make this idea a bit more specific by introducing a very plausible principle, called the "confirmation principle". According to the **confirmation principle,** one way to *confirm* (increase the degree of credibility of) universal generalizations of the form "All P's are Q's" is to find things that are both P's and Q's, and one way to *disconfirm* a universal generalization of this form is to find things that are P's but not Q's. For example, according to this principle, evidence that there are black ravens confirms the universal generalization "All ravens are black" (the more ravens observed, the higher the *degree* of confirmation), and evidence that there are ravens that are not black disconfirms that generalization.

Equally plausible is the **equivalence principle,** which states that whatever confirms a given sentence equally confirms all logically equivalent sentences. This principle is accepted by many philosophers because they believe that there is a sense in which sentences that are equivalent say the very same thing, only in different words. For instance, the equivalent sentences "It is not the case that it will both rain and snow" (in symbols $\sim(R \cdot S)$) and "Either it won't rain or it won't snow" (in symbols $\sim R \vee \sim S$) seem to say the very same thing, only in different words. Thus, it appears to be plausible to suppose that whatever confirms $\sim(R \cdot S)$ equally confirms $\sim R \vee \sim S$, and vice versa.

But when we put these two apparently plausible principles together, and become precise about the correct symbolizations of universal generalizations, we immediately get into difficulty. Consider the sentence "All nonblack things are nonravens". Using the notation of predicate logic, it seems plausible to symbolize that sentence as $(x)(\sim Bx \supset \sim Rx)$, where Bx = "x is black", and Rx = "x is a raven". According to the confirmation principle, that sentence is confirmed by observations of nonblack nonravens; the more such observations the better the confirmation. The trouble is that the sentence $(x)(\sim Bx \supset \sim Rx)$ *is logically equivalent* to the sentence $(x)(Rx \supset Bx)$ (in English, "All ravens are black"), so that according to the equivalence principle whatever confirms the former equally confirms the latter. Thus, observations of brown shoes, green desk blotters, white chalk, and blue walls, all nonblack nonravens, which confirm $(x)(\sim Bx \supset \sim Rx)$ according to the confirmation principle, also equally confirm the logically equivalent sentence $(x)(Rx \supset Bx)$, according to the equivalence principle. We seem able to confirm the hypothesis that all ravens are black without ever examining ravens for color. Attractive as this sort of "indoor ornithology" may be, the natural inclination is to suspect that something must be wrong. The whole process seems paradoxical (indeed in the literature it is referred to as "the paradox of the ravens" or "the paradox of confirmation"). The problem is to remove the paradox while doing the least violence to our other philosophical assumptions.

Notice that this confirmation problem is a problem in *inductive* not deductive logic. It is not a question of going from true premises to a false conclusion by apparently valid means, because in inductive logic valid rules of inference (such as the confirmation principle—assuming that it is valid) are not supposed to *guarantee* that one cannot infer from true premises to a false conclusion. Nevertheless, the paradox does pose a perplexing problem, and (hopefully) one on which light can be shed by using the apparatus of predicate logic.

The most widely held solution to the raven paradox* is that our intuition against the confirmation of a hypothesis like "All ravens are black" by evidence such as the examination of nonblack nonravens is mistaken. Advocates of this view claim that the more closely we examine the process in question the less paradoxical it will seem. For instance, it will appear to be less paradoxical to confirm "All ravens are black" by examination of a nonblack nonraven once we notice that *taken by itself* this evidence not only confirms that hypothesis but also the hypotheses "All ravens are nonblack", "All things are nonblack", "All things are nonravens", and so on.

We tend to forget some of these other hypotheses because we know that they are false from other evidence. For instance, we know that the hypothesis "All things are nonblack" is false because we know that there are many black things. And since any hypothesis that is disconfirmed is automatically rejected, we reject this hypothesis, thus overlooking the fact that *taken by itself* evidence concerning a nonblack nonraven confirms it. And, proponents of this view claim, the seeming paradox vanishes when we notice that the hypotheses "All ravens are black" and "All ravens are nonblack" are *contraries,* so that (on the assumption that some ravens exist—whatever their color) one of these two hypotheses must be false. To decide between them, and thus to obtain any useful

---

* See, for instance, Carl Hempel, "Studies in the Logic of Confirmation", *Mind,* n.s., vol. 54 (1945), pp. 1–26, 97–120, which also contains the classic presentation of the problem.

knowledge concerning the color of ravens, we still have to observe ravens for color.

Proponents of this view also claim that the feeling of paradoxicality arises partly from the use of information not explicitly stated as evidence. For instance, confirmation of the hypothesis "All ravens are black" by examination of, say, a brown shoe, seems paradoxical partly because we know ahead of time that shoes, whatever their color, are not ravens. But suppose we are not told that the thing examined is a brown shoe but only that something was observed that was nonblack, and that that thing turned out to be a nonraven. Then surely this ought to count as confirming evidence for the hypothesis "All ravens are black", because if the nonblack thing had turned out to be a *raven,* instead of a shoe, then this information would have disconfirmed the hypothesis in question. After all, accepting the hypothesis that all ravens are black leads one to expect that if something is not black then it is not a raven; the thing examined was not black, and as predicted by the hypothesis, it turned out to be not a raven.*

Only a very few philosophers have proposed that we solve the raven paradox by rejecting the equivalence principle, and only a handful have suggested that we reject the confirmation principle.

Finally, there is the popular view that it is the use of predicate logic itself, in particular the use of *material implication,* that generates the problem. Advocates of this view deny that the use of a truth-functional logic sheds any light on the raven paradox, the problems of dispositionals and counterfactuals, or any similar problems. Rather, they claim that it is the very use of this logic in the symbolization of certain English sentences that *generates* these problems. Recall that in the discussion of material implication in Chapter Two we indicated that many uses of "if ______ then _ _ _ _ _ " and its synonyms in English are not truth functional, so that translations of such sentences by "$\supset$" at best capture only *part* of their meaning. Those who believe material implication is the cause of the problem claim that the part of their meaning lost in the translation process is vital in certain cases, and that if more adequate translations were used, problems such as the raven paradox, dispositionals, and counterfactuals would not arise.

But this line of reasoning can't be entirely correct. For instance, someone who asserts that "All ravens are black" at least *implies* that all nonblack things are nonravens, and someone who asserts the sentence "All nonblack things are nonravens" at least *implies* that all ravens are black. In other words, two sentences of this type (that is, two sentences that are contrapositives) are *logically equivalent.* (This was recognized by logicians long before the development of modern predicate logic.) But then,

---

* If you're interested in hearing the author's reasons for rejecting Hempel's solution, write to him for his unpublished paper, "Hempel and Goodman on the Ravens".

no matter how we symbolize contrapositives, just so long as their symbolizations are equivalent, the raven paradox will be generated. For example, the evidence that a brown shoe is nonblack and not a raven, which confirms the hypothesis "All nonblack things are nonravens", will equally confirm the equivalent hypothesis "All ravens are black". Thus the paradox arises without the express use of material implication. Modern logic doesn't generate the problem. It just makes it harder to overlook.

Exercise 16-1:

1. a. What is the distinction between an empirical hypothesis and a theory?
   b. Do you think this distinction is useful or important? Explain.
2. **McBird:** Tom took a couple of whiffs of the stuff in this bottle and went out like a light. What's in that bottle that put him out like that?
   Jane: Oh, that bottle; it contains a soporific.
   McBird: Oh, I see.
   Critically evaluate Jane's explanation.
3. Why don't disconfirming instances of a statistical hypothesis falsify it?
4. Why suppose that the larger the class of possible confirming instances, the smaller the degree of confirmation furnished by any particular confirming instance?
5. Suppose someone asks why that bird over in the cornfield is black, and receives the answer that it's a crow and all crows are black.
   a. Does this constitute an acceptable explanation according to the account in the text?
   b. Critically discuss what you think is the most likely reason for deciding that the above explanation is not adequate.
6. New Hebrides natives, having noticed that in all observed cases those infected with lice have good health, while sick people eventually become lice-free, have concluded that good health is the reason why a person has lice. When asked what caused the local missionary, John McNash, to be lice-free, a native replied that a person who doesn't have lice must be in poor health, so the missionary obviously isn't in good health.
   Critically discuss the native's answer.
7. Briefly identify the following, giving an (original) example of each:
   a. Auxiliary hypothesis.
   b. Probabilistic explanation.
   c. Deductive nomological explanation.
8. Explain in your own words what the problem is in trying to justify induction. Use original examples where they will help show you understand the problem.
9. Argue for or against the view that the problem of the justification of induction is a pseudo-problem.
10. Argue for or against the view that the problem of the justification of induction is solved by keeping track of the success rate of inductions, thus proving that induction *works.*
11. True or false: The confirmation paradoxes arise when we try to symbolize statements of the form "All P's and Q's" by means of "$\supset$"; stop using a truth-functional implication and the problem will disappear. Defend your answer.
12. True or false: The confirmation principle states (in part) that the only way to confirm an hypothesis of the form "All P's are Q's" is to find P's that are Q's. Explain.

Exercise 16-2:

Evaluate each of the following for inductive correctness and deductive validity.

1. We can confirm that the Earth is roughly a sphere and not flat in several different ways:
   a. We can travel west (or east) and eventually come back to our starting point, traveling a longer distance in doing so the closer we get to the equator.
   b. We can go down to the sea and observe ships coming into harbor. If we do, we'll see the tops of ships first, indicating that the Earth isn't flat, but curved somehow, since if it was flat, we should be able to see all of the ship above the water line at once.
   c. In an eclipse, the shadow of the surface of the Moon always has the shape of all or part of a disc, exactly as it would be if the Earth were a sphere casting that shadow.
2. The fact that fish are able to remain motionless under water is a conclusive reason for thinking that the material of their bodies has the same specific gravity as that of water; accordingly, if in their makeup there are certain parts which are heavier than water there must be others which are lighter, for otherwise they would not produce equilibrium.—Galileo, *Two New Sciences*
3. When asked whether he accepted the "twenty-five-year itch" theory about war, according to which it takes 25 years or so for memories of the horrors of war to fade and for a new generation to grow up who've never experienced those horrors, Herman Kahn, member of a noted "think tank", stated: ". . . I don't think it's accurate. I suspect the analogy is drawn from one single instance—the time that elapsed between 1914 and 1939, and I for one would hesitate to generalize from one observation. If one goes further back in history: In the Napoleonic wars, young men in France had been bloodied over and over again but were still willing to go to war. They liked war in some real sense. In America, on the other hand, 25 or 30 years after the Civil War there was no sign of any generational unrest, any thirst for a fresh conflict coming to the surface".
4. Ignatz Semmelweis discovered the cause of *childbed fever,* which was killing large numbers of expectant mothers in nineteenth-century European hospitals. At first, he couldn't account for the fact that women attended to by doctors had a death rate about five times higher than those looked after by midwives (10 percent compared to 2 percent). Then a colleague died, exhibiting symptoms of childbed fever after being cut on the finger by a medical student's scalpel during an autopsy. Since the doctors and medical students usually just happened to spend time in the autopsy room before examining patients, Semmelweis guessed that some sort of "cadaverous material" was being transmitted by the doctors to their patients, causing their deaths. To test this guess, he had the doctors wash their hands with chlorinated lime, a strong disinfectant, before examining patients, and quickly reduced the death rate from childbed fever to below 2 percent.
5. By the early 1800s, Newtonian physics was able to account for and predict the motions of the various planets and moons. But it was noticed that the orbit of Uranus, the outermost planet known at the time, didn't quite conform to Newtonian predictions. Either Newton's theory wasn't true throughout the universe or some as yet unknown force or body was at work. Since Newton's laws were known to account for an extremely large number of very different kinds of observations and experimental results, scientists weren't inclined to give them up easily. Finally, in 1843, Adams and Le Verrier independently calculated, using Newtonian principles, that the observed motion of Uranus could be accounted for on the assumption that there was another planet further out—as yet unobserved—causing the observed deviations from the expected path of Uranus. They also calculated just where astronomers should look to find it. In 1846, the planet, named Neptune by Le Verrier, was in fact observed. (A similar scenario was repeated in the early twentieth century, leading to the discovery of Pluto in 1930.)
6. After the discover of Uranus in the nineteenth century, it was noticed that the orbit of Mercury, the planet closest to the sun, didn't quite square with predictions made by Newtonian physics. Astronomers assumed that, as in the case of Uranus, there must be a planet (this time closer to the sun) causing the deviation, and calculated where it should be. But re-

peated attempts to actually observe this planet, named Vulcan, failed, as did several ingenious attempts to explain Mercury's deviations. Nevertheless, since Newton's laws explain so many things, the continued failure to explain the orbit of Mercury should not have been held as a disconfirmation, much less refutation, of the Newtonian theory.

7. However solid things are thought to be, you may yet learn from this that they are of rare body: in rocks and caverns the moisture of water oozes through and all things weep with abundant drops; food distributes itself through the whole body of living things; trees grow and yield fruit in season, because food is diffused through the whole from the very roots over the stem and all the boughs. Voices pass through walls and fly through houses shut, stiffening frost pierces to the bones. Now if there are no void parts, by what way can the bodies severally pass? You would see it to be quite impossible. Once more, why do we see one thing surpass another in weight though not larger in size? For if there is just as much body in a ball of wool as there is in a lump of lead, it is natural it should weigh the same, since the property of body is to weigh all things downwards, while on the contrary the nature of void is ever without weight. Therefore when a thing is just as large, yet is found to be lighter, it proves sure enough that it has more of void in it; while on the other hand that which is heavier shows that there is in it more of body and that it contains within it much less of void. Therefore that which we are seeking with keen reason exists sure enough, mixed up in things; and we call it void.—Lucretius, *On the Nature of Things,* Book I

8. In 1610, Galileo discovered four of the moons of Jupiter. First, he observed three stars, as he thought, very close to Jupiter, two to the east, one to the west of that planet. The next night, he was surprised to observe that all three were to the west, closer to each other than before, and two nights later that there were just two stars, this time both to the east of the planet.

   Since it was impossible for Jupiter to move from west to east one day and from east to west two days later, he concluded that it was the stars that moved, not Jupiter, although he didn't know how this was possible. Finally, on the next night, he observed two stars to the east of Jupiter, but now one was twice the size of the other, although on the previous night they had been the same size. He concluded that "there were in the heaven three stars which revolved round Jupiter, in the same manner as Venus and Mercury revolved round the sun". And on the next night, he observed a fourth star, or as he now concluded, a fourth planet revolving round Jupiter, as our moon revolves around the Earth. The import of his discovery was very great in his day (even though today it has much less significance), because it overturned the Aristotelian theory of the heavens that had held sway in the Western world for over 1500 years (perhaps the reason why clerics refused to look through his telescope to see the moons, since on their Aristotelian theory such moons could not exist).

Key Terms Introduced in Chapter Sixteen

Antecedent condition: An instance of the antecedent of some general hypothesis. An example is the state of affairs that a given match is well made and heated in the presence of oxygen, antecedent conditions of the hypothesis that all well-made matches heated in the presence of oxygen light.

Auxiliary hypothesis: A sentence or proposition, usually a report of some observation or particular event, used with an inductive generalization to infer a conclusion. An example is the report that Art is intelligent, used in conjunction with the inductive generalization that all intelligent students graduate, to conclude that Art will graduate.

Confirmation principle: The principle that states that one way to *confirm* a hypothesis of the form "All *P*'s are *Q*'s" is by finding things that are both *P*'s and *Q*'s, and one way to *disconfirm* a hypothesis of that form is to find things that are *P*'s but *not Q*'s.

Confirming instance: An instance of a general hypothesis that makes it more probable.

Deductive nomological explanation: An explanation in which a description of what is explained follows *deductively* from the general hypotheses plus antecedent conditions used to explain it.

Degree of confirmation (of a hypothesis): The degree of evidential support (for that hypothesis).

Eliminative theory of confirmation: The theory that a hypothesis is confirmed by only those of its instances that also disconfirm competing hypotheses.

Empirical entity: Something that can be directly observed via the senses. *Antonym:* **Theoretical entity.** *Synonym:* **Observable entity.**

Empirical hypothesis: A hypothesis that is a mere inductive generalization from its evidence, making no reference to any kind of entity not mentioned by the evidence. An example is the empirical hypothesis that all ravens are black, based on the evidence that all observed ravens are black.

Equivalence principle: The principle that whatever confirms a given hypothesis equally confirms all logically equivalent hypotheses.

Instance variety: Variety among confirming instances of a hypothesis. The more instance variety, the greater the confirming power of given instances.

Observable entity: (See **Empirical entity**).

Probabilistic explanation: An explanation in which a description of what is explained follows only *probably* from the general hypothesis plus antecedent conditions used to explain it.

Simplicity: A nonevidential criterion of confirmation acceptance. The simpler of two theories equally supported by the evidence is the better confirmed, the more acceptable.

Theoretical entity: An unobservable entity postulated by some theory. *Antonyms:* **Empirical entity; observable entity.**

Theoretical hypothesis: A hypothesis that makes reference to unobservable (theoretical) entities of a kind not referred to in the evidence for the hypothesis. An example is the sea of air hypothesis, which makes reference to *air pressure,* which is not directly observable.

Part Five

More on
Symbolic Logic

Chapter Seventeen

The Truth
Tree Method

The **truth tree method** is a strictly mechanical, or automatic, method for proving arguments valid or invalid, and for proving whether sentences are consistent or inconsistent. Although it isn't a complete method, that is, it won't work in every case, it can be used in virtually every case we're likely to come across outside of a logic textbook. (By way of contrast, the predicate logic proof technique introduced in Part Two of this text is complete, but it isn't a mechanical method—we may fail to find a proof even though one exists, because we lack sufficient ingenuity.) Let's see how the sentential logic truth tree method works, see why it works, and then look into the predicate logic truth tree method.

1 *The Sentential Logic Indirect Truth Tree Method*

The basic truth tree method combines the idea of an *indirect proof* (*reductio ad absurdum* proof) with that of truth table analysis. Take a very simple argument, say

$A \vee B$
$\sim A \quad /\therefore B$

The first step in the truth tree method is to add the negation of the conclusion of the argument to the set of its premises, just as we do in an ordinary indirect proof, to obtain what we might call its *expanded set of premises:*

$A \vee B$
$\sim A$
$\sim B$

We can think of these statements as forming the trunk of an upside down tree.

Now check (or cross out) the disjunction $A \vee B$, and **decompose** it into its parts A and B, placed on branches jutting out from the trunk of the tree, like this:

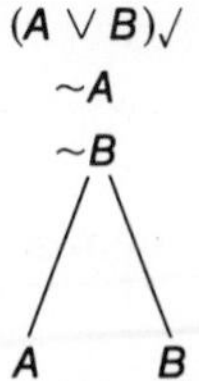

This gives us two paths, one running through the trunk of the tree and then branching to the left (containing $\sim A$, $\sim B$, and A), the other running through the trunk and branching to the right (containing $\sim A$, $\sim B$, and B).

Notice that both the right and left paths of the tree contain an explicit contradiction. (The contradiction in the left branch is $\sim A$ and A, and in the right branch is $\sim B$ and B.) We take note of these contradictions by placing an x at the end of each path that contains an explicit contradiction, so that our tree looks like this:

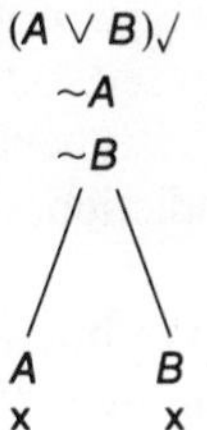

A path marked by an x is said to be a **closed path.** If every path in a truth tree is closed, the argument in question is *valid*. So the argument we've been considering is valid.

Now consider a simple invalid argument, say the argument

$A \vee B$
$A \quad /\therefore B$

It's truth tree looks like this:

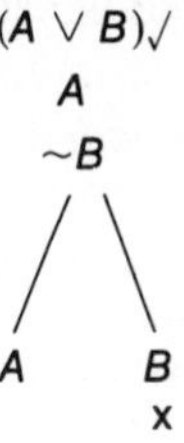

In this case, only the right path is closed. The left path is said to be an **open path,** because it doesn't contain an explicit contradiction. If even one path in a truth tree is open, the argument it diagrams is *in*valid. So the argument in question is invalid.

Now consider an argument containing a premise that is a conjunction, say the trivial argument

$A \cdot B$
$\sim C \quad /\therefore A$

First, we add the negation of its conclusion to the set of its premises, to form a tree trunk, like this:

$A \cdot B$
$\sim C$
$\sim A$

Then, we check the conjunctive premise, $A \cdot B$, and decompose it into its components, placed at the bottom of the column that forms the trunk of the tree, like this:

$(A \cdot B)\surd$
$\sim C$
$\sim A$
A
B
x

Since the one path in this tree contains an explicit contradiction, indicated by placing an *x* at its end, the argument is valid.

Notice that we don't place *A* and *B* into the tree by means of branches, as we did in the previous case. Branching is used to decompose disjunctions, and in this case we want to decompose a conjunction. The rule for decomposing conjunctions is to place each conjunct into the tree trunk one under the other as we have done in this case.*

Now consider an example involving implication, say the argument

$A \supset B$
$A \quad /\therefore B$

In this case, after adding the negation of the conclusion to its truth tree, we check the premise, $A \supset B$, and replace it with its disjunctive equiva-

* In more complicated cases, where the conjunction occurs in a branch of the tree, the conjuncts get placed one below the other on that branch. See the example on page 363. In cases where the conjunction occurs in the trunk of the tree but the tree already has branches, the conjuncts get placed one below the other on each open path. See the footnote on page 362.

lent, $\sim A \vee B$, handling that disjunction as explained before so as to get a tree that looks like this:

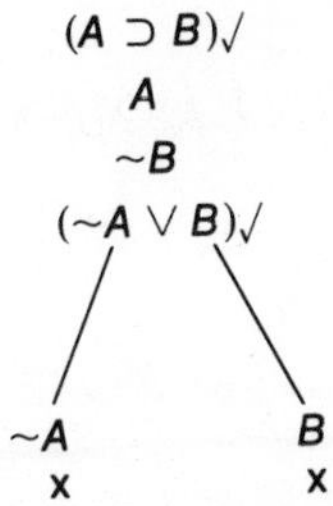

The two x's indicate that each of the two paths in this tree are closed (contain an explicit contradiction), and so the argument is valid.

We can, of course, handle more complicated arguments containing, say, conjunctions *and* disjunctions. Here is an example:

$A \supset B$
$A \cdot B \quad /\therefore B$

First, as usual, we add the negation of the conclusion to the trunk of the tree. Then, we decompose the conjunctive premise, $A \cdot B$, and add its parts to the tree trunk, so that, up to this point, our tree looks like this:

$(A \supset B)$
$(A \cdot B)\surd$
$\sim B$
A
B
x

And then we replace the premise $A \supset B$ by its equivalent, $\sim A \vee B$, and decompose $\sim A \vee B$ into its parts, placing them on branches of the tree and marking all closed paths:

$(A \supset B)\surd$
$(A \cdot B)\surd$
$\sim B$
A
B
$(\sim A \vee B)\surd$

$\sim A$ B
x   x

Since both paths are closed, the argument is valid.*

By way of contrast, consider the invalid argument

$A \supset B$
$A \cdot B \quad /\therefore \sim B$

Its truth tree looks like this:

```
(A ⊃ B)√
(A · B)√
   B†
   A
   B
(~A ∨ B)√
  /     \
~A       B
 x
```

In this case, one path is closed, but the other path is open. Since there is even one path open, the argument is *in*valid.

Next consider an argument containing an equivalence, say the argument

$A \equiv B$
$A \quad /\therefore B$

After adding the negation of the conclusion to the premises, we replace the equivalence, $A \equiv B$, with its logical equivalent, $(A \cdot B) \vee (\sim A \cdot \sim B)$, so that our tree looks like this:

---

* In general, conjunctions should be decomposed before disjunctions. If we do it the other way around, the decomposed conjuncts must be placed into both branches. For the argument in question, that sort of tree would look like this:

```
(A ⊃ B)√
(A · B)√
  ~B
(~A ∨ B)√
  /     \
~A       B
 A       A
 B       B
 x       x
```

† Technically, we should write $\sim\sim B$, but let's be informal in our use of *double negation*.

```
        (A ≡ B)✓
           A
          ~B
    (A · B) ∨ (~A · ~B)
```

Then, we check the unchecked disjunction and decompose it into its two disjuncts, $(A \cdot B)$ and $(\sim A \cdot \sim B)$:

```
        (A ≡ B)✓
           A
          ~B
    (A · B) ∨ (~A · ~B)✓
          /       \
         /         \
   (A · B)       (~A · ~B)
```

And finally, we decompose each of the two conjunctions, and place an x at the end of each closed path:

```
          (A ≡ B)✓
             A
            ~B
    [(A · B) ∨ (~A · ~B)]✓
            /       \
           /         \
   (A · B)✓       (~A · ~B)✓
      A               ~A
      B               ~B
      x                x
```

This tree has two paths. The left path (ignoring checked lines) contains A, $\sim B$, A, and B, and the right path A, $\sim B$, $\sim A$, and $\sim B$. Since both paths are closed, the argument is valid.

Finally, consider a case involving negation over a large unit:

```
A
B  /∴ A · B
```

Adding the negation of the conclusion to the premises, we get

```
     A
     B
  ~(A · B)
```

To decompose the negated statement, we first replace it with a logical equivalent, namely $\sim A \vee \sim B$, to get:

```
     A
     B
  ~(A · B)✓
  ~A ∨ ~B
```

Then we decompose $\sim A \vee \sim B$ in turn, to get the branching tree:

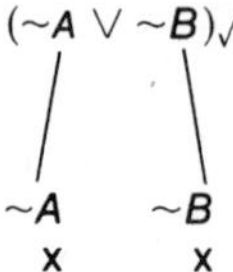

Again, both branches are closed; so the argument is valid.

We should note that all sorts of combinations can occur, resulting in a tree with no branches or with more than two. Consider the invalid argument

$A \supset B$
$B \supset C$
$C \quad /\therefore A$

Its tree starts out like this:

```
 (A ⊃ B)√
 (B ⊃ C)√
     C
    ~A
 (~A ∨ B)√
   ~B ∨ C
    /   \
  ~A     B
```

Up to this point, we've replaced both premises with logically equivalent disjunctions and decomposed the first one, $\sim A \vee B$. Now we decompose the other one, $\sim B \vee C$, being careful to branch out its parts along *both* open paths, like this:

```
     (A ⊃ B)√
     (B ⊃ C)√
         C
        ~A
     (~A ∨ B)√
     (~B ∨ C)√
      /      \
    ~A        B
   /  \      /  \
 ~B    C   ~B    C
            x
```

Since this completed tree has an open path (in fact, three open paths), the argument is invalid.

Next let's take a look at the tree for the valid argument

$\sim A \vee B$
$\sim B \vee C$
$\sim C \quad /\therefore \sim A$

Its tree starts out

$(\sim A \vee B)\surd$
$(\sim B \vee C)$
$\sim C$
A

$\sim A \qquad B$
x

Since the left path already contains a contradiction, even without the information contained in the premise $\sim B \vee C$, we close that path. And when we decompose the premise $\sim B \vee C$, we don't have to deal further with that closed path. The completed tree thus will look like this:

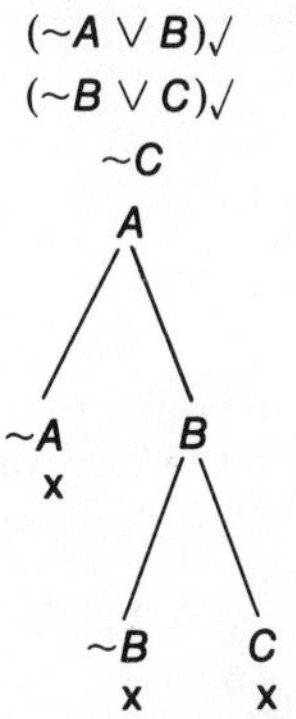

All three paths are closed, and so the argument is valid.

Let's now summarize the sentential logic indirect truth tree procedure:

1. Add the negation of the conclusion of the argument to be tested to the set of its premises, to form the expanded set of premises for that argument.

2. Replace any compound sentence in the expanded set that is either an implication or an equivalence or contains a negated compound expression by an equivalent conjunction or disjunction.

3. Decompose any conjunctions, placing their parts one under the other in the trunk of the tree.

4. Decompose any disjunctions, placing their parts on separate branches of the tree.

In complicated cases, the third and fourth steps often have to be performed more than once, in various orders, either grafted onto the trunk of the tree or onto one or more of its branches. For example, after decomposing the disjunction $(A \cdot B) \vee (C \cdot D)$, the conjunction $A \cdot B$ has to be decomposed in the left branch, and $C \cdot D$ has to be decomposed in the right branch.

Since certain steps in the truth tree method almost always occur together, truth tree rules are generally written so as to combine them. For instance, *implications* have to be first replaced by equivalent disjunctions, which are then decomposed. So an implication decomposition rule is generally introduced combining both of these steps. That is, instead of constructing the following tree:

```
(A ⊃ B)√
    A    /∴ B
   ~B
(~A ∨ B)
   /  \
 ~A    B
  x    x
```

we can construct this one:

```
(A ⊃ B)√
   A  /∴ B
  ~B
  /  \
~A    B
 x    x
```

The implication decomposition rule then looks like this:

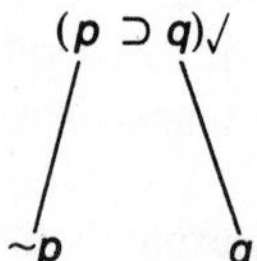

Similarly, we can write combined rules for decomposing equivalences, and so on, so that our complete set of truth tree rules for sentential logic becomes:

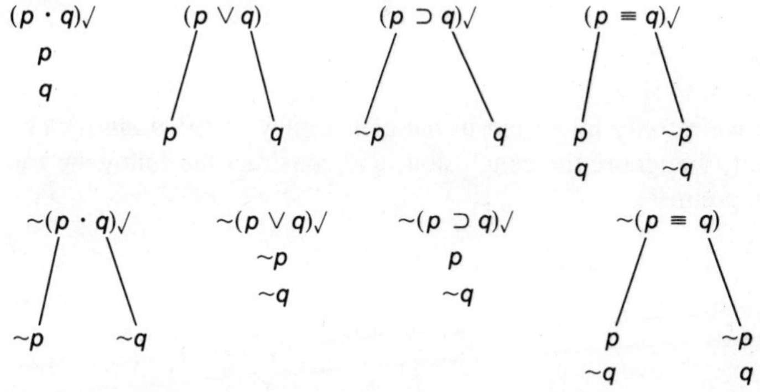

```
(p · q)✓        (p ∨ q)          (p ⊃ q)✓          (p ≡ q)✓
   p             /    \           /    \            /    \
   q            p      q        ~p      q          p     ~p
                                                   q     ~q

~(p · q)✓       ~(p ∨ q)✓        ~(p ⊃ q)✓          ~(p ≡ q)
  /    \           ~p               p                /    \
~p      ~q         ~q              ~q               p     ~p
                                                   ~q      q
```

Exercise 17-1:

Use the truth tree method to determine the validity/invalidity of each of the following arguments:

(1) 1. $A \cdot B$
2. $B \supset C$ /∴ C

(2) 1. $C \supset A$
2. $A \supset (B \cdot D)$
3. C /∴ B

(3) 1. $(A \cdot B) \supset C$
2. A /∴ $B \supset C$

(4) 1. $R \vee N$
2. $L \supset N$
3. R /∴ $\sim N$

(5) 1. $A \equiv B$ /∴ $\sim B \vee A$

(6) 1. $(A \cdot B) \vee (C \cdot D)$
2. $\sim A$ /∴ C

(7) 1. $F \supset G$
2. $(G \cdot H) \vee K$ /∴ F

(8) 1. $A \supset B$
2. $C \supset D$
3. $B \vee C$ /∴ $A \vee D$

(9) 1. $\sim(A \vee \sim B)$
2. $C \supset A$ /∴ $C \supset D$

(10) 1. $F \supset (G \supset H)$
/∴ $(\sim H \cdot K) \supset (G \supset \sim F)$

The truth tree method also can be used to determine whether sentences or sets of premises are consistent or inconsistent. Take the simplest contradiction, $A \cdot \sim A$. Its tree looks like this:

```
(A · ~A)✓
   A
  ~A
   x
```

Since the only path in this tree is closed, the sentence is inconsistent.

Or consider the more complicated example:

$(A \vee B) \supset C$
$A \cdot \sim C \quad /\therefore B$

Since we're only interested in the consistency of the *premises* of the argument, we ignore the conclusion, and construct the following truth tree for its premises:

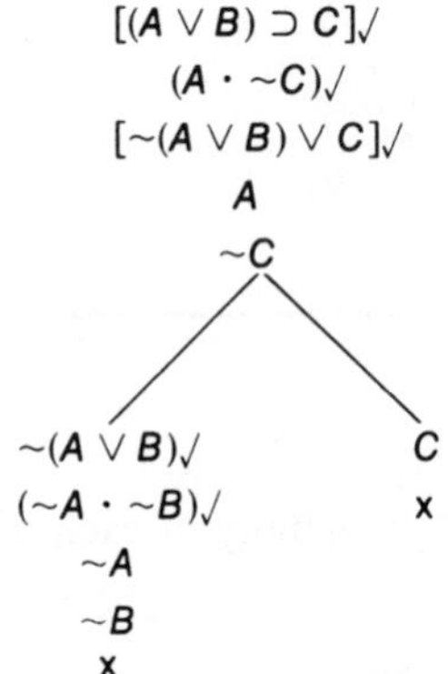

Since every path on this tree is closed, the premises of this argument are inconsistent.

Now consider an argument with consistent premises:

$\sim A \vee B$
$C \vee \sim B$
$\sim C \quad /\therefore \sim A$

Again, since we're only interested in the premises of the argument, we ignore its conclusion and construct a tree for its premises:

$(\sim A \vee B)\surd$
$(C \vee \sim B)\surd$
$\sim C$

$\sim A$ | B

C x | $\sim B$ | C x | $\sim B$ x

Since there is one open path, the premises of the argument are consistent. (Notice that the premise $C \vee \sim B$ had to be decomposed into two different paths.)

Exercise 17-2:

Use the truth tree method to prove that the arguments in Exercise 5-6 (page 98) have inconsistent premises. Then use the truth tree method to prove that the arguments in Exercise 5-7 (page 100) have consistent premises.

2 *Rationale Behind the Indirect Truth Tree Method*

The sentential logic truth tree method is just a graphic version of a more ordinary proof procedure based on the fact that any given sentence or conjunction of sentences can be cast into a logically equivalent sentence having what we might call *standard truth tree form*. Roughly speaking, a sentence is in **standard truth tree form** if it is either (1) a single letter, or a single letter negated (*examples:* A, B, $\sim C$, $\sim B$); (2) a simple conjunction (*examples:* $A \cdot B$, $\sim C \cdot D$, $\sim B \cdot \sim F$); (3) a simple disjunction (*examples:* $A \vee B$, $\sim A \vee B$, $\sim A \vee \sim B$); or (4) any combination of these (*examples:* $(A \cdot B) \vee C$, $A \vee (\sim B \vee C)$; $(C \cdot D) \vee (A \cdot B)$). Sentences containing an implication, equivalence, or a negated compound sentence are *not* in standard truth tree form (*examples:* $A \supset \sim B$, $C \equiv D$, $\sim(A \vee \sim B)$, $\sim(A \cdot B) \cdot C$).

Now recall our truth tree proof of the validity of the argument

$A \vee B$
$\sim A \quad /\therefore B$

It looked like this:

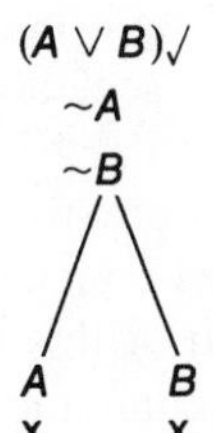

This tree contains two paths, the left path consisting of $\sim A$, $\sim B$, and A, the right path of $\sim A$, $\sim B$, and B. If we think of the items in a truth tree path as forming a conjunction, and branching as illustrating disjunction, then in effect this truth tree is a diagram of the disjunction $[(\sim A \cdot \sim B) \cdot A] \vee [(\sim A \cdot \sim B) \cdot B]$, which happens to be a standard truth tree form sentence logically equivalent to the expanded set of premises for the argument in question. (The expanded set is $A \vee B$, $\sim A$, and $\sim B$, and we can easily prove that the conjunction of these items, namely $(A \vee B) \cdot (\sim A \cdot \sim B)$, is logically equivalent to the standard form sentence $[(\sim A \cdot \sim B) \cdot A] \vee [(\sim A \cdot \sim B) \cdot B]$, by Comm and DeM.)

Notice that each disjunct of this standard form sentence contains an explicit contradiction. This means that the disjunctive sentence as a whole also is contradictory (because if every disjunct of a disjunction is contradictory, then, obviously, the whole disjunction must be contradictory). And since this contradictory disjunction is logically equivalent to the expanded set of premises for the argument in question, that set of premises also must be contradictory. Thus, by the rule of *indirect proof,* we're entitled to conclude that the argument itself is valid.

In other words, we can prove an argument is valid, without constructing a truth tree, simply by proving that the expanded set of its premises (containing the argument's premises plus the negation of its conclusion) is equivalent to a disjunction each of whose disjuncts contains a contradiction. The truth tree construction itself is just a heuristic device and isn't actually needed to prove argument validity.

Now recall the invalid argument

$A \vee B$
$A \quad / \therefore B$

and its truth tree:

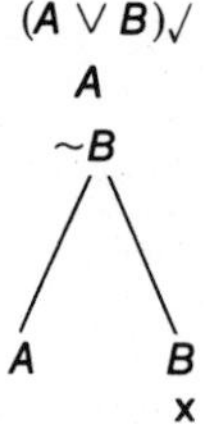

The left path of this tree contains A, $\sim B$, and A, and the right path A, $\sim B$, and B. The analogous standard truth tree form sentence is $[(A \cdot \sim B) \cdot A] \vee [(A \cdot \sim B) \cdot B]$, which is logically equivalent (by DeM) to $(A \cdot \sim B) \cdot (A \vee B)$, the conjunction of the expanded set of premises for this argument. Notice, however, that only the right disjunct contains an explicit contradiction, mirroring the fact that the right path of this truth tree is closed, while the left disjunct does not contain a contradiction, mirroring the fact that the left path of the truth tree is open. Since only one of the two disjuncts of the disjunction contains an explicit contradiction, the disjunction as a whole is consistent. Therefore, the argument in question is invalid.

In like manner, any argument of sentential logic can be evaluated by constructing a standard truth tree form sentence logically equivalent to the expanded set of premises for that argument, then determining whether that standard form sentence is contradictory or not. If it is, the argument is valid; if it isn't, the argument is invalid.

Exercise 17-3:

Construct a standard truth tree form sentence for each of the illustrative examples in Section 1 of this chapter, and determine, without constructing a truth tree, which arguments are valid, which invalid.

3 *The Direct Coupled Tree Method*

The truth tree method just introduced is an *indirect* method, in that it mirrors proofs using the argument form Indirect Proof **(IP).** But there is also a direct truth tree method—the coupled tree method.

In the indirect method, we start by adding the negation of the conclusion to the given premises (all put into standard truth tree form). If every path closes, the argument is valid (because a closed path is a contradictory path). If one or more paths are open, the argument is invalid (because an open path is a consistent path—the premises plus the conclusion then do not imply a contradiction).

In the direct method, using *coupled trees,* we start with the premises and work toward the conclusion while at the same time working from the conclusion up toward the premises. (Recall the strategy hint about working backward from the conclusion as well as forward from the premises.) We do not negate the conclusion.

Take the following valid argument:

$A \supset B \quad /\therefore \sim B \supset \sim A$

Here is its coupled tree, one part moving from the premise down toward the conclusion, the other from the conclusion up toward the premise:

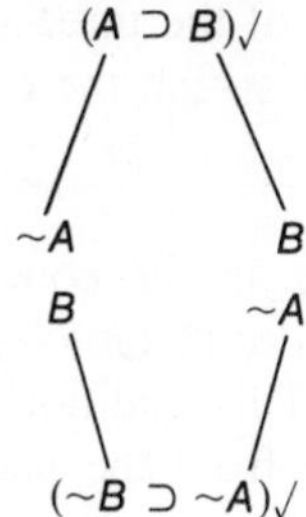

In this simple example, it's obvious that every sentence in the right path of the lower tree (there happens to be just one, namely $\sim A$) also is in the left path of the upper tree, and similarly for the other path. Both upper paths thus *cover* a lower path. We indicate this pattern for our example tree by linking the paired paths of the two trees:

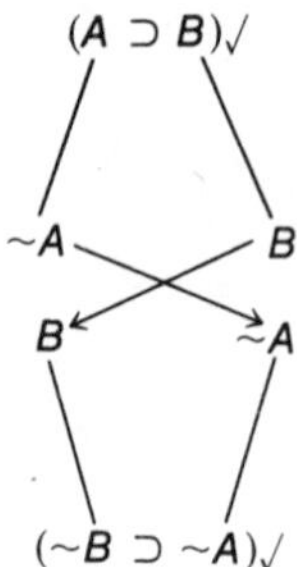

Since every path in the upper tree thus covers a path in the lower tree, the argument is valid.

When the conclusion is a single letter or a negated single letter, a coupled tree looks a bit different, as the following case illustrates:

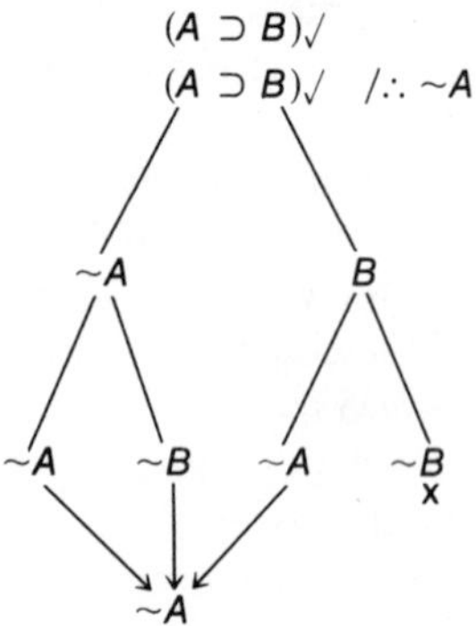

Note first that the path farthest to the right is closed (because it contains a contradiction), and so can't represent a possible case. Then notice that each one of the three open paths covers the conclusion. This display shows that each one of the three ways in which both premises might be true also are ways in which the conclusion is true. The argument therefore is valid.

If a letter appears in the conclusion of an argument but not in its premises, we need to add a tautology to the premises to make the coupled tree method work. This addition is legitimate because we can always prove any tautology from the null set of premises, so that we always could prove the addition of the added tautology if we wanted to. In the typical case, the tautology to be added is an instance of the law of the excluded middle, that is, $A \vee \sim A$, $B \vee \sim B$, and so on. (Sometimes, several such tautologies need to be added.) If the letter C, say, appears in the conclusion but not the premises of an argument, then we want to add the tautology $C \vee \sim C$ to the premises. Here is an example showing how we add a tautology to a tree by adding two branches, in this case one branch is B and the other $\sim B$:

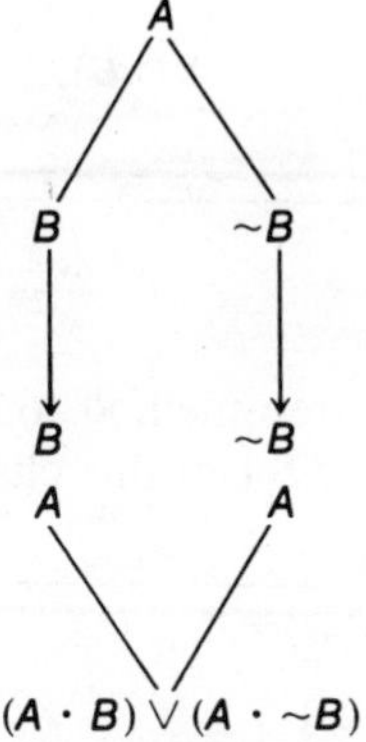

Since every open branch in the upper tree covers a branch in the lower, the argument A /∴ $(A \cdot B) \vee (A \cdot \sim B)$ is valid.

Now let's see what a coupled tree looks like when it proves *in*validity. Take the following example:

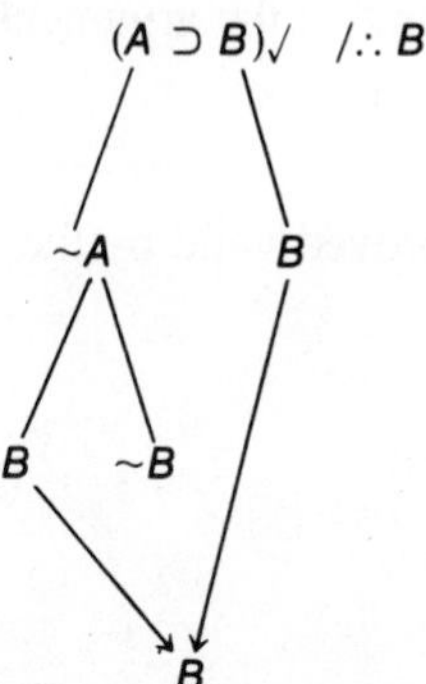

Since there is an open path of the upper tree (namely $\sim A$, $\sim B$) that covers no branch of the lower, the argument is invalid. In this case, introduction of the tautology $B \vee \sim B$ failed to bridge the gap between upper and lower trees.

Finally, it should be noted that a valid tree may have an uncovered lower path. What makes it valid is rather that every upper path covers some lower path or other, as the following illustrates:

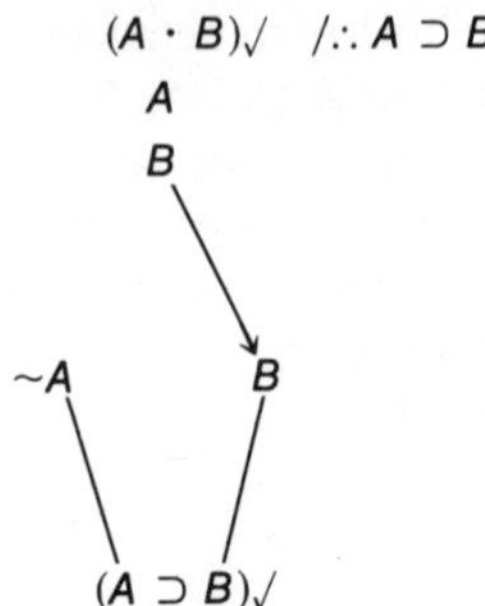

Exercise 17-4:

Use the coupled tree method to determine the validity/invalidity of the items in Exercise 17-1 of this chapter.

---

4 *The Predicate Logic Truth Tree Method*

Perhaps the most important reason for introducing the truth tree method is to deal with the quantified arguments of predicate logic that we can't prove by truth table analysis. (Any argument of predicate logic that can be proved by truth table analysis also can be proved by the truth tree method.) An example is the argument:

$(x)Fx \vee (x)Gx$
$\sim(x)Fx \quad /\therefore (x)Gx$

This argument is proved valid by the following truth tree:

$[(x)Fx \vee (x)Gx]\surd$
$\sim(x)Fx$
$\sim(x)Gx$

$(x)Fx$	$(x)Gx$
x	x

Since both paths are closed, the argument is valid.

The general predicate logic truth tree procedure consists in the sentential logic procedure to which the quantifier rules **UI, EI,** and **QN** have been added.* Although the predicate logic truth tree procedure unfortu-

---

* See Chapter Six, Section 5, for an explanation of rules **UI** and **EI,** and Chapter Seven, Section 3, for an explanation of rule **QN.**

nately doesn't work in every case, it does work in almost every case we're likely to run across, and it does tell us when it isn't going to work.

Consider the following argument:

$(x)(Fx \vee Gx)$
$\sim Fa \quad /\therefore Ga$

First, we add the negation of the conclusion to the premises, and then, in this case, use **UI** on the first premise:

1. $(x)(Fx \vee Gx)$
2. $\sim Fa$
3. $\sim Ga$
4. $Fa \vee Ga$ — 1, **UI**

Then, we check the disjunction, $Fa \vee Ga$, and decompose it as in the sentential logic procedure, closing all paths that contain a contradiction:

4. $(Fa \vee Ga)\surd$ — 1, **UI**

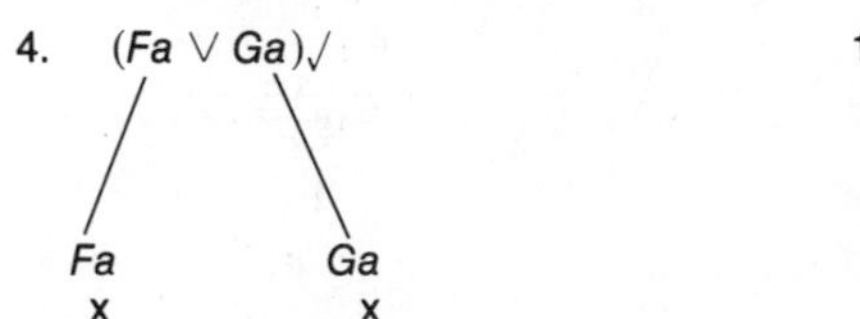

Since both paths are closed, the argument is valid.

Notice, however, that we didn't check the first line when we applied **UI** to it. The reason is that this use of **UI** extracts only part of the content of line 1. It ignores, for instance, the information $Fb \vee Gb$, $Fc \vee Gc$, and so on. In this case, we don't need any of this additional information, but in some other cases we do. Here is an example:

1. $(x)(Fx \vee Gx)$
2. $\sim Fa$
3. $\sim Fb \quad /\therefore Gb$

Its tree continues:

4. $\sim Gb$ — **AP**
5. $Fa \vee Ga$ — 1, **UI**

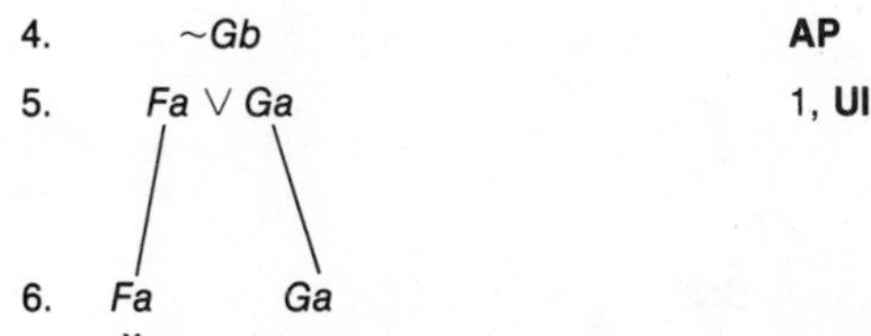

Suppose that after applying **UI** to line 1 we had checked off that line, making it unavailable for further use in the proof. Then we wouldn't have been able to close the right path of the tree and determine, correctly, that the argument in question is valid. Instead, we would have had to conclude, erroneously, that the argument is invalid. By not checking line 1 after applying **UI** to it, we leave open the possibility of applying

UI to it again, and again, as often as we need to. In this case, we need to apply it once more, because another individual constant, *b*, appears in the proof in addition to *a*. So the next step in constructing a truth tree for this argument is to apply **UI** again to line 1, this time getting:

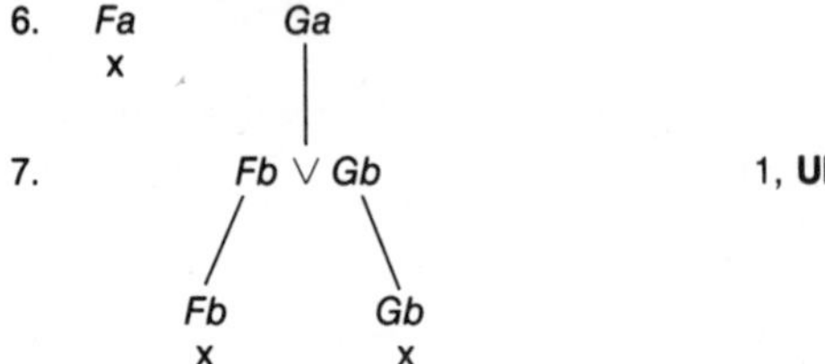

All paths on this tree are closed, and so the argument is valid. (Notice we don't have to bother adding $Fb \vee Gb$ to the left path of the tree, since that path already was closed.)

Here is the truth tree for another argument, listing justifications to the right of each line:

1.	$(\exists x)(y)Fxy\checkmark$	$/\therefore (y)(\exists x)Fxy$
2.	$\sim(y)(\exists x)Fxy$	**AP**
3.	$(\exists y)(x)\sim Fxy\checkmark$	2, **QN** (Twice)
4.	$(y)Fxy$	1, **EI**
5.	$(x)\sim Fxy$	3, **EI**
6.	Fxy	4, **UI**
7.	$\sim Fxy$ x	5, **UI**

Since the only path in this very sparse tree is closed, the argument is valid. (Notice that this nonbranching tree is just an ordinary *indirect proof*.)

Examples:

(1)

1.	$(x)(Fx \supset Gxx)$	
2.	$\sim(x)Gxx\checkmark$	$/\therefore \sim(x)Fx$
3.	$(x)Fx$	**AP**
4.	$(\exists x)\sim Gxx\checkmark$	2, **QN**
5.	$\sim Gxx$	4, **EI**
6.	Fx	3, **UI**
7.	$(Fx \supset Gxx)\checkmark$	1, **UI**

$\sim Fx$ (x) $\quad$ Gxx (x)

Since both paths are closed, the argument is valid.

(2)	1.	$(x)(Fx \supset Gxx)$	
	2.	$\sim(x)Gxx$	$/\therefore (\exists x)Fx$
	3.	$\sim(\exists x)Fx$	**AP**
	4.	$(x)\sim Fx$	3, **QN**
	5.	$(\exists x)\sim Gxx\checkmark$	2, **QN**
	6.	$\sim Gxx$	5, **EI**
	7.	$\sim Fx$	4, **UI**
	8.	$(Fx \supset Gxx)$	1, **UI**
	9.	$\sim Fx$ / Gxx x	

Since one path is open, the argument is invalid.

(3)	1.	$(x)[(\exists y)Lxy \supset (y)Lyx]$	
	2.	Laa	$/\therefore Lba$
	3.	$\sim Lba$	**AP**
	4.	$[(\exists y)Lay \supset (y)Lya]$	1, **UI**
	5.	$\sim(\exists y)Lay$ / $(y)Lya$	
	6.	Lba x (right branch)	5, **UI**
	7.	$(y)\sim Lay$	5, **QN**
	8.	$\sim Laa$ x	7, **UI**

Both paths are closed, and so the argument is valid.

(4)	1.	$(x)(Fx \supset Gx)$	
	2.	$(x)(Gx \supset Hx)$	$/\therefore (x)(Fx \supset Hx)$
	3.	$\sim(x)(Fx \supset Hx)$	**AP**
	4.	$[\exists x)\sim(Fx \supset Hx))\checkmark$	3, **QN**
	5.	$\sim(Fx \supset Hx)\checkmark$	3, **EI**
	6.	Fx	5*
		$\sim Hx$	5
	7.	$Fx \supset Gx$	1, **UI**

---

* Up to now, we haven't been keeping track of the lines obtained by the truth tree rules for decomposing sentences. But now it will sometimes be useful to at least cite the line from which the decomposed material has been obtained.

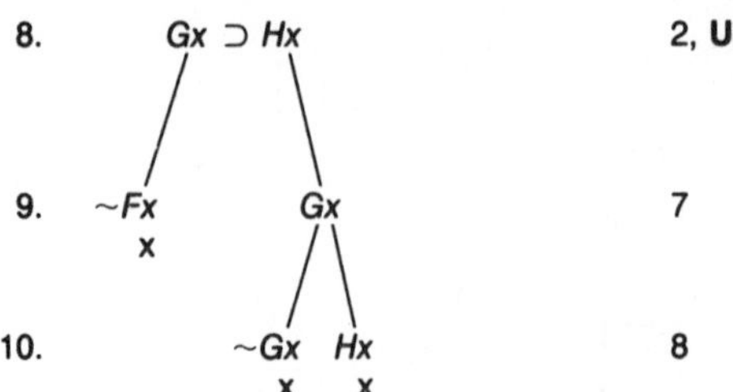

All paths are closed, and so the argument is valid. (Note how much simpler an ordinary proof would be.)

(5) 1. (x)~Fxx

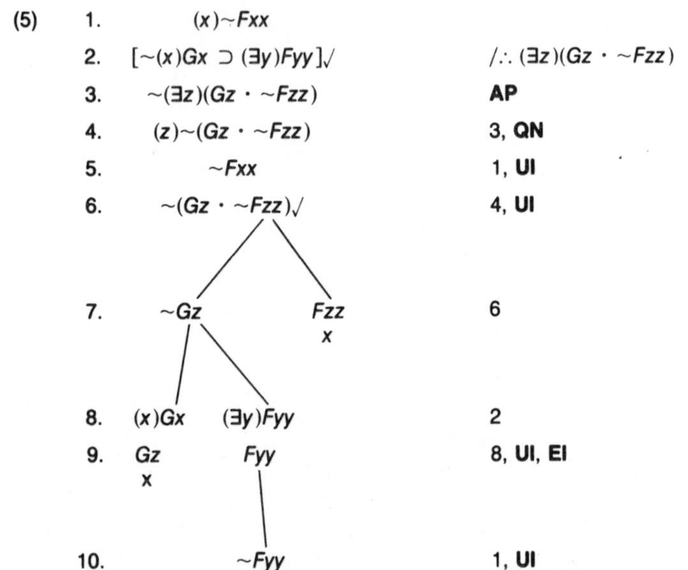

2. [~(x)Gx ⊃ (∃y)Fyy]√ /∴ (∃z)(Gz · ~Fzz)
3. ~(∃z)(Gz · ~Fzz) AP
4. (z)~(Gz · ~Fzz) 3, QN
5. ~Fxx 1, UI
6. ~(Gz · ~Fzz)√ 4, UI
7. ~Gz Fzz 6
x
8. (x)Gx (∃y)Fyy 2
9. Gz Fyy 8, UI, EI
x
10. ~Fyy 1, UI
x

All paths are closed. So the argument is valid.

Unfortunately, some truth trees can never be completed. Suppose we want to find out whether the sentence $(x)(\exists y)Fxy$ is consistent or inconsistent. If its tree contains all closed paths, it is inconsistent, and if its tree contains an open path, it is consistent. Following the general procedure, we start the tree as follows:

1. (x)(∃y)Fxy
2. (∃y)Fxy √ — 1, UI
3. Fxz — 2, EI

Since z now occurs free on line 3, it seems that we need to apply **UI** to line 1 again:

4. $(\exists y)Fzy$ ✓ 1, **UI**

And then apply **EI** again:

5. Fzw 4, **EI**

But doing so just introduces a new letter free into the proof; so we again have to apply **UI** and then **EI**:

6. $(\exists y)Fwy$ ✓ 1, **UI**
7. Fwv 4, **EI**

And so on, indefinitely.

A branch like the one just considered that never closes or ends is called a **nonterminating** branch. If a tree contains a nonterminating branch, then the sentence or sentences that generate the tree are consistent (and if the tree diagrams an argument then the argument is invalid). In this case, we're intuitively sure that the tree will never stop; so we can be sure that the sentence $(x)(\exists y)Fxy$ is consistent.

Unfortunately, there is no effective way to determine in every case whether a branch is nonterminating or will close at some later point. So the predicate logic truth tree method will not get us an answer in every case. It so happens, however, that many trees containing a nonterminating branch when constructed one way don't contain such a branch when constructed another way. The trick in these cases is to not spin our wheels concentrating on lines derived from one sentence, but to move back and forth from that sentence to others, as in this example:

1. $(x)(\exists y)Fxy$ /∴ $(\exists x)Fax$
2. $\sim(\exists x)Fax$

If we concentrate on line 1 and lines derived from line 1, we get an apparently never-ending tree, like this:

3. $(\exists y)Fay$ ✓ 1, **UI**
4. Faz 3, **EI**
5. $(\exists y)Fzy$ ✓ 1, **UI**
6. Fzw 5, **EI**
7. $(\exists y)Fwy$ ✓ 1, **UI**
8. Fwv 7, **EI**

And so on, indefinitely. But if we mix in lines following from line 2, we get a quickly closing tree:

3. $(\exists y)Fay$ ✓ 1, **UI**
4. Faz 3, **EI**
5. $(x)\sim Fax$ 2, **QN**
6. $\sim Faz$ 5, **UI**

x

Exercise 17-5:

Use the truth tree method to determine which of the following arguments are valid and which invalid (noting the one argument whose tree is inconclusive):

(1) 1. $(x)(Fx \supset Gx)$
2. $(\exists x){\sim}Gx$ $/\therefore (\exists x){\sim}Fx$

(2) 1. $(x)[Fx \supset (y)Gy]$
2. Fa $/\therefore (x)Gx$

(3) 1. $(x)(Ax \supset Bx)$
2. $(x)({\sim}Ax \supset Cx)$ $/\therefore (x)({\sim}Bx \supset {\sim}Cx)$

(4) 1. $(\exists x)Fx$
2. $(x)({\sim}Gx \supset {\sim}Fx)$
3. $(x)Mx$ $/\therefore (\exists x)Gx \cdot (\exists x)Mx$

(5) 1. $(\exists x)[Fx \cdot (y)(Gy \supset Lxy)]$
2. $(x)[Fx \supset (y)(My \supset {\sim}Lxy)]$
$/\therefore (x)(Gx \supset {\sim}Mx)$

(6) 1. $(x)(Ax \supset Fx)$
2. $(\exists x)Fx \supset {\sim}(\exists y)Gy$
$/\therefore (x)[(\exists y)Ay \supset {\sim}Gx]$

(7) 1. $(\exists x)(Ax \cdot {\sim}Bx)$
2. $(\exists x)(Ax \cdot {\sim}Cx)$
3. $(\exists x)({\sim}Bx \cdot Dx)$
$/\therefore (\exists x)[Ax \cdot ({\sim}Bx \cdot Dx)]$

(8) 1. $(x){\sim}Fxx$
2. ${\sim}(x)Gx \supset (\exists y)Fya$
$/\therefore (\exists z)(Gz \cdot Fzz)$

(9) 1. $(\exists x)(Ax \vee {\sim}Bx)$
2. $(x)[(Ax \cdot {\sim}Bx) \supset Cx]$
$/\therefore (\exists x)Cx$

(10) 1. $(x)(\exists y)(Fx \cdot Gxy)$
$/\therefore (\exists y)(x)(Fx \cdot Gxy)$

Key Terms Introduced in Chapter Seventeen

Closed path: A path, or branch, of a truth tree containing an explicit contradiction (and marked with an *x* to signify that fact).

Coupled tree method: A truth tree method that works from the conclusion up to the premises as well as from the premises down to the conclusion.

Decompose (a formula): Divide a formula into smaller parts, then place appropriately on a truth tree.

Nonterminating (branch of a truth tree): A branch that never closes.

Open path: A path, or branch of a truth tree that does *not* contain an explicit contradiction. (See also **closed path.**)

Standard truth tree form: A formula that is either (1) a single letter (alone or negated); (2) a simple conjunction; (3) a simple disjunction; or (4) any combination of these (thus not containing any occurrences of "⊃", "≡", or negated compounds).

Truth tree method: A method for diagramming arguments to determine whether they are valid or invalid (also usable to determine the consistency-inconsistency of premises).

Chapter Eighteen

Rationale Behind the Precise Formulation of the Quantifier Rules

Although the general idea behind the use of the four quantifier rules introduced in Part Two of this text is fairly simple (and intuitive), as we saw in Chapter Seven, their precise formulation turns out to be quite complicated, and in a few cases nonintuitive (but never counterintuitive). There are eighteen kinds of inferences that the four quantifier rules must handle correctly. An example is presented to illustrate each of them.

The first concerns uses of rule **EI** such as this one:

(1) 1. $(\exists x)Hx$ p
2. Ha 1, **EI** (invalid)

This use of **EI** clearly is invalid. Although it follows from line 1 that *some entity or other* has the property *H*, it surely does not follow that whatever is named by the individual constant *a* is that entity. For instance, if *H* is the property of being heavy, and *a* names some light object, say a certain piece of chalk, then line 1 is true, since there surely is *some* entity that is heavy, but line 2 is false, since the piece of chalk in question is not heavy. The moral of this example is that *when* **EI** *is used to drop an existential quantifier, the variables thus freed cannot validly be replaced by individual constants*. Instead, *they must be replaced by individual variables*.

Now consider the proof

(2) 1. $(\exists x)Fx$ p
2. $(\exists x)Gx$ p /∴ $(\exists x)(Fx \cdot Gx)$
3. Fx 1, **EI**
4. Gx 2, **EI** (invalid)
5. $Fx \cdot Gx$ 3,4 **Conj**
6. $(\exists x)(Fx \cdot Gx)$ 5, **EG**

Suppose Fx = "x is a fox" and Gx = "x is a goose". Then premise 1 asserts that something is a fox, which is true, and premise 2 that something is a goose, which also is true. But the conclusion, line 6, asserts that something is *both* a fox *and* a goose, which obviously is false. The trouble occurs at line 4, which results from line 2 by **EI.** Although 2 justifies the assertion that *some x or other* is a goose, it does *not* justify the assertion that *the x that is a fox is a goose*. But use of the same free variable on 4 that already occurred free on 3 permits derivation of this unwarranted conclusion. The moral this time is that *a variable introduced free into a proof by* **EI** *must not occur free previously in the proof.* (Of course, we could have used some variable other than x on 4. For instance, we could have used the variable y, to obtain Gy on that line, since y does not occur free previously in the proof.)

Now consider the use of **UG** in the following proof:

(3)	1.	Fa	p
	2.	$(x)Fx$	1, **UG** (invalid)

Suppose Fa = "Art is friendly", and assume that in fact Art *is* friendly. Then the use of **UG** in the above argument moves us from the true statement that Art is friendly to the patently false one that everything is friendly. Hence that use of **UG** is invalid. The moral this time is that *we cannot use* **UG** *on a constant.*

Next, consider another invalid use of **UG:**

(4)	1.	$(\exists x)Fx$	p /∴ $(x)Fx$
	2.	Fy	1, **EI**
	3.	$(x)Fx$	2, **UG** (invalid)

Assuming again that Fx = "x is friendly", line 1 asserts that *something* is friendly, while line 3 asserts the falsehood that *everything* is friendly. The trouble here is that the y on line 2 resulted from an application of **EI** to line 1, so that in generalizing on y to obtain line 3 we generalized on a variable obtained by **EI.** Surely it is incorrect to assert that because *some* entity has a certain property, *every* entity does. Consequently, we must forbid uses of **UG** (such as the one to line 3 of this proof) that permit the passage from "some" to "all". In other words, *we cannot use* **UG** *on a variable introduced free into a proof by* **EI.**

Now we have to consider a more difficult example.

(5)	1.	$(x)(\exists y)Lyx$	p /∴ $(\exists y)(x)Lyx$
	2.	$(\exists y)Lyx$	1, **UI**
	3.	Lyx	2, **EI**
	4.	$(x)Lyx$	3, **UG** (invalid)
	5.	$(\exists y)(x)Lyx$	4, **EG**

Suppose Lxy = "y is larger than x", and the universe of discourse has been restricted to numbers only. Then premise 1 asserts the arithmetic truth that given any number x, there is some number y that is larger than x; that is, 1 asserts that whichever number we choose, there is some number larger than that number, or that there is no largest number. So the premise of this argument is true.* But its conclusion, line 5, is false, since it asserts that there is some number y that is larger than all numbers. This must be false, since no number is larger than itself, and because (as the premise of this argument asserts) there is no largest number. So in going from 1 to 5 we have passed from a true premise to a false conclusion.

It is rather difficult to see what went wrong in this proof, and in particular what is wrong with the inference from line 3 to line 4. After all, the x free on 3, to which **UG** was applied, does not result from an application of **EI**, as in the previous invalid proof. Rather it results from an application of **UI** to line 1, so that we seem to be simply dropping and then adding the same universal quantifier. This *seems* as harmless as the similar process in the proof

1.	$(x)Fx$	p
2.	Fx	1, **UI**
3.	$(x)Fx$	2, **UG**

But the use of **UG** in proof (5) is not harmless by any means. The mere fact that x is free on line 3 of that proof, *a line obtained by* **EI**, is sufficient to make the application of **UG** to x invalid. It is as though (to use a metaphor) the "taint" of **EI** placed on the y variable in line 3 "rubbed off" the y variable onto the other variable, x, free on that line. The moral is that *we cannot use* **UG** *on a variable free in a line obtained by* **EI**, whether that variable became free by using **EI** or not. (Notice that by forbidding such applications of **UG** we eliminate not only the invalid use of **UG** in proof (5), but also the invalid use of **UG** in proof (4).)

This restriction on **UG** introduces a nonintuitive element into our discussion for the very first time, for taken in isolation it is neither intuitive nor counter-intuitive. Its justification is that without it, or some similar restriction, we would be able to go from true premises to false conclusions, whereas with it we cannot do so.

Next consider the following proof:

---

*This assertion is a truth of arithmetic because the series of numbers has no end. We know intuitively that this must be true, because we know that we can always add one to any number, no matter how large, to obtain a larger number, then add one more to obtain an even larger number, and so on, indefinitely.

(6)

→1.	Fy	**AP** /∴ $(z)[Fz \supset (x)Fx]$
2.	$(x)Fx$	1, **UG** (invalid)
3.	$Fy \supset (x)Fx$	1–2, **CP**
4.	$(z)[Fz \supset (x)Fx]$	3, **UG**

Suppose Fy = "y is friendly". Then the conclusion, which depends on no premises whatever, asserts that if anything is friendly, then everything is friendly, an obviously false statement. The moral is that *within the scope of an assumed premise we cannot use* **UG** *on a variable free in that assumed premise*. This restriction rules out the use of **UG** on line 2 of the above proof, because it occurs within the scope of the assumed premise 1. But it does not rule out the valid use of **UG** that yields line 4, because 4 is outside the scope of that assumed premise.

To some extent, this restriction on **UG** is nonintuitive, just like the previous one. It, too, is justified by the fact that without it we could go from true premises to false conclusions.

Notice, however, that this restriction does not rule out all uses of **UG** within the scope of an assumed premise. It forbids only those uses where the Universal Generalization takes place on a variable free in the assumed premise itself. Thus, the restriction does *not* rule out the use of **UG** in the following proof:

1.	$(x)(Fx \supset Gx)$	p /∴ $(x)Fx \supset (x)Gx$
→2.	$(x)Fx$	**AP**
3.	Fx	2, **UI**
4.	$Fx \supset Gx$	1, **UI**
5.	Gx	3,4 **MP**
6.	$(x)Gx$	5, **UG** (valid)
7.	$(x)Fx \supset (x)Gx$	2–6, **CP**

One might naïvely characterize a particular application of **EI** or **UI** as a process in which a quantifier is dropped and all of the variables thus freed are replaced by a particular variable.* Thus, in the following use of **EI**,

1.	$(\exists x)(Fx \cdot Gx)$	p
2.	$(Fy \cdot Gy)$	1, **EI**

the quantifier $(\exists x)$ is dropped, and each x thus freed is replaced by a free y. (Of course we could just as well have replaced each x by itself.) The

---

*In the remaining examples we will sometimes refer to the variables thus freed as x variables, and their replacements in the resulting formulas as y variables. An analogous x and y notation will be used in discussing **UG** and **EG**.

important point is that there is a *one-to-one correspondence* between the x's freed by dropping the $(\exists x)$ quantifier and the free y's that replaced them; that is, to each x freed by dropping the $(\exists x)$ quantifier in line 1, there corresponds a y free in line 2; *and* to each y free in line 2, there corresponds an x in line 1 that is freed by dropping the $(\exists x)$ quantifier.

The question naturally arises as to whether all valid uses of **UI, EI, UG,** and **EG** require one-to-one correspondences of this kind. Surprisingly, it turns out that there are two cases in which this one-to-one correspondence *cannot* be required, if our logic is to be complete.

The first case concerns **UI.** Consider the argument

(7)			
	1.	$(\exists y)(x)Lyx$	p /∴ $(\exists x)Lxx$
	2.	$(x)Lyx$	1, **EI**
	3.	Lyy	2, **UI** (valid)
	4.	$(\exists x)Lxx$	3, **EG**

Suppose the domain of discourse is limited to human beings only, and suppose Lyx = "y loves x". Then the premise of this argument asserts that there is someone who loves everyone, while its conclusion asserts that there is someone who loves himself. Now this premise may be true or it may be false. But *if* it is true, *then* surely the conclusion is true also, for if it is true that someone loves everyone then it follows that that person loves himself. So we must have a way to infer from the premise of this argument to its conclusion, and the most intuitive way is to permit inferences like the one on line 3. Notice that there is *not* a one-to-one correspondence between free y variables on line 3 and bound x variables on line 2. Since we must allow the step from line 2 to line 3, it follows that *we cannot require a one-to-one correspondence between x and y variables in the application of* **UI.**

The other case in which we cannot require a one-to-one correspondence concerns **EG.** Consider the argument:

(8)			
	1.	$(x)Fxx$	p /∴ $(x)(\exists y)Fxy$
	2.	Fxx	1, **UI**
	3.	$(\exists y)Fxy$	2, **EG** (valid)
	4.	$(x)(\exists y)Fxy$	3, **UG**

Suppose Fxx = "x is identical with x". Then the premise of this argument asserts that everything is identical with itself, which is true, and its conclusion that given any x, there is something (y) identical with x, which is true also, since the y in question for any particular x is that x itself. Clearly, if 1 is true, and it is, then 4 must be true also. We must permit a step such as the one from 2 to 3 to enable us to draw the conclusion on line 4. So in general, *we cannot require a one-to-one correspondence between x and y variables in the application of* **EG.**

The eight possibilities we have just considered comprise a catalogue of cases that might puzzle students, or concerning which they might incline toward error. Before going on to the more technical cases, let's summarize what the eight examples were designed to prove:

1. When **EI** is used to drop an existential quantifier, the variables thus freed cannot validly be replaced by individual constants.
2. A variable introduced free into a proof by **EI** must not occur free previously in the proof.
3. We cannot use **UG** on a constant.
4. We cannot use **UG** on a variable introduced free into a proof by **EI.**
5. We cannot use **UG** on a variable free in a line obtained by **EI.**
6. Within the scope of an assumed premise we cannot use **UG** on a variable free in that assumed premise.
7. We cannot require a one-to-one correspondence between x and y variables in the application of **UI.**
8. We cannot require a one-to-one correspondence between x and y variables in the application of **EG.**

Now let's consider the ten remaining possibilities. Although not of great importance in learning how to use the quantifier rules, since the errors they deal with are ones students are unlikely to commit, they are of some theoretical interest.

The primary aim in the use of **UI** and **EI** is to drop a quantifier and *free* the variables that it bound. Consequently, we must forbid uses of **UI** and **EI** in which the variable that is supposed to be freed ends up bound. The following is an example involving **UI:**

(9)	1.	$(x)(\exists y)Lyx$	p
	2.	$(\exists y)Lyy$	1, **UI** (invalid)

Suppose Lyx = "y is larger than x", and x and y range over numbers only. Then the premise of this argument asserts the true statement that given any number x, there is some number larger than x, while its conclusion asserts the falsehood that there is some number larger than itself. The trouble is that the x variable in 1, which the application of **UI** is supposed to free, is replaced in 2 by a *bound* y variable.

Similarly, the use of **EI** in the following proof is invalid:

(10)	1.	$(\exists x)(y){\sim}Dxy$	p
	2.	$(y){\sim}Dyy$	1, **EI** (invalid)

Suppose Dxy = "x dislikes y", and the domain of discourse is restricted to human beings. Then the premise of this argument asserts that there is someone who doesn't dislike anyone, which is true (surely there is a newborn baby somewhere who doesn't dislike anyone), while its conclusion asserts that no one dislikes himself, which (unfortunately) is false.

The moral of all this is that *when a quantifier is dropped by* **UI** *or* **EI,** *all the variables thus freed must be replaced by free variables* (or, in the case of **UI,** by free variables or constants).

Now let's consider a slightly different case concerning **UG** and **EG.** When we use **UG** or **EG,** we want the occurrences of the appropriate *y* variables to be bound by the newly introduced quantifier. We definitely do *not* want any of the occurrences of that variable to be bound by some *other* quantifier that just happens to occur in the resulting formula. For instance, we don't want to allow the following use of **UG:**

(11)	1.	$(x)(\exists y)Lyx$	p
	2.	$(\exists y)Lyx$	1, **UI**
	3.	$(y)(\exists y)Lyy$	2, **UG** (invalid)

Suppose again that Lyx = "*y* is larger than *x*", and the domain of discourse is restricted to numbers. Then 1 asserts the truth that given any number *x*, there is some number larger than *x*, while 3 asserts the falsehood that some number is larger than itself.*

The case is just the same for **EG,** as this example illustrates:

(12)	1.	$(\exists x)(y)Dxy$	p
	2.	$(y)Dxy$	1, **EI**
	3.	$(\exists y)(y)Dyy$	2, **EG** (invalid)

This time, let Dxy = "*x* dislikes *y*", with the domain of discourse restricted to humans. Then 1 asserts that someone dislikes everyone, which may well be true, while 3 asserts that everyone dislikes everyone (again the initial quantifier is vacuous), which undoubtedly is false.

The moral is that *in using* **UG** *or* **EG,** *the variables to be quantified by the newly introduced quantifier must not be bound by some other quantifier*.

When we add an existential quantifier, we want to quantify (bind) occurrences of one variable only, and not two. Thus we don't want to allow the use of **EG** in the following proof:

(13)	1.	$(\exists y)(\exists x)Fxy$	p
	2.	$(\exists x)Fxy$	1, **EI**
	3.	Fxy	2, **EI**
	4.	$(\exists y)Fyy$	3, **EG** (invalid)

---

*The universal quantifier on line 3 is said to be a *vacuous* quantifier, because the closer existential quantifier binds the *y* variables that follow it.

This time, let Fxy = "x is the father of y" and restrict the domain of discourse to human beings. Then 1 asserts (truly) that someone is the father of someone (or other), while 4 asserts (falsely) that someone is the father of himself. The trouble is that the added existential quantifier on line 4 binds not only the y that replaces the free x on line 3, but also an extra y that just happens to be free on line 4.

Similarly, when we add a *universal quantifier,* we want to quantify occurrences of one variable only, and not two. The unhappy consequence of capturing occurrences of two different variables is illustrated by the following example:

(14)	1.	$(\exists y)(x)Lyx$	p
	2.	$(x)Lyx$	1, **EI**
	3.	Lyx	2, **UI**
	4.	$(y)Lyy$	3, **UG** (invalid)

Suppose this time that Lyx = "y loves x", and the domain of discourse is restricted to persons. Then 1 asserts that someone loves every person, while 4 asserts that every person loves himself. Since 1 could be true when 4 is false, the proof is not valid. The trouble is that in generalizing on the x variable in 3, we also quantified the y variable that is free on that line. The moral of this and the previous example is that *in using* **EG** *or* **UG,** *the replacements for the occurrences of only one variable in the original formula are to be bound in the resulting formula by the newly introduced quantifier.*

We stated previously that when applying **UI** we cannot require a one-to-one correspondence between bound x variables in the original formula and free y variables in the resulting formula, because this would block perfectly valid inferences, such as the one in example (7) from $(x)Lyx$ to Lyy. In that proof, one x variable was freed when we dropped the universal quantifier, and yet we ended up with two free y variables. So we ended up with more variables free than were bound in the original formula.

But what about the reverse process? What about dropping a quantifier by **UI** and replacing, say, only one of two variables thus freed by some other variable? The answer is that such a use of **UI** is invalid, as the following example illustrates:

(15)	1.	$(x)(Ox \lor Ex)$	p
	2.	$(Ox \lor Ey)$	1, **UI** (invalid)
	3.	$(y)(Ox \lor Ey)$	2, **UG**
	4.	$(x)(y)(Ox \lor Ey)$	3, **UG**

Suppose Ox = "x is odd" and Ex = "x is even", and the domain of discourse is restricted to positive whole numbers. Then 1 asserts (truly) that every number x is either odd or even, while 4 asserts (falsely) that given *any* two numbers, x and y, either x is odd or y is even. (That 4 is false can be seen by considering the substitution instance of 4 obtained by replacing x by 2 and y by 1, since this substitution instance asserts the falsehood that either 2 is odd or 1 is even.)

The moral this time is that *if one occurrence of some variable x is freed by* **UI** *and replaced by a free y variable, then all x variables freed by this application of* **UI** *must be replaced by free y variables.*

Whether a similar restriction must also be placed on **EI** depends on how the restrictions on **UG** have been worded. Consider the following example:

(16)	1.	$(\exists x)Ixx$	p
	2.	Iyx	1, **EI** (?)

Should we allow the step from 1 to 2 by **EI,** even though only one of the x variables freed by dropping the existential quantifier from line 1 is replaced by a y variable? The answer is that it depends on how we have restricted **UG.** The essential thing is to forbid passage from 1 to

3. $(x)Iyx$ 2, **UG**

and then to

4. $(\exists y)(x)Iyx$ 3, **EG**

Let Iyx = "y is identical with x", and it becomes obvious that we must block the inference from 1 to 4, since 1 then asserts that something is identical with itself, while 4 says that something is identical with everything.

It turns out that we can block this inference either by putting a restriction on **UG,** forbidding the inference from 2 to 3, or on **EI,** forbidding the inference from 1 to 2. Most sets of quantifier rules place the restriction on **EI.** However, it happens that the set of rules to be presented in the next section places appropriate restrictions on both **EI** and **UG** (because to do otherwise would make the statement of the rules slightly more complicated).

We said above that we must permit uses of **UI** such as the one from $(x)Lyx$ to Lyy. But what about similar uses of **EI,** such as the one inferring from $(\exists x)Fxy$ to Fyy? Should we allow these also? The answer is no; all such uses of **EI** are invalid. But it turns out that all cases in which such inferences might arise are forbidden by the restriction (already mentioned) that a free variable introduced into a proof by **EI** must not occur free previously in the proof. The following argument contains an example:

(17)	1.	$(\exists y)(\exists x)Txy$	p
	2.	$(\exists x)Txy$	1, **EI**
	3.	Tyy	2, **EI** (invalid)
	4.	$(\exists x)Txx$	3, **EG**

Suppose *Txy* = "*x* is taller than *y*" and the domain of discourse is restricted to persons. Then the premise of this argument, line 1, asserts that someone is taller than someone, which clearly is true, while its conclusion, line 4, asserts that someone is taller than himself, which obviously is false.

We also said above that we must permit uses of **EG** like the one from *Fxx* to $(\exists y)Fxy$. But what about similar uses of **UG,** such as the one from *Fxx* to $(y)Fxy$? The answer is that such inferences are invalid, as the following example illustrates:

(18)			
	1.	$(x)Ixx$	p
	2.	Ixx	1, **UI**
	3.	$(y)Ixy$	2, **UG** (invalid)
	4.	$(x)(y)Ixy$	3, **UG**

Suppose *Ixy* = "*x* is identical with *y*". Then line 1 states the truth that everything is identical with itself, while line 4 states the falsehood that everything is identical with everything.

So our last moral is that *in the use of* **UG,** *if a free x in the original formula is replaced by a y that becomes bound in the resulting formula, then all free occurrences of x in the original formula must be replaced by bound y variables in the resulting formula.*

The above constitutes a catalogue of the kinds of inferences we must forbid (as well as two kinds we must permit). The four quantifier rules (**EI, UI, EG, UG**) presented in Chapter Seven (page 135) were designed so that they forbid all of the kinds of inferences that we've just seen must be forbidden, while permitting the two kinds we've found must be permitted.

Thus, the first kind of inference discussed in this appendix is forbidden by the first restriction on **EI;** the second by the second restriction on **EI;** the third by the first restriction on **UG;** the fourth and fifth by the second restriction on **UG;** and the sixth by the third restriction on **UG.** The seventh and eighth kinds are *permitted* because of the precise working of the instructions for using rules **UI** and **EG** (which do not require a one-to-one correspondence between the relevant variables free in (. . . *u* . . .) and in (. . . *w* . . .)). The ninth and tenth are forbidden by the precise wording of the instructions for using **UI** and **EI** (requiring variables in (. . . *u* . . .) intended to be freed by dropping quantifiers to actually be free in (. . . *w* . . .)); the eleventh and twelfth by the precise wording of the instructions for using **UG** and **EG,** requiring that the free variables in (. . . *u* . . .) intended to be bound by a newly introduced quantifier not be bound by a quantifier occurring within (. . . *w* . . .); the thirteenth by the (only) restriction on **EG;** the fourteenth by the fourth restriction on **UG;** the fifteenth and sixteenth by the precise wording of the instructions for using **UI** and **EI** (requiring that all occurrences of *u* in (. . . *u* . . .) be replaced by occurrences of *w* free in (. . . *w* . . .)); (the sixteenth also is forbidden by the fourth restriction on **UG;** the seventeenth by the second restriction on **EI**); and finally, the eighteenth kind of inference discussed in this chapter is forbidden by the fourth restriction on **UG** and also by the precise wording of the instructions for using **UG,** which require that (. . . *w* . . .) result from replacing *all* free occurrences of *u* in (. . . *u* . . .) by *w*'s *free* in (. . . *w* . . .).

There are, of course, many other ways to write the quantifier rules so that they correctly handle all eighteen of these cases. The formulation in this book was chosen for simplicity and relative ease of comprehension.

Part Six

Modal, Epistemic, and Deontic Logic

Chapter Nineteen

Modal Logic

The predicate logic developed in Part Two of this text, many claim, cannot adequately deal with sentences containing **modal terms,** that is, terms like "possible", "necessary", and their variants. As a result, special modal systems have been devised, which encompass the ordinary sentential and predicate logic.* Here is the outline of one such **modal logic.**

1 *Symbols and Expressions*

To extend sentential logic to handle modal sentences, we must add at least one symbol denoting a modal term. Let's introduce the diamond symbol "◇" as the **possibility operator,** used to symbolize sentences expressing possibilities. For instance, using the possibility operator, we can symbolize "*A* is possible" as $\Diamond A$.

Examples:

Here are some basic sentences that can be symbolized using the possibility operator (letting S = "Snow is white"):

Symbolization	English Sentence
1. $\Diamond S$	1. It's possible that snow is white.

*For more details on modal logic than are presented in this book, see G. E. Hughes and M. J. Cresswell, *Introduction to Modal Logic* (London: Methuen, 1968), and (particularly for the so-called "Lewis systems") C. I. Lewis and C. H. Langford, *Symbolic Logic*, 2nd edition (New York: Dover Publications, 1959).

2. $\Diamond{\sim}S$	2. It's possible that snow isn't white.
3. ${\sim}\Diamond S$	3. It's not possible that snow is white.
4. ${\sim}\Diamond{\sim}S$	4. It's not possible that snow isn't white.

After one modal symbol has been introduced, others can be defined in terms of it. For instance, we can define the **necessity operator** "$\Box$" by the following definition:

$\Box p$ = df ${\sim}\Diamond{\sim}p$

To say, for instance, that it's not possible that snow *isn't* white, in symbols ${\sim}\Diamond{\sim}S$, is, after all, to say exactly that it's necessary that snow *is* white. $\Box S$, then, has the same meaning as ${\sim}\Diamond{\sim}S$.

Similarly, to say that it's impossible that snow is white is to say that it's necessary that snow isn't white. So the formula ${\sim}\Diamond S$ is logically equivalent to $\Box{\sim}S$.

In fact, as should be apparent from the above, the possibility and necessity operators are linked in exactly the same way as are the existential and universal quantifiers of predicate logic.

Examples:

Here are four logical equivalences relating the existential and universal quantifiers and the analogous equivalences relating the possibility and necessity operators:

Quantifier Equivalences	Modal Equivalences
1. $(x)p \equiv {\sim}(\exists x){\sim}p$	1. $\Box p \equiv {\sim}\Diamond{\sim}p$
2. $(\exists x)p \equiv {\sim}(x){\sim}p$	2. $\Diamond p \equiv {\sim}\Box{\sim}p$
3. $(x){\sim}p \equiv {\sim}(\exists x)p$	3. $\Box{\sim}p \equiv {\sim}\Diamond p$
4. $(\exists x){\sim}p \equiv {\sim}(x)p$	4. $\Diamond{\sim}p \equiv {\sim}\Box p$

2 *Strict Implication*

There are different kinds of possibilities and necessities. For instance, we might mean by "necessarily p" that p is **logically necessary** (true because of the laws of logic) or that it is **physically necessary** (true because of the laws of nature). Modal logic systems have been developed to capture the ideas of logical necessity, logical possibility, and logical impossibility. In particular, a modal logic seems to be needed to capture the concepts of **logical entailment** (or **logical implication**) and **logical equivalence.**

Take the notion of logical implication, or entailment. If p logically implies q, we can't symbolize that fact as $p \supset q$, because $p \supset q$ is too weak. It might be true, for instance, simply because p is false, and not because its truth logically implies the truth of q.

But by using modal operators, we can symbolize statements of logical implication quite easily. For *p logically implies q if, and only if, p ⊃ q is a theorem of logic,* and thus necessarily true.* Letting the symbol "⥽" stand for logical implication, or as it is usually called, **strict implication,** we can introduce the following definition:

$p ⥽ q = \text{df}\square(p \supset q)$

Examples:

Here are some sentences and their correct symbolizations using first the necessity operator and then the symbol for strict implication:

1. $(A \cdot B)$ logically entails A.

   $\square[(A \cdot B) \supset A]$

   $(A \cdot B) ⥽ A$

2. $(B \supset C)$ logically implies $({\sim}C \supset {\sim}B)$.

   $\square[(B \supset C) \supset ({\sim}C \supset {\sim}B)]$

   $(B \supset C) ⥽ ({\sim}C \supset {\sim}B)$

3. $[A \vee (B \cdot C)]$ entails $[(A \vee B) \cdot (A \vee C)]$.

   $\square\{[A \vee (B \cdot C)] \supset [(A \vee B) \cdot (A \vee C)]\}$

   $[A \vee (B \cdot C)] ⥽ [(A \vee B) \cdot (A \vee C)]$

4. $(A \supset B)$ logically implies $(B \supset A)$.

   $\square[(A \supset B) \supset (B \supset A)]$

   $(A \supset B) ⥽ (B \supset A)$

(Of course, this last sentence is false, but we must be able to symbolize false sentences, also.)

It is important that the difference between "⥽" and "⊃" be grasped quite clearly, and that it be understood why "⊃" does not capture the

*Or in the case of sentence forms, if, and only if, all of its substitution instances are true.

sense of logical implication. Take the modal sentence "'Art is smart' logically implies 'Betsy is beautiful'". Letting A = "Art is smart", and B = "Betsy is beautiful", we can symbolize that sentence as "$A \prec B$". Now if A and B both are true, then $A \supset B$ will be true. But $A \prec B$ is false, no matter what the truth values of A and B, since A does not *logically* imply B. That is, $A \prec B$ is false because "A /∴ B" is not a valid deductive argument (even if A and B both happen to be true).*

Now let's introduce a symbol for logical equivalence, bearing in mind that two sentences are *logically equivalent* if, and only if, they logically imply each other. Letting the four bar symbol "≣" represent logical equivalence, we can introduce the following definition:

$$p \equiv q = \text{df } (p \prec q) \cdot (q \prec p)$$

Examples:

Here are some equivalences and their translations using the symbol for logical equivalence:

1. $(A \cdot B)$ is logically equivalent to $(B \cdot A)$.

   $(A \cdot B) \equiv (B \cdot A)$

2. $(A \supset B)$ is logically equivalent to $(\sim B \supset \sim A)$.

   $(A \supset B) \equiv (\sim B \supset \sim A)$

3. $(A \cdot B)$ is logically equivalent to A.

   $(A \cdot B) \equiv A$

(Of course, this last sentence is false.)

---

3 *Modal Axioms*

The philosopher C. I. Lewis constructed the first axiom systems for sentential modal logic. Indeed, he constructed several nonequivalent modal systems.

The fact that *nonequivalent* systems have been proposed and argued about illustrates a difference in status between the ordinary truth-func-

---

*This account of the logical necessity captured by the " $\prec$ " symbol avoids the controversy over semantic analytic truths. Most philosophers want the notion of logical implication to be wide enough to make, say, "(Art is a bachelor) $\prec$ (Art is unmarried)" a true modal statement, but some do not. See Appendix A for more on semantic analytic truths.

tional logic and non-truth-functional modal logic; modal logic is much more controversial than ordinary truth-functional logic. It is true that some argue against sentential or predicate logic on the grounds that they cannot adequately handle some of the non-truth-functional sentences of natural languages. But no one would argue that any of the axioms of an axiomatized sentential or predicate logic are *false*. Yet that is precisely the situation for modal logic. Modal axioms have been proposed whose very truth is in question.

Let's now examine the Lewis modal axioms (passing over the technical details of his systems). Here are thirteen of his axioms, the first eleven being used by Lewis in developing his modal systems S1 through S5 (along with their sentential logic analogues):*

	Modal Axiom	**Sentential Logic Analogue**	
(1)	$(p \cdot q) \prec (q \cdot p)$	$(p \cdot q) \supset (q \cdot p)$	**(Comm)**
(2)	$(p \cdot q) \prec p$	$(p \cdot q) \supset p$	**(Simp)**
(3)	$p \prec (p \cdot p)$	$p \supset (p \cdot p)$	**(Taut)**
(4)	$[(p \cdot q) \cdot r] \prec [p \cdot (q \cdot r)]$	$[(p \cdot q) \cdot r] \supset [p \cdot (q \cdot r)]$	**(Assoc)**
(5)	$p \prec \sim\sim p$	$p \supset \sim\sim p$	**(DN)**
(6)	$[(p \prec q) \cdot (q \prec r)] \prec (p \prec r)$	$[(p \supset q) \cdot (q \supset r)] \supset (p \supset r)$	**(HS)**
(7)	$[p \cdot (p \prec q)] \prec q$	$[p \cdot (p \supset q)] \supset q$	**(MP)**
(8)	$\Diamond(p \cdot q) \prec \Diamond p$		
(9)	$(p \prec q) \prec (\sim\Diamond q \prec \sim\Diamond p)$		
(10)	$\Box p \prec \Box\Box p$		
(11)	$\Diamond p \prec \sim\Diamond\sim\Diamond p$		
(12)	$p \prec \sim\Diamond\sim\Diamond p$		
(13)	$\Diamond\Diamond p$		

The system S1 contains the first seven axioms (axiom (5) incidentally, can be derived from the others and is thus superfluous); S2 the first seven plus (8); S3 the first seven plus (9); S4 the first seven plus (10); and S5 the first seven plus (11). It has been proved that every theorem of S1 is a theorem of S2, every theorem of S2 a theorem of S3, and so on (but not vice versa). Thus, as you go up the Lewis modal ladder, the systems get stronger and stronger. (The problem is just how strong the *right* system should be.)

Axioms (10) and (13) are contraries. So on the assumption that there is at least one necessary proposition, we must reject either (10) or (13). This is unfortunate, because many have found both of these axioms, taken alone, to be intuitively plausible.

In addition, axiom (10) itself has generated a great deal of controversy.

---

* With minor changes.

Take as an example the necessary sentence "Snow is white or it isn't". Clearly that sentence is necessary, since it is a logical truth. But is it *necessary* that it is necessary? Opinions seem to differ. (It should also be noted that adoption of S5 leads to the interesting consequence that all modal propositions will be either necessarily true or necessarily false, a consequence that some find unacceptable.)

4 *Modal Theorems*

There is a very close resemblance between the theorems (counting axioms as theorems) of modal logic and the theorems of sentential logic that correspond to the valid argument forms discussed in Part One. With three exceptions, these theorems parallel one another. For instance, corresponding to the theorem we might by extension call *Modus Ponens,* namely $[p \cdot (p \supset q)] \supset q$, is the modal theorem $[p \cdot (p \prec q)] \prec q$. The three exceptions are *Implication, Exportation,* and one version of *Equivalence*. (In particular, $(p \prec q) \equiv (\sim p \vee q)$, the modal parallel to *Implication,* is *not* a modal theorem.) However, for each of these there are slightly altered parallels. Thus for *Implication* there is $(p \prec q) \prec (\sim p \vee q)$, for *Exportation* there is $[(p \cdot q) \prec r] \equiv [p \prec (q \supset r)]$, and for *Equivalence* there is $(p \equiv q) \prec [(p \cdot q) \vee (\sim p \cdot \sim q)]$.

Here are some other interesting theorems of modal logic, all provable in S5, although some are not provable in S4, S3, S2, or S1, and thus are controversial:

1. $(p \prec q) \prec (p \supset q)$
2. $(p \equiv q) \prec (p \equiv q)$
3. $\Box(p \equiv q) \equiv (p \equiv q)$
4. $(p \prec q) \supset (\Box p \prec \Box q)$
5. $\Box p \prec \Diamond p$
6. $\Box\Box p \equiv \Box\Box\Box p$
7. $\Diamond p \equiv \Diamond\Diamond p$
8. $\Box(p \cdot q) \equiv (\Box p \cdot \Box q)$
9. $\Diamond(p \vee q) \equiv (\Diamond p \vee \Diamond q)$
10. $\Diamond(p \cdot q) \prec (\Diamond p \cdot \Diamond q)$ [But not vice versa.]
11. $(\Box p \vee \Box q) \prec \Box(p \vee q)$ [But not vice versa.]

5 *Modal Paradoxes*

When he developed his modal systems, Lewis pointed out that there are apparently paradoxical theorems in modal logic analogous to the alleged paradoxes of material implication.* One example is the theorem:

$\sim\Diamond p \prec (p \prec q)$

But Lewis felt that this theorem is acceptable, in spite of its apparent paradoxicality. For it merely states the principle behind the rule of *indirect proof (reductio ad absurdum)*—that what is contradictory (not possible) logically implies anything and everything.

Another theorem that appears paradoxical is this one:

$\Box p \prec (q \prec p)$

Lewis felt this theorem also is acceptable, because it merely states the principle that we can deduce a tautology (necessarily true sentence) from any sentence whatever, which must be accepted since a tautology can be deduced even from the null set of premises.

6 *A Philosophical Problem*

At the beginning of this chapter, we introduced the topic of modal logic by saying that it is *claimed* by many that we need a special logic to deal with sentences containing modal terms. The word "claimed" was inserted because some deny that a special modal logic is needed at all.†

One objection is that if "$\Box p$" *means* the same as "p is a theorem of logic", or "p is provable", then the statements of modal logic all become statements expressible in the *meta-language* of any given system without the need to introduce special modal symbols.†† But lurking behind the dispute is the more serious question of exactly what necessity, possibility, etc., consist in. One view is that necessity is a purely linguistic concept. A theorem is provable, according to this view, precisely because of linguistic conventions. That is, a theorem is true just because of the meanings of its terms. (This theory is consistent with the view that theorems of logic and logical truths are provable from the null set of premises precisely because they are empty of factual content.)

On the other side are those who insist that necessity is more than merely linguistic, that necessities are real and independent of language conventions or even the existence of language users.

---

* For instance, it is sometimes held to be paradoxical that a false sentence materially implies any sentence (that is, paradoxical that if p is false, then $p \supset q$ is true, no matter what q happens to be), and that a true sentence is materially implied by any sentence (that is, paradoxical that if q is true, then $p \supset q$ is true, no matter what p happens to be).

† See, for instance, Gustav Bergmann, "The Philosophical Significance of Modal Logic", *Mind*, vol. 69 (1960), pp. 466–485.

†† Another is that in any event the term "modal *logic*" is a misnomer, because the axioms of modal logic are not *logical* truths, containing as they do nonlogical constants such as "$\Box$" and "$\Diamond$".

Those who hold the latter view tend to accept the principle that $\Box p \equiv \Box\Box p$ (sometimes called the *axiom of reiterated necessity*). Those who hold the former view (that necessity is essentially linguistic) deny that principle, because if "$\Box p$" *means* the same as "p is a theorem of logic", then the axiom of reiteration would appear false. (For to be true it would have to be the case that the statement "p is a theorem of sentential logic" is itself a theorem of sentential logic, which it is not.)

7 *Modal Predicate Logic*

So far, we have been discussing modal extensions of sentential logic, a fairly controversial topic. Now let's very briefly discuss modal *predicate* systems, an even more controversial area.

There are two important problems with modal predicate logic systems, in addition to the ones it inherits from modal sentential logic. The first concerns the validity in modal logic of the four quantifier rules, as well as the rule of *identity* **(ID)**.*

Consider the following argument (where a = "the number of planets"):

1.	$(x)[(x = 9) \supset \Box(x > 7)]$	p
2.	$a = 9$	p /∴ $\Box(a > 7)$
3.	$(a = 9) \supset \Box(a > 7)$	1, UI
4.	$\Box(a > 7)$	2,3 MP

It appears that both premises are true, and the conclusion false (since it isn't *necessary* that the number of planets be greater than seven). And yet the conclusion follows from the premises by the normal inference rules of predicate logic (in this case **UI** and **MP**).

Examples of this kind have elicited several different responses. One, of course, is simply to reject modal predicate logic entirely, as ill conceived. Another is to devise restrictions on the four quantifier rules (as well as the rule of identity, to handle related problems arising from the use of that rule). For instance, we seem able to block undesirable consequences of the kind just illustrated by placing a new restriction on the general schema for **UI:**†

$(u)(\ldots u \ldots)$

/∴ $(\ldots w \ldots)$

Proviso: No u free in $(\ldots u \ldots)$ is within the scope of a necessity operator, unless $(\ldots w \ldots)$ is necessary (that is, unless $\Box(\ldots w \ldots)$).

---

* See, for instance, W. V. Quine, "Notes on Existence and Necessity", *The Journal of Philosophy*, vol. 40 (1943), pp. 113–127.

† See Richard L. Purtill, *Logic for Philosophers* (New York: Harper & Row, 1971), pp. 289–291.

This seems to eliminate the troublesome use of **UI** in the above example because the x in the phrase "$x > 7$" on line 1 is within the scope of a necessity operator. (But it doesn't rule out the legitimate use of **UI** in the inference from, say, $(x)[(x = 9) \supset \Box(x > 7)]$ to $(3^2 = 9) \supset \Box(3^2 > 7)$, because the latter is necessarily true.)

Finally, another way out of the problem is to argue that in spite of appearances, rule **UI** is universally valid in modal predicate logic. Take the example in question. Either a (the expression "the number of planets") designates the number 9, or it does not. If it does, then premise 2 is true. *But so is the argument's conclusion,* since the number 9 necessarily is greater than 7. So if a designates the number 9, the argument in question does not take us from true premises to a false conclusion, and we haven't proved the inference pattern invalid.

Now suppose that a does *not* designate the number 9. Then premise 2 is false, since it asserts that a is identical with the number 9, which must be false if a does not designate the number 9. (Obviously, only the number 9 is identical with the number 9, so if a does not designate that number what it does designate cannot be identical with the number 9.) So if a does not designate the number 9, one of the premises is false, we have not gone from true premises to a false conclusion, and thus have not proved that the argument schema is invalid in modal predicate logic. It may well be valid after all.

A second important problem for modal predicate logic is simply to decide which of the many plausible candidates should be accepted as *theorems* of modal predicate logic. Let's end our very brief discussion of modal logic by listing a few theorem candidates, then explaining why some of them are controversial (letting p and q be any well-formed formulas and "(u)" and "$(\exists u)$" be respectively any universal or existential quantifiers):

(A) $(\exists u)\Box p \prec \Box(\exists u)p$

(B) $\Diamond(u)p \prec (u)\Diamond p$

(C) $(\exists u)\Diamond p \equiv \Diamond(\exists u)p$

(D) $\Box(u)p \equiv (u)\Box p$

(E) $\Box(u)(p \supset q) \supset \Box[(u)p \supset (u)q]$

(F) $(u)\Box(p \supset q) \supset \Box[(u)p \supset (u)q]$

The first two of these formulas, while intuitively unobjectionable, are interesting because they generally are believed *not* to hold in the opposite direction. Take the reverse of (A), namely $\Box(\exists u)p \prec (\exists u)\Box p$, and consider the substitution instance $\Box(\exists x)Nx \prec (\exists x)\Box Nx$, where Nx = "x is the number of planets". The antecedent of this expression states that necessarily some x is the number of planets, which is true, because even if there were no planets there still would of necessity be some number of planets (namely zero). But the consequent of this expression seems to be false, because there is no number that *necessarily* is the number of planets (since the actual number of planets is a contingent and not a necessary fact—logic does not dictate that there be exactly nine planets).

Now consider the reverse of (B), namely $(u)\Diamond p \prec \Diamond(u)p$, and consider the substitution instance $(x)\Diamond Nx \prec \Diamond(x)Nx$, where again Nx = "x is the number of planets". The antecedent of this expression states that given any x, it is possible that x is the number of planets, which is true because logic does not require that there be any certain number of planets (instead of nine there might have been eight or seven or a million, so far as logic is concerned). But the consequent of this expression is false because it is not possible that *every* number be the actual number of planets.

While (A) and (B), above, are generally accepted, and their reverses generally rejected, (C) seems more problematic. Consider, for instance, the substitution instance $(\exists x)\Diamond Fx \equiv \Diamond(\exists x)Fx$, where Fx = "x is on fire".* If we suppose that $(\exists x)\Diamond Fx$ translates back into English as "There is something which may be on fire", and $\Diamond(\exists x)Fx$ as "There may be something on fire", then clearly the two do not strictly imply each other. So if we want to accept (C) as a legitimate modal theorem, we must find some other translation for the substitution instance in question.†

Theorem (D) above is also extremely controversial. Specifically, the controversy centers on a particular consequence of (D), namely the formula $(u)\Box p \supset \Box(u)p$, called the **Barcan Formula.**††

At first glance, this formula seems acceptable. But consider one of its instances, say the sentence $(x)\Box Tx \supset \Box(x)Tx$, where Tx = "x is triangular". In the actual universe, the antecedent of this statement is false, and hence the whole statement is true. But logical principles have to be valid in all possible universes, not just the real one. So imagine a universe containing nothing but trilaterals. Then, since all triangles are necessarily also trilaterals, the left hand side of the Barcan substitution instance, namely $(x)\Box Tx$, will be true. But the right hand side, namely $\Box(x)Tx$, appears to be false. For even though *in fact* all x's would be triangular in the world we have just imagined, it wouldn't be *necessary* that all things in that universe be triangular; it *might* have contained some squares, circles, or other non-triangles.

Hence, it is argued that the Barcan Formula is not acceptable. (Since the Barcan Formula can be derived as a theorem in any modal predicate

---

* The example is from W. Kneale and M. Kneale, *The Development of Logic* (London: Oxford University Press, 1962), p. 615.

† For instance, see Purtill, pp. 263–265.

†† After Ruth Barcan Marcus. See her article "A Functional Calculus of First Order Based on Strict Implication", *Journal of Symbolic Logic*, vol. II (1946), p. 2.

logic containing the Lewis system S5 as its sentential component, those who reject the Barcan Formula also have to reject S5. Conversely, those who accept the Barcan Formula are almost certainly committed to accepting S5.)

Key Terms Introduced in Chapter Nineteen

Barcan Formula: The disputed modal theorem $(u)\Box p \supset \Box(u)p$.

Logical entailment: An implication that is a theorem of logic. *Synonyms:* **Logical implication, Strict implication.**

Logical equivalence: An equivalence that is a theorem of logic.

Logical implication: (See **Logical entailment.**)

Logical necessity: A statement that is true because of the laws of logic—a theorem of logic. Example: "It will rain or it won't".

Modal logic: A logic designed to handle statements and arguments containing modal operators, such as "It is necessary that ___".

Modal terms: Terms (operators) expressing necessity, possibility, and so on.

Necessity operator: The symbol "□", used to express the concept of necessity.

Physical necessity: A statement that is true because of the laws of nature. Example: "All copper conducts electricity".

Possibility operator: The symbol "◇", used to express possibilities.

Strict implication: (See **Logical entailment.**) The symbol " ⥽ " is used to express strict implication.

Chapter Twenty

Epistemic Logic: The Logic of Knowledge and Belief

In discussing the limitations of predicate logic (Chapter Nine), we pointed out that it is not clear whether predicate logic can adequately handle sentences containing so-called belief contexts, such as the sentence "Art believes he'll go to the show". Attempts to develop a logic of knowledge and belief, an **epistemic logic,** are intended to extend predicate logic so that it can deal with such cases.

1 *Predicate Logic Rules in Epistemic Contexts*

The application of the standard rules of predicate logic to epistemic contexts is in doubt, just as is their application in modal contexts. Here is an example in which the rule of *identity,* **ID,** seems to fail when used in an epistemic context:

	1.	Art believes that Mark Twain wrote Huck Finn.	p
	2.	Mark Twain = Samuel Clemens.	p
/∴	3.	Art believes that Samuel Clemens wrote Huck Finn.	1,2 **ID**

If we let Bxy = "x believes that y", t = "Mark Twain", c = "Samuel Clemens", h = "Huckleberry Finn", and Wxy = "x wrote y", then we can symbolize the above argument as:

	1.	$Ba(Wth)$	p
	2.	$t = c$	p
/∴	3.	$Ba(Wch)$	1,2 **ID**

The problem with this example is this. Suppose Art happens to be ignorant of the fact that Mark Twain and Samuel Clemens are the same person. Then it seems possible for premises 1 and 2 of this argument both to be true when the conclusion 3 is false. If so, then it is possible to go from true premises to a false conclusion by the rule of *identity*, something no valid system may permit.

Now let's look at an example where it is claimed that the quantifier rule **EG** gets us into trouble:*

	1.	Philip is unaware that Tully denounced Cataline.	p
/∴	2.	Some *x* is such that Philip is unaware that *x* denounced Cataline.	1, **EG**

Letting Uxy = "x is unaware that y", and using other obvious abbreviations, we can symbolize this argument as:

	1.	$Up(Dtc)$	p
/∴	2.	$(\exists x)Up(Dxc)$	1, **EG**

Suppose we assume that Philip really is not aware that Tully denounced Cataline, but is aware that Cicero did, even though (unknown to Philip) Tully = Cicero. Then, it has been argued, although 1 is true, 2 is false. For who is the x who denounced Cataline without Philip learning of that fact? Tully, that is, Cicero? No, because this would conflict with the fact that the statement "Philip is unaware that Cicero denounced Cataline" is false. Hence, the inference from 1 to 2, it is claimed, is invalid.

Finally, consider one more example. Suppose it is true that some little child, say Johnny, believes that Santa Claus comes down his (Johnny's) chimney every Christmas bringing toys. Then using rule **EG,** we can construct the following apparently invalid argument (letting Cx = "x comes down Johnny's chimney on Christmas", j = "Johnny", and c = "Santa Claus"):

	1.	$Bj(Cc)$	p
/∴	2.	$(\exists x)Bj(Cx)$	1, **EG**

Again, we seem hard pressed to find an x that would make 2 a true

---

* The example is from W. V. Quine, "Notes on Existence and Necessity", *Journal of Philosophy*, vol. 40 (1943), pp. 117–118. Quine claims that this example shows rule **EG** must be restricted in epistemic contexts.

statement. In particular, *Santa Claus* does not seem to be such an x, since, sad to relate, Virginia, there *is* no Santa Claus.

While we can't go into all the claims and counterclaims concerning the use of **ID** and **EG** in epistemic contexts, let's just mention one defense of the use of **ID** and **EG** in epistemic contexts, since it parallels an argument we discussed before defending the use of **UI** in modal contexts (on page 400).

Consider again the argument

	1.	$Ba(Wth)$	p
	2.	$t = c$	p
/∴	3.	$Ba(Wch)$	1,2 **ID**

Either c designates the person Mark Twain or it does not. Suppose it does. (We're assuming, of course, that the term t designates the person Mark Twain.) Then if premise 1 is true (if Art believes the person Mark Twain wrote Huck Finn), then so is the conclusion true (that Art believes the person Sam Clemens (also known as *Mark Twain*) wrote Huck Finn). We thus will have moved from true premises to a true conclusion, and so the argument will be valid. Therefore this case can't be an example of the failure of **ID** in epistemic contexts.

Now suppose c does not designate the person Mark Twain. Then the second premise of this argument, which states that $t = c$, will be false (given that t does designate Mark Twain). We thus will not have moved from true premises to a false conclusion, and so this case can't be an example of the failure of **ID** in epistemic contexts.

In like manner, it is claimed, all of the varied examples alleged to illustrate the invalidity of rule **ID** in epistemic contexts can be successfully rebutted.

It also is claimed that some (but not all) of the alleged counterexamples to the legitimacy of rule **EG** in epistemic contexts can be easily disposed of. Recall the one above about Philip being unaware that Tully denounced Cataline:

	1.	$Up(Dtc)$	p
/∴	2.	$(\exists x)Up(Dxc)$	1, **EG**

It was objected that although 1 is true, 2 is false, since there seems to be no x who denounced Cataline without Philip learning of that fact.

But surely, if there is no such x, then premise 1 is false (and so we will not have moved from true to false). After all, for Philip to be unaware that Tully was the denouncer, there must be an x, namely Tully, whose actions Philip is unaware of; if there is no such x, then Philip can't be unaware of his actions, and premise 1 will be false. (What is true, of course, is that Philip is unaware that the person he knows as *Cicero* also was known as *Tully*.)

2 Epistemic Theorems

A second problem for epistemic logic, again paralleling modal predicate logic, is the difficulty in deciding which epistemic statements we want to be theorems of epistemic logic. Here are a few of the obvious candidates (letting *Kap* = "*a* knows that *p*"; and *Bap* = "*a* believes that *p*"):

1. $Kap \supset Bap$
2. $Ka{\sim}p \supset {\sim}Bap$
3. ${\sim}Kap \supset Ba{\sim}p$
4. $Kap \supset p$
5. $Bap \supset p$
6. $Kap \supset KaKap$
7. $Bap \supset BaBap$
8. $Bap \supset KaBap$
9. $Kap \supset BaKap$

Of these, (3) and (5) clearly are inadmissible. From the fact that Art doesn't know that Sophia is the capital of Bulgaria, it doesn't follow that he believes it isn't the capital of Bulgaria. So (3) must be rejected. And from the fact that Johnny believes Santa Claus comes down his chimney, it doesn't follow that Santa actually does so. So (5) must be rejected.

On the other hand, (1) clearly is acceptable; you can't know something without believing it. But all the others, however plausible they may initially appear, are open to doubt, or at least some have thought so.

Take (6), often called the **KK thesis,** according to which if you know something, it follows that you know you know that thing. One argument against the *KK* thesis is this:* For a person *a* to know something, *a* must *understand* that thing. Hence, to know *p*, *a* has to understand *p*. But for *a* to know that he knows *p*, *a* must understand not only *p* but also the sentence "*Kap*". It seems possible for *a* to understand *p*, but not understand "*Kap*", and hence possible that he knows *p*, but does not know that he knows *p*.

Since similar remarks seem to apply to believing, formulas (7), (8), and (9) also appear to be fairly doubtful.

Now let's consider (2), which states that if *a* knows ~*p*, then he doesn't believe *p*. If knowing *p* entails believing *p*, and if no one can believe contradictory propositions, then (2) has to be accepted. But there are those who claim that it is possible to believe contradictory propositions. And if this is possible, then (2) must be rejected. For then someone might know ~*p* and still believe *p*.

Finally, there are a few who might reject even (4), which says that if you know *p*, then *p* must be the case. The idea behind this formula is that

---

* The argument is given by Arthur C. Danto in "On Knowing That We Know", in Avrum Stroll, ed., *Epistemology* (New York: Harper & Row, 1967), pp. 32–53.

one cannot know something that is false. But some pragmatists* have denied that one cannot know something that is false, because their pragmatic explication of the concept of knowledge does not make the truth of a sentence a necessary condition for knowing that sentence.

Key Terms Introduced in Chapter Twenty

Epistemic logic: A logic designed to deal with statements containing epistemic contexts. *Example:* Enrique believes that now is the time to sell real estate.

KK thesis: The thesis that if someone knows some *x*, then that person knows that he knows *x*.

* For instance, Robert J. Ackermann, who in effect argued against the validity of (4) in his paper "A Pragmatic Analysis of Knowledge", delivered to the American Philosophical Association, Western Division, May 1972. Ackermann argued that because we can never be sure a statement is true and hence (if truth is a component of knowledge) can never know that we know anything whatever, it is useless to make truth a component of knowledge. He thus advised that we adopt a conception of knowledge which has no truth component, making it possible to know *x* in some cases even though *x* later turns out to be false.

Chapter Twenty-one

Deontic Logic

Predicate logic, modal logic, and epistemic logic all can be said to be **operator logics,** because they deal with operators (we called them quantifiers when we discussed predicate logic) which bind parts of expressions. Recently, attempts have been made to develop a similar system for another area of philosophy, namely certain kinds of reasoning in ethics. The result is **deontic logic,** which deals with the ethical notions of permission, obligation, and the like.

1 *A Typical Deontic System*

Several different deontic systems have been proposed. Most of them are fairly similar. To illustrate the problems and complexities they all face let's concentrate on part of a typical system, namely the one proposed by Nicholas Rescher* (which we will refer to as RDL, for "Rescher's Deontic Logic").

RDL has seven axioms, written in the notation of modal predicate logic together with one new operator. The new operator is the **permission operator,** defined as:

$P(p/c)$ = df (Action p is permitted in circumstance c)

Here are the axioms of RDL:

1. $P(p \vee \sim p/c)$
2. $P(p \vee q/c) \equiv [P(p/c) \vee P(q/c)]$

---

*In his article "An Axiom System for Deontic Logic", *Philosophical Studies,* vol. IX (1958), pp. 24–30.

3. $(p \prec q) \prec [P(p/c) \prec P(q/c)]$
4. $P(p \cdot q/c) \prec P(p/c \cdot q)$
5. $[P(p/c) \cdot P(q/c \cdot p)] \prec P(p \cdot q/c)$
6. $P(p/c \vee {\sim}c) \prec P(p/d)$
7. $P(p/d) \prec P(p/c \cdot {\sim}c)$

All of these axioms have an initial plausibility. The first says that tautologies are always permitted, which sounds fairly trivial but surely not fallacious; the second that $(p \vee q)$'s being permitted in some circumstance c is logically equivalent to either p's being permitted in that circumstance or q's being so permitted; the third that if p entails q, then that entails that p's being permitted in some circumstance c in turn entails that q is permitted in that circumstance; and so on.

From the axioms, many plausible permission theorems can be derived. For instance, here is a proof that $P(p/c) \vee P({\sim}p/c)$, or in English that in any circumstance either p is permitted or ${\sim}p$ is permitted (important because it assures that in every circumstance there is *something* that you're permitted to do):

1.	$P(p \vee {\sim}p/c)$	**Axiom (1)**
2.	$P(p \vee {\sim}p/c) \equiv [P(p/c \vee P({\sim}p/c)]$	**Axiom (2)**
3.	$\{P(p \vee {\sim}p/c) \prec [P(p/c) \vee P({\sim}p/c)]\} \cdot$ $\{[P(p/c) \vee P({\sim}p/c)] \prec P(p \vee {\sim}p/c)\}$	**2, Strict Equiv.***
4.	$P(p \vee {\sim}p/c) \prec [P(p/c) \vee P({\sim}p/c)]$	**3, Simp**
5.	$P(p/c) \vee P({\sim}p/c)$	**1,4 Strict MP†**

Here are some other plausible theorems:

(8) ${\sim}P(p/c) \prec P({\sim}p/c)$
(9) $P(p \cdot q/c) \prec [P(p/c) \cdot P(q/c)]$
(10) $P(p \cdot q/c) \prec [P(p/c) \cdot P(q/c \cdot p)]$
(11) $[P(p/c) \cdot P(q/c \cdot p)] \prec P(q/c)$
(12) $P(p/c \cdot q) \prec P(p \vee {\sim}q/c)$
(13) $[P(p/c) \cdot {\sim}P(q/c)] \prec P(p \cdot {\sim}q/c)$
(14) $P(p/c) \prec [P(q/c) \vee P(p/c \cdot {\sim}q)]$

In addition, Rescher introduces several other deontic operators, defined in terms of the permission operator. For instance, he defines the **obligation operator** as:

$O(p/c) = \text{df} \; {\sim}P({\sim}p/c)$

---

* The modal equivalent of $(p \equiv q) :: [(p \supset q) \cdot (q \supset p)]$.

† The modal equivalent of $p, p \supset q \; / \therefore \; q$.

This says that "p is obligatory in circumstance c" means the same as "$\sim p$ is not permitted in circumstance c". Some theorems concerning this operator are:

(15) $O(p/c) \dashv P(p/c)$

(16) $O(p \cdot q/c) \equiv [O(p/c) \cdot O(q/c)]$

(17) $(p \dashv q) \dashv [O(p/c) \dashv O(q/c)]$

(18) $[O(p/c) \vee O(q/c)] \dashv O(p \vee q/c)$ [But not vice versa.]

2 Problems with Deontic Systems

There is a great deal of controversy concerning most of the axioms proposed for deontic systems. For instance, one objection raised against RDL is that axioms 3 and 5 (plus appropriate rules and theorems of modal logic), yield the following theorem:*

$[P(p/c) \cdot P(\sim p/c \cdot p)] \dashv P(q/c)$

This theorem states that permission to do p in c and permission to do $\sim p$ in $c \cdot p$ entails permission to do any q whatever in c. Thus, if one is permitted to smoke and permitted to not smoke in the circumstance that one is smoking in a railroad smoking car, one is permitted to do anything (murder, for instance) in that smoking car.

Obviously, this theorem is not acceptable if it yields such results, so Rescher replaced Axiom 5 with what he called "A5*":

A5* $\{[P(p/c) \cdot P(q/c \cdot p)] \cdot \Diamond(p \cdot q)\} \dashv P(p \cdot q/c)$

Since $p \cdot \sim p$ is not possible, the counterexample just discussed cannot be derived in RDL when A5* replaces A5.

But other suspicious theorems can be derived. For example, from A5* plus A3 we can derive the theorem:†

$\{[P(p/c) \cdot P(q/c \cdot p)] \cdot \Diamond(p \cdot q)\} \dashv [P(p/c) \cdot P(q/c)]$

But if c is, for instance, the circumstance of being in an honors program, p the action of taking Philosophy 1H, and q the action of taking Philosophy 2H, where 1H is a prerequisite for 2H, then this theorem yields an unacceptable result. For it says that if one is permitted to take Philosophy 1H, in the circumstance that one is in the honors program, and permitted to take Philosophy 2H, in the circumstance of being in the honors pro-

---

* For proof, see Alan Ross Anderson, "On the Logic of Commitment", *Philosophical Studies,* vol. X (1959), pp. 23–27.

† For more on this counterexample, see John Robison, "Further Difficulties for Conditional Permission in Deontic Logic", *Philosophical Studies,* vol. XVIII (1967), pp. 27–30.

gram *and* having taken Philosophy 1H, and if it is possible to take both 1H and 2H, then all of this entails that in the circumstance of being an honors student one is permitted to take 1H, and in the same circumstance (with or without the added circumstance of having taken 1H) one is permitted to take 2H. This is unacceptable of course, since in the example only those honors students who take 1H are permitted to take 2H.

In addition to objections to its axioms, RDL has been objected to because one of its *definitions* seems to yield questionable consequences. The definition objected to* is the one defining the obligation operator:

$$O(p/c) =_{df} \sim P(\sim p/c)$$

For this definition (plus several RDL axioms), yields the following theorem:

$$O(p/d) \dashv\!\exists\, O(p/c \vee \sim c)$$

And this entails (using Castañeda's example, if women's liberationists will *permit* it) that if in the circumstance that you're married to Jane you ought to support her, then this entails that you ought to support her in any circumstance ($c \vee \sim c$). But surely we can't accept this result, and so we must reject either the definition of obligation (as Castañeda suggests) or else one of the axioms used in the proof.

Objections of the kind just discussed have led some to reject deontic logic, as some reject modal or epistemic logic. Some even claim, though for other reasons, that these operator systems, unlike predicate logic, are not real *logic* systems at all.

But whatever the merits of this last claim, this much seems certain. It would be very useful indeed if we had generally acceptable modal, epistemic, and deontic rules, so that when philosophers argued about ethics, or whatever, they could say (as Leibniz hoped we might some day be able to) "Come, let us calculate".

Key Terms Introduced in Chapter Twenty-one

Deontic logic: A logic that deals with the ethical notions of obligation, permission, and so on.

Obligation operator: The operator "*O*", used to express obligation.

Operator logic: A logic dealing with operators that bind all or parts of expressions.

Permission operator: The operator "*P*", used to express permission.

* By Hector-Neri Castañeda, "The Logic of Obligation", *Philosophical Studies,* vol. X (1959), pp. 17–23.

Appendix A

Logic and a Traditional Problem in Philosophy

Many of the most important and controversial questions in philosophy center on the very nature of knowledge itself. In recent times* much of this controversy has been concerned with four key concepts, namely the *a priori, a posteriori, analytic,* and *synthetic*.

Because of their controversial nature, no precise definition or characterization of these key concepts can be given that would be acceptable even to a majority of present-day philosophers. There is no "neutral" way to talk about them. The characterization presented here is, perhaps, as standard as any.

1 *The A Priori and the A Posteriori*

Given that a sentence or proposition† is taken as "known", we can ask, first, *how it is known,* and second, *what kind of sentence or proposition it is that is known*. The terms *a priori* and *a posteriori* concern the first question—how things are, or can be, known.

Take the sentence "Either it will rain tomorrow (at a particular place) or it won't", in symbols $R \vee \sim R$. We can determine that this sentence is true by going to that particular place and seeing whether or not it rains there. But we need not do so. By truth table analysis we can determine that it is true *prior* to such an empirical investigation. Hence, the sen-

---

* Since the time of Immanuel Kant (1724–1804), who introduced two of the key terms, *analytic* and *synthetic*. See, for instance, the Preamble on the Peculiarities of All Metaphysical Knowledge, in his *Prolegomena to Any Future Metaphysic*.

† Again, we beg the question of whether we should be speaking about *sentences* or *propositions* (or even, as Kant claimed, *judgments*).

tence $R \vee \sim R$ is said to be knowable *a priori*. A sentence or proposition is said to be knowable **a priori** if it can be known to be true without the need to experience any of the things that the sentence is about.

At least some of our knowledge surely is *a priori*. Theorems of logic are examples. But some knowledge is not. Take the belief that all of the books in Art's library are logic books (let's suppose that this happens to be true). Unlike the case for the belief that it either will or won't rain, we cannot know *a priori* that the sentence "All of the books in Art's library are logic books" is true. To justify our belief that it is true, we (or someone) must actually examine the contents of his library. So this sentence is said to be knowable *a posteriori,* or after inspection of the thing known. A sentence or proposition is said to be knowable only **a posteriori** if its truth value cannot be known before experience of things of the kind that the sentence or proposition is about. We require empirical (observable) evidence of some kind or other to determine the truth value of an *a posteriori* proposition.*

2 *The Analytic and the Synthetic*

In addition to the question of *how* we can know the truth values of sentences or propositions, there is the question of *what kinds* of sentences or propositions we can know. A sentence is said to be **analytic** if the meaning of its grammatical predicate is all or part of the meaning of its grammatical subject, and **synthetic** if it is not.

Take the sentence "All bachelors are unmarried". If we assume that the term "bachelor" means "unmarried adult male", then clearly the meaning of the predicate term "unmarried" is part of the meaning of the subject term "bachelor". Hence, the sentence "All bachelors are unmarried" is analytic. Using more traditional language, we can say that the judgment or proposition that all bachelors are unmarried is analytic because unmarriedness is part of the concept of bachelorhood.

Now consider the sentence "All bachelors weigh more than 50 pounds". Assuming again that the term "bachelor" means "unmarried adult male", it is clear that the meaning of the predicate expression "weighs more than 50 pounds" is *not* part of the meaning of the subject term "bachelor". Hence, the sentence "All bachelors weigh more than 50 pounds" is synthetic. Using more traditional language, we can say that the judgment or proposition that all bachelors weigh more than 50 pounds is synthetic because the concept of weighing more than 50 pounds is not contained in the concept of bachelorhood.

---

*The distinction between the *a priori* and the *a posteriori* corresponds roughly to the distinction between *relations of ideas* and *matters of fact,* made by the philosopher David Hume (1711–1776), and to the distinction between *truths of reason* and *truths of fact,* made by the philosopher G. W. Leibniz (1646–1716).

3 Semantic and Syntactic Analyticity

It has become customary to divide analytic propositions into two kinds, namely *syntactic* and *semantic*.

A proposition is **syntactic analytic** if it derives its analyticity from its *form* (plus the meanings of its logical terms), and not from the meanings of its nonlogical terms. For example, the syntactic analytic proposition "All bachelors are bachelors" is true because all propositions of the form "All ______ are ______" are true.

A proposition is **semantic analytic** if it derives its analyticity not simply from its form but also from the meanings of its *nonlogical terms*. Only some of the propositions having the form "All ______ are ------" (the form of "All bachelors are unmarried") are true, or analytic, or knowable *a priori*. To determine the truth value of the semantic analytic truth "All bachelors are unmarried", we must know not only its form, but also the meanings of the nonlogical terms "bachelor" and "unmarried", and hence know that unmarriedness is part of the concept of bachelorhood.

4 The Synthetic A Priori

We now have divided sentences, propositions, and judgments into four kinds, *a priori, a posteriori,* analytic, and synthetic. But these divisions are not mutually exclusive. For instance, the proposition "All bachelors are bachelors" is not only analytic, but also *a priori,* since we can know that it is true without examining any bachelors. And the proposition "All bachelors weigh more than 50 pounds" is not only synthetic, but also *a posteriori,* since we can discover its truth value only by an actual examination of bachelors. Clearly then, there are *analytic a priori* and *synthetic a posteriori* propositions.

But are there also *analytic a posteriori* or *synthetic a priori* propositions? It would seem that there are not. In the first place, there cannot be any analytic *a posteriori* propositions, because if a sentence is analytic, then mere knowledge of the meanings of its subject and predicate terms will enable us to determine its truth value, without any empirical observations being required. And second, it would seem that there cannot be any synthetic *a priori* propositions, because if a proposition is synthetic then no mere *mental process,* such as comparing the meanings of its subject and predicate terms, will be sufficient to enable us to determine its truth value.

As a matter of fact, practically all philosophers agree that there are no analytic *a posteriori* propositions. But they disagree violently as to the existence of synthetic *a priori* propositions.

The most obvious reason for supposing that there are synthetic *a priori* propositions or judgments is that they seem to exist. Examples are "If something is red (all over), then it is not green", "Seven plus five equals twelve", and "A cube has twelve edges".

Take the proposition "If something is red (all over), then it is not green". It is argued that this proposition is *synthetic,* because the concept of being red does not contain within it the concept of being nongreen, and also *a priori,* because we can know that it is true without actually examining red things to determine if they are green or not. So it is claimed that this proposition is **synthetic a priori.**

Similarly, it is argued that the proposition "Seven plus five equals twelve" is *synthetic,* because the concept of adding seven and five does not contain within it the concept of being twelve, and also *a priori,* because we can know that it is true without actually examining the results of adding seven things to five things to see if we obtain a collection of twelve things.

And it is argued that the proposition "A cube has twelve edges" is *synthetic,* because the concept of being a cube does not contain within it the concept of having twelve edges (for instance, we might conceive of a cube as a solid figure containing exactly six square surfaces), and also *a priori,* because we can know that it is true without actually examining cubes to determine if they have twelve edges. (The existence of these and other apparent cases of synthetic *a priori* propositions is why Kant thought that the fundamental question is how synthetic *a priori* propositions are possible, not whether there are synthetic *a priori* propositions.)

5 *Current Positions*

Some present-day philosophers accept Kant's view more or less as he originally formulated it. They believe that some propositions are analytic *a priori* (for instance, the propositions "All bachelors are bachelors" and "All bachelors are unmarried"), some synthetic *a posteriori* (for instance, the propositions "John is tall" and "All men have hearts"), and some synthetic *a priori* (for instance, the propositions "If something is red (all over), then it is not green" and "A cube has twelve edges").

But some believe that there are no synthetic *a priori* propositions, instead believing that all propositions can be classified as either analytic *a priori* or as synthetic *a posteriori*. This has always been the position of philosophers called *empiricists*.

Take the proposition "If something is red (all over), then it is not green", which is alleged to be synthetic *a priori*. An empiricist would argue that either the concept of being red does contain within it the idea of being nongreen, in which case this proposition is analytic, or else the concept of being red does not contain within it the concept of being nongreen, in which case the proposition in question is *a posteriori*. In either case, the proposition "If something is red (all over), then it is not green" is not synthetic *a priori*.

No doubt the empiricists are right that the proposition in question is analytic *if* the concept of being red contains within it the concept of being nongreen. But the claim that it is *a posteriori* if the concept of being red does not contain within it the concept of being nongreen needs to be argued for. Empiricists would be likely to argue for it by claiming that in general it is the very containment of one concept in another that permits us to know *a priori* that a proposition about these concepts is true. For instance, we can know *a priori* that the proposition "All bachelors are unmarried" is true *precisely because* unmarriedness is part of the concept of bachelorhood. In other words, empiricists would claim that it is the *analytic* nature of propositions that makes them knowable *a priori*.*

In the twentieth century, the controversy concerning the existence of synthetic *a priori* propositions has taken a back seat to the controversy over which propositions, if any, are analytic, and which synthetic.

Some, while believing that there are *syntactic* analytic propositions, deny that there is a sharp division between *semantic* analytic propositions and synthetic propositions. (At least they deny this for propositions expressed in a natural language such as English. "Artificial" or "constructed" languages are another matter.)

One reason for their denial is the *vagueness* of the concepts denoted by most terms in natural languages. Take the term "bachelor". In some ways, the concept of bachelorhood is quite precise. For example, it is clear that *unmarriedness* is part of that concept. But in other ways, it is not precise. For instance, the *age requirement* for bachelorhood is not precise. Clearly, anyone five years of age is too young to be called a bachelor. The same is true for age ten. But what about ages 15, 20, and 25? For these age brackets, we cannot answer with any degree of certainty. Bachelorhood has no minimum age requirement. It follows then, that we cannot say for certain whether a proposition such as "All bachelors are over 20 years old" is analytic or synthetic.

This lack of a sharp division between the semantic analytic and the synthetic has resulted in at least three closely related positions on the subject.

(1) It has been argued that there is a continuous ordering of propositions from the most analytic (least synthetic), such as the propositions "All bachelors are unmarried" and "All women are human", through more and more doubtful cases, such as the propositions "All copper conducts elec-

---

* In addition, empiricists reject Kant's account (for example, in *The Critique of Pure Reason*) of how it is possible to know synthetic propositions *a priori*.

tricity", "Grass is green", "Sugar tastes sweet", and "Mark Twain wrote *Huck Finn*", to the least analytic (most synthetic), such as the propositions "Art is tall", "Art is taller than Betsy", "All bachelors are over five feet tall", and "Over seven million people reside in New York City".

According to this view, when we say that a given proposition is a semantic analytic proposition, either what we say is false, or else it is a way of stating the relative position of the proposition on the continuous analytic-synthetic scale (just as saying that something is hot is a way of stating its relative position on the hot-cold—that is, temperature—scale).

(2) Others argue that the vagueness of most concepts and terms in everyday use necessitates the introduction of a new category, say the "borderline case" category, placed between the semantic analytic and the synthetic categories, to take account of such propositions as "All bachelors are over 20 years of age", which are neither analytic nor synthetic. (Working this out yields what is sometimes called *ambiguous logic*.)

(3) Finally, some argue that the whole idea of semantic analytic propositions is mistaken. They would be inclined to dispense with this category entirely, lumping all of its alleged members together with the clearly synthetic propositions. In other words, they would divide all propositions into those that are *syntactic analytic* and those that are *synthetic*.

Whichever of these three views is correct,* it certainly is true that most of the words and concepts in daily use are vague, so that no sharp division between the semantic analytic and the synthetic can be made for the propositions expressed in the language of everyday life. However, this does not exclude the possibility of constructing *artificial* languages (so-called "logically perfect" languages) in which such a division can be made, and does not exclude the possibility of *deliberately sharpening* the key terms of a natural language to permit a sharp *enough* division between the semantic analytic and the synthetic to be drawn. Indeed, there is reason to suppose that the key terms of a natural language can be deliberately sharpened in this way, since the various sciences often do so quite successfully.

6 *The Use of Logic to Clarify the Problem*

We said before that a proposition is analytic if the meaning of its grammatical predicate is all or part of the meaning of its grammatical subject.

---

* There are a few philosophers who reject the analytic-synthetic distinction altogether, even denying that there is a sharp distinction between *syntactic* analytic sentences and synthetic sentences. The complexity of the arguments for and against this view precludes their discussion here.

But many propositions do not have a subject-predicate form. Compound sentences, for instance, do not. So we need to extend the notion of analyticity to cover propositions that are not in subject-predicate form.

First, let's consider *syntactic* analyticity. The key to syntactic analyticity is the idea of the *form* of a sentence or proposition. So we can say that *any proposition* (whether in subject-predicate form or not) *that is true solely because of its form* (plus the meanings of its logical terms) *is a syntactic analytic proposition.*

Once we do this, all of the *tautologous sentences* of sentential logic become syntactic analytic truths. An example is the sentence "Either Art will go to the show or he won't", in symbols $A \vee \sim A$, which is true by virtue of its form (since every sentence of the form "_______ $\vee$ $\sim$_______" is true).

In addition, all of the so-called logical truths* of predicate logic become syntactic analytic truths,† because they too are true by virtue of their form (plus the meanings of their logical terms). An example is the logical truth, "All things are either red or not red", in symbols $(x)(Rx \vee \sim Rx)$, which is true because of its form (since every sentence of the form "All things are either _______ or not _______" is true). Another is the more complicated logical truth, "If everyone who went to the show received a door prize, then everyone who didn't get a door prize didn't go to the show", in symbols $(x)[(Px \cdot Sx) \supset Dx] \supset (x)[(Px \cdot \sim Dx) \supset \sim Sx]$, which also is true because of its form.

All of the logical truths involving *identity* also become syntactic analytic truths by this criterion of syntactic analyticity. An example is the sentence "Art is Art", in symbols $a = a$, since clearly every sentence of the form $x = x$ is true.

Having extended the notion of syntactic analyticity by "mapping it" onto the concept of logical truth, we must now treat the concept of *semantic* analyticity.

In the first place, we have to accept the view that we cannot make a sharp division between the propositions expressible in a natural language that are semantically analytic and those that are synthetic. Nevertheless, we must admit that some of these propositions clearly *are* semantic analytic (for example, "All bachelors are unmarried"), and some clearly synthetic (for example, "All bachelors weigh more than 50 pounds").

Next, let's use the fact that we can deliberately sharpen a term or con-

---

* Sentences expressible in predicate logic notation that are provable from the null set of premises.

† The expression "syntactic analytic truth" is apt here, because by extension we can speak of "syntactic analytic falsehood", meaning by that expression a sentence or proposition that is false because of its form (plus the meaning of its logical terms). Similarly, we can speak of "a priori falsehoods", meaning sentences or propositions that can be known in advance to be false. According to empiricists, only contradictions can be syntactic analytic falsehoods.

cept to enable any given proposition to be classifiable either as semantically analytic or as synthetic. For instance, by sharpening the concept of being a bachelor (or by redefining the term "bachelor") so that to be a bachelor one must be over 20 years of age, we can make the proposition "All bachelors are over 20 years of age" a semantic analytic proposition.

Next, let's make explicit a principle we have been using implicitly, namely the principle that *if replacement of a term (or terms) in a sentence by its definition results in a syntactic analytic sentence, then the given sentence is a semantic analytic sentence*. For example, we implicitly used this principle in concluding that the sentence "All bachelors are unmarried" is semantically analytic because replacement of its subject term "bachelor" by its definition "unmarried male over 20 years of age" results in the syntactic analytic sentence "All unmarried males over 20 years of age are unmarried".

Now let's expand the notion of analyticity to cover the axioms and theorems of certain axiom systems.* The key principle is that *all theorems of an axiom system that deductively follow from analytic axioms are analytic*. In other words, we want all logical consequences of analytic sentences to be analytic.

The problem, of course, lies with the status of the axioms themselves, in particular the axioms of systems for arithmetic and geometry, as well as the empirical sciences. Are they analytic or synthetic? Kantians, and most "rationalists", believe that all of the axioms of arithmetic and geometry, and some of those of certain sciences (such as physics), are synthetic (and also *a priori*). They thus believe in a synthetic *a priori*.

On the other hand, empiricists tend to believe that all of the axioms of arithmetic and of so-called pure geometry are analytic (and also *a priori*), whereas those of empirical sciences and so-called applied geometry† are synthetic (and also *a posteriori*). They thus deny the existence of a synthetic *a priori*.

Indeed, it is plausible to characterize the dispute between rationalists and empiricists, which has been a central philosophical argument for most of the past three hundred years, as a dispute over the synthetic *a priori*.†† The problem for rationalists is to explain how synthetic *a priori* knowledge is possible, and for empiricists why the apparent cases of synthetic *a priori* knowledge are either not synthetic or not *a priori*.

---

* Roughly, an axiom system is composed of one or more statements (the axioms), one or more rules of inference, and statements (theorems) that follow from the axioms according to the rules of inference. See Appendix B for a discussion of axiom systems.

† For more on the distinction between pure and applied geometry, see Han Reichenbach, *Rise of Scientific Philosophy* (Berkeley: University of California Press, 1951).

†† Phrasing the problem roughly in the way suggested to me by Arthur Skidmore.

Exercise A-1:

Briefly identify the following, give an original example of each, and explain why it is an example.

1. Analytic *a priori* proposition.
2. Semantic analytic proposition.
3. Syntactic analytic proposition.
4. Synthetic *a posteriori* proposition.

Exercise A-2:

Which of the following are analytic and which synthetic? (Defend your answers, and if you have doubts, explain.)

1. The moon is made of blue cheese.
2. All dogs are canines.
3. Absence makes the heart grow fonder.
4. The class of right actions consists exactly in those actions one ought to do.
5. South Carolina is south of North Carolina.
6. Long after all life has ceased to exist, distant galaxies will still be moving away from our galaxy.
7. If equals are added to equals, their sums are equal.
8. The square on the hypotenuse is equal to the sum of the squares on the other two sides.
9. Every proposition is either analytic or synthetic.

Key Terms Introduced in Appendix A

A posteriori: That which cannot be known prior to, or without the need of, experience of the thing known. That which requires experience, or empirical evidence, of some kind to be known.

A priori: That which can be known before, and without the need of, experience of the thing known.

Analytic: Traditionally, a proposition whose grammatical predicate is all or part of the meaning of its grammatical subject.

Semantic analytic: Traditionally, roughly a proposition whose predicate is part of its subject, as being *unmarried* is part of being a *bachelor.*

Syntactic analytic: Traditionally, roughly a proposition whose predicate merely repeats its subject, as in the proposition "All bachelors are bachelors".

Synthetic: A sentence or proposition is *synthetic* if the meaning of its grammatical predicate is not part of the meaning of its grammatical subject.

Synthetic a priori: A sentence or proposition is *synthetic a priori* if it is both synthetic and *a priori.* (The existence of a synthetic *a priori* constitutes one of the most important and controversial questions in modern philosophy.)

Appendix B

Axiom Systems

One way to *systematize* a given area of knowledge is to use an **axiom system.**

1 The Nature of an Axiom System

An axiom system has three main elements: **symbols** (or words), **formulas,** and **inference rules.** Symbols divide into **defined symbols,** for which explicit definitions are presented, and **primitive (undefined) symbols,** for which no definitions are presented. For instance, in an axiom system for anthropology we might introduce the terms "parent" and "male" as primitives, and then define the term "father" to mean "male parent". Symbols also divide into **logical symbols,** such as "and", "not", "some", and so on, and **extralogical** or **nonlogical symbols,** which vary depending on the area of knowledge to be systematized.

Formulas break down into **sentences** and **sentence forms** (or functions).* They also divide into **axioms,** for which no justification is provided within the system, and **theorems,** which can be derived from the axioms by means of the inference rules of the system. Indeed, one of the main reasons for constructing axiom systems is to derive theorems from axioms.

Formulas also can be divided into **well-formed formulas,** such as $p \supset q$ and $\sim[(A \vee B) \supset \sim C]$, and those that are not, such as $(pq \vee$ and $AB) \vee$. (This distinction will be explained in more detail later.) And

---

* This is not quite true for what are called *uninterpreted* systems, because it is inappropriate to speak of the formulas of such systems as sentences or sentence forms.

finally, inference rules divide into **primitive inference rules,** for which no justification is provided within the system, and **derived inference rules,** for which a justification *is* provided.

Of course, every system need not have all of these elements. For instance, we can have an axiom system without defined symbols or derived rules. But to be complete, an axiom system must have symbols, formulas, and inference rules.

One of the primary motives for constructing axiom systems is *rigor*. We want symbols precisely defined, and theorems rigorously proved. Consequently, it might be supposed that to include *undefined* symbols, *unproved* axioms, and *unjustified* inference rules is to settle for something less than the ideal. But this is an illusion. It is impossible to define *all* symbols, prove *all* sentences, or justify *all* inference rules within a given system, except either circularly or by an infinite (and useless) series of definitions or proofs. (For example, it would be useless to define "automobile" as "car" and then to define "car" as "automobile". And it would be useless to attempt to present an infinite series of definitions, because to understand it one would have to run through the entire series, something it is impossible to do.) So we must settle for at least some undefined symbols, unproved axioms, and unjustified inference rules.*

Of course, undefined symbols must be understood, and the axioms and inference rules must be acceptable. Clearly, some symbols will not do as primitives in a rigorous system. But the question of *which* symbols and *which* axioms and inference rules are acceptable as primitives is in dispute. For instance, some claim that the axioms of an axiom system for deductive logic must be *intuitively acceptable,* or *self-evidently true,* while others say that, theoretically, any theorems of logic can be axioms, the choice being made to obtain the smallest possible set of axioms from which all theorems can be derived. But all agree that (other things being equal) it is desirable to have very few axioms or primitive rules of inference, and very few undefined symbols.

It should be noted that the undefinability *within a system* of all terms of that system does not entail the inherent *undefinability* of any terms of that system. It may be that no terms are undefinable.

Most of us are familiar with at least one axiom system, Euclidean geometry, although it is normally presented only in a semirigorous form. (For instance, usually only a partial list of inference rules is provided.) But it is clear how such a system can be made more rigorous, and so we can take Euclidean geometry as our model of an axiom system.

---

* It is sometimes possible to reduce the number of axioms to zero by increasing the number of primitive inference rules. But we can never reduce the number of axioms *and* primitive inference rules in a given system to zero.

2 Interpreted and Uninterpreted Systems

An **uninterpreted axiom system** is one in which the primitive symbols not only are not defined *within* the system, but are given no meaning or interpretation whatever. (Of course, those who construct uninterpreted axiom systems generally have particular interpretations in mind. For instance, anyone who constructs an uninterpreted axiom system for sentential logic obviously has sentential logic in mind; otherwise there would be no point in calling it an uninterpreted system *for sentential logic*.)

The point of an uninterpreted system is to enable us to concentrate on form or structure without being distracted by content, and to make it less likely that we will tacitly use knowledge not contained in the axioms of the system. For example, dealing with an uninterpreted axiom system for geometry makes it less likely that we will tacitly appeal to geometric intuitions not explicitly stated in the axioms and inference rules of the system. (In fact, Euclid himself made tacit use of information about geometry not explicitly stated in his system.)

An **interpreted axiom system** is one for which all of the primitive terms are assigned a meaning or interpretation. In some axiom systems the formulas when interpreted are sentences, in others they are sentence forms.

Notice that it is one thing to define a term within a system, and another to assign a meaning to a primitive term. A term defined within a system is defined by the primitive terms of the system (or other terms so defined). Primitive terms are assigned meanings in other ways. For example, in applied geometry the primitive term "straight line" may be taken to refer to the path of a light ray.

Although there is some dispute about which terms are usable as primitives, other things being equal, terms whose meanings we clearly understand (however we obtain this understanding) are preferable to those that are vague or figurative.

3 Properties of Axiom Systems

Good axiom systems themselves have several important properties, in particular *consistency* and *completeness*.

Consistency

The most important requirement for an acceptable axiom system is *consistency*. An axiom system is **consistent** *iff** contradictory formulas can-

---

* That is, *if and only if*.

not be derived from its axioms by means of its rules of inference. An axiom system that fails to satisfy this requirement, so that a contradiction is derivable as a theorem, is said to be *inconsistent* and is obviously unsatisfactory.

Example:

A system containing the two axioms

(A1) $p \supset \sim p$

(A2) p

plus the two inference rules

(R1) If p and $p \supset q$, then we can infer q. (Modus Ponens)

(R2) If p and q, then we can infer $p \cdot q$. (Conjunction)

is inconsistent, since we can derive a contradiction in such a system, as follows:

1.	$p \supset \sim p$	**Axiom**
2.	p	**Axiom**
3.	$\sim p$	1,2 **MP**
4.	$p \cdot \sim p$	2,3 **Conj**

The general procedure for proving that an axiom system is *inconsistent* is the same as the one for proving a set of premises inconsistent, namely the derivation of an explicit contradiction. But failure to derive a contradiction does not prove that a given axiom system is consistent, for we may have failed through lack of ingenuity. Instead, the general procedure for proving that an axiom system is consistent is to prove that a formula exists that is not derivable as a theorem of that system. This proves that a given axiom system is consistent because inconsistent systems permit the derivation of any and every expressible formula (since a *contradiction* logically entails any and every expressible formula). Hence, if there is some formula that cannot be derived as a theorem, then no contradiction can be derived either, and the system must be consistent.*

---

*This criterion of consistency, known as "Post's consistency criterion", after its inventor, E. L. Post, works only for *complete* systems. Incomplete systems that also are inconsistent may be such that there are formulas expressible in the system that are not provable.

Expressive Completeness

An axiom system is **expressively complete** *iff* its language is rich enough to express everything that the system is intended to express. For example, the usual axiom systems for Euclidean geometry are expressively complete, because they permit every statement (true or false) concerning geometry. But an axiom system for Euclidean geometry would be expressively incomplete if, say, it contained no method for stating sentences about circles.

Completeness

There is another kind of completeness, more frequently discussed in the literature than expressive completeness and much more difficult to state. This kind concerns the *provability* or *derivability* of formulas. Perhaps the best criterion we can give for this kind of completeness is that an axiom system is **complete** in this sense *iff* all of the formulas we *desire* to prove as theorems of the system in fact are provable as theorems of that system.

Although it is quite difficult to state precisely what this kind of completeness consists of *in general,* it is less difficult to characterize it for three of the more important kinds of axiom systems:

(1) An axiom system for sentential logic is complete *iff* every tautologous sentence or sentence form expressible in the system is provable as a theorem of the system.

(2) In Chapter Eight, sentence forms all of whose substitution instances are true sentences were called *theorems of logic*. Adopting this terminology, we can say that an axiom system for predicate logic is complete *iff* every theorem of logic is provable as a theorem of that system. (Notice that we cannot use the same criterion of completeness for predicate logic that we used for sentential logic because many theorems of predicate logic are not tautologies.)

(3) An axiom system for *arithmetic* is complete *iff* every sentence expressible in the system is such that either it or its negation is a theorem of the system. To see that this criterion is adequate, consider several kinds of typical sentences of arithmetic.

First, consider *unquantified* sentences, such as $2 + 2 = 4$, $7 + 1 = 3$, and so on. Clearly, every such sentence is either true, in which case it is a theorem of arithmetic, or false, in which case its negation is a theorem of arithmetic. (An example of the latter would be the sentence $\sim(7 + 1 = 3)$, which is a theorem of arithmetic.)

Next, consider *quantified* sentences, such as $(x)(y)[(x + y) = (y + x)]$, $\sim(x)(x = x)$, and so on. Once again, it is clear that every such sentence is either true, in which case it is a theorem of arithmetic, or false, in which case its negation is a theorem of arithmetic.

Notice that the kind of completeness required of an axiom system for arithmetic is stronger than that required for sentential or predicate logic. We cannot require such a strict kind of completeness for logic, because axiom systems for logic contain either *contingent sentences* or *contingent sentence forms,* and neither they nor their negations are theorems of logic.

Axiom Independence

An axiom of a given system is **independent** of the other axioms *iff* it cannot be derived from them using the inference rules of that system. Otherwise, an axiom is dependent.

Example:

We can prove that the axioms contained in the system discussed in the footnote on page 69 are not independent by showing, for instance, the dependence of the axiom $(p \supset q) \equiv (\sim q \supset \sim p)$. And we can show this by deriving it as a theorem of the system, as follows:

→1.	$p \supset q$	**AP**
2.	$\sim p \vee q$	1, **Impl**
3.	$q \vee \sim p$	2, **Comm**
4.	$\sim\sim q \vee \sim p$	3, **DN**
5.	$\sim q \supset \sim p$	4, **Impl**
6.	$(p \supset q) \supset (\sim q \supset \sim p)$	1–5, **CP**
→7.	$\sim q \supset \sim p$	**AP**
8.	$\sim\sim q \vee \sim p$	7, **Impl**
9.	$\sim p \vee \sim\sim q$	8, **Comm**
10.	$\sim p \vee q$	9, **DN**
11.	$p \supset q$	10, **Impl**
12.	$(\sim q \supset \sim p) \supset (p \supset q)$	7–11, **CP**
13.	$[(p \supset q) \supset (\sim q \supset \sim p)] \cdot [(\sim q \supset \sim p) \supset (p \supset q)]$	6, 12 **Conj**
14.	$(p \supset q) \equiv (\sim q \supset \sim p)$	13, **Equiv**

Naturally, the above proof does *not* use Contraposition, since that would make the proof viciously circular, and hence useless.

We can prove that a given axiom is *dependent* by deriving it from the other axioms of a system. But failure to find such a proof does not constitute a proof that an axiom is independent; we may simply have overlooked the proof.

To prove that an axiom is *independent* of a given set of axioms, it suffices to show that there is some characteristic or property possessed by every axiom in the given set, and also possessed by every formula derivable from that set of axioms, which is *not* possessed by the axiom in question. This proves independence because any particular axiom that does not have a property possessed by every formula derivable from a given set of axioms itself cannot be derivable from that set, and hence itself must be independent of that set.

Decision Procedure

A **decision procedure** is a mechanical method for determining in a finite number of steps whether or not a given formula is a theorem of an axiom system. For example, truth table analysis is a decision procedure for sentential logic, since it enables us to determine in a finite number of steps whether or not a given formula is a tautology, and hence a theorem of sentential logic.

The existence of a decision procedure for a given axiom system renders all questions about the theorems of that system *routinely* answerable, without the need for ingenuity in the construction of proofs. This has the advantage that all questions and disputes about whether a particular formula is a theorem of the system can be settled by the mere manipulation of symbols of the kind that computers can be programmed to perform.

Axiom systems for which there is no decision procedure are generally of more interest to logicians and mathematicians, since questions and disputes about alleged theorems of these systems, even if in principle soluble, require genius (or a good deal of luck) for their solution. Indeed many such questions may go unanswered forever.

4 *Outline of an Axiom System for Sentential Logic*

Object Language—Metalanguage

We now present the bare outline of an axiom system for sentential logic. However, to do so, we must *talk about* that system. Since there is a sense in which that axiom system itself constitutes a language, we need some other language to talk about it. And since the sentential logic axiom system, "SL" for short, is the *object* of discussion, we can refer to it as the **object language,** and refer to the language used to talk about SL as the **metalanguage.**

The terms "object language" and "metalanguage" are relative. For instance, if we use German to talk about English, then German is the metalanguage. But if we use English to talk about German, then English is the metalanguage. Of course, the same language can be both object and metalanguage. For instance, in an English grammar class conducted in English, English is used to talk about itself, and hence is both object and metalanguage. (However, problems arise when we use a language to talk about its own *semantic* properties. The liar paradox discussed in Chapter Nine is an example.)

Quotation marks often are used to distinguish between *talk about* (or *mention of*) a language, and *use of* a language. For instance, we can use English sentences to talk about, or mention, the state of Kansas. But we also can talk about, or mention, the *words used* to talk about the state of Kansas. In talking about the state of Kansas, we use its English name without quotes; in talking about the word that is the name of the state, we put that word, "Kansas", in quotes. Thus, we can say that "Kansas" has six letters, whereas Kansas is a state roughly in the center of the continental United States. We can also go one step further and talk about the name of the name of Kansas. Thus, we can say that "'Kansas'" contains quotation marks, whereas "Kansas" does not, and that "Kansas" is the name of a state, whereas Kansas is not (since it *is* a state). In other words, the device of quotation marks provides a convenient and automatic way for generating names of linguistic entities.

Another device used for generating names of linguistic entities is boldface and lightface type. For instance, we can use the term **w** in the object language SL and *w* in the metalanguage when we wish to talk about "**w**".

From the point of view of logic, many other methods for naming words would do just as well as the above two. For instance, we might refer to the word "Kansas" by the name "Art". And then we could say (truthfully) that Art has six letters, the first one "K", the second "a", and so on. But such a notation would be inconvenient to say the least.

We shall adopt ordinary English (suitably fortified with special terms to refer to the symbols of SL) as the metalanguage both of SL and of itself. But in our informal exposition, we also shall refer to many terms and expressions of SL and its metalanguage simply by placing them in quotation marks.

Syntax, Semantics, Pragmatics

The **syntactic properties** of a language are its *structural* properties, that is, those properties it has in abstraction from the meanings of its terms (other than the logical terms). For instance, the English sentence "John is tall" has the syntactic property of containing ten letters. And the sentence "Art is smart *and* Betsy is beautiful" has the syntactic property of being a *conjunction*.

The **semantic properties** of a language are those properties that it possesses by virtue of the *meanings* of its terms. For instance, English has the semantic property of containing sentences stating arithmetic truths, such as "two plus two equals four", a semantic property that SL lacks. And the sentence "Snow is white" has the semantic property of containing a color term, namely the term "white". (Notice that uninterpreted systems have no semantic properties whatever, because their symbols have no meanings.)

The **pragmatic** properties of a language are those that it has in relation to its speakers (or users). For example, the English sentence "Snow is white" has the pragmatic property of *being believed* by many English-speaking people. And English itself has the pragmatic property of being spoken by most citizens of the United States.

Another way to look at the difference between syntax, semantics, and pragmatics is to say that the syntax of a language concerns the relationships between the elements of the language (such as letters, words, sentences, and so on), semantics the relationships between the elements of a language and the things that the language can talk about, and pragmatics the relationships between the elements of a language, the things it talks about, and the users of the language.

Little will be said here about the pragmatic properties of SL. However, we should bear in mind that in considering only the syntax and semantics of a language we are abstracting from the total language-use situation, which by its very nature must include language users. A "language" that no one ever uses or understands is no language at all.

Similarly, we should bear in mind that in discussing the syntax of an interpreted system, we are abstracting not only from its pragmatic properties, but also from its semantic properties.*

The Symbols of SL

An axiom system for sentential logic can be either interpreted or uninterpreted.† The axiom system SL, to be outlined here, is an interpreted system. This means that although the primitive terms are not defined in the system, they are taken to have their usual meanings.

All of the symbols of SL are primitive symbols. Among these symbols we distinguish **logical primitives** and **extralogical primitives.** (But there is no indication *within* SL whether a symbol is a logical or extralogical primitive. This distinction is made in the metalanguage.)

SL contains exactly four logical primitives, namely "$\sim$", "$\supset$", "(",

---

*However, in syntactic analyses, we generally do not abstract from the meanings of the *logical* terms of a system. This fact is frequently overlooked.

†Although some would deny that it makes sense to speak of an uninterpreted axiom system for any given area.

and "**)**", in boldface type (the last two to be used as left- and right-hand parentheses respectively).

In addition, SL contains indefinitely many *sentence variables,* ***p, q, r,*** and so on, as extralogical primitives.

Notice that the usual logical connectives "**.**", "$\vee$", and "$\equiv$" do not occur in SL. They are omitted to simplify the number of primitive symbols and the number of axioms. However, their counterparts will be introduced later as *defined* terms in the metalanguage.

Definition of WFF

Among all possible finite strings of terms of SL, some are *well formed,* such as **((p ⊃ q) ⊃ p)**, **(p ⊃ ~q)**, and so on, and some not, such as **(pp ⊃ ~)**, **)(((p**, and others. Intuitively, it is clear that all of the well-formed formulas ("WFF" for short) of SL are sentence forms. So we could define "WFF of SL" to mean "sentence form of SL". This would be a *semantic* definition of WFF. But we cannot always provide semantic definitions of WFF. For instance, we cannot do so for uninterpreted axiom systems, since they do not have semantic properties. The definition of WFF for an uninterpreted system must therefore be *syntactic*. And since we want SL to serve as an example, we shall provide a purely syntactic definition of "WFF of SL".

Of course, the definition of WFF occurs in the metalanguage, not in SL itself. So we need to introduce certain terms into the metalanguage to talk about the formulas of the object language SL. For this purpose, we introduce into the metalanguage the symbols *P*, *Q*, *R*, and so on, as *formula variables,* that is, as symbols in the metalanguage for which formulas in the object language can be substituted. Thus, in a given use, a formula variable denotes any formula of the object language (subject to the usual rule concerning the use of variables, which requires that in a single context every occurrence of a given variable must denote the same formula).

We also introduce the symbols "⊃", "~", "(", and ")", in lightface type, and stipulate (roughly) that these symbols denote the boldface type symbols "**⊃**", "**~**", "**(**", and "**)**" of the object language. (We also have available in the metalanguage the lightface type symbols *p*, *q*, *r*, and so on, that is, symbols that name particular formulas of the object language. However, these symbols are not used in the definition of WFF.)

Finally, to facilitate talk about the object language, we introduce the symbols "$\vee$", "$\cdot$", and "$\equiv$" as *defined terms* of the metalanguage:

(D1): "$(P \vee Q)$" is defined as an abbreviation for "$(\sim P \supset Q)$".

(D2): "$(P \cdot Q)$" is defined as an abbreviation for "$\sim(\sim P \vee \sim Q)$".

(D3): "$(P \equiv Q)$" is defined as an abbreviation for "$(P \supset Q) \cdot (Q \supset P)$".

These defined terms are sometimes useful in talking about the WFF's of SL, but they are not used in the definition of "WFF of SL" itself.

We now are ready to define the term "WFF of SL":

1. All sentence variables of SL are WFF's of SL.
2. If a formula P is a WFF of SL, then so is $\sim(P)$.
3. If P and Q are WFF's of SL, then so is $(P \supset Q)$.

We further state that no formula is a WFF of SL unless it is according to lines 1 through 3 above.

This definition provides an effective mechanical procedure for recognizing the WFF's of SL. If a formula is a WFF of SL, repeated application of the above definition will reveal this fact.* An infinite number of formulas of SL are WFF's according to this definition.

To illustrate how this definition works, consider the formula $(\sim(\boldsymbol{p} \supset \boldsymbol{p}) \supset \boldsymbol{q})$. According to line 1 of the definition, $\boldsymbol{p}$ and $\boldsymbol{q}$ both are WFF's. Therefore, according to line 3, $(\boldsymbol{p} \supset \boldsymbol{p})$ is a WFF; and according to line 2, $\sim(\boldsymbol{p} \supset \boldsymbol{p})$ is a WFF. Consequently, according to line 3, $(\sim(\boldsymbol{p} \supset \boldsymbol{p}) \supset \boldsymbol{q})$ is a WFF.

The Axioms and Inference Rules of SL†

We stipulate three WFF's as the axioms of SL:

(A1): $(\boldsymbol{p} \supset (\boldsymbol{q} \supset \boldsymbol{p}))$

(A2): $((\boldsymbol{p} \supset (\boldsymbol{q} \supset \boldsymbol{r})) \supset ((\boldsymbol{p} \supset \boldsymbol{q}) \supset (\boldsymbol{p} \supset \boldsymbol{r})))$

(A3): $((\sim\boldsymbol{q} \supset \sim\boldsymbol{p}) \supset ((\sim\boldsymbol{q} \supset \boldsymbol{p}) \supset \boldsymbol{q}))$

We also stipulate two rules of inference for SL. However, these two rules are formulated in the *metalanguage*, not in SL itself:

(R1): If $(P \supset Q)$ and P are either axioms or theorems of SL, then Q may be inferred from them.

(R2): If P is an axiom or theorem of SL, then any WFF may be substituted for any variable in P, provided the substitution is made for every occurrence of that variable in P.

(R1) already is familiar, since it is simply Modus Ponens. (R2) also should be familiar, since it simply states *explicitly* the rule of substitution used *implicitly* in the sentential and predicate logics presented earlier. For instance, (R2) permits inferences from $(\boldsymbol{p} \supset (\boldsymbol{q} \supset \boldsymbol{p}))$ to $(\boldsymbol{r} \supset (\boldsymbol{q} \supset \boldsymbol{r}))$, and to $((\boldsymbol{s} \supset \boldsymbol{t}) \supset (\boldsymbol{q} \supset (\boldsymbol{s} \supset \boldsymbol{t})))$, and so on.

We now define a **proof of SL** as a sequence of WFF's, all of which are axioms of SL or are inferable from the axioms by repeated applica-

---

* However, it does not provide an effective mechanical procedure for determining in general *whether* a formula is a WFF of SL; that is, it does not provide a method for determining that a non-WFF is not a WFF of SL. But such a procedure can be provided.

† For details of a system just like SL, see Eliot Mendelson, *Introduction to Mathematical Logic* (Princeton, N.J.: Van Nostrand, 1964).

tions of (R1) and/or (R2). For example, all sequences of WFF's of the object language having the forms

$(P \supset (Q \supset P))$
$(\sim P \supset (Q \supset \sim P))$

are proofs of SL. An example would be the sequence of formulas

$(\mathbf{p} \supset (\mathbf{q} \supset \mathbf{p}))$
$(\sim\mathbf{p} \supset (\mathbf{q} \supset \sim\mathbf{p}))$

which constitutes a proof of SL because the second WFF follows from the first by an application of (R2), and the first is an axiom of SL.

Another example of a proof having this form is the following sequence of formulas:

$(\mathbf{p} \supset (\mathbf{q} \supset \mathbf{p}))$
$(\sim(\mathbf{r} \supset \mathbf{s}) \supset (\mathbf{q} \supset \sim(\mathbf{r} \supset \mathbf{s})))$

which also constitutes a proof because the second WFF follows from the first by an application of (R2).

Proofs of SL tend to be quite long and very difficult to construct, which is the price we have to pay for having so few axioms and inference rules. The following is a more complex proof of SL:

$(\mathbf{p} \supset (\mathbf{q} \supset \mathbf{p}))$
$(\mathbf{p} \supset ((\mathbf{q} \supset \mathbf{p}) \supset \mathbf{p}))$
$((\mathbf{p} \supset (\mathbf{q} \supset \mathbf{r})) \supset ((\mathbf{p} \supset \mathbf{q}) \supset (\mathbf{p} \supset \mathbf{r})))$
$((\mathbf{p} \supset ((\mathbf{q} \supset \mathbf{p}) \supset \mathbf{p})) \supset ((\mathbf{p} \supset (\mathbf{q} \supset \mathbf{p})) \supset (\mathbf{p} \supset \mathbf{p})))$
$((\mathbf{p} \supset (\mathbf{q} \supset \mathbf{p})) \supset (\mathbf{p} \supset \mathbf{p}))$
$(\mathbf{p} \supset \mathbf{p})$

This constitutes a proof of SL because the first and third lines are axioms of SL, the second line follows from the first by (R2), the fourth line from the third by (R2), the fifth line from the second and fourth by (R1), and the sixth line from the first and fifth by (R1).

We now define a **theorem of SL** as a WFF for which a proof can be given in SL. Thus, the WFF $(\sim\mathbf{p} \supset (\mathbf{q} \supset \sim\mathbf{p}))$ is a theorem of SL, since it follows from the axiom $(\mathbf{p} \supset (\mathbf{q} \supset \mathbf{p}))$ by an application of (R2), and consequently a proof for it can be given in SL. (Of course, the *fact* that it is a theorem of SL, and the *fact* that the two above formulas constitute a proof of SL, cannot be stated within SL itself, but must be stated in the metalanguage.)

Properties of SL

Earlier, we discussed the properties, such as completeness, consistency, expressive completeness, and so on, that we want axiom systems to possess. The question arises as to which of these properties are possessed by SL, and the answer is that SL possesses *all* of them.

It has been proved that SL is complete (in the sense that every tautology is a theorem of SL), consistent, and expressively complete. In addition, it has been proved that there is a decision procedure for SL (namely truth table analysis), and that its axioms are independent.*

5 Axiom Systems for Predicate Logic

Axiom systems for first-order predicate logic are quite similar to those for sentential logic. (Indeed, to be complete a system for predicate logic must contain a system for sentential logic as a part.) Let's briefly examine a particular system of this kind, which we'll call "QL" (for quantifier logic).

The Symbols of QL

The primitive symbols of QL will be those of SL plus a set of predicate symbols ***F***, ***G***, ***H***, and so on, a set of variables ***x***, ***y***, ***z***, and so on, and the symbol ***U***, used to denote the *universal quantifier*.

In addition, we introduce the symbol *U* into the metalanguage to denote the symbol ***U*** of the object language, the symbol *u* as a metalanguage variable ranging over the object language variables **x**, **y**, **z**, and also the symbol "∃", which is introduced by means of the following definition:

"$(\exists u)P$" is defined as an abbreviation for "$\sim(Uu)\sim P$".

The Axioms of QL

Let's take infinitely many formulas as axioms of QL, and introduce five axiom patterns in the metalanguage, using the letters *P*, *Q*, and *R* as formula variables, as before, and the letters *u* and *w* as metalinguistic variables ranging over the object language individual variables ***x***, ***y***, ***z***, and so on:

(A1): $(P \supset (Q \supset P))$

(A2): $((P \supset (Q \supset R)) \supset ((P \supset Q) \supset (P \supset R)))$

(A3): $((\sim Q \supset \sim P) \supset ((\sim Q \supset P) \supset Q))$

(A4): $(Uu)(P \supset Q) \supset (P \supset (Uu)Q)$, where *P* contains no free occurrence of the variable *u*.

(A5): $(Uu)P \supset Q$, where *Q* results from *P* by the replacement of all free occurrences of *u* in *P* by *w*, and *w* occurs free in *Q* at all places at which *u* occurs free in *P*.†

---

* It is possible to construct a simpler axiom system for sentential logic, but the cost is even lengthier proofs and formulas.

† (A5) corresponds to the rule **UI** introduced in Chapter Six.

The Inference Rules of QL

We introduce (into the metalanguage) two rules of inference for QL:

(R1): If $(P \supset Q)$ and P are either axioms or theorems of QL, then Q may be inferred from them.

(R2): If P is an axiom or theorem of QL, then $(Uu)P$ may be inferred from P.*

Properties of QL

It has been proved that QL is complete (in the sense that all sentence forms expressible in QL that are theorems of logic are provable as theorems of QL), consistent, and expressively complete. In addition, it has been proved that the axioms of QL are independent. However, not only is there no known decision procedure for QL, but it has been proved that *there cannot be such a decision procedure.*† This fact is of vital importance, because the existence of a decision procedure for predicate logic would make possible the construction of a machine capable of answering all questions about predicate logic in a purely mechanical way.

6 Other Kinds of Axiom Systems

Some philosophers have held that axiom systems are the ideal way to systematize in the *sciences,* just as in logic or mathematics, although as a matter of fact very few axiom systems for science have been attempted.

Axiom systems for science differ from those for logic in several respects, the most important of which is the nature of their axioms. For instance, all the axioms of sentential logic are *tautologies* and are established without resort to observable (empirical) information or test. But the axioms of a system for a particular *science* cannot be established without making some observations. At least some axioms of a system for a physical science must be *contingent* sentences, whereas those for sentential logic all are tautologies.

Axiom systems for arithmetic are very much like those for deductive logic in some respects. For instance, they both can be established without resort to observation. But they differ from those for logic in several ways:

(1) As stated previously, we want an axiom system for arithmetic to be complete in a different sense than is required for logic. The difference stems from the fact that (roughly) systems for logic can express *contin-*

---

* (R2) of QL corresponds to the rule **UG** introduced in Chapter Six. Since QL contains infinitely many axioms, it doesn't have to contain a rule of inference similar to the rule (R2) of SL.

† The proof was first given by Alonzo Church. For details on this and related topics, see S. C. Kleene, *Introduction to Meta-Mathematics* (New York: Van Nostrand, 1952).

gent sentences while those for arithmetic cannot. And since they cannot, all of their well-formed formulas that are sentences will be either *truths of arithmetic* or *negations of truths of arithmetic*. Hence, to be complete, an axiom system for arithmetic must be such that every sentence expressible in the system is either a theorem of that system or the negation of a theorem of that system.

(2) There are axiom systems for sentential and predicate logic that have been proved to be complete. Unfortunately, not only has no completeness proof been discovered for arithmetic, but it has been proved that *there cannot be a complete axiom system for all of arithmetic*.* No matter how many axioms and theorems such a system contains, we can always find some truth of arithmetic that is not a theorem of that system. Indeed, having found such a truth, it won't help matters to add it to the list of axioms of the system, for it has been proved that no matter how many times we do this, there will always be other truths of arithmetic discoverable that are still not axioms or theorems of the system.

The proof that we cannot have a complete axiom system for arithmetic is widely regarded as one of the most important proofs about arithmetic ever constructed.†

(3) It also has been proved that *there can be no decision procedure for axiom systems for arithmetic*. Thus, just as in the case of predicate logic, we can never construct a computer that will solve all of the problems of arithmetic in a purely mechanical way.

(4) Perhaps there is some consolation in the fact that proofs of consistency have been constructed for axiom systems for certain parts of arithmetic, and that decision procedures also have been devised for portions of arithmetic.

7 *Objections to Axiom Systems*

Finally, let's note that some philosophers are less than enthusiastic concerning the construction of axiom systems. One reason for this lack of enthusiasm is that the construction of an axiom system (at least for logic) involves a certain amount of *vicious circularity*.

---

* More precisely, what has been proved is that there cannot be a complete and consistent axiom system for arithmetic. Obviously, an inconsistent system could be constructed which would be complete, but such a system would be worthless. The proof that arithmetic is essentially incomplete is by Kurt Gödel. For details, see S. C. Kleene, *Introduction to Meta-Mathematics*.

† However, it should be noted that various philosophers, including this writer, deny the significance of Gödel's proof—for different reasons that are beyond the scope of this text.

Take an axiom system for predicate logic. Suppose we want to prove that such a system is *consistent*. The trouble is that a proof of consistency (in the metalanguage) unavoidably uses the very "tools of reasoning" (such as Modus Ponens) that are taken as inference rules in the system itself. Now if these "tools of reasoning" themselves are consistent, then a proof that the object language system is consistent is worthwhile. However, if they are inconsistent, then such a proof is worthless. So no progress is made by constructing a consistency proof, since we have to believe ahead of time in the consistency of the very rules of inference that the consistency proof establishes as consistent.*

* The same is true for the *axioms* of the system. Indeed, to be precise, we should speak of the consistency of the rules of inference *and* axioms, taken as a unit.

Answers to Even-Numbered Exercise Items*

Exercise 1-1:

Items 2, 6, and 8 do not contain arguments. (Don't be fooled by the "thus" in item 8.)

4. At the present rate of consumption, the oil will be used up in 20–25 years (premise). And we're sure not going to reduce consumption in the near future (premise). So we'd better start developing solar power, windmills, and other "alternative energy sources" pretty soon (conclusion).

10. [Six-month bank certificates] are insured by an agency of the federal government (premise). [Such] a certificate enables you to lock up your 9 percent, or whatever rate you are getting for the next six months (premise). . . . someone might buy a six-month bank certificate (conclusion).

    —Richard Blodgett, *McCalls* magazine

12. You can choose to fight them in the morning—they'll kill you or enslave you (premise). You can choose to hide from them—they'll find you [and kill or enslave you] (premise). Or you can take their victory from them [commit suicide]. They will remember you (premise). [Therefore, commit suicide and be remembered] (implied conclusion).

Exercise 1-2:

2. Yes, because the conclusion of such an argument makes a claim not contained in its premises.
4. Yes, if one or more of its premises are false.
6. No. A deductively valid argument with true premises guarantees the truth of its conclusion, because the conclusion already is said (usually implicitly) in saying the premises.
8. No, because a sound argument is one that is deductively valid and has all true premises, and a deductively valid argument containing all true premises must have a true conclusion.
10. Conclusions. *Example:* Since John will go if Lisa does, and Lisa is going to go (premises), it *must* be that John will go (conclusion).
12. The context of discovery has to do with how we think of or discover conclusions; the context of justification with how we *justify* accepting conclusions. Only the latter is the domain of logic.

Exercise 2-1:

2, 6, and 10 are correctly symbolized by the dot.

---

* Except where inappropriate to supply answers.

Exercise 2-2:

2. a, b, d
4. a, b, d, h, j
6. a, b, d, e, k, l
8. a, b, c, f, g, o
10. a, b, c, f, n

Exercise 2-3:

2. p, $p \vee q$, $p \vee (q \cdot r)$
4. p, $\sim p$, $\sim (p \supset q)$
   $\sim[(p \equiv q) \supset r]$
6. p, $p \supset q$, $\sim p \supset q$, $p \supset (q \supset r)$
   $\sim p \supset (q \supset r)$, $\sim p \supset (q \supset p)$

Exercise 2-4:

2. Yes. For example, the sentence $A \vee B$ is a substitution instance of p and of $p \vee q$.
4. *But, however,* and many others.
6. *Compound.* It says the same thing as "Archie Leach is a public figure, and Cary Grant is a public figure."
8. *Atomic.*

Exercise 3-1:

2. $(R \cdot A) \vee (\sim R \cdot \sim A)$
4. $(\sim A \cdot \sim R) \supset C$
6. $C \equiv (\sim R \cdot \sim A)$
8. $[(\sim R \supset \sim A) \cdot (\sim A \supset \sim R)] \cdot C$
10. $(S \cdot \sim W) \supset (M \cdot D)$
12. $(S \cdot M) \equiv (A \vee R)$
14. $(\sim R \cdot \sim A) \supset [(\sim M \cdot D) \cdot \sim L]$

Exercise 3-2:

Remember, of course, that there are many other correct answers. For example, another correct answer for item 6 would be "Jerry watched neither the LLF nor Dallas".

2. Jerry either didn't watch the "*Late Late Flick*" or he did watch "*Dallas*".
4. It isn't true that Jerry watched either the "*LLF*" or "*Dallas*".
6. Jerry didn't watch the "*LLF*", and he didn't watch "*Dallas*" either.
8. Jerry didn't watch the "*LLF*" or he didn't watch "*Dallas*".
10. If Jerry speaks grammatically, he doesn't say "He don't".
12. If Jerry isn't a male chauvinist, then he doesn't always pay on dates.
14. If Jerry always pays on dates, then he's a male chauvinist, but Freda will go out with him anyway.
16. If Jerry isn't a male chauvinist and doesn't pay on dates, then Freda won't go out with him and he'll watch the "*LLF*".
18. If Jerry always pays on dates but Freda won't go out with him, then he's a male chauvinist.
20. If Jerry doesn't speak grammatically or if he doesn't always pay on dates, then Freda won't go out with him.
22. Supposing Jerry says "He don't" and doesn't always pay on dates, then he doesn't always speak grammatically and isn't a male chauvinist.

24. If Jerry doesn't say "He don't" and always pays on dates, then it isn't true both that he speaks ungrammatically and is a male chauvinist, *and* Freda will go out with him.

Exercise 3-3:

2. $H \supset J$
4. $J \supset H$
6. $P \equiv \sim N$
8. $\sim D \equiv \sim(P \vee \sim N)$

Exercise 3-4:

2. True
4. False
6. True
8. False
10. False

Exercise 3-5:

2. Contradictory
4. Contingent
6. Contingent
8. Contradictory
10. Tautologous

Exercise 3-6:

2. F-true: 2 is true
   F-false, G-true: 2 is false
   /∴ 2 is a material conditional
4. F-true: 4 is true
   F & G false: 4 is false
   /∴ 4 is a material conditional
6. M true: 6 is true
   M false: 6 is true
   /∴ 6 is a logical conditional
8. M-true: 8 is false
   M & K false: 8 is true
   /∴ 8 is a material conditional
10. 10 is true under all four truth possibilities.
    /∴ 10 is a logical equivalence

Exercise 3-7:

2. No.
4. (1) Whole 3rd line of truth table analysis (p-false, q-true) omitted.
   (2) Line 1: first p-true, 2nd p-false. both should be true.
   (3) Line 2: first p-true, 2nd p-false. both should be true.
   (4) Line 4: first p-false, 2nd p-true both should be false.
   (5) Line 4: (false $\supset$ false) should be true, not false.

Exercise 4-1:

(2) 5. 1,3 **DS**
6. 2,5 **MP**
7. 4,6 **DS**

(4) 6. 1,3 **HS**
7. 5,6 **MP**
8. 2,4 **DS**
9. 7,8 **MT**

(6) 5. 3,4 **DS**
6. 2,5 **MP**
7. 3,6 **MP**
8. 1,7 **MT**

Exercise 4-2:

(2)	4.	$\sim R$	1,3 **MT**
	5.	$\sim T$	2,4 **MT**
(4)	5.	$A \vee B$	1,4 **MP**
	6.	A	2,5 **DS**
	7.	D	3,6 **MP**
(6)	5.	$\sim D$	2,4 **DS**
	6.	$\sim D \supset (B \supset C)$	1,3 **HS**
	7.	$B \supset C$	5,6 **MP**
	8.	$\sim B$	2,7 **MT**

Exercise 4-3:

(2) 4. 2, **Simp**
5. 1,3 **HS**
6. 4,5 **MP**
7. 2, **Simp**
8. 6,7 **Conj**

(4) 4. 2, **Simp**
5. 1,4 **MT**
6. 3,5 **DS**

(6) 5. 1,4 **HS**
6. 2, **Add**
7. 5,6 **MP**
8. 3,7 **DS**
9. 2,8 **Conj**

Exercise 4-4:

(2)	4.	A	1,3 **MP**
	5.	$B \cdot D$	2,4 **MP**
	6.	B	5, **Simp**
(4)	4.	$F \supset G$	1,3 **DS**
	5.	$\sim F$	2,4 **MT**
(6)	4.	$A \vee \sim D$	2, **Add**
	5.	$R \cdot S$	3,4 **MP**
	6.	$(R \cdot S) \vee B$	5, **Add**
(8)	5.	D	1,3 **DS**
	6.	$D \vee U$	5, **Add**
	7.	C	4,6 **MP**
	8.	$C \vee A$	7, **Add**
	9.	L	2,8 **MP**
(10)	6.	$\sim(D \cdot E)$	2, **Simp**
	7.	$\sim A$	4,6 **DS**
	8.	$\sim A \cdot \sim(D \cdot E)$	6,7 **Conj**
	9.	$B \supset \sim D$	1,8 **MP**
	10.	$B \vee E$	5,6 **MP**
	11.	$\sim D \vee F$	3,9,10 **CD**

Exercise 4-5:

(2)
4. 1, **DN**
5. 3, **Comm**
6. 4,5 **MT**
7. 2, **DeM**
8. 6,7 **DS**

(4)
3. 1, **Assoc**
4. 2, **Dist**
5. 4, **Simp**
6. 4, **Simp**
7. 3,5 **DS**
8. 7, **Comm**
9. 6,8 **Conj**
10. 9, **Dist**

Exercise 4-6:

(2)
4. 2,3 **Conj**
5. 4, **DeM**
6. 1, **DN**
7. 6, **Contra**
8. 7, **Impl**
9. 8, **DN**
10. 5,9 **MT**

(4)
4. 1, **Equiv**
5. 2, **Impl**
6. 5, **DN**
7. 3, **Comm**
8. 6,7 **Conj**
9. 8, **Dist**
10. 9, **DN**
11. 10, **DN**
12. 11, **DeM**
13. 4,12 **DS**
14. 13, **Simp**

Exercise 4-7:

(2)	3.	$\sim(R \cdot S)$	1, **DeM**
	4.	$\sim A$	2,3 **MT**
(4)	3.	$\sim B \vee \sim\sim C$	2, **DeM**
	4.	$\sim B \vee C$	3, **DN**
	5.	$B \supset C$	4, **Impl**
	6.	$A \supset C$	1,5 **HS**
(6)	4.	$\sim H \vee \sim G$	2, **DeM**
	5.	$\sim\sim H$	3, **DN**
	6.	$\sim G$	4,5 **DS**
	7.	$\sim F$	1,6 **MT**
(8)	2.	$(M \supset N) \cdot (N \supset M)$	1, **Equiv**
	3.	$N \supset M$	2, **Simp**
	4.	$\sim N \vee M$	3, **Impl**
(10)	4.	$\sim A$	1,3 **DS**
	5.	$\sim A \vee \sim\sim B$	4, **Add**
	6.	$\sim(A \cdot \sim B)$	5, **DeM**
	7.	$\sim C$	2,6 **MP**
(12)	4.	$[(A \vee B) \supset C] \cdot [C \supset (A \vee B)]$	2, **Equiv**
	5.	$C \supset (A \vee B)$	4, **Simp**
	6.	$\sim A \cdot \sim B$	1,3 **Conj**
	7.	$\sim(A \vee B)$	6, **DeM**
	8.	$\sim C$	5,7 **MT**
	9.	$\sim C \vee \sim D$	8, **Add**
	10.	$\sim(C \cdot D)$	9, **DeM**

(14)	5.	$\sim(B \vee D)$	3,4 **MT**
	6.	$\sim B \cdot \sim D$	5, **DeM**
	7.	$\sim B$	6, **Simp**
	8.	$\sim A$	1,7 **MT**
	9.	$\sim D$	6, **Simp**
	10.	$\sim C$	2,9 **MT**
	11.	$\sim A \cdot \sim C$	8,10 **Conj**
	12.	$\sim(A \vee C)$	11, **DeM**

Exercise 4-8:

(2)	2.	$(A \cdot B) \supset C$	1, **Exp**
	3.	$\sim C \supset \sim(A \cdot B)$	2, **Contra**
	4.	$\sim\sim C \vee \sim(A \cdot B)$	3, **Impl**
	5.	$[\sim\sim C \vee \sim(A \cdot B)] \vee \sim D$	4, **Add**
	6.	$\sim D \vee [\sim\sim C \vee \sim(A \cdot B)]$	5, **Comm**
	7.	$(\sim D \vee \sim\sim C) \vee \sim(A \cdot B)$	6, **Assoc**
	8.	$(\sim\sim C \vee \sim D) \vee \sim(A \cdot B)$	7, **Comm**
	9.	$\sim(\sim C \cdot D) \vee \sim(A \cdot B)$	8, **DeM**
	10.	$(\sim C \cdot D) \supset \sim(A \cdot B)$	9, **Impl**
	11.	$(\sim C \cdot D) \supset (\sim A \vee \sim B)$	10, **DeM**
	12.	$(\sim C \cdot D) \supset (\sim B \vee \sim A)$	11, **Comm**
	13.	$(\sim C \cdot D) \supset (B \supset \sim A)$	12, **Impl**
(4)	4.	$(D \cdot B) \supset W$	2, **Exp**
	5.	$(B \cdot D) \supset W$	4, **Comm**
	6.	$B \supset (D \supset W)$	5, **Exp**
	7.	$D \supset (D \supset W)$	1,6 **HS**
	8.	$(D \cdot D) \supset W$	7, **Exp**
	9.	$D \supset W$	8, **Taut**
	10.	$D \supset (W \supset S)$	1,3 **HS**
	11.	$(D \cdot W) \supset S$	10, **Exp**
	12.	$(W \cdot D) \supset S$	11, **Comm**
	13.	$W \supset (D \supset S)$	12, **Exp**
	14.	$D \supset (D \supset S)$	9, 13 **HS**
	15.	$(D \cdot D) \supset S$	14, **Exp**
	16.	$D \supset S$	15, **Taut**
(6)	3.	$\sim(R \vee S) \vee T$	2, **Impl**
	4.	$(\sim R \cdot \sim S) \vee T$	3, **DeM**
	5.	$T \vee (\sim R \cdot \sim S)$	4, **Comm**
	6.	$(T \vee \sim R) \cdot (T \vee \sim S)$	5, **Dist**
	7.	$T \vee \sim R$	6, **Simp**
	8.	$\sim R \vee T$	7, **Comm**
	9.	$R \supset T$	8, **Impl**
	10.	$[K \cdot (L \vee M)] \supset R$	1, **Exp**

	11.	$[(L \vee M) \cdot K] \supset R$	10, **Comm**
	12.	$(L \vee M) \supset (K \supset R)$	11, **Exp**
	13.	$\sim(L \vee M) \vee (K \supset R)$	12, **Impl**
	14.	$(\sim L \cdot \sim M) \vee (K \supset R)$	13, **DeM**
	15.	$(K \supset R) \vee (\sim L \cdot \sim M)$	14, **Comm**
	16.	$[(K \supset R) \vee \sim L] \cdot [(K \supset R) \vee \sim M]$	15, **Dist**
	17.	$(K \supset R) \vee \sim M$	16, **Simp**
	18.	$\sim M \vee (K \supset R)$	17, **Comm**
	19.	$M \supset (K \supset R)$	18, **Impl**
	20.	$(M \cdot K) \supset R$	19, **Exp**
	21.	$(M \cdot K) \supset T$	9,20 **HS**
	22.	$(K \cdot M) \supset T$	21, **Comm**
	23.	$K \supset (M \supset T)$	22, **Exp**
(8)	3.	$\sim A \vee B$	1, **Impl**
	4.	$(\sim A \vee B) \vee D$	3, **Add**
	5.	$\sim A \vee (B \vee D)$	4, **Assoc**
	6.	$(B \vee D) \vee \sim A$	5, **Comm**
	7.	$\sim C \vee D$	2, **Impl**
	8.	$(\sim C \vee D) \vee B$	7, **Add**
	9.	$\sim C \vee (D \vee B)$	8, **Assoc**
	10.	$\sim C \vee (B \vee D)$	9, **Comm**
	11.	$(B \vee D) \vee \sim C$	10, **Comm**
	12.	$[(B \vee D) \vee \sim A] \cdot [(B \vee D) \vee \sim C]$	6,11 **Conj**
	13.	$(B \vee D) \vee (\sim A \cdot \sim C)$	12, **Dist**
	14.	$(\sim A \cdot \sim C) \vee (B \vee D)$	13, **Comm**
	15.	$\sim(A \vee C) \vee (B \vee D)$	14, **DeM**
	16.	$(A \vee C) \supset (B \vee D)$	15, **Impl**
(10)	4.	$\sim E \cdot \sim F$	2, **DeM**
	5.	$\sim E$	4, **Simp**
	6.	$C \supset (\sim\sim E \vee A)$	3, **DN**
	7.	$C \supset (\sim E \supset A)$	6, **Impl**
	8.	$(C \cdot \sim E) \supset A$	7, **Exp**
	9.	$(\sim E \cdot C) \supset A$	8, **Comm**
	10.	$\sim E \supset (C \supset A)$	9, **Exp**
	11.	$C \supset A$	5,10 **MP**
	12.	$\sim C \vee A$	11, **Impl**
	13.	$(\sim C \vee A) \vee B$	12, **Add**
	14.	$\sim C \vee (A \vee B)$	13, **Assoc**
	15.	$(A \vee B) \vee \sim C$	14, **Comm**
	16.	$\sim D \vee \sim\sim(E \vee B)$	1, **DeM**

17.	$\sim D \vee (E \vee B)$	16, **DN**
18.	$(E \vee B) \vee \sim D$	17, **Comm**
19.	$E \vee (B \vee \sim D)$	18, **Assoc**
20.	$(B \vee \sim D)$	5,19 **DS**
21.	$(B \vee \sim D) \vee A$	20, **Add**
22.	$A \vee (B \vee \sim D)$	21, **Comm**
23.	$(A \vee B) \vee \sim D$	22, **Assoc**
24.	$[(A \vee B) \vee \sim C] \cdot [(A \vee B) \vee \sim D]$	15,23 **Conj**
25.	$(A \vee B) \vee (\sim C \cdot \sim D)$	24, **Dist**
26.	$(A \vee B) \vee \sim(C \vee D)$	25, **DeM**
27.	$\sim\sim(A \vee B) \vee \sim(C \vee D)$	26, **DN**
28.	$\sim(\sim A \cdot \sim B) \vee \sim(C \vee D)$	27, **DeM**

Exercise 4-9:

2. Equivalence argument forms may be used on parts of lines because in doing so we replace part of a line with another formula having the same truth value, so that the truth value of the whole line remains the same.

4. Because some substitution instances of some invalid argument forms are valid, since they also are substitution instances of some valid argument form or other. *Example:* The valid argument $A \supset B$, A /∴ B, a substitution instance of the invalid form p, q /∴ r, also is a substitution instance of the valid argument form *Modus Ponens.*

Exercise 5-1:

(2)	1.	$A \supset (B \cdot C)$	/∴ $A \supset C$
	→2.	A	**AP**
	3.	$B \cdot C$	1,2 **MP**
	4.	C	3, **Simp**
	5.	$A \supset C$	2–4, **CP**
(4)	1.	$A \supset (B \supset C)$	
	2.	$\sim C$	/∴ $A \supset \sim B$
	→3.	A	**AP**
	4.	$B \supset C$	1,3 **MP**
	5.	$\sim B$	2,4 **MT**
	6.	$A \supset \sim B$	3–5, **CP**
(6)	1.	$A \supset (B \supset C)$	
	2.	$A \supset B$	/∴ $A \supset C$
	→3.	A	**AP**
	4.	B	2,3 **MP**
	5.	$B \supset C$	1,3 **MP**
	6.	C	4,5 **MP**
	7.	$A \supset C$	3–6, **CP**

(8)

1.	$(A \cdot B) \supset C$	
2.	$(B \cdot C) \supset D$	$/\therefore (A \cdot B) \supset D$
→3.	$A \cdot B$	**AP**
4.	C	1,3 **MP**
5.	B	3, **Simp**
6.	$B \cdot C$	4,5 **Conj**
7.	D	2,6 **MP**
8.	$(A \cdot B) \supset D$	3–7, **CP**

(10)

1.	$A \supset (B \supset C)$	
2.	$C \supset D$	$/\therefore A \supset (B \supset D)$
→3.	A	**AP**
→4.	B	**AP**
5.	$B \supset C$	1,3 **MP**
6.	C	4,5 **MP**
7.	D	2,6 **MP**
8.	$B \supset D$	4–7, **CP**
9.	$A \supset (B \supset D)$	3–8, **CP**

Exercise 5-2:

(2)

1.	$A \supset (B \supset C)$	$/\therefore (\sim C \cdot D) \supset (B \supset \sim A)$
→2.	$\sim C \cdot D$	**AP**
3.	$\sim C$	2, **Simp**
4.	$(A \cdot B) \supset C$	1, **Exp**
5.	$\sim(A \cdot B)$	3,4 **MT**
6.	$\sim A \vee \sim B$	5, **DeM**
7.	$\sim B \vee \sim A$	6, **Comm**
8.	$B \supset \sim A$	7, **Impl**
9.	$(\sim C \cdot D) \supset (B \supset \sim A)$	2–8, **CP**

(4)

1.	$D \supset B$	
2.	$D \supset (B \supset W)$	
3.	$B \supset (W \supset S)$	$/\therefore D \supset S$
→4.	D	**AP**
5.	$B \supset W$	2,4 **MP**
6.	B	1,4 **MP**
7.	$W \supset S$	3,6 **MP**
8.	W	5,6 **MP**
9.	S	7,8 **MP**
10.	$D \supset S$	4–9, **CP**

(6)	1.	$K \supset [(L \vee M) \supset R]$	
	2.	$(R \vee S) \supset T$	$/\therefore K \supset (M \supset T)$
	3.	K	**AP**
	4.	M	**AP**
	5.	$(L \vee M) \supset R$	1,3 **MP**
	6.	$M \vee L$	4, **Add**
	7.	$L \vee M$	6, **Comm**
	8.	R	5,7 **MP**
	9.	$R \vee S$	8, **Add**
	10.	T	2,9 **MP**
	11.	$M \supset T$	4–10, **CP**
	12.	$K \supset (M \supset T)$	3–11, **CP**

(8)	1.	$A \supset B$	
	2.	$C \supset D$	$/\therefore (A \vee C) \supset (B \vee D)$
	3.	$A \vee C$	**AP**
	4.	$B \vee D$	1,2,3 **CD**
	5.	$(A \vee C) \supset (B \vee D)$	3–4, **CP**

(10)	1.	$\sim[D \cdot \sim(E \vee B)]$	
	2.	$\sim(E \vee F)$	
	3.	$C \supset (E \vee A)$	$/\therefore \sim(\sim A \cdot \sim B) \vee \sim(C \vee D)$
	4.	$\sim A \cdot \sim B$	**AP**
	5.	$\sim E \cdot \sim F$	2, **DeM**
	6.	$\sim(E \vee A) \supset \sim C$	3, **Contra**
	7.	$(\sim E \cdot \sim A) \supset \sim C$	6, **DeM**
	8.	$\sim E$	5, **Simp**
	9.	$\sim A$	4, **Simp**
	10.	$\sim E \cdot \sim A$	8,9 **Conj**
	11.	$\sim C$	7,10 **MP**
	12.	$\sim D \vee \sim\sim(E \vee B)$	1, **DeM**
	13.	$\sim D \vee (E \vee B)$	12, **DN**
	14.	$(\sim D \vee E) \vee B$	13, **Assoc**
	15.	$\sim B$	4, **Simp**
	16.	$\sim D \vee E$	14,15 **DS**
	17.	$\sim D$	8,16 **DS**
	18.	$\sim C \cdot \sim D$	11,17 **Conj**
	19.	$\sim(C \vee D)$	18, **DeM**
	20.	$(\sim A \cdot \sim B) \supset \sim(C \vee D)$	4–19, **CP**
	21.	$\sim(\sim A \cdot \sim B) \vee \sim(C \vee D)$	20, **Impl**

Exercise 5-3:

(2)

(2)	1.	$\sim A \supset B$	
	2.	$\sim(\sim A \cdot B)$	$/ \therefore A$
	→3.	$\sim A$	**AP**
	4.	B	1,3 **MP**
	5.	$\sim\sim A \vee \sim B$	2, **DeM**
	6.	$A \vee \sim B$	5, **DN**
	7.	$\sim B$	3,6 **DS**
	8.	$B \cdot \sim B$	4,7 **Conj**
	9.	A	3–8, **IP**
(4)	1.	$A \vee (\sim B \cdot C)$	
	2.	$B \supset \sim A$	$/ \therefore \sim B$
	→3.	B	**AP**
	4.	$\sim A$	2,3 **MP**
	5.	$\sim B \cdot C$	1,4 **DS**
	6.	$\sim B$	5, **Simp**
	7.	$B \cdot \sim B$	3,6 **Conj**
	8.	$\sim B$	3–7, **IP**
(6)	1.	$(A \cdot B) \supset C$	
	2.	$\sim A \supset C$	
	3.	B	$/ \therefore C$
	→4.	$\sim C$	**AP**
	5.	$\sim\sim A$	2,4 **MT**
	6.	A	5, **DN**
	7.	$A \cdot B$	3,6 **Conj**
	8.	C	1,7 **MP**
	9.	$C \cdot \sim C$	4,8 **Conj**
	10.	C	4–9, **IP**
(8)	1.	$A \supset (B \supset C)$	
	2.	$A \supset B$	
	3.	$\sim C \supset (A \vee D)$	$/ \therefore C \vee D$
	→4.	$\sim(C \vee D)$	**AP**
	5.	$\sim C \cdot \sim D$	4, **DeM**
	6.	$\sim C$	5, **Simp**
	7.	$A \vee D$	3,6 **MP**
	8.	$\sim D$	5, **Simp**
	9.	A	7,8 **DS**
	10.	B	2,9 **MP**
	11.	$B \supset C$	1,9 **MP**
	12.	C	10,11 **MP**

	13.	$C \cdot \sim C$	6,12 **Conj**
	14.	$C \vee D$	4–13 **IP**
(10)	1.	$C \supset [D \vee \sim(A \vee B)]$	
	2.	$\sim A \supset B$	$/\therefore \sim D \supset \sim C$
	→3.	$\sim(\sim D \supset \sim C)$	**AP**
	4.	$\sim(\sim\sim D \vee \sim C)$	3, **Impl**
	5.	$(\sim\sim\sim D \cdot \sim\sim C)$	4, **DeM**
	6.	$\sim D \cdot C$	5, **DN** (twice)
	7.	C	6, **Simp**
	8.	$D \vee \sim(A \vee B)$	1,7 **MP**
	9.	$\sim D$	6, **Simp**
	10.	$\sim(A \vee B)$	8,9 **DS**
	11.	$\sim A \cdot \sim B$	10, **DeM**
	12.	$\sim A$	11, **Simp**
	13.	B	2,12 **MP**
	14.	$\sim B$	11, **Simp**
	15.	$B \cdot \sim B$	13,14 **Conj**
	16.	$\sim D \supset \sim C$	3–15, **IP**

Exercise 5-4:

(2) Without **IP**:

1.	$H \supset (A \supset B)$	
2.	$\sim C \supset (H \vee B)$	
3.	$H \supset A$	$/\therefore C \vee B$
4.	$(H \cdot A) \supset B$	1, **Exp**
5.	$(A \cdot H) \supset B$	4, **Comm**
6.	$A \supset (H \supset B)$	5, **Exp**
7.	$H \supset (H \supset B)$	3,6 **HS**
8.	$(H \cdot H) \supset B$	7, **Exp**
9.	$H \supset B$	8, **Taut**
10.	$\sim C \supset (B \vee H)$	2, **Comm**
11.	$\sim C \supset (\sim\sim B \vee H)$	10, **DN**
12.	$\sim C \supset (\sim B \supset H)$	11, **Impl**
13.	$(\sim C \cdot \sim B) \supset H$	12, **Exp**
14.	$(\sim C \cdot \sim B) \supset B$	9,13 **HS**
15.	$\sim C \supset (\sim B \supset B)$	14, **Exp**
16.	$\sim C \supset (\sim\sim B \vee B)$	15, **Impl**
17.	$\sim C \supset (B \vee B)$	16, **DN**
18.	$\sim C \supset B$	17, **Taut**
19.	$\sim\sim C \vee B$	18, **Impl**
20.	$C \vee B$	19, **DN**

(2) With **IP**:

1.	$H \supset (A \supset B)$	
2.	$\sim C \supset (H \vee B)$	
3.	$H \supset A$	$/\therefore C \vee B$
→4.	$\sim(C \vee B)$	**AP**
5.	$\sim C \cdot \sim B$	4, **DeM**
6.	$\sim C$	5, **Simp**
7.	$H \vee B$	2,6 **MP**
8.	$\sim B$	5, **Simp**
9.	H	7,8 **DS**
10.	A	3,9 **MP**
11.	$A \supset B$	1,9 **MP**
12.	B	10,11 **MP**
13.	$B \cdot \sim B$	8,12 **Conj**
14.	$C \vee B$	4–13, **IP**

(4) Without **IP**;

1.	$(A \vee B) \supset (C \supset {\sim}D)$	
2.	$(D \vee E) \supset (A \cdot C)$	$/\therefore {\sim}D$
3.	${\sim}(D \vee E) \vee (A \cdot C)$	2, **Impl**
4.	$({\sim}D \cdot {\sim}E) \vee (A \cdot C)$	3, **DeM**
5.	$(A \cdot C) \vee ({\sim}D \cdot {\sim}E)$	4, **Comm**
6.	$[(A \cdot C) \vee {\sim}D] \cdot [(A \cdot C) \vee {\sim}E]$	5, **Dist**
7.	$(A \cdot C) \vee {\sim}D$	6, **Simp**
8.	${\sim}D \vee (A \cdot C)$	7, **Comm**
9.	$({\sim}D \vee A) \cdot ({\sim}D \vee C)$	8, **Dist**
10.	${\sim}D \vee A$	9, **Simp**
11.	$({\sim}D \vee A) \vee B$	10, **Add**
12.	${\sim}D \vee (A \vee B)$	11, **Assoc**
13.	$D \supset (A \vee B)$	12, **Impl**
14.	$D \supset (C \supset {\sim}D)$	1,13 **HS**
15.	$(D \cdot C) \supset {\sim}D$	14, **Exp**
16.	$(C \cdot D) \supset {\sim}D$	15, **Comm**
17.	$C \supset (D \supset {\sim}D)$	16, **Exp**
18.	${\sim}D \vee C$	9, **Simp**
19.	$D \supset C$	18, **Impl**
20.	$D \supset (D \supset {\sim}D)$	17,19 **HS**
21.	$(D \cdot D) \supset {\sim}D$	20, **Exp**
22.	$D \supset {\sim}D$	21, **Taut**
23.	${\sim}D \vee {\sim}D$	22, **Impl**
24.	${\sim}D$	23, **Taut**

(4) With **IP**:

1.	$(A \vee B) \supset (C \supset {\sim}D)$	
2.	$(D \vee E) \supset (A \cdot C)$	$/\therefore {\sim}D$
→3.	${\sim}{\sim}D$	**AP**
4.	D	3, **DN**
5.	$D \vee E$	4, **Add**
6.	$A \cdot C$	2,5 **MP**
7.	A	6, **Simp**
8.	$A \vee B$	7, **Add**
9.	$C \supset {\sim}D$	1,8 **MP**
10.	C	6, **Simp**
11.	${\sim}D$	9,10 **MP**
12.	$D \cdot {\sim}D$	4,11 **Conj**
13.	${\sim}D$	3–12, **IP**

(6) Without **IP**:

1.	$(L \vee N) \supset (F \cdot P)$	p
2.	$F \supset (H \cdot K)$	p
3.	$H \supset ({\sim}L \cdot M)$	p $/\therefore {\sim}L$
4.	${\sim}(L \vee N) \vee (F \cdot P)$	1, **Impl**
5.	$[{\sim}(L \vee N) \vee F] \cdot [{\sim}(L \vee N) \vee P]$	4, **Dist**
6.	${\sim}(L \vee N) \vee F$	5, **Simp**
7.	$F \vee {\sim}(L \vee N)$	6, **Comm**
8.	$F \vee ({\sim}L \cdot {\sim}N)$	7, **DeM**
9.	$(F \vee {\sim}L) \cdot (F \vee {\sim}N)$	8, **Dist**
10.	$F \vee {\sim}L$	9, **Simp**
11.	${\sim}L \vee F$	10, **Comm**
12.	$L \supset F$	11, **Impl**
13.	$L \supset (H \cdot K)$	2,12 **HS**

(6) With **IP**:

1.	$(L \vee N) \supset (F \cdot P)$	p
2.	$F \supset (H \cdot K)$	p
3.	$H \supset ({\sim}L \cdot M)$	p $/\therefore {\sim}L$
→4.	L	**AP**
5.	$L \vee N$	4, **Add**
6.	$F \cdot P$	1,5 **MP**
7.	F	6, **Simp**
8.	$H \cdot K$	2,7 **MP**
9.	H	8, **Simp**
10.	${\sim}L \cdot M$	3,9 **MP**
11.	${\sim}L$	10, **Simp**
12.	$L \cdot {\sim}L$	4,11 **Conj**
13.	${\sim}L$	4–12 **IP**

14.	$\sim L \vee (H \cdot K)$	13, **Impl**
15.	$(\sim L \vee H) \cdot (\sim L \vee K)$	14, **Dist**
16.	$\sim L \vee H$	15, **Simp**
17.	$L \supset H$	16, **Impl**
18.	$L \supset (\sim L \cdot M)$	3,17 **HS**
19.	$\sim L \vee (\sim L \cdot M)$	18, **Impl**
20.	$(\sim L \vee \sim L) \cdot (\sim L \vee M)$	19, **Dist**
21.	$\sim L \vee \sim L$	20, **Simp**
22.	$\sim L$	21, **Taut**

Exercise 5-5:

(2) *R*, *L*, *N*—True

(4) *A*—False
B, *C*, *D*—True

(6) *P*, *R*, *S*—False
Q—True

(8) *A*, *B*, *C*, *E*—False
D—True

(10) *R*, *T*—True
Q, *S*, *W*, *N*—False
P—True or False

Exercise 5-6:

(2)	1.	$\sim A \vee B$	*p*
	2.	$\sim B \vee \sim A$	*p*
	3.	A	*p*
	4.	$\sim\sim A$	3, **DN**
	5.	B	1,4 **DS**
	6.	$\sim B$	2,4 **DS**
	7.	$B \cdot \sim B$	5,6 **Conj**
(4)	1.	$\sim R \cdot \sim S$	*p*
	2.	$S \vee (\sim S \cdot T)$	*p*
	3.	$\sim(R \vee S) \supset \sim(S \vee T)$	*p*
	4.	$\sim(R \vee S)$	1, **DeM**
	5.	$\sim(S \vee T)$	3,4 **MP**
	6.	$\sim S \cdot \sim T$	5, **DeM**
	7.	$\sim S$	6, **Simp**
	8.	$\sim S \cdot T$	2,7 **DS**
	9.	T	8, **Simp**
	10.	$\sim T$	6, **Simp**
	11.	$T \cdot \sim T$	9,10 **Conj**
(6)	1.	$A \supset (C \supset B)$	*p*
	2.	$(B \cdot C) \vee A$	*p*
	3.	$C \vee (B \cdot A)$	*p*
	4.	$B \supset \sim C$	*p*
	5.	$D \vee B$	*p*

	6.	$B \cdot \sim A$	p
	7.	B	6, **Simp**
	8.	$\sim C$	4,7 **MP**
	9.	$B \cdot A$	3,8 **DS**
	10.	A	9, **Simp**
	11.	$\sim A$	6, **Simp**
	12.	$A \cdot \sim A$	10,11 **Conj**
(8)	1.	$A \supset (B \supset C)$	p
	2.	$\sim[\sim C \vee (A \vee \sim D)]$	p
	3.	$\sim\{\sim A \vee [C \supset (B \cdot D)]\}$	p
	4.	$\sim\sim A \cdot \sim[C \supset (B \cdot D)]$	3, **DeM**
	5.	$\sim\sim A$	4, **Simp**
	6.	$\sim\sim C \cdot \sim(A \vee \sim D)$	2, **DeM**
	7.	$\sim(A \vee \sim D)$	6, **Simp**
	8.	$\sim A \cdot \sim\sim D$	7, **DeM**
	9.	$\sim A$	8, **Simp**
	10.	$\sim A \cdot \sim\sim A$	5,9 **Conj**

Exercise 5-7:

(2) *A*—True
B, *C*—False

(4) *A*, *C*, *D*—True
E—True (or false)

(6) *P*, *Q*—False
R—True
D—True (or false)

(8) *A*, *B*—True

Exercise 5-8:

(2) $p \cdot (q \cdot r) :: r \cdot (p \cdot q)$

$p \cdot (q \cdot r)$		$r \cdot (p \cdot q)$
T(T) TTT		T(T) TTT
T F TFF		F F TTT
T F FFT		T F TFF
T F FFF		F F TFF
F F TTT		T F FFT
F F TFF		F F FFT
F F FFT		T F FFF
F F FFF		F F FFF

Since the only line (line 1) that has a **T** on the left has one on the right, and the only line (again line 1) that has a T on the right has one on the left, the argument form cannot lead us from true to false, and so is a valid argument form.

(4) $p \vee \sim q :: p \supset \sim q$

$p \vee \sim q$		$p \supset \sim q$
T T FT		T F FT
T T TF		T T TF
F F FT		F T FT
F T TF		F T TF

Since there is a line (line 1) that has a T on the left and an F on the right, the argument form may lead us from true to false, and so is invalid. (Similarly, since there is a T on the *right* of line 3, but an F on the left of that line, the argument form is invalid.)

(6)

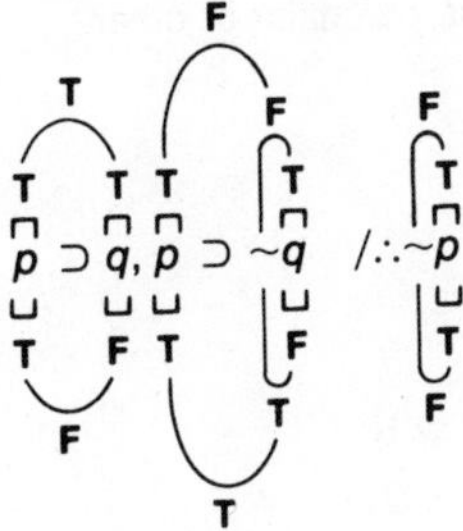

The only way the conclusion can be false is if *p* is true. But then, whether *q* is true or false, at least one premise has to be false, and so we cannot go from true premises to a false conclusion. The argument form is valid.

Exercise 5-9:

2. If the premises of an argument are *in*consistent, then (1) at least one of the premises must be false, so that we're not justified in being persuaded by the argument to accept its truth; and (2) the argument is valid, since from a contradiction, everything follows.

4. At least one of its premises must be false, since from a valid argument with all true premises only true conclusions follow.

6. If every sentence of the form $\sim(p \vee A)$ is false, then every sentence of the form $(p \vee A)$ is true. Among the sentences having this form are many in which the sentence substituted for *p* is false. An example is the sentence $(F \vee A)$, where *F* is "San Francisco is in Illinois". In such a case, since *F* is false, *A* must be true; otherwise $(F \vee A)$ would be false, and so $\sim(F \vee A)$ would be true (contrary to the supposition of the problem).

Exercise 6-1:

2. Mm

4. $\sim Mfm$

6. $Mf \supset Mm$

8. $Mfm \vee Mfc$

10. $\sim(Mcf \cdot Mcj)$

Exercise 6-2:

2. (1) x is bound.
   (2) a is an individual constant; F and G are property constants.
   (3) No free variables; a *is* within the scope of the (x) quantifier.
4. (1) y and the first x variable (not counting the x that is part of the quantifier) are bound; the second x variable is free.
   (2) No individual constants; F and G are property constants.
   (3) Free x variable is within the scope of the (y) quantifier.
6. (1) Both y variables and the first x variable are bound. The last 3 x variables are free.
   (2) F and G serve as property constants; a as an individual constant.
   (3) The three free x variables are within the scope of the (y) quantifier. Every individual constant is within the scope of some quantifier or other.

Exercise 6-3:

2. $(x)(Ex \supset Cx)$
4. $(x)(Ex \supset \sim Cx)$
6. $(x)[(Ex \cdot Cx) \supset Nx]$
8. $(x)[Cx \supset (Nx \cdot Ex)]$
10. $(x)[Ex \supset (Nx \vee \sim Cx)]$

Exercise 6-4:

2. $(x)(Sx \supset \sim Lx)$
4. $(x)(Lx \supset \sim Px)$
6. $\sim(x)(Sx \supset Lx) \supset \sim(x)(Sx \supset \sim Px)$
8. $(x)(Px \supset \sim Sx) \supset (\sim Lj \supset Sj)$
10. $(\sim Pj \cdot \sim Lj) \supset [\sim(x)(Sx \supset Px) \cdot \sim(x)(Sx \supset Lx)]$

Exercise 6-5:

2. $(\exists x)(Ax \cdot \sim Ox)$
4. $(\exists x)[(Ox \cdot Mx) \cdot \sim Ax]$
6. $(\exists x)[Mx \cdot (Ox \cdot Ex)] \cdot (\exists x)(Mx \cdot Ox)$
8. $(\exists x)[(Mx \cdot \sim Ax) \cdot (\sim Ex \cdot \sim Ox)]$
10. $\sim[(\exists x)(Ax \cdot Ox) \supset (\exists x)(Ax \cdot \sim Ex)]$

Exercise 6-6:

2. $(Fa \vee Ga) \vee (Fb \vee Gb)$
4. $[Fa \cdot (Ga \vee Ha)] \vee [Fb \cdot (Gb \vee Hb)]$
6. $\sim(Fa \cdot Ga) \vee \sim(Fb \cdot Gb)$
8. $\sim[(Fa \vee Ga) \vee (Fb \vee Gb)]$
10. $[Fa \supset \sim(Ga \cdot Ha)] \cdot [Fb \supset \sim(Gb \cdot Hb)]$

Exercise 6-7:

2. Some TV newscasters are not political experts.
4. No TV newscasters are political experts.
6. No political experts who lack a pleasant personality are TV newscasters.
8. Some TV newscasters have either a pleasant personality or political expertise.
10. If Walter Cronkite is a TV newscaster, then all TV newscasters with pleasant personalities are not political experts.

12. If all TV newscasters have pleasant personalities and are political experts, then neither Walter Cronkite nor Howard Cosell are TV newscasters.

Exercise 6-8:

2. $(x)[(Px \cdot Rx) \supset {\sim}Hx]$
4. $(x)[(Px \cdot Rx) \supset Hx]$ or $\sim(\exists x)[(Px \cdot Rx) \cdot {\sim}Hx]$
6. $(\exists x)[(Px \cdot {\sim}Rx) \cdot {\sim}Hx]$
8. $(x)\{[(Px \cdot {\sim}Rx) \cdot {\sim}Hx] \supset Wx\}$
10. $(x)[(Px \cdot Hx) \supset {\sim}Rx] \supset (\exists x)[(Px \cdot Rx) \cdot {\sim}Hx]$
12. $(x)[(Px \cdot {\sim}Hx) \supset Rx] \supset {\sim}(x)[(Px \cdot Rx) \supset Hx]$

Exercise 6-9:

2. $(\exists x)(\exists y)Sxy$
   $(Saa \vee Sab) \vee (Sba \vee Sbb)$
4. $(x)(\exists y)Sxy$
   $(Saa \vee Sab) \cdot (Sba \vee Sbb)$
6. $\sim(\exists x)(y)Sxy$
   $\sim[(Saa \cdot Sab) \vee (Sba \cdot Sbb)]$
8. $(\exists x)(y)Syx$
   $(Saa \cdot Sba) \vee (Sab \cdot Sbb)$

Exercise 6-10:

(2) 5. Invalid. The (x) quantifier did not quantify the whole line.

6. Invalid. Antecedent of line 5 does not match line 3.

7. Invalid. Can't universally generalize from a constant.

(4) 5. Invalid. Can't universally generalize from a variable introduced by **EI**.

Exercise 6-11:

2. Because $(x)(Wx \cdot Lx)$ symbolizes the completely different sentence "Everything is both an atomic war and will be lost". "All atomic wars will be lost" says in effect that if something is an atomic war, then it will be lost: $(x)(Wx \supset Lx)$.
4. Because $(\exists x)(Wx \supset Lx)$ symbolizes "There is something such that if it is an atomic war, then it is lost," an awkward sentence seldom uttered in everyday life. "Some atomic wars will be lost," says in effect that there is something that is an atomic war and will be lost: $(\exists x)(Wx \cdot Lx)$.

Exercise 7-1:

(2) 1. Inference to line 4 violates the second restriction on **EI**.

2. Inference to line 6 is invalid, because the x on line 6, supposedly obtained by **EG**, is in fact free.

(4) 1. Inference to line 3 is invalid because the y on line 3 that replaces the x on line 1 is not free.

2. Inference to line 5 is invalid because if Fy is substituted for p in a given use of **MP** we cannot also substitute Fx for p in that same use.

3. Inference to line 8 violates the restriction on **EG**, since there are not 2 y variables free in line 7 corresponding to the 2 w variables free in $(Fw \supset Gw)$.

4. Inference to line 9 is invalid because the scope of the $(\exists w)$ quantifier has been extended to cover Gy.

Exercise 7-2:

(2)	1.	$(x)(Fx \supset Gx)$	
	2.	$(x)(Ax \supset Fx)$	
	3.	$(\exists x){\sim}Gx$	$/\therefore (\exists x){\sim}Ax$
	4.	${\sim}Gx$	**3, EI**
	5.	$Ax \supset Fx$	**2, UI**
	6.	$Fx \supset Gx$	**1, UI**
	7.	$Ax \supset Gx$	5,6 **HS**
	8.	${\sim}Ax$	4,7 **MT**
	9.	$(\exists x) \sim Ax$	**8, EG**
(4)	1.	Ka	
	2.	$(x)[Kx \supset (y)Hy]$	$/\therefore (x)Hx$
	3.	$Ka \supset (y)Hy$	**2, UI**
	4.	$(y)Hy$	1,3 **MP**
	5.	Hy	**4, UI**
	6.	$(x)Hx$	**5, UG**
(6)	1.	$(\exists x)(Ax \cdot Bx)$	
	2.	$(y)(Ay \supset Cy)$	$/\therefore (\exists x)(Bx \cdot Cx)$
	3.	$Ax \cdot Bx$	**1, EI**
	4.	$Ax \supset Cx$	**2, UI**
	5.	Ax	**3, Simp**
	6.	Cx	4,5 **MP**
	7.	Bx	**3, Simp**
	8.	$Bx \cdot Cx$	6,7 **Conj**
	9.	$(\exists x)(Bx \cdot Cx)$	**8, EG**
(8)	1.	$(x)[(Fx \vee Rx) \supset {\sim}Gx]$	
	2.	$(\exists x){\sim}({\sim}Fx \cdot {\sim}Rx)$	$/\therefore (\exists y){\sim}Gy$
	3.	${\sim}({\sim}Fx \cdot {\sim}Rx)$	**2, EI**
	4.	${\sim}{\sim}Fx \vee {\sim}{\sim}Rx$	**3, DeM**
	5.	$Fx \vee Rx$	**4, DN**
	6.	$(Fx \vee Rx) \supset {\sim}Gx$	**1, UI**
	7.	${\sim}Gx$	5,6 **MP**
	8.	$(\exists y){\sim}Gy$	**7, EG**
(10)	1.	$(x)[(Rx \cdot Ax) \supset Tx]$	
	2.	Ab	
	3.	$(x)Rx$	$/\therefore Tb \cdot Rb$
	4.	Rb	**3, UI**
	5.	$(Rb \cdot Ab) \supset Tb$	**1, UI**
	6.	$Rb \cdot Ab$	2,4 **Conj**

	7.	Tb	5,6 **MP**
	8.	$Tb \cdot Rb$	4,7 **Conj**

Exercise 7-3:

(2)	1.	$(x)(Hx \supset \sim Kx)$	$/\therefore \sim(\exists y)(Hy \cdot Ky)$
	2.	$Hx \supset \sim Kx$	1, **UI**
	3.	$\sim Hx \vee \sim Kx$	2, **Impl**
	4.	$\sim(Hx \cdot Kx)$	3, **DeM**
	5.	$(y)\sim(Hy \cdot Ky)$	4, **UG**
	6.	$\sim(\exists y)(Hy \cdot Ky)$	5, **QN**
(4)	1.	$\sim(\exists x)Fx$	$/\therefore Fa \supset Ga$
	2.	$(x)\sim Fx$	1, **QN**
	3.	$\sim Fa$	2, **UI**
	4.	$\sim Fa \vee Ga$	3, **Add**
	5.	$Fa \supset Ga$	4, **Impl**
(6)	1.	$\sim(x)(Hx \vee Kx)$	
	2.	$(y)[(\sim Ky \vee Ly) \supset My]$	$/\therefore (\exists z)Mz$
	3.	$(\exists x)\sim(Hx \vee Kx)$	1, **QN**
	4.	$\sim(Hx \vee Kx)$	3, **EI**
	5.	$\sim Hx \cdot \sim Kx$	4, **DeM**
	6.	$\sim Kx$	5, **Simp**
	7.	$(\sim Kx \vee Lx) \supset Mx$	2, **UI**
	8.	$\sim Kx \vee Lx$	6, **Add**
	9.	Mx	7,8 **MP**
	10.	$(\exists z)Mz$	9, **EG**
(8)	1.	$(x)(Gx \supset Hx)$	
	2.	$(\exists x)(Ix \cdot \sim Hx)$	
	3.	$(x)(\sim Fx \vee Gx)$	$/\therefore (\exists x)(Ix \cdot \sim Fx)$
	4.	$Ix \cdot \sim Hx$	2, **EI**
	5.	$\sim Fx \vee Gx$	3, **UI**
	6.	$Gx \supset Hx$	1, **UI**
	7.	$Fx \supset Gx$	5, **Impl**
	8.	$Fx \supset Hx$	6,7 **HS**
	9.	$\sim Hx$	4, **Simp**
	10.	$\sim Fx$	8,9 **MT**
	11.	Ix	4, **Simp**
	12.	$Ix \cdot \sim Fx$	10,11 **Conj**
	13.	$(\exists x)(Ix \cdot \sim Fx)$	12, **EG**

(10)	1.	$(x)[(Rx \vee Qx) \supset Sx]$	
	2.	$(\exists y)(\sim Qy \vee \sim Ry)$	
	3.	$(\exists z)\sim(Pz \vee \sim Qz)$	$/\therefore (\exists w)Sw$
	4.	$\sim(Px \vee \sim Qx)$	3, **EI**
	5.	$\sim Px \cdot \sim\sim Qx$	4, **DeM**
	6.	$\sim\sim Qx$	5, **Simp**
	7.	Qx	6, **DN**
	8.	$Qx \vee Rx$	7, **Add**
	9.	$Rx \vee Qx$	8, **Comm**
	10.	$(Rx \vee Qx) \supset Sx$	1, **UI**
	11.	Sx	9,10 **MP**
	12.	$(\exists w)Sw$	11, **EG**
(12)	1.	$(x)[Px \supset (Ax \vee Bx)]$	
	2.	$(x)[(Bx \vee Cx) \supset Qx]$	$/\therefore (x)[(Px \cdot \sim Ax) \supset Qx]$
	3.	$Px \supset (Ax \vee Bx)$	1, **UI**
	4.	$(Bx \vee Cx) \supset Qx$	2, **UI**
	→5.	$Px \cdot \sim Ax$	**AP**
	6.	Px	5, **Simp**
	7.	$Ax \vee Bx$	3,6 **MP**
	8.	$\sim Ax$	5, **Simp**
	9.	Bx	7,8 **DS**
	10.	$Bx \vee Cx$	9, **Add**
	11.	Qx	4,10 **MP**
	12.	$(Px \cdot \sim Ax) \supset Qx$	5–11, **CP**
	13.	$(x)[(Px \cdot \sim Ax) \supset Qx]$	12, **UG**

Exercise 7-4:

(2)	1.	$(\exists x)[Fx \cdot (y)(Gy \supset Hxy)]$	$/\therefore (\exists x)[Fx \cdot (Ga \supset Hxa)]$
	2.	$Fx \cdot (y)(Gy \supset Hxy)$	1, **EI**
	3.	Fx	2, **Simp**
	4.	$(y)(Gy \supset Hxy)$	2, **Simp**
	5.	$Ga \supset Hxa$	4, **UI**
	6.	$Fx \cdot (Ga \supset Hxa)$	3,5 **Conj**
	7.	$(\exists x)[Fx \cdot (Ga \supset Hxa)]$	6, **EG**
(4)	1.	$(x)(Ax \supset Hx)$	
	2.	$(\exists x)Ax \supset \sim(\exists y)Gy$	$/\therefore (x)[(\exists y)Ay \supset \sim Gx]$
	→3.	$(\exists y)Ay$	**AP**
	4.	Ay	3, **EI**
	5.	$(\exists x)Ax$	4, **EG**

	6.	$\sim(\exists y)Gy$	2,5 **MP**
	7.	$(y)\sim Gy$	6, **QN**
	8.	$\sim Gx$	7, **UI**
	9.	$(\exists y)Ay \supset \sim Gx$	3–8, **CP**
	10.	$(x)[(\exists y)Ay \supset \sim Gx]$	9, **UG**
(6)	1.	$(x)[Ax \supset (Bx \supset \sim Cx)]$	
	2.	$\sim(\exists x)(Cx \cdot Dx) \supset (x)(Dx \supset Ex)$	$/\therefore \sim(\exists x)[Dx \cdot (\sim Ax \vee \sim Bx)] \supset (x)(Dx \supset Ex)$
	→3.	$\sim(x)(Dx \supset Ex)$	**AP**
	4.	$\sim\sim(\exists x)(Cx \cdot Dx)$	2,3 **MT**
	5.	$(\exists x)(Cx \cdot Dx)$	4, **DN**
	6.	$Cx \cdot Dx$	5, **EI**
	7.	$Ax \supset (Bx \supset \sim Cx)$	1, **UI**
	8.	Cx	6, **Simp**
	9.	$\sim\sim Cx$	8, **DN**
	10.	$(Ax \cdot Bx) \supset \sim Cx$	7, **Exp**
	11.	$\sim(Ax \cdot Bx)$	9,10 **MT**
	12.	$\sim Ax \vee \sim Bx$	11, **DeM**
	13.	Dx	6, **Simp**
	14.	$Dx \cdot (\sim Ax \vee \sim Bx)$	12,13 **Conj**
	15.	$(\exists x)[Dx \cdot (\sim Ax \vee \sim Bx)]$	14, **EG**
	16.	$\sim\sim(\exists x)[Dx \cdot (\sim Ax \vee \sim Bx)]$	15, **DN**
	17.	$\sim(x)(Dx \supset Ex) \supset \sim\sim(\exists x)[Dx \cdot (\sim Ax \vee \sim Bx)]$	3–16, **CP**
	18.	$\sim(\exists x)[Dx \cdot (\sim Ax \vee \sim Bx)] \supset (x)(Dx \supset Ex)$	17, **Contra**
(8)	1.	$(x)[(\exists y)(Ay \cdot Bxy) \supset Cx]$	
	2.	$(\exists y)\{Dy \cdot (\exists x)[(Ex \cdot Fx) \cdot Byx]\}$	
	3.	$(x)(Fx \supset Ax)$	$/\therefore (\exists x)(Cx \cdot Dx)$
	4.	$Dz \cdot (\exists x)[(Ex \cdot Fx) \cdot Bzx]$	2, **EI**
	5.	$(\exists x)[(Ex \cdot Fx) \cdot Bzx]$	4, **Simp**
	6.	$(Ew \cdot Fw) \cdot Bzw$	5, **EI**
	7.	$Ew \cdot Fw$	6, **Simp**
	8.	Fw	7, **Simp**
	9.	$Fw \supset Aw$	3, **UI**
	10.	Aw	8,9 **MP**
	11.	$(\exists y)(Ay \cdot Bzy) \supset Cz$	1, **UI**
	12.	Bzw	6, **Simp**
	13.	$Aw \cdot Bzw$	10,12 **Conj**
	14.	$(\exists y)(Ay \cdot Bzy)$	13, **EG**
	15.	Cz	11,14 **MP**

	16.	Dz	4, **Simp**
	17.	$Cz \cdot Dz$	15,16 **Conj**
	18.	$(\exists x)(Cx \cdot Dx)$	17, **EG**
(10)	1.	$(\exists x)Fx \supset (x)[Px \supset (\exists y)Qxy]$	
	2.	$(x)(y)(Qxy \supset Gx)$	/∴ $(x)[(Fx \cdot Px) \supset (\exists y)Gy]$
	→3.	$\sim(x)[(Fx \cdot Px) \supset (\exists y)Gy]$	**AP**
	4.	$(\exists x)\sim[(Fx \cdot Px) \supset (\exists y)Gy]$	3, **QN**
	5.	$\sim[(Fx \cdot Px) \supset (\exists y)Gy]$	4, **EI**
	6.	$\sim[\sim(Fx \cdot Px) \vee (\exists y)Gy]$	5, **Impl**
	7.	$\sim\sim(Fx \cdot Px) \cdot \sim(\exists y)Gy$	6, **DeM**
	8.	$\sim\sim(Fx \cdot Px)$	7, **Simp**
	9.	$Fx \cdot Px$	8, **DN**
	10.	Fx	9, **Simp**
	11.	$(\exists x)Fx$	10, **EG**
	12.	$(x)[Px \supset (\exists y)Qxy]$	1,11 **MP**
	13.	$Px \supset (\exists y)Qxy$	12, **UI**
	14.	Px	9, **Simp**
	15.	$(\exists y)Qxy$	13,14 **MP**
	16.	Qxy	15, **EI**
	17.	$(y)(Qxy \supset Gx)$	2, **UI**
	18.	$Qxy \supset Gx$	17, **UI**
	19.	Gx	16,18 **MP**
	20.	$\sim(\exists y)Gy$	7, **Simp**
	21.	$(y)\sim Gy$	20, **QN**
	22.	$\sim Gx$	21, **UI**
	23.	$Gx \cdot \sim Gx$	19,22 **Conj**
	24.	$(x)[(Fx \cdot Px) \supset (\exists y)Gy]$	3–23, **IP**

Exercise 7-5:

(2)	1.	$\sim(\exists x)Fx$	/∴ $Fa \supset Ga$
	2.	$(x)\sim Fx$	1, **QN**
	3.	$\sim Fa$	2, **UI**
	4.	$\sim Fa \vee Ga$	3, **Add**
	5.	$Fa \supset Ga$	4, **Impl**
(4)	1.	$(y)[Fy \vee (\exists x)Gx]$	
	2.	$(x)\sim Fx$	/∴ $(\exists x)Gx$
	3.	$Fy \vee (\exists x)Gx$	1, **UI**
	4.	$\sim Fy$	2, **UI**
	5.	$(\exists x)Gx$	3,4 **DS**

(6)	1.	Ka	
	2.	$(x)[Kx \supset (y)Hy]$	$/\therefore (x)Hx$
	→3.	$\sim(x)Hx$	**AP**
	4.	$(\exists x)\sim Hx$	3, **QN**
	5.	$\sim Hx$	4, **EI**
	6.	$Ka \supset (y)Hy$	2, **UI**
	7.	$(y)Hy$	1,6 **MP**
	8.	Hx	7, **UI**
	9.	$Hx \cdot \sim Hx$	8,5 **Conj**
	10.	$(x)Hx$	3–9 **IP**

(8)	1.	$\sim(\exists x)Ax$	$/\therefore (\exists x)(Ax \supset Gx)$
	→2.	$\sim(\exists x)(Ax \supset Gx)$	**AP**
	3.	$(x)\sim(Ax \supset Gx)$	2, **QN**
	4.	$(x)\sim Ax$	1, **QN**
	5.	$\sim Ax$	4, **UI**
	6.	$\sim(Ax \supset Gx)$	3, **UI**
	7.	$\sim(\sim Ax \vee Gx)$	6, **Impl**
	8.	$\sim\sim Ax \cdot \sim Gx$	7, **DeM**
	9.	$\sim\sim Ax$	8, **Simp**
	10.	$\sim Ax \cdot \sim\sim Ax$	5,9 **Conj**
	11.	$(\exists x)(Ax \supset Gx)$	2–10 **IP**

(10)	1.	$(\exists x)Rx$	
	2.	$(x)(\sim Gx \supset \sim Rx)$	
	3.	$(\exists x)Mx$	$/\therefore (\exists x)Gx \cdot (\exists x)Mx$
	→4.	$\sim[(\exists x)Gx \cdot (\exists x)Mx]$	**AP**
	5.	$\sim(\exists x)Gx \vee \sim(\exists x)Mx$	4, **DeM**
	6.	Rx	1, **EI**
	7.	$\sim Gx \supset \sim Rx$	2, **UI**
	8.	$\sim\sim Rx$	6, **DN**
	9.	$\sim\sim Gx$	7,8 **MT**
	10.	$\sim\sim(\exists x)Mx$	3, **DN**
	11.	$\sim(\exists x)Gx$	5,10 **DS**
	12.	$(x)\sim Gx$	11, **QN**
	13.	$\sim Gx$	12, **UI**
	14.	$\sim Gx \cdot \sim\sim Gx$	13,9 **Conj**
	15.	$(\exists x)Gx \cdot (\exists x)Mx$	4–14 **IP**

Exercise 7-6:

(2)	1.	$(\exists y)(x)Fxy$	$/\therefore (x)(\exists y)Fxy$
	→2.	$\sim(x)(\exists y)Fxy$	**AP**
	3.	$(\exists x)(y)\sim Fxy$	2, **QN** (twice)

	4. (y)~Fxy	3, EI
	5. (x)Fxy	1, EI
	6. Fxy	5, UI
	7. ~Fxy	4, UI
	8. Fxy · ~Fxy	6,7 **Conj**
	9. (x)(∃y)Fxy	2–8 **IP**
(4)	1. (x)[Fx ⊃ (∃y)Gxy]	
	2. (∃x)Fx	/∴ (∃x)(∃y)Gxy
	→3. ~(∃x)(∃y)Gxy	**AP**
	4. (x)(y)~Gxy	3, **QN** (twice)
	5. Fx	2, **EI**
	6. Fx ⊃ (∃y)Gxy	1, **UI**
	7. (∃y)Gxy	5,6 **MP**
	8. Gxy	7, **EI**
	9. ~Gxy	4, **UI** (twice)
	10. Gxy · ~Gxy	8,9 **Conj**
	11. (∃x)(∃y)Gxy	3–10 **IP**
(6)	1. (∃x)Ax ⊃ ~(∃y)Gy	/∴ (x)[(∃y)Ay ⊃ ~Gx]
	→2. ~(x)[(∃y)Ay ⊃ ~Gx]	**AP**
	3. (∃x)~[(∃y)Ay ⊃ ~Gx]	2, **QN**
	4. ~[(∃y)Ay ⊃ ~Gx]	3, **EI**
	5. ~[~(∃y)Ay ∨ ~Gx]	4, **Impl**
	6. (∃y)Ay · Gx	5, **DeM, DN**
	7. (∃y)Ay	6, **Simp**
	8. Ay	7, **EI**
	→9. ~(∃x)Ax	**AP**
	10. (x)~Ax	9, **QN**
	11. ~Ay	10, **UI**
	12. Ay · ~Ay	8,11 **Conj**
	13. (∃x)Ax	9,12 **IP**
	14. ~(∃y)Gy	1,13 **MP**
	15. (y)~Gy	14, **QN**
	16. ~Gx	15, **UI**
	17. Gx	6, **Simp**
	18. Gx · ~Gx	16,17 **Conj**
	19. (x)[(∃y)Ay ⊃ ~Gx]	2,18 **IP**

Exercise 8-1:

(Assume the domain of discourse to be positive integers.)

(2) Let $Fx = x > 10$, $Gx = x > 5$, $Ex = x < 15$

T 1. $(x)[(x > 10) \supset (x > 5)]$
T 2. $(x)[\sim(x > 10) \supset (x < 15)]$
F /∴ $(x)[\sim(x > 5) \supset \sim(x < 15)]$

(4) Let $Px = x$ is odd, $Qx = x$ is even, $Rx = x > 10$

T 1. $(x)\{[(x \text{ is odd}) \cdot (x \text{ is even})] \supset (x > 10)\}$
T 2. $(\exists x)[(x \text{ is even}) \cdot \sim(x > 10)]$
T 3. $(\exists x)[(x \text{ is odd}) \cdot \sim(x > 10)]$
F /∴ $(\exists x)[\sim(x \text{ is odd}) \cdot \sim(x \text{ is even})]$

(6) Let $Mx = x > 25$, $Nx = x > 20$, $Px = x > 15$, $Qx = x > 10$

T 1. $(x)\{(x > 25) \supset [(x > 20) \supset (x > 15)]\}$
T 2. $(x)[\sim(x > 10) \supset \sim(x > 15)]$
F /∴ $(x)\{\sim(x > 10) \supset [(x > 25) \lor (x > 20)]\}$

(8) Let $Ax = x > 10$, $Bx = x > 10$, $Cx = x > x$

T 1. $(\exists x)[(x > 10) \lor \sim(x > 10)]$
T 2. $(x)\{[(x > 10) \cdot \sim(x > 10)] \supset (x > x)\}$
F /∴ $(\exists x)(x > x)$

(10) Let $Fx = x = 10$, $Gxy = x > y$

T 1. $(x)[(x = 10) \supset (\exists y)(x > y)]$
T 2. $(\exists x)(x = 10)$
T 3. $(\exists x)(\exists y)(x > y)$
F /∴ $(x)(\exists y)(x > y)$ (because not true of number one).

(12) Let $Fxy = x > y$, $Gxy = x \geqq y$, $Fx = x$ is even

T 1. $(x)(y)[(x > y) \supset (x \geqq y)]$
T 2. $(\exists x)[(x \text{ is even}) \cdot (\exists y)(y \geqq x)]$
F /∴ $(x)(y)\{[(x > y) \supset (x \geqq y) \cdot (y \geqq x)]\}$

Exercise 8-2:

(2) **Consistent**

Let $Rx = x < 5$, $Mx = x > 10$

T 1. $(\exists x)[(x < 5) \lor (x > 10)]$
T 2. $(x)[(x > 10) \supset \sim(x < 5)]$

(4) **Inconsistent**

1.	$(\exists x)\sim Bx$	p
2.	$(\exists x)Bx$	p
3.	$\sim(\exists x)Kx$	p
4.	$(x)(\sim Kx \supset \sim Bx)$	p
5.	Bx	2, **EI**
6.	$(x)\sim Kx$	3, **QN**
7.	$\sim Kx$	6, **UI**
8.	$\sim Kx \supset \sim Bx$	4, **UI**
9.	$\sim Bx$	7,8 **MP**
10.	$Bx \cdot \sim Bx$	5,9 **Conj**

(6) **Inconsistent**

1.	$\sim(x)[Dx \supset (\sim Fx \lor Gx)]$	p
2.	$\sim(\exists x)[Fx \cdot (Dx \lor \sim Fx)]$	p
3.	$(x)\sim[Fx \cdot (Dx \lor \sim Fx)]$	2, **QN**
4.	$(\exists x)\sim[Dx \supset (\sim Fx \lor Gx)]$	1, **QN**
5.	$\sim[Dx \supset (\sim Fx \lor Gx)]$	4, **EI**
6.	$\sim[\sim Dx \lor (\sim Fx \lor Gx)]$	5, **Impl**

7.	$\sim\sim Dx \cdot \sim(\sim Fx \vee Gx)$	6, **DeM**
8.	$\sim\sim Dx \cdot (\sim\sim Fx \cdot \sim Gx)$	7, **DeM**
9.	$\sim[Fx \cdot (Dx \vee \sim Fx)]$	3, **UI**
10.	$\sim Fx \vee \sim(Dx \vee \sim Fx)$	9, **DeM**
11.	$\sim Fx \vee (\sim Dx \cdot \sim\sim Fx)$	10, **DeM**
12.	$(\sim Fx \vee \sim Dx) \cdot (\sim Fx \vee \sim\sim Fx)$	11, **Dist**
13.	$\sim Fx \vee \sim Dx$	12, **Simp**
14.	$\sim\sim Dx$	8, **Simp**
15.	$\sim Fx$	13,14 **DS**
16.	$\sim\sim Fx \cdot \sim Gx$	8, **Simp**
17.	$\sim\sim Fx$	16, **Simp**
18.	$\sim Fx \cdot \sim\sim Fx$	15,17 **Conj**

(8) **Inconsistent**

1.	$(x)(\exists y)(Fxy \supset Gx)$	p
2.	$\sim(x)[(y)Fxy \supset Gx]$	p
3.	$(\exists x)\sim[(y)Fxy \supset Gx]$	2 **QN**
4.	$\sim[(y)Fxy \supset Gx]$	3, **EI**
5.	$(\exists y)(Fxy \supset Gx)$	1, **UI**
6.	$Fxy \supset Gx$	5, **EI**
7.	$\sim[\sim(y)Fxy \vee Gx]$	4, **Impl**
8.	$(y)Fxy \cdot \sim Gx$	7, **DeM, DN**
9.	$(y)Fxy$	8, **Simp**
10.	Fxy	9, **UI**
11.	Gx	6,10 **MP**
12.	$\sim Gx$	8, **Simp**
13.	$Gx \cdot \sim Gx$	11,12 **Conj**

Exercise 8-3:

2. $(x)[(Dx \cdot Bx) \supset Nx]$
4. $\sim(x)(Wx \supset Fx)$
6. $(x)(Lx \supset \sim Dx)$
8. $(x)[(\exists y)(Fy \cdot Dxy) \supset Rx]$ or $(x)(y)[(Fy \cdot Dxy) \supset Rx]$
10. $(x)[(\exists y)(Fy \cdot Dxy) \supset Rx]$ or $(x)(y)[(Fy \cdot Dxy) \supset Rx]$
12. $(x)[(Jx \cdot Wx) \supset \sim Ex]$
14. $(x)[Dx \supset (Ix \equiv Mx)]$
16. $(x)\{[Px \cdot (\exists y)(Sy \cdot Cxy)] \supset Ex\}$
18. $(x)[Px \supset (\exists y)(\exists z)(Py \cdot Oxzy)]$
20. $(\exists x)\{Px \cdot (y)[Py \supset (\exists z)Oxzy]\}$
22. $(x)\{Px \supset (y)[Py \supset (\exists z)Oxzy]\}$

Exercise 8-4:

2. $(x)[(Sx \cdot Fx) \supset (\exists y)(Jy \cdot Tyx)]$
4. $(x)(Sx \supset Fx) \supset [(\exists x)(Sx \cdot Ix) \supset (\exists x)(Sx \cdot Ox)]$
6. Ambiguous: Either $(x)[(Px \cdot Hgx) \supset Hxx]$ or $(x)[Px \supset (Hgx \equiv Hxx)]$
8. $(x)\{\{Px \cdot (\exists y)(\exists z)[(Py \cdot Tz) \cdot Sxyz]\} \supset (w)(Tw \supset Sxgw)\}$

Exercise 8-5:

2. Some people believe in God.
4. Not everyone believes in God.
6. Anyone who doesn't vote is disenfranchised.
8. Not all nonvoters are disenfranchised.
10. Some people don't have any redeeming features.
12. All redeeming features are lacked by somebody (or other).
14. No one has any redeeming features.
16. If Art doesn't vote, then if everyone who doesn't vote is disenfranchised, then Art is disenfranchised.
18. Anyone who votes is the master of someone who doesn't vote.

Exercise 8-6:

(2)	→1.	$(x)Gy$	**AP**
	2.	Gy	1, **UI**
	3.	$(x)Gy \supset Gy$	1–2, **CP**
	→4.	Gy	**AP**
	5.	$(x)Gy$	4, **UG**
	6.	$Gy \supset (x)Gy$	4–5, **CP**
	7.	$[(x)Gy \supset Gy] \cdot [Gy \supset (x)Gy]$	3,6 **Conj**
	8.	$(x)Gy \equiv Gy$	7, **Equiv**
(4)	→1.	$(\exists x)(y)Fxy$	**AP**
	2.	$(y)Fxy$	1, **EI**
	3.	Fxy	2, **UI**
	4.	$(\exists x)Fxy$	3, **EG**
	5.	$(y)(\exists x)Fxy$	4, **UG**
	6.	$(\exists x)(y)Fxy \supset (y)(\exists x)Fxy$	1–5, **CP**
(6)	→1.	$(x)Fx \vee (x)Gx$	**AP**
	→2.	$\sim Fx$	**AP**
	3.	$(\exists x)\sim Fx$	2, **EG**
	4.	$\sim(x)Fx$	3, **QN**
	5.	$(x)Gx$	1,4 **DS**
	6.	Gx	5, **UI**
	7.	$\sim Fx \supset Gx$	2–6, **CP**

8.	$\sim\sim Fx \vee Gx$	7, **Impl**
9.	$Fx \vee Gx$	8, **DN**
10.	$(x)(Fx \vee Gx)$	9, **UG**
11.	$[(x)Fx \vee (x)Gx] \supset (x)(Fx \vee Gx)$	1–10, **CP**

(8)

1.	$(\exists x)(Fx \cdot Gx)$	**AP**
2.	$Fx \cdot Gx$	1, **EI**
3.	Fx	2, **Simp**
4.	$(\exists x)Fx$	3, **EG**
5.	Gx	2, **Simp**
6.	$(\exists x)Gx$	5, **EG**
7.	$(\exists x)Fx \cdot (\exists x)Gx$	4,6 **Conj**
8.	$(\exists x)(Fx \cdot Gx) \supset [(\exists x)Fx \cdot (\exists x)Gx]$	1–7, **CP**

(10)

1.	$(x)Fx \cdot P$	**AP**
2.	$(x)Fx$	1, **Simp**
3.	Fx	2, **UI**
4.	P	1, **Simp**
5.	$Fx \cdot P$	3,4 **Conj**
6.	$(x)(Fx \cdot P)$	5, **UG**
7.	$[(x)Fx \cdot P] \supset (x)(Fx \cdot P)$	1–6, **CP**
8.	$(x)(Fx \cdot P)$	**AP**
9.	$Fx \cdot P$	8, **UI**
10.	Fx	9, **Simp**
11.	$(x)Fx$	10, **UG**
12.	P	9, **Simp**
13.	$(x)Fx \cdot P$	11,12 **Conj**
14.	$(x)(Fx \cdot P) \supset [(x)Fx \cdot P]$	8–13, **CP**
15.	$7 \cdot 14$	7,14 **Conj**
16.	$[(x)Fx \cdot P] \equiv (x)(Fx \cdot P)$	15, **Equiv**

(12)

1.	$(x)(P \supset Fx)$	**AP**
2.	P	**AP**
3.	$P \supset Fx$	1, **UI**
4.	Fx	2,3 **MP**
5.	$(x)Fx$	4, **UG**
6.	$P \supset (x)Fx$	2–5, **CP**
7.	$(x)(P \supset Fx) \supset [P \supset (x)Fx]$	1–6, **CP**
8.	$P \supset (x)Fx$	**AP**
9.	P	**AP**
10.	$(x)Fx$	8,9 **MP**
11.	Fx	10, **UI**

12.	$P \supset Fx$	9–11, **CP**
13.	$(x)(P \supset Fx)$	12, **UG**
14.	$[P \supset (x)Fx] \supset (x)(P \supset Fx)$	8–13, **CP**
15.	$7 \cdot 14$	7,14 **Conj**
16.	$(x)(P \supset Fx) \equiv [P \supset (x)Fx]$	15, **Equiv**

(14)

→1.	$(\exists x)(P \cdot Fx)$	**AP**
2.	$P \cdot Fx$	1, **EI**
3.	P	2, **Simp**
4.	Fx	2, **Simp**
5.	$(\exists x)Fx$	4, **EG**
6.	$P \cdot (\exists x)Fx$	3,5 **Conj**
7.	$(\exists x)(P \cdot Fx) \supset [P \cdot (\exists x)Fx]$	1–6, **CP**
→8.	$P \cdot (\exists x)Fx$	**AP**
9.	P	8, **Simp**
10.	$(\exists x)Fx$	8, **Simp**
11.	Fx	10, **EI**
12.	$P \cdot Fx$	9,11 **Conj**
13.	$(\exists x)(P \cdot Fx)$	12, **EG**
14.	$[P \cdot (\exists x)Fx] \supset (\exists x)(P \cdot Fx)$	8–13, **CP**
15.	$7 \cdot 14$	7,14 **Conj**
16.	$(\exists x)(P \cdot Fx) \equiv [P \cdot (\exists x)Fx]$	15, **Equiv**

(16)

→1.	$(\exists x)(Fx \supset P)$	**AP**
→2.	$(x)Fx$	**AP**
3.	$Fx \supset P$	1, **EI**
4.	Fx	2, **UI**
5.	P	3,4 **MP**
6.	$(x)Fx \supset P$	2–5, **CP**
7.	$(\exists x)(Fx \supset P) \supset [(x)Fx \supset P]$	1–6, **CP**
→8.	$\sim(\exists x)(Fx \supset P)$	**AP**
9.	$(x)\sim(Fx \supset P)$	8, **QN**
10.	$\sim(Fy \supset P)$	9, **UI**
11.	$\sim(\sim Fy \vee P)$	10, **Impl**
12.	$\sim\sim Fy \cdot \sim P$	11, **DeM**
13.	$Fy \cdot \sim P$	12, **DN**
14.	Fy	13, **Simp**
15.	$(x)Fx$	14, **UG**
16.	$\sim P$	13, **Simp**
17.	$(x)Fx \cdot \sim P$	15,16 **Conj**
18.	$\sim\sim(x)Fx \cdot \sim P$	17, **DN**

19.	~[~(x)Fx ∨ P]	18, **DeM**
20.	~[(x)Fx ⊃ P]	19, **Impl**
21.	~(∃x)(Fx ⊃ P) ⊃ ~[(x)Fx ⊃ P]	8–20, **CP**
22.	[(x)Fx ⊃ P] ⊃ (∃x)(Fx ⊃ P)	21, **Contra**
23.	7 · 22	7,22 **Conj**
24.	(∃x)(Fx ⊃ P) ≡ [(x)Fx ⊃ P]	23, **Equiv**

Exercise 8-7:

2. *(x)(Tx ⊃ Rx)* symbolizes the different idea that all TV programs reach a mass audience, which might be true even though some radio programs also reach a mass audience. But "Only TV programs reach a mass audience" is false if some radio programs do. So it's correctly symbolized as *(x)(Rx ⊃ Tx)*.

4. *False.* Although it won't work in most cases, some quantified theorems of logic can be proved by truth table analysis. *Example:*

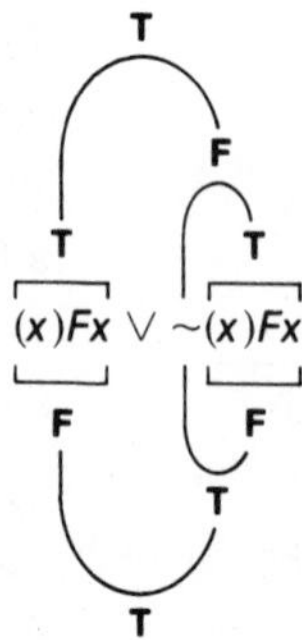

6. (1) Everyone is a better hockey player than someone (or other).

   (2) No one is a better hockey player than Wayne Gretsky.

   (3) If someone is a better hockey player than everyone, then Wayne Gretsky is a better player than himself.

Exercise 9-1:

(2)

1.	(x)(Px ⊃ Qx)	
2.	(x)(Qx ⊃ Rx)	
3.	Pa · ~Rb	/∴ ~(a = b)
→ 4.	~~(a = b)	**AP**
5.	a = b	4, **DN**
6.	Pa ⊃ Qa	1, **UI**
7.	Qa ⊃ Ra	2, **UI**
8.	Pa ⊃ Ra	6,7 **HS**
9.	Pa	3, **Simp**
10.	Ra	8,9 **MP**
11.	~Rb	3, **Simp**

	12.	$\sim Ra$	5,11 **ID**
	13.	$Ra \cdot \sim Ra$	10,12 **Conj**
	14.	$\sim(a = b)$	4–13, **IP**
(4)	1.	$(\exists x)(y)\{[\sim Fxy \supset (x = y)] \cdot Gx\}$	$/\therefore (x)\{\sim Gx \supset (\exists y)[(\sim y = x) \cdot Fyx]\}$
	2.	$\sim(\exists y)[\sim(y = z) \cdot Fyz]$	**AP**
	3.	$(y)\sim[\sim(y = z) \cdot Fyz]$	2, **QN**
	4.	$(y)\{[\sim Fwy \supset (w = y)] \cdot Gw\}$	1, **EI**
	5.	$[\sim Fwz \supset (w = z)] \cdot Gw$	4, **UI**
	6.	$\sim[\sim(w = z) \cdot Fwz]$	3, **UI**
	7.	$(w = z) \vee \sim Fwz$	6, **DeM, DN**
	8.	$\sim(w = z) \supset \sim Fwz$	7, **DN, Impl**
	9.	$\sim Fwz \supset (w = z)$	5, **Simp**
	10.	$\sim(w = z) \supset (w = z)$	8,9 **HS**
	11.	$(w = z) \vee (w = z)$	10, **Impl, DN**
	12.	$w = z$	11, **Taut**
	13.	Gw	5, **Simp**
	14.	Gz	12,13 **ID**
	15.	$\sim\sim Gz$	14, **DN**
	16.	$\sim(\exists y)[\sim(y = z) \cdot Fyz] \supset \sim\sim Gz$	2–15, **CP**
	17.	$\sim Gz \supset (\exists y)[\sim(y = z) \cdot Fyz]$	16, **Contra**
	18.	$(x)\{\sim Gx \supset (\exists y)[\sim(y = x) \cdot Fyx]\}$	17, **UG**
(6)	1.	$(x)[Fx \supset (x = a)]$	
	2.	$(x)[Mx \supset (x = b)]$	
	3.	$(\exists x)(Fx \cdot Mx)$	$/\therefore a = b$
	4.	$Fx \cdot Mx$	3, **EI**
	5.	$Fx \supset (x = a)$	1, **UI**
	6.	Fx	4, **Simp**
	7.	$x = a$	5,6 **MP**
	8.	$Mx \supset (x = b)$	2, **UI**
	9.	Mx	4, **Simp**
	10.	$x = b$	8,9 **MP**
	11.	$a = b$	7,10 **ID**

Exercise 9-2:

2. $(x)[(Sx \cdot Px) \supset (x = r)]$
4. $(x)(y)[\{[(Fx \cdot Rx) \cdot (Fy \cdot Ry)] \cdot (x \neq y)\} \supset (z)\{(Fz \cdot Rz) \supset [(z = x) \vee (z = y)]\}]$
6. $(Pr \cdot Sr) \cdot (x)[(Px \cdot Sx) \supset (x = r)]$

Exercise 9-3:

2. $(\exists x)\{Sx \cdot (y)\{[Sy \cdot x \neq y)] \supset Ixy\}\}$

4. $Sb \cdot (x)\{[Sx \cdot (x \neq b)] \supset Ibx\}$
6. $(Ib \cdot Sb) \cdot (x)\{(Ix \cdot Sx) \supset [\sim(x = b) \supset Bbx]\}$
8. $(\exists x)(\exists y)\{\{[(Cx \cdot Cy) \cdot (x \neq y)] \cdot (Rxcs \cdot Rycs)\} \cdot (z)\{Cz \supset [(z = x) \vee (z = y)]\}\}$
10. $(\exists x)\{(Sx \cdot Rxmn) \cdot (y)\{[Sy \cdot (x \neq y)] \supset Ixy\}\}$

Exercise 9-4:

2. Asymmetrical, intransitive, irreflexive
4. Asymmetrical, transitive, irreflexive
6. Symmetrical, transitive, totally reflexive
8. Nonsymmetrical, nontransitive, nonreflexive

Exercise 9-5:

2. Some say that the levels of language theory solves this paradox. For we can think of a bibliography as a very long conjunction, each entry in the bibliography being a conjunct of that conjunction. Suppose (*N*) is a bibliography of this kind. Then, on the levels of language theory, no conjunct in (*N*) can refer to itself—to talk of (*N*) itself we need to go one flight up, to a higher level language, where we can have a bibliography listing all bibliographies on a lower level. So on the levels of language theory, there cannot be a bibliography that lists all bibliographies that do not list themselves, nor indeed a bibliography that does list itself.
4. Some claim the simple theory of types solves this paradox. For on that theory, a class must be of a higher type than its members; thus there is neither a class of all classes that are members of themselves nor of all classes that are not.

Exercise 9-6:

2. (Not appropriate to answer.)
4. (Not appropriate to answer)
6. (1) *Observed*—manifest
   (2) *Solubility*—dispositional
   (3) *Green*—both
   (4) *Teach*—maniifest: *teachable*—dispositional
   (5) *Dangerous*—dispositional
   (6) *Dependable*—dispositional
   (7) *Character*—dispositional

Exercise 10-1:

2. All poor are lazy. (*PAL*, or $P\overline{L} = O$)
4. No porno flicks are erotic. (*PEE*, or $PE = O$)
6. No amateurs are professionals. (*AEP*, or $A\overline{P} = 0$)
8. Some prescription drugs are harmful. (*PIH*, or $PH \neq O$)
10. Some children are available to play the part. (*CIA*, or $CA \neq O$)
12. No persons who have dry wits are drinkers. (*WED*, or $WD = O$)
14. All persons who forget the past are sufferers from amnesia. (*FAS*, or $F\overline{S} = O$)
15. Some omnivores are not vegetarians. (*OOV*, or $O\overline{V} \neq O$)

Exercise 10-2:

(2) 1. Can't infer to the truth value of *PIM*.

2. *PEM* could be either true or false (because if one of two contraries is false, the other sometimes is true, sometimes false).

3. *POM* is true (because *PAM* and *POM* are contradictories).

(4) 1. *CES* is true (because *CIS* and *CES* are contradictories).

2. *COS* is true (because *CIS* and *COS* are subcontraries).

3. *CAS* is false (because its subalternate, *CIS*, is false).

Exercise 10-3:

(2) 2, 4—True; 3, 5—False

(4) 2, 3—Indeterminate; 4—False; 5—True

Exercise 10-4:

(2) 1, 2—True; 3, 4, 5—Indeterminate; 6—False

(4) 1, 2, 4, 5, 7, 9—Indeterminate; 3, 6—False; 8—True

Exercise 10-5:

2. a. *PEM*
   b. $PM = O$

4. a. *MOA*
   b. $M\overline{A} \neq O$

6. a. *PAJ*
   b. $P\overline{J} = O$

8. a. *LID*
   b. $LD \neq O$

Exercise 10-6:

2. a. *CEM*
   b. $CM = O$

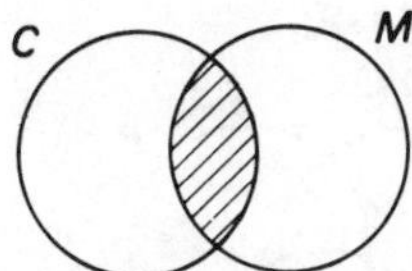

4. a. $ME\overline{C}$
   b. $M\overline{C} = O$

6. a. *TES*
   b. $TS = O$

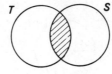

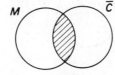

8. a. *CIP*
   b. $CP \neq O$

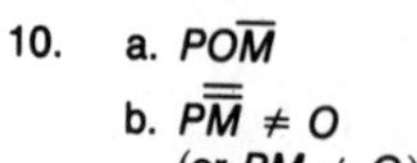

10. a. $PO\overline{M}$

    b. $P\overline{\overline{M}} \neq O$
    (or $PM \neq O$)

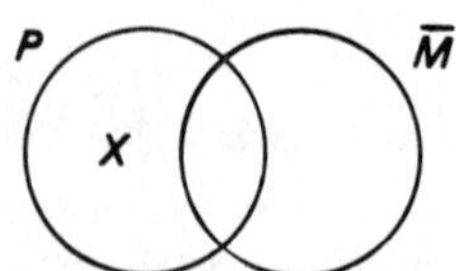

12. a. $BI\overline{H}$

    b. $B\overline{H} \neq O$

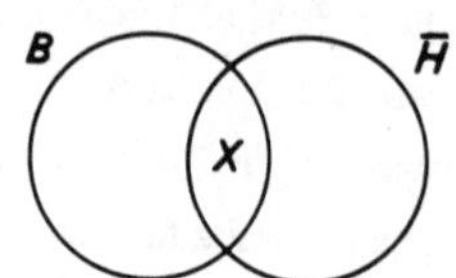

Exercise 10-7:

2. (1) and (3), since they work in both directions.

Exercise 11-1:

2. *GAR*
   GIC   *AII*-III
   /∴ *CIR*

4. *RED*
   POR   *EOI*-I
   /∴ *PID*

6. *MEJ*
   SOM   *EOO*-1
   /∴ *SOJ*

8. *SEB*
   BAC   *EAE*-IV
   /∴ *CES*

Exercise 11-2:

2. *GAR*
   GIC
   /∴ *CIR*

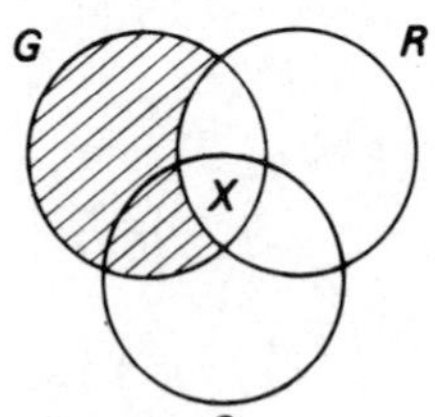

Valid: *X* is in *CR* slot

4. *RED*
   POR
   /∴ *PID*

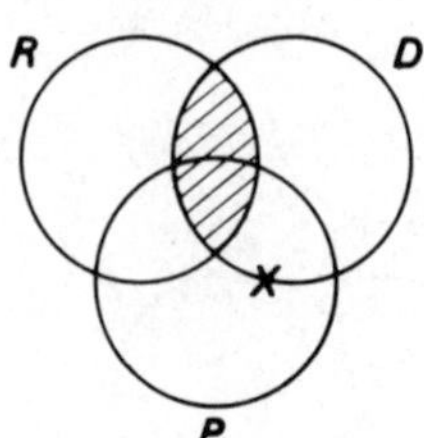

Invalid: No *X* in *PD* slot. Violates rules 3 and 4.

6. *MEJ*
SOM
/∴ *SOJ*

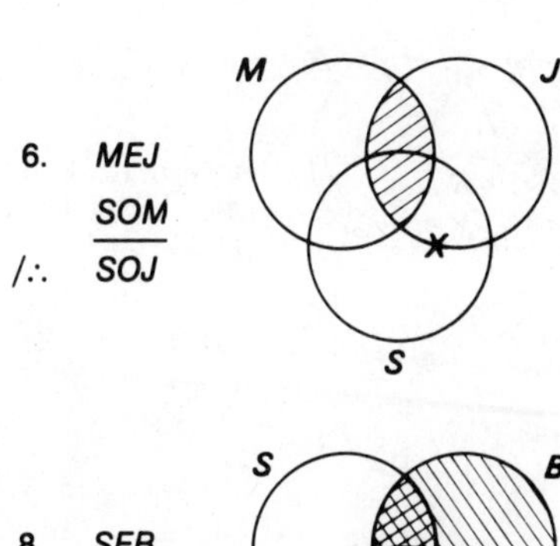

Invalid: No *X* in the $S\overline{J}$ slot. Violates rule 3.

8. *SEB*
BAC
/∴ *CES*

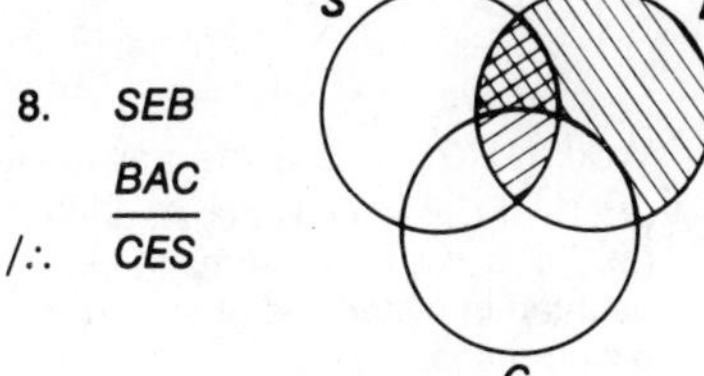

Invalid: All of the *CS* slot is not shaded out. Violates rule 2.

Exercise 11-3:

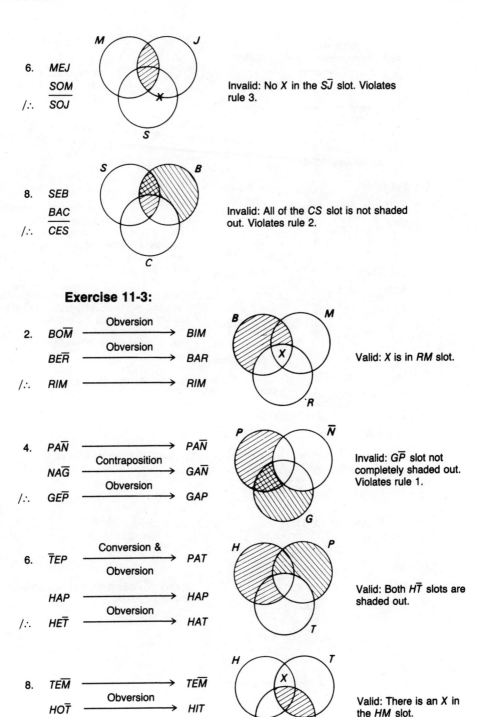

2. $BO\overline{M}$ —Obversion→ *BIM*
$BE\overline{R}$ —Obversion→ *BAR*
/∴ *RIM* → *RIM*

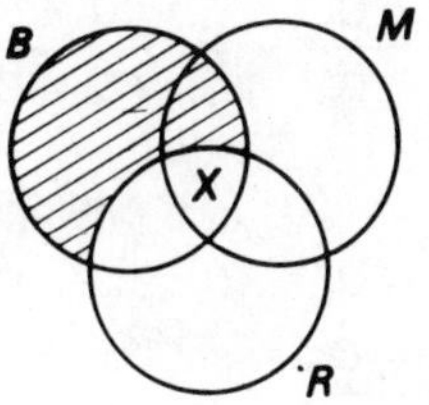

Valid: *X* is in *RM* slot.

4. $PA\overline{N}$ → $PA\overline{N}$
$NA\overline{G}$ —Contraposition→ $GA\overline{N}$
/∴ $GE\overline{P}$ —Obversion→ *GAP*

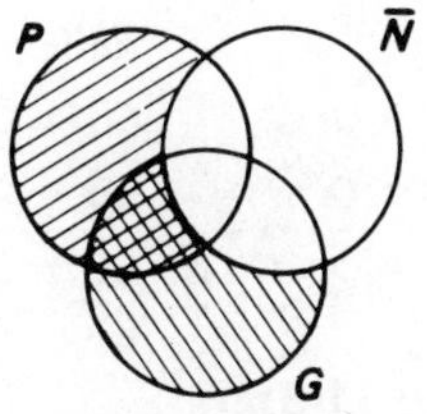

Invalid: $G\overline{P}$ slot not completely shaded out. Violates rule 1.

6. $\overline{T}EP$ —Conversion & Obversion→ *PAT*
HAP → *HAP*
/∴ $HE\overline{T}$ —Obversion→ *HAT*

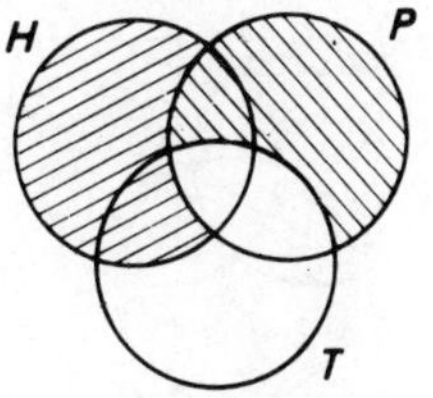

Valid: Both $H\overline{T}$ slots are shaded out.

8. $TE\overline{M}$ → $TE\overline{M}$
$HO\overline{T}$ —Obversion→ *HIT*
$HO\overline{M}$ → $HO\overline{M}$

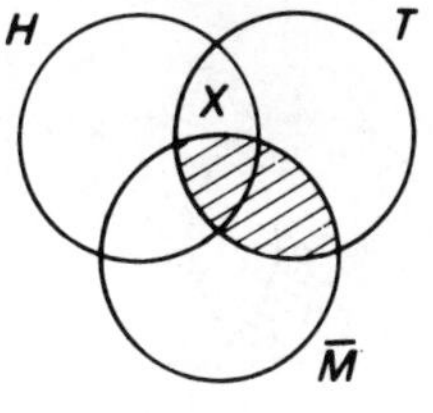

Valid: There is an *X* in the *HM* slot.

10.

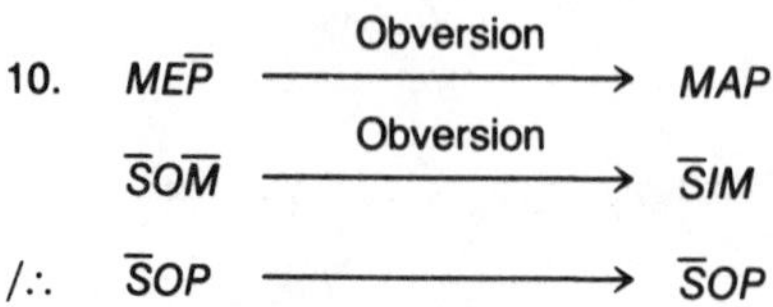

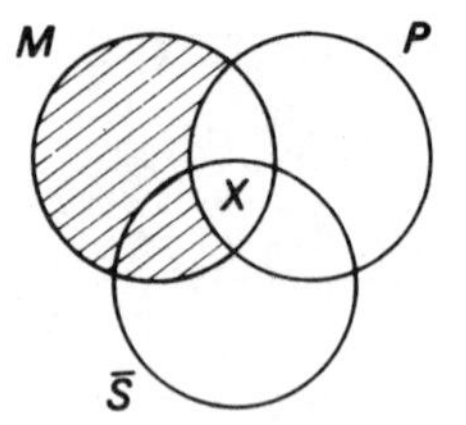

Invalid: No X in the $\overline{S}\overline{P}$ slot. Violates rules 2 and 4.

Exercise 11-4:

2.

Syllogism		Antilogism
GAR	$G\overline{R} = O$	$G\overline{R} = O$
GIC	$GC \neq O$	$GC \neq O$
∴ CIR	∴ $CR \neq O$	∴ $CR = O$

Valid. (1) $GC \neq O$ is the only inequality. (2) R, of $CR = O$, is negated in $G\overline{R} = O$. (3) Each of the two terms in $GC \neq 0$ is not negated in either one of its two occurrences.

4.

Syllogism		Antilogism
RED	$RD = O$	$RD = O$
POR	$P\overline{R} \neq O$	$P\overline{R} \neq O$
∴ PID	∴ $PD \neq O$	∴ $PD = O$

Invalid. Violates 2nd criterion (no term unnegated in one equality is negated in the other); and violates 3rd criterion ($\overline{R}$ is negated in the inequality $P\overline{R} \neq O$ but not in $RD = O$).

6.

Syllogism		Antilogism
MEJ	$MJ = O$	$MJ = O$
SOM	$S\overline{M} \neq O$	$S\overline{M} \neq O$
∴ SOJ	∴ $S\overline{J} \neq O$	∴ $S\overline{J} = O$

Invalid. Violates 3rd criterion.

8.

Syllogism		Antilogism
SEB	$SB = O$	$SB = O$
BAC	$B\overline{C} = O$	$B\overline{C} = O$
∴ CES	∴ $CS = O$	∴ $CS \neq O$

Invalid. Violates 3rd criterion.

Exercise 11-5:

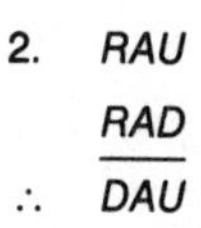

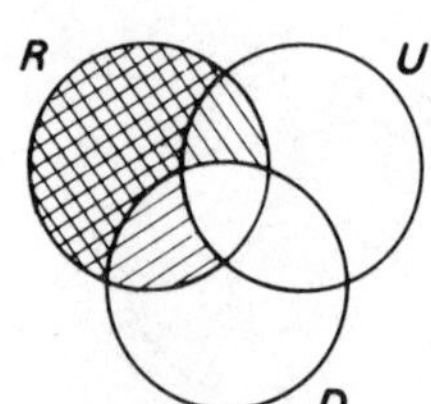

Invalid: $D\overline{U}$ slot is not completely shaded out. Violates rule 2.

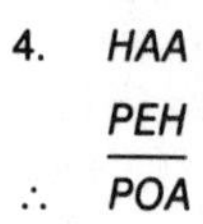

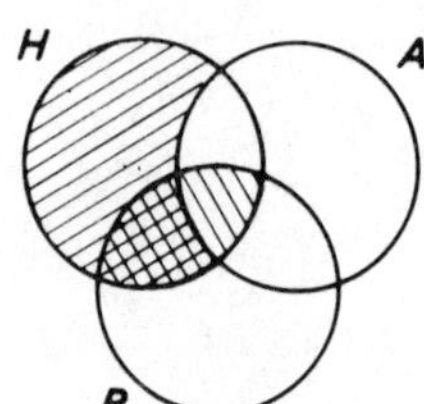

Invalid: No X in *the* $P\overline{A}$ slot. Violates rules 2 and 5.

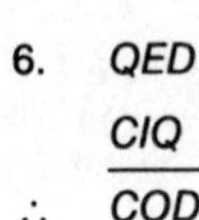

6. *QED*
   CIQ
   ∴ *COD*

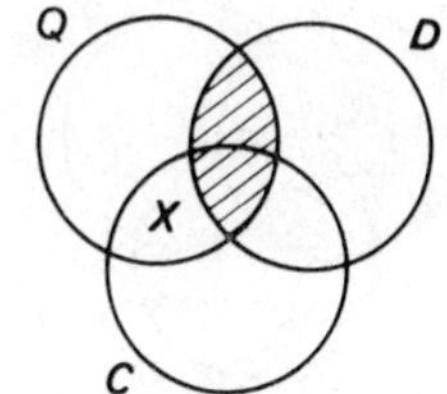

Valid: There is an *X* in the $C\overline{D}$ slot.

8. *TED*
   TOB
   ∴ *BOD*

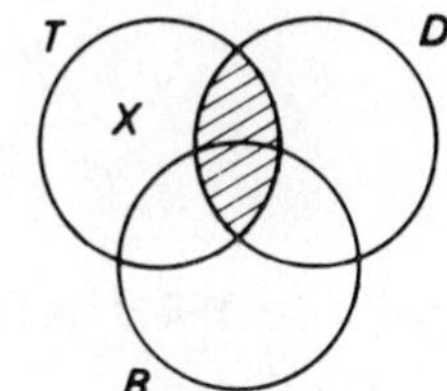

Invalid: There is no *X* in the $B\overline{D}$ slot. Violates rule 3.

10. *MIC*
    AIM
    ∴ *AIC*

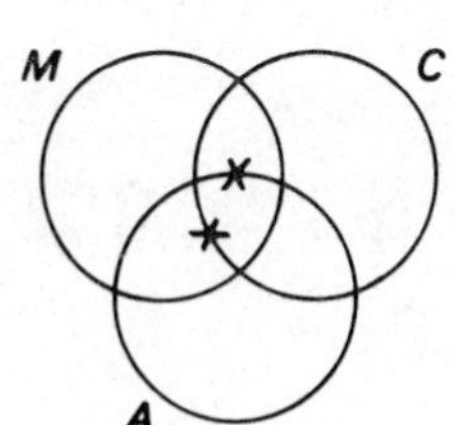

Invalid: There is no *X* in the *AC* slot. Violates rule 1.

Exercise 11-6:

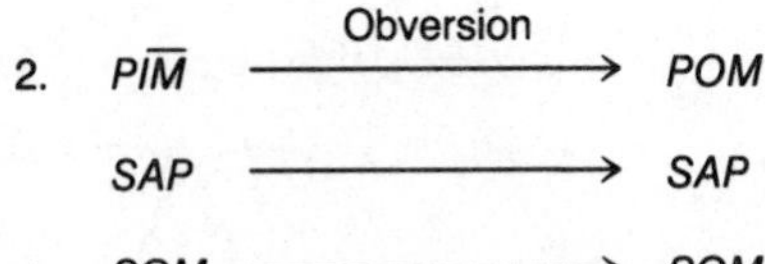

2. $PI\overline{M}$ → *POM*
   SAP → *SAP*
   ∴ *SOM* → *SOM*

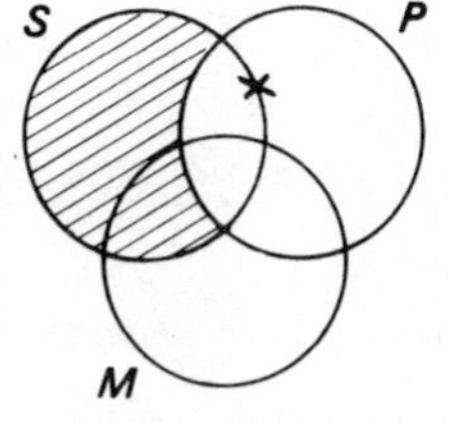

Invalid: No *X* in the $S\overline{M}$ slot. Violates rule 1.

4. *IAM*
   WEI
   ∴ *WEM*

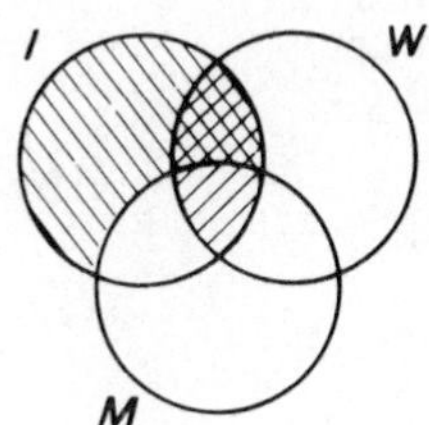

Invalid: *WM* slot is not completely shaded out. Violates rule 2.

6. *LAI*
   LIH
   ∴ *HII*

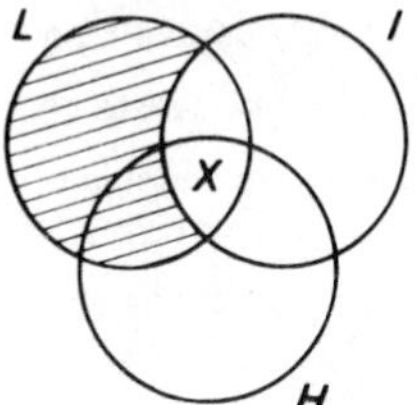

Valid: There is an *X* in the *HI* slot.

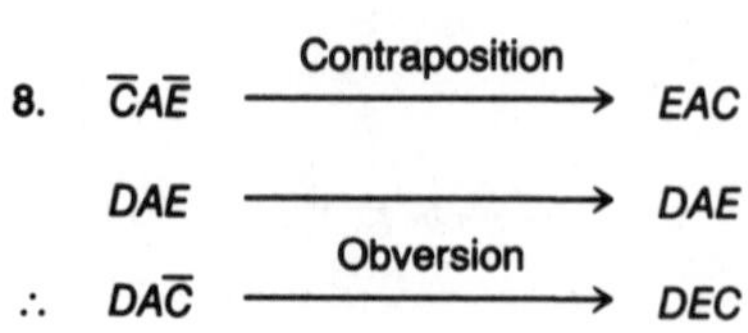

8. $\overline{C}A\overline{E}$ Contraposition → EAC
DAE → DAE
∴ $DA\overline{C}$ Obversion → DEC

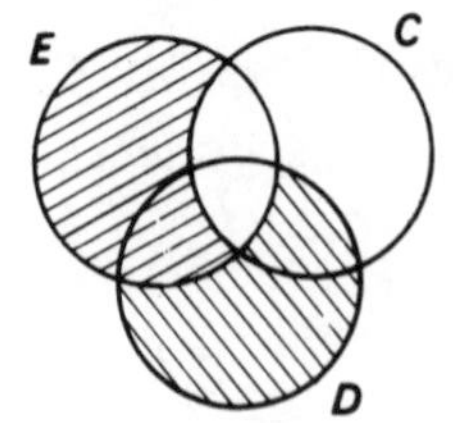

Invalid: The *DC* slot is not completely shaded out. Violates rules 2 and 4.

10. *HAM*
JAH
∴ *JAM*

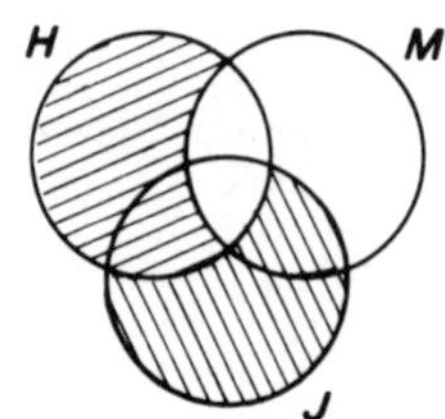

Valid: The *JM* slot is shaded out.

12. *PIL*
PIS
∴ *SIL*

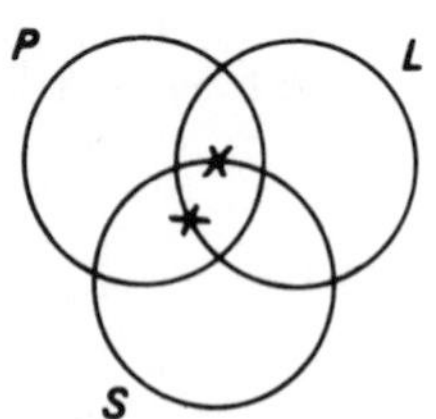

Invalid: There is no *X* in the *SL* slot. Violates rule 1.

14. *TAD* (All times are times when we have death and taxes.)
DEG (No times when we have death and taxes are times when we give up without a fight.)
∴ *TEG* (No times are times when we give up without a fight.)

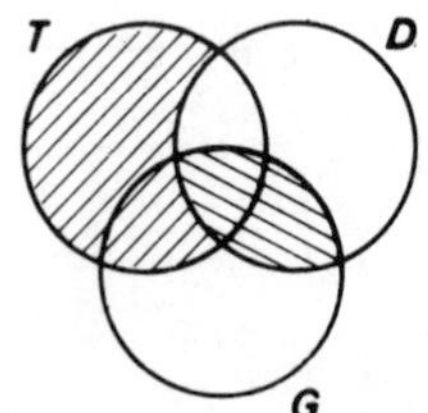

Valid: The *TG* slot is shaded out.

Exercise 11-7:

2. Taking the life of a fetus is taking the life of a human being.
4. Anyone who eats plenty of brown rice is in pretty good shape.
6. If you listen to superficial accounts of the news, you waste your time.
8. Anyone who's smarter than lots of college grads is capable of holding a high-level management position.
10. A lot of people who've taken LSD have scrambled brains.

Exercise 11-8:

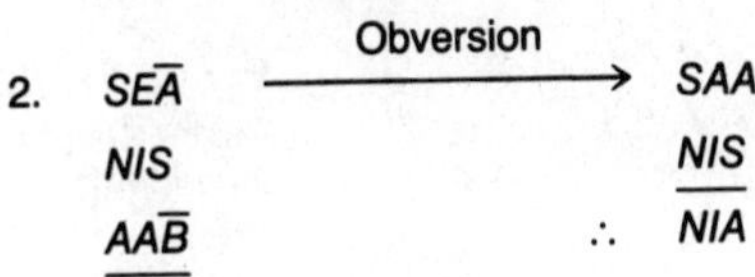

2. $SE\overline{A}$
   NIS
   $AA\overline{B}$
   ∴ $NI\overline{B}$

Obversion →

SAA
NIS
∴ NIA

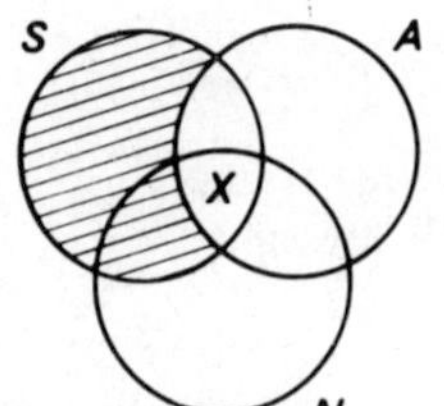

Valid: There is an X in the *NA* slot.

$AA\overline{B}$
NIA
∴ $NI\overline{B}$

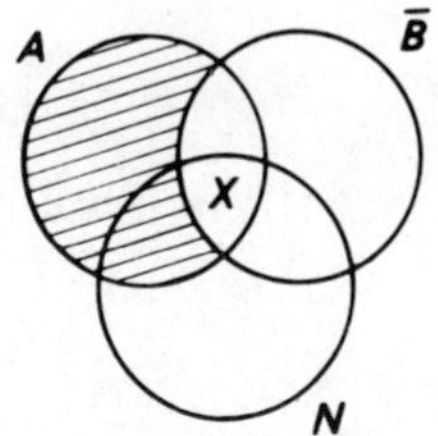

Valid: There is an X in the $N\overline{B}$ slot.

4. $SE\overline{M}$
   GAF
   MEF
   ∴ GES

Obversion →

MEF
SAM
∴ SEF

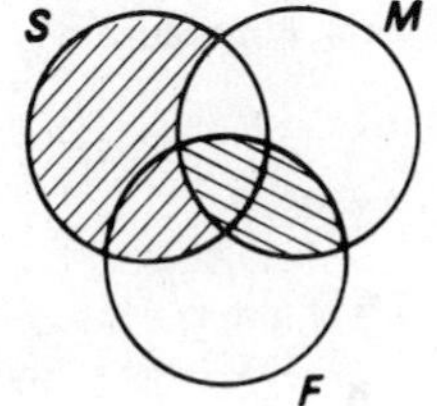

Valid: *SF* slot is shaded out.

SEF
GAF
∴ GES

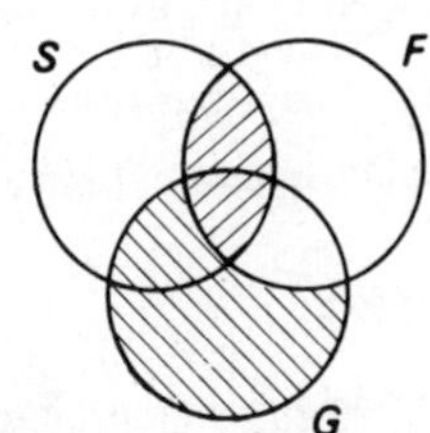

Valid: *GS* slot is shaded out.

6. IED
   $PE\overline{G}$
   OAP
   IEG
   ∴ OAD

Obversion →

IED
PAG
OAP
IEG
∴ OAD

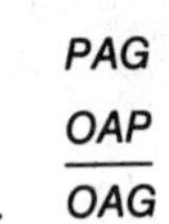

PAG
OAP
∴ OAG

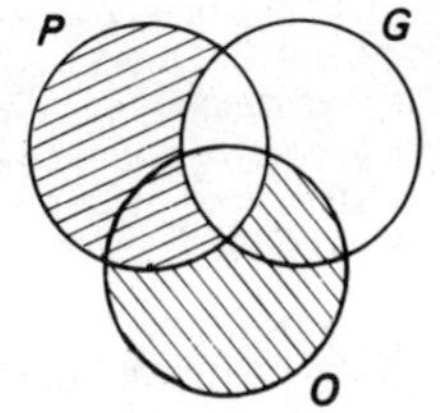

Valid: $O\overline{G}$ slot is shaded out.

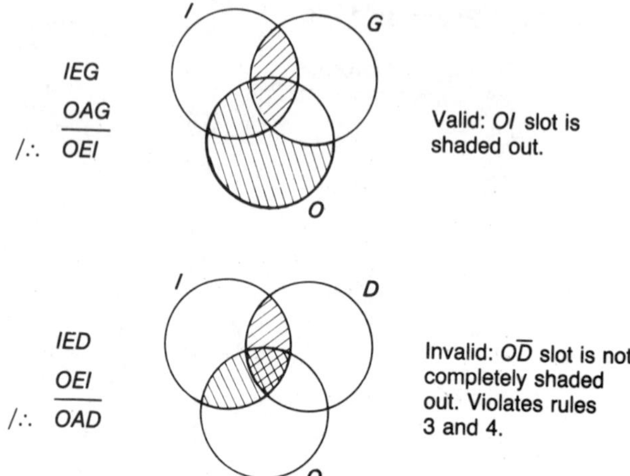

(There are other possibilities, all invalid. A *complete* proof would cover all these possibilities. But it is clear the sorites is invalid because one of its premises is negative, and yet its conclusion is affirmative.)

Exercise 11-9:

2. *True.* Because this shows that the conclusion already is contained in its premises, as they have to be in a deductively valid argument.
4. A categorical proposition distributes a term if it says something about every member of the class designated by that term. A proposition of the form "No *S* are *P*" says of all *S*'s that they are not P's, and of all P's that they are not S's, and so distributes both *S* and *P*. But "Some *S* are *P*" says something about *some* S's and P's, but obviously not all.
6. (Not appropriate to answer.)

Exercise 12-1:

2. **Unwarranted statement:** How did the good doctor come by all these "facts"?
4. **Inconsistency:** Jane first says of American medicine "Who needs it?" and then moans that the poor aren't getting their share of its "important benefits".
6. **Unwarranted statement:** How does Juliano know that the addicts he arrested all started out on pot? (We surely ought to doubt that he asked every one of them and received a truthful answer.)
   Suppressed evidence: A good deal of evidence exists indicating that the use of marijuana does not invariably or even usually lead to heroin use. If it did, we would have many millions more heroin addicts than in fact we do, since millions more have smoked dope than there are heroin addicts. (Add up the figures!)
8. **Ambiguity:** The Lipton Company wants you to think that salad dressing is the only thing made by the company that makes *Wishbone* salad dressing (unlike, say, competitor Kraft); the fact is that *Wishbone* is a name Lipton puts on only salad dressing, but it's a *brand name,* not the name of the company (which also makes Lipton Tea, for instance). Also, perhaps, **suppressed evidence,** since Lipton failed to tell us they make products sold under different names.
10. **Inconsistency** (or **unwarranted statement**)**:** Buckley says marijuana is dangerous, but then states its effects on health haven't been established.

12. **Suppressed evidence:** Although no aspirin product reduces fever better, none reduces it worse, since all aspirin products of the same strength reduce fever the same.

14. **Suppressed evidence:** It's the milk that gives you the most useable food value, not the *Cap'n Crunch.* For instance, a glass of milk and a slice of whole wheat bread beat *Cap'n Crunch* and milk for nutritional value.

Exercise 12-2:

2. **Questionable cause** or **accidental correlation,** and **faulty comparison:** Before concluding even tentatively that getting an Oscar causes marital problems, we need to know how many female Oscar winners there were in the past twelve years; perhaps six is a small percentage of that number. We also need to know the rate of marital difficulties among actresses in general, so we can compare it with the rate for female Oscar winners; perhaps six is an average amount for actresses in general. We also need to know how soon after receiving the award the marital difficulties started.

4. **False dilemma:** There aren't just two economic systems to choose from. For instance, the United States today works under neither a capitalistic nor a socialistic system (as Knight defined them).

6. a. **Hasty conclusion:** Even supposing brushing removes plaque, and tooth decay can't occur without plaque present, it doesn't follow that fluorides, etc., aren't of value. For it may be that even in the presence of plaque, teeth fortified with a fluoride tend to resist tooth decay, and as we all know, it's rather difficult to remove plaque promptly and completely all the time. In addition, it is plausible to assume, in the absence of proof to the contrary, that children in poor areas have poorer diets, perhaps lower in calcium; and this may be the cause of their greater amount of tooth decay.

   b. **Suppressed evidence:** There is a not insignificant amount of evidence (which those doing research in the field should be familiar with) supporting the theory that plaque, while perhaps a necessary condition of tooth decay, is not a sufficient condition. And there is some evidence that when certain trace minerals are present in large quantities, *no* tooth decay takes place.

8. **Begging the question:** Earned run averages in one league can't be compared with those in the other unless other evidence is used first to rate the batters in both leagues. But the latter is exactly what was at issue. (Earned run averages only show how the pitchers in a given league compare to the batters in that league. A low average earned run average for a league might mean that the pitchers are better than usual or that the batters are poorer than usual.)

10. **Suppressed evidence** (*biased statistics*): If 23,000,000 Americans joined, then many more didn't join.

12. **Unknowable statistic:** There were no IQ tests in Mill's day, so how can we assign a value of 185 to his intelligence? That he would have done well on an IQ test is not in question. But exactly 185?

14. **False dilemma:** Omits alternative of life imprisonment with no possible parole.

16. **Appeal to authority:** (1) Doctors disagree on the issue, so only their *reasons* are relevant. (2) Whether a fetus is a *person,* a human being, is not a medical question.

18. a. **Small sample:** We're talking about a sample of six presidents.

   b. **Suppressed evidence:** There is plenty of "background" information explaining election results and auto production in terms of more relevant factors. For example, Adlai Stevenson wasn't victimized by peculiarities in auto production, but by the fact that Eisenhower was an extremely popular war hero, a fine father figure, and so on.

20. **False dilemma:** Marital intercourse could have been intended to serve both functions, not necessarily just one or the other. (Whether statements about what a Creator might or might not do constitute *unwarranted statements* is a question in theology, or philosophy proper, and is best passed over in a logic text.)

22. **Faulty comparison** (and *suppressed evidence*): Michener failed to mention how many play football in the U.S., and how few fight bulls in bullfight country. He also failed to consider here that the main objection to bullfighting is the brutality of killing innocent bulls for sport.

24. **Faulty comparison:** This example illustrates the problem of bringing background information to bear. The author of this text knew that infant mortality is higher in winter than spring, but failed to think of that when reading the quoted figures. *The Nation* writer had to point that out to him, and show the true comparison between April–June 1978 and April–June 1979, showing a great increase in infant mortality for the latter three months over the former.

26. **Inconsistency:** The principal reason to save executive time is the same as saving any salaried person's time, namely money paid out in salary. (Lots of big-time executives would dispute this one, however.)

Exercise 13-1:

2. **Too broad:** That would make kangaroos, australopithecines, and tyrannosaurus rex human beings, not to mention plucked chickens.
4. While very suggestive, this "definition" violates several rules, in particular the one against figurative or obscure language.
6. A reasonably good definition.
8. A good extensional definition.
10. **Vague:** *Which* part of what philosophers write and say? Also, in the absence of an accompanying definition of "philosopher", this definition is circular. (Still, in the case of a notoriously difficult word like "philosophy", such an inadequate definition has a certain merit.)

Exercise 13-2:

No answers are provided because the questions call for original examples.

Exercise 13-3:

2. Not a definition by genus and difference; "porpoise" and "dolphin" are synonyms.
4. A reasonably good definition; the genus is college undergraduate, the difference being in the first year of study.
6. **Too Broad:** For instance, Israeli Premier Golda Meir and Indian Prime Minister Indira Gandhi were rulers (in the sense of heads of state) but not queens.
   Too narrow: Queens whose husbands are monarchs do not rule.
8. Not a definition by genus and difference. Still, it could serve as a definition in the sense of a good explanation of the term "sibling".

Exercise 13-4:

2. **Pro:** steed; **Con:** nag
4. **Pro:** superintendent
6. **Pro:** sanitation engineer; **Con:** garbage collector
8. **Pro:** defense force
10. **Pro:** tax relief; **Con:** tax loophole
12. **Con:** whitey, the man

14. **Pro:** memorial park;
Con: boneyard, boot hill

16. **Pro:** inn, pub, tavern; **Con:** grog shop

18. **Pro:** bathroom tissue

20. **Pro:** pugilist, boxer;
Con: pug, brawler

22. **Pro:** loved one

Exercise 13-5:

2. **Neutral:** take; **Positive:** select
4. **Negative:** jug, can, hoosegow, slammer; **Positive:** correctional facility
6. **Neutral:** odor; **Positive:** fragrance
8. **Neutral:** overcome; **Positive:** vanquish, surmount, hurdle, master
10. **Negative:** finicky, fussy; **Neutral:** particular

Exercise 14-1:

2. **Increase strength:** d (because McBird may be better able to take the trauma)
Decrease strength: a, b, c, and e (because tenure gives Jane financial security, which removes one factor tying her to McBird)

Exercise 14-2:

2. **Strong analogy:** It calls our attention to a feature of military conquest we might otherwise overlook, and the one analogical instance it presents is convincing.
4. Although weak in itself because it has only one analogical instance, it is still very strong, because it is enthymematic for an analogy that mentions the constant nature of as many animals as we wish, since all are constant.
6. **Weak analogy:** LBJ taking care of daughters and the U.S. government protecting freedom everywhere are two vastly different undertakings depending on totally different factors, namely Johnson's economic position and the power of the U.S. relative to its enemies.
8. Although weak in itself, because it has only one analogical instance, it still is very strong because it is enthymematic for an analogy that mentions lots of cases where we note a correlation between our inner sensations and overt appearance and behavior. However, this argument from analogy to the existence of other streams of consciousness notoriously differs from most cases in that we can never check up directly to see if our conclusion is correct, because we cannot experience another person's experience (behaviorists and others obviously disagree in one way or another). (This last point is relevant also to question 7.)

Exercise 14-3:

2. Theoretical
4. *Attention*—theoretical; *neutrinos*—probably theoretical
6. Both: ". . . looked red"—observable; ". . . he wasn't sure" that it *was* red—theoretical.

Exercise 14-4:

2. Concomitant variation (negative)
4. Difference
6. Agreement (negative)
8. Concomitant variation

10. Agreement (negative) and agreement (positive)
12. Agreement and difference
14. Agreement and difference

Exercise 14-5:

2.	False	4.	True	6.	True	8.	True
10.	False	12.	True	14.	True		

Exercises 15-1 and 15-2:

No answers are provided because the importance of these exercises lies in the way students explain and defend their answers.

Exercise 15-3:

2. a. $p = 1/2 \times 1/2 = 1/4$ b. $p = 1/2 \times 1/2 \times 1/2 = 1/8$
4. Probability of even number $= 3/6$

   Probability of number less than 3 $= 2/6$

   Probability of even number less than 3 $= 3/6 \times 2/6 = 1/6$

   Probability of either even number or number less than 3 (or both) $=$ $3/6 + 2/6 - 1/6 + 4/6 = 2/3$
6. $P(p \cdot q) = P(p) \times P(q) = \frac{1}{10} \times \frac{1}{10} = \frac{1}{100}$ or $P(p \cdot q) = \frac{1}{10}$
   (This item is ambiguous.)
8. Probability of *HHT* (or *HTH* or *THH*) $= 1/2 \times 1/2 \times 1/2 = 1/8$
   Probability of exactly two heads out of three $= 1/8 + 1/8 + 1/8 = 3/8$
10. a. Probability of ace on first draw $= 1/13$
    Probability of ace on second draw $= 3/51$
    Probability of two aces in a row $= 1/13 \times 3/51 = 1/221$

    b. Probability of at least one ace $= 1/13 + 3/51 - 1/221 = 29/221$

    c. Probability of first spade $= 1/4$
    Probability of second space $= 12/51$
    Probability of two spades $= 1/4 \times 12/51 = 1/17$

    d. Probability of first black ace $= 1/26$
    Probability of second black ace $= 1/51$
    Probability of two black aces $= 1/26 \times 1/51 = 1/1326$

Exercise 16-1:

2. There is *some* explanatory force to Jane's "explanation", but not much. McBird learned from it only that Tom's blacking out was not accidental, but rather (as McBird suspected) the result of taking a whiff of what was in the bottle. He didn't find out what sort of soporific it was (for example, chloroform), much less what makes it a soporific.
6. Given the background information available to the natives, the answer is perfectly acceptable. However, if the natives are good scientists, they will check up on McNash's health directly, since if they can find no direct evidence of poor health, he would constitute a disconfirming case for their theory that good health is the cause of lice infestation.
12. False. It states that this is *one way* to confirm "all P's are Q's."

    No answers are provided for problems 4, 8, and 10 because the importance of these exercises lies in the way students explain and defend their answers.

Exercise 16-2:

No answers are given for this exercise set because the importance of the exercise rests with the way students explain their answers.

Exercise 17-1:

(2)

$(C \supset A)\surd$
$[A \supset (B \cdot D)]\surd$
C $\quad /\therefore B$
$\sim B$

Left: $\sim C$, x
Right: A
- Left: $\sim A$, x
- Right: $(B \cdot D)$, B, D, x

(Valid because all paths are closed.)

(4)

$(R \vee N)\surd$
$(L \supset N)\surd$
R $\quad /\therefore \sim N$
N

Left: R
- $\sim L$
- N

Right: N
- $\sim L$
- N

(Invalid, because there are open paths on this completed tree.)

(6)

$[(A \cdot B) \vee (C \cdot D)]\surd$
$\sim A$ $\quad /\therefore C$
$\sim C$

Left: $(A \cdot B)\surd$, A, B, x
Right: $(C \cdot D)$, C, D, x

(Valid, because all paths are closed.)

(8)

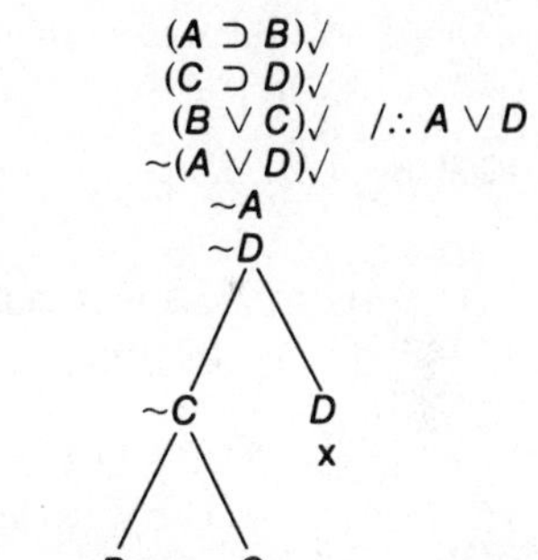

$(A \supset B)\surd$
$(C \supset D)\surd$
$(B \vee C)\surd$ $\quad /\therefore A \vee D$
$\sim(A \vee D)\surd$
$\sim A$
$\sim D$

Left: $\sim C$
- Left: B
  - $\sim A$
  - B
- Right: C, x

Right: D, x

(Invalid, because the completed tree has an open path.)

(10)

$[F \supset (G \supset H)]\surd$ $\quad /\therefore (\sim H \cdot K) \supset (G \supset \sim F)$
$\sim[(\sim H \cdot K) \supset (G \supset \sim F)]\surd$
$(\sim H \cdot K)\surd$
$\sim(G \supset \sim F)\surd$
$\sim H$
K
G
$\sim\sim F$

Left: $\sim F$, x
Right: $(G \supset H)\surd$
- Left: $\sim G$, x
- Right: H, x

(Valid, because all paths are closed.)

Exercise 17-2:

(2)

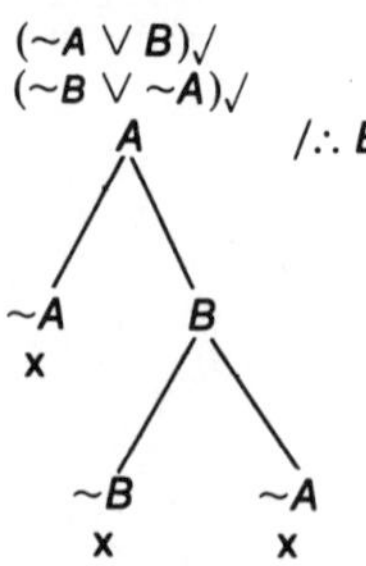

(Inconsistent premises, because all paths are closed. Notice that we do not add the negation of the conclusion to the tree, because we're trying to prove whether the *premises* are consistent or inconsistent.)

(4)

(~R · ~S)√
[S ∨ (~S · T)]√
[~(R ∨ S) ⊃ ~(S ∨ T)]√ /∴ R
~R
~S

S   (~S · T)
x   ~S
T

(R ∨ S)   ~(S ∨ T)
~S
~T
x

R   S
x   x

(Inconsistent—all paths are closed.

(6)

[A ⊃ (C ⊃ B)]
[(B · C) ∨ A]√
[C ∨ (B · A)]
(B ⊃ ~C)√
(D ∨ B)
(B · ~A)√ /∴ B ∨ (A ⊃ D)
B
~A

~B   ~C
x

(B · C)   A
B   x
C
x

(Inconsistent, because all paths are closed. This example is interesting because it shows that the set of three checked premises is inconsistent, and therefore that the whole set of six premises is inconsistent, without bothering about the unchecked premises.)

(8)

[A ⊃ (B ⊃ C)]
~[~C ∨ (A ∨ ~D)]√
~{~A ∨ [C ⊃ (B · D)]}√

C
~(A ∨ ~D)√
~A
D
A
~[C ⊃ (B · D)]
x

(The one path is closed, so the premises are inconsistent. Notice we didn't have to bother with premise 1.)

(2)

(A · ~B)√
(B ∨ ~C)√
~(~C · B)√ /∴ ~(A · B)
A
~B

B   ~C
x

~~C   ~B
x

(The premises are consistent, because there is an open path on this completed tree.)

(4)

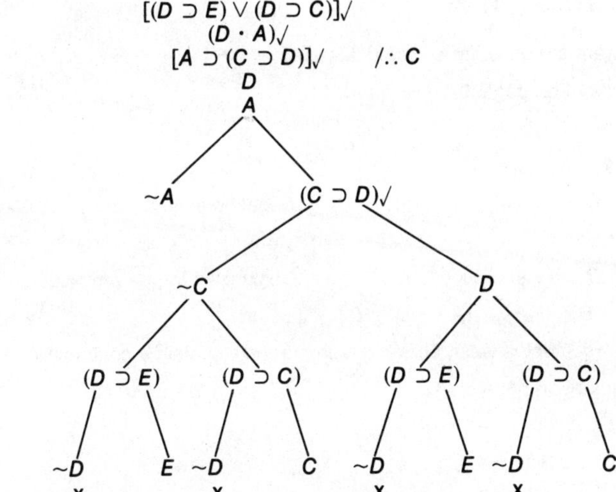

(Premises are consistent, because there is an open path in the completed tree. Note that we could have stopped the tree after finding one open path.)

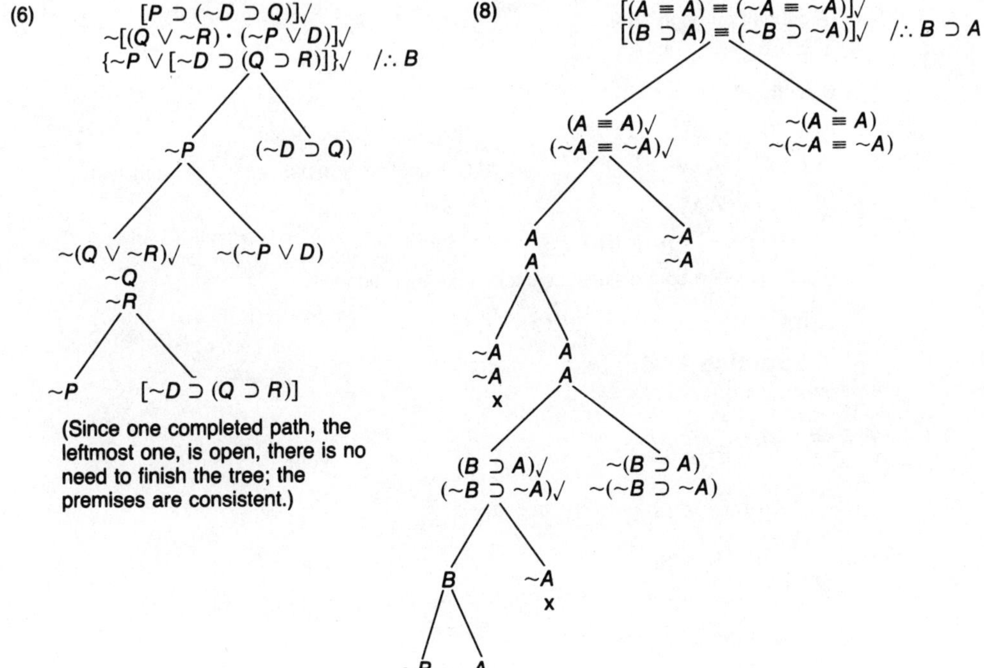

(Since one completed path, the leftmost one, is open, there is no need to finish the tree; the premises are consistent.)

(Since there is one completed path that is open, the premises are consistent.)

Exercise 17-3:

(Answers are given for selected items.)

(Argument on page 361):

1.	$A \supset B$	
2.	A /∴ B	
3.	$\sim B$	(Negation of conclusion)
4.	$\sim A \vee B$	1, **Impl**
5.	$(A \cdot \sim B) \cdot (\sim A \vee B)$	(Conjunction of the premises)
6.	$[(A \cdot \sim B) \cdot \sim A] \vee [(A \cdot \sim B) \cdot B]$	5, **Dist**

(The argument is valid, because both disjuncts contain a contradiction.)

(Argument on page 362):

1.	$A \supset B$	
2.	$A \cdot B$ /∴ $\sim B$	
3.	B	(Negation of conclusion)
4.	$\sim A \vee B$	1, **Impl**
5.	$[(A \cdot B) \cdot B] \cdot (\sim A \vee B)$	(Expanded set of premises plus *Implication* on first premise)
6.	$\{[(A \cdot B) \cdot B] \cdot \sim A\} \vee \{[(A \cdot B) \cdot B] \vee B\}$	5, **Dist**

(Invalid, because the right disjunct is not contradictory.)

(Argument on page 351):

1.	A	
2.	B /∴ $A \cdot B$	
3.	$\sim(A \cdot B)$	(Negation of conclusion)
4.	$(A \cdot B) \cdot \sim(A \cdot B)$	(Conjunction of expanded set of premises)
5.	$(A \cdot B) \cdot (\sim A \vee \sim B)$	4, **DeM**
6.	$[(A \cdot B) \cdot \sim A] \vee [(A \cdot B) \cdot \sim B]$	5, **Dist**

(Valid, because both disjuncts contain a contradiction.)

Exercise 17-4:

2.

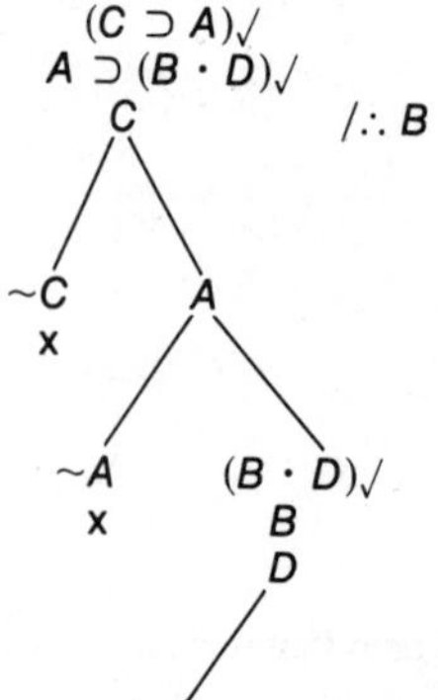

(Since every open path in the upper tree, namely the one on the right, covers a path (there is just one) in the lower tree, the argument is valid.)

4.

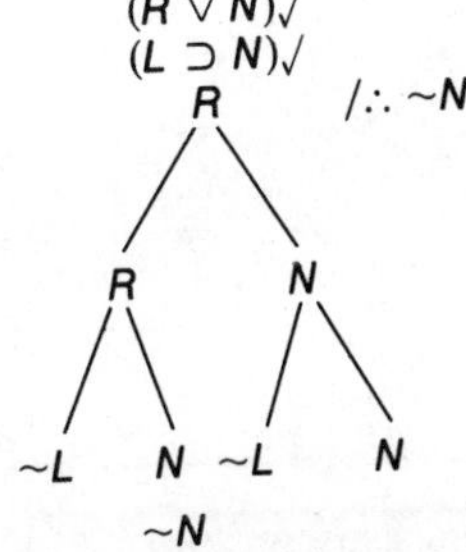

(Since there is an open path in the upper tree that does not cover the one path in the conclusion (in fact, there are four), the argument is invalid.)

6.

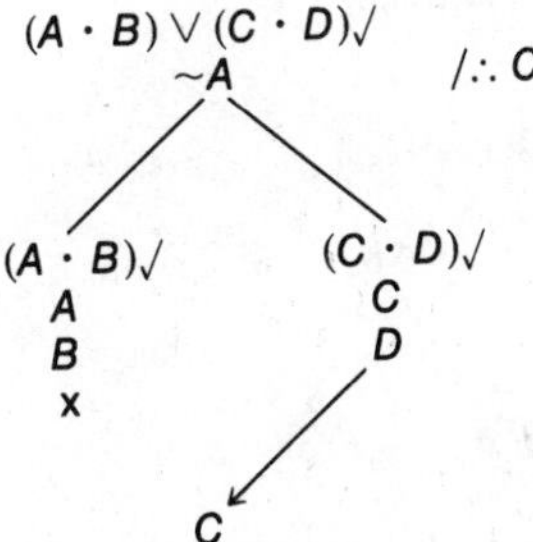

(Since the one open upper path covers the one lower path, the argument is valid.)

8.

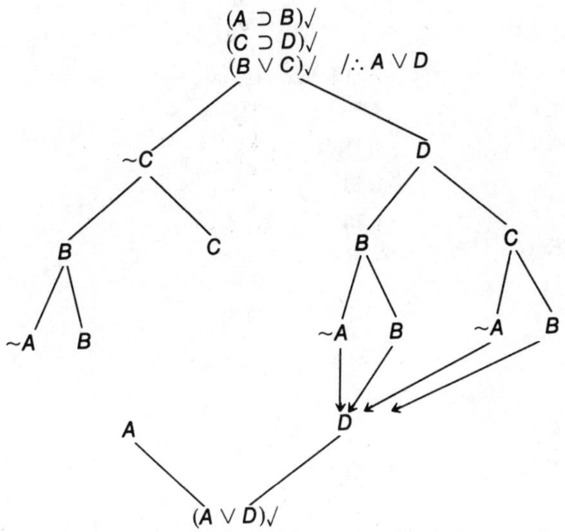

(Since there is at least one open upper path that does not cover a lower path, the argument is invalid.)

10. $[F \supset (G \supset H)]\checkmark \quad /\therefore (\sim H \cdot K) \supset (G \supset \sim F)$

$\sim F \qquad (G \supset H)\checkmark$

$\sim G \qquad H$

$H \qquad \sim K \qquad \sim G \qquad \sim F$

$\sim(\sim H \cdot K) \qquad (\sim G \vee \sim F)\checkmark$

$[(\sim H \cdot K) \supset (G \supset \sim F)]\checkmark$

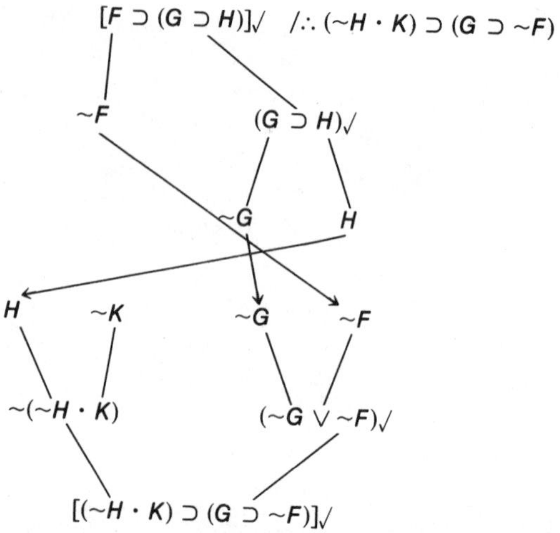

(Since all three upper paths cover a lower path, the argument is valid.)

Exercise 17-5:

(2)

	1.	$(x)[Fx \supset (y)Gy]$	
	2.	Fa	$/\therefore (x)Gx$
→	3.	$\sim(x)Gx$	**AP**
	4.	$(\exists x)\sim Gx$	3, **QN**
	5.	$[Fa \supset (y)Gy]\checkmark$	1, **UI**
	6.	$(\exists x)\sim Gx\checkmark$	3, **QN**
	7.	$\sim Gb$	6, **EI**
	8.	$\sim Fa$ x $(y)Gy$	5
	9.	Gb x	8, **UI**

(Valid, because all paths are closed.)

(4)

	1.	$(\exists x)Fx$	
	2.	$(x)(\sim Gx \supset \sim Fx)$	
	3.	$(x)Mx$	$/\therefore (\exists x)Gx \cdot (\exists x)Mx$
→	4.	$\sim[(\exists x)Gx \cdot (\exists x)Mx]\checkmark$	**AP**
	5.	$[\sim(\exists x)Gx \vee \sim(\exists x)Mx]\checkmark$	4, **DeM**
	6.	Fx	1, **EI**
	7.	Mx	3, **UI**
	8.	$(\sim Gx \supset \sim Fx)\checkmark$	2, **UI**
	9.	$\sim\sim Gx$ $\sim Fx$ x	8
	10.	$\sim(\exists x)Gx$ $\sim(\exists x)Mx$	5
	11.	$(x)\sim Gx$ $(x)\sim Mx$	10, **QN**
	12.	$\sim Gx$ x $\sim Mx$ x	11, **UI**

(Valid, because all paths are closed.)

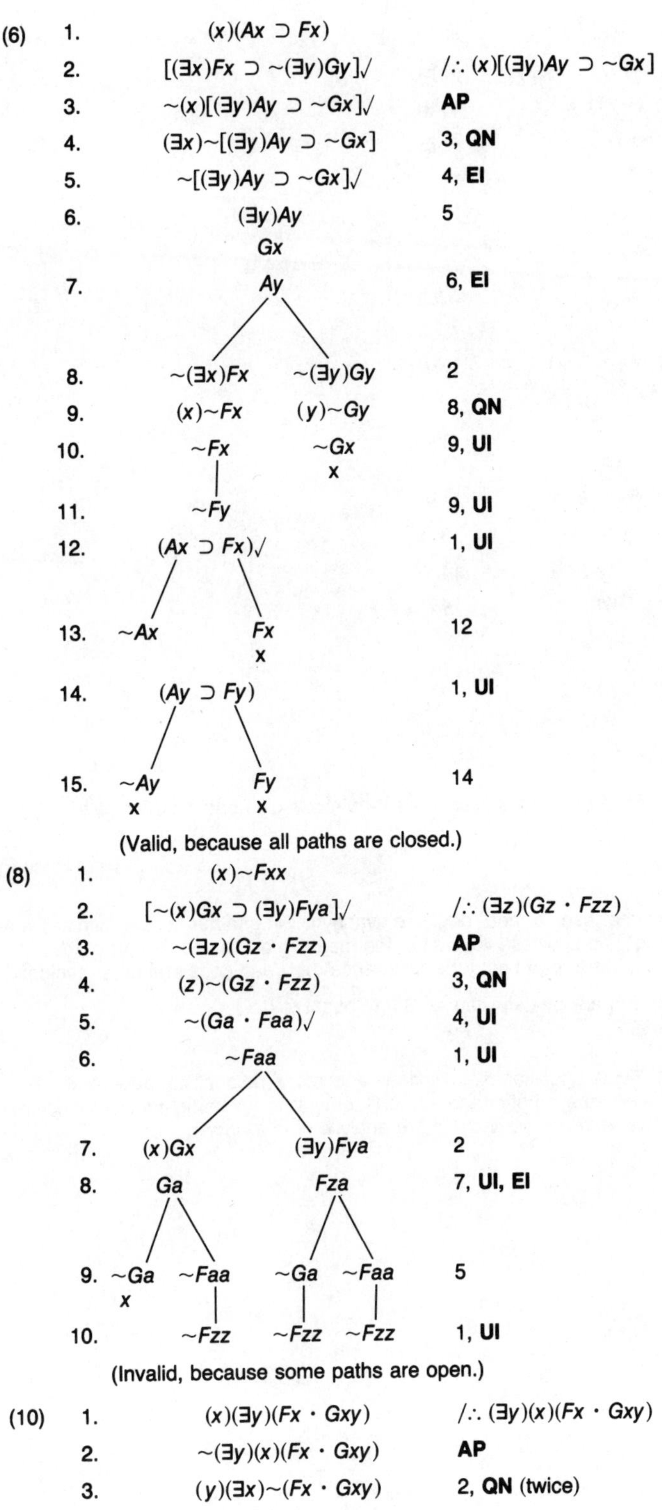

(6)

1. $(x)(Ax \supset Fx)$
2. $[(\exists x)Fx \supset \sim(\exists y)Gy]\checkmark$ — $/\therefore (x)[(\exists y)Ay \supset \sim Gx]$
3. $\sim(x)[(\exists y)Ay \supset \sim Gx]\checkmark$ — **AP**
4. $(\exists x)\sim[(\exists y)Ay \supset \sim Gx]$ — 3, **QN**
5. $\sim[(\exists y)Ay \supset \sim Gx]\checkmark$ — 4, **EI**
6. $(\exists y)Ay$, Gx — 5
7. Ay — 6, **EI**
8. $\sim(\exists x)Fx$ | $\sim(\exists y)Gy$ — 2
9. $(x)\sim Fx$ | $(y)\sim Gy$ — 8, **QN**
10. $\sim Fx$ | $\sim Gx$ x — 9, **UI**
11. $\sim Fy$ — 9, **UI**
12. $(Ax \supset Fx)\checkmark$ — 1, **UI**
13. $\sim Ax$ | Fx x — 12
14. $(Ay \supset Fy)$ — 1, **UI**
15. $\sim Ay$ x | Fy x — 14

(Valid, because all paths are closed.)

(8)

1. $(x)\sim Fxx$
2. $[\sim(x)Gx \supset (\exists y)Fya]\checkmark$ — $/\therefore (\exists z)(Gz \cdot Fzz)$
3. $\sim(\exists z)(Gz \cdot Fzz)$ — **AP**
4. $(z)\sim(Gz \cdot Fzz)$ — 3, **QN**
5. $\sim(Ga \cdot Faa)\checkmark$ — 4, **UI**
6. $\sim Faa$ — 1, **UI**
7. $(x)Gx$ | $(\exists y)Fya$ — 2
8. Ga | Fza — 7, **UI, EI**
9. $\sim Ga$ x | $\sim Faa$ | $\sim Ga$ | $\sim Faa$ — 5
10. $\sim Fzz$ | $\sim Fzz$ | $\sim Fzz$ — 1, **UI**

(Invalid, because some paths are open.)

(10)

1. $(x)(\exists y)(Fx \cdot Gxy)$ — $/\therefore (\exists y)(x)(Fx \cdot Gxy)$
2. $\sim(\exists y)(x)(Fx \cdot Gxy)$ — **AP**
3. $(y)(\exists x)\sim(Fx \cdot Gxy)$ — 2, **QN** (twice)

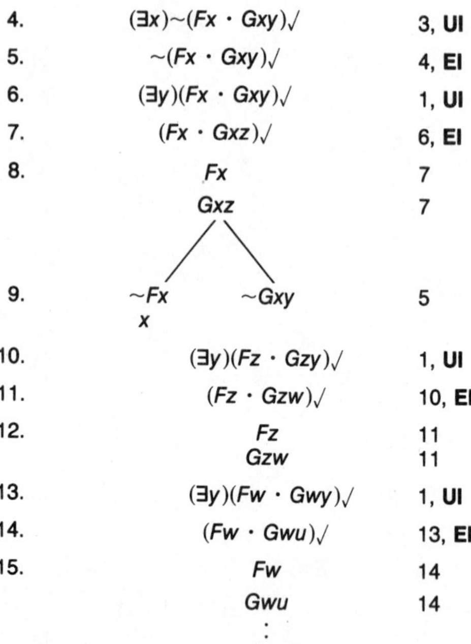

4.	(∃x)~(Fx · Gxy)✓	3, **UI**
5.	~(Fx · Gxy)✓	4, **EI**
6.	(∃y)(Fx · Gxy)✓	1, **UI**
7.	(Fx · Gxz)✓	6, **EI**
8.	Fx	7
	Gxz	7
9.	~Fx ~Gxy	5
	x	
10.	(∃y)(Fz · Gzy)✓	1, **UI**
11.	(Fz · Gzw)✓	10, **EI**
12.	Fz	11
	Gzw	11
13.	(∃y)(Fw · Gwy)✓	1, **UI**
14.	(Fw · Gwu)✓	13, **EI**
15.	Fw	14
	Gwu	14
	⋮	

(Inconclusive truth tree.)

Exercise A-1:

No answers are provided because students are required to give original examples.

Exercise A-2:

2. **Analytic:** In one sense "canine" and "dog" are synonyms; in another sense, "canine" is a genus of which "dog" is a species—thus all of the meaning of "canine" is part of the meaning of "dog", the other part being the "difference" between dogs and other canines.
4. **Analytic:** Right actions are by definition what one ought to do.
6. **Synthetic.**
8. Very controversial. Some (for example, Kantians and lots of rationalists) believe all theorems of geometry are synthetic (and *a priori*); others (for example, most empiricists, and the author of this text) believe they all are analytic (and *a priori*).

Bibliography

The following is a selected list of books and articles dealing with material covered in this book. Starred items are mentioned in the body of the text.

Parts One, Two, and Five

Bochenski, I. M. *A History of Formal Logic*. (transl. and edited by Ivo Thomas). New York: Chelsea, 1970.

*Church, Alonzo. *Introduction to Mathematical Logic*. Princeton, N.J. Princeton University Press, 1956.

*Copi, Irving. *Symbolic Logic*, Sixth Edition. New York: Macmillan, 1982.

*Fitch, Frederick B. *Symbolic Logic*. New York: The Ronald Press, 1952.

Kleene, Stephen C. *Mathematical Logic*. New York: John Wiley, 1967.

Kneale, W., and M. Kneale. *The Development of Logic*. Oxford: Clarendon Press, 1962.

Lemmon, E. J. *Beginning Logic*. (revised by G. N. D. Barry). Indianapolis: Hackett, 1978. London: Thomas Nelson, 1965.

*Purtill, Richard L. *Logic for Philosophers*. New York: Harper & Row, 1971.

Reichenbach, Hans. *Elements of Symbolic Logic*. New York: Macmillan, 1947. (Reprinted in a Dover edition.)

*Russell, Bertrand. *Principles of Mathematics*. Cambridge: Cambridge University Press, 1903.

*Russell, Bertrand. "On Denoting". *Mind,* n.s., vol. 14 (1905). Reprinted in Robert C. Marsh, ed., *Logic and Knowledge*. New York: MacMillan, 1956.

*Russell, Bertrand. "Mr. Strawson on Referring", in *My Philosophical Development*. London: Allen and Unwin, 1959.

*Strawson, P. F. "On Referring". *Mind,* n.s., vol. 59 (1950).

*Suppes, Patrick, *Introduction to Logic*. Princeton, N.J.: Van Nostrand, 1957.

*Tarski, Alfred. "Semantic Conception of Truth". *Philosophy and Phenomenological Research,* vol. 4 (1944).

*Wittgenstein, Ludwig. *Tractatus Logico Philosophicus*. New York: Harcourt Brace, 1922.

Part Three

*Barker, Stephen. *Elements of Logic,* Fourth Edition. New York: McGraw Hill, 1985.

*Baum, Robert. *Logic,* Second Edition. New York: Holt, Rinehart and Winston, 1981.

Bird, Otto, *Syllogistics and Its Extensions*. Englewood Cliffs, N.J.: Prentice-Hall, 1964.

*Blair, J. Anthony, and Johnson, Ralph H. *Informal Logic: The First International Symposium*. Inverness, Calif.: Edgepress, 1980.

*Cadwallader, Eva H. "Christine Ladd-Franklin's Antilogism". *Newsletter on the Teaching of Philosophy,* Fall 1980.

*Carroll, Lewis. *Symbolic Logic and the Game of Logic*. New York: Dover, 1958

Cohen, Morris R., and Ernest Nagel. *An Introduction to Logic*. New York: Harcourt, 1962.

*Copi, Irving. *Introduction to Logic,* Sixth Edition. New York: Macmillan, 1982.

*Dodgson, C. L. (Lewis Carroll). *Symbolic Logic,* 1896.

Eaton, Ralph M. *General Logic*. New York: Charles Scribner's Sons, 1931.

*Gensler, Harry. "Star Test". *Notre Dame Journal of Formal Logic,* vol. 14 (1973).

*Kahane, Howard. *Logic and Contemporary Rhetoric,* Fourth Edition. Belmont, Calif.: Wadsworth, 1984.

*Oliver, James W. "Formal Fallacies and Other Invalid Arguments". *Mind,* n.s., vol. 76 (1967).

Orwell, George. "Politics and the English Language", in *Shooting an Elephant and Other Essays*. New York: Harcourt Brace, 1945.

*Ruby, Lionel. *The Art of Making Sense,* Second Edition. New York: J. B. Lippincott, 1954.

*Sanford, David. "Contraries and Subcontraries". *Nous,* vol. 2 (1968).

*Suppes, Patrick. *Introduction to Logic*. Princeton: Van Nostrand, 1957.

Part Four

*Ayer, A. J. *Language, Truth and Logic*. New York: Dover.

*Carnap, Rudolf. "On the Application of Inductive Logic". *Philosophy and Phenomenological Research,* vol. 8 (1947).

*Carnap, Rudolf. *The Continuum of Inductive Methods*. Chicago: University of Chicago Press, 1952.

*Carnap, Rudolf. *Logical Foundations of Probability,* Second Edition. Chicago: University of Chicago Press, 1962.

*Copi, Irving. *Introduction to Logic,* Sixth Edition. New York: Macmillan, 1982.

*Gierre, Ronald. *Understanding Scientific Reasoning,* Second Edition. New York: Holt, Rinehart and Winston, 1984.

*Goodman, Nelson. *Fact, Fiction, and Forecast,* Third Edition. Indianapolis: Bobbs-Merrill, 1973.

*Hempel, Carl. *Philosophy of Natural Science*. Englewood Cliffs, N.J.: Prentice-Hall, 1966.

*Hempel, Carl. "Studies in the Logic of Confirmation". *Mind,* n.s., vol. 54 (1945).

*Hume, David. *An Enquiry Concerning Human Understanding*.

*Hume, David. *A Treatise of Human Nature*.

*Kahane, Howard. "Baumer on the Confirmation Paradoxes". *British Journal for the Philosophy of Science,* vol. 18 (1967).

*Kahane, Howard. "Eliminative Confirmation and Paradoxes". *British Journal for the Philosophy of Science,* vol. 20 (1969).

*Kahane, Howard. "Hempel and Goodman on the Ravens." (Private paper)

*Kahane, Howard. "Pathological Predicates and Projection". *American Philosophical Quarterly,* vol. 8 (1971)

*Mill, John Stuart. *Systems of Logic*.

Nagel, Ernest. *The Structure of Science*. New York: Harcourt, 1961.

*Peirce, Charles. "Induction as Experimental and Self-correcting". *Collected Papers of Charles Sanders Peirce*. vol. VI, ed. by Charles Hartshorne and Paul Weiss. Cambridge, Mass.: Harvard University Press, 1935.

*Pole, Nelson. "A Deductive Argument with a Specific Premise and a General Conclusion". *Notre Dame Journal of Formal Logic,* vol. XVI (1975).

*Popper, Karl. *The Logic of Scientific Discovery*. New York: Basic Books, 1959.

*Quine, Willard V. *From a Logical Point of View*. Cambridge, Mass.: Harvard University Press, 1953.

*Ramsey, Frank. *The Foundations of Mathematics*. London: Routledge, Keegan Paul, 1931.

*Reichenbach, Hans. *Nomological Statements and Admissible Operations*. Amsterdam: North Holland Publ., 1954.

*Reichenbach, Hans. *Rise of Scientific Philosophy*. Berkeley: University of California Press, 1951.

*Reichenbach, Hans. *The Theory of Probability*. Berkeley: University of California Press, 1949.

Reichman, William J. *Use and Abuse of Statistics*. New York: Oxford University Press, 1962.

Salmon, Wesley C. *The Foundations of Scientific Inference*. Pittsburgh: University of Pittsburgh Press, 1967.

Salmon, Wesley C. *Scientific Explanation and the Causal Structure of the World*.

*Skyrms, Brian. *Choice and Chance,* Third Edition. Belmont, Calif.: Wadsworth, 1985.

*von Wright, G. H. *Logical Problems of Induction,* Second Rev. Edition. New York: Barnes & Noble, 1965.

*Woozley, A. D. "Universals". *Encyclopedia of Philosophy,* ed. by Paul Edwards. New York: Collier MacMillan, 1967.

Part Five

Bergmann, Merrie; Moor, James; and Nelson, Jack. *The Logic Book*. New York: Random House, 1980.

Jeffrey, Richard. *Formal Logic: Its Scope and Limit,* Second Edition. New York: McGraw Hill, 1981.

Part Six

*Anderson, Allan Ross. "On the Logic of Commitment". *Philosophical Studies,* vol. X (1959).

*Barcan Marcus, Ruth. "A Functional Calculus of First Order Based on Strict Implication". *Journal of Symbolic Logic,* vol. II (1946).

*Bergmann, Gustav. "The Philosophical Significance of Modal Logic". *Mind,* n.s., vol. 69 (1960).

*Castañeda, Hector-Neri. "The Logic of Obligation". *Philosophical Studies,* vol. 10 (1959).

*Danto, Arthur C. "On Knowing That We Know", in Avrum Stroll, ed., *Epistemology*. New York: Harper and Row, 1967.

*Quine, Willard V. "Notes on Existence and Necessity". *Journal of Philosophy,* vol. 40 (1943).

*Rescher, Nicholas. "An Axiom System for Deontic Logic". *Philosophical Studies,* vol. IX (1958).

*Robison, John. "Further Difficulties for Conditional Permission in Deontic Logic". *Philosophical Studies,* vol. XVIII (1967).

Appendix A

Barker, Stephen F. *The Philosophy of Mathematics*. Englewood Cliffs, N.J.: Prentice-Hall, 1964.

*Hume, David. *An Enquiry Concerning Human Understanding*.

*Hume, David. *A Treatise of Human Nature*.

*Kant, Immanuel. *Prolegomena to any Future Metaphysic*.

*Quine, Willard V. *From a Logical Point of View*. Cambridge, Mass: Harvard University Press, 1953.

*Reichenbach, Hans. *Rise of Scientific Philosophy*. Berkeley: University of California Press, 1951.

Appendix B

Church, Alonzo. *Introduction to Mathematical Logic*. Princeton, N.J.: Princeton University Press, 1956.

Copi, Irving. *Symbolic Logic,* Sixth Edition. New York: Macmillan, 1982.

*Kleene, S. C. *Introduction to Meta-Mathematics*. New York: Van Nostrand, 1964.

*Mendelson, Elliot. *Introduction to Mathematical Logic,* Second Edition. Princeton, N.J.: Van Nostrand, 1979.

Special Symbols

Symbol	Introduced on Page
/∴ (also ∴)	3fn.
· (also &)	15
~	19
(), [], {}	20
∨	21
⊃ (also →)	25
≡	27
::	63
┌→	83
(x), (y), etc.	111
(∃x), (∃y), etc.	115
=	165
≠	166
A, *E*, *I*, *O*	199
$\overline{P}$, $\overline{S}$, etc.	206
O	210
=*df*	271

Symbol	Introduced on Page
P	321
/ \\ *A* *B* (etc.)	359
x	
◇	392
□	393
⥽	394
≣	395
RDL	408
$P(p/c)$	408
$O(p/c)$	409
SL	430
WFF	431
QL	434
(Uu)	434
(∃u)	434

Index

Five Rules for Valid Syllogisms

All valid syllogisms must have

1. A middle term which is distributed at least once.
2. No term distributed in its conclusion which is not distributed in a premise.
3. At least one affirmative (nonnegative) premise.
4. A negative conclusion if and only if one of its premises is negative.
5. At least one particular premise if the conclusion is particular.

Antilogism Rules for Valid Syllogisms

1. Construct the antilogism by replacing the syllogism's conclusion by its negation.
2. The syllogism is valid if and only if its antilogism meets the following conditions:
   a. Exactly one of its three statements is an inequality.
   b. One of the two equalities has a term negated in the other equality.
   c. Each of the two terms in the inequality is either negated in both of its occurrences or in neither.

Truth Tables for Sentence Connectives

p	q	$p \cdot q$	$p \vee q$	$p \supset q$	$p \equiv q$
T	**T**	**T**	**T**	**T**	**T**
T	**F**	**F**	**T**	**F**	**F**
F	**T**	**F**	**T**	**T**	**F**
F	**F**	**F**	**F**	**T**	**T**

p	$\sim p$
T	**F**
F	**T**

Rules for Sentential Logic Truth Trees

$(p \cdot q)\checkmark$
p
q

$(p \vee q)\checkmark$
/ \
p | q

$(p \supset q)\checkmark$
/ \
$\sim p$ | q

$(p \equiv q)\checkmark$
/ \
p, q | $\sim p$, $\sim q$

$\sim(p \cdot q)\checkmark$
/ \
$\sim p$ | $\sim q$

$\sim(p \vee q)\checkmark$
$\sim p$
$\sim q$

$\sim(p \supset q)\checkmark$
p
$\sim q$

$\sim(p \equiv q)\checkmark$
/ \
p, $\sim q$ | $\sim p$, q